THE HISTORY OF THE COLONY AND PROVINCE OF MASSACHUSETTS–BAY

VOLUME I

LONDON: HUMPHREY MILFORD

OXFORD UNIVERSITY PRESS

The History of the Colony and Province of Massachusetts-Bay

BY

THOMAS HUTCHINSON

EDITED FROM THE AUTHOR'S OWN COPIES OF VOLUMES
I AND II AND HIS MANUSCRIPT OF VOLUME III,
WITH A MEMOIR AND ADDITIONAL NOTES

BY

LAWRENCE SHAW MAYO

CAMBRIDGE, MASSACHUSETTS

HARVARD UNIVERSITY PRESS

1936

PRINTED AT THE HARVARD UNIVERSITY PRESS

CAMBRIDGE, MASS., U. S. A.

EDITOR'S INTRODUCTION

A FEW years ago Mr. Charles E. Goodspeed, knowing that a new edition of Hutchinson's *History of Massachusetts-Bay* was being contemplated, kindly sent me an interesting memorandum that had come into his possession. It is endorsed thus: "Dr. Wm. Jencks [*sic*] handed me this about the time Mr. Savage went to England. (1842.)," and runs as follows:

HUTCHINSON'S HIST. MASS. in
4 vols. 8vo.

Portrait — from painting of Mass. Hist. Soc., &
Memoir — of the Author.

Preface & Introduction —
As Mr. S. pleases —

Portraits of
Gov. Edw. Winslow — Hist. Soc.
" Josias Winslow — D°.
" John Winthrop, sen. — State house.
" John Endicott — D°.
Rev. John Wilson — Hist. Soc.
Gov. Simon Bradstreet — State house.
" William Burnet — D°.
Rev. Increase Mather — Hist. Soc.
Gov. John Leverett — State house.

To be published — with copious notes & illustrations, by the
Hon. Ja[s]. Savage, Esq.

This memorandum suggests that more than ninety years ago the editor of John Winthrop's *History of New England* and compiler of the *Genealogical Dictionary of the First Settlers of New England* was approached in regard to preparing a new edition of Governor Hutchinson's well-known work. Why the project was not carried into effect we know not. Possibly Savage felt that the days of "Fifty-four forty, or fight" were not an auspicious time for bringing out a

Tory governor's history of Massachusetts. If so, he was probably right; for even fifty years later there were educated men in the Bay State to whom the name of Thomas Hutchinson was still anathema. Or it may be that he wished to devote all his time and energy to the stupendous task of compiling the *Genealogical Dictionary*. However it may have been, I cannot but feel that the historical world would have been richer if James Savage had loosed his erudition, wit, and assurance upon Hutchinson's annals. Therefore, I am all the more conscious of my own limitations for the task I have undertaken, and wish to offer an explanation of the method I have adopted.

There are already in existence three editions of the *History of Massachusetts-Bay*, or rather there are three editions of the first and second volumes and one of the third.[1] Volume I was first printed in Boston in 1764. An English edition (a part of which was erroneously dated MDCCLX) came out in London in the following year. Volume II first appeared in Boston in 1767, and was reprinted in London in 1768. In 1795 a third edition (second American) of these two volumes was printed at Salem, Massachusetts, for "Thomas and Andrews, No. 45, Newbury-Street, Boston."[2] This was virtually a reprint of the first American edition, with a few additional footnotes by the anonymous editor and the occasional use of italics in the text to emphasize "Mr. Hutchinson's sentiments respecting allegiance and the political connexion of this country with Great Britain." Volume III was published in London in 1828, almost fifty years after the death of the author; it was edited by John Hutchinson, a grandson of the Governor.

In the Chapin Library at Williamstown, Massachusetts, are Governor Hutchinson's own copies of volumes I and II, and the original manuscript of volume III. Inasmuch as the author's copies of the earlier volumes contain many corrections in his own hand in the margins of the pages and are interleaved with a considerable amount of new material in manuscript, they constitute Hutchinson's final

---

[1] Although there was but one edition of the third volume, it was issued in two forms and with different title-pages: one was for English readers, the other for Americans. The English form appeared as a separate *History of the Province of Massachusetts-Bay from 1749 to 1774*, with a dedication to Lord Lyndhurst, a son of John Singleton Copley, and a preface — both written by the editor, John Hutchinson. The American form was issued as volume III of the *History*, and without dedication or preface. James Savage had secured subscriptions in America for five hundred copies, an achievement which may have led the editor to feel that no further introduction would be necessary in that part of the world.

[2] A so-called third edition appeared serially in the *Royal American Magazine* (Boston) in 1774-75. It is incomplete, consisting of only 152 pages of volume I, and "is the rarest of the editions of this history." Joseph Sabin, *Dictionary of Books relating to America*, IX, 24.

revision of this part of his *History*. These corrections and additions have never been printed. The manuscript of volume III is equally important because it gives us the text exactly as the author wrote it, and not as it appeared after it had been edited by his grandson for publication in 1828.

In preparing the present edition, I have, of course, followed Hutchinson's final revision of volumes I and II and the original manuscript of volume III. To call the reader's attention to the author's additions, I have enclosed those phrases, sentences, paragraphs, and notes in brackets. His corrections are sometimes so indicated; and sometimes I have used an editor's footnote to remark upon a change of this kind in the text. As the basis for his final revision the author used the second edition (London, 1765 and 1768). He made a few corrections before the London edition of volume I was printed;[1] but the English printer added errors of his own, some of which inevitably escaped the eye of the author when he was engaged upon his final revision. Some of these I have corrected by substituting the word given in the first edition; in other cases I have employed a footnote to call the reader's attention to the variation in the texts. Probably many have escaped my eye as they escaped Hutchinson's. If so, I trust that the reader will be charitable.

For the modern reader the chief handicap in reading Hutchinson's narrative lies in the fact that oftentimes persons appear in his pages without their full names or other means of identification. In general, the author has favored the more important figures with biographical footnotes; but even so there are scores that come and go under their surnames only — occasionally adorned with the title "Mr.," which helps little except perhaps to place them socially. To identify these individuals and to give them background and life has been my chief purpose in adding footnotes of my own; and I hope that at least part of the pleasure I have found in becoming acquainted or reacquainted with various men and women of early Massachusetts will be passed on to the reader. As Hutchinson employed printer's marks to indicate his notes, I have used Arabic numerals for my own; thus the reader need never be in doubt as to whether the note is the author's or the editor's. In the absence of any citation it may be assumed that Savage's *Genealogical Dictionary*

---

[1] This statement is sustained by the following comment by the author: "Mr. Condy to whom I gave the copy, finding the book was in demand here, ordered immediately a large impression in England. I am sorry for it, because I had not opportunity enough to make several amendments I should have chosen to have made. Care is taken of the typographical errors which are numerous, as also some inaccuracies." Thomas Hutchinson to Ezra Stiles, January 15, 1765. The letter is printed in *New England Historical & Genealogical Register*, XXVI, 163–164.

or some equally obvious source of information is the authority upon which my notes rest. If Hutchinson has sufficiently identified an individual, either in the text or in a footnote, I have chosen, as a rule, not to add a note of my own, in spite of the fact that we of the twentieth century may possess many additional facts. Now and then a bibliographical note will suggest where one may learn more of this person or of that, but these references are merely incidental and do not pretend to be complete.

The idea of a new edition of Hutchinson's *History* originated with the late Mr. Harold Murdock, Director of the Harvard University Press, and for his friendly encouragement and wise guidance I shall always be grateful. Another inspiring friend and counselor was Professor Edward Channing, who was ever ready to turn from his own pursuits to lend a hand to the inexperienced and sometimes perplexed editor.

L. S. M.

MEMOIR OF THOMAS HUTCHINSON

THE story of the life of Thomas Hutchinson has been so well told by James Kendall Hosmer in his sympathetic biography of him that the editor of this edition of Hutchinson's *History of Massachusetts-Bay* feels that he cannot do better than to base this Memoir on that work. Hosmer wrote his account in the last decade of the nineteenth century, when it required both discernment and courage to present a true portrait to the American public. The old antipathy of our ancestors had been resurrected and given new intensity by the pen of George Bancroft, whose patriotism appears to have blinded him to the good there was in the men whose political views differed from those of the leaders of the American Revolution. A corrective was needed; and fortunately for us Dr. Hosmer, who had written a biography of Samuel Adams for the *American Statesmen* series, was the man who undertook the delicate task.

Thomas Hutchinson, the last American-born royal governor of the province of Massachusetts-Bay, was a great-great-grandson of that Anne Hutchinson who was banished from the colony in 1638 because of her incorrigible liberalism. Curiously enough, one hundred and forty years later her distinguished descendant was banished — and his property confiscated — because of his uncompromising conservatism. The time may come when someone will give us a Hutchinson saga that will narrate in detail the vicissitudes of the family during that century and a half, incidents and developments that can be only sketched here. There was, for instance, Captain Edward Hutchinson, son of the independent-thinking Anne; he was great-grandfather of the Governor. The liberal tendency showed itself in Edward when Quakerism was the latest and most dangerous heresy to menace the established order in the Bay Colony. The General Court took the problem in hand and voted that any Quaker who ventured to return to Massachusetts after banishment should be put to death. Edward Hutchinson, who was one of Boston's representatives at that time, was so strongly opposed to the passage of this law that he asked to have his dissent entered upon the records.[1] Yet no one can say that Edward Hutchinson was not a loyal son of the Bible Commonwealth. He amply proved his devotion to it when he went

---

[1] George Bishop, *New England Judged by the Spirit of the Lord* (Philadelphia, 1885), p. 83.

into the western country to negotiate with the Nipmuck Indians in King Philip's War and lost his life in the service of the colony.[1] Edward's son Elisha may have been less of a dissenter than his immediate forebears, but it is clear that he was one of the most useful public citizens of his time. Though relatively unsuccessful as a merchant, he possessed the kind of character, physique, and personality that attracted to him many responsibilities and honors. He was a member of the Council, colonel of the Boston regiment, and a judge of the Court of Common Pleas for Suffolk County. And his funeral in 1717 was attended with a degree of solemnity and display that made it memorable even in that era of mortuary extravagances.[2]

The succeeding head of the house of Hutchinson was Thomas, son of Colonel Elisha and father of the Governor. He contributed more of the romantic to the family history. When a young man he accompanied the officer who arrested Captain Kidd at his lodgings in Boston, and it was he who stayed the pirate's arm when he attempted to draw his sword.[3] In later years Thomas Hutchinson, Jr., was for a quarter of a century a member of the Council. He acquired a handsome fortune, and lost most of it by not selling his shipping when it ceased to be profitable. "What will become of all the people in my employ, if I should sell all my vessels?" he asked his son. The future governor's reply is not recorded, but his high regard for his father as a public servant appears in a footnote in his *History of Massachusetts-Bay*: "Regardless of the frowns of the people he spoke and voted according to his judgment, attaching himself to no party any further than he found their measures tended to promote the public interest."[4] We shall soon see how closely the son followed his father's example in his own political career.

Thomas Hutchinson, the author of this *History of Massachusetts-Bay*, was born in his father's handsome mansion on Garden Court Street, Boston, Massachusetts, September 9 (O. S.), 1711. His mother was Sarah Foster Hutchinson. As a small boy he attended the North Grammar School, and at the age of twelve he entered Harvard College. He appears to have been a precocious and serious youngster with a marked fondness for reading, especially for reading history. Upon graduation from the College he became a merchant apprentice in his father's counting-room, and through ventures of

---

[1] George Madison Bodge, *Soldiers in King Philip's War* (1906), pp. 29–30, 106–112.
[2] *Diary and Letters of Thomas Hutchinson*, edited by Peter Orlando Hutchinson, II, 466.
[3] Thomas Hutchinson, *History of Massachusetts-Bay*, II, 89.
[4] *Ibid.*, II, 297.

his own he had acquired between £400 and £500 by the time he was twenty-one. The pursuit of wealth did not occupy all his time, however; he continued to study, going on with his Latin and taking up French with Le Mercier, the Huguenot minister. Early in his twenties he married, and from every point of view he married well. His bride was Margaret Sanford, the youngest daughter of Governor Sanford of Rhode Island; she was in her seventeenth year and an heiress. Few marriages, if any, have been happier than this turned out to be. For nineteen years Thomas and Margaret were devoted to each other; and when death separated them, her dying words were: "Best of husbands."

In 1737 Hutchinson was elected a selectman of Boston, and in the same year his native town chose him one of its representatives to the General Court. When he took his seat in the House on May 31, he was not yet twenty-six years old. From the outset of his political career it was clear to Thomas Hutchinson that the greatest need of the province was the abolition of paper currency and the substitution of hard money. He proposed to accomplish this by borrowing in England a sum in silver equal to all the paper money then extant, redeem the bills, and then gradually pay off the debt over a period of years by provincial taxation. Today few will doubt the soundness of his proposal, but in the seventeen-thirties those who clamored for paper money and more paper money were in the saddle. After two years in the House of Representatives he was dropped by his constituents. But those in high places had already recognized the character and ability of the man, and in 1740 he was entrusted with a mission to England, where he was to endeavor to recover for Massachusetts a large tract of land which the province had lost through a recent determination of New Hampshire's southern boundary. Hutchinson went to London, did his best with a difficult claim, accomplished nothing, and after a year of disappointment and homesickness returned to Boston. One might have guessed that this fruitless errand would have ended his public career, but it was not so to be.

In 1742 Hutchinson was again elected to the General Court, and continued to serve in that body until 1749; in 1746, 1747, and 1748 he was Speaker of the House. Towards the end of this period he had the great satisfaction of seeing the provincial currency placed on a hard-money basis. In 1748 Parliament reimbursed the province for its expense in the Louisbourg expedition of 1745 and sent over £183,649 2s 7d in Spanish dollars and coined copper. As this amount would almost exactly wipe out the local paper money, if the latter were redeemed at a given rate, Hutchinson proposed that such a course be adopted. At first he was almost alone in advocating this measure, but after an initial defeat his bill was supported by men of influence and at last it was passed. The hostility of the common people was bitter, almost riotous in fact, but in a very short time the good effect of the change to hard money became apparent to all and a revulsion of popular feeling took place. For once, and perhaps for the only time in his career, Thomas Hutchinson found himself a favorite of the people.

While the cloud of unpopularity was over him, in 1749, Hutchinson failed of re-election to the General Court; but the Court itself was with him and at once elected him a member of the Council. In his new office he distinguished himself from the outset as a commissioner to settle various provincial boundary disputes. The first of these concerned the line between Massachusetts-Bay and Connecticut; the next determined the Rhode Island boundary; and at a much later time the province turned to him again to negotiate with New York on a similar question. In 1752 he was appointed Judge of Probate and Justice of the Common Pleas for the County of Suffolk, succeeding an uncle in both offices. When a convention of the colonies was held at Albany, in 1754, to devise ways and means of combating the encroachments of the French, Thomas Hutchinson headed the five deputies sent by Massachusetts-Bay. At the Albany Congress, as it is usually called, he prepared a representation of the state of the colonies while Benjamin Franklin submitted a plan for union. Except as a forerunner of more productive continental congresses the Albany gathering has little historical significance, but the fact that its chief business was entrusted to these two men suggests that Hutchinson was already recognized as one of the master minds in British America. And it may well have been his services at Albany that led to his appointment as Lieutenant-Governor in 1758.

When Chief Justice Sewall died, in 1760, there was much speculation as to who would be his successor. Colonel James Otis of Barnstable, the father of James Otis of Revolutionary renown, probably did not aspire to such elevation, but he was personally interested in the situation because Governor Shirley had promised him some years earlier that if a vacancy should occur in the Superior Court he should be appointed to fill it. Assuming that one of the members of that court would now be made Chief Justice, he not unnaturally anticipated a vacancy and his consequent appointment. But in 1760 Shirley was no longer governor of Massachusetts-Bay, and Bernard, his successor, had plans of his own for the judiciary. Instead of promoting any of the judges of the Superior Court he chose to appoint the Lieutenant-Governor, Thomas Hutchinson. When this intention was rumored about town, the Otises, father and son, — especially the latter, — were enraged. Indeed it was common report that James Otis, Jr., declared "that he would set the province in flames, though he perished in the fire." [1] In the light of subsequent events it is not surprising that Hutchinson wrote in his *History*, "From so small a spark a great fire seems to have been kindled." Up to this time the Otises had been friendly to the administration. Hutchinson was appointed Chief Justice. Thereafter the Otises were among the most active and implacable enemies of those who represented royal authority in Massachusetts-Bay. Perhaps Judge Trowbridge, a contemporary of those immediately concerned, was right when he gave it as his opinion that the American Revolution "would have been put off many years if Governor H. had not been made Chief Justice." [2]

Long before 1760 Hutchinson had inherited his father's mansion in Boston, which was acknowledged to be one of the finest residences in the town. One can easily believe that there was none more magnificent. Besides this he had a country place in Milton, where during many months of the year he and his family of five children — three boys and two girls — delighted in comparative seclusion and all the other charms of rural life. From the commodious house on Milton Hill one could gaze eastward down the valley of the widening Neponset, out to the blue harbor with its single lighthouse, and beyond to the broad Atlantic. In the other direction the landscape fell away in farms and woodland until it rose once more in the romantic outline of the Blue Hills. It is not to be wondered that Thomas Hutchinson loved his seat at Milton more than any other place. Few mortals have been more blessed in their places of residence than was he who now held the offices of Lieutenant-Governor and Chief Justice of the province of Massachusetts-Bay. Milton gave him relaxation, refreshment, opportunity to reflect or even to dream. Boston meant ambition, work, responsibility, and, as a compensating factor, the stimulation that comes of contact with other minds. In town he kept his excellent library and also the many papers relating to the history of his native province which he had collected in one way or another over a period of years. It was in town, therefore, that he sat down to the self-imposed task of writing a history of Massachusetts-Bay. Probably he began work upon it in 1763, for the first

[1] William Tudor, *Life of James Otis*, p. 54.
[2] John Eliot, *Biographical Dictionary*, p. 274, note.

volume was published in Boston in 1764, and one of his letters tells us that the time he spent on it was spread over "about twelve months." "I never had time to write two sheets at a sitting without avocations by public business," he explained to his friend Ezra Stiles, the future president of Yale College, "but was forced to steal a little time in the morning and evening while I was in town, and then leave it for weeks together, so that I found it difficult to keep any plan in mind." To the modern reader the first volume of Hutchinson's *History* is undeniably dry reading. But our ancestors either possessed tougher mental fibre or liked their reading dry. Certain it is that the Boston edition of Hutchinson's first volume sold so readily that the printer, Mr. Condy, hurried the copy to London for an English edition which appeared there in 1765.[1] In fact he acted too precipitately to suit the author, who complained that he was not given sufficient time to make "several amendments," though he did succeed in correcting numerous typographical errors, "as also some inaccuracies."

Encouraged by the reception accorded his first volume, Hutchinson pressed on with the second which should bring the story down to the year 1750. The first had ended with the arrival of the new charter and the accession of Governor Phips in 1692. By the summer of 1765 about two-thirds of the new volume had been written. Then occurred a catastrophe which would have disheartened a less resolute author from going on with his work. On the evening of August 26, 1765, a mob, bent upon indiscriminate vengeance for the enforcement of the new customs laws, attacked his town house with unbelievable fury. Hutchinson happened to be in the mansion with his children, having come in from Milton that morning. Sensing danger, he directed the children to fly to a place of safety, then locked up the house and stood his ground. Only when his eldest daughter returned and refused to leave unless he went with her did he quit the house and go to a neighbor's. The mob fell upon the mansion, broke down the doors with axes, tore away wainscot and hangings, beat down partitions, and even knocked off the cupola. All night the vandalism continued. The garden house was laid flat and his trees were "broke down to the ground." Money to the amount of £900 was carried off. His library, the manuscript of his second volume, and all his precious historical documents were thrown into the street, and he who wishes to do so may see the Boston mud of 1765 still

---

[1] For bibliographical and critical studies of the *History of Massachusetts-Bay*, see Charles Deane's *Hutchinson Bibliography* (1857) and Lawrence Shaw Mayo's paper in the American Antiquarian Society's *Proceedings*, New Series, XLI (1931), 321–339.

clinging to various pages of the manuscript, which is preserved in the Massachusetts archives. Happily for Thomas Hutchinson, and for us, his neighbor the Reverend John Eliot rescued what books and papers he could on the following day and took them to his own house for safe-keeping.

How Hutchinson or any other man could have felt any interest in the history of Massachusetts-Bay after being treated thus by some of his fellow citizens is not easy to understand. Yet he does not appear to have become embittered to this extent. He completed his second volume within a few months; it was printed in Boston in 1767, and in London a year later. In 1769 he put together the more significant historical documents that had survived the destruction of his house and published them in a single volume entitled *A Collection of Original Papers relative to the History of the Colony of Massachusets-Bay.*

Governor Bernard returned to England in July, 1769, leaving to Hutchinson, the Commissioners of Customs, and two regiments of British regulars the task of keeping in order the ungovernable Yankees. Hutchinson had no desire to become Governor; he preferred the less wearing office of Chief Justice. But pending the appointment of Bernard's successor he, as Lieutenant-Governor, had no choice but must serve as the chief magistrate. The trend of events seemed to conspire against peace in the province. Early in September James Otis was savagely beaten by one of the Commissioners of Customs; a non-importation agreement came into being; mobs went about making life miserable for this man or that; not only the House of Representatives but the Council as well refused to join the Lieutenant-Governor in measures for repressing lawlessness; and finally, in March, 1770, came a brawl between a few inhabitants of Boston and the British soldiers stationed in the town — the Boston Massacre. In that episode a handful of exasperated soldiers fired into a crowd that had been annoying them, killed three persons outright and mortally wounded others. At once the town was in an uproar. On the following morning the citizens met in the Old South Meeting-House and demanded of Hutchinson that the British regiments be transferred to the Castle, three miles from town and out in the harbor. It was useless for the Lieutenant-Governor to point out that under his commission he had no authority over the British soldiery. Something had got to be done, and the people of Boston expected Hutchinson to do it. All things considered he did not do badly. Without exceeding his authority he persuaded Colonel Dalrymple to remove the more objectionable regiment to the Castle; and when the town insisted that this was not enough, he prevailed upon him to remove both. A royal governor who was a skilful politician could have brought this to pass in such a way that he would have emerged from the situation the savior and hero of the populace. But this was the kind of thing that Thomas Hutchinson could not or would not do. We do not know that he was ungracious, but we do know that Samuel Adams, the chief spokesman for the town of Boston, carried off all the glory on that occasion.

Soon after the Boston Massacre Hutchinson begged the authorities in England to relieve him of his office and to appoint in his stead "a person of superior powers of body and mind." But Lord Hillsborough, the secretary for colonial affairs, and his advisers, were entirely satisfied that he was the right man to head the administration in Massachusetts-Bay; and in March, 1771, Hutchinson was inaugurated as Governor of the turbulent province. Peter Oliver, whose son had married Hutchinson's daughter Sarah, succeeded him as Chief Justice; and Andrew Oliver, a brother-in-law of Mrs. Hutchinson, became Lieutenant-Governor.

For a year or two Hutchinson must have felt increasingly cheerful about the office which had been thrust upon him. After the repeal of most of the new taxes in 1770, the hostility of the Boston merchants and the lawlessness of the Boston populace subsided to such an extent that in 1772 there was comparative peace and good order in the province. John Hancock's enthusiasm for Samuel Adams and his schemes had cooled considerably, and the two men were now on terms that were barely friendly. Even James Otis had come to the conclusion that opposition to Hutchinson had gone far enough, if not too far. To many it must have looked as if the days of conflict were over and an era of peace and prosperity was beginning for the British colonies in North America. Samuel Adams was one of the few who were still bent on agitation. To keep the spark of opposition alive he seized upon a minor issue and goaded the town of Boston into formulating a statement of the rights of the colonists. This was communicated to the other towns of Massachusetts-Bay "and to the world," with a request for replies. The stroke was almost unaccountably successful. As if by clockwork the principal towns responded immediately with manifestoes denying the right of Parliament to tax the colonies and with votes instructing their representatives in the General Court to combat all infringement of their rights under the Charter.

If Governor Hutchinson had had more political wisdom and less conscience he would have ignored this artificial burst of patriotism.

Unfortunately he felt called upon to prove the soundness of the doctrine of the supremacy of Parliament, and did so — to his own satisfaction at least — in an address to the General Court. The Court was on the defensive at once and, thanks to the combined talents of Samuel Adams, Dr. Joseph Warren, and John Adams, made an admirable reply. Hutchinson rejoined with a rebuttal, and the Court answered his rebuttal. Neither side convinced the other; but each summarized its position so well that historians should be forever grateful to Thomas Hutchinson for having occasioned a perfect presentation of both sides of the perplexing constitutional question that underlay the American Revolution. In the winter of 1773, however, the net result of the exchange of views was merely to stir up feeling that had become dormant and to increase unnecessarily and immeasurably the unpopularity of Governor Hutchinson.

Before the hostility engendered by the unfortunate controversy had died down Hutchinson became the victim of a bit of underhanded work that makes unpleasant reading. In the difficult days of the Bernard administration he had used his personal correspondence with a friend in England as a safety valve for his opinions and emotions. The friend appears to have been Thomas Whately. In some mysterious way, after Whately's death, these letters came into the possession of Benjamin Franklin, who was then in England acting as Agent for the province of Massachusetts-Bay. Franklin read them and found them interesting. In one passage, for instance, the writer remarked, "There must be an abridgment of what are called English liberties"; in another, "I doubt whether it is possible to project a system of government in which a colony 3000 miles distant from the parent state shall enjoy all the liberty of the parent state." Franklin knew full well the sensation these opinions over Hutchinson's signature would create if read by the leaders of the opposition in Boston; he knew also that the letters were private and personal. Nevertheless, he sent them across the water and salved his conscience by stating that it was understood that they were not to be printed or copied, — they were merely to be shown to a few leading persons. Inevitably they reached the hands of Samuel Adams, who promptly made the most of them. In June, 1773, he read them to the House of Representatives, and it was not long before they were printed and circulated throughout the province. From that moment the usefulness of Thomas Hutchinson as royal governor was no more.

About this time Parliament, with the best of intentions, passed a bill calculated to improve the financial situation of the East India Company. This act relieved the Company from paying various duties in England on tea that was reshipped to the colonies. To English eyes it was clear that this measure would enable the great company to undersell all competitors in the American market and so dispose of its large overstock of tea. Incidentally the Americans would be able to buy their tea at a lower price than that to which they were accustomed. What could be a happier arrangement for all concerned? All might have been well if the Company had not chosen for its agents in the colonies merchants who were known to be friendly to the British government. In Massachusetts-Bay, for instance, two of the favored few were Thomas and Elisha Hutchinson, sons of Governor Hutchinson; another was the Governor's nephew, Richard Clarke. From the point of view of our ancestors these men were granted a virtual monopoly of the tea trade, for they would undoubtedly be able to undersell all other dealers, even those who sold smuggled tea. The "independent" merchants did not intend to allow this. Accordingly they fused their grievance with the latent objection to the existing duty on all teas, and raised a new hullabaloo. When the first of the ships bearing the monopoly tea came into Boston harbor, towards the end of November, 1773, Samuel Adams and his associates prevented her cargo from being landed and instructed the owner of the ship to have her put to sea. This the owner was willing to do, but customs regulations stood in his way. If a vessel had been entered, she could not be granted a clearance until the duty on her cargo had been paid or secured. The collector of the port refused to make an exception in this case, and the local British naval officer sustained him by refusing to give a permit for the vessel to pass the Castle. As a last resort the town required the owner to go to Governor Hutchinson, who was at Milton, and ask him to cut the Gordian knot by issuing the requisite pass. In retrospect it is easy to see that in such a situation an executive should exceed his authority, prevent a cataclysm, and hope to be able to satisfy his superiors that he had acted for their best interest. But Thomas Hutchinson could not take that view. All he could, or would, see was that his commission gave him no power to grant such a permit unless the vessel had been regularly cleared at the customhouse. He gave this answer on the afternoon of December 16. In the evening a band of Bostonians, disguised as Indians, overran the tea ships (two more had come into the harbor) and broke open and emptied overboard three hundred and forty-two chests of tea. "Such barbarity," wrote Hutchinson to a Tory friend, "none of the Aborigines were ever guilty of."

For several months the Governor had felt the need of going to

England to talk over with his superiors the state of affairs in Massachusetts-Bay. Permission to do so arrived in the winter of 1773, and he would have gone at once if there had been anyone to take his place. The death of Lieutenant-Governor Oliver, which occurred early in March, made it imperative that Hutchinson remain in the province till a substitute should be appointed. Towards the middle of May relief came and he found himself superseded by Governor Gage, whose duty it would be to put into execution the Boston Port Act and other innovations that Parliament brought into being as a result of the Tea Party. It was understood, however, that Gage's appointment was only temporary and that Hutchinson might return to the office of governor before long, if he chose to do so. As Hutchinson's departure was now imminent, one hundred and twenty merchants and gentlemen of Boston, and other representative groups of citizens, sent him respectful addresses in which they expressed their approval of him as a governor and as a man. On June 1, Hutchinson, accompanied by his youngest daughter Peggy, left his loved country seat at Milton, and a few hours later sailed for England in the *Minerva*.

"How do you do, Mr. Hutchinson, after your voyage?"

"Much reduced, Sir, by sea-sickness; and unfit upon that account, as well as by my New England dress, to appear before your Majesty."

After this manner began a conversation between George III and Thomas Hutchinson which lasted nearly two hours. The former governor had just arrived in London and had had about an hour's talk with Lord Dartmouth, the secretary for colonial affairs. The day was July 1, 1774. As the King was at St. James's Palace and would not be there again until the middle of the following week, Dartmouth persuaded Hutchinson to go, just as he was, with him to see his Majesty. It was his first meeting with royalty, but if he conducted himself as well as he appears to have done in his own account of the interview he did exceedingly well. George III asked many intelligent questions and received equally intelligent replies. Naturally enough the King had difficulty in differentiating Samuel Adams and John Adams; nor could he quite understand why Thomas Cushing, the Speaker of the Massachusetts House, was not the great disturber of the peace rather than Samuel Adams who was only a member. Furthermore, he was surprised to learn that the Yankees were Congregationalists; he had thought them to be Presbyterians. But on the whole his Majesty kept up his end pretty well, and when he was able to change the topic of conversation to agriculture he fairly shone. While they were still discussing political affairs the King asked how the people received the news of the late measures of Parliament; to which Hutchinson replied, "When I left Boston we had no news of any Act of Parliament, except the one for shutting up the port, which was extremely alarming to the people." Apparently the King had already formed his opinion on this point, for immediately after the interview he wrote to Lord North, "I have seen Mr. Hutchinson, late Governor of Massachusetts, and am now well convinced they will soon submit. He owns the Boston Port Bill has been the only wise and effectual method."

The first year or two of Hutchinson's exile — for it was little less than that — was comparatively enjoyable. Massachusetts-Bay was very much in the public eye and the former governor of the unruly province was an object of interest and of sympathy. Lord Dartmouth was especially kind. Among the other prominent persons to show him attention were the Earl of Hillsborough, the Archbishop of Canterbury, the Bishops of London and of Oxford, and Lords Mansfield, Rockingham, Hardwicke, Loughborough, and Townshend. Hutchinson and his lovely daughter Peggy were much invited and much noticed. Although he found London an expensive place of residence, he was far from destitute, for the government provided him with a handsome pension. A baronetcy was offered him, but he declined it. Much more to Hutchinson's taste was the honorary degree of Doctor of Civil Law which the University of Oxford conferred upon him on July 4, 1776.

Besides the flattering attentions of the great there were pleasant contacts with other New Englanders who chanced to be in London. These meetings with old friends and acquaintances Hutchinson seldom failed to record in his Diary. For regular occupation he turned again to writing the history of his native land. Volume II had brought the narrative down to the year 1750. Picking up the thread at that point he wrote the story of the next twenty-four years, closing it with his own departure for England in 1774. Other historians sought his society. There was, for instance, Dr. William Robertson of Edinburgh, whose *History of Scotland during the Reigns of Mary and James VI* and *History of the Reign of the Emperor Charles V* are still read. And on at least one occasion Thomas Hutchinson dined with Gibbon.

In the spring of 1776 the atmosphere began to change. Mr. Hutchinson was no longer a novelty; but that was not the only reason. There were too many Americans in London. Many of those who left Boston with the British army in March, 1776, turned up in England sooner or later, and most of these were in straitened circumstances.

One distinguished refugee may be interesting, even exciting; but a swarm of poverty-stricken refugees is certain to be embarrassing and depressing. Even before this time Hutchinson had recorded in his Diary, "Americans are plenty here and very cheap. Some of us, at first coming, are apt to think ourselves of importance, but others do not think so; and few, if any of us, are much consulted or inquired after." The former governor of Massachusetts-Bay fared much better than did most of his fellow expatriates, but Fate was hardly kind even to him. If England and the English had tired of him, it was no less true that he had tired of them. He longed for New England sights and sounds and ways as only the homesick heart can long. A visit at Wimpole Hall, the magnificent seat of Lord Hardwicke, left him cold. "This is high life," he wrote in his pathetic Diary, "but I would not have parted with my humble cottage at Milton for the sake of it." The town of Bristol was the haven of many American loyalists, and Hutchinson has probably given us the reason for their congregating there. "I think," he wrote, "take in all circumstances, I should prefer living there to any place in England. The manners and customs of the people are very like those of the people of New England, and you could pick out a set of Boston Selectmen from any of their churches."

Homesickness by itself is a sufficient affliction for most New Englanders, but Thomas Hutchinson had to bear more than this, more and more and more. First came the news that his property in Milton and Boston had been appropriated by the rebels, and he estimated that at least £1100 worth of movables had been taken out of his house and off the farm. 'Twas said that General Washington now rode in his coach. In 1778 the revolutionary government forbade his ever returning to Massachusetts-Bay; and in the following year all his American estates were confiscated. His pension, which at first had seemed ample for his needs, now had to meet the necessities of twenty-five persons, for all his sons and daughters and their households had come to England and were dependent upon him for support.

When the Declaration of Independence was published in England, Hutchinson wrote a thoughtful criticism of it entitled *Strictures upon the Declaration of the Congress at Philadelphia; in a Letter to a Noble Lord, etc.* It appeared as an anonymous pamphlet, and was reprinted in Almon's *Remembrancer* (for the year 1776, Part III, pp. 25–42). But even the severance of the colonies from the mother country did not diminish his passion for New England. "I prefer the *natale solum* to all other," he wrote to a friend in 1777; and as the war dragged on, the thought that he would probably die and be buried elsewhere than in New England oppressed him with increasing intensity. If this indicates that he was morbid, one must admit that he had sufficient cause for being so. Peggy, his beloved daughter and constant companion, had not been well since their arrival in London in the summer of 1774; and as the years passed, it became evident that she was the victim of consumption. In September, 1779, she passed away and was buried at Croydon. Less than six months later, his youngest son Billy succumbed to the same malady. Billy had been in England since 1766; and though he may not have been the most dutiful of sons, he appears to have been especially dear to his father's heart. There was little left for Thomas Hutchinson to live for. To him it must have seemed as if everything he loved or believed in had gone or was slipping from his grasp. In America the tedious war had clearly turned against England. There was little or no prospect of his ever seeing Boston and Milton again. Peggy had gone. Billy had gone. And now London itself was at the mercy of rioters, for those were the days of the Gordon Riots. When and how would it all end? For him the end came on June 3, 1780. He was buried beside Peggy at Croydon.

THE
HISTORY
OF THE
COLONY
OF
MASSACHUSET'S BAY,

FROM THE

FIRST SETTLEMENT THEREOF

IN 1628,

UNTIL ITS INCORPORATION

WITH THE

Colony of PLIMOUTH, Province of MAIN, &c.

BY THE

Charter of King WILLIAM and Queen MARY,

IN 1691.

By MR. HUTCHINSON,
Lieutenant-Governor of the MASSACHUSET'S Province.

Hiftoria, non oftentationi, fed fidei, veritatique componitur.
Plin. Epift. L. 7. E. 33.

THE SECOND EDITION.

LONDON:
Printed for M. RICHARDSON, in Pater-nofter Row.

M DCC LXV.

CONTENTS.

APPENDIX.

THE

PREFACE.

THE repeated destruction of ancient records and papers, by
fire in the town of Boston, first inclined me to endeavour the
preservation of such materials as remained proper for an history of the Massachusets colony. Many such came to me from my
ancestors, who, for four successive generations, had been principal
actors in public affairs: among the rest, a manuscript history of Mr.
William Hubbard,[1] which is carried down to the year 1680, but after
1650 contains but few facts. The former part of it has been of great
use to me: It was so to Dr. Mather in his history,[2] of which Mr.
Neale's [3] is little more than an abridgement. I made what collection
I could of the private papers of others of our first settlers, but in this
I have not had the success I desired. The descendants of some of
them are possessed of many valuable letters and other manuscripts,
but have not leisure or inclination to look into them themselves, and
yet will not suffer it to be done by others. I am obliged to no person
more, than to my friend and brother the Reverend Mr. Mather,[4]
whose library has been open to me, as it had been before to the

[1] William Hubbard (1621–1704), minister of Ipswich. His *General History of New
England* was first printed by the Massachusetts Historical Society in 1815. A second
edition, prepared by William Thaddeus Harris, was published in 1848. The original
manuscript is not extant, but an ancient contemporary copy, occasionally corrected in
Hubbard's hand, is preserved by the Massachusetts Historical Society.

[2] Cotton Mather (1663–1728), minister of the North Church in Boston. His *Magnalia Christi Americana: or the Ecclesiastical History of New England* was published in
London in 1702.

[3] Daniel Neal (1678–1743) published in two volumes a *History of New England* to the
year 1700. It was printed in London in 1720. He acknowledged his indebtedness to
Cotton Mather, but explained in his Preface, "Had the Dr. put his Materials a little
closer together, and disposed them in another Method, his Work would have been more
acceptable to this Part of the World." Neal was an English clergyman. His most ambitious work was a *History of the Puritans*.

[4] Samuel Mather (1706–1785) was the son of Cotton and the grandson of Increase
Mather. At one time he was pastor of the North Church, later of the church in North
Bennett St. One of his works was a *Life of Cotton Mather*, published in 1729. He mar-
ried a sister of Governor Hutchinson. Horace E. Mather, *Lineage of Rev. Richard
Mather*, p. 110.

Reverend Mr. Prince,[1] who had taken from thence the greatest and most valuable part of what he had collected.

SEVERAL gentlemen have given us encouragement to expect from them an history of the colony. Mr. Prince gave us the chronology of two or three years, and there left it. Mr. Prat,[2] the late chief justice of New York, has often mentioned to me his intention to prepare and publish such an history. Death has put it out of his power. Another gentleman,[3] of the first character at the bar, whose talents for it will not be called in question, has proposed the same thing. Want of leisure for it has probably prevented.

I AM sensible that whoever appears in print should be able to dispose his matter in such order, and cloath it with such stile and language, as shall not only inform but delight the reader; therefore I would willingly have delivered over every thing I have collected to a person of genius for such a work. But seeing no prospect of its being done by any other, I engaged in it myself; being very loth, that what had cost me some pains to bring together, should be again scattered and utterly lost.

I AM sensible of many defects in this performance, and that it stands in need of all the apologies I am capable of making for it. It cannot be expected that the affairs of a colony should afford much matter, interesting or entertaining to the world in general. I write for the sake of my own countrymen, and even to many of them I expect some facts will be thought of too little importance; and yet I

---

[1] Thomas Prince (1687–1758) was the pastor of the Old South Church. In the tower of the church edifice he deposited and preserved many manuscripts and books relating to the history of New England. This collection was partly destroyed by the British in 1775–76. He began a *Chronological History of New England* in the form of annals; the first volume was published in 1736, and two numbers of the second in 1755.

[2] Benjamin Pratt (1710–1763) was born in Cohasset, represented Boston in the General Court, 1737–50, and through the friendship of Governor Pownall was appointed chief justice of New York. He made extensive collections with the intention of writing a history of New England.

[3] This may have been Peter Oliver (1713–1791), who succeeded Hutchinson as chief justice of Massachusetts-Bay in 1771. He "collected something of a library and had transcribed several MS. local histories. Among them was a MS. copy of Rev. Mr. Hubbard's history of New England." "Scholars from all parts of the colony came to consult his books and manuscripts, and for such information as he only could give them in matters of history, literature and art." Thomas Weston, Jr., *Peter Oliver*, reprinted from the *New England Historical and Genealogical Register*, July and October 1886.

The editor of the third edition (1795) of the present work assures the reader, "The gentleman here meant was Oxenbridge Thacher, esquire, who died the next year after this Volume was first published, viz. in 1765." Upon what authority this statement was made the present editor has been unable to discover.

have omitted many such as have been judged proper for the press by former historians. In general, we are fond of knowing the minutiæ which relate to our own ancestors. There are other facts, which, from the nature of them, will afford but a dull and heavy narration. My chief design is to save them from oblivion.

ALL historians profess a sacred regard to truth. I have found some difficulty in guarding against every degree of prejudice, in writing the history of my own country. I hope, by shunning one extreme, I have not run upon the other.

THE Massachusets colony may be considered as the parent of all the other colonies of New-England. There was no importation of planters from England to any part of the continent, northward of Maryland, except to the Massachusets, for more than fifty years after the colony began. In the first ten years, about twenty thousand souls had arrived in the Massachusets. Since then, it is supposed more have gone from hence to England than have come from thence hither. Massachusets-Bay, New-Hampshire, Connecticut, and Rhode-Island, at this day, probably contain five hundred thousand souls.[1] A surprising increase of subjects of the British crown!

BARBADOS and the leeward islands owed very much of their growth to the supplies of lumber, horses and provisions, with which they were furnished, at the beginning of their settlements, from this colony, in as great plenty as they desired.

THE addition of wealth and power to Great Britain, in consequence of this first emigration of our ancestors, exceeds all expectation. They left their native country with the strongest assurances that they and their posterity should enjoy the privileges of free natural born English subjects. May the wealth and power of Britain still increase, in proportion to the increase of her colonies; may those privileges never be abused; may they be preserved inviolate to the latest posterity.

[1] Franklin Bowditch Dexter's study of colonial population (American Antiquarian Society's *Proceedings*, October 1887) confirms Hutchinson's estimates.

CHAP. I.

The History of the Colony of *Massachusets-Bay*, from the first Settlement until the Year 1660.

THE discovery of America by Columbus, and of the northern continent by the Cabots, in the 15th century, and the several voyages of English and French, in the 16th, I pass over, and begin with the voyage made by Bartholomew Gosnold,[1] an Englishman, in the year 1602, to that part of North America since called New-England. (It is not certain that any European had been there before. Hackluit [2] mentions the landing of some of Sir H. Gilbert's [3] men upon some part of the continent; but, it is probable, that was farther eastward, upon what is now called Nova-Scotia.) He landed first on the eastern coast, which he calls Mavoshen.* After some commerce with the natives, he sailed southward, and landed upon one of the islands called Elizabeth islands.† He gave them that name in honour to Q. Elizabeth, who was living when he left England, and they have retained it ever since. He built a fort, and intended a settlement upon the island, or the con-

---

* About 43 degrees North.

† A little Southward of Cape Cod. He gave the name also to Martha's Vineyard.

---

[1] A "relation" of Gosnold's voyage by Gabriel Archer, a member of the expedition, was included by Purchas in his *Pilgrimes*. It is reprinted in Massachusetts Historical Society *Collections*, Third Series, vol. VIII. Gosnold was one of the founders of Jamestown, where he died in 1607.

[2] Richard Hakluyt (1552?–1616), "Master of Artes and Student sometime of Christ-Church in Oxford," published in 1589 *The Principall Navigations, Voiages, and Discoveries of the English Nation.* Ten years later he enlarged this work into three volumes. Vol. III contains the story of Gilbert's expedition as related by Edward Hayes, one of the survivors.

[3] Sir Humphrey Gilbert (1539?–1583) was stepbrother to Sir Walter Raleigh. In June 1583, he sailed with a fleet of five ships to discover and occupy advantageous places on the Northwest Passage. After landing at Newfoundland, of which he took possession for Elizabeth, he sailed southward seeking a site for his colony. His vessel was lost and Gilbert went down with it. See *Sir Humfrey Gylberte and his Enterprise of Colonization in America*, edited by Carlos Slafter and issued by the Prince Society.

tinent near it; but he could not persuade his people to remain there, and they all returned to England before winter.*

In 1603, De Monts [1] obtained a patent from Henry the 4th of France, for all the country, from the 40th to the 46th degree, by the name of Cadie or Acadie. In 1604 De Monts ranged along the sea coast, from St. Lawrence to Cape Cod, and to the south of it. He went far up Kenebeck river, and into divers other rivers, bays and harbours.†

In 1606, King James, the first, granted all the continent, from 34 to 45 degrees; which he divided into two colonies, viz. the Southern, or Virginia, to certain merchants of London; the Northern, or New-England, to merchants of Plymouth.

In 1607, some of the patentees of the Northern colony began a settlement at Sagadehoc.[2] They laid the plan of a great state.‡ The president died the first winter, which was extreme cold. Sir John Popham his brother, the great promoter of the design, and Sir John Gilbert the admiral's brother, died the same year in Europe, and the next year, 1608, the whole number which survived the winter returned to England. Their design of a plantation was at an end. Both English and French continued their voyages to the coast, some for fishing, and some for trade with the natives; and some feeble attempts were made, by the French, towards plantations, but they were routed by the English in 1613.[3] There was no spirit in the people of either nation for colonizing. Favourable accounts were

* This I suppose is what Josselyn,[4] and no other author, calls the first colony of New-Plimouth, for he says it was begun in 1602, and near Narraganset bay.

† He did not go into the Massachusets bay, but struck over from some part of the eastern shore to Cape Ann, and so to Cape Cod, and sailed further southward. *Champ.*[5]

‡ The following persons were sent over to begin the colony, George Popham, president; Rawleigh Gilbert, admiral; Edward Harlow, master of the ordnance; Robert Davies, serjeant major; Ellis Best, marshal; —— Seaman, Secretary; James Davies commander of the fort; Gome Carew, searcher; and about one hundred commonalty.

---

[1] Pierre du Guast, Sieur de Monts, visited and named Mount Desert Island — "Isle des Monts deserts" — in 1604. His activities in North America are admirably narrated in Francis Parkman, *Pioneers of France in the New World.*

[2] Sagadehoc, the region about the mouth of the Kennebec. That river was then known as the Sagadahoc. For a good brief account of this unsuccessful enterprise see Edward Channing, *History of the United States*, I, 170–172.

[3] For the best account of Samuel Argall's expedition against the French settlements on the coast of Maine and in Nova Scotia see Francis Parkman, *Pioneers of France in the New World.*

[4] John Josselyn, *An Account of Two Voyages to New England* (London, 1675). It has been reprinted by the Massachusetts Historical Society in its *Collections*, Third Series, III, 211–396.

[5] Samuel de Champlain, *The Voyages of Sieur de Champlain.*

published of the continent, by Capt. Smith [1] and others, but who would remove, and settle in so remote and uncultivated a part of the globe, if he could live tolerably at home? * The country would afford no immediate subsistance, and therefore was not fit for indigent persons. Particular persons or companies would have been discouraged from supporting a colony, by the long continued expence and outset, without any return.† No encouragement could be expected from the public. The advantages of commerce from the colonies were not then foreseen, but have been since learned by experience. Virginia in its infancy was struggling for life; and what its fate would have been, if the fathers of it in England had not seen the rise and growth of other colonies near it, is uncertain.‡ God in his providence bringeth good out of evil. Bigotry and blind zeal prevailed, among christians of every sect or profession. Each denied to the other, what all had a right to enjoy, liberty of conscience. To this we must ascribe, if not the settlement, yet at least the present flourishing state of North America. Persecution drove one Mr. Robinson [2] and his church from England to Holland, about the year 1608. They stayed about a year at Amsterdam, and then removed to Leyden. In 1617 they began to think of removing to America. They laid great stress upon their peculiar [religious] tenets, but this did not lessen their regard to morality. The manners of the Dutch were too licentious for them. Their children left them; some became soldiers, and others sailors, in the Dutch service. In a few years their posterity would have been Dutch, and their church extinct. They were at a loss whether to remove to Guiana § or to Virginia, but the majority were in favour of the latter. The Dutch

* Quis porro, præter periculum horridi & ignoti maris, Asiâ aut Africâ aut Italiâ relictâ, Germaniam peteret informem terris, asperam cælo, tristem cultu aspectuq; nisi si patria sit. Tac. de mor. Germ.

† Sir Ferdinando Gorges and Capt. Mason spent twenty thousand pounds each, in attempts for settlement, and each of them thought it adviseable to give over their designs and sit down with the loss.

‡ Whether Britain would have had any colonies in America at this day, if religion had not been the grand inducement, is doubtful. One hundred and twenty years had passed, from the discovery of the northern continent by the Cabots, without any successful attempt. After repeated attempts had failed, it seems less probable that any should undertake in such an affair, than it would have been if no attempt had been made.

§ Sir Walter Rawleigh had raised the fame of Guiana about this time.

---

[1] Captain John Smith (1580–1631), of Virginia fame, explored the New England coast in 1614 and published, two years later, *A Description of New England.*

[2] John Robinson (1575?–1625), the pastor of the Pilgrims in the Old World. He appears frequently in the pages of William Bradford's *History of Plymouth Plantation,* and is the subject of at least three biographies, notably one by Ozora S. Davis.

laboured to persuade them to go to Hudson's river and settle under
their West-India company; but they had not lost their affection
for the English, and chose to be under their government and protection. They applied to the Virginia company for a patent for part
of the country. To render it probable that their undertaking would
not, like all former, be abortive, they gave among others these
special reasons: "That they were well weaned from the delicate
milk of their mother country, and inured to the difficulties of a
strange land. That they were knit together in a strict and sacred
bond, by virtue of which they held themselves bound to take care
of the good of each other, and of the whole. That it was not with
them as with other men, whom small things could discourage, or
small discontents cause to wish themselves at home again." The
Virginia company were very much pleased with the application, and
some of the chief of them addressed the King to grant the petitioners
liberty in religion, under the great seal; but this was refused. He
promised to connive, and not molest them; but this would not do
for them at that time. They laid aside the design for that year. In
1619 they renewed their application and resolved to venture, tho'
they could not have a special grant, from the King, of liberty of conscience. They hoped their remote situation would put them out of
danger of the ecclesiastical courts. The affairs of the Virginia company were in great confusion, and it was the latter end of the year
before the patent was granted. It was taken out, under the company's seal, to John Wincob. He lived in the family of the Countess
of Lincoln, and not removing with the rest, they never took any
benefit from the patent. Mr. Weston [1] and other merchants of
London engaged, some to adventure their money, and some to go
over with them. They therefore made the necessary preparations,
and in July 1620 the principal of them went over to Southhampton,
where two ships were ready to take them on board. They sailed the
beginning of August, but were obliged, repeatedly, to put back, and
to leave one of their ships behind, with part of their company at last.
They intended for Hudson's river or the coast near to it; but the
Dutch had bribed their pilot,[2] and he carried them farther north-

---

[1] Thomas Weston. For his negotiations with the Pilgrims, see William Bradford's
History of Plymouth Plantation. A very readable account of his enterprise at Wessa-
gusset (Weymouth, Massachusetts) may be found in Charles Francis Adams, *Three
Episodes of Massachusetts History*, I, 45–104. For a brief account see Charles Knowles
Bolton, *The Real Founders of New England*, pp. 43–48.

[2] This tradition first appears in Nathaniel Morton's *New England's Memorial* (1669).
Besides a statement in the body of the text, Morton wrote in a footnote: "Of this
plot, betwixt the Dutch and Mr. Jones, I have had late and certain intelligence."

ward, so that they fell in about Cape Cod, and arrived in that harbour the 11th of November. The harbour is good, but the country is sandy and barren. This was discouraging, but it was too late in the year to put to sea again. They coasted about, in their boat, until they found a place more agreeable to them for a plantation, though not so good a harbour. Here they brought their ship, and determined to take up their abode. They gave it the name of New-Plimouth. Capt. Smith happened to give the name of Plimouth to the same place, in 1614. A very circumstantial account of the beginning and progress of this colony, wrote by Mr. Edward Winslow,[1] one of the principal undertakers, is to be found among Purchase's collections.*

THE project, of settling America, revived again, and a new patent was granted, bearing date Nov. 3d, 1620; incorporating the adventurers to the northern colony, by the name of the Council for the affairs of New-England; the bounds of the country were expressed, between 40 and 48 deg. N.;† Sir Ferdinando Gorges[2] and Capt. John Mason[3] were two of the most active members of this

---

* In 1629 they obtained a patent from the Council of Plimouth.

† [This Company was not fully satisfied with a Charter from *the King* and in the year 1622 had determined to apply to *Parliament* for a confirmation or for a new Grant. In case of a judicial proceeding it might be made a question whether *the King* had not exceeded his prerogative and complaint was actually made in Parliament against this Charter as a Monopoly which the King had not authority to grant; but the authority of Parliament the supreme legislative power is not to be called in question in a judicial process, and that power only which made the grant can annul or reassume it. A doubt arose whether a new Charter from the Parliament would not occasion the proceedings of the Company during the two years they had acted under a Charter from the King to be called in question and this stopped the application. *Book of Records of Council of Plymouth.*]

---

[1] Edward Winslow (1595–1655) was governor of the Plymouth Colony in 1633, 1636, and 1644. The reference is to the condensed version of *Mourt's Relation* (1622) and of *Good Newes from New England* (1624) which Purchas included in the fourth volume of his *Pilgrimes* in 1625.

[2] Sir Ferdinando Gorges (1566?–1647) appears to have become interested in American colonization in 1605, when George Weymouth returned from the New World bringing with him five American Indians. They landed at Plymouth, England, where Gorges was "governor of the forts and island." Thereafter he engaged in various enterprises of exploration and colonization, and in 1620 organized the Council for New England, which received a grant of the territory between latitudes 40° and 48°. The charter was given up in 1635. Four years later Gorges obtained a new grant which made him lord proprietary of the province of Maine. The best study of his life is by James Phinney Baxter in *Sir Ferdinando Gorges and his Province of Maine*, published by the Prince Society.

[3] John Mason (1586?–1635), "the founder of New Hampshire." "Mason was a merchant of London, but became a sea-officer, and, after the peace, governor of Newfoundland, where he acquired a knowledge of America, which led him, on his return to

council. All the sea coast, at one time or other, has been granted or pretended to be granted by this council, and some parts several times over, partly from defects in form in preceding grants, and partly from unacquaintedness with the geography of the country. The first grant, within the bounds of the Massachusets, was obtained by Mr. Weston, who in the summer of 1622, sent over two ships with 50 or 60 men, to begin a plantation at Wessagusset, since called Weymouth. They were sickly when they arrived, and received necessaries and refreshment from their neighbours at New-Plimouth. They were a dissolute crew, soon brought themselves to poverty, then robbed the Indians and offered other abuses to them. The Indians made their complaints to the colony of New-Plimouth; but the abuses continuing, the next year they laid a plot for the destruction of all Weston's company.* The plot was discovered to the New-Plimouth people, who sent some of their men and prevented the execution of it, by the surprizal of those who were to be the principal actors. Mr. Weston coming over to visit his plantation, was cast away in Ipswich bay, and stripped by the Indians of every thing but his shirt. Being thus rendered incapable of affording any relief to his colony, it came to an end, after one year's continuance.

CAPTAIN Robert Gorges obtained a patent from the council of Plimouth dated Dec. 13, 1622, 10 miles in breadth, and 30 miles into the land, on the northeast side of Massachusets bay. This was loose

---

* It was this plantation, which gave occasion to the author of Hudibras to make merry with New-England in general, for hanging a bed rid weaver, instead of a useful cobler. The Plimouth people, their neighbours, allowed that there was some foundation for the story. Several had been concerned in a theft. The Indians insisted that the ringleader should be put to death. They hanged one, who was less culpable and not like to live, in his stead. Others say they deceived the Indians, and hanged up one who died, of sickness or famine, a little while before. *Hubbard.* [Morton who was one of the company and must be supposed to know best says that the offender was a strong young fellow and that many were for putting his clothes on an impotent old man and hanging him instead of the other, and it seemed to be concluded on until one more scrupulous than the rest was the means of hindering it. They then persuaded this young fellow to be bound in jest, and hanged him in earnest, otherwise with a weapon, when at liberty, he would have put them to a non plus. *Mortons N. English Canaan.*]

England, into a close attachment to those who were engaged in its discovery; and upon some vacancy in the council, he was elected a member and became their secretary; being also governor of Portsmouth in Hampshire." Jeremy Belknap, *History of New Hampshire* (1784), I, 7. In 1629 he received a grant of all the land between the Merrimac and the Piscataqua, and named it "New Hampshire."

Almost everything known about Mason has been collected and published by the Prince Society in a volume entitled *Capt. John Mason.* It contains an excellent memoir by Charles Wesley Tuttle.

Wollaston to Merry Mount, set all the servants free, erected a may-pole, and lived a life of dissipation, until all the stock, intended for trade, was consumed. He was charged with furnishing the Indians with guns and ammunition, and teaching them the use of them. At length, he made himself so obnoxious to the planters in all parts, that, at their general desire, the people of New-Plimouth seized him by an armed force, and confined him, until they had an opportunity of sending him to England. In the fall of 1626, Roger Conant, and some, if not all, of his company removed from Cape-Ann to a neck of land upon Naumkeak river.[1] I find mention made of planters at Winsimet [2] about the same time, who probably removed there from some of the other plantations. This is all the account we have of any settlements, or attempts for settlements in the Massachusets bay, until the year 1627. Mr. White,[3] the minister of Dorchester, had encouraged Conant and his company to remain in New-England, and promised them men, provisions, &c.

In 1627, March 19, the Council of Plimouth sold to Sir Henry Roswell, Sir John Young, Thomas Southcoat, John Humphry, John Endicot, and Simon Whetcomb, who lived about Dorchester in England, their heirs and associates, all that part of New-England, three miles to the south of Charles river, and three miles north of Merrimack river, from the Atlantick to the South Sea. All the lesser grants which have been mentioned within those limits (the settle-ment of the country being entirely neglected by the grantees) were, without doubt, looked upon to be forfeited or void. The conditions or tenor of none of them appear at this day. It is very likely, the three persons, first named in this grant, had nothing more in view by the purchase, than a settlement for trade with the natives, or for fishery, or other advantageous purposes. As soon as a colony for

---

[1] In the third edition, and often in the first edition, this name appears as "Naum-keag," the modern spelling. Conant's settlement was merged with Endicott's and be-came Salem.

[2] Winisimet, more frequently spelled Winnisimett, is the old name for Chelsea, Massachusetts.

[3] John White (1575–1648), "the Patriarch of Dorchester," was an Oxford graduate. As rector of Holy Trinity at Dorchester, England, he did a great deal of good among his parishioners. In 1624 he undertook to send a colony of Dorset non-conformists to Massachusetts. This led to the formation of the Massachusetts-Bay Company. When Winthrop sailed in 1630 White held a service on board the *Arbella*. To him are attrib-uted *The Humble Request of his Majesties loyall Subjects, the Governour and the Com-pany late gone for New-England* (London, 1630) and *The Planters Plea* (London, 1630). See Samuel Eliot Morison's admirable essay in his *Builders of the Bay Colony*, chapter II; also a biography, *John White, Founder of Massachusetts*, by Frances Rose-Troup. *The Planters Plea* has recently been reprinted in Massachusetts Historical Society *Proceedings*, LXII, 367–425.

religion was projected, we hear no more of them.* The other three remained. Mr. White managed a treaty, between Sir Richard Saltonstall, Matthew Cradock and John Venn, Esquires, and divers others in and about London, and the original patentees. A purchase was made, and the same summer Mr. Endicot,† one of the original patentees, was sent over to Naumkeak with planters and servants, and all the affairs of the colony committed to his care. The patent, from the council of Plimouth, gave a good right to the soil, but no powers of government. A royal charter was necessary. This passed the seals, March 4, 1628. Matthew Cradock was appointed the first governor, and Thomas Goffe, deputy governor. Two days before, March 2d, some affairs of the colony requiring it, there had been a meeting of the company, at which both governor and deputy are named as such. The day, for the annual election of officers by charter, being the last Wednesday in Easter term, on the 13th of May 1628, Mr. Cradock was chosen governor by the company, and Mr. Goffe deputy governor, and Sir Richard Saltonstall, Isaac Johnson, Samuel Aldersey, John Venn, John Humfrey, Simon Whetcomb, Increase Nowell, Richard Perry, Nathanael Wright, Samuel Vassall, Theophilus Eaton, Thomas Adams, Thomas Hutchins, George Foxcroft, William Vassall, William Pincheon, John Pocock, and Christopher Coulson, assistants. William Burgis was chosen secretary, in the room of John Washburne. At this court it was determined, that every one of the company, who had

* Some of the principal of the liberal speakers in parliament, being committed to the tower, others to other prisons, this took away all hope of reformation of church government from many not affecting episcopal jurisdiction, nor the usual practice of the common prayers of the church; thereof there were several sorts, though not agreeing among themselves, yet all of like dislike of those particulars. Some of the discreeter sort, to avoid what they found themselves subject to, made use of their friends to procure, from the council for the affairs of New England, to settle a colony within their limits. — In a very short time, numbers of people, of all sorts, flocked thither in heaps; that, at last, it was especially ordered by the King's command, that none should be suffered to go without licence; so that, what I long before prophesied, when I could hardly get any for money to reside there, was now brought to pass. *Ferd. Gorges Hist. of New-England.*[1]

† His instructions were dated London, May 30, 1628, and signed by John Venn, Matthew Cradock, George Harwood, John Humphry, Richard Perry, George Hewson, Samuel Aldersley,[2] Thomas Stevens, Joseph Caxon, Thomas Webb, Increase Nowell, Hugh Peters, John White, and Abraham Palmer. His first letters from Naumkeak were dated Sept. 13, 1628.

[1] Ferdinando Gorges, *A Briefe Narration of the Originall Undertakings of the Advancement of Plantations into the parts of America. Especially, Shewing the begining, progress and continuance of that of New England.*

[2] In the first edition this name is spelled "Aldersey," which is correct.

subscribed fifty pounds, should have 200 acres of land assigned, and in proportion for a greater or lesser sum as the first dividend. The names of all the adventurers, and the sums subscribed, were sent over to Mr. Endicot, who was appointed their governor in the plantation. A second embarkation, of planters and servants, had been determined at a meeting April 30, to be made with all speed.* Four ministers were provided. Three of them, Francis Higginson, Samuel Skelton, and Francis Bright, were readily accepted by the company, and had all due encouragement promised them; the fourth, Ralph Smith, was required to give under his hand, that he would not exercise his ministry within the limits of the patent without the express leave of the governor upon the spot.† Five ships were provided for this embarkation. Mr. Higginson says in his journal,[1] that he sailed from the Isle of Wight the 11th of May, and arrived at Cape-Ann the 27th of June, and at Naumkeag the 29th. They found at Naumkeag about 100 planters,‡ 8 houses, besides a fair house built for Mr. Endicot. The old and new planters together were about 300, of which, 100 removed to Charlestown, where

* Mr. Endicot sent three brethren, Ralph, Richard and William Sprague, to explore the country westward. Between Mistick and Charles rivers they find a body of Indians settled, called Aberginians, and one English house, thatched and possessed by Thomas Walford, a smith. The Indian name of the neck was Mishawun, now Charlestown. The first travellers,[2] with the consent of the Indians, took up their abode there. Some of their posterity remain there, and in other parts of the colony to this day.

† Mr. Bright, one of these ministers, is said, by Hubbard, to have been a conformist. He went, soon after his arrival, to Charlestown, and tarried about a year in the country. Mr. Smith seems to have been of the separation in England, which occasioned the caution used with him. He was a little while at Nantasket, and went from thence to Plimouth, where he was their minister several years.

‡ [Roger Conant was the principal person. After one years trial in the Fishery at Cape Ann the Adventurers were discouraged and on the next year Cape Ann was deserted and Mr. Conant with several others removed to Naumkeak and intimated to his friends in England that it would be a convenient place for such as upon the account of Religion would be willing to begin a foreign Plantation. Whereupon Mr. White wrote to Mr. Conant to persuade him not to desert the business and promised that if he and three more, whom he knew to be honest and prudent men, viz. Tho. Woodbury, John Balch and Peter Palfrey employed by the Adventurers would stay at Naumkeak he would obtain a Patent for them and send them such provisions and goods as they should write for. Answer was returned that they would all stay on those terms. But the Patent to Sir Henry Rosewell et al. comprehended the land, where Conant was settled, and he became a planter. *Hubbard.*]

[1] Francis Higginson (1587–1630). His journal is printed in Hutchinson's *Collection of Original Papers* and in Massachusetts Historical Society *Proceedings*, LXII, 285–299; also, but with modernized spelling, in Alexander Young's *Chronicles of Massachusetts*. There is a *Life of Francis Higginson* by his descendant Thomas Wentworth Higginson.

[2] The first edition gives "these first travellers" instead of "the first travellers." The third edition (1795) follows the first.

there was a house built; the rest remained at Salem. Mr. Endicot had corresponded with the settlers at Plimouth, [particularly with Samual Fuller who had been a deacon of Mr. Robinson's Independent or Separate church in Holland,] who satisfied him, that they were right in their judgments of the outward form of worship, being much like to that of the reformed churches in France, &c.* On the 20th of July, Mr. Higginson and Mr. Skelton,[1] after fasting and prayer, were first elected by the company for their ministers, the first, teacher, the other, pastor; each of them, together with three or four grave members, laying their hands on the other, with solemn prayer. Nothing is said of any church being then formed; but on the 6th of August, the day appointed for the choice and ordination of elders and deacons, thirty persons entered into a covenant in writing, which is said to be the beginning of the church, and that the ministers were ordained or instituted anew. The repetition of this form they probably thought necessary, because the people were not in a church state before. It is difficult to assign any other reason. Messengers or delegates, from the church of Plimouth, were expected to join with them, but contrary winds hindered them in their passage, so that they did not arrive until the afternoon, but time enough to give the right hand of fellowship. Two of the company, John Brown, and Samuel Brown, one a lawyer, the other a merchant, both men of good estates, and of the first patentees and of the council, were dissatisfied. They did not like, that the common prayer and service of the church of England should be wholly laid aside, and therefore drew off, with as many as were of their sentiments, from the rest, and set up a separate society. This offended the

* Mr. Hubbard, in his M. S. history, remarks upon this occasion; "It is certainly known, that the old non-conformists and good old puritans, of Queen Elizabeth's and King James's time, did in many things not symbolize with the separatists; the one endeavouring only a reformation of some corruptions retained or crept into the church (as they thought) either before or after its reformed state; the other, not contented therewith, stood, as stiffly, to maintain a necessity of disannulling their former church state, as that like a vessel, once infected with leprosy, it must be broken in pieces to be new cast. —— It is affirmed, that Mr. Hildersham advised Mr. Higginson and other ministers, looking this way, to agree upon their form of church government before they came away from England; which counsel, if it had been attended, might have prevented some inconvenience that hath since fallen out, or, at least, have saved some of the succeeding ministers from the imputation of departing from their first principles, because they were not publickly declared in the beginning of things." *M. S. History.*

[1] Samuel Skelton (1584–1634) had been a preacher in Lincolnshire, England, where he was persecuted for non-conformity. He received his formal education at Clare Hall, Cambridge, and was awarded the degrees of A.B. in 1611 and A.M. in 1614. In church polity he appears to have been a Separatist.

governor, who caused the two members of his council to be brought before him; and judging, that this practice, together with some speeches they had uttered, tended to sedition, he sent them back to England. The heads of the party being removed, the opposition ceased.*

WHILST these things were doing in the colony, the company in England were projecting a much larger embarkation, and the transfer of the corporation itself, from Old England to New. Several gentlemen of figure and estate, Isaac Johnson, John Winthrop, Thomas Dudley, and divers others, who were dissatisfied with the arbitrary proceedings both in church and state, pleased themselves with the prospect of liberty in both, to be enjoyed in America, and proposed to the company at London to remove with their families; but upon this condition only, that the patent and charter should remove with them. This proposal was first communicated July the 28th, 1629. A committee was appointed to consider of it, and to advise with counsel learned in the law, and to make report. The adventurers had been at great expence, without any returns made to them, and had no rational prospect of any profit from the plantation in the way they were in. The principal objection seems to have arose, from a doubt whether such a transfer was legal. The report of the committee is not recorded. Mr. White,[1] a counsellor at law, was one of the company, and great stress was laid upon his opinion; and, on the 29th of August, it was determined, "by the general consent of the company, that the government and patent should be settled in New-England." [It is difficult to conceive any reasons in support of this opinion.] It is evident from the charter,

---

* They applied to the company, upon their arrival in England, for recompence for the damages they had sustained, and the matter was referred to Samuel Vassall, William Vassall, Simon Whetcomb and William Pynchon, chosen by the complainants, and John White, John Davenport, Isaac Johnson, and John Winthrop, chosen by the company. The letters which the Browns had sent over to their private friends, were stopped by the company in England, and opened and publickly read, to prevent any prejudice to the plantation. *Mass. Rec.* It does not appear, by the records, how the dispute was finally issued.

"It is a principle, that every religion which is persecuted, becomes itself persecuting; for assoon as, by some accidental turn, it arises from persecution, it attacks the religion which persecuted it," &c. *Spirit of Laws.*

---

[1] John White (1590–1645) did not emigrate to New England. He was elected a member of Parliament in 1640. "The first charter of the Massachusetts Colony was probably procured under his advice, and written by him." Lemuel Shattuck, "Memorials of the Whites," Massachusetts Historical Society *Collections*, Fourth Series, II, 217–220. In the records of the Company he appears as "Mr. Whyte, the Councellor," to differentiate him from "Mr. Whyte, the Preacher," who was the Reverend John White of Dorchester.

that the original design of it was to constitute a corporation in England, like to that of the East-India and other great companies, with powers to settle plantations within the limits of the territory, under such forms of government and magistracy as should be fit and necessary. The first step, in sending out Mr. Endicot, appointing him a council, giving him commission, instructions, &c. was agreeable to this construction of the charter.

IN consequence of this new resolution, the members of the corporation, which remained in England, were to retain a share, in the trading stock and the profits of it, for the term of seven years. The management of it was committed to five persons, who were going over, viz. J. Winthrop, Sir Richard Saltonstall, I. Johnson, T. Dudley, and J. Revel, and to five who were to remain, M. Cradock, N. Wright, T. Eaton, T. Goffe, and J. Young, and, at the expiration of the term, the stock, with the profits, was to be divided to each man, in proportion to his adventure. All other powers and privileges were to remain with the planters upon the spot. We have no account of any dividend ever made, nor indeed of any trade ever carried on for the company. There was another article; that one half the charge of fortifications and support of the ministers should be paid out of the joint stock, but no notice was taken of it in the colony.

THE 20th of October, at a general court of governor, deputy and assistants, and the generality, a new choice was made of governor, &c. consisting of such persons as had determined to go over with the patent. John Winthrop was elected governor, John Humfrey deputy governor, Sir Richard Saltonstall, Isaac Johnson, Thomas Dudley, John Endicot, Increase Nowell, William Vassall, William Pynchon, Samuel Sharp, Edward Rossiter, Thomas Sharp, John Revell, Mathew Cradock, Thomas Goffe, Samuel Aldersey, John Venn, Nathaniel Wright, Theophilus Eaton, and Thomas Adams, assistants.* They did not all go over. From time to time until the

---

* I have endeavoured to obtain as particular account, as can be now had, of the character and circumstances of the principal undertakers.

Mr. Winthrop, the governor, was of Groton in Suffolk, descended from reputable ancestors. One of them, Adam Winthrop, is said to have been an eminent lawyer, and also a great favourer of the gospel in the reign of Henry the eighth. Mr. Winthrop was a justice of peace at the age of eighteen, and very early in life was exemplary for his polite as well as grave and christian deportment. He had an estate of six or seven hundred pounds a year, which he turned into money, and embarked his all to promote the settlement of New-England. It is a very full evidence of the esteem he was in, that when many gentlemen of character, some of them of noble alliance, were concerned in the same undertaking with him, he, by a general voice, was placed at their head. He was eleven times chosen governor, and spent his whole estate in the public service, the stipend being small, and his hospitality great, and his bayliff unfaithful. His son and grandson were successively governors of Connecticut colony. His great grandson,

general embarkation, as any one declined, some other person was

John Winthrop, Esq; died in London about 12 or 14 years ago. He was known there by the name of Governor Winthrop, a Fellow of the Royal Society, and one volume of the Philosophical Transactions is dedicated to him. And his posterity have been ever since respected and honoured, both in Connecticut and in the Massachusets. Mr. Winthrop was about forty-three years of age when he removed.

Mr. Dudley's father, Capt. Roger Dudley, lost his life in the service of his country, leaving no other son. Mr. Dudley, early in life, engaged in the same service. In 1597, he raised a company of volunteers, received a captaincy from Queen Elizabeth, went over to France, and was at the siege of Amiens under Henry the fourth. After his return to England, he married a gentlewoman of good family and estate, and settled near North-ampton, in the neighbourhood of Mr. Dod, Hildersham, and other celebrated puritan ministers, was a devout attendant upon their ministry, and (although he had been an officer) became a sober non-conformist. Lord Say and Seal recommended him to the Earl of Northampton. The Earl when he came to his estate, found it encumbered and entangled; but putting his affairs under the care of Mr. Dudley, he, by his prudent management, very happily extricated them. After which, leaving the service of the Earl, he removed to Boston, where he became acquainted with Mr. Cotton. He was soon desired to return to the Earl's family, where he continued until he came to New-England. He was far advanced in life for such an undertaking, being fifty-four years of age. He was chosen into the magistracy every year of his life afterwards, four years governor, and often deputy governor. He married a second time in his old age, and had a new set of children; and it is very remarkable, that he was a captain in 1597, and in 1764 two of his grand children are living, viz. one elderly lady at New-London, in Connecticut colony, the widow of John Winthrop, Esq; great grandson of the first governor, and another at Newbury in the Massachusets, Mrs. Atkins.

Mr. Humphrey was early engaged. He was one of the six original patentees from the council of Plimouth. He was prevented from coming over with the charter. He married the Lady Susan, daughter to the Earl of Lincoln, and brought her, with their children, to New-England in 1632, and was immediately chosen an assistant. He settled at Saugus, now Lynn, about 12 miles from Boston. Ebenezer Burril, Esq; late of the council, lived on part of his farm. Upon an invitation from Lord Say he intended, in the year 1640, to have removed to the Bahama islands; but the island of Providence being taken by the Spaniards, he gave over that design. Soon after, having met with great losses by fire, and his estate being much impaired, he sold his plantation at Saugus to Lady Moody [Dowager of a Sir Henry Moody] and returned to England.

Sir Richard Saltonstall was the first named associate to the six original patentees. [His family was of Killingley Yorkshire in England, and flourished there several ages.] Al-though he remained but a short time in New-England, yet his heart was set upon pro-moting the colony. He sent over two of his sons, one of which was chosen into the magistracy and continued in it, except while he was absent in England, until after the year 1680. Sir Richard was son or grandson of Sir Richard Saltonstall, Lord Mayor of London in 1597. He lived many years after his return to England. I have seen his name among the commissioners for the trial of Lilburn, or some other offender against the state. By a will made in 1658, he gave a legacy to the college in New-England. His great grandson, Gurdon Saltonstall, was many years governor of Connecticut, and some of his posterity, in that colony and the Massachusets, are in esteem and honour to this day. Sir John Foche, a city knight in King William's reign, married his great grand daughter.

Mr. Johnson, in a will uncancelled, and which remains on the Massachusets files, executed April 28, in the 5th of King Charles the first, calls himself of Clipsham in the county of Rutland, son of Abraham Johnson, Esq; and grandson of Robert Johnson. Doctor Chaderton was his mother's father. He had much the largest estate of any of the undertakers. It lay in Rutland, Northamptonshire and Lincolnshire. He values his interest, at that time, in the New-England adventure, at six hundred pounds. He

chosen in his stead. First Roger Ludlow was chosen, instead of

had no children. After providing for his lady, he gave a great number of legacies to his friends, and to pious and charitable uses; his lands he gave to his father and brethren. To Mr. Cotton, from whom, to the praise of God's grace, he acknowledges to have received much help and comfort in his spiritual estate, he gave thirty pounds and a gown cloth. The advowson and right of patronage of the parish church of Clipsham, he gave to Mr. Dudley and Mr. Cotton. He limitted his funeral charges to 250 l. As providence ordered it, a small part of that sum sufficed. His heart was set on the New-England concern, and he ordered his executors to carry on his share or part in it. He made another will before his death, and appointed John Hampden, Esq; one of his executors, with Winthrop and Dudley. Upon his death-bed, he is said to have rejoiced that he had lived to see a church of Christ gathered in America, and professed that he thought his life better spent than in any other way. He was buried, at his own request, in part of the ground upon Trimontain or Boston, which he had chosen for his lot, the square between School-street and Queen-street. He may be said to have been the idol of the people, for they ordered their bodies, as they died, to be buried round him; and this was the reason of appropriating for a place of burial, what is now called the old burying-place, adjoining to King's chapel. He married the Lady Arabella, another daughter of the Earl of Lincoln.

Mr. Endicot, the next named, was among the most zealous undertakers, and the most rigid in principles, as will appear in the course of the history. This disposition distinguished him, more than his other mental accomplishments or his outward condition in life. I have seen a letter, from the Secretary of State in King Charles the second's time, wherein is this expression, "The King would take it well, if the people would leave out Mr. Endicot from the place of governor." Some of his posterity remain at or near Salem.

Mr. Nowell was nephew to Alexander Nowell, Dean of St. Paul's in Queen Elizabeth's reign, or else the Dean was his great uncle. He was a ruling elder, some time, of the church at Charlestown; but that place and a place in the civil order were thought, in that day, not well to consist, and therefore he quitted it, chusing the places of assistant and secretary. [Archbp Usher in a letter from London in 1613 to Dr Chaloner at Dublin says "Mr Therwood hath written to the Provost for (*in favour of*) one Increase Nowel of the age of 19 years, of good sufficiency in learning and religion; he looketh to have your furtherance also in his admitting." It is very probable this was the person.]

Mr. William Vassall, as well as his brother Samuel Vassall, were gentlemen of good circumstances in England, but do not seem to have been fully of the same sentiment in matters of religion with the planters in general; and altho' William came over with the first company, yet he soon went back to England. He returned a few years after to New-England, and settled at Scituate in Plimouth colony, not because they were reputed more rigid than the Massachusets people. When Jamaica was taken, by Cromwell, he laid the foundation of several fine estates there, enjoyed by his posterity to the present time.

Mr. Pynchon was a gentleman of learning as well as religion. He laid the foundation of Roxbury, but soon removed to Connecticut river, was the father of the town of Springfield, where his family hath flourished ever since.

Edward Rossiter was of a good family in the West of England. He died the first year. His son lived afterwards at Combe. His grandson Edward Rossiter, in the year 1682, was deacon of Mr. Joseph Alleine's church in Taunton. He says in a letter, dated March 28, 1682, that his grandfather, a pious gentleman of good estate, left England for the sake of religion.

Thomas Sharp and John Revell made but a short stay in New-England.

Mr. Eaton was an East country merchant. His father was a minister in Coventry. He did not come to New-England until 1637. And then settled New-Haven colony, of which he was governor all his life after. His correspondence, both with the governor

Samuel Sharp.* [1] Whilst they were at Southampton, (March 18) Sir Bryan Jansen, William Coddington and Simon Bradstreet,

of the Massachusets and with the Dutch governor of Manhadoes, or New-York, discover a good understanding and virtuous mind.

Mr. Coddington was of Lincolnshire, zealous to a great degree, was afterwards the father of Rhode Island colony, where his zeal abated, and he promoted a general toleration. He was many years their governor, and would gladly have joined in confederacy with the other colonies, but different sentiments upon religion prevented.

Mr. Bradstreet was of Emanuel College Cambridge, from whence he removed to the family of the Earl of Lincoln as his steward, and afterwards he lived in the same capacity with the Countess of Warwick. He married one of Mr. Dudley's daughters, and, after her death, a sister of Sir George Downing. He lived to be the Nestor of New-England, was born the beginning of the century in 1603, and wanted but three or four years of compleating it. I suppose Sir Simon Bradstreet and Dudley Bradstreet, of the kingdom of Ireland, are descended from him.

Mr. Venn, commonly called colonel Venn, was in the design from the beginning, and intended to have removed, but never did. Upon the change of affairs in England he made a figure there, being one of the members for the city in the long parliament, and among the most active in the opposition to the court, and was one of the King's judges.

Mr. Cradock was more forward in advancing out of his substance than any other, being generally the highest in all subscriptions. He was an eminent merchant in London, and continued, divers years, to carry on a trade in the colony by his servants, but he never came over. His son or grandson Samuel Cradock, was a dissenting minister at Wickambrook in 1690. George Cradock, Esq; now in publick posts in the colony, is descended from him.

I can give no account of the other assistants.

Sir William Brereton was one of the company, and seems to have been preparing to come over, but he found employment also in the long parliament and in the army, was at the head of the forces which reduced Chester. Several others, as Mr. Blackhouse, Mr. Whichcote, Captain Waller, Mr. Pocock, Mr. Harwood, and other persons of note, were of the company, and great promoters of the plantation. Lincolnshire contributed greatly, and more of our principal families derive their origin from thence than from any part of England, unless the city of London be an exception. The Countess of Warwick was a benefactor. In 1634, the general court voted, "that there should be letters of thankfulness signed by the court and sent to the Countess of Warwick, Mr. Paynter, Mr. Wood, and others that have been benefactors to this plantation." The Earl of Warwick, her son, was a patron of the colony, and was very able as well as willing to do kind offices to it as long as he lived. Some of the ministers were of families of distinction. Mr. Bulkley from Bedfordshire, of an honourable family there. Samuel Whiting, who was minister of Lynn, married a daughter of Oliver St. John. She came with him to New-England. John Shearman, minister of Watertown, married a grand daughter of Earl Rivers. Her father, Mr. Laume, was a gentleman of 1400 l. a year. She was alive in 1697, the mother of 20 children. [Vincent Potter came to Boston but returned to England and was one of the Kings Judges.]

* Samuel Sharp came over afterwards, and lived at Salem, but was never restored to the magistracy. *Mass. Rec.*

---

[1] Roger Ludlow (1590–?) was a brother-in-law of John Endicott. He was made Deputy-Governor in 1634 but was not re-elected in the following year. Displeased with the government of the Bay Colony, he moved to Windsor, Connecticut, and later to Fairfield. In Connecticut he was many times elected Deputy-Governor, and distinguished himself chiefly by codifying the laws in 1650. For various reasons he tired of his environment and in 1654 returned to England *via* Virginia. Cromwell placed him on the first Irish commission, 1654–58; it is believed that he died in Ireland between 1664 and 1668. See John M. Taylor, *Roger Ludlow, the Colonial Lawmaker.*

were chosen in the room of Mr. Wright, Eaton and Goffe, and yet Sir Bryan never came to New-England. Even after they had embarked, at a court on board the Arabella, Mr. Dudley was chosen deputy governor, in the room of Mr. Humfrey who staid behind. It is not matter of wonder that they discovered so great want of resolution. It is strange that so many persevered. It shews some little fortitude, in a man in health and vigour, who goes through the fatigues of a long voyage, and spends but a few months in a wilderness, among Savages, and in a climate more severe than he had ever experienced. What must we think, then, of persons of rank and good circumstances in life bidding a final adieu to all the conveniencies and delights of England, their native country, and exposing themselves, their wives and children, to inevitable hardships and sufferings, in a long voyage across the Atlantick, to land upon a most inhospitable shore, destitute of any kind of building to secure them from the inclemency of the weather, and of most sorts of food to which they had been always used at their former home? The sickness and mortality which prevailed the first winter, they did not foresee. It is an observation, since made, that most parts of America have proved unhealthy (except where the country is cleared) until persons have had a seasoning in it.

ELEVEN ships, which sailed from different ports in England, arrived in New-England before the end of July. Six more arrived before the end of the year. They brought above 1500 passengers. The Arabella,[1] on board which was the governor and several of the assistants, left Yarmouth between the 7th and 10th of April. On the 7th the governor, and divers others on board, signed a paper [2] directed to their brethren of the church of England, to remove suspicions or misconstructions, and to ask their prayers. This paper has occasioned a dispute, whether the first settlers of the Massachusets were of the church of England or not.* However problematical it may be, what they were while they remained in England, they left no room for doubt after they arrived in America. The Arabella

---

* [Mr. White after his friends had left England and before there could be any account of their arrival in America, published a vindication of them from several charges which had been brought against them one of which was seperation from the Church of England, and he addresses this paper as an evidence that they did not intend to seperate.]

---

[1] "This vessel had been appropriately renamed for Lady Arabella Johnson." Edward Channing, *History of the United States*, I, 330.

[2] See Appendix, No. I, of this volume.

arrived at Salem the 12th of June.* The common people immediately went ashore, and regaled themselves with strawberries, which are very fine in America, and were then in perfection. This might give them a favourable idea of the produce of the country, but the gentlemen met with enough to fill them with concern. The first news they had, was of a general conspiracy, a few months before, of all the Indians as far as Naraghanset, to extirpate the English. Eighty persons, out of about three hundred, had died in the colony the winter before, and many of those that remained were in a weak sickly condition. There was not corn enough to have lasted above a fortnight, and all other provisions were very scant. They were obliged to give all the servants,† they had sent over, their liberty, that they might shift for themselves, although they had cost from sixteen to twenty pounds a head. They had not above three or four months to look out proper places for settlements, and to provide shelter against the severity of the winter. With this prospect of difficulties, great enough for them to encounter, sickness began among them. Being destitute of necessary accommodations, they dropped away one after another. Among others, the lady Arabella, who, to use Mr. Hubbard's words, "came from a paradise of plenty and pleasure, in the family of a noble Earl, into a wilderness of wants, and although celebrated for her many virtues, yet was not able to encounter the adversity she was surrounded with, and in about a month after her arrival she ended her days at Salem where she first landed." Mr. Johnson, her husband, highly esteemed for his piety and wisdom, overcome with grief, survived her a short time only, and died at Boston the 30th September, to the great loss of the colony. Mr. Rossiter, another of the assistants, died soon after. Before December they had lost two hundred of their number, including a few who died upon their passage.

THE governor and some of the principal persons left Salem the 17th of June, and travelled through the woods to Charlestown, about 20 miles, to look out for a convenient place for their chief town, which they had determined should be in some part of the bay or harbour between Nantasket and Cambridge. At first, they pitched upon the north side of Charles river, or rather northwest, by the major voice; but a number of the principal gentlemen having fixed their cottages (shelters intended for one winter only) upon the opposite side of the river, the governor and most of the assistants

* Masconomco, the Sagamore of Cape-Ann, came on board the next morning after the governor's arrival to bid him welcome. *Hub.*

† The whole number sent over was 180. This was a heavy loss.

removed to them in November. They were, however, undetermined where to build in the spring. A fortified town, at least palisadoed, was thought necessary to defend them against the natives, and they could not agree upon the most convenient place for that purpose.

THEY found, when they arrived, a few families scattered about in several parts of the bay. Mr. Maverick,[1] who will often appear in the course of this history, lived upon Noddle's island, a grant or confirmation of which he afterwards obtained from the court. He had built a small fort, and had four cannon mounted there. At a point upon Shawmut or Trimontaine, since Boston,* lived Mr. Blaxton,[2] who had left England, being dissatisfied there, and not a thorough conformist; but he was more dissatisfied with the non-conformity of the new-comers. He told them, he came from England because he did not like the Lords Bishops, but he could not join with them because he did not like the Lords Brethren. He claimed the whole peninsula upon which Boston is built, because he was the first that slept upon it. He had a grant of a very handsome lot there at the west part of the town, but he chose to quit all and removed to the southward, at or near what is since called Providence,† where he lived to old age. There were also several families at Mattapan, since called Dorchester, or rather Dorchester

---

* Said to be called so from respect to Mr. Cotton, minister of Boston in England, who they expected to follow them.

† One Mr. Blakestone, a minister, went from Boston, having lived there 9 or 10 years, because he would not join with the church. He lives near Mr. Williams,[3] but is far from his opinion. *Lechford.*[4]

---

[1] Samuel Maverick (*c.* 1602–*c.* 1670) may have been a son of the Rev. John Maverick mentioned on the following page, but Savage considers this attribution "against all probability." First and last he made much trouble for the rulers of the Bay Colony, and they for him. He came to New England in 1624, according to his own statement (*New England Historical and Genealogical Register*, XXXIX, 46); Charles Francis Adams endeavored to prove that Maverick and Blackstone were remnants of the Wessagusset (Weymouth) colony of 1623. Massachusetts Historical Society *Proceedings*, XVI, 194–206.

[2] William Blaxton, or Blackstone (1595–1675), "was bred at Emanuel, often called the Puritan College, Cambridge, where had his degrees 1617, and 1621, and was probably ordained in England but had no known cure, came in unknown ship at uncertain time, for undiscovered cause, and sat down, alone, on the peninsula, now the chief part of Boston, where he continued some four or five years after the arrival of the Governor and company and was admitted freeman 18 May 1631, having requested that benefit in October preceding." James Savage, *Genealogical Dictionary*, I, 198.

[3] Presumably Roger Williams.

[4] Thomas Lechford, *Plain Dealing: or Newes from New-England* (London, 1642). Lechford was "a lawyer from one of the Inns of Court at London." He came to Boston in 1637, and "left here after vain attempt to earn bread" in 1641. His book is an unsympathetic view of the New England he knew.

neck; here * Mr. Ludlow and Mr. Rossiter pitched, with two ministers, Mr. Warham [1] and Mr. Maverick.[2] On the north of Charles river (Charlestown) were the remains of those who had moved the last year from Salem; here Mr. Nowell and some of his friends made their pitch, but considered themselves and Boston, at first, as but one settlement and one church, with Mr. Wilson [3] for their minister. When he went to England in the spring, Charlestown became a distinct church and town, and took Mr. James [4] for their minister. Sir Richard Saltonstall chose a place some miles up Charles river, which has taken the name of Watertown. His company took Mr. Phillips [5] for their minister. Mr. Pynchon was at the head of another company who settled between Dorchester and Boston. Their town took the name of Roxbury. They had Mr. Elliot † [6] for their minister. Medford and Mistick were then distinct places, tho' not so at present. At Medford,‡ which I take to have been a small village at the lower part of Mistick river, now called Neck of Land, where

* They arrived at Nantasket, the 30th of May, from Plymouth in England.
† He did not come over until 1631. Mr. Weld was his colleague.
‡ *Wood.*[7]

---

[1] John Warham had been a minister at Exeter, England. From Dorchester he moved to Windsor, Connecticut, in 1635, and died there in 1670. See *Memoirs of Captain Roger Clap*.

[2] John Maverick died February 3, 1636. "He was a man of a very humble spirit, and faithful in furthering the work of the Lord here, both in the churches and civil state." John Winthrop, *History of New England*.

[3] John Wilson (1588–1667) was educated at Eton and at Christ's College, Cambridge. Though he "went to England" at this time (April 1631), he returned in 1632. There is a memoir of him in Cotton Mather's *Magnalia*, Book III, but the outline of his life in Savage's *Genealogical Dictionary* is probably more reliable.

[4] Thomas James was educated at Emmanuel College, Cambridge. "Being a very melancholick man, and full of causeless jealousies," he got into difficulty with his flock and was dismissed in 1636. After a few years he went to New Haven. Hubbard says he ultimately returned to England and was minister at Needham, in Suffolk. *History of New England*, p. 191.

[5] George Phillips (1593–1644) was the ancestor of the distinguished Massachusetts family which bears his name. He was a graduate of Gonville and Caius College, Cambridge. Before coming to America he "had been minister of the gospel at Bocksted, in Essex." Hubbard, *History of New England*, p. 133. There is an excellent paper on Phillips by Henry Wilder Foote in the Massachusetts Historical Society *Proceedings*, LXIII, 193–227.

[6] John Eliot (1603–1690) was a graduate of Cambridge, Jesus College He came to Boston in November, 1631, preached there in the absence of the Rev. John Wilson, and a year later was established as teacher (minister) of the church at Roxbury. He is remembered chiefly for his philanthropic work among the Indians. His translation of the Bible into the Indian language was a notable achievement. Convers Francis, *Life of John Eliot* is in Sparks's *Library of American Biography*, First Series, vol. V. See also Samuel Eliot Morison's excellent study in his *Builders of the Bay Colony*, chapter X.

[7] William Wood, *New-England's Prospect*.

a creek also ran into Charles river, it was intended a settlement should be made for Mr. Cradock and the people he was sending and had sent over. Here, by his agents, he built several vessels of burden. At these several places, together with Salem, the whole company were settled for the first winter. They had little time enough to provide their huts. As soon as December came, their out-door work was over. On the 6th of December, the governor and assistants met, and agreed to fortify the neck between Boston and Roxbury, and orders were given for preparing the materials; but at another meeting, on the 21st, they laid that design aside, and agreed on a place * about three miles above Charlestown, and most of them engaged to build houses there the next year. The weather held tolerable until the 24th of December, but the cold then came on with violence. Such a Christmas eve they had never seen before. From that time, to the 10th of February, their chief care was to keep themselves warm, and as comfortable in other respects as their scant provisions would permit. The poorer sort were much exposed, lying in tents and miserable hovels, and many died of the scurvy and other distempers. They were so short of provisions, that many were obliged to live upon clams, mussels and other shell-fish, with ground-nuts and acorns instead of bread. One, that came to the governor's house to complain of his sufferings, was prevented, being informed that, even there, the last batch was in the oven. Some instances are mentioned of great calmness and resignation in this distress. A good man, who had asked his neighbour to a dish of clams, after dinner returned thanks to God who had given them to suck of the abundance of the seas and of treasure hid in the sands.† They had appointed the 22d of February for a fast, but on the 5th, to their great joy, the ship Lyon, Capt. Pierce, one of the last year's fleet, returned laden with provisions from England, which were distributed according to the necessities of the people. They turned their fast into a thanksgiving.

In the spring of 1631, they pursued their design of a fortified town at Newtown. The governor set up the frame of a house; the deputy governor finished his house and removed his family. About this time, Chicketawbut, the chief of the Indians near Boston, came to visit the governor and made high professions of friendship. The apprehensions of danger lessened by degrees, the design of a forti-

---

* First called Newtown, since Cambridge.

† [Alluding to the clams which ly buried in the sands. Clams are not common in England. I have seen them at Manning Wee. Upon enquiry I was informed at the Inn that poor people sometimes digged them up for food.]

fied town went off in the same proportion, until it was wholly laid aside. The governor took down his frame and carried it to Boston. Mr. Dudley, the deputy, was offended, and persisted for some time in his first determination of residing at Newtown, but at length removed to Roxbury.

THIS scheme, of a fortified town, was well enough while they were uncertain what the temper of the natives would be. Their design was to make improvements, and to extend their settlements in the several parts of the country. Unless they were upon such terms with the Indians, that they could do this with safety, the colony could not long subsist. If they were upon such terms, fortified towns were unnecessary.*

THE high price of provisions, this year in England, impoverished the colony. Every bushel of wheat meal cost, including the freight, 14 s. sterling; every bushel of pease 10 s. and Indian corn, imported from Virginia, sold at 10 s.† Some were discouraged and returned to England, viz. Sir Richard Saltonstall, Thomas Sharpe, &c. and never came back; but others, in hopes of better times, went over to fetch their families and returned with them, viz. Mr. Wilson, Coddington,‡ &c. They went in the Lyon, which brought their supply. In the same ship, Sir Christopher Gardner [1] was sent home under confinement. He was a knight of the sepulchre, but concealed his true character, and came over last year under pretence of separating himself from the world, and living a life of retirement and devotion.

---

* Mr. Dudley says, they laid aside all thought of a fort, because upon any invasion when they should retire to it, they must necessarily lose their houses. *Letter to Countess of Lincoln.* There was the same objection to a fortified town, if the inhabitants of other towns and villages should retire to it.

† It was the year 1633, before they knew they should be able to raise English grain, if we may credit Johnson.[2] "This year, a small glean of rye was brought to the court, as the first fruits of English grain, at which, this poor people greatly rejoiced to see the land would bear it." *Johnson* 1633.

‡ The following paragraph, in a letter to Mr. Cotton from Mr. Coddington, London June 4, 1632, shews with what zeal he had embarked in this undertaking. "I am, I thank God, in bodily health, yet not enjoying that freedom of spirit, being withheld from that place which my soul desireth and my heart earnestly worketh after; neither, I think, shall I see it till towards the next spring, my wife being with child, and all her friends unwilling she should go in that condition."

---

[1] In his monograph, *Sir Christopher Gardiner, Knight*, Charles Francis Adams points out that Hutchinson is in error when he states that Gardiner was sent off in the *Lyon*. "Gardiner had no occasion to complain against us, for he was kindly used, and dismissed in peace, professing much engagement for the great courtesy he found here." John Winthrop, *History of New England* (1853), II, 232.

[2] Edward Johnson in his *History of New-England,* which is more often referred to as *Wonder-working Providence of Sions Saviour in New England.*

He offered to join to several of the churches, but he was suspected to be an immoral man, and not received. He had a comely young woman, who travelled with him. He called her his cousin. For some miscarriages in the Massachusets, he fled to the Indians. They carried him to Plimouth, having first used him pretty roughly From thence he was sent to Boston. He joined afterwards, with Gorges, Mason and others, in complaints against the colony.

Mr. Wilson left the church on the south side of the river without a minister. At his parting he recommended them to the care of the governor, deputy-governor and other godly and able christians, to carry on the worship of God, on the Lord's day, by prophesying until his return.

So much of their attention was necessary in order to provide for their support, that little business was done by the assistants or by the general court. The removal of the charter made many new regulations necessary, which were settled by degrees. The first court of assistants was at Charlestown, Aug. 23d, about two months after their arrival. A beadle, a corporation officer, was appointed. It was then ordered, that the governor and deputy for the time being, should be justices of the peace, four of the then assistants were also appointed justices. All justices whatsoever were to have the same power, for reformation of abuses and punishing offenders, which justices have in England, but no corporal punishment to be inflicted except by an assistant. In high offences, the governor and assistants sat as a court, as well as in civil matters. There was a trial by a jury this year for murder, and the person charged was acquitted. The first general court was held the 19th of October, not by a representative, but by every one, that was free of the corporation, in person. None had been admitted freemen since they left England. The governor and assistants had a great influence over the court. It was ordered, that, for the future, the freemen should chuse the assistants, and the assistants, from among themselves, chuse the governor and deputy governor. The court of assistants were to have the power of making laws and appointing officers. This was a departure from their charter. One hundred and nine freemen were admitted at this court. Maverick, Blackstone, and many more who were not of any of the churches, were of this number. This was all that was transacted, that was any thing material, the first year. The next general court was the court of election for 1631. The scale was now turned, and the freemen resolved to chuse both governor, deputy and assistants, notwithstanding the former vote, and made an order, that, for the time to come, none should be admitted to the freedom of the body politick but such as were church members.*

THIS was a most extraordinary order or law, and yet it continued in force until the dissolution of the government, it being repealed, in appearance only,† after the restoration of King Charles the second. Had they been deprived of their civil privileges in England by an act of parliament, unless they would join in communion with the churches there, it might very well have been the first in the roll of grievances. But such were the requisites to qualify for church membership here, that the grievance was abundantly greater.

THE scarcity of the former year excited the inhabitants to make the greater improvements, by tillage, as soon as the spring advanced, and it pleased God to give them such favourable seasons, that they had a very plentiful harvest; and Indian corn,‡ which could not be purchased with money the year before, at the end of this year was made a tender in discharge of all debts, except money or beaver had been specially agreed for. Cattle were extremely dear, a great part of what had been shipped from England being dead, and a milch cow was valued at 25 to 30 l. sterling.

THE same governor and deputy governor and such of the assistants of 1630, as were living and in the colony, were re-elected for the year 1631.§ They continued to make the same choice for 1632, with the addition of Mr. John Humfrey, who had been deputy governor in England, but was prevented coming the first year, and John Winthrop, jun. the governor's eldest son, who, with his wife, mother, and some others of the family, arrived in October the year before. [The Governor and Assistants made a levy this year upon the inhabitants to defray Publick charges. At Watertown they had

---

* None may now be a freeman of that company, unless he be a church member among them. None have voice in elections of governor, deputy and assistants, none are to be magistrates, officers or jurymen, grand or petit, but freemen. The ministers give their votes in all elections of magistrates. Now the most of the persons at New-England are not admitted of their church, and therefore are not freemen; and when they come to be tried there, be it for life or limb, name or estate, or whatsoever, they must be tried and judged too by those of the church who are, in a sort, their adversaries. How equal that hath been or may be, some by experience do know, others may judge. *Lechford.*

† The minister was to certify, that the candidates for freedom were of orthodox principles and of good lives and conversations.

‡ This however was mean diet, and distasteful to Europeans in general. "The want of English grain, wheat, barley and rye, proved a sore affliction to some stomachs who could not live upon Indian bread and water, yet were they compelled to it." *Johnson.*

§ *Hubbard.* This year, and this only, the assistants chosen are not named in the colony records.

a ruling Elder Richard Browne who had given them trouble in
church affairs, but being overruled in them, he attempted civil disturbance and succeeded there, for the town of Watertown refused
payment of their proportion of the tax alledging that the Governor
and Assistants were like the Mayor and Aldermen of a corporation
in England and had no power to make laws or raise taxes without
the people. The delinquents were called before the Governor and
told that as the Gov[ernor] and Assistants were chosen by the people
annually they were rather of the nature of a Parliament and Watertown submitted, but divers persons of other towns made their objections and a day was set for their compliance or otherwise to appear and answer for their neglect. They all except one complied
before the day came, and he after a censure complied also.]* They
were frequently alarmed this year † by the Indians, which put them
into confusion; happy for them, that in this their feeble infant state
they were only alarmed. A company of Eastern Indians called
Tarretines, about an hundred in number, assaulted the wigwams of
the Sagamore of Agawam.‡ They came by water in 30 canoes, slew
seven Indians and wounded two Sagamores who lived near Boston,
and carried away captives one of their wives with divers other Indians. The governor likewise received advice from the governor of
Plimouth of a broil between some English of that colony and some
of the Naraganset Indians, who set upon the English house at
Sowam; § also of motions made by the Pequods, which caused the
Dutch governor of Manhadoes to give notice to the English to be
upon their guard. A shallop belonging to Dorchester having been
missing all the winter, it appeared, this summer, that the crew, consisting of five men, had been secretly murdered by the Eastern Indians. However, the Sagamores, near Boston, made professions of
friendship, and on the 5th of August this year, Miantinomo, one of
the great Sachems of the Naragansets, the most numerous of all the
Indians between Boston and Hudson's river, came down to Boston,
whether out of fear or love they could not tell, to enter into a league
of friendship with the colony. He and his followers were invited to
attend the public worship, but three of them withdrew in sermon
time, and to satisfy their hunger, broke into an English house to get
victuals. The Sagamore, who was a very high spirited fellow, could

---

* [*Hubbard.*]

† There was an alarm in 1631 at Saugus or Lynn. Lieut. Walker, then upon the
watch, was shot through his cloaths by two arrows, but by an immediate discharge of
a culverin it was supposed the Indians withdrew. *Johnson*, &c.

‡ Ipswich.   § In part of what is now Bristol.

hardly be persuaded to order them any corporal punishment; but he was so ashamed of his attendants, that he ordered them out of town, and followed them himself soon after.

THE French also occasioned some uneasy apprehensions. They had been drove from Accady by Sir Samuel Argall in 1613. The people of New-Plimouth had set up a trading house, at Penobscot,[1] about the year 1627. Intelligence was brought this year to the Massachusets, that in 1630 or 1631 Sir William Alexander had sold the country of Nova-Scotia to the French, and that the fort, with all the ammunition and stores, was delivered to them; that Cardinal Richlieu had ordered some companies there, and that more were expected the next year with priests, Jesuits, &c. This news alarmed the governor and council, and put them upon consultations for their defence. They determined to finish a fort which was begun at Boston, to build another at Nantasket, and to hasten the settlement of Agawam (Ipswich,) it being one of the best places both for pasture and tillage, lest an enemy should take possession and prevent them. Mr. Winthrop, the governor's son, was accordingly sent to begin a plantation there.* It appears that their apprehensions of the French designs, to take possession of some part or other of the coast, were not ill founded; for they sent a ship, this year, to Penobscot, as a

---

* The Tarrateen, or Eastern Indians, who had a spight against the Indians of Agawam, and had attacked them and drove them from their settlement, intended mischief against the English also, as appears by the following account, preserved among the papers of Mr. Cobbett, the minister of Agawam or Ipswich:

"At the first planting of Ipswich, as a credible man informed me, namely Quartermaster Perkins, the Tarrateens or Easterly Indians had a design to have cut them off at the first, when they had but between 20 and 30 men, old and young, belonging to the place; and, at that instant, most of them gone into the bay about their occasions, not hearing of any intimations thereof. It was thus: One Robin, a friendly Indian, came to this John Perkins, then a young man, living then in a little hut upon his father's island on this side of Jeoffry's neck, and told him, on such a Thursday morning, early, there would come four Indians, to draw him to go down the hill to the water side, to truck with them, which, if he did, he and all near him would be cut off, for there were 40 birchin canoes would lie out of sight at the brow of the hill, full of armed Indians for that purpose. Of this he forthwith acquainted Mr. John Winthrop, who then lived there in a house near the water, who advised him, if such Indians came, to carry it ruggedly towards them, and threaten to shoot them if they would not be gone, and when their backs were turned, to strike up a drum he had with him besides his two muskets, and then discharge them, that so 6 or 8 young men, who were in the marshes hard by a mowing, keeping their guns ready charged by them, might take the alarm, and the Indians would perceive their plot was discovered and haste away to sea again; which accordingly was so acted and took like effect, for he told me, he presently after discerned 40 such canoes shove off from under the hill and make as fast as they could to sea."

---

[1] Palfrey defines "Penobscot" as Point Bagaduce (Castine). John Gorham Palfrey, *History of New England* (1858), I, 338, note 1.

prelude to what was to come after. Governor Bradford of Plimouth gives this account of it.

This year the house at Penobscot is robbed by the French in this manner: While the master of the house, and part of the company with him, is come with one vessel to the westward to fetch a supply of goods brought over for us, a small French vessel, having a false Scot aboard, goes into the harbour, pretends they are newly come from sea, knows not where they are, that the vessel is very leaky, and desires they may haul her ashore and stop her leaks, making many French complements and congées: And seeing but three or four simple men, who are servants, and, by the Scotchman, understanding the master and the rest of the company are gone from home, fall to commending the guns and muskets which lie on the racks by the wall side, take them down to look on them, asking if they were charged, and when possessed of them, one presents a loaded piece against the servants, another a pistol, they bid them not to stir but deliver the goods, and made them help in carrying them all aboard, to the value of four or five hundred pounds sterling, prime cost; three hundred weight of beaver, the rest in trading goods, as coats, rugs, blankets, &c. then set the servants at liberty and go away with this taunting message, Tell your master, when he returns, that some of the Isle of Rhée gentlemen have been here.

It appears that the Massachusets people took possession of the country at a very critical time. Richlieu, in all probability, would have planted his colony nearer the sun, if he could have found any place vacant. De Monts and company had acquired a thorough knowledge of all the coast from Cape Sables beyond Cape Cod in 1604; indeed it does not appear that they then went round or to the bottom of Massachusets bay. Had they once gained footing there, they would have prevented the English. The frenchified court of King Charles the first would, at the treaty of Saint Germains, have given up any claim to Massachusets bay as readily as they did to Acadie; for the French could make out no better title to Penobscot, and the other parts of Acadie, than they could to Massachusets. The little plantation at New-Plimouth would have been no greater bar to the French in one place than in the other. The Dutch, the next year, would have quietly possessed themselves of Connecticut river, unless the French, instead of the English, had prevented them. Whether the people of either nation would have persevered is uncertain. If they had done it, the late contest for the dominion of North America [1] would have been between France and Holland, and the commerce of England would have borne a very

---

[1] The Seven Years' War, 1756–1763.

different proportion to that of the rest of Europe from what it does at present.

THE new settlers were in perils also from their own countrymen. Sir Ferdinando Gorges and Capt. Mason, two of the council of Plimouth, who with a view to the advancement of their fortunes, had expended large sums to little purpose in attempts to settle colonies in New-England, beheld the Massachusets with an envious eye. They intended, for themselves, all that part of the colony which lies to the Eastward of Naumkeag. Gardiner and Morton,* to revenge the affronts they had received, joined with them in a complaint to the King in council against the colony. At this time they failed of success, and an order was made in council 19th of January 1632,

* Morton wrote the following letter to one Jeffries in New-England: "My very good gossip! If I should commend myself to you, you would reply with this proverb, *propria laus sordet in ore*, but to leave impertinent salutes and really proceed, you shall hereby understand, that altho' when I was first sent to England, to make complaint against Ananias and the brethren, I effected the business but superficially (thro' the brevity of time) I have at this time taken deliberation, and brought the matter to a better pass, and it is brought about, that the King hath taken the matter into his own hands. The Massachusets patent, by an order of council, was brought in view, the privileges therein granted well scanned, and at the council board, in presence of Sir R. Saltonstall and the rest, it was declared, for manifold abuses therein discovered, to be void. The King hath re-assumed the whole business into his own hands, and given order, for a general governor for the whole territory, to be sent over. The commission is passed the privy seal, I saw it, and the same was sent to my Lord Keeper, to have it pass the great seal, and I now stay to return with the governor, by whom all complainants shall have relief. So that now, Jonas being set ashore, may safely cry, Repent ye cruel schismaticks, repent, there are yet but 40 days. If Jove vouchsafe to thunder, the charter and the kingdom of the separatists will fall asunder. — My lord of Canterbury, with my lord privy seal, having caused all Mr. Cradock's letters to be viewed and his apology for the brethren particularly heard, protested against him and Mr. Humfries that they were a couple of imposturous knaves, so that, for all their great friends, they departed the council chamber in our view with a pair of cold shoulders. I have staid long, yet have not lost my labour. The brethren have found themselves frustrated, and I shall see my desire upon mine enemies. —— Of these things I thought good, by so convenient a messenger, to give you notice, lest you should think I died in obscurity, as the brethren vainly intended I should. As for Ratcliffe, he was comforted by their lordships with the cropping of Mr. Winthrop's ears, which shews what opinion is held, amongst them, of king Winthrop with all his inventions and his Amsterdam and fantastical ordinances, his preachings, marriages and other abusive ceremonies, which exemplify his detestation of the church of England, and contempt of his Majesty's authority and wholsome laws. I rest your loving friend,

May 1, 1634.   Thomas Morton."

Morton came to New-England again, in 1643, when this letter and a book he had wrote, full of invectives, were produced against him. He was truly called the accuser of the brethren. [He came first to New Haven and bro't letters from the Earl of Carlisle and Mr. Rigby which did not protect him. He went from thence to Boston where] the court fined him 100 l. He was poor and unable to pay it. Nothing but his age saved him from the whipping-post. He went to Acamenticus,[1] and there died a year or two after.

---

[1] Acamenticus became York, Maine.

declaring the fair appearances and great hopes which there then were, that the country would prove beneficial to the kingdom, as well as profitable to the particular persons concerned; and that the adventurers might be assured, that if things should be carried on as was pretended when the patents were granted and according as by the patent is appointed, his Majesty would not only maintain the liberties and privileges heretofore granted, but supply any thing further which might tend to the good government, prosperity and comfort of the people there.*

In the year 1633, the people still continued the administration of government in the same hands. Fresh supplies of inhabitants had been brought from England, from time to time, in the course of the two former years, but there were many who were willing to see the success of the first adventurers before they embarked themselves. The reports carried over were very encouraging, so that, this year, there was a very great addition made, ships arriving all summer, in some months twelve or fourteen in a month; an exportation so great and of such sort of persons, that it produced the following order of the King in Council, 21st February 1633.

Whereas the board is given to understand of the frequent transportation, of great numbers of his Majesty's subjects out of this kingdom, to the plantation of New-England, among whom divers persons known to be ill affected, discontented not only with civil but ecclesiastical government here, are observed to resort thither, whereby such confusion and distraction is already grown there, especially in point of religion, as, beside the ruin of the said plantation, cannot but highly tend to the scandal both of church and state here. And whereas it was informed in particular, that there are, at this present, divers ships, in the river of Thames, ready to set sail thither, freighted with passengers and provisions; it is thought fit and ordered, that stay should be forthwith made of the said ships until further order from this board. And the several masters and freighters of the same should attend the board, on Wednesday next in the afternoon, with a list of the passengers and provisions in each ship. And that Mr. Cradock, a chief adventurer in that plantation now present before the board, should be required to cause the letters patent for the said plantation to be brought to this board.†

Mr. Hubbard says, that this order was the effect of a new complaint preferred by Gardiner, Morton and others, of their hardships and sufferings from the severity of the government, and that such of the company as were in England were called before the committee of council, and delivered an answer in writing, and that, upon reading thereof, it pleased God so to work with the Lords of the council

* Hubbard.   † Hubbard.

and afterwards with the King's Majesty, that when the whole matter was reported to him by Sir Thomas Jermayne (one of the council who had been present at the three days of hearing, and spake much in commendation of the governor, both to the Lords and after to his Majesty) the King said, he would have such severely punished as should abuse his governor and the plantation, and the defendants were dismissed, with a favourable order for their encouragement; being assured, from some of the council, that his Majesty did not intend to impose the ceremonies of the church of England upon them, for that it was considered, it was for the sake of freedom from those things that people went over thither. It is certain, a stop was not put to the emigration. There came over, amongst many others in this year 1633, Mr. Haynes [1] of the civil order, Mr. Cotton,* [2] Mr Hooker, [3] and Mr. Stone, [4] three of the most famous men of the religious order. Mr Cotton is supposed to have been more instru-

---

* Mr. Cotton's removal was hastened by letters missive, which were out against him to convent him before the high commission court for nonconformity. His friends advised him to keep close, until he had an opportunity of embarking. *MS. letter Sam. Whiting.*

---

[1] John Haynes (d. 1654), the third Governor of Massachusetts-Bay and the first Governor of Connecticut. He was "a gentleman of easy fortune" and a native of the county of Essex, in England, where he possessed an elegant seat called Copford Hall. He came to New England in the *Griffin* in the summer of 1634 in company with John Cotton, Richard Hooker, and Samuel Stone. He was Governor of the colony in 1635-36. In 1637 he migrated to Hartford, Connecticut, where he became Governor of the new colony in 1640. Among other activities he was instrumental in bringing about the New England Confederation in 1643. There is a biographical sketch of him in Jacob Bailey Moore, *Memoirs of American Governors*, I, 297-312.

[2] John Cotton (1585-1652) arrived in the *Griffin*, Sept. 4, 1633. He was a graduate of Cambridge and preached at Boston, Lincolnshire, for twenty-one years before coming to New England. Savage calls him "the most distinguished divine that came from England in the first age." A *Life of John Cotton* by A. W. M'Clure (Boston, 1846) appears to be the most comprehensive account of his career.

[3] Thomas Hooker (1586?-1647) was a graduate of Cambridge, Emmanuel College. In England his Puritanism brought him into disfavor with Archbishop Laud and he found it prudent to withdraw to the Netherlands. Thence he came to New England in 1633. Soon after his arrival he was chosen pastor of the church at Newtown (Cambridge). In June 1636 Hooker and the greater part of his flock moved to Hartford, Connecticut. The best account of his life is in George Leon Walker, *History of the First Church in Hartford.*

There are at least two biographies of Hooker: Edward William Hooker, *Life of Thomas Hooker* (1849), and George Leon Walker, *Thomas Hooker* (1891).

[4] Samuel Stone (1602-1663) was born in Hertford, England, and Hartford, Connecticut, was named for his birthplace. He graduated from Cambridge, Emmanuel College, in 1623 and was a Puritan lecturer before coming to New England in 1633. At Newtown (Cambridge, Massachusetts) he was chosen teacher in the church of which Thomas Hooker was pastor. When the majority of the community migrated to the Connecticut River, Stone accompanied it. In 1637 he took part in the Pequot War.

mental, in the settlement of their civil as well as ecclesiastical polity, than any other person: The church of Boston, by advice of the governor and council and of the elders in the colony, received him for their teacher; to which office he was ordained the 17th October. Mr. Thomas Leverett,[1] an ancient member of Mr. Cotton's church in England, was at the same time ordained a ruling elder. The circumstances and order of proceeding, in Mr. Cotton's ordination, were intended as a precedent, and the congregational churches in New-England have generally conformed thereto ever since. Mr. Hooker and Mr. Stone, with their friends, settled at Newtown (Cambridge.*)

* In the year 1633, the small pox made terrible havock among the Indians of Massachusets. Whether or no their food and irregular diet furnishes greater quantities of the morbific matter, than in more temperate persons, I leave to physicians. They were destitute of every thing, proper for comfort and relief, and died in greater proportion than is known among the English. John Sagamore of Winesimet, and James of Lynn, with almost all their people, died of the distemper. All writers agree, that, a few years before the English came to New-Plimouth, a mortal contagious distemper swept away great numbers of Indians, so that some tribes were in a manner extinct; the Massachusets, particularly, are said by some to have been reduced from thirty thousand to three hundred fighting men. The small pox proving since so fatal to Indians, caused some to suppose that to have been the distemper, but the Indians themselves always gave a very different account, and, by their description, it was a pestilential putrid fever. In one of the voyages, collected by Purchas, it is said to have been the plague, and that some of the Indians which recovered shewed the scars of the boil. An instance of mortality among the Indians of Nantucket, in the year 1763, strengthens the probability of their account of the distemper itself and of the amazing effects of it.

In the beginning of October there were belonging to the island of Nantucket about 320 Indians, of every age and sex, in 90 families. A fever then began among them, and, before the end of January, between 260 and 270 persons had been seized with it, of which number 6 men and 9 women only recovered, and but 15 families and about 85 souls remained, 15 of which had wintered in the straits of Belleisle and escaped the distemper. A physician of note supposed this mortality to be occasioned by a dearth among the Indians the two preceding years, so that they had but little corn or any other farinaceous food, and this year had been some months without, which caused them to fall upon their pompions, squoshes, &c.[2] before they were ripe; and this food brought their blood into a putrid and broken state. It is remarkable, that the English inhabitants were free from the distemper, and not one person died of it. The infection was supposed, by some, to be taken from an Irish brigantine; but Mr. Timothy Folger,[3] a sensible gentleman of the island, from whom I received the foregoing account, assured me there was no room to suppose so, or that it came from abroad.

Our ancestors supposed an immediate interposition of providence in the great mor-

---

[1] Thomas Leverett (d. 1650) was an alderman of Boston, Lincolnshire, before he came to New England. Soon after his arrival in Boston, Massachusetts, he was chosen an elder of the church and a selectman. There is a good notice of Leverett and his family by Dr. Nathaniel B. Shurtleff in *New England Historical and Genealogical Register*, IV, 121-136.

[2] In the third edition, "pumpkins, squashes, &c."

[3] Timothy Folger (b. 1706) was a cousin of Benjamin Franklin. Franklin's mother was Abiah Folger.

In the year 1634, they thought proper to give their governor some respite, Mr. Dudley being chosen in his stead, and Roger Ludlow deputy governor.

Mr. Haynes, who had lately come over, was chosen to the place of assistant. The governor and assistants kept the powers of government, both legislative and executive, very much in their hands the three first years. The people began to grow uneasy, and the number of freemen being greatly multiplied, an alteration of the constitution seems to have been agreed upon or fallen into by a general consent of the towns; for at a general court for elections in 1634, twenty four of the principal inhabitants appeared as the representatives of the body of freemen, and, before they proceeded to the election of magistrates, the people asserted their right to a greater share in the government than had hitherto been allowed them, and resolved,

That none but the general court had power to make and establish laws, or to elect and appoint officers, as governor, deputy governor, assistants, treasurer, secretary, captains, lieutenants, ensigns, or any of like moment, or to remove such upon misdemeanour, or to set out the duties and powers of these officers —— That none but the general court hath power to raise monies and taxes, and to dispose of lands, viz. to give and confirm proprieties.

After these resolutions, they proceeded to the election of magistrates. Then they further determined,

That there shall be four general courts held yearly, to be summoned by the governor for the time being, and not to be dissolved without the consent of the major part of the court —— That it shall be lawful for the freemen of each plantation to chuse two or three before every general court, to confer of and prepare such business as by them shall be thought fit to consider of at the next court; and that such persons, as shall be hereafter so deputed by the freemen of the several plantations to deal in their behalf in the affairs of the commonwealth, shall have the full power and voices of all the said freemen derived to them for the making and establishing of laws, granting of lands, &c. and to deal in all other affairs of the commonwealth, wherein the freemen have to do, the matter of elec-

---

tality among the Indians, to make room for the settlement of the English. I am not inclined to credulity, but should not we go into the contrary extreme if we were to take no notice of the extinction of this people in all parts of the continent? In some, the English have made use of means the most likely to have prevented it, but all to no purpose. Notwithstanding their frequent ruptures with the English, very few comparatively have perished by wars. They waste, they moulder away, and, as Charlevoix says of the Indians of Canada, they disappear.

tion of magistrates and other officers only excepted, wherein every free-man is to give his own voice.*

— And, to show their resentment, they imposed a fine upon the court of assistants for going contrary to an order of the general court.†

The freemen were so increased, that it was impracticable to debate and determine matters in a body, it was besides unsafe, on account of the Indians, and prejudicial to their private affairs, to be so long absent from their families and business; so that this representative body was a thing of necessity, but no provision had been made for it in their charter.

Thus they settled the legislative body, which, except an alteration of the number of general courts which were soon reduced to two only in a year, and other not very material circumstances, continued the same as long as the charter lasted. This I suppose was the second house of representatives in any of the colonies. There was, as has been observed, no express provision for it in the charter, they supposed the natural rights of Englishmen, reserved to them, implied it. In Virginia, a house of burgesses met first in May 1620. The government in every colony, like that of the colonies of old Rome, may be considered as the *effigies parva* of the mother state.

There was great disturbance in the colony this year, occasioned by Roger Williams, minister of Salem. He had been three or four years at Plimouth, and for some time was well esteemed, but at length advanced divers singular opinions, in which he did not meet with a concurrence, whereupon he desired a dismission to the church of Salem, which was granted him. That church had invited him, upon his first coming to New-England; but the governor and council interposed with their advice, and prevented his settlement at that time. He had refused to join in communion with the church at Boston, because they would not make a public declaration of their repentance for holding communion with the church of England whilst they lived there. He was charged with divers exceptionable

* [Most of these regulations were made without any authority from their charter. The removal of the corporation from England was the first instance of departure from the charter and in a most essential point. In America they were less scrupulous than they would have been in England. Although the charter makes the corporation to consist of Governor, Deputy Governor and eighteen Assistants, six of which assistants with the Governor or Deputy are made a quorum, they nevertheless in March 1630 determined that when there should be less than nine assistants in the colony the major part of them should be a quorum and their acts as valid as if there had been seven or more, and at the election in 1632 instead of eighteen assistants they would chuse only eight.]

† Mass. Records.

tenets, as "that it is not lawful for a godly man to have communion, in family prayer or in an oath, with such as they judge unregenerate, and therefore he refused the oath of fidelity and taught others so to do — that it is not lawful for an unregenerate man to pray — that the magistrate has nothing to do in matters of the first table"; another tenet is added, which ought not to have been ranked with the former, viz. "that to punish a man for any matters of his conscience is persecution." * The magistrates sent a second time to the church of Salem to desire them to forbear calling him to office, but they refused to hearken to their advice, and proceeded to ordain him, Mr. Skelton, their former minister, dying a little before. Mr. Williams caused the church of Salem to send their letters of admonition to the church at Boston, and to several other churches, accusing the magistrates, which were members of them, of divers heinous offences, [and] would admit no church to be pure but the church of Salem; but at length, because the members of that church would not separate not only from all the churches in Old England, but from all in New-England also, he separated from them; and, to make compleat work of it, he separated from his own wife, and would neither ask a blessing nor give thanks at his meals if his wife was present, because she attended the publick worship in the church of Salem.† But what gave just occasion to the civil power to interpose, was his influencing Mr. Endicot, one of the magistrates and a member of his church, to cut the cross out of the King's colours, as being a relique of antichristian superstition.‡ A writer of the history of those times questions whether his zeal would have carried him so far, as to refuse to receive the King's coin because of the cross upon it. Endeavours were used to reclaim him, but to no purpose, and at length he was banished the jurisdiction. He removed to the southward, to look out for a new settlement among the Indians, and fixed upon a place called by them Moshawsick, but by him Providence.§ After all that has been said of the actions or tenets of this person while he was in the Massachusets, it ought for ever to be remembred to his honor, that, for forty years after, instead of shewing any revengeful resentment against the colony from which he had been banished, he seems to have been continually employed in acts of kindness and benevo-

---

* Hubbard.   † *Hubbard.*

‡ Many of the militia refused to train with the mangled defaced colours. This scruple afterwards prevailed, and the cross was left out of the colours, and generally condemned as unlawful.

§ The inhabitants have a veneration for a spring which runs from the hill into the river above the great bridge. The sight of this spring caused him to stop his canoe and land there.

lence, giving them notice, from time to time, not only of every motion of the Indians over whom he had very great influence, but also of the unjust designs of the English within the new colony, of which he himself had been the founder and governor, and continued the patron.*

MR. Endicot was sentenced by the court "for his rashness, uncharitableness, indiscretion, and exceeding the limits of his commission, to be sadly admonished, and also disabled for bearing any office

* Mr. Calender,[1] in his century sermon at Rhode Island, questions Mr. Williams's ever professing himself a baptist: but Mr. Hubbard says, he was rebaptized at Providence by one Holman, and that Mr. Williams in return baptized him and ten more, but afterwards renounced this baptism, not being able to derive the authority of it from the apostles but through the ministers of the church of England, whom he judged to be antichristian. He refused communion with all christians of every profession, and conceived that God would raise up new apostles, and expected to be one himself, but afterwards changed from these principles, and would preach and pray with all that would hear him without any distinction. In the year 1677, he published a defence of some fundamental doctrines of christianity against the quakers. In 1643 he went to England, and, by the interest of Sir Henry Vane, obtained from the Earl of Warwick a charter of incorporation of Providence plantation in Narraghanset bay. He seems to have been well respected in England. He brought a letter to the governor of Massachusets bay, of which the following is a copy.[2]

To the right worshipful the governor and assistants and the rest of our worthy friends in the plantation of Massachusets bay.

Our much honour'd friends,

TAKING notice, some of us, of long time, of Mr. Roger Williams his good affections and conscience, and of his sufferings by our common enemy and oppressors of God's people the prelates; as also of his great industry and travels in his printed Indian labours in your parts (the like whereof we have not seen extant from any part of America) and in which respect it hath pleased both houses of parliament to grant unto him and friends with him a free and absolute charter of civil government for those parts of his abode, and withal sorrowfully resenting, that amongst good men (our friends) driven to the ends of the world, exercised with the trials of a wilderness, and who mutually give good testimony each of the other (as we observe you do of him and he abundantly of you) there should be such a distance. We thought it fit, upon divers considerations, to profess our great desires of both your utmost endeavours of nearer closing and of ready expressing those good affections (which we perceive you bear each to other) in the actual performance of all friendly offices. The rather because of those bad neighbours you are likely to find too too near you in Virginia, and the unfriendly visits from the West of England and from Ireland. That howsoever it may please the Most High to shake our

[1] John Callender (1706–1748) was born in Boston, and graduated from Harvard in 1723. After 1731 he was settled over the First Baptist Church in Newport, Rhode Island. In 1738 the centennial of the purchase of Aquidneck island was celebrated and Callender delivered an address entitled *An Historical Discourse, on the Civil and Religious Affairs of the Colony of Rhode-Island and Providence Plantations, from the First Settlement to the end of the First Century* (Boston, 1739). It is reprinted in vol. IV of the *Collections* of the Rhode Island Historical Society (1838). For over a century this was the only history of Rhode Island.

[2] This document was quoted by Hubbard in his *General History of New England.* See Massachusetts Historical Society *Collections,* Second Series, VI, 348.

in the commonwealth for the space of a year next ensuing." He protested against the proceeding of the court, and an order passed for his commitment, but upon his submission he was dismissed.

Mr. Winthrop's conduct had been such, from his first associating with the company in England until his being dropped this year from his place of governor, that unless the ostracism of the ancient Greeks had been revived in this new commonwealth, it was reasonable to expect that he should be out of all danger of so much as the least thought to his prejudice, and yet he had a little taste of what, in many other popular governments, their greatest benefactors have taken a large potion. After he was out of the chair, he was questioned in such a manner, as appears to have been disagreeable to him, concerning his receipts and disbursements for the publick during his administration. Having discharged himself with great honor, he concludes his declaration and account in these words: *

In all these things, which I offer, I refer myself to the wisdom and justice of the court, with this protestation, that it repenteth me not of my cost or labour bestowed in the service of this commonwealth, but do heartily bless the Lord our God, that he hath pleased to honour me so far, as to call for any thing he hath bestowed upon me for the service of his church and people here, the prosperity whereof and his gracious acceptance shall be an abundant recompence to me.

I conclude with this one request (which in justice may not be denied me) that as it stands upon record, that upon the discharge of my office I was called to account, so this my declaration may be recorded also, lest hereafter, when I shall be forgotten, some blemish may lye upon my posterity, when there shall be nothing to clear it.

Sept. 4, 1634.†   John Winthrop.

foundations, yet the report of your peaceable and prosperous plantations may be some refreshings to

Your true and faithful friends

Cor. Holland	Oliver St. John	Northumberland
John Blackistow	Gilbert Pickering	P. Wharton
Isaac Pennington	Robert Harley	Tho. Barrington
Miles Corbett	John Gurdon	William Masham

This letter produced a profession of readiness to all officers of christian love and mutual correspondence; but, unless he could be brought to lay down his dangerous principles of separation, they saw no reason why to concede to him, or any so perswaded, free liberty of ingress and egress, lest the people should be drawn away with such erroneous opinions. He died in 1682, forty eight years after his banishment.

* He might have torn his books of accounts, as Scipio Africanus did, and given the ungrateful populace this answer. A colony, now in a flourishing estate, has been led out and settled under my direction. My own substance is consumed. Spend no more time in harangues, but give thanks to God.

† Mr. Winthrop, about this time, received a letter from the Earl of Warwick, congratulating the success of the plantation, and offering his assistance in their proceedings. *Hubbard.*

In the year 1635,* there was a great addition made to the number of inhabitants; among others Mr. Vane,[1] afterwards Sir Henry Vane, was admitted to the freedom of the colony on the 3d of March; and at the same time Mr. Harlakenden,[2] a gentleman of good family and estate. There were many others, as Mr. Bellingham,[3] Mr. Dummer,[4] of the magistrates; Mr. R. Mather,[5] Mr. Norton,[6] Mr. Shepard,[7] and Mr. Peters,[8] of the ministers, who came over in this and the last year, determined to take up their abode, and many other persons of figure and distinction were expected to come over, some

* Mr. Maverick, the minister of Dorchester, died the third of February 1635, aged about 60. *Hubbard*.

In the spring of 1634, they first turned their thoughts to fortifying the harbour of Boston. Mr. Winthrop, the governor, and 8 or 10 of the principal men, went down to what is now called castle island in a boat, the day being warm and pleasant, the winter as they supposed breaking up, but they were surprized by a north-wester, and the cold so great as to freeze all up, so as that for a day and a night they could not get off the island, and were forced to lodge upon the ground and in heaps to prevent freezing. *Johnson*.

[1] Henry Vane (1613–1662) was sent over by his father "in the hope of curing him of puritanism" (Samuel Eliot Morison, *Builders of the Bay Colony*, p. 118). The biography of Vane by James Kendall Hosmer is probably the best.

[2] Roger Harlakenden (1611–1638) was the "most dear friend" of Thomas Shepard. His sister Mabel was the second wife of Governor Haynes. See Samuel Eliot Morison, *Builders of the Bay Colony*, pp. 109–111, 189.

[3] Richard Bellingham (1592?–1672) was recorder of Boston, Lincolnshire, before migrating to New England. He was frequently elected governor of the Bay Colony and held that office uninterruptedly from 1665 until his death. There is a brief biography of him by E. H. Goss in the *Magazine of American History*, XIII, 262–268.

[4] Richard Dummer (1599?–1678) was the father of Jeremiah Dummer, the goldsmith, and the grandfather of William Dummer, who was lieutenant-governor of the province. He was an Assistant in 1635–36, favored Wheelwright in the Antinomian controversy, went to England in 1636, but came back in the following year and resumed his residence at Newbury.

[5] Richard Mather (1596–1669) was the father of Increase Mather and the grandfather of Cotton Mather. His life, written by Increase Mather, was printed in 1670 and is reprinted in Alexander Young's *Chronicles of the First Planters of Massachusetts*.

[6] John Norton (1606–1663) was the minister at Ipswich. After the death of John Cotton he was called to Boston, where he was installed in 1656. He was a graduate of Cambridge, Peterhouse. Cotton Mather includes a Life of Norton in his *Magnolia*, Book III, Part I, chapter II.

[7] Thomas Shepard (1605–1649), a graduate of Cambridge, Emmanuel College, was the first minister of the First Church of Cambridge, Massachusetts. His was not the greatest intellect in New England, but he was one of the best loved men. See Samuel Eliot Morison's *Builders of the Bay Colony*, chapter IV.

[8] Hugh Peters or Peter (1599–1660), the fourth minister of the church at Salem, was a graduate of Cambridge, Trinity College. Returning to England in 1641, he engaged actively in the Civil War. He was "a popular preacher of the militant type and later became chaplain to General Sir Thomas Fairfax." In 1660 he was executed. There is a memoir of Peter (1851) by Joseph B. Felt. See also "Hugh Peter in Literature" by William S. Appleton in Massachusetts Historical Society *Proceedings*, Second Series, VIII, 118–122.

of which are said to have been prevented by express order of the King, as Mr. Pym, Mr. Hampden, Sir Arthur Haslerigg,[1] Oliver Cromwell, &c. I know this is questioned by some authors, but it appears plainly by a letter from Lord Say and Seal [2] to Mr. Vane, and a letter from Mr. Cotton to the same nobleman, as I take it, though his name is not mentioned, and an answer to certain demands made by him, that his Lordship himself and Lord Brooke [3] and others were not without thoughts of removing to New-England, and that several other persons of quality were in treaty about their removal also, but undetermined whether to join the Massachusets or to settle a new colony. By the charter, the number of assistants might be eighteen, but hitherto they had chosen a less number, from 6 to 9, which left room, as any gentleman of distinction came over, to admit him to a share in the government without leaving out any of the former assistants.

It appears, by the demands just mentioned, that some of the nobility and principal commoners, of that day, had what appears, at this day, to be very strange apprehensions of the relation they should stand in to Great Britain, after their removal to America. Many of the proposals were such, as imply that they thought themselves at full liberty, without any charter from the crown, to establish such sort of government as they thought proper, and to form a new state as fully to all intents and purposes as if they had been in a state of nature, and were making their first entrance into civil society. The importance of the colonies to the nation was not fully understood and considered. Perhaps the party, which then prevailed in England, would have been content to have been rid of the heads of what was deemed a faction in the government, and to have had no further connexion with them. Be that as it may, this sentiment, in persons of such figure and distinction, will in a great measure excuse the same mistake which will appear to have been made by our first settlers, in many instances in the course of our history. The answer made to the demands seems not to have been satisfactory, for these Lords and gentlemen, soon after, again turned

[1] Sir Arthur Haslerigg or Hesilrige (d. 1661) played a prominent part in the Civil War and after. At the Restoration he was placed in the Tower and died there.

[2] Lord Say and Seal. William Fiennes (1582–1662), first Viscount Saye and Sele, was a prominent Puritan. At this time he was much interested in New England, and acquired land in Connecticut and New Hampshire. Saybrook, Connecticut, was named partly for him. He declined to come to Massachusetts, for reasons which will appear.

[3] Lord Brooke. Robert Greville (1608–1643), like Lord Saye and Sele, was a Puritan member of the House of Lords. Their names are combined in that of the town of Saybrook, Connecticut, which was founded by John Winthrop, Jr., under a commission from them. He took an active part in the Civil War and was killed at Lichfield.

their thoughts to Connecticut, where they were expected to arrive every year, until after 1640.*

MR. Haynes was chosen governor for this year, and Mr. Bellingham deputy governor; Mr. Dummer and Mr. Haugh [1] were added to the assistants.† The inhabitants of the plantation, being so much increased, found it difficult to pitch upon convenient places for settlements. Mr. Hooker and Mr. Cotton were deservedly in high esteem; some of the principal persons were strongly attached to the one of them, and some to the other. The great influence, which Mr. Cotton had in the colony, inclined Mr. Hooker and his friends to remove to some place more remote from Boston than Newtown. Besides, they alledged, as a reason for their removal, that they were straitened for room, and thereupon viewed divers places on the sea-coast, but were not satisfied with them. Three or four persons, had, some time before,‡ travelled westward into the country an hundred miles upon discovery, until they struck a great river, which afterwards they found to be Connecticut or the fresh river, where there were many spots of interval land, and land in other respects to be desired for settlement. The Dutch at the Manhados [2] had some knowledge of this place, and had given intimations of it to the people of new Plimouth with whom they had commerce, but Plimouth government kept their intelligence secret.§ A letter from Mr. Winslow of New-Plimouth Sept. 26, 1633, mentions their having been up the river. They forbad the Dutch making any settlements there, and set up a trading house themselves.‖ The governor of the Massachusets also, this year 1635, sent a bark round the cape to the Dutch governor, to acquaint him that the King had granted the river and country of Connecticut to his own subjects, and desired him to for-

* See the Appendix [Nos. II and III].

† Mr. Ludlow aiming at the governor's place the year before, and being disappointed, had protested against the choice; which so offended the freemen, that this year they left him out of the magistracy. He removed soon after to Connecticut.

‡ In the year 1633. These were John Oldham before-mentioned, Samuel Hall and others. *Hubbard.*

§ The commissioners of the united colonies, in a declaration against the Dutch in 1653, say, that "Mr. Winslow, one of the commissioners for Plimouth, discovered the fresh river when the Dutch had neither trading house nor any pretence to a foot of land there."   ‖ *Hubbard.*

[1] Atherton Haugh or Hough (*d.* 1650) had been mayor of Boston, Lincolnshire, and was an alderman there when he decided to emigrate. Hough's Neck in Quincy was granted to him in 1637. See William S. Pattee, *History of Old Braintree and Quincy.*

[2] The Manhados, as used by Hutchinson, appears to be the Hudson River rather than Manhattan Island. In a document of 1632 the West India Company speaks of "the North River (commonly called the Manhattos)." *Documents relative to the Colonial History of New York,* I, 51.

bear building any where thereabouts. This river Mr. Hooker and his friends pitched upon as the most likely place to accommodate them. The latter end of the last year (1634) they intended to remove, and applied to the court for leave.* Of 21 members of the lower house, 15 were for their removal; but of the magistrates, the governor and two assistants only were for it, the deputy governor Mr. Winthrop and the rest of the assistants against it; but still, as the lower house was so much more numerous than the upper, the major part of the whole court was for it. This division was the occasion of first starting the question about the negative voice. The deputies or representatives insisted that the voice of a major part of the assistants was not necessary. The assistants refused to give up their right, and the business was at a stand. The whole court agreed to keep a day of humiliation and prayer, to seek the divine direction in all the congregations in the colony, and to meet again the next week after. At the opening of the court, Mr. Cotton preached from Hag. II. 4. "Yet now be strong O Zerubbabel, saith the Lord, and be strong O Joshua the son of Josedech the high priest, and be strong all ye people of the land, saith the Lord, and work, for I am with you, saith the Lord of hosts." His sermon was as pertinent to the occasion as his text, and prevailed upon the deputies to give up the point at that time.† Here was a crisis, when the patricians, if I may so stile them, were in danger of losing great part of their weight in the government. It may seem a matter of less consequence than it would have been, if the office of assistant had by charter been hereditary or even for life; but the assistants, aided by the elders who had great influence with the people, were in a good measure secure of their places. It was by the same aid that they now carried the point against the plebeians. There was no occasion for prodigies or other arts of the priests of old Rome. A judicious discourse from a well chosen text was more rational, and had a more lasting effect.

THERE were some circumstances very discouraging; particularly the neighbourhood of the Dutch on the one side, and some intelligence received of the designs of the Pequod ‡ Indians on the other,

---

* It was the general sense of the inhabitants, that they were all mutually bound to one another by the oath of a freeman as well as the original compact, so as not to be at liberty to separate without the consent of the whole.

† *Hubbard.*

‡ I suppose the chief country of the Pequods to be at or near the mouth of the river at Stonington, towards New-London, which is situated at the mouth of what was properly Pequod river. The chief Sachem was called Tatobam, a very stout fellow. Tatobam hated the English, and was ever moving the other Indians to join with him against them. *Wins. ans. to Gorton.*[1]

---

[1] *"Wins. ans. to Gorton"* is Edward Winslow's *Hypocrisie Unmasked.*

and of their having killed Capt. Stone [1] and his company as he was going up the river; but they could not be satisfied until they had accomplished their intentions and obtained the leave of the court.

THEY met with a new company, which arrived this year, who purchased their estates and settled at Newtown in their stead, with Mr. Shepard for their minister. They did not take their departure until June the next year, and then about an hundred persons in the first company, some of them had lived in splendour and delicacy in England, set out on foot to travel an hundred and twenty or thirty miles with their wives and children, near a fortnight's journey, having no pillows but Jacob's, and no canopy but the heavens, a wilderness to go thro' without the least cultivation, in most places no path nor any marks to guide them, depending upon the compass to steer by, many hideous swamps and very high mountains, beside five or six rivers or different parts of the same winding river (the Chickapi) not every where fordable, which they could not avoid. The greatest part of the lands, they were going to, were evidently without the jurisdiction of the Massachusets; nevertheless they took a commission from the authority of that colony to govern in Connecticut. There are other instances, which shew that they supposed they retained some authority over their inhabitants, even when out of the limits of the colony.*

THE Plimouth people, notwithstanding the French piracy in 1632, kept possession of their house at Penobscot, and carried on trade with the Indians; but in 1635, Rossillon, commander of a French fort

---

* They were reduced to great extremity, the first winter; their provisions being detained at the river's mouth, by the severity of the weather, the stream being frozen all the way. Some scattered down towards the mouth of the river, others ventured thro' the woods back to the Bay, one or two of whom perished. A few only remained to look after the cattle, many of which were lost. *Hubbard.*

Several authors, and Douglass among the rest, suppose this settlement to have been began by the more rigid brethren who separated from the rest. I question whether they had any grounds for their supposition. The peculiar tenets of Mr. Vane and Mrs. Hutchinson did not prevail until 1636. Mr. Hooker opposed them. "A copy of Mr. Vane's expressions at Roxbury, I desire to see and receive by the next messenger. — I have heard my brother Eliot is come about to this opinion; I have writ to him about it. I would fain come to a bandy, where I might be a little rude in the business, for I do as verily believe it to be false, as I do believe any article of my faith to be true. *Hooker to Shepard.*

---

[1] Captain John Stone (*d.* 1633), of Virginia, was forever in trouble in New England, both with the Bay Colony and with the Plymouth people. See Winthrop's *History of New England* (1853), I, 124, 132; and Nathaniel Morton's *New England's Memorial*, p. 119.

at La Have upon the Nova Scotia shore, sent a French man of war to Penobscot, which took possession of the trading house and all the goods. The French gave their bills for the goods, and sent away all the men. The commander wrote to the governor of Plimouth, that he had orders to displace all the English as far as Pemaquid, but to those westward he would shew all courtesy. The Plimouth government, who supposed they had good right to the place, were not willing to put up the injury quietly, and hired a large ship of some force, the Hope of Ipswich in England, —— Girling,[1] commander, to displace the French. Girling was to have two hundred pounds if he effected it. A barque with 20 men was sent with him as a tender. But the French, having notice of the design, fortified the place, and Girling having near spent his ammunition, sent the barque to the Massachusets for aid. Two persons came from Plimouth also to treat about it, and the court agreed to assist their neighbours by a subscription among themselves; but provision was so scarce, that there could not sufficient be had, suddenly, to fit out an expedition of an hundred men only; so the matter was deferred to a further time, and Girling returned, leaving the French in possession, which they continued until 1654.

THE situation the colony was in at this time must have given them a threatning prospect; the French on their borders on one side, the Dutch on the other, the Indians in the midst restrained only by want of union among themselves from breaking up all settlements, they being utterly defenceless.

THIS year Mr. Winthrop, jun.[2] returned from England, whither he had gone the year before, and brought a commission,* from the Lord Say and Seal, and Lord Brook and others, to be their governor of their plantation at Connecticut.† A fort was built at the mouth of the river, known by the name of Saybrook fort. He brought also

---

* How can we account for it that they should imagine they had a right to settle colonies and establish what form of government they pleased? Ten years after, it might well enough be supposed, but this was several years before the confusions in England began.

† [They obtained a grant from the Council of Plymouth.]

---

[1] —— Girling. For a vivid account of this unsuccessful enterprise, see William Bradford's *History of Plymouth Plantation* (Original Narratives edition), pp. 318–320.

[2] John Winthrop, Jr. (1606–1676), son of Governor Winthrop, came over in the *Lion* in the autumn of 1631. He was one of the founders of Ipswich, Massachusetts, and later of New London, Connecticut, whither he removed. He was Governor of Connecticut in 1657, and served again in that capacity from 1659 until his death in 1676. His personality and interests are well set forth in Samuel Eliot Morison's *Builders of the Bay Colony*, chapter IX.

a number of men with arms ammunition and stores, and two thousand pounds in money to bring forward a settlement. The commission interfered with the intended settlements by the Massachusets; notwithstanding that, as a number of the inhabitants of Watertown had possessed themselves of a fine piece of meadow at Weathersfield below Hartford where Mr. Hooker and his company settled, the agents for the Lords, being well disposed to promote the general good, permitted these settlers quietly to enjoy their possessions. The fortress below struck terror into the Indians, and quieted the minds of the English. Plimouth was dissatisfied with being thus supplanted by the Massachusets (the Dorchester men as I suppose having pitched upon the spot where Plimouth had built a trading house, and, as they alledged, had purchased the lands of the Indians) and demanded an hundred pounds or part of the land. There was great danger of a warm contention between the two colonies, but at length the Dorchester men made such offers of satisfaction that Plimouth accepted them. The Dutch also sent home to Holland for instructions, intending to maintain their claim to the river or the place where they had possession; but upon a treaty afterwards with the commissioners of the united colonies, they quitted all claim to all parts of the river, resigning it up to the English.*

SIR Ferdinando Gorges and Capt. Mason, having been at more expence and taken more pains than any other members of the grand council of Plimouth, and perceiving no prospect of any equivalent return, and fearing from the great clamour in the nation against monopolies that they should e'er long be forced to resign up their grand charter, they entered this year upon a new project, viz. to procure a general governor for the whole country of New-England to be forthwith sent over, and because the Massachusets charter stood in their way they endeavoured a revocation of it, that so the whole from St. Croix to Maryland might be brought under the same form of government. The settlement of the Dutch at Manhados, which lay within those limits, both then and at all other times was considered by the English court as an intrusion, as indeed it was.† In June, letters were received from Lord Say, advising that petitions had been

---

* Hubbard.

† In 1609 Henry Hudson an Englishman, from some misunderstanding between the East-India company and him, engaged in the Dutch service. On his return from the straights and bay which bear his name, he made the first discovery of Hudson's river and went up as far as Aurania (Albany) or near to it. The Dutch, a few years after, built a small house or fort there for the sake of trade, pretending no title to the country. It has been observed, that the English who came to New Plimouth intended in 1620 to have settled there. Neglected by the English court, the Dutch began a settlement soon after. It has been sometimes urged, that the line of the Massachusets charter which

prefered to the King and to the Lords of the council, by the Duke of Lenox, Marquis of Hamilton and divers other noblemen, together with Sir Ferdinando Gorges and Capt. Mason, but conceived to be the project of Sir F. Gorges only. That, to the Lords, was as follows, viz.

May it please your Lordships,

WHEREAS it pleased your Lordships to give orders to Sir Ferdinando Gorges to confer with such as were chiefly interested in the plantation of New England, to resolve whether they would resign wholly to his Majesty the patent of New-England, and to leave to his Majesty and his council the sole management of the public affairs, with reservation of every man's right formerly granted; or whether they would stand to the said patent, and prosecute the business among themselves, and have the said patent renewed, with the reformation or addition of such things as should be found expedient. We whose names are here underwritten, being interested in that business, do humbly submit to his Majesty's pleasure to do therewith as he pleaseth. But withal we humbly desire, that, upon our resignation of our said patent, his Majesty being to dispose of the whole country severally and immediately from himself, those divisions upon the sea-coast, that are hereunder designed, may be instantly confirmed and bestowed by new grants from his Majesty unto us, to be holden of his Majesty, paying the fifth part, &c. and with the privilege of the said patent and such further royalties as the Lord of Baltimore hath in his patent for the country of Maryland; saving only, that we should submit ourselves to the general governor now presently to be established by his Majesty for the whole country, and after his decease or other determination of his office, that then, from the Lords of his province, there may be an election of three by lot, which said three persons so so elected shall be presented to the King, that out of the number, one may be chosen by his Majesty to succeed in the place of the general governor, who shall, in person, or by his sufficient deputy, reside in the country during the space of three years only, and so from three years to three years another governor to be chosen successively, and the old governor to be left out of the lot of choice.

---

extends to the South Sea or until it meets the settlements of some other christian prince or state, was so expressed, from a particular regard to this Dutch settlement, and that a line to extend to the Spanish settlements was too extravagant to have been intended; but the Dutch were never allowed by the English to have any title to the country, and at the time of granting the charter, there were only a few stragglers there. Cromwell and the parliament before him considered them as intruders, and blamed the English colonies that they had not extirpated them. The geography of this part of America was less understood than it is at present. A line to the Spanish settlements was imagined to be much shorter than it really was. Some of Champlain's people, in the beginning of the last century, who had been but a few days on a march from Quebeck, returned with great joy, supposing that from the top of a high mountain they had discovered the South-Sea.

THE proposed divisions of the twelve provinces were as follows: The first, was from St. Croix to Pemaquid; the second, from Pemaquid to Sagadehoc; the third, contained the land between the rivers Amarascoggin and Kenebeck; the fourth, along the sea-coast from Sagadehock to Piscataqua; the fifth, from Piscataqua to Naumkeak; the sixth, from Naumkeak, round the sea-coast by Cape Cod, to Naraganset; the seventh, from Naraganset to the half-way bound betwixt that and Connecticut river, and so fifty miles up into the country; the eighth, from the half-way bound to Connecticut river, and so fifty miles into the country; the ninth, from Connecticut river along the sea-coast to Hudson's river, and so up thirty miles; the tenth, from the thirty miles end to cross up forty miles eastward; the eleventh, from the west side of Hudson's river thirty miles up the country towards the 40th degree, where New England beginneth; the twelfth, from the end of the 30 miles up the said river, northward thirty miles further, and from thence to cross into the land forty miles. And out of every one of these provinces was 5000 acres to be granted to certain persons there named, in lieu of some former grants made to each of them in those divisions which they were now to surrender, and to hold to each man his 5000 acres in fee of the Lord of the province. And the Lord of every one of those twelve provinces was to send the same year ten men, with the general governor, well provided.

To all which was added,

IT is humbly desired that your Lordships would be pleased to order these things following:

1. THAT the patent for the plantation of the Massachusets-Bay may be revoked, and that all those who have any other grants within any of these provinces, whether they have planted or not upon any part of the same, yet they shall enjoy their lands, laying down their jura regalia, if they had any, and paying some reasonable acknowledgment as freeholders to the Lord of the province of whom they are now to take new grants of their said lands; and in case any of their lands shall be found, having exorbitant bounds, to have been unlawfully obtained, they shall be reduced to a lesser proportion, as may be fit for the grantor who is undertaker, under the direction of Sir Ferdinando Gorges. And if the grantee shall be any ways refractory, and refuse to surrender and hold anew of the said Lord of the province, that then your Lordships will take order by such course, as law will permit, to make void the same.

2. THAT every river, which parts two provinces, shall equally belong half way over to the provinces they lie contiguous unto.

3. THAT the islands upon the sea-coast, or within the river of any

province being not here named, shall belong to the province they lie nearest unto.

4. THAT there is offered to your Lordships consideration the building of a city for the seat of the governor; unto which city forty thousand acres of land may be allotted besides the divisions above mentioned. And that every one, who is to have any of these provinces, shall be at the charge of sending over with the governor ten men, towards the building of the said city, wherein every such adventurer shall not only have his share of the trade and buildings, but also shall have all other fruit of the ten men's labour sent as aforesaid.

MOREOVER, there is humbly dedicated, to the foundation of a church in the said city and maintenance of clergymen to serve in the said church, 10,000 acres of land near adjoining to the said city.

THE petition to the King was of this form:

May it please your Majesty,

IT is humbly desired by the Duke of Lenox, &c. ancient patentees and adventurers in the plantation of New-England, that forasmuch as they are now presently to join in the surrender to your Majesty of the grand patent of their corporation, that your royal Majesty will be graciously inclined to give order to your attorney general, to draw several patents of such parcels of land as by their mutual consent have been allotted to them, and to have the same patents prepared fit for your royal signature, with such titles, privileges and immunities as have been heretofore granted, either to them or to any other by your Majesty or by your late royal father King James of blessed memory, with reservations of appeal to the governor or lieutenant of the territories, in cases reasonable; that, they knowing their own interest, may be the better able to plant and govern them to your Majesty's honour, their particular profit, and their people's civil government and faithful obedience to the laws of your sacred Majesty.*

April 6, 1635.

A COPY of some grant or agreement concerning one of the provinces to Capt. Mason was sent over, signed Lenox, Hamilton, Arundel and Surry, Carlisle, Stirling, Edward Gorges, Ferd. Gorges. Attested by Thomas Maydwell, Not. Pub. It has been said, that the Marquis of Hamilton and the Earl of Stirling both, obtained the like instruments, and it is possible all the others might also. It is not material, at this day, whether they did or not. It is certain, that above an hundred years are past, and no possession taken, or improvements made by them or their assigns in consequence thereof; and all the territory is either included in other grants, some made before this surrender, by the council itself, and some made since by

* Gorges — Hubbard.

the crown, or has been purchased of the natives, which, if done *bonâ fide*, so far as respects the property, has been thought by some to be the best title.*

In the year 1636, Mr. Vane was chosen governor, Mr. Winthrop deputy governor, and Mr. Harlakenden, who came in the same ship with Mr. Vane, was added to the assistants. The people of the colony very early discovered that they were not without disposition to novelty and change. It was not merely out of policy to encourage others, that they took early notice of such as came over from year to year. Besides this motive, they were easily captivated with the appearance of wisdom and piety, professions of a regard to liberty and of a strong attachment to the public interest. Mr. Haynes, who seemed to stand most in the way of Mr. Winthrop, had left the colony and was settled at Connecticut, and Mr. Winthrop would have had a good prospect of recovering his former share of the people's favour, if Mr. Vane's grave solemn deportment, although he was not then above 24 or 25 years of age, had not engaged almost the whole colony in his favour. There was a great friendship between Mr. Cotton and him, which seems to have continued to the last.† He had great respect shewn him at first. He took more state upon him than any governor had ever done before. When he went, either to court or to church, four serjeants walked before him with their halberds. His administration for several months met with great applause. Towards the end of the year, the people grew discontented. He perceived it, and grew weary of the government. Receiving letters from London in December, urging his return home, he first communicated them to the council, and then called the general court together to ask their consent to his quitting the administration. He declared to them the necessity of his departure, and such of the council, as had seen the letters, affirmed that the reasons were very urgent, but not fit to be imparted to the whole court. The court took time until the morning to consider, when one of the assistants lamenting the loss of such a governor in a time of such danger, both from French and Indians, the governor burst into tears and professed that howsoever the causes propounded for his departure did concern the utter ruin

---

* Mention is made by Hubbard of a storm Aug. 15, 1635, which by his description was more violent than any that has ever happened since. Many houses were blown down, and many more uncovered, the Indian corn every where beat down to the ground so as not to rise again: The tide rose twenty feet perpendicular. At Naraganset, the Indians were obliged to betake themselves to the trees, and yet many of them were drowned, the tide of flood returning before the usual time for it.

† A small house which he lived in, at the side of the hill above Queen-street, he gave to Mr. Cotton, who made an addition to it after Mr. Vane went away, and lived and died there.

of his outward estate, yet he would rather have hazarded all than gone from them at such a time, if something else had not pressed him more, viz. the inevitable danger of God's judgments, which he feared were coming upon them for the differences and dissentions which he saw amongst them, and the scandalous imputation brought upon himself, as if he should be the cause of all, and therefore he thought it was best for him to give place for a time. The court did not think fit to consent to his going for such reasons. He found he had gone too far, and recalled himself, professing that the reasons which concerned his own estate were sufficient to satisfy him, and therefore desired he might have leave; the other passage slipped from him out of passion, not judgment. Whereupon the court agreed that it was necessary to give way to his departure, and ordered another meeting of the general court to make choice of a governor and deputy governor,* and as it was in the midst of winter (15 December) the freemen had liberty to send their votes in writing, if they did not come in person. Some of the church of Boston, loth to part with the governor, met together and agreed that it was not necessary, for the reasons alledged, that the governor should depart, and sent some of their number to signify as much to the court. The governor pretended to be overpowered, and expressed himself to be such an obedient son of the church, that notwithstanding the licence of the court, yet without the consent of the church he durst not go away. A great part of the people, who were informed of this transaction, declared their purpose still to continue him; and it was thought adviseable, when the day appointed for election came, to adjourn the court to May, the time of the annual choice.†

THERE came over with Mr. Cotton, or about the same time, Mr. Hutchinson,[1] and his family, who had lived at Alford in the neighbourhood of Boston. Mr. Hutchinson had a good estate and was of good reputation. His wife, as Mr. Cotton says, "was well beloved, and all the faithful embraced her conference and blessed God for her fruitful discourses." ‡ After she came to New England, she was

---

* In case the deputy should be chose governor as was expected.
† Mass. records — *Hubbard*.　　　　　　　　　‡ Answer to Bailey.[2]

---

[1] William Hutchinson (1586–1642) and his wife Anne (1590–1643) were the great-great-grandparents of Governor Thomas Hutchinson. This fact makes more remarkable the judicial attitude maintained by the Governor in his treatment of Mrs. Hutchinson in the narrative. There are various biographies of Anne Hutchinson, but for maximum satisfaction one should turn to Charles Francis Adams's *Three Episodes of Massachusetts History* and to the volume entitled *Antinomianism in the Colony of Massachusetts Bay* which Mr. Adams edited for the Prince Society.

[2] John Cotton, *The Way of Congregational Churches Cleared.*

treated with respect, and much notice was taken of her by Mr. Cotton and other principal persons, and particularly by Mr. Vane the governor. Her husband served in the general court, several elections, as a representative for Boston, until he was excused at the desire of the church.* So much respect seems to have increased her natural vanity. Countenanced and encouraged by Mr. Vane and Mr. Cotton, she advanced doctrines and opinions which involved the colony in disputes and contentions; and being improved, to civil as well as religious purposes, had like to have produced ruin both to church and state. The vigilance of some, of whom Mr. Winthrop was the chief, prevented, and turned the ruin from the country upon herself and many of her family and particular friends. Mr. Wheelwright,[1] a zealous minister, of character for learning and piety, was her brother-in-law and firmly attached to her, and finally suffered with her. Besides the meetings for public worship on the Lord's day, the stated lecture every Thursday in Boston, and other occasional lectures in other towns, there were frequent private meetings of the brethren of the churches for religious exercises. Mrs. Hutchinson thought fit to set up a meeting of the sisters also, where she repeated the sermons preached the Lord's day before, adding her remarks and expositions. Her lectures made much noise, and sixty or eighty principal women attended them. At first, they were generally approved of. After some time, it appeared she had distinguished the ministers and members of churches through the country; a small part of them under a covenant of grace, the rest under a covenant of works. The whole colony was soon divided into two parties; and however distant one party was from the other in principle, they were still more so in affection. The two capital errors, with which she was charged, were these, "That the Holy Ghost dwells personally in a justified person; and that nothing of sanctification can help to evidence to believers their justification." From these two, a great number of

---

* Mr. William Hutchinson was discharged from assisting at the particular courts at the request of the church. *Mass. Rec. Dec.* 1636.

---

[1] John Wheelwright (1592?–1679) was a graduate of Cambridge, Sidney College, and had been the vicar of Bilsby, Lincolnshire, for about ten years. For his second wife he took Mary Hutchinson, a sister of William Hutchinson. He embarked for New England early in April 1636, and landed at Boston May 26. Some of his admirers attempted to have him associated with John Cotton and John Wilson as a third minister of the Boston church, but Winthrop objected and he was made pastor of the church at Braintree instead. Charles H. Bell's "Memoir," which is included in the Prince Society's *John Wheelwright*, gives a good account of his life, but should be supplemented by Charles Francis Adams's "The Antinomian Controversy" in his *Three Episodes of Massachusetts History*, and by a paper by Edmund M. Wheelwright in the *Publications* of the Colonial Society of Massachusetts, I, 271–303.

others were said to flow, which were enumerated and condemned at a synod held the next year. The ministers of the several parts of the country, alarmed with these things, came to Boston while the general court was sitting, and some time before the governor, Mr. Vane, asked his dismission. They conferred with Mr. Cotton and Mr. Wheelwright upon those two points. The last, they both disclaimed, so far as to acknowledge that sanctification did help to evidence justification; the other, they qualified, at least by other words; they held the indwelling of the person of the Holy Ghost, but not strictly a personal union, or as they express it, not a communicating of personal proprieties. The governor not only held with Mr. Cotton, but went further or was more express, and maintained a personal union. Mr. Winthrop, the deputy governor, denied both, and Mr. Wilson, the other minister of Boston, and many of the ministers in the country, joined with him. A conference or disputation was determined on, which they agreed should be managed in writing, as most likely to tend to the peace of the church. When they could not find that the scriptures nor the primitive church, for the first 300 years, ever used the term $\pi\rho\sigma\hat{\omega}\pi\sigma\varsigma$, or person, of the Holy Ghost, they generally thought it was best it should be forborn, as being of human invention. Upon the other question, Mr. Cotton in a sermon, the day the court met, had acknowledged that evident sanctification is a ground of justification, and went on to say, that in cases of spiritual desertion, true desire of sanctification was found to be sanctification, as divines usually held; and further, if a man was laid so flat upon the ground, as that he could see no desires, but only as a bruised reed did wait at the foot of Christ, yet here was matter of comfort, for this was found to be true sanctification in the root and principle of it. Mr. Vane and he both denied that any of these or any degree of sanctification could be evident without a concurrent sight of justification.* The town and country were distracted with these subtleties, and every man and woman who had brains enough to form some imperfect conceptions of them, inferred and maintained some other point, such as these; "a man is justified before he believes; faith is no cause of justification; and if faith be before justification, it is only a passive faith, an empty vessel, &c. and assurance is by immediate revelation only." The fear of God and love of our neighbour seemed to be laid by and out of the question. All the church of Boston, except four or five, joined with Mr. Cotton. Mr. Wilson, the other minister, and most of the ministers in the country, opposed him.

* *Hubbard.*

To increase the flame, Mr. Wheelwright preached a sermon
(Jan. 19) in which, besides carrying antinomianism to the heighth,
he made use of some expressions which were laid hold of by the
court as tending to sedition; for which he was sent for and examined
whilst Mr. Vane was in office, but a full enquiry and determination
was suspended until a more convenient time.

WHILST these contentions were thus increasing within, the Pequods, the most warlike of all the Indians, were plotting destruction
from without. After Stone and his company were murdered, they
sent messengers to Boston to make peace, pretending that the murder was committed by a few bad fellows who had fled to the Dutch.
Their ambassadors were courteously treated, and the terms of peace
were agreed on. In confidence of their fidelity, John Oldham, of
whom mention has been made before, went in a small bark to trade
with the Indians at Block Island. They murdered him, but spared
two boys and two Naraganset Indians who were of his company.
The murderers were discovered by the crew of a small vessel, one
Gallop master from Connecticut, which happened to come upon
them soon after the fact. Gallop had with him only one man and
two boys, and no arms except two muskets and two pistols. Altho'
the deck was full of Indians who had guns, swords, &c. yet, as they
were then not much used to them, they made but little resistance,
and when he boarded the vessel they jumped into the sea and many
of them were drowned. He found Oldham's body not cold, his brains
beat out and his limbs hacked off. Block Island was under the Naraganset Indians, but they denied their having any concern in the
murder. The murderers were sheltered and protected by the Pequods, who at the same time surprized divers English in Connecticut
river. These proceedings caused the Massachusets to send fourscore
men, by water, under Captain Endicot, who had instructions to offer
peace to the Indians upon their delivering up the murtherers; if they
refused to do it, then to attack them. A great number of them entered into some sort of parley by a messenger and interpreter, keeping at a great distance themselves; but, assoon as they knew the
terms, they fled into the woods. Winter was approaching, and Mr.
Endicot thought it adviseable to return home in order to prepare for
a more general attack the next summer. There were some severe
reflections cast upon him for not pursuing the enemy at that time.
The Pequods, in the winter, attempted an union with the Naragansets. There had been a fixed inveterate enmity between the two
tribes, but on this occasion the Pequods were willing to smother it,
their enmity against the English being the strongest of the two; and

although they had never heard the story of Polyphemé and Ulysses, yet they artfully urged that the English were come to dispossess them of their country, and that all the Naragansets could hope for from their friendship, was, the favour of being the last devoured; whereas, if the Indians would unite, they might easily destroy the English, or force them to leave the country, without being exposed themselves to any hazard. They need not come to open battles: Firing their houses, killing their cattle, and lying in wait for them as they went about their ordinary business, would soon deprive them of all means of subsisting. But the Naragansets * preferred the present pleasure of revenge upon their mortal enemies, to the future happiness of themselves and their posterity.† They are said to have wavered at first, but at length Myantinomo, their chief sachem, with 20 attendants went to Boston, where all the magistrates and ministers were called together to receive them, and a guard of 20 musketeers sent to Roxbury to attend them. They proposed to join in war against the Pequods, and that neither English nor Indians should make peace with them but utterly destroy them. The governor, for form sake, took time, until the next morning, to give an answer, and then the following articles were agreed to.

1. A FIRM and perpetual peace betwixt them and the English.

2. NEITHER party to make peace with the Pequods without the consent of the other.

3. THAT the Naragansets should not harbour any Pequods.

4. THAT they should put to death or deliver up any murderers of the English.

5. THAT they should return fugitive servants.

6. THE English to give them notice when to go out against the Pequods, and the Naragansets to furnish guides.

7. FREE trade to be carried on between the parties.

8. None of the Naragansets to come near the English plantation, during the war with the Pequods, without some Englishman or Indian known to the English.

CUSHAMAQUIN, a sachem of the Massachusets Indians, also became a party to the treaty.

INDIAN fidelity is proverbial in New-England, as Punick was in Rome. The Naragansets are said to have kept to the treaty until

* The Naraganset sachem, and Uncas, sachem of the Moheges, sent to the English and offered their service to join with them against the Pequods. *Winslow's answ. to Gorton.*

† MS. Journal.

the Pequods were destroyed, and then they grew insolent and treacherous.

Towards the end of the year religious heats became more violent, and the civil affairs more sensibly affected by them. The people of Boston, in general, were in favour of Mr. Vane the governor, the rest of the towns, in general, for Mr. Winthrop the deputy governor. At a sessions of the court in March, it was moved that the court of elections for 1637 should not be held in Boston but in Newtown (Cambridge.) Nothing could be more mortifying to the governor, and as he could not hinder the vote by a negative, he refused to put the question. Mr. Winthrop the deputy governor, as he lived in Boston, excused himself, and the court required Mr. Endicot one of the assistants to do it. It was carried for the removal.

The more immediate occasion of the court's resentment against Boston, was a petition signed by a great number of the principal inhabitants of that town, together with some belonging to other towns, judging and condemning the court for their proceedings against Mr. Wheelwright. At this session, Mr. Vane the governor could not prevent a censure upon one Stephen Greensmith, for saying that all the ministers except Mr. Cotton, Mr. Wheelwright, and he thought Mr. Hooker preached a covenant of works. He was required to make an acknowledgment to the satisfaction of the magistrates and ministers, was fined forty pounds, &c.*

At the opening the court of election for 1637, which was not done until one a clock, (May 17th) a petition was again offered, from many of the town of Boston, which the governor, Mr. Vane, would have had read, but Mr. Winthrop the deputy governor opposed it as being out of order; this being the day, by charter for elections, and the inhabitants all convened for that purpose, if other business was allowed to take up the time the elections would be prevented; after the elections were over, the petition might be read. The governor, and those of his party would not proceed unless the petition was read. The time being far spent, and many persons calling for election,† the deputy governor called to the people to divide, and the greater number should carry it; which was done, and the ma-

---

* Mass. Records.

† Mr. Wilson, the minister, in his zeal gat up upon the bough of a tree (it was hot weather, and the election, like that of parliament men for the counties in England, was carried on in the field) and there made a speech, advising the people to look to their charter and to consider the present work of the day, which was designed for the chusing the governor, deputy governor and the rest of the assistants for the government of the commonwealth. His speech was well received by the people, who presently called out, Election, election, which turned the scale. *MS. Life of J. Wilson.*

jority was for proceeding. Still the governor refused, until the deputy governor told him they would go on without him. This caused him to submit. Mr. Winthrop was chosen governor, Mr. Dudley deputy governor, Mr. Saltonstall,*[1] son of Sir Richard, and Mr. Stoughton [2] new assistants; and Mr. Vane and his friends of the same persuasion, Dummer, Haugh and Coddington, left out of the magistracy. There was great danger of a violent tumult that day. The speeches on both sides were fierce, and they began to lay hands on one another, but the manifest majority, on one side, was a restraint to the other.† Boston waited the event of this election of magistrates, before they would chuse their representatives for the other business of the general court, and the next morning they chose Mr. Vane, the late governor, Mr. Coddington and Mr. Haugh. This election of Boston was immediately determined, by the court, to be undue. The reason is not assigned in the record, but it is said,‡ this reason was given, that all the freemen were not notified. A warrant issued for a new choice, and Boston returned the same men again, and then they were not rejected. The serjeants, who used to attend Mr. Vane, laid down their halberds and went home as soon as the new governor was elected,§ and they refused to attend him to and from the meetings on the Lord's days as had been usual. They pretended, this extraordinary respect was shewn to Mr. Vane as a person of quality. The court would have appointed others, but Mr. Winthrop took two of his own servants to attend him. Mr. Vane professed himself ready to serve the cause of God in the meanest

* [He left New England in 1672 and died at Hulme in England April 20th 1694. *MS.*]

† Hubbard — Mass. Records.

‡ *Hubbard.*

§ The military companies elected their officers, otherwise the court would undoubtedly have appointed other serjeants.

---

[1] Richard Saltonstall (1610–1694) attended Emmanuel College, Cambridge, before coming to New England with his father in 1630. He returned to England in 1631, married there, and then came back to America, settling at Ipswich. He revisited England several times and, as it happened, died there. See *Ancestry and Descendants of Sir Richard Saltonstall*, pp. 86–94.

[2] Israel Stoughton (*d.* 1645) was the father of Lieutenant-Governor William Stoughton who presided at the witchcraft trials in 1692 and was chief-justice 1695–1701. Israel, a man of property and distinction, resided in Dorchester. He objected to the veto power of the Assistants and circulated a brief which set forth his views. The Assistants were aggrieved, and the General Court was induced to disqualify him from office-holding for three years. This was in 1635. In the following year he was restored to his former capacity and, as we see, became an Assistant in 1637. Returning to England in 1643, he served as lieutenant-colonel in the Parliamentary army and died at Lincoln in 1645. See *History of Dorchester, Mass.*, pp. 83–86.

capacity. He was notwithstanding much mortified, and discovered his resentment. Although he had sat at church among the magistrates from his first arrival, yet he, and those who had been left out with him, placed themselves with the deacons, and when he was invited by the governor to return to his place, he refused it.

An extraordinary act, made by the general court this session, very much heightened the discontent. Many persons of the favourite opinions in Boston were expected from England; a penalty therefore was laid on all persons who should entertain, in their houses, any stranger who came with intent to reside, or should allow the use of any lot or habitation above three weeks, without liberty from one of the standing council or two other assistants. The penalty on private persons was forty pounds, and twenty pounds besides for every month they continued in the offence. And any town, which gave or sold a lot to such stranger, was subject to 100 *l.* penalty, but if any inhabitant of such town should enter his dissent with a magistrate, he was to be excused his part of the fine.* This was a very severe order, and was so disliked by the people of Boston, that upon the governor's return from court they all refused to go out to meet him or shew him any respect.† Mr. Winthrop, however firm and resolute in the execution of his office and steady to his principles, yet in private life behaved with much moderation. He was obliging and condescending to all, and by this means, in a short time, recovered their affections and was in greater esteem than ever. Indeed, while Boston thus slighted him, the other towns increased their respect; and in travelling, the same summer, to Ipswich, he was guarded from town to town with more ceremony than he desired.‡

Mr. Vane, in company with Lord Leigh, son of the Earl of Marlborough, who came to see the country, sailed for England the beginning of August, where he had a much larger field opened. The nation at that time was disposed to receive, very favorably, men of his genius and cast of mind. The share he had in the revolution there,

* Mass. Records.

† [Master Williams told me that he was imployed to buy from the Savages for the late Governour and Master Cotton with their followers a proportion of land without the English Plantation whither they might retire and live according to their own mind exempt from the Jurisdiction Civil and Ecclesiastick of all others. M. Williams was in so great friendship with that late Governor, when he told me so much, that I believe he would have been loth to have spoken any untruth of him. *Bayley's Dissuasive etc.*] Mr. Cotton was so dissatisfied with this law, that he says, he intended to have removed out of the jurisdiction to Quinnypiack, since called New-Haven; but finding the law was not improved to exclude such persons as he feared it would be, he altered his mind. *Ans. to Bailey.*[1]   ‡ *Hubbard.*

[1] John Cotton, *The Way of Congregational Churches Cleared.*

and his unhappy fate upon the restoration of King Charles the second, are too well known to need any notice here. He came into New-England under peculiar advantages. His father was one of the privy council. He himself had the friendship of the Lord Say and Seal, who was in the highest esteem in the colony. He made great professions of religion, and conformed to the peculiar scruples of that day. I have seen a long letter wrote to him while he was on shipboard, by one of the passengers in the same ship, applauding him for honouring God so far as to shorten his hair upon his arrival in England from France, and urging a compleat reformation by bringing it to the primitive length and form. It was with much difficulty he could obtain his father's consent to come over, but his inclination was so strong, that, at length, he had leave of absence for three years. It is said, that the King being acquainted with Mr. Vane's disposition, commanded the father, who had no great affection for the religion of New-England, to gratify him.* However this may have been, it was believed in New-England to be true, and, with the other circumstances mentioned, strongly recommended him. Part of his business was the settlement of Connecticut, in conjunction with Mr. Winthrop the governor's son, as agents for Lord Say and Seal and Lord Brooke, &c.† The most valuable places for townships had been taken up before, by people from the Massachusets, as we have already observed; and the agents, not being willing to disturb them, contented themselves, at present, with the possession of the mouth of the river, and Mr. Vane was stopped, by the general desire of the colony, in order to his being elected governor. The administration of a young and unexperienced, but obstinate and self-sufficient, governor, could not but be disliked by the major part of the people; and, at the next election, they not only would not so much as chuse him an assistant, but made an order, that no man for the time to come should be qualified for the place of governor, until he had been, at least, one whole year in the country.‡ A letter, wrote from New-England, shews the sense they had of him after they had made trial.

* *Hubbard.*

† The Earl of Warwick obtained a grant of the sea coast, from Naraganset river to the south-west 40 leagues, to keep the breadth to the south sea. This he assigned, in 1631, to Lord Say and Seal, Lord Brook, Lord Rich, Charles Fiennes, Sir Nathaniel Rich, Sir Richard Saltonstall, Richard Knightly, John Pym, John Hampden, John Humfrey, and Herbert Pelham, Esq; These, with their associates, are the noblemen and gentlemen often mentioned in private letters to be expected over every year; and Mr. Fenwick kept possession, and would not suffer settlements, until affairs in England had taken such a turn, that persons of their character had no occasion for an asylum.

‡ I do not find this order in the records. It is mentioned by Mr. Hubbard, who was then on the spot.

Mr. Vane, coming from England a young gentleman, was presently elected governor, and before he was half warm in his seat, to show his spirit, began to broach new tenets drawn from the lees of one Mr. Wheelwright, agitated with such violence, as if they had been matters of that consequence that the peace and welfare of New-England must be sacrificed, rather than they should not take place. Divisions are always dangerous, never safe, never more dangerous than in a new settled government. Yet this man, altogether ignorant of the art of government, thinks it not enough to set the house on fire, but must add oil to the flame, and so far had the bandying of these things proceeded, that it was of God's great mercy it ended not in our destruction. It is fit that something should be said of the man that put us into this danger. Truly, by his aspect, you would judge him a good man. Yet I am persuaded he hath kindled those sparks among us, which many ages will not be able to extinguish. But the wisdom of the state put a period to his government before he had run out his circuit. They were necessitated to undo the work of their own hands, and leave a blemish upon that rash undertaking, for posterity to descant upon, and a caveat to us, that all men are not fit for government, and none so dangerous, when he is up, as one that makes his affection his rule. But this disgrace took so deep an impression, that partly from a sense of it, and partly from a consciousness how ill he had deserved of us through his heat of indiscretion, he exchanged New-England for Old.

Lord Say and Seal speaking of him, after his arrival in England, in a letter to Mr. Cotton, says:

For the young man, Mr. Vane, whom your love followeth, and its well it doth so, for he may be recovered, I have not been wanting to do my endeavour to shew him the danger of his way, and what hath been the sad issue thereof in others; from whence I think it cometh, and whither Satan's aim is to drive it, as might have appeared to you by my letters, written to him unto New-England, when I first did perceive his delusions, if he had shewn my letters to you. I shall be glad to do my best to that end still; but I have not that frequent converse with his family, now, as heretofore, whereof there are the most in Holland, and the rest will shortly be there also.*

* After all that has been said to the disadvantage of Mr. Vane's character, it ought to be remembered to his honour, that notwithstanding the slights put upon him by the colony, he shewed a truly christian spirit of forgiveness; for when, in the year 1644, an attachment was made of the effects of alderman Berkley of London, in the Massachusets colony, at the suit of the Lady La Tour, and judgment given for 2000 *l.* sterling and no appeal admitted, a heavy complaint was made against the government, and they were threatened with the loss of their privileges, Sir H. Vane stood their friend, and, by his great interest with the parliament, appeased their resentment, and laid the storm which was gathering and hung over them. *MS. letter.*

The author of the life and death of Sir Henry Vane, printed in 1662, says — "That it was suggested by the bishops to the then King concerning him, that the heir of a con-

THE party in New-England lost their head. Mrs. Hutchinson, notwithstanding, continued her lectures. The court, for the present, took no notice of her conduct, nor of any erroneous opinions, but waited the determination of the churches in a general council; ac-

siderable family about his Majesty was grown into dislike of the discipline and ceremonies of the church of England, and that his Majesty might do well to take some course about him. On this, the then bishop of London took him to task, who seemed to handle him gently in the conference, but concluded harshly enough against him in the close. In fine, seeing himself on all hands in an evil case, he resolved for New-England. In order to this, striking in with some nonconformists which intended that way, his honourable birth, long hair, and other circumstances of his person, rendered his fellow travellers jealous of him as a spy to betray their liberty rather than any way like to advantage their design. But he, that they thought at first sight to have too little of Christ for their company, did soon after appear to have too much for them. For he had not been long in New-England, but he ripened into more knowledge and experience of Christ, than the churches there could bear the testimony of. Even New-England could not bear all his words, though there was no King's court or King's chapel. Then he returns for Old England."

The following letter was wrote, by a person of quality, to a near relation of Sir Henry Vane, about a week after his execution.

"Madam,

If I do, later than others, give you an account of the share I have in the loss of your generous kinsman, it is because I would not rudely disturb the motions of so just a sorrow; but I hope that you are assured I have so real a concern in all that relates to you, that it was not necessary, by an early haste, to send you an information of it. I have, Madam, whilst I own a love to my country, a deep interest in the publick loss which so many worthy persons lament. The world is robbed of an unparallelled example of virtue and piety. His great abilities made his enemies persuade themselves, that all the revolutions in the last age were wrought by his influence, as if the world was moved only by his engine. In him they lodged all the dying hopes of the party. There was no opportunity that he did not improve for the advantage of his country. And when he was in his last and much deplored state, he strove to make the people in love with that freedom they had so foolishly and lavishly thrown away. —— He was great in all his actions, but to me he seemed greatest in his sufferings, when his enemies seemed to fear that he alone should be able to acquaint them with a change of fortune. In his lowest condition, you have seen him the terror of a great prince, strengthened by many potent confederates and armies. You have seen him live in high estimation and honour, and certainly he died with it. Men arrive at honours by several ways. The martyrs, though they wanted the glittering crowns the princes of those ages dispensed, have rich ones in every just man's esteem. — Virtue, though unfortunate, shines in spite of all its enemies, nor is it in any power to deface those lasting monuments your friend hath raised, of his, in every heart that either knew him or held any intelligence with his fame. But, Madam, I trespass too long upon your patience. This is a subject I am apt to dwell on, because I can never say enough of it. I shall now only desire you to make use of that fortitude and virtue that raised your friend above the power and malice of his enemies, and do not, by an immoderate sorrow, destroy that which was so dear to him, yourself, but live the lively representation of his virtue, the exercise of which hath made you always the admiration of

Your humble servant, &c."

The 21st June 1662.

Life of Sir H. Vane.[1]

---

[1] [George Sikes,] *The Life and Death of Sir Henry Vane.*

cordingly a synod was appointed to be held at Newtown, the 30th
of August, where were present, not only the ministers and messengers of churches, but the magistrates also, who, Mr. Weld [1] says,
(I suppose he was a member) were not only hearers but speakers also,
as they thought fit. Mr. Cotton, although at the head of the ministers, was too much a party to be proper for a moderator, and Mr.
Hooker and Mr. Bulkley [2] were chosen. Three weeks were spent in
disputing, *pro* and *con.* and at length above fourscore points or opinions, said to have been maintained by some or other in the country,
were condemned as erroneous, and the result was signed by all the
members but Mr. Cotton. He had expressed his dislike of most of
them, but declined condemning them all, maintaining, that union to
Christ preceded faith in him, but at the same time declared, that the
other new opinions were heretical, absurd, and some of them blasphemous, and promised to bear testimony against them.* This general agreement struck a damp upon the opinionists, and gave further
life and vigor to the other party. Mr. Hooker at first disapproved of
determining the points in controversy by a synod. He writes to
Mr. Shepard of Newtown, April 8, 1636. (It should be 37)

For your general synod, I cannot yet see either how reasonable or how
suitable it will be for your turn, for the settling and establishing the truth
in that honourable way as were to be desired. My ground is this. They
will be chief agents in the synod who are chief parties in the cause, and for
them only, who are prejudiced in the controversy, to pass sentence against
cause or person, how improper! how unprofitable! My present thoughts
run thus: That such conclusions which are most extra, most erroneous,
and cross to the common current, send them over to the godly learned to
judge in our our own country, and return their apprehensions. I suppose
the issue will be more uncontroulable. If any should suggest this was the
way to make the clamour too great and loud, and to bring a prejudice
upon the plantations, I should soon answer, there is nothing done in corners here but it is openly there related, and in such notorious cases, which

* Hubbard — Johnson.

---

[1] Thomas Weld (1590?–1662) was the pastor of the church at Roxbury. He was a
graduate of Trinity College, Cambridge, and came to Massachusetts in 1632. In 1641
he was sent to England as one of the agents of the Colony. He did not return to New
England, but continued to practise his gift for controversy in the old country. The
passage referred to by Hutchinson is in Weld's Preface to John Winthrop's *Short Story
of the Rise, Reign and Ruin of the Antinomians.* See *Antinomianism in the Colony of
Massachusetts Bay* (edited by Charles Francis Adams for the Prince Society), p. 86.
[2] Peter Bulkley (1583–1659) was the first minister of Concord, Mass. He was a
graduate of St. John's College, Cambridge, and came to Massachusetts in 1635. After
residing a year or two in Cambridge he was installed at Concord, April 6, 1637. See
Cotton Mather, *Magnalia,* Book III, Part II, chap. X.

cannot be kept secret, the most plain and naked relation ever causeth the truth most to appear, and prevents all groundless and needless jealousies, whereby men are apt to make things more and worse than they are.

ALTHOUGH two of the elders were the moderators, or prolocutors of the assembly, yet Mr. Winthrop seems to have had a controuling power. An anonymous writer of a manuscript, sent from New-England the same year, gives this account of it.

The synod being met, much time is spent in ventilation and emptying of private passions; at length, divers truths are concluded upon, as, the nature of grace and faith, the necessity of repentance and good works, the perfection of the scriptures, and like truths of common allay were assented unto by common suffrage: But when they came to the nature of the covenant, the qualifications preceding it, the use of it, the seal of the Spirit, the Helenæs for which they strive, there they were as different as ever, resolved in nothing but this, that no one would be resolved by another; but therein was the wisdom and excellent spirit of the governor seen, silencing passionate and impertinent speeches as another Constantine, desiring the divine oracles might be heard speak and express their own meaning, adjourning the assembly when he saw heat and passion, so that, through the blessing of God, the assembly is dissolved, and jarring and dissonant opinions, if not reconciled, yet are covered; and they who came together with minds exasperated, by this means depart in peace, and promise, by a mutual covenant, that no difference in opinion shall alienate their affections any more, but that they will refer doubts to be resolved, by the great God, at that great day when we shall appear at his tribunal.

The synod being thus over, the minds of the people were prepared for a further proceeding against the opinionists.* The court at their sessions, the 2d of November, took notice of the petition, presented and called seditious, in March preceding. They expelled two of their own members, Aspinwall [1] and Coggeshall,[2] one for signing and the other for justifying it, and sent a warrant to the town of Boston to

* This spiritual court did not pronounce particular persons to be hereticks, but it determined what was heresy, and made the way plain for the secular power to proceed.

---

[1] William Aspinwall had come over in the fleet with Winthrop and was now a deputy from Boston. Disarmed, disfranchised, and banished, he went to Rhode Island, where he was elected Secretary of the Colony. Thence to New Haven for a year or two. Forgiven by the General Court, he returned to Massachusetts and served as Recorder of the Suffolk County Court, 1644–1651. Ultimately he went back to England, where he printed an extraordinary book predicting the coming of the millennium in twenty years. See *Records relating to the Early History of Boston*, XXXII, i–x.

[2] John Coggeshall came over in the *Lion* in 1632. He was a mercer and lived at first in Roxbury. When banished he was a deputy from Boston. He migrated to Rhode Island, where, ten years later, he was chosen President of the Colony!

return two other deputies in their room. The town agreed to send them back, but Mr. Cotton hearing of it, went to the meeting and prevented it; and they chose two others, one of which had signed the petition, and was therefore dismissed.* The court then sent for Mr. Wheelwright, and requiring of him an acknowledgment of his offence, he refused it and justified his conduct; but the court resolved, that it tended to disturb the civil peace, disfranchised and banished him, allowing 14 days to settle his affairs, &c.†

MRS. Hutchinson was next called to her trial, before the whole court and many of the elders. An ancient manuscript, of the trial at large, having been preserved, discovers nothing in her conduct but what might naturally be expected from a high degree of enthusiasm.[1] Her notions of revelations do not seem to have been altogether discountenanced by Mr. Cotton himself. Her sentence upon record stands thus:

Mrs. Hutchinson, the wife of Mr. William Hutchinson, being convented for traducing the ministers and their ministry in the country, she declared voluntarily her revelations, and that she should be delivered and the court ruined with their posterity, and thereupon was banished; and, in the mean while, was committed to Mr. Joseph Weld [2] (of Roxbury) until the court shall dispose of her.

Having received her sentence from the court, she had a further trial to go through in the church. She was first admonished. Mr. Cotton says, that Mr. Davenport and he imagined they had convinced her of her errors, and she presented what was called a recantation under her hand, but at the same time professed that she never was of any other judgment than what she now held forth. The recantation is not preserved. She had, no doubt, some fine spun distinctions, too commonly made use of in theological controversies, to serve as a subterfuge, if there be occasion; ‡ and perhaps, as many other enthusiasts have done, she considered herself divinely commissioned for some great purpose, to obtain which, she might think those windings, subtleties and insinuations lawful, which will hardly consist

* *Hubbard.*
† Mass. Records.
‡ Mr. Cotton, in a letter to Mr. Stone at Hartford, says, "Mrs. Hutchinson, of whom you speak, though she publickly revoked the errors, yet affirming her judgment was never otherwise, though her expressions were contrary, she was excommunicated by the whole church, *nem. con.* Some other of the members, that joined with her, were gone away before," &c.

---

[1] It is printed in vol. II, Appendix, No. 2.
[2] Joseph Weld was a brother of Thomas Weld, the minister of Roxbury.

with the rules of morality. No wonder she was immoderately vain, when she found magistrates and ministers embracing the novelties advanced by her. The whole church of Boston, a few members excepted, were her converts. At length, she forsook the public assemblies, and set up what she called a purer worship in her own family. It is not improbable she was encouraged herein by Mr. Vane, who, some years after, fell into the same practice in England. Mr. Hooker, who had been charged by her with want of soundness in the faith, in return expresses himself with some acrimony concerning her.

The expression of providence against this wretched woman hath proceeded from the Lord's miraculous mercy, and his bare arm hath been discovered therein from first to last, that all the churches may hear and fear. I do believe, such a heap of hideous errors, at once to be vented by such a self-deluding and deluded creature, no history can record; and yet, after recantation of all, to be cast out as unsavory salt that she may not continue a pest to the place, that will be for ever marvellous in the eyes of all the saints. It will not get out of my mind and heart but there is a mystery in the closure and upshot of this business; but he, that carries the wisdom of the crafty headlong, is able to lay open that also in his season. At the first reading of your relation I could not but suspect so much, may be it is but my melancholick suspicion, but these three things presented themselves, in open view, to my mind, 1. That it was never intended she should be excommunicated. 2. That her recantation was still with so much reservation, as sinks the mind of such who would have made way for her escape, viz. That our election is first evidenced. 3. That this conceit is a nest egg to breed and bring in many other false imaginations, if it be stretched to its breadth. Add also hereunto, that there is no odds from herself but only in some expressions and misprisions that way, as she would have men think, and then you have the whole cause, where it was conceived in a narrower compass and under a double vizard, that the appearance of it may suit every purpose as the occasion fits.[1]

Mr. Hutchinson, her husband, sold his estate and removed, with his wife and family, first to Aquidneck * (Rhode Island) being one of the purchasers of that island from the Indians; where, by the influence of his wife,† the people laid aside Mr. Coddington and three other magistrates, and chose him for their sole ruler; but he dying, about the year 1642, and she being dissatisfied with the people or

* Canonicus, Chief Sachem of Naraganset and Niantic, sold the island to William Coddington and his associates, March 29, 1637. *MS.*

† *Hubbard.*

[1] At this point in his own copy Hutchinson has written "† Appendix." His reference is to No. II of the Appendix to vol. II, "The Examination of Mrs. Ann Hutchinson at the court at Newtown."

place, removed to the Dutch country [1] beyond New-Haven; and, the next year, she and all of her family which were with her, being 16 persons, were killed by the Indians, except one daughter whom they carried into captivity.*

THE confusion in the colony, occasioned by these religious disputes, was very great; and it appears, from the letters then wrote from England, that they made great noise there; but after all, it is highly probable that if Mr. Vane had remained in England, or had not craftily made use of the party which maintained these peculiar opinions in religion, to bring him into civil power and authority and draw the affections of the people from those who were their leaders

* For the falshood of her declaration she was excommunicated. Some writers mention the manner of her death, as being a remarkable judgment of God for her heresies. Her partizans charged the guilt of the murder upon the colony. Mr. Weld says, she was delivered of as many unformed fœtuses at a birth as she maintained errors, and that another actress was delivered of a monster, and that all the women were seized with a violent vomiting and purging; stories, as credible as that of the Flanders Countess, who is said to have as many children at a birth, as there are days in the year.

The author of a little tract, published in 1676, under the title of *A Glass for the People of New-England*, by S. G. (it seems by the language and the malevolent spirit to be Samuel Gorton [2]) says, "The next piece of wickedness I am to mind you of, is your barbarous action committed against Mrs. Ann Hutchinson, whom you first imprisoned, then banished, and so exposed her to that desolate condition that she fell into the hands of the Indians, who murdered her and her family except one child; and, after that, made a notorious lie on the destroyed woman, which Samuel Clark, priest of London, taking the lie out of his brother Weld's short story, must needs put into his book, called, God's Judgments against heresy. — The woman before-mentioned, having been by the priests and professors pumped and sifted to get something against her, laying their snares to entrap her, and taking their opportunity when her husband and friends, as it was said, were absent, examined and banished her. — So she goes by water, with many others, who perceived they must go to pot next, and providentially fell in with Rhode Island, where they made a cave or caves, and in them lived until the cold winter was past, in which time it was known to the professors where they were, and that they had bought the island of the Indians. And the professors began to stir and endeavour to bring the island within the compass of their patent; so the poor molested woman, it is like, left in fear, and thought she would go far enough from their reach; so going southward to seek a place to settle upon, where she and her family might live in quietness, fell upon a piece of land that was in controversy between the Dutch and the Natives, and the Natives, being in a heat, came upon them and were the executioners of what the New-England priests, magistrates and church members, were the occasion, through their wicked and cruel proceedings, in forcing them to flee from their rage and fury. —— So, reader, thou mayst see the rage and envy of this professing generation; for they imprisoned and banished this tenderly bred woman in or towards winter, and, what with fears and tossings to and fro, the woman miscarried, upon which they grounded their abominable untruth. Many witnesses might be produced to prove this, and to disprove their abominable frequently told slander, and also printed by priests and New-England professors and their confederates here in England."

---

[1] The present Pelham, New York.

[2] Nowadays this rare tract is attributed to Samuel Groome (*d.* 1683). It was reprinted (1929) in *The Magazine of History*, vol. 37, no. 3.

into the wilderness, these, like many other errors, might have prevailed a short time without any disturbance to the state, and, as the absurdity of them appeared, silently subsided, and posterity would not have known that such a woman as Mrs. Hutchinson ever existed.* We may suppose that they, who from the beginning had gone along with her in her errors, were not displeased at a good pretence for getting rid of her without condemning themselves. It is difficult to discover, from Mr. Cotton's own account of his principles, published ten years afterwards, in his answer to Bailey, wherein he differed from her. Her warm imagination was more wrought upon by the enthusiastic tenet than his placid temper. He seems to have been in danger when she was upon trial. Mr. Dudley, the Deputy governor, bore hard upon him; Hugh Peters shewed that he was well disposed to bring him upon trial. The other ministers treated him coldly, but Mr. Winthrop, whose influence was now greater than ever, protected him. Not long after, in a sermon at a fast Dec. 13, 1638, he confessed and bewailed the churches and his own security and credulity, by means whereof so many dangerous errors had spread, and shewed how he came to be deceived; the errors being formed, in words, so near the truth which he had preached, and the falshood of the maintainers of them being such that they usually would deny to him what they had maintained to others.† His con-

---

* A great number of the principal inhabitants, most of them being disarmed and deprived of their civil privileges, removed. Mr. Coddington and Dummer had been assistants, Mr. Hutchinson, Aspinwall and Coggeshall, representatives; Rainsford,[1] Sanford,[2] Savage,[3] Eliot,[4] Easton,[5] Bendall,[6] Denison,[7] were all persons of distinction. About 60 were disarmed in Boston besides.

† *Hubbard.*

---

[1] Edward Rainsford (*d.* 1680) came in the fleet with Winthrop, became a deacon and ruling elder of the First Church in Boston, and one of the founders of the Third Church. An island in Boston harbor still bears his name.

[2] John Sanford went to Rhode Island with Coddington, Hutchinson, and others, and was chosen President of the Colony in 1653.

[3] Thomas Savage (1608?–1682) came to New England in 1635 and married a daughter of Mr. and Mrs. Hutchinson in 1637. With them he went to Rhode Island, but remained there only a few months. He returned to Boston, where he became a prominent citizen and the father of a large family.

[4] Jacob Eliot (*d.* 1651) was an elder brother of the celebrated Rev. John Eliot of Roxbury.

[5] Nicholas Easton, of Ipswich and Newbury, went to Rhode Island and was there chosen an Assistant.

[6] Edward Bendall (*d.* 1682) was "one of uncommon enterprise, projected and used a diving bell to remove from the channel the wreck of a ship before the dock called Bendall's, being the chief place of trade." Savage.

[7] William Denison (*d.* 1654), of Roxbury, was the father of Major-General Daniel Denison of Ipswich.

duct, in this day of temptation, was forgotten and he soon recovered; and, to his death, preserved the esteem and respect of the whole colony.

MR. Wheelwright went to New-Hampshire, and laid the foundation of the town and church of Exeter; and afterwards removed to Hampton, and from thence to Salisbury. He was restored in 1644, upon a slight acknowledgment. He was in England in 1658, and in favour with Cromwell, as appears by a letter to the church at Hampton. He lived to be the oldest minister in the colony; which would have been taken notice of, if his persecutors had not remained in power.*

THE court, to prevent tumults, required about sixty of the inhabitants of Boston to deliver up their arms and ammunition of every sort, under penalty of 10 l. upon each person neglecting, and laid the like penalty upon every one of them who should afterwards borrow any arms or ammunition. And, at the same time, made a law to punish any person by fine, imprisonment or banishment, who should defame any court or any of their sentences.

A GREAT number removed out of the jurisdiction, some of them being banished, some disfranchised; more to Rhode Island than to any other place. In a short time, most of them were permitted to return and were restored to their former privileges. The most of those errors, which were condemned by the synod, it's probable, they never would have owned as their principles, and they appear rather to be deduced, by some of the synod, as naturally following from the capital opinions, than to have been advanced by the opinionists themselves; or perhaps may have been unguardedly dropped by particular persons, in the heat of their disputes, or during an enthusiastick frenzy; and in others may have been the effect of a fond fancy for paradoxical tenets. They were charged indeed with principles which admit and introduce all kinds of immorality, and which make no distinction between virtue and vice. So are fatalists and predestinarians. Many of them were afterwards employed in posts of honour and trust, were exemplary in their lives and conversations, and their letters and private papers shew that they were pious and devout, and with the name of antinomians paid the strictest regard to moral virtue. The opinionists were punished for being deluded enthusiasts. The other side were deluded also by a [fond opinion that the honour of God required them to punish his creatures for differing] from themselves. It is evident, not only by Mrs. Hutchinson's

* He died in 1680. His son, grandson, and great grandson have been of the council for the province.

trial, but by many other public proceedings, that inquisition was made into men's private judgments as well as into their declarations and practice. Toleration was preached against as a sin in rulers which would bring down the judgments of heaven upon the land.*

THIS unhappy controversy did not take off the attention of the government from their necessary defence against the Pequod Indians, who continued their hostilities. Governor Vane had sent Capt. Underhill,[1] the winter before, to strengthen the garrison at Saybrook fort,[2] which they laid siege to for several weeks together. The three colonies, Massachusets, Plimouth and Connecticut, agreed, with their joint forces, to go into the Indian country and attempt their entire destruction. Massachusets sent 160 men under the command of Capt. Stoughton.[3] The number raised by each town gives us some idea of the proportion which the several settlements bore to one another at this time.† Connecticut men being settled near the Indian country, it was expected they would be early in action; the first of the Massachusets men that could be raised were therefore ordered to march. This party consisted of 40 men. Capt. Patrick,‡ who had the command of them, by letters dispatched from

* Mr. Dudley died with a copy of verses in his pocket, wrote with his own hand. The following two lines made part of it:
> Let men of God, in court and churches, watch
> O'er such as do a toleration hatch.
This was the prevailing doctrine many years, and until their eyes were opened by a fresh persecution coming upon themselves from King James. This made his declaration for a general liberty of conscience welcome, and they thanked the King for allowing to them what they before thought themselves bound in conscience to deny to others.

† Boston 26, Charlestown 12, Roxbury 10, Dorchester 13, Weymouth 5, Hingham 6, Medford 3, Newbury 8, Ipswich 17, Salem 18, Saugus (Lyn) 16, Watertown 14, Newtown 19, Marblehead 3.

‡ Patrick had served in Holland, in the Prince of Orange's guard, and was sent for to instruct the people of the colony in military discipline. In order to his being made a freeman, he was admitted a member of the church at Watertown, but the strict manners of the New-England men did not agree with a Dutch soldier. He soon removed to the Dutch at New Netherland. He was shot dead by a Dutchman at Stamford in 1643. *Hubbard.*

---

[1] Capt. John Underhill (*d.* 1672) wrote his own account of the Pequot War in a tract entitled *Newes from America* (London, 1638). It is reprinted in the *Collections* of the Massachusetts Historical Society, Third Series, vol. VI. Curiously enough, soon after he returned victor from the war he was disarmed by the Colony because he was a follower of Wheelwright and Mrs. Hutchinson. He withdrew to Dover, New Hampshire, where he was governor for nearly two years. Thence he moved to New Haven, and in 1643 to New Netherland. Expelled from New Netherland in 1653, he went to Rhode Island. After the conquest of New Netherland in 1664, he moved to Oyster Bay, Long Island, where he spent the remainder of his days.

[2] At the mouth of the Connecticut River.

[3] Israel Stoughton. See editor's note 2 on p. 55.

Providence, acquainted Capt. Mason [1] the commander of the Connecticut men, that he was hastening to join him. The body of the Indians were in two forts or inclosures, which on all sides they had rendered as defensible as they could by pallisadoes, their skill in fortification carrying them no farther. Sassacus, the chief sachem, was in one of them, and to that the English intended. Capt. Mason went with about 80 English (20 of which, under Capt. Underhill of the Massachusets, he had taken from Saybrook fort) and 100 river * Indians, by water, to the Naragansets country, where 200 of that tribe joined him. He would gladly have waited for Patrick's company, but was afraid the friend Indians would attribute the delay to want of courage, and therefore, on the 24th of May, he began his march for Sassacus's fort. The Naraganset Indians were struck with terror at the name of Sassacus, and endeavoured to dissuade Mason, but finding him determined, many of them left him, and near an hundred of them went back to Providence, where they reported that the Pequods had killed all the English. This report was carried to Boston, and must have caused great concern there. † Soon after, one of Underhill's men fell lame, and the rest of the company, wearied in travelling, being loaded with arms, ammunition and provisions, and Sassacus's fort being eight miles further distant, they resolved to attack the Indians in the other which was called Mistick fort.‡ Wequash,§ originally a Pequod, who was born at Mistick but now lived with the Naragansets, was their guide to the destruction of his own countrymen and nearest relations. They sent him forward to reconnoitre, and he returned with intelligence, that the Pequods

* Connecticut river.

† *MS. letter.*

‡ A manuscript journal says, that Underhill, upon his man's lameness, resolved that he and his company should go to Mistick, reading God's mind by that providence; and that Mason, unwilling to part, conformed, but Hubbard says, they were both of a mind for the other reasons mentioned. Underhill was one of the forwardest of the Boston enthusiasts.

§ Wequash became a christian and an apostle among his own people, travelling up and down to make converts; and when he died, gave his soul to Christ, and his only child to the English, hoping it would know more of Christ than its poor father ever did. *Mr. Shepard's letter to London.*

[1] Capt. John Mason (1600–1672) came to Massachusetts about 1632 and represented Dorchester in General Court in 1634 and 1635. In the latter year he migrated to Windsor, Connecticut. After the Pequot War he settled at Saybrook, moving later to Norwich. In 1660 he was elected Deputy-Governor of Connecticut. He was also chief judge of the county court, 1664–1670.

Mason's *Brief History of the Pequot War* may be found in the *Collections* of the Massachusetts Historical Society, Second Series, vol. VIII. There is an adequate biography by George E. Ellis in Sparks's *Library of American Biography*, Second Series, vol. III.

had taken great store of bass that day and were in a high feast, singing dancing and blessing their god * for that the English were gone away. They had seen the vessels pass by their river, from Saybrook towards Naraganset, and supposed they were gone off. Some of the English advanced, and heard the Indians at their revels until midnight. The next morning (May 26) about break of day, after a march of three or four miles from the place where they halted the night before, they came within sight of the fort which was upon a hill. Wequash piloted them to the gate. The centinel happened just then to be gone into a wigwam to light his pipe. The Indians were all in a deep sleep. One of their dogs, barking at the approach of the English, caused a discovery. The Indians within the fort began their tremendous yell, and the Indians without, who were in the English rear and afraid to come up, seconded them. No sound that was ever made can be more horrid than the Indian yell. The English immediately fired into the fort, the palisadoes not being so close as to hinder the muzzles of their guns going between. Not being able easily to enter at the gate, Mason went round to the other side of the fort, where was another opening or entrance barred with branches of forked trees only; at which he entred, with those that were with him. His lieutenant and the rest of the English entred, at the same time, by other parts. The Indians, who had no arms but bows, tomahawks and English hatchets, made stout resistance at first, and wounded many of the English. Mason intended to have spared the wigwams, but finding his men thus distressed, he entred one of them, and with a firebrand he found there, set it on fire. While he was doing it, an Indian was drawing his bow and would undoubtedly have killed him, if his serjeant, coming in, had not cut the bowstring with his hanger. The fire spread to the rest of the wigwams, and the English all retreated without the fort and surrounded it. The Indians, some climbed to the top of the palisadoes to avoid the fire and so exposed themselves to the English bullets, others forced their way out of the fort, and if any of them brake through the English the allied Indians were in a ring at some little distance; so that few if any escaped. There were about 60 or 70 wigwams in the fort or inclosure, and, it was imagined, four or five hundred Pequods men women and children. Three of the English were slain, and many, both English and Indians their friends, wounded with arrows, and some very badly. The army was in distress, notwithstanding their victory. The morning was cold. They had no sort of refreshment, not so much as water, nor any shelter for their wounded. They had

* This may be the conjecture of the journalist.

no intelligence of their vessels, which had been ordered to come from Naraganset to Pequod river. Many Indians were in the woods, who were not of the party in the fort. In the midst of this perplexity, they espied their vessels at a distance, sailing towards them. They then took up their wounded upon mats fastened to poles, some with the heads of the arrows in their bodies, and marched to the vessels six miles through the woods and swamps, the Indians lying in wait at every convenient place, and, with their arrows, wounding many more; but many of the Indians were slain in their attempts upon the English. They put their wounded into one of the barks, which set sail the same night and reached Saybrook fort. Patrick came in a pinnace from Providence to Naraganset soon after the forces marched, and, with the other vessels, went forward, taking Myontinomo, the sachem of Naraganset with them; but their arrival was prevented by contrary winds until the morning of the action, after it was over. Most of the English and all the Indians marched through what was called Nianticut's country, to Saybrook fort, their vessels also arriving there the next day. The Indians, in alliance with the English, had taken eighteen captives, ten males and eight females, four of the males were disposed of, one to each of four sachems, the rest put to the sword. Four of the females were left at the fort, the other four carried to Connecticut, where the Indians challenged them as their prize; the English not agreeing to it they were sacrificed also to end the dispute. The policy, as well as the morality of this proceeding, may well be questioned. The Indians have ever shewn great barbarity to their English captives, the English in too many instances have retaliated it. This has only enraged them the more. Besides, to destroy women and children, for the barbarity of their husbands and parents, cannot easily be justified.

SASSACUS, the sachem, after the taking of Mistick fort and so many of his warriors being slain, broke down his own fort, burnt all their wigwams, put his goods into canoes, and men, women and children forsook their country and went away by land to Quinnipiack.[1] The forces under Capt. Stoughton arrived at Saybrook the latter end of June. They pursued the Indians, meeting now and then two or three at a time, whom they killed or took prisoners; at length, they were informed of a great body of Indians in a swamp,* which they surrounded. They seem to have been of other tribes as well as Pequods. One of the sachems came out with 99 men, women

* Mr. Hubbard says, near Fairfield or Stratford.

---

[1] Quinnipiack was the Indian name for the site of New Haven.

and children, and delivered themselves up to the English. Wampum he said he had none, nor had he ever killed any English. The garment he had on, which was of black beaver skin, he presented. An Indian was sent in to tell the rest, that if they would come out and deliver up their arms and clear themselves from having murdered any English they should fare the better. After a short parley, they determined, that as they had lived together they would die together. Twelve of the murtherers were among them. They were about eighty in all. The English fired upon them, and having surrounded the swamp all night, entered in the morning, but found great part had escaped. Some of the Indians had guns and fired upon the English. This is the first account we have of their making use of guns. Sassacus fled to the Mohawks, by whom it was reported he was murdered. It is more probable, that he and his company incorporated with them. Many of the captives were sent to Bermudas and sold for slaves. The Pequod tribe was wholly extinguished. The Naragansets took charge of some of them, and promised to pay the English for their service; the few that remained never dared own they belonged to that tribe, but mixed with the Naraganset and other tribes. We have been more particular in relating this action, it being the first between the English and Indians, many circumstances not having been published before, and the rest of the Indians being thereby brought to be more afraid of the English, and restrained from open hostilities near forty years together.* [1]

* [It is worth observing that a controversy subsisted among the conquerors for some years after the conquest not only concerning the proportion of the right to the Prisoners but also to the conquered lands. Traces of this controversy appear many years after in the proceedings of the "united colonies," and I believe the right to private property takes its origin in many instances from the settlement then made and it appears from the papers of the Commissioners from K[ing] Charles the second that the Massachusets made a grant or donation of a tract of these conquered lands on the Eastern side of Pawcatuck river now in Rhode Island Colony 20 years after the conquest. An English Colony derives no right to lands conquered by it from its Charter, which is circumscribed by certain limits. In 1675 the Massachusets Colony had the principal share in the conquest of the Narraganset Country which lyes within the limits of Rhode Island Colony and the jurisdiction and property remained to that Colony. In 1690 the Massachusets alone conquered Nova Scotia, and the territory by a grant from the Crown was soon after with other territories erected into a province. In 1745 the Massachusets forces, under the Commission of the Governor, being joined by His Majesty's Ships, conquered Cape Breton. The territory was immediately considered as an acquisition to the Crown. The Army seems to have had an equitable right to their proportion of all other effects considered as prize and to the valuable captures consequent upon the surrender of the territory but their claim was never prosecuted.]

[1] Four contemporary accounts of the Pequot War have been collected in a single volume by Charles Orr — *The Pequot War*. They are Mason's, Underhill's, Vincent's and Gardener's. All four are reprinted from the *Collections* of the Massachusetts Historical Society.

THIS year, 1637, a number of the Puritan ministers in England wrote over to the ministers of New-England, informing them of reports that they had embraced new opinions which they disliked formerly, and which they in England still judged to be groundless and unwarrantable, viz.

That a stinted form of prayer and set liturgy is unlawful. That the children of godly and approved christians are not to be baptized until their parents be set members of some particular congregations. That the parents themselves, though of approved piety, are not to be received to the Lord's supper until they be admitted set members. That the power of excommunication is in the body of the church, though the minister should be of another mind. That upon a minister's being dismissed, though unjustly, from his particular congregation, he ceaseth to be a minister. That one minister cannot perform a ministerial act in any but his own congregation. That members of one congregation may not communicate in another.

They add,

that letters in New-England had influenced many in Old to leave their assemblies, because of a stinted liturgy, and to absent themselves from the Lord's supper because such as ought to be were not debarred from it.

They therefore requested that a seasonable review might be taken of the grounds and reasons that had swayed, and sent over, and if they were found to have weight they would be ready to give the right hand of fellowship; if otherwise they would animadvert upon them, so far as they varied from the truth, &c. The famous puritan, John Dod,[1] joined in the request.* Mr. Hooker, upon the occasion of this letter, writes thus to Mr. Shepard:

I confess freely to thee my fears that the first and second questions, touching a stinted form of prayer, will prove very hard to make any handsome work upon; and I do sadly suspect a troublesome answer may be returned to all the arguments. This to yourself, wherein I crave silence.

AN answer was wrote by Mr. Cotton, and a more full answer afterwards printed. In some of the points, I suppose the two last, the ministers in England were misinformed. In some of the others, particularly those which it was thought most difficult to answer, in a few years after the clergy in England fully concurred with their brethren in New-England.

* MS. original letters and papers.

---

[1] John Dod (1549?–1645) was an early and ardent non-conformist who remained in England.

IN June 1637, two large ships arrived from England with passengers. Mr. Eaton [1] and Mr. Hopkins,* two London merchants, Mr. Davenport [2] a minister of great character for learning and piety, and many others of good note and condition were of this company. Great pains were taken to persuade them to stay in the jurisdiction. The court offered them any place they would pitch upon, The town of Newbury offered to give up their settlement to them. Quinnipiack, and the country between that and the Dutch, was represented as a very fruitful place and well situated for trade and navigation. They flattered themselves, but upon what grounds does not appear, that there they should be out of the reach of a general governor, with which the country was from time to time threatned. These were the reasons publickly given for removing there. Besides, the principal men of the new company would be at the head of the government there; here, it was natural to expect, the old standers would be considered as their superiors. They laid the foundation of a flourishing colony, of which Quinnipiack, or New-Haven, was the chief town. They agreed among themselves upon a model of government in church and state, very like to that of the Massachusets, and continued a distinct colony and government until the year 1665,† when Connecticut and New-Haven, having three years before been incorporated by a charter from King Charles the second, united under

* Mr. Hopkins had been a Turkey merchant in London, of good credit and esteem, but of puritan principles; and for the sake of an undisturbed enjoyment of the worship of God, agreeable to those principles, came to New-England. He married Mr. Eaton's daughter-in-law. When Mr. Eaton removed to New-Haven, Mr. Hopkins went to Hartford, the chief town of Connecticut, and was chosen their governor several years, at length, returned to England and was chosen member of parliament, was warden of the fleet, a commissioner of the navy and of the admiralty. He had, notwithstanding, thoughts of returning to New-England, having an affection for the country, but death put an end to those thoughts. He died at London, in March 1657. He left a legacy to Harvard College, which was unpaid until 1710, when it was received by virtue of a decree in chancery.

† Connecticut charter was brought over by Mr. Winthrop in 1662, but New-Haven refused to submit to it. At a general meeting at New-Haven, 4th Nov. 1662, Mr. Davenport being present insisted 1. That the colony of New-Haven was not within the patent. 2. That it was not lawful to join, and they unanimously concluded to stand to their own combination. *Goffe's Journal.* But in 1665, upon commissioners coming over to enquire into the state of the colonies, they wisely changed their resolution, and of a colony became a county, and so have remained ever since.

[1] Theophilus Eaton (1590–1658). See Hutchinson's footnote on p. 16. There is a memoir of Eaton by Jacob Bailey Moore in the *Collections* of the New York Historical Society, Second Series, II, 467–493.

[2] John Davenport (1597–1670). See Hutchinson's footnote on p. 74.

one governor.* The people in the Massachusets soon after reflected upon the favour of providence, in not gratifying them with the continuance of this company among them. It appeared that the Dutch were designing to take possession of this country, and they opposed the English in the settlement even of New-Haven itself, threatning hostilities against them. Mr. Eaton, being a man of good abilities,

* The heads of the combination or agreement were these, viz.

That none shall be admitted to any office in the government, civil or military, or have a voice in any election, except he be a member of one of the churches in New-England.

That all the freemen, without summons, shall yearly meet, the last fourth day in May, and vote in the election of governor, deputy governor, magistrates and other officers; such as cannot attend in person may vote by proxy, or send their votes sealed.

That there be a general court, consisting of governor, deputy governor and magistrates, and two deputies for each plantation where there is a church and freemen orderly admitted; every member of the court to have a voice, and all determinations to be by the major vote of the magistrates and the major vote of the deputies. This court to sit the last fourth day of May in every year of course, and on other occasions to be summoned by the governor, or in his absence by the deputy governor, or in the absence of both by two magistrates. To declare, publish and establish the laws of God the supreme legislator, and to make and repeal orders for smaller matters not particularly determined in scripture, according to the general rules of righteousness. To order all affairs of war and peace, and all matters relative to the defending or fortifying the country. To receive and determine all appeals, civil or criminal, from any inferior courts, in which they are to proceed according to scripture light, and laws and orders agreeing therewith.

That there be a court of magistrates, to meet or be held twice every year, to determine all weighty causes, civil or criminal, above those limited to plantation courts, and to receive and try all appeals from plantation courts. In this court, when the voices are equal, the governor, or in his absence the deputy governor, shall have a casting voice.

That there be a court in each plantation, in which there shall be one or more magistrates; the freemen to chuse two, three or four deputies to assist the magistrate for the trial of civil causes, not exceeding twenty pounds, and criminal, the penalty not exceeding stocks, whipping, or five pounds fine.

Their laws and judicial proceedings varied in very few circumstances from the Massachusets; one indeed was material, that they had no jury, neither in civil nor criminal cases. All matters of fact, as well as law, were determined by the court.

Mr. Davenport, the minister who came over with Mr. Eaton, had been a preacher of great note in Colman-street, London, and for his noncompliance in ecclesiastical matters absconded and came over privately. Many of his principal hearers accompanied him, and formed a church at New-Haven. [Doctor Mather in the life of this Mr. Davenport takes notice of his fleeing to Holland about the year 1633 and that he did not succeed there, because he declined baptizing children whose parents or sureties were ignorant or scandalous. But there is a passage in a letter from Archbp. Laud to Vossius Feb. 24, O. S 1633 which if the Doctor had seen he would not have omitted mentioning. *Vidi nuperrime literas tuas ad Golfum etc. Merum figmentum est, Episcopos Angliae jurisdictionem suam in Ecclesias vestras velle extendere. Id quidem illis ne per somnium accidit. Poeta, ad minimum, Davenportus, si dicat, fingit. Nam hoc vult Rex Serenisimus, ne mercatores alii que subditi sui Forbesium similemve alium Ecclesiae Anglicanae praeferant. Ideoque Forbesio dimisso, Golfus ad quem scripsisti vir doctus & disciplinae nostrae prudens assertor, omnium suffragiis substituitur. Quid hoc ad Ecclesias vestras? Sed quoniam "facina" isthaec Davenportum subolet, habebis viri apud nos res gestas. Triennio, plus minus abhinc, coram me Episcopo tum Londinensi sistebatur etc. Si ideo gratus sit vestris Amstelodamensibus quod Ecclesiae suae, et Reformatae, desertor*

was a fit person to resist them; and, finally, in the year 1650, the other colonies uniting in the cause with New-Haven, they were by treaty limited to Greenwich, said to be ten or twelve miles on a

sit, fruatur ille fortunae suae, vos illo! [1]] Another company came from Kent, Suffolk, and Surry in England, among whom was Mr. William Leet, then a young man (after Mr. Eaton's death, governor) and after the colonies were united, some time governor of Connecticut. These, with Mr. Whitfield their minister, chose a place about 16 miles East of New-Haven, since called Guildford.[2] Another company removed from Hartford with Mr. Peter Prudden for their minister, and settled a little West from New-Haven and called the place Milford. Brainford on the East, and Stamford near forty miles West of New-Haven, were both settled by people who removed from Weathersfield on account of disturbances in the church there. These towns, together with a plantation upon the East end of Long-Island called Southold, are said to have been all that were concerned in the combination which was first formed. The colony chose their leader Mr. Eaton for their first governor, and continued him every year until he died, which was 14 years after the foundation. Their chief view was trade; and, to be better accommodated, they built on small house-lots near the sea, and fairer and more commodious houses than those in the other colonies. They built vessels for foreign voyages, and set up trading-houses upon lands which they purchased at Delaware Bay for the sake of beaver, but were unsuccessful, and their stocks sunk very fast, and in five or six years they were much exhausted. Unwilling to give over, they exerted themselves, as a last effort, in building a ship for the trade to England, in which they put their whole stock of money, plate, and all the proper goods they could procure, to make a more valuable adventure. In her went passenger Mr. Grigson, one of the magistrates, in order to solicit a patent, and eight or ten more considerable persons, who, to use Mr. Cotton's expression, all went to heaven by water, the ship never being heard of after their sailing. The loss of this ship entirely broke them up as traders, and they

---

[1] Professor Paul Birdsall of Williams College has kindly given the editor the following translation of Laud's letter:

"I have very recently seen your letters to Goffe, etc. It is sheer imagination to assume that the Bishops of England wish to extend their jurisdiction over your churches. That does not occur to them even in their sleep. Davenport, who at least possesses a poetic imagination, is romancing if he says this. For our most serene highness the King desires that neither his merchants nor others of his subjects grant preferment to Forbes or to any other like him in the English Church. Therefore when Forbes was dismissed, Goffe — to whom you have written — a learned man and discreet spokesman of our faith — was substituted for him by the votes of every one. What has this to do with your churches? But since that workshop reeks of Davenport, you shall have evidence of the man in his relations with us. Three years ago, more or less, he was tried in my presence when I was Bishop of London, etc. If as a traitor to his church and to the Reformed Church he is the more acceptable to your Amsterdam congregation, then may he enjoy his good fortune, and may you enjoy him!"

Forbes appears to have been John Forbes (1568?–1634), minister of Alford, Aberdeenshire, who was banished in 1606. In 1611 he was settled as pastor of a British congregation at Middelburg, and later of the British church at Delft. "In 1628 Charles I, influenced by Laud, began to interfere with the worship and discipline of the English and Scots churches in the Netherlands, and Forbes was ultimately removed from his charge." *Dictionary of National Biography*.

Goffe was presumably Stephen Goffe, D.D. (1605–1681). About 1633 he was a chaplain to the regiment of Colonel Horace Vere in the Low Countries. Later he was appointed one of Charles I's chaplains. *Dictionary of National Biography*.

[2] In the first edition this name is spelled "Guilford," which is the accepted spelling today. The third edition follows the first.

strait line distant from Hudson's river. Indeed the suffering them to extend thus far was mere favour and indulgence, but there had been a good correspondence always kept up between the English colonies and these intruders. They had mutual trade and commerce, and although the Dutch at that day, whatever they may now do, did not esteem godliness to be the greatest gain, yet their form of worship, their principles as to discipline and ceremonies were more agreeable to the New-Englanders than those of the high party in England. New-Haven was a barrier to the colony of Connecticut, and caused its increase. To which we may add, that the Massachusets, by the removal of this company, were enabled to provide the better for the immediate acommodation of the great number of passengers which unexpectedly came over the next year;

For in 1638, notwithstanding the clamour against the plantation was revived in England, and a design was on foot to revoke and annul the charter, there arrived about 20 ships and three thousand passengers. These ships were the more welcome to the colony, because they were afraid, that in consequence of the complaints against them, a stop would be put to any more passengers coming from England. In 1635, a commission had been granted to several of the nobility, and great officers of the crown for the regulation of the colonies.* The archbishop of Canterbury [Laud] kept a jealous eye over New-England. One Burdett [1] of Piscataqua was his correspondent. A copy of a letter to the archbishop, wrote by Burdett, was found in his study, and to this effect, viz.

---

turned to husbandry for their support. The manner of their settlement, upon small lots, was inconvenient for husbandmen, and the soil was not the best, so that they were much discouraged and several projections were made for their removal in a body. They made further purchases of large tracts of land at Delaware bay, but were obstructed and discouraged by opposition from the Dutch. They had offers from Ireland, after the wars were over, and were in treaty for the purchase of lands there for a small distinct province by themselves, and when Jamaica was conquered by Cromwell, proposals were made to them to remove there in a body; but as the first generation went off, and the second came on with the attachment natural to the place of their birth and education, they became more reconciled to their situation, and although they have never been remarkable for foreign commerce, the first intention of the settlement, yet their improvements in husbandry have been equal to any of their neighbours. The ancient colony of New-Haven is at this day a principal part of the colony of Connecticut, on many accounts respectable, and to be placed with those of the first rank.

* Appendix. [No. 4]

---

[1] George Burdett, a popular preacher, flourished in Salem 1635–37 and then moved to Dover, New Hampshire. There he got into various quarrels, moved on to York, Maine, and finally back to England. As Savage remarks, "the criminal proceedings of the courts under Gorges's government, for adultery and other charges, make it plain that New England was not the right place for him." See Jeremy Belknap's *History of New Hampshire*, I, 33–36.

That he delayed going to England, that he might fully inform himself of the state of the place as to allegiance, for it was not new discipline which was aimed at, but sovereignty; and that it was accounted perjury and treason, in their general court, to speak of appeals to the King.

By the first ships which came this year, a letter was brought from the archbishop to Burdett, rendering him thanks for the care of his Majesty's service, and assuring him, that he would take a time for the redress of the disorders which he informed them of; but, by reason of much business which lay upon them, they could not at that time accomplish his desire. This letter to Burdett was, by some means or other not mentioned, shewn to the governor of the Massachusets. A *quo warranto* had been brought by Sir John Banks, attorney-general, a year or two before, against the governor, deputy-governor and assistants of the corporation of the Massachusets. This was never served upon any persons in New-England. Some, which were or had been of the corporation, and who remained in England, appeared and disclaimed the charter; and there was a determination, that the liberties and franchises of the corporation should be seized into the King's hands; but, it is said, judgment was never entered in form against the corporation.* It is agreed, that there was an order of the King in council May 3d 1637, that the attorney-general be required to call for the patent of the Massachusets, and this year (1638) Mr. Winthrop received a letter from Mr. Meautis, clerk of the council, accompanied with an order from the Lords of the council of April 4th 1638, requiring the governor, or any other person who should have the letters patent in their power or custody, without fail to transmit the same by the return of the ship which carried the order, and in case of contempt their Lordships would move his Majesty to re-assume into his hands the whole plantation. An answer was drawn up and transmitted, as appears by the files of the court; † in which, after professing their loyalty, they say, that they were never called to answer to the *quo warranto*; if they had been, they should have had a good plea against it, that they came over with their families and estates, with his Majesty's licence and encouragement, had greatly enlarged his dominions, and if their

* Mr. Hubbard says, judgment was given, &c. but the government themselves, in some of the declarations in King Charles their second's time, say, that the process was never compleated. — Judgment was entered against so many as appeared, and they which did not appear were outlawed.[1]

† The records of the session take no notice of it. Appendix [No. 5].

---

[1] The course of the proceedings against the colony is traced carefully by Charles Deane in Justin Winsor's *Memorial History of Boston*, I, chapter X.

charter should be taken away they should be forced to remove to
some other place or return to their native country; that the other
plantations would be broke up, and the the whole country fall into
the hands of the French or Dutch, and that all men would be discouraged from such undertakings in confidence of a royal grant; that
the common people, if cast off by his Majesty, might confederate
under some new form of government, which would be of evil example and might expose the court to his Majesty's displeasure;* and
for these reasons, they pray their Lordships that they may be suffered to live in this wilderness; that their liberties may not be restrained, when others are enlarged; and that men of abilities may
not be hindred from coming to them, when they are encouraged to
go to other plantations. It was never known what reception this
answer met with. It is certain, that no further demand was made.
In a short time, the archbishop, and several other of the Lords of the
council who were present at this order, lost their authority and influence. They were as much perplexed, when called to account for
their own conduct, as the colony could have been for theirs, had it
been more exceptionable than it was. We may make some conjec-
tures what would have been the consequence of taking away the
charter at this time. It is pretty certain, the body of the people
would have left the country. Two years after, merely from a dissatisfaction with the soil and the climate, many did remove, and
many more were on tiptoe and restrained only by the consideration
of their engagements to stand by and support one another; but
where they would have removed, is the question. It would not have
been to the French. This would have been going further from the
sun. They were too far northward already. Besides, they might
well expect a heavier yoke under the romish hierarchy, than what
they complained of under the protestant. They would not have removed to any plantation or territory claimed by the King of England. What assurance could they have of security, for the enjoyment of privileges, in any other part, stronger than they had when
they came here? After they had spent their substance, and many
that came with them their lives, in possessing and improving a country, in confidence that they should enjoy their charter privileges,
they and their posterity for ever, they would not have trusted to
promises if any had been made them a second time. It is most likely
they would have gone to the Dutch at Hudson's river. They had
always kept up a friendly correspondence with them. In their religious principles and form of worship and church government, they

* For being the occasion of it, by giving up the charter.

were not very distant from one another. The Dutch were not generally very nice upon those points. The only difficulty would have been, to have obtained those privileges in matters of government from the Dutch, which they had from the English; and I think the Dutch would have been politic enough to have granted them. If they had failed with the Dutch, such was their resolution, that they would have sought a *vacuum domicilium*, (a favourite expression with them) in some part of the globe where they would, according to their apprehensions, have been free from the controul of any European power. In their first migration, most of them could say, *omnia mea mecum porto*. All the difference, as to the second would have been, that so far as they had lessened their substance, so much less room would have been necessary for the transportation of what remained. Such a scheme would have consisted very well with their notions of civil subjection, as we shall see in many instances. I do not say their notions were just. Allegiance in an English born subject is said to be perpetual, and to accompany him wherever he goes.

THE same governor, deputy governor and assistants were chosen for 1638, as had been for 1637. The settlements were extended this year beyond Merrimack river. Salisbury and Hampton had a great quantity of salt meadows. They were an inducement to people to sit down there, although the upland was a light sandy soil and not very inviting. Rowley and Sudbury were both settled this year also.

THE inhabitants of Lynn being desirous of larger accommodations, many of them removed to Long Island, near the west end; Lord Stirling, by his agent there, having sold or quit claimed to them a tract for a plantation; but they were soon disturbed by the Dutch, and some of them were imprisoned under a pretence of an affront offered to the Prince of Orange's arms, which they had taken down from a tree where the Dutch had hung them up. Not being able to keep their ground, they removed to the east end, and settled a church and town (Southampton) and entered into a civil combination, intending to be independent of any of the colonies. Another distinct government was forming at the mouth of Connecticut river by the agent of Lord Say and Seal and Lord Brooke, who, with other persons of distinction, were still expected in New-England, and other companies who were intending to remove, intended likewise to form into separate governments. But this humour did not last long. In a few years, all the colonies found an union or confederacy necessary for their defence, not only against the Indians, but against the French and Dutch; and there could be no encouragement for small bodies of men to sit down any where, independant or unconnected.

All that had begun any settlements between the Massachusets and the Dutch (the Rhode Islanders excepted, who were covered, except on the sea, by the other colonies) joined with Connecticut or New-Haven, and all to the eastward, whether in New-Hampshire, Province of Main or the country further east, applied to the Massachusets that they might incorporate with them.

THE year 1638 was memorable for a very great earthquake throughout New-England. The shake, by the printed accounts of it, and from manuscript letters, appears to have been equal to that in 1727, the pewter in many places being thrown off the shelves, and the tops of chimnies in some places shook down, but the noise, though great, not so surprizing as that of the last mentioned. The course of it was from west to east. This was a remarkable æra. So long after the earthquake was as common an expression with the people of New-England, for many years, as it seems to have been heretofore with the children of Israel.*

HARVARD College takes its date from the year 1638. Two years before, the general court gave four hundred pounds towards a public school at Newtown, but Mr. John Harvard,[1] a worthy minister of Charlestown, dying this year and having given a great part of his estate, between seven and eight hundred pounds to the same use, the school took the name of Harvard College by an order of Court.†

* *Johnson. — Hubbard.*

† The first master of the college was Nathaniel Eaton, who was a good scholar, but had not the other qualities requisite for the instruction and government of youth. He was charged with avarice, in withholding necessary or convenient commons, and with cruelty, in beating his usher with a cudgel whilst two of his servants held him out by the legs and arms. His conduct having been enquired into by the court, in 1639, he was thereupon displaced, fined 100 marks and ordered to pay thirty pounds to Mr. Briscoe[2] whom he had cruelly beat. After the sentence of the court, he was excommunicated from the church at Cambridge. He complained that the church had enquired into his case before, and fully understood it and passed no censure upon him; but when they knew the opinion of the court, they conformed to that. He went to Virginia. After the restoration he was in England, conformed and had a living, and is said to have revenged himself upon all nonconformists, being greatly instrumental in their persecutions. He was educated under Dr. Ames in Holland, and known to Mr. Hooker whilst there, who says he did not approve of his spirit, and feared the issue of his being received here, &c. He was succeeded by Mr. Henry Dunstar,[3] well esteemed for his learning, piety and spirit of government.

---

[1] John Harvard (1607–1638) graduated from Emmanuel College, Cambridge, in 1632, and took his master's degree there three years later. He did not come to Massachusetts until the spring of 1637. What little is known of Harvard's life is succinctly told by Samuel Eliot Morison in his *Builders of the Bay Colony*, pp. 189–190.

[2] Nathaniel Briscoe was a son of Nathaniel Briscoe of Watertown, a rich tanner. He was usher at Harvard College under Eaton. Later he moved to Milford, Massachusetts.

[3] Henry Dunster (1609–1660) was a graduate of Magdalene College, Cambridge.

IN 1639, the former governor and deputy governor were continued, and the same assistants, except Mr. Harlakenden, who died in the colony, and I suppose the last year.

STRAITS and difficulties, at the beginning of the colony, had produced industry and good husbandry, and then they soon raised provisions enough for their own support, and an overplus for exportation. We hear but little of trade for the first seven years, except a small traffick with the natives by barter of toys, and the few utensils, tools and cloathing they at first thought necessary, in exchange for furs and skins. What the planters brought with them consisted, principally, of materials for their buildings, necessary tools for their husbandry, stock for their farms, and cloathing for themselves and families; and those who had more estate than was sufficient for these purposes, were country gentlemen and unacquainted with commerce, as Winthrop, Dudley, Bellingham, Bradstreet, &c. and never employed themselves in it, (Mr. Winthrop built a small barque called the Blessing,[1] which was employed to import corn from the southern Indians when the colony was in want, but she was soon cast away) and people in general turned their minds to provide comfortable lodgings, and to bring under improvement so much land as would afford them necessary support, and this was enough to employ them. After a few years, by hard labour and hard fare, the land produced more than was consumed by the inhabitants; the overplus was sent abroad to the West-Indies, the Wine-Islands,[2] &c. Returns were made in the produce of the respective countries and in bullion, the most of which, together with the furs procured from the natives, went to England to pay for the manufactures continually necessary from thence. As hands could be spared from husbandry and labour in providing their houses, they were taken off, and some employed in sawing boards, splitting staves, shingles and hoops, others in the fishery, and as many as were capable of it in building small vessels for the fishery and for coasting and foreign trade. Thus gradually and insensibly they seem to have fallen into that trade

---

He came to Massachusetts in 1640 and did an excellent piece of work in establishing Harvard College upon a sound basis. Later he became a Baptist, and accordingly gave up the presidency of the College. He retired to Scituate, where he spent his remaining years.

There is a life of Dunster by Jeremiah Chaplin (1872), but at present the most satisfactory account of his life and estimate of his achievements will be found in Samuel Eliot Morison's *Builders of the Bay Colony*. Chapter VI is entitled "Henry Dunster."

[1] The full name of this bark was the *Blessing of the Bay*. See John Winthrop's *History of New England* (1853), I, 69.

[2] The Wine Islands: the Canary Islands, the Azores, and Madeira.

most natural to the country and adapted to their peculiar circumstances, without any premeditated scheme or projection for that purpose. The primary views, in their removal, were the enjoyment of civil and religious liberty. Merchants, and others for the sake of gain when they saw a prospect of it afterwards, came over and incorporated with them, and caused a great increase of commerce, and led the legislators to measures for the further improvement of it. For encouraging the fishery, an act was made, this year, to free all estates, employed in catching making or transporting fish, from all duties and public taxes; and all persons were restrained, by penalty, from using any cod or bass fish for manuring the ground; and all fishermen during the season for business, and all ship-builders, were by the same act excused from trainings. Sumptuary laws were made for restraining excess in apparel and other expences; a spirit of industry and frugality prevailed; and those who lived in the next age speak of this as the *aurea ætas* in which religion and virtue flourished: But it was not long before many became discontented and encouraged projects for their removal.

IN the year 1640, Mr. Dudley was governor and Mr. Bellingham deputy governor; Mr. Winthrop, the former governor, one of the assistants; the rest the same as the last year. The importation of settlers now ceased. The motive to transportation to America was over, by the change in the affairs of England. They, who then professed to be able to give the best account, say, that in 298 ships, which were the whole number from the beginning of the colony, there arrived * 21200 passengers, men women and children, perhaps about 4000 families.† Since which, more persons have removed out of New-England to other parts of the world than have come from other parts to it; and the number of families, at this day, in the four governments may be supposed to be less rather than more than the natural encrease of four thousand. This sudden stop had a surprizing effect upon the price of cattle. They had lost the greatest part of what they intended for the first supply, in the passage from

---

* Mr. Neale supposes this to be impossible, but the number is not great for so many ships. If we allow half of them for transporting goods, and 140 souls to each of the other, it will make the number. Many of the ships were large, in the first fleet especially.

† A modest computation then made of the whole charge of transportation of the persons, their goods, the stock of cattle, provisions until they could support themselves, necessaries for building, artillery, arms and ammunition, amounts to 192,000 l. sterling. *Johnson*. A dear purchase, if they had paid nothing before to the council of Plimouth, and nothing afterwards to the sachems of the country. Well might they complain, when the titles to their lands were called in question by Sir Edmond Andros; their labour in clearing and improving them was of more value than the lands after they were improved, and this other expence might be out of the question.

Europe. As the inhabitants multiplied, the demand for the cattle increased, and the price of a milch cow had kept from 25 to 30 l. but fell at once this year to 5 or 6 l. A farmer, who could spare but one cow in a year out of his flock, used to cloath his family with the price of it at the expence of the new comers; when this failed they were put to difficulties. Although they judged they had 12000 neat cattle, yet they had but about 3000 sheep in the colony.

The year 1641 afforded not so pleasing a prospect. As soon as the country ceased to be necessary, as an asylum for oppressed people in England, some of those who had been the greatest benefactors there not only discouraged any further transportation, but endeavoured to induce such as had gone over to remove. Had the same changes happened in England six or eight years sooner, the continent of North America would in all probability have been at this day in a far less flourishing estate than it is. Some of the principal men wavered, but others were more resolute, and determined not to forsake their undertaking.*

Lord Say and Seal had turned his thoughts to a more southern settlement in the Bahama islands. He had engaged Mr. Humfries,[1] one of the assistants of the Massachusets colony, in the design, with a promise of being the governor of the new settlement. A new plan of government was framed, wholly aristocratical, and the magistracy to be hereditary; but exceptions being taken to this form by the people, it was altered and brought nearer to that of the Massachusets.† Mr. Winthrop (the usual governor and always considered

* Mr. Richard Salstonstall about this time, and I suppose upon this occasion, made a vow to God that he would not leave the country whilst the ordinances of God continued there in purity. Some years after, his wife was in a bad state of health and it was thought she might have relief by physicians in England. He applied to Mr. Cotton, not to absolve him, but to satisfy his doubting conscience. Mr. Cotton convinced him that the marriage vow was the most binding. *MS. J. Cotton.*

† It is observable that all the colonies, before the reign of King Charles the second, Maryland excepted, settled a model of government for themselves. Virginia had been many years distracted under the government of presidents and governors, with councils in whose nomination or removal the people had no voice, until in the year 1620 a house of burgesses broke out in the colony; the King nor the grand council at home not having given any powers or directions for it. — The governor and assistants of the Massachusets at first intended to rule the people, and, as we have observed, obtained their consent for it, but this lasted two or three years only; and although there is no colour for it in the charter, yet a house of deputies appeared suddenly, in 1634, to the surprize of the magistrates and the disappointment of their schemes for power. — Connecticut soon after followed the plan of the Massachusets. — New-Haven, altho' the people had

[1] "Mr. Humfries" was John Humfry. Hutchinson spells his name in a number of ways, and the various editions are correspondingly casual. See Hutchinson's footnote about him on p. 15.

abroad as the head of the colony) had wrote to Lord Say, representing to his Lordship that it seemed evident that God had chosen New-England to plant his people in, and that it would be displeasing unto him that this work should be hindered; and that such as had been well inclined, if not with their persons yet with their substance,

---

the highest reverence for their leaders and for near 30 years in judicial proceeding submitted to the magistracy (it must however be remembred that it was annually elected) without a jury, yet in matters of legislation the people, from the beginning, would have their share by their representatives. —— New-Hampshire combined together under the same form with Massachusets. —— Lord Say tempts the principal men of the Massachusets, to make them and their heirs nobles and absolute governors of a new colony; but, under this plan, they could find no people to follow them. — Barbadoes and the leward islands, began in 1625, struggled under governors and councils and contending proprietors for about 20 years. Numbers suffered death by the arbitrary sentences of courts martial, or other acts of violence, as one side or the other happened to prevail. At length, in 1645, the first assembly was called, and no reason given but this, viz. That, by the grant to the Earl of Carlisle, the inhabitants were to enjoy all the liberties, privileges and franchises of English subjects, and therefore, as it is also expressly mentioned in the grant, could not legally be bound or charged by any act without their own consent. This grant, in 1627, was made by Charles the first, a Prince not the most tender of the subjects liberties. After the restoration there is no instance of a colony settled without a representative of the people, nor any attempt to deprive the colonies of this privilege, except in the arbitrary reign of King James the second. The colonies, which are to be settled in the new acquired countries, have the fullest assurance, by his Majesty's proclamation, that the same form of government shall be established there. Perhaps the same establishment in Canada, and the full privileges of British subjects conferred upon the French inhabitants there, might be the means of firmly attaching them to the British interest; and civil liberty tend also to deliver them by degrees from their religious slavery. The inhabitants of Acadie or Nova-Scotia lived, above forty years after the reduction of Port Royal, under the government of their priests. No form of civil government was established, and they had no more affection for England than for Russia. The military authority served as a watch to prevent confederacies or combinations. The people indeed chose more or less deputies from each canton or division, but their only business seems to have been to receive orders from the governor, and to present petitions to him from the people. Temporal offences, unless enormous, and all civil controversies were ordinarily adjudged and determined by their spiritual fathers. I asked some of the most sensible of the Acadians, what punishment the priests could inflict to answer the ends of government. They answered me by another question. What can be a greater punishment than the forfeiture of our salvation? In no part of the romish church the blind persuasion, of the power of the priest to save or damn, was ever more firmly riveted; and although these Acadians have, for eight years past, been scattered through the English colonies, yet I never could hear of one apostate or so much as a wavering person among them all; and if the Canadians are treated in the same manner, they will probably remain under the same infatuation. [The priests of other regions have assumed the same power. Caesar says of the Druids — that they decided all publick and private controversies — all disputes concerning inheritance, or the bounds of lands, as well as murder, manslaughter and other heinous deeds are judged and determined by them — they appoint rewards, they pronounce punishments: Whoever abides not by their decrees is excommunicated from all sacrifices, which with them is deemed the severest penalty, for all under this interdiction are treated as the most wicked and atheistical — all men avoid talking or meeting with them lest they should receive infection from them — they are denied the benefit of the law and are rendered incapable of sustaining any office.]

to encourage it, should desist and discourage it by insinuating that there was no possibility of subsistance there; and added, that God would never have sent so many of his people thither, if he had not seen the place sufficient to maintain them or intended to make it so. His Lordship answered, that he could not deny great part of what was written, particularly the evidence of God's owning his people in the country of New-England; but alledged, that it was a place appointed for a present refuge only, and a better place being now found out they ought all to remove there.*

IT is certain that a great part of the colony was under great doubts as to their subsistance. All could not be traders. Much labour was necessary to the clearing a new country for pasture or tillage; after three or four years improvement of a piece of ground, they found they had exhausted the goodness of the soil and were obliged to go upon new improvements. They never used such manure as would keep it in heart. The common practice, of manuring with fish, left the land in a worse state than it would have been in if they had used no manure at all, or than any other manure, even lime, would have left it. This caused many of them to have an unfavourable opinion of the country and to despair of obtaining a livelihood in it, and great numbers had determined to remove. Some were persuaded to alter their resolution, but others persisted. A church had been gathered at Providence, and news came, that Mr. Sherwood the pastor, with another minister, had been sent home prisoners by Carter the deputy governor, and that the magistrates were inclined to persecution. This is not incredible, even in the year 1641, when they could not have expected that these measures would be approved in England, for Virginia persisted in opposition to the parliament many years after.† Whilst some in New-England were discouraged by this advice, others were the more confirmed, looking upon it their duty to go over and strengthen their brethren. Mr. Humfries had met with great losses by fire, the year before, and was detained in New-England by his private affairs for this year; but a company embarked with Capt. William Pierce,[1] who was of the first fleet which came over with the charter, and a very noted commander. Upon their

* *Hubbard.*

† [Vonner the cooper who headed an Insurrection in England soon after the Restoration and suffered death, was concerned in this undertaking. *Magn.*]

---

[1] Capt. William Pierce. The surname is spelled "Peirce" in the first edition. The third follows the first. Savage calls him "a distinguished shipmaster," and adds "made more voyages than any other person in the same years to and from Boston, was killed by the Spaniards at Providence in the Bahamas, 13 July 1641."

arrival at Providence, they found the island in the possession of the Spaniards. They had shot in under the command of the fort before they discovered their danger; and in coming about, Pierce was slain from the fort, but the vessel got clear and returned to New England, and the designs of the rest, of course, were at an end. The Lords, and others concerned in this attempt to settle the Bahama islands, spent sixty thousand pounds sterling, which was entirely lost by the island's being taken.*

THE difficulties particular persons were under, and the difference of sentiment upon private affairs, had an influence upon the public affairs. The election this year (1641), notwithstanding the great number of voters, was determined in favour of Mr. Bellingham for governor, Mr. Winthrop being his competitor, by a majority of six votes only. Mr. Endicot was chosen deputy governor. It was disputed whether they had the majority, and it was some time, Mr. Hubbard says, long, before either of them were admitted to their places. The choice seems not to have been agreeable to the general court, for the first order they made, was to repeal a standing law for allowing one hundred pounds annually to the governor.

THE court, this year, expecting great revolutions were at hand in England, sent over, as their agents, two of the ministers, Mr. Thomas Weld, and Mr. Hugh Peters,† and one of the representatives, Mr. William Hibbins,[1] in order to establish the interest of the colony. Their particular instructions have not been preserved.

THIS year also, the plantation at Springfield, upon Connecticut river, returned to the jurisdiction of the Massachusets. In the year 1636, as has been observed, the towns or settlements on Connecticut river began. A more particular account of the settlement of that colony will perhaps be expected. The inhabitants of the towns of Roxbury, Dorchester, Cambridge and Watertown, in the Massa-

* *Hubbard.*

† [Neither] Weld nor Peters ever returned to New-England.[2] The first, as appears by some of his letters, had a living at Gatesend in the Bishoprick of Durham. He went to Ireland with Lord Forbes, but came back to England and was ejected in King Charles the second's reign. The latter, by busying himself too much with politicks, came to a tragical end, which he would have been in no danger of if he had returned to his church again. His wife, whom he married in New-England, was supported after his death by a collection of 30 l. a year until 1671. *MS. letter.*

[1] William Hibbins (*d.* 1654), of Boston, was chosen an Assistant in 1643 and continued in that office until his death. His widow, Ann Hibbins, who was a sister of Richard Bellingham, was condemned for being a witch and was executed in June 1656. She was excommunicated by the Boston church in 1641.

[2] The variation of the text of this sentence is peculiar in the three editions. The first edition gives "Weld nor Peters never"; the third "Weld and Peters never."

chusets, laid the foundation of the colony of Connecticut. Mr. William Pynchon, being the principal person among those from Roxbury who had pitched upon a place higher up the river than the rest, called by the Indians Agawam, he changed the name to Springfield.* His mansion house was at a town, of that name in England, near to Chelmsford in Essex. Those from Dorchester pitched upon a place below, called by the Indians Mattaneaug or Cushankamaug. Mr. Ludlow was the principal person who removed with them. Mr Warham their minister and the whole church followed the next year. They called their settlement Windsor. The Cambridge people, with Mr. Hooker and Mr. Stone their ministers, and Mr. Haynes who the year before had been governor at their head, were seated next below at a place called Suckiang, which they changed into Hartford, the place of Mr. Stone's nativity in England. A few miles below, there was another tract of interval land called by the Indians Pauquiang, which those of Hartford intended to have included in their settlement; but a few of the Watertown people were too quick for them. They gave it the name of Weathersfield. The commission, which they took from the Massachusets, was of a pretty extraordinary nature. The preamble to it acknowledges, that the lands, which they intended to take possession of, were without the commonwealth and body of the Massachusets, and that certain noble personages in England, by virtue of a patent, challenged the jurisdiction there; but their minds not being known as to a form of government, and there being a necessity that some authority should be established, they therefore appoint Roger Ludlow, Esq; &c.† with full power and authority to hear and determine, in a judicial way, all matters in difference between party and party, to inflict corporal punishment, imprisonment and fines, and to make and decree orders for the present as shall be necessary for the plantation, relative to trading, planting, building, military discipline and defensive war, if need require, and to convene the inhabitants in general court if it shall be thought meet. The commission to continue no longer than one year, and to be recalled if a form of government could be agreed upon between the noble personages, the inhabitants, and the commonwealth of the Massachusets, &c.

* At first they called the new settlements by the names of the towns they had left in the bay.

† The others were William Pynchon, Esq; John Steele, William Swaine, Henry Smith, William Phelpes, William Westwood, and Andrew Warner.

Mr. Ludlow, in a letter from Hartford, 1st of the 8th Month, 1638, to the Massachusets general court, observes they had desired that Connecticut would forbear exercising jurisdiction at Agawam.

THERE would be no accounting for this stretch of power were it not for a principle at that time generally received, and which upon a question was determined some years after by the general court, some of the members dissenting, that the oath of fidelity to the commonwealth was binding even though the person should no longer reside within the limits.

NOTWITHSTANDING this commission, they soon after entered into an agreement or combination, by virtue of which they called themselves a body politick formed and established by mutual consent, and framed such laws and constitutions as they thought necessary; the most material point in which they differed from the Massachusets, was the not making membership of their churches necessary to freedom in the civil government or to the holding any offices therein. Upon the petition of Mr. Pynchon and others to the court to receive them again, an order passed asserting the court's right, and a commission was granted to Mr. Pynchon to hold courts there,* from whose judgments an appeal lay to the court of assistants.†

---

* Mass. Records.

† George Fenwick, Esq; a worthy pious gentleman and of a good family and estate, came from England with design to take possession of the lands upon Connecticut river for the Lords Say and Brook, &c. The lands between Connecticut river and the Naraganset country, sixty miles in length and breadth, were assigned by the council of Plimouth, in 1635, to the Marquiss of Hamilton. The Lords Say, &c. had a patent from the Earl of Warwick, including all that part of New-England in America from Naraganset river forty leagues upon a strait line near the sea shore towards the southwest, west and by south or west, as the coast lies towards Virginia, and all lands within the breadth aforesaid, from the western ocean to the south sea, so that the two grants or claims interfered. The Connecticut people purchased the title of the Lords, of Mr. Fenwick, December 5, 1644. The thoughts of removing were then at an end, and Fenwick joined with the colony and was chosen an assistant. The colony went on exercising the powers of government until the restoration, when they applied, by Mr. Winthrop [1] their agent, to King Charles II. in 1661, for a charter, which was granted in 1662, with as ample privileges as they could desire. Mr. Winthrop had been many years an assistant in the Massachusets. He was sensible of the defects in the charter; and besides, this colony being in America at the time of granting the charter, the powers granted them would naturally be better adapted to their circumstances. Mr. Winthrop, it is said, presented the King with a ring which had been given by Charles the first to his grandfather, and that the King was much pleased with it. When they were finding fault with the Massachusets, they notwithstanding established another government, much of the same form and the same sort of people. Rhode-Island about the same time obtained the like charter. Certain powers, assumed by the Massachusets, not mentioned in their charter, by these new charters are expresly granted to the two colonies. Had these applications been delayed two or three years longer they would hardly have succeeded. Plimouth, which had as much reason to expect such a favour, never could obtain it. They kept solliciting, one time after another, and were amused with general promises of favour until they were comprehended in a commission to Sir Edmund Andros, which

---

[1] John Winthrop, Jr.

THE settlers at Piscataqua, about the same time, submitted themselves to the Massachusets government. The submission and agreement upon record is as follows:

The 14th of the 4th month, 1641.

WHEREAS some Lords, Knights, Gentlemen and others did purchase, of Mr. Edward Hilton and some merchants of Bristol, two patents, the one called Wecohamet or Hilton's point, commonly called or known by the name of Dover or Northam, the other patent set forth by the name of the south part of the river Pascataquack, beginning at the sea side or near thereabouts, and coming round the said land by the river side unto the falls of Quamscot,[1] as may more fully appear by the said grant. And whereas others also,[2] residing at present within the limits of both the said grants, have, of late and formerly, complained of the want of some good government amongst them, and desired some help in this particular from the jurisdiction of the Massachusets bay, whereby they may be ruled and ordered according unto God both in church and common weal; and for avoiding of such unsufferable disorders whereby God hath been much dishonoured amongst them, these gentlemen whose names are here specified, George Willys,[3] gent. Robert Saltonstall,[4] gent. William Whiting,[5] Ed-

---

put an end to their expectations. — Mr. afterwards Colonel Fenwick, above-mentioned, by his last will, proved in Sussex in England, April 27, 1657, gave five hundred pounds to the public use of the country of New-England, if his loving friend Mr. Edward Hopkins should think fit, and to be employed as he should order and direct. Mr. Hopkins died a day or two before Colonel Fenwick, and by his will left at least 2000 l. to be employed for breeding youth at the grammar school and university in New-England. The question was, whether the 500 l. mentioned in Mr. Fenwick's will, be not recoverable from the executrix of the said will. This was proposed to Serjeant Maynard. Ans. The disposition to the charitable use being with condition of Mr. Hopkins's approvement, and Mr. Hopkins dying before the testator, is impossible, and the charitable use becomes absolute and ought now to be performed. John Maynard. I never heard that any part of this legacy was recovered. Mr. Hopkins's, or part of it, was decreed by Lord Chancellor Cowper, as we have before observed, and the college estate in Hopkinton was purchased therewith. *MS. letters.*

---

[1] Quamscot. The falls of the Squamscot or Exeter river are at Exeter, New Hampshire.

[2] The third edition changes this phrase to "whereas also the inhabitants."

[3] George Willys (*d.* 1645), "a gentleman from Fenny Compton, County of Warwick," came to New England in 1638 and secured immediate recognition at Hartford. In the following year he was elected an Assistant; in 1641, Deputy-Governor; and in 1642, Governor.

[4] Robert Saltonstall (*d.* 1650) was a son of Sir Richard Saltonstall. He was the superintendent of his father's interests in this country. *Ancestry and Descendants of Sir Richard Saltonstall*, p. 107.

[5] William Whiting (*d.* 1647) was an Assistant and Treasurer of the Connecticut colony from 1643 until his death. "A wealthy merchant who had been engaged in a patent for lands at Swamscot with Lord Say and Lord Brook." Savage.

ward Holioke,[1] Thomas Makepeace,[2] partners in the said patent, do, in the behalf of the rest of the patentees, dispose of the lands and jurisdiction of the premises as followeth; being willing to further such a good work, have hereby, for themselves and in the name of the rest of the patentees, given up and set over all that power or jurisdiction of government of the said people dwelling or abiding within the limits of both the said patents unto the government of the Massachusets bay, by them to be ruled and ordered in all causes criminal and civil, as inhabitants dwelling within the limits of Massachusets government, and to be subject to pay in church and commonwealth as the said inhabitants of Massachusets Bay do, and no other; and the freemen of the said two patents to enjoy the like liberties as other freemen do within the said Massachusets government; and that there shall be a court of justice kept within one of the two patents, which shall have the same power that the courts at Salem and Ipswich have. Provided always, and it is hereby declared, that one of the said patents, that is to say, that on the south side of the river Piscataquack, and in the other patent one third part of the land with all improved land in the said patent to the Lords and gentlemen and owners shall be and remain, unto them their heirs and assigns forever, as their proper right, as having true interest therein, saving the interest of jurisdiction to the Massachusets. And the said patent of Wecohamet shall be divided, as formerly is expressed, by indifferent men, equally chosen on both sides, whereby the plantation may be furthered and all occasion of difference avoided. And this honoured court of the Massachusets doth hereby promise to be helpful to the maintenance of the right of the said patentees in both the patents all legal courses in any part of their jurisdiction.

Subscribed by the aforenamed gentlemen, in the presence of the general court assembled, the day aforewritten.*

THE river of Newichewannock, or Piscataqua, is said to have been first discovered by Capt. Smith or some employed by him in 1614 or 1615. De Monts, ten years before, had been at Kennebeck and Saco, and some leagues further westward along shore; but struck over from some part of Welles, by the description he gives of the coast, to Cape Ann, which he calls Cape Louis, and from thence to Cape Blanc,

* Mass. Records.

---

[1] Edward Holioke (d. 1660) came to Lynn, Massachusetts, about 1636, from Tamworth in the County of Stafford. Later he settled at Rumney Marsh (now Chelsea) and was frequently elected a member of the General Court. He was the grandfather of President Edward Holyoke of Harvard College.

[2] Thomas Makepeace (d. 1666) came over in 1635 probably and settled in Dorchester, Mass. He appears to have been a man of some importance and of liberal sentiments. Because of "his novel disposition" he was informed that Massachusetts-Bay would "weary of him, unless he reform." This hint seems to have been sufficient. *History of Dorchester, Massachusetts*, p. 67.

which must be Cape Cod. In the year 1623, several gentlemen, merchants and others in the west of England, belonging to Bristol, Exeter, Dorchester, Shrewsbury, Plimouth, &c. having obtained patents from the council of Plimouth for several parts of New-England, and being encouraged by the plantation of New-Plimouth, and the reports of fishermen who had made voyages upon the coast, projected and attempted a fishery about Piscataqua, and sent over David Thompson,[1] together with Edward Hilton and William Hilton,[2] who had been fishmongers in London, and some others, with all necessaries for their purpose. The Hiltons set up their stages some distance above the mouth of the river, at a place since called Dover. Some others of the company, about the same time, seized on a place below at the mouth of the river, called Little Harbour, where they built the first house. Sir Ferdinando Gorges and Capt. John Mason were of this company, and the place where this house was built with three or four thousand acres of land for a manor or lordship, by consent of the rest of the undertakers, was assigned to Capt. Mason, and the house took the name of Mason-hall.*

THESE settlements went on very slowly for seven years after; and in 1631, when Edward Colcott † first came over, there were but three houses in all that side of the country adjoining to Piscataqua river. There had been some expence besides about salt works. The affairs of the great council of Plimouth, from first to last, were carried on in a confused manner. There have been six or seven several grants of the lands between Merrimack and Kennebeck. Whether any of them, besides those to Gorges and the Massachusets, are at this day of any validity I will not determine.‡ In 1629, Gorges and Mason are said to have taken a patent together for all the lands between the two rivers; and by mutual agreement, and by a distinct

* The Chimney and part of the stone wall were standing in the year 1680. *Hubbard*.

† He was afterwards chose, by some of the planters about Dover,[3] their head or governor. *Hubbard*.

‡ Benighton's patent, upon Saco river, was early, and divers persons hold under it.

---

[1] David Thompson came to New England in 1623 and settled at Piscataqua. About 1626 he removed to the island in Boston harbor which still bears his name. Probably all that is known about Thompson is contained in Charles Deane's paper in the Massachusetts Historical Society *Proceedings*, XIV (1875–76), 358–385.

[2] William Hilton came to Plymouth in 1621 and removed to Dover before 1627. Edward Hilton is said to have come directly to Piscataqua in 1623. After living there twenty years he removed to Exeter. See Charles Deane's paper in Massachusetts Historical Society *Proceedings*, XIV (1875–76), 358–385; also Elwyn L. Page's "A.D. 1623" in the *Granite Monthly*, XXIV (1922), 205–211.

[3] The first edition gives "above Dover" instead of "about Dover." The third edition gives "at Dover."

patent, all the lands from Piscataqua to Merrimack were assigned to Mason.* Gorges seems to have laid no great stress upon his title, for in 1639, he obtained a patent under the great seal from King Charles the first. The Lord [1] Say and Brooke, who were very general adventurers, purchased the Bristol men's share, which was two thirds of the first company's interest. Some persons of Shrewsbury held the other third. Capt. Wiggan was made the agent for the Shrewsbury men. In the year 1630, Captain Neale, with three others, came over to Piscataqua to superintend the affairs of Sir Ferdinando Gorges, Mason, and the rest, but principally to discover a new country, to which they gave the name of Laconia, and which in Gorges's history is very pompously described. Champlain, many years before this, had given his own name to Lake Iroquois, and the English, it may be, were informed by the Indians something of the geography of the country, and of other lakes on the back of New-England, and no doubt the rumour was carried over to England. Neale spent three years in searching out his new country, but could not find it and so returned. Nothing else memorable is mentioned of Neale, except that he forbad Wiggan settling a point of land betwixt Dover and Exeter. Wiggan went on, and determined to defend his right by the sword. The other threatned as high, and from what might have happened, the disputed land took the name of Bloody Point, which it retains to this day. The Lords Say and Brooke also, made Wiggan their agent for the term of seven years; during which time the interest was not greatly advanced, the whole being sold to him, at the expiration of the term, for six hundred pounds.

Soon after the year 1631, one Mr. Williams came over from England, sent also by Gorges and Mason to take care of their salt-works. Mr. Chadburne,† with several other planters and traders, came over with him. These began the settlement of Strawberry bank (Portsmouth) and after Neale went away they are supposed either to have entered into an agreement and to have chosen Williams for their governor, who is said to have been a discreet sensible man and a gentleman, or else he was appointed by the company in England. There was a grant of a sum of money for building a parsonage house and a chapel, and for a glebe of 50 acres of land to be annexed, made by the inhabitants of Strawberry bank to Thomas Walford and

---

* *Hubbard.*

† Mr. Chadburne had the direction of the artificers who built what was called the great house at Strawberry bank. His posterity are settled on the other side the river in the province of Main.

---

[1] In the first edition "Lord" is pluralized, as it obviously should be.

Henry Sherburn, church wardens, and their successors, &c. and this was signed by Francis Williams governor, Ambrose Gibbons assistant, and 18 inhabitants, dated May 25, 1640. Williams soon after removed to Barbados. The first who enterprized the settlement of Piscataqua had some religious as well as civil views, and a puritan minister Mr. Leveridge, a worthy man, came over with Capt. Wiggan in 1633, but not being supported he removed to the southward and was succeeded by Mr. Burdet, who has not left so good a character. Not contented with his sacred function, he invaded the civil government, and thrust out Capt. Wiggan, and assumed the place of governor himself.

IN the mean time, the Lords, and others concerned, had prevailed upon several persons of good estates and who made profession of religion, to transplant themselves and families to Piscataqua, so as to be able to make inhabitants enough for a considerable township; and having no charter commission or power of government from the crown, they were under necessity of entring into a combination or agreement among themselves, which was in the following form:

WHEREAS sundry mischiefs and inconveniencies have befallen us, and more and greater may, in regard of want of civil government, his gracious Majesty having settled no order for us to our knowledge, we whose names are under written, being inhabitants upon the river Piscataqua, have voluntarily agreed to combine ourselves into a body politic, that we may the more comfortably enjoy the benefit of his Majesty's laws; and do hereby actually engage ourselves to submit to his royal Majesty's laws, together with all such laws as shall be concluded by a major part of the freemen of our society, in case they be not repugnant to the laws of England, and administred in behalf of his Majesty And this we have mutually promised and engaged to do, and so to continue till his excellent Majesty shall give other orders concerning us. In witness whereof we have hereunto set our hands Octob. 22.[1] in the 16th year of the reign of our sovereign Lord Charles, by the grace of God, King of Great-Britain, France and Ireland, defender of the faith, &c.

Signed by Thomas Larkham, Richard Waldron,
William Waldron, with thirty eight more.

ABOUT the same time, viz. in 1638, Mr. Wheelwright, the minister who had been banished from the Massachusets, with a number of persons who adhered to him, began a plantation on the south side of the great bay up Piscataqua river, to which they gave the name of Exeter. They thought it necessary likewise to form themselves into a body politic, in order to enable them to carry on the affairs of their

---

[1] The third edition inserts "1640" at this point.

plantation. The instrument which they determined upon, was of the following form:

WHEREAS it hath pleased the Lord to move the heart of our dread Sovereign Charles, &c. to grant licence and liberty to sundry of his subjects to plant themselves in the western parts of America: We his loyal subjects, members of the church of Exeter, situate and lying upon the river Piscataqua, with other inhabitants there, considering with ourselves the holy will of God and our own necessity, that we should not live without wholsome laws and civil government amongst us, of which we are altogether destitute, do, in the name of Christ and in the sight of God, combine ourselves together to erect and set up among us such government as shall be, to our best discerning, agreeable to the will of God; professing ourselves subject to our Sovereign Lord King Charles, according to the liberty of the English colony of the Massachusets, and binding ourselves solemnly, by the grace and help of Christ and in his name and fear, to submit ourselves to all such christian laws as are established in the realm of England, to our best knowledge, and to all other such laws which shall upon good grounds be made and enacted among us according to God, that we may live quietly and peaceably together in all godliness and honesty. October 4, 1639, John Wheelwright, William Wentworth, George Walton,

with 32 more. Captain Underhill, an enthusiast who obtained his assurance, as he expressed himself before the church of Boston, while he was taking a pipe of the good creature tobacco,* and who was at the same time a very immoral man, and for adultery had been excommunicated,[1] joined Mr. Wheelwright's company, and played his card so well, that he obtained the place of governor over them, and also over the other company at Dover, they having quarrelled with Mr. Burdet the minister, who removed to York. There was a strong party against Underhill, which caused great disturbance and confusion. At the same time they were as much divided in their ecclesiastical affairs. They at Dover had one Mr. Knolles for their minister, but Mr. Larkham arriving there from Northam near Barnstable in England, many people were taken with him and determined to dismiss Knolles; but his party stood by him, and he and his company excommunicated Larkham. He in return laid violent hands on Knolles. The magistrates took part, some on one side and some on the other; but Larkham's party, being weakest, sent to Williams the governor below for assistance, who came up with a company of armed men, beset Knolles's house, where Underhill the gov-

* *Hubbard*, &c.

---

[1] The third edition abbreviates the remainder of this sentence to "obtained the place of governor at Dover."

ernor then was, called him to account, set a fine upon him and some others who had been concerned in the riot, and obliged them to remove from the plantation. Knolles was a rigid antinomian; his practice was agreeable to his principles. He was charged with being too familiar with some of his female domesticks, and found it necessary to depart. Larkham, a zealous churchman, soon followed him for an offence of the same nature.* Thus we see three distinct colonies and independent governments formed upon Piscataqua river.

DURING these transactions, the Massachusets people were enquiring into the bounds of their patent. In 1639, they sent persons to find out the northermost part of Merrimack river. A line to run east, from three miles north of the head of the river, will take in the whole of New-Hampshire.† They determined therefore that it came within their jurisdiction, and from that time they allowed plantations to be settled, particularly at Hampton, as readily as in any other part of the colony, and exercised jurisdiction over them; but they left those upon the river to their liberty; and it was their inability to preserve order among themselves which occasioned the application and submission which has already been mentioned. At their session in October the court passed the following order:

WHEREAS it appeareth that, by the extent of the line according to our patent, the river of Piscataquack is within the jurisdiction of the Massachusets, and conference being had at several times with the said people and some deputed by the general court for the settling and establishing of order in the administration of justice there; it is now ordered by the general court, holden at Boston this 9th day of the 8th month 1641, and with the consent of the inhabitants of the said river, as followeth. Imprimis, That from henceforth the said people, inhabiting there, are and shall be accepted and reputed under the government of the Massachusets, as the rest of the inhabitants within the said jurisdiction are. Also, that they shall have the same order and way of administration of justice, and way of keeping courts as is established at Ipswich and Salem.‡ Also they shall be exempted from all publick charges, other than those that shall arise for or from among themselves, or from any action or course that may be taken to procure their own good or benefit. Also they shall enjoy all such lawful liberties of fishing, planting and felling timber, as formerly they have en-

---

* I have taken the principal facts, relative to the settlement of Piscataqua, from Hubbard's and other original antient manuscripts.

† The bounds in the charter being three miles south of Charles river and all and every part thereof, and three miles north of Merrimack and all and every part thereof, and all lands within the limits aforesaid in latitude and breadth, and in length and longitude, &c. they supposed they had a right to stretch their line east from the head of Merrimack to the ocean.

‡ Parts of the Massachusets nearest to Piscataqua.

joyed in the same river. Mr. Simon Broadstreet, Mr. Israel Stoughton, Mr. Samuel Simonds, Mr. William Tyng, Mr. Francis Williams, and Mr. Edward Hilton, or any four of them, whereof Mr. Broadstreet, or Mr. Stoughton to be one, these shall have the same power that the quarter courts at Salem and Ipswich have. Also, the inhabitants there are allowed to send two deputies from the whole river to the court at Boston. Also Mr. Broadstreet, Mr. Stoughton, and the rest of the commissioners, shall have power at the court at Piscataquack to appoint two or three to join with Mr. Williams and Mr. Hilton to govern the people as the magistrates do here, till the next general court, or till the court take further order. It is further ordered, that until our commissioners shall arrive at Piscataquack, those men who already have authority, by the late combination, to govern the people there, shall continue in the same authority and power, to be determined at the coming of the said commissioners, and not before.

Although nothing is said of Strawberrybank in the submission, yet all the settlements seem to have concurred, and Williams, the governor below, was made one of the magistrates.

THE Massachusets, by thus extending its wing over the inhabitants of New-Hampshire, nourished and cherished them for near 40 years; and to this must be attributed the growth and the present flourishing state of that colony. The principal inhabitants, when the benefit was recent, in 1680, made a public and grateful acknowledgment of it. Upon this construction of the charter, the whole province of Main is taken into the Massachusets as well as New-Hampshire; but no application being made by the people there, nothing was done concerning them. Mr. Wheelwright and others, who had been banished from the Massachusets, soon after removed to the province of Main from New-Hampshire.

MR. Winthrop was elected governor in 1642, and Mr. Endicot deputy governor, and Mr. Thomas Flint * added to the assistants, together with Mr. Pynchon, who, upon his removal to Springfield, had been left out whilst the jurisdiction was doubtful.

THE college at Cambridge was this year put upon a more respectable footing than it had been. The governor, deputy governor and magistrates, and the ministers of the six next adjacent towns, with the president, were made a corporation for ordering and managing the affairs of the college, and nine young gentlemen,† at a public

---

* Mr. Flint was a gentleman of a fair estate in England, which he laid out in forwarding the plantation, arriving in New England about the year 1635. *Johnson.* A large tract of land, which he owned in Concord, still retains the name of Flint's farm.

† Most of them soon after went over to England, and before 1651 (as appears by a letter from Mr. Samuel Mather, who received a degree the next year, and was a celebrated preacher in Dublin) made some figure there. Benjamin Woodbridge, the first-

commencement this year, received the degree of batchelor of arts. The Thesis, with a particular account of the whole proceeding, was published in England. I know of but two copies extant, and as my chief design is to preserve from oblivion every transaction, which

---

born of Harvard-College, was successor to Doctor Twisse at Newberry; and though inclined to presbyterianism, to use Mr. Mather's words, not malignantly affected. George Downing went into the army, and was scout-master general of the English army in Scotland. He was afterwards in great favour with Cromwell, who sent him ambassador to the States, and upon the restoration he turned with the times, and was sent or kept by the King in the same employ, had the merit of betraying, securing and sending over several of the regicides (he had been captain under one of them, Col. Okey) was knighted and in favour at court, and died in 1684. His character runs low with the best historians in England; it was much lower with his countrymen in New-England; and it became a proverbial expression, to say of a false man who betrayed his trust, that he was an arrant George Downing. Oliver Cromwell, when he sent him agent or ambassador to the States, in his letter of credence says, "George Downing is a person of eminent quality, and after a long trial of his fidelity, probity and diligence in several and various negotiations, well approved and valued by us. Him we have thought fitting to send to your Lordships, dignified with the character of our agent," &c. (Milton's letters.) In his latter days he is said to have been very friendly to New-England, and when the colony was upon the worst terms with King Charles the second. An article of news from England, in 1671, says, "Sir George Downing is in the Tower, it is said because he returned from Holland, where he was sent ambassador, before his time: As it is reported, he had no small abuse offered him there. They printed the sermons he preached in Oliver's time and drew three pictures of him. 1. Preaching in a tub, over it was wrote, *This I was.* 2. A treacherous courtier, over it, *This I am.* 3. Hanging on a gibbet, and over it, *This I shall be.*" Prints of that sort were not so common in England in that day as they have been the last twenty years.

"Downing was sent to make up the quarrel with the Dutch, but coming home in too great haste and fear, is now in the prison where his master lay that he betrayed." *MS. letter Lond. March* 4, 1671–2. By his master, no doubt Okey is intended. His son was one of the Tellers in the Exchequer in 1680. Sir George died in 1684. He was brother-in-law to governor Bradstreet, and kept up a correspondence with him.

John Bulkley (son of Peter Bulkley, minister of Concord, who was of a very reputable family, and had been esteemed for his learning and piety in England) was a settled minister at Fordham in Essex, and after his ejectment, in 1662, practised physic in London.

Henry Saltonstall, who I suppose was a grandson of Sir Richard Saltonstall, was a doctor of physic and a fellow of New college Oxford.

Nathanael Brewster was a settled minister in Norfolk, and of good report.

Samuel Bellingham received the degree of doctor of physic at Leyden. Two others of the class, William Hubbard and John Wilson, were ministers settled in New England and in high esteem there. Several of the succeeding classes went over to England soon after their taking their batchelors degree. John Allen, whose friends lived in Suffolk. William Ames, who was son of doctor Ames, settled at Wrentham. Jeremiah Holland, who first settled near London, but soon after removed into Northamptonshire, where he had a living of between two and three hundred pounds a year. Jacob Ward, who had a fellowship in Maudlin college Oxford. John Birden and Abraham Walver, who were both preachers in the counties where their friends lived; and Sampson Eyton, who I suppose left Harvard college before he had his degree, was made a fellow in one of the universities in England. Leonard Hoar went to Cambridge and took the degree of doctor in physic. Mr. Mather writes very pressing for others to come over to England, where they might be assured of encouragement and preferment.

posterity may think of any importance, I shall give it a place in the appendix.[1]

THERE was a general design this year, among the Indians, against the English.* Miantinomo, the sachem of the Naragansets, was supposed to be the author and chief promoter, and to have drawn many other sachems to join with him. The Indians began to make use of fire-arms, and had procured a great number, together with powder and shot, from English traders in the eastern parts, as well as from the Dutch. A constant watch was ordered to be kept from sun-set to sun-rising, and a place of retreat to be provided, in each plantation, for the women and children and for the security of ammunition. Beacons were erected and ordered to be fired upon an alarm, and all smiths were required to lay aside all other business until all the arms in the colony were put into good order; for which payment was promised by the government. Mr. John Leverett † and Mr. Edward Hutchinson ‡ were sent to Miantinomo with articles of complaint, and to require him to come himself, or to send two of his chief counsellors to the governor in order to give satisfaction. Connecticut proposed to fall upon the Indians immediately, and offered, if the Massachusets would send 120 men to Saybrook, to join a proportionable number. But the Massachusets court doubted whether they had sufficient proofs of the designs of the Indians to justify a war. However, the governor with the magistrates, before the court met, thought it necessary to disarm the Indians within the colony, which they readily submitted to. Miantinomo came in person to the court, and demanded that his accusers should be brought face to face, and if they failed in their proof that they should suffer the same punishment he would have deserved himself if he had been guilty, viz. death. His behaviour was grave, and he gave his answers with great deliberation and seeming ingenuity. He would never speak but in the presence of two of his counsellors, that they might be witnesses of every thing which passed. Two days were spent in

* Intelligence was given by some of the Indians themselves, and letters were dispatched from New Haven and Connecticut to give advice. Under pretence of trade, in small companies at the English houses, while some secured the arms the others were to perpetrate the massacre; the time appointed for which was immediatel yafter the harvest should be over.

An Indian of Providence attempted a rape upon an English woman, the wife of Nicholas Wood of Dorchester, and was protected by Miantinomo. This, if true, is a rare instance.

† Afterwards governor.

‡ Son of the famous Mrs. Hutchinson.

[1] See Appendix, No. VI.

treaty. He denied all he was charged with, and pretended, the reports to his disadvantage were raised by Uncas, sachem of the Mohegins, or some of his people. He was willing to renew his former engagements, that if any of the Indians, even the Nianticks, who he said were as his own flesh and blood, should do any wrong to the English, so as neither he nor they could satisfy without blood, he would deliver them up and leave them to mercy. The people of Connecticut put little confidence in him, and could hardly be kept from falling upon him, but were at last prevailed upon, by the Massachusets, to desist for the present.* The minds of men were filled with fear from these rumours of a general conspiracy, and every noise in the night was alarming. A poor man, in a swamp at Watertown,† hearing the howling of a kennel of wolves, and expecting to be devoured by them, cried out for help, which occasioned a general alarm through all the towns near Boston.‡ The Indians, being thus prevented from surprizing the English, remained quiet.§

THE House of Commons this year passed a memorable resolve in favour of the Massachusets colony, which was transmitted to the governor by the clerk of the house, and ordered by the court to be entered upon the publick records, that it might remain to posterity.

VENERIS 10 MARCH 1642.

WHEREAS the plantations in New-England have, by the blessing of the Almighty, had good and prosperous success, without any public charge to this state,‖ and are now likely to prove very happy for the

---

* Records of the united colonies.

† Sept. 19th, 1642.

‡ *Hubbard.*

§ One Darbyfield,[1] an Irishman, with some others travelled this year to the white hills, supposed to be the highest in these parts of America. They reported that they had been to the top, where is a plain of 60 feet square; that on the west side is a very steep precipice, and all the country round about appeared like a level much beneath them. The glistering appearance of the rocks, as they came near them, caused an expectation of something valuable, but they found nothing. *Hubbard.*

The growth of the several parts of the colony, at different periods, will be thought by some worth observing. In 1642 a tax of 800 *l.* was apportioned as follows: Hingham 20 *l.* Weymouth 14 *l.* Braintree 14 *l.* Dorchester 58 *l.* 10 *s.* Roxbury 50 *l.* Boston 120 *l.* Dedham 20 *l.* Concord 25 *l.* Watertown 55 *l.* Cambridge 67 *l.* 10 *s.* Charlestown 60 *l.* Salem 75 *l.* Lynn 45 *l.* Ipswich 82 *l.* Newbury 30 *l.* Salisbury 12 *l.* 10 *s.* Hampton 5 *l.* Rowley 15 *l.* Sudbury 15 *l.* Medford 10 *l.* Glocester 6 *l.* 10 *s.*

‖ I transcribe this part of the order with pleasure. The merit of our ancestors, many of whom were personally known to the principal members of parliament, was fresh in

---

[1] Darby Field (*d.* 1649). Hutchinson appears to have misread Hubbard's manuscript, as others have done, making one name from two. Field was at Exeter in 1638. In 1644 he removed to Oyster River (now Durham), where he prospered. All that is known about him has been set forth by Warren W. Hart in *Appalachia*, XI, no. IV (June 1908).

propagation of the gospel in those parts, and very beneficial and commodious to this kingdom and nation. The commons, now assembled in Parliament, do for the better advancement of those plantations and the encouragement of the planters to proceed in their undertaking, ordain, that all merchandizing goods, that by any person or persons whatsoever, merchant or other, shall be exported out of this kingdom of England into New-England to be spent, used or employed there, or being of the growth of that kingdom,* shall be from thence imported hither, or shall be laden or put on board any ship or vessel for necessaries in passing to and fro, and all and every the owner or owners thereof shall be freed and discharged of and from paying and yielding any custom, subsidy, taxation, or other duty for the same, either inward or outward, either in this kingdom or New-England, or in any port, haven, creek, or other place whatsoever, until the House of Commons shall take further order therein to the contrary. And all and singular customers, farmers and collectors of customs, subsidies and imposts, and other officers, ministers and subjects whatsoever, are hereby required and injoined, that they and every of them, upon the shewing forth unto them this order, or a true copy thereof under the hand of the clerk of the House of Commons, without any other writ or warrant whatsoever, do make full, whole and entire, and due allowance and clear discharge unto the said owners of the said goods and merchandize, their factors, servants and agents, according to the tenor and true meaning of this order.

H. Elssing, Cler. Parl. D. Com.

In the year 1642, letters came to Mr. Cotton of Boston, Mr. Hooker of Hartford, and Mr. Davenport of New-Haven, signed by several of the nobility, divers members of the house of commons, and some ministers, to call them or some of them, if all could not come, to assist in the assembly of divines at Westminster.† Such of the

---

their remembrance. Length of time has not lessened the merit. Consequences so advantageous to the nation have followed it, that in reason it ought to strike stronger now than it did then.

* Inaccurately, for those colonies.

† I have the original papers which accompanied these letters. The following is an exact copy.

"The expression of the desires of those honourable and worthy personages, of both houses of parlament, who call and wish the presence of Mr. Cotton, Mr. Hooker and Mr. Davenport to come ovar with all possible speed, all or any of them, if all cannot. The condityon whearein the state of things in this kingdom doth now stand, wee suppose you have from the relations of others; whearby you cannot but understand how greate need there is of the healp of prayer and improvement of all good meanes, from all parts for the seatlinge and composeing the affaires of the church. Wee therefore present unto you our earnest desires of you all. To shewe whearein or howe many wayes you may be useful would easely bee done by us, and fownd by you, weare you present with us. In all likelyhood you will finde opportunity enough to draw forth all that healpefullness that God shall affoard by you. And wee doubt not these advantages will

magistrates and ministers, as were near Boston, met together, and most of them were of opinion that it was a call of God, but Mr. Hooker did not like the business, and thought it was not a sufficient call to go a thousand leagues to confer about matters of church government. Mr. Davenport thought otherwise, but his church, having but one minister, would not spare him. Mr. Cotton thought it a clear call, and would have undertaken the voyage if others would have gone with him. Soon after, other letters were received, which diverted them from any thoughts of proceeding.* Mr. Hooker was about that time preparing for the press a vindication of congregational churches, or rather framing a system or plan of church government, which he designed for the New-England churches, let the determination at Westminster be what it would. Had the churches of New-England appeared there by their representatives, or any of the principal divines appeared as members of the assembly, greater exception might have been taken to their building after a model of their own framing. Several persons who came from England, in 1643, made a muster to set up presbyterian government, under the authority of the assembly at Westminster; but a New-England assembly, the general court, soon put them to the rout.

The governor and deputy governor for the last year were re-elected in 1643. Samuel Symonds † and William Hibbins ‡ were added to the assistants. The colony had so increased, that it was

---

be sutch, as will fully answer all inconveniencies your sealves, churches or plantations may sustaine in this your voyage and short absence from them. Onely the sooner you come the bettar.
                                                    Warwick
                        W. Say & Seale   Ph. Wharton
                              Mandeville
                             Rob. Brooke

Nath. Fiennes	Wm. Stricland	Tho: Hoyle	
Gilbᵗ Gerrard	Henry Darley	Cor: Holland	
Tho: Barrington	Valentine Walton	Anth. Stapley	
Richard Browne	Willᵐ Cawleys	Humfrey Salway	
Henry Martin	John Gurdon	William Hay	
Oliver Cromwell	John Blakiston	J. Wastill	
A. Haselrig	Godfrey Rosseville		
Wm. Masham	H. Ruthin	Gilbert Pickering	Alex. Bence
Mart. Lumley	Ro. Cooke	Ol. St. John	
Nath. Barnardiston	Sam. Lake	Isaac Pennington	
Ar. Goodwin	John Francklyn	Miles Corbett	Wm. Spurstowe."

* *Hubbard.*

† Mr. Symonds was a gentleman of an ancient family and good estate in England. He came from Yeldham in Essex. *Hubbard.*

‡ Mr. Hibbins was a principal merchant in the colony, but soon after met with great losses in his trade. I know of none of their descendants of the same names in New-England.

divided this year into four counties or shires, Essex, Middlesex, Suffolk and Norfolk.*

A NEW sect, springing from the ashes of the antinomians, made great disturbance about this time. Samuel Gorton,[1] a citizen of London, who came from Boston in 1636, was at the head of it. Mr. Cotton says,† his principles were the very dregs of familism. It is certain that he was artful enough to explain them in such a manner, that his judges in the Massachusets were divided in opinion whether they were heretical or no. He staid not long in the Massachusets, but went to Plimouth, and, disturbing the church there, he was whipped and required to find sureties for his good behaviour, which not being able to do he removed, Mr. Winslow [2] says was driven ‡ to Rhode-Island. There he treated the court with contempt, and by order of the governor, Mr. Coddington, was first imprisoned and afterwards whipped. From Rhode-Island he went to Providence, where Roger Williams with his usual humanity, although he disliked his principles and behaviour, gave him shelter. Here he found several of his own disposition, fond of novelties in religion, and they first sat down at Patuxet near Providence; but some of the inhabitants there applied to the Massachusets that they and their lands might be received into protection, and complained that Gorton and his company, under pretence of purchase from the Indians, were going about to deprive them of their estates, of which for several years they had been in the lawful possession. The governor and three of the assistants signed what was called a warrant, or notification, to all the people of Providence, requiring them to submit to the jurisdiction of the Massachusets. This was dated in October 1642. Gorton sent a very contemptuous answer, and told them they had no

* ESSEX contd.	MIDDLESEX.	SUFFOLK.	NORFOLK.
Salem	Charlestown	Boston	Salisbury
Linn	Cambridge	Roxbury	Hampton
Enon (Wenham)	Watertown	Dorchester	Haverhill
Ipswich	Sudbury	Dedham	Exeter
Rowley	Concord	Braintree	Dover
Newbury	Woburn	Weymouth	Strawberry-Bank
Glocester	Medford	Hingham	(Portsmouth.)
Chochichawick	Linn Village	Nantasket (Hull)	

† Bloody Tenet washed, &c. p. 5 & 8.
‡ Answer to Gorton.

---

[1] Samuel Gorton (1592–1677). There are a number of biographies and biographical sketches of Gorton, notably Adelos Gorton, *Life and Times of Samuel Gorton.*
[2] Edward Winslow (1595–1655), in his *Hypocrisy Unmasked* (London, 1646). To Winslow, then in London, was entrusted the task of defending the Plymouth and Massachusetts colonies against the accusations of Gorton.

authority over the people of Providence. But either for the sake of being more out of the reach of the Massachusets, or from discord among themselves, Gorton and 11 more purchased of Miantinomo, the Naraganset sachem,* a tract of land called Showamet [1] and removed thither. The price they paid was 144 fathom of wampum.†
Showamet was then claimed by Plimouth government, as within their jurisdiction. Two of the chief of the Indians who dwelt there and at Patuxet, and who were called sachems, Pomham and Sachonoco, came to Boston with their interpreter to complain of Gorton and his company for taking their lands from them, and offered to subject themselves and their country to the Massachusets, which by an instrument, under their hands, was accordingly done in the form following.

THIS writing is to testify, that we Pomham, sachem of Showamet, and Sachonoco, sachem of Patuxet, have and by these presents do voluntarily and without any constraint or persuasion, but of our own free motion, put ourselves, our subjects, lands and estates under the government and jurisdiction of the Massachusets, to be governed and protected by them according to their just laws and orders, so far as we shall be made capable of understanding them; and we do promise, for ourselves and our subjects and all our posterity, to be true and faithful to the government and aiding to the maintenance thereof to our best ability; and from time to time to give speedy notice of any conspiracy, attempt, or evil intention of any which we shall know or hear of against the same, and do promise to be willing from time to time to be instructed in the knowledge of the worship of God. In witness whereof, we have hereunto put to our hands the 22d of the 4th month, 1643.

The γ mark   The ⊕ mark
of Saconocho.   of Pomham.

MIANTINOMO was likewise sent for to Boston, but did not make out his right to the Indian country to the satisfaction of the court. It does not appear that he relinquished it, and Gorton says in his defence, that Pomham and Sachonoco were the natural subjects of Miantinomo and influenced by the Massachusets to withdraw from him. He being the greatest and most powerful sachem in New-England, it is probable that these were dependants upon him or tributaries to him. Be that as it may, the Massachusets sent a message

---

* Pomham, a petty sachem who lived upon the lands, joined in the sale, but alledged that he had no consideration for it. *Winslow.*

† A fathom of wampum was one string of Indian beads, six feet or a fathom in length, which was valued at 5s. 8d. sterling.

---

[1] Showamet is now Warwick, Rhode Island.

to Gorton and his company, acquainting them that they were still within their jurisdiction by virtue of the submission of Pomham and Sachonoco, and requiring them to appear at the court of Boston to answer to complaints against them for injuries done to the Indians, &c. and promising them safe-conduct, &c. This was dated the 12th of the 7th month 1643. They sent back by the messenger a verbal answer, that they were out of the Massachusets jurisdiction, and would acknowledge subjection to none but the state and government of Old England. Upon the receipt of their answer, viz. on the 19th of the same month, another message was sent to acquaint them, that the court had appointed commissioners * to hear and determine the controversy upon the spot, and if they refused, to bring them to Boston by force. After some small resistance, Gorton and several others were taken and carried to Boston and imprisoned.† Being

* The commissioners were, Capt. George Cooke, Lieut. Hump. Atherton, and Edward Johnson, who had also military commissions, and 40 men to attend them. Cooke was afterwards a colonel in the wars in Ireland. *Johnson.*

† If we may give credit to Gorton's account, Mr. Ward,[1] a minister, came to the prison window and called to him one of the prisoners who had been his neighbour in Essex in England, and desired him, if he had done or said any thing he could with good conscience renounce, that he would recant, and probably the court would be merciful; and added, that this would be no disparagement, for the reverend Mr. Cotton ordinarily preacheth that publickly one year, that the next year he publickly repents of before the congregation, &c. Mr. Winslow, in his answer, will not allow this to be true. This Mr. Ward was author of The Simple Cobler of Agawam, and several other witty performances. The ruling passion would frequently shew itself in instances which would have been liable to some exception in those days of great gravity, if his principles had not been orthodox and his general behaviour serious and guarded. Many of his witty facetious turns are handed down to posterity. A letter of his, I find among Mr. Cotton's papers, discovers something of his cast of mind.

"Salutum in Xto nostro.

Reverend and dear friend,

I was yesterday convented before the bishop, I mean to his court, and am adjourned to the next term. I see such giants turn their backs, that I dare not trust my own weak heart. I expect measure hard enough, and must furnish apace with proportionable armour. I lack a friend to help buckle it on. I know none but Christ himself, in all our coast, fit to help me, and my acquaintance with him is hardly enough to hope for that assistance my weak spirit will want and the assaults of tentation call for. I pray therefore, forget me not, and believe for me also if there be such a piece of neighbourhood among Christians. And so blessing God with my whole heart, for my knowledge of you and immerited interest in you, and thanking you entirely for that faithful love I have found from you in many expressions of the best nature, I commit you to the unchangeable love of God our Father in his son Jesus Christ, in whom I hope to rest for ever.

Stondon Mercy,   Your's in all truth of heart,
Dec. 13, 1631.

                                                                Nath¹ Warde."

---

[1] Nathaniel Ward (1578?–1652) was the minister of Ipswich, Massachusetts. He was a graduate of Cambridge, Emmanuel College, and had practised law in London before he entered the ministry. His Puritanism got him into trouble with Bishop Laud

brought before the court, the charge exhibited against them was in the following words:

UPON much examination, and serious consideration of your writings, with your answers about them, we do charge you to be a blasphemous enemy of the true religion of our Lord Jesus Christ and his holy ordinances, and also of civil authority among the people of God, and particularly in this jurisdiction.

THEIR writings were produced in evidence against them; and they explained them, in such a manner, that the governor, Mr. Winthrop, said he could agree with them in their answer, tho' he could not in their writings; but Mr. Dudley stood up, much moved, and said he would never consent to it, while he lived, that they were one with them in those answers. The governor then asked Gorton what faith was? he answered, in the words of the apostle, that faith is the substance of things hoped for, and the evidence of things not seen; the governor told him that was true, but he could say more of faith than that. He desired to be excused, and Mr. Bradstreet, prudently enough, excepted to such questions, unless he was free to speak to them; and thereupon they were dismissed and remanded to prison.* Their sentences were cruel. Gorton ordered to be confined to Charlestown, there to be kept at work, and to wear such bolts and irons as might hinder his escape; and if he broke his confinement, or by speech or writing published or maintained any of the blasphemous abominable heresies wherewith he had been charged by the general court, or should reproach or reprove the churches of our Lord Jesus Christ in these united colonies, or the civil government, &c. that upon conviction thereof, upon trial by a jury, he should suffer death.† The rest were confined to different towns, one in a town, and upon the same conditions with Gorton; their cattle were seized and ordered to be sold, and the charge of fetching them and

---

* *Gorton.*[1]

† Gorton says, they cast a lot for their lives, putting it to the major vote of the court whether they should live or die; and that God in his providence ordered it by a majority of two votes only, in favour of their lives.

---

and he came to New England in 1634. His great contribution to the development of the Colony was the Body of Liberties which he drew up. This code, adopted in 1641, gave the Bay colonists a government of laws rather than of men. But he is remembered chiefly as the witty author of *The Simple Cobbler of Agawam* (London, 1647), a treatise aimed at manners and theories of which he disapproved. Samuel Eliot Morison has an excellent chapter on Ward in his *Builders of the Bay Colony*. There is a good memoir by John Ward Dean.

[1] Samuel Gorton, *Simplicities Defence against Seven-headed Policy.*

the expence attending the trial and imprisonment to be paid out of the proceeds, and the overplus to be reserved for their future maintenance during their confinement.* As all who have published any

* After being confined one winter, they were banished the jurisdiction and from the lands purchased of the Indians, upon pain of death. Gorton soon after went to England and obtained an order from the Governor in chief, the lord high admiral and commissioners appointed by the parliament for the English plantations in America, directed to the governor and assistants of the Massachusets, and to all other governors and other inhabitants of New-England and all others whom it may concern, requiring them to suffer Gorton and the rest quietly to enjoy their lands in Naraganset bay, and to land at any port in New-England in their way thither, &c. This order was sent to the governor by Randall Holden, one of Gorton's adherents, who with others arrived at Boston, 13th Sept. 1646. Having desired leave to land, the governor, Mr. Winthrop, answered that he could not give them leave by his own authority, as it would dispense with an order of the general court, but the council being to meet in two or three days he would impart the order, and intimated that he should not trouble himself about them in the mean time. The council were not all of a mind, but the majority agreed to suffer them to pass quietly for the present, and that when the court met, further consideration should be had of their possessing the land they claimed. The court thought proper to send Mr. Edward Winslow to England, in order to give satisfaction to the commissioners for plantations. He carried with him a remonstrance and petition against Gorton, and in vindication of the colony, asserted their right by charter finally to determine all causes, without admitting of appeals to England; and alledged that the lands lay in Plimouth colony, and produced an act of the commissioners of the four colonies, of which Plimouth was one, impowering the Massachusets to proceed as they thought proper. The commissioners for plantations, in their answer, say, "they intended not to encourage any appeals from their justice, which it might be very inconvenient to admit, nor to restrain the bounds of their jurisdiction to a narrower compass, but they supposed the Naraganset bay (the thing in question) was without the bounds of their patent; but as they had received advertisement that the place was within the patent of New-Plimouth, and the ground of their proceedings was a joint authority from the four governments, of Massachusets, Plimouth, Connecticut, and New-Haven, if these things should be proved, it would much alter the state of the question; but at that distance these points could not be settled, and must be left to be determined upon the place if there should be occasion, for there the boundaries would be best known; and if it should appear that the said tract was within any of the New-England patents, they should leave the same and the inhabitants thereof to the jurisdiction of that government under which they fell; nevertheless, inasmuch as the petitioners had transplanted their families thither and settled at great charge, they commend it to the government within whose jurisdiction they shall appear to be, not only not to remove them from the plantations, but also to encourage them with protection and assistance and in all fit ways, whilst they should demean themselves peaceably, &c. *Hubbard.*

Gorton came again to Boston in the spring of 1648. The court, upon his arrival, ordered that he should be apprehended; but producing a letter from the Earl of Warwick, desiring that he might have liberty to return home, the court recalled the order and gave him a week's liberty to provide for his departure.

After this time, the Gortonists considered how to make their peace, and making their application in sober language, they remained unmolested and quietly enjoyed their possessions at Showamet, to which, in honour to their patron and benefactor, they gave the name of Warwick, which it retains to this day; and the posterity of several of them are persons of reputation and esteem in that colony.

Gorton published an account of his sufferings. Mr. Winslow, the agent for the Massachusets, answered him. In 1665 he preferred his petition to the commissioners, sent over by King Charles the second, for recompence for the wrongs done him by the

thing concerning Gorton, except Mr. Calender in his century sermon, set him in an infamous light, it will be but just to publish a letter which he wrote to Mr. Morton,[1] in 1669, vindicating himself from the charges against him in New England's memorial which was first printed in that year.*

THE dangers to which the colonies in New-England were exposed, from domestic and foreign enemies, first induced them to think of an alliance and confederacy for their mutual defence and safety. Those of Aquidnick or Rhode Island were willing enough to have joined with the rest, but the Massachusets refused to admit commissioners from that colony, to treat with the commissioners from the rest, upon the terms of the agreement. The other four, settled articles of confederation, May 19, 1643. They have been published at large by Doctor Mather, Mr. Neale, &c. and are in substance as follows: —

THE united colonies of New-England, viz. Massachusets, Plimouth, Connecticut and New-Haven, enter into a firm and perpetual league, offensive and defensive.

EACH colony to retain a distinct and separate jurisdiction; no two colonies to join in one jurisdiction without the consent of the whole; and no other colony to be received into the confederacy without the like consent.

THE charge of all wars, offensive or defensive, to be borne in proportion to the male inhabitants between 16 and 60 years of age in each colony.

UPON notice, from three magistrates of any colony, of an invasion, the rest shall immediately send aid; the Massachusets 100, and each of the other 45 men, and if a greater number be necessary, the commissioners to meet and determine upon it.

TWO commissioners from each government, being church members, to meet annually the first Monday in September; the first

Massachusets, alledging that, besides his other sufferings, he and his friends had 80 head of cattle taken and sold. The Massachusets in their answer charge him with heretical tenets, both in religion and civil government, and with an unjust possession of the Indian lands in the vicinity of the colonies for the sake of disturbing their peace; and add, that the goods which they seized did not amount to the charge of their prosecution; but they do not sufficiently vindicate their seizing their persons or goods without the limits of their jurisdiction, and conclude with hoping that his Majesty will excuse any circumstantial error in their proceedings, &c.

* Appendix. [No. 20]

[1] Nathaniel Morton (1613–1685) was a nephew of Governor Bradford of Plymouth and was Secretary of the Plymouth Colony for forty years. His *New England's Memorial* (1669) is for the most part an abbreviation of Bradford's *Plymouth Plantation*.

meeting to be held at Boston, then at Hartford, New-Haven and Plimouth, and so yearly in that order, saving that two meetings successively be held at Boston.

ALL matters, wherein six shall agree, to be binding upon the whole; and if there be a majority, but under six, the matter in question to be referred to the general court of each colony, and not to be obligatory unless the whole agree to it.

A PRESIDENT, for preserving order, to be chosen by the commissioners each year out of their number.

THE commissioners shall have power to establish laws or rules of a civil nature and of general concern for the conduct of the inhabitants, viz. relative to their behaviour towards the Indians, to fugitives from one colony to another, and the like.

No colony to engage in war, except upon a sudden exigency; and, in that case, to be avoided as much as possible, without the consent of the whole.

IF a meeting be summoned upon any extraordinary occasion, and the whole number of commissioners do not assemble, any four who shall meet may determine upon a war, when the case will not admit of delay, and send for the agreed proportion of men out of each jurisdiction; but not less than six shall determine the justice of the war, or have power to settle bills of charges, or make levies for the same.

IF any colony break any article of the agreement, or any ways injure another colony, the matter shall be considered and determined by the commissioners of the other colonies.

THESE articles were ratified by Massachusets, Connecticut and New-Haven, May 19, 1643. Plimouth commissioners had not then full powers, but they acceded, at the first meeting for business, September 7th following.

THIS confederacy had been in agitation for several years. In 1638, articles were drawn up which were referred until 1639. Mr. Haynes and Mr. Hooker, from Connecticut, tarried several weeks in the Massachusets soliciting it. They had reason to expect trouble from the Dutch, who kept a trading house at Hartford, after that place was under the jurisdiction of Connecticut, and broils frequently happened there, and the Dutch at Manhadoes were ready to have taken advantage of the least breach or alienation between the colonies; but, by reason of several obstructions from time to time, nothing could be perfected until 1643, when commissioners came from all the several colonies to Boston, whilst the general court was sitting, viz. Mr. Haynes and Mr. Hopkins from Hartford; Mr. Eaton and Mr.

Grigson [1] from New-Haven; besides Mr. Fenwick the governor of Saybrook fort; Mr. Winslow [2] and Mr. Collier [3] from Plimouth. The Massachusets appointed Mr. Winthrop, Mr. Dudley and Mr. Bradstreet of the magistrates; Mr. Hawthorne,[4] Mr. Gibbons [5] and Mr. Tyng [6] of the deputies.*

* This union subsisted, with some alterations, until the year 1686, when all the charters were in effect vacated by a commission from King James the second. For many years, commissioners met annually in September, and occasionally at other times. In the latter part of the union the meetings were triennial. A special and principal part of their business, after the first years, was the care of gospelizing the Indians. The society established by the parliament for propagating the gospel in New-England among the Indians, of which we shall hereafter take further notice, made the commissioners their correspondents and agents for dispensing the charitable donations; and, after a grant of a new charter by King Charles the second, the same powers and trust were continued. A particular account of all their proceedings in this capacity is preserved in their records. This confederacy was acknowledged and countenanced by the authority in England from its beginning until the restoration; and in letters from King Charles the second, notice is taken of it without any exception to the establishment.

July 23, 1643, a vessel of about 100 tons, belonging to the Earl of Warwick, arrived at Boston from Trinadada, in order to transport passengers to people the island, but none could be prevailed upon to remove. One Chaddock, son to the governor of Bermudas, was commander of this ship. He was a loose profligate man, and had a crew like himself. Five or six of them were blown up, by two barrels of powder taking fire in the pinnace where they were, near the castle. Some time after, strange sights were seen about the castle and at Governor's island, in form like a man casting out flame and sparks of fire, and a voice was heard in several parts of the harbour, crying, "Boy, boy, come away, come away"; of all which divers sober persons were eye and ear witnesses, and these sights and noises were supposed to have a special reference to the place where the pinnace was blown up. One of the men, it was said, had been acquainted with the black art.

From manuscripts and printed accounts I could collect as many prodigies, in one part of the country and another, at different times, as would fill a small volume; guns fired in the air, great quantities of clay cast up in form of bullets out of the earth, and the like; but I shall take no notice of any other than this, which is related by one of the

[1] Thomas Grigson came over with Eaton and Davenport in 1637, and became one of the chief men of the New Haven Colony. The ship in which he sailed for London in 1646 was never heard from.

[2] Edward Winslow (1595–1655) had been Governor of the Plymouth Colony in 1633 and 1636; and was to be Governor again in 1644.

[3] William Collier, of Duxbury, was a London merchant before coming to the Plymouth Colony in 1633. For twenty-eight years between 1634 and 1665 he was an Assistant. He died in 1670.

[4] William Hawthorne (d. 1681), an ancestor of Nathaniel Hawthorne, came over in the Arbella with Winthrop. He established himself in Salem, was now and then Speaker of the House of Deputies, and an Assistant 1662–79.

[5] Edward Gibbons (d. 1654). Hutchinson has an interesting footnote on Gibbons on p. 137.

[6] William Tyng (d. 1653) was a prominent merchant of Boston. He was a member of the House of Deputies 1639–1644, and Treasurer of the Colony 1640–44. Later he moved to Braintree and represented that town in the General Court. At his death he left a larger estate than any other in this country at that time.

ABOUT this time, much division and disturbance in the colony was occasioned by the French of Acadie and Nova-Scotia. It is necessary to look back upon the state of those countries. After Argall dispossessed the French in 1613, they seem to have been neglected both by English and French, until the grant to Sir William Alexander in 1621. That he made attempts and began settlements in Nova-Scotia has always been allowed, the particular voyages we have no account of. It appears from Champlain,* that many French had joined with the English or Scotch, and adhered to their interest. Among the rest, La Tour [1] was at Port Royal in 1630, where out of seventy Scots, thirty had died the winter before from their bad accommodations. La Tour, willing to be safe, let the title be in which it would, English or French, procured from the French King a grant of the river St. John, and five leagues above and five below, and ten leagues into the country; this was in 1627.† At the same time he was connected with the Scotch, and first obtained leave to improve lands and build within the territory, and then, about the year 1630, purchased Sir William Alexander's title. La Tour's title is said to have been confirmed to him under the great seal of Scotland,‡ and that he obtained also a grant of a baronettage of Nova-Scotia, Penobscot, and all the country westward and southward, was at this time in the possession of the English.

IN 1632, La Tour obtained from the French King a grant of the river and bay of St. Croix and islands and lands adjacent, twelve leagues upon the sea and twenty leagues into the land.§ By the

best historians || with great seriousness, as if he had no doubt of the truth of it. This turn of mind was not peculiar, at this time, to the people of New England. It was prevalent in England. If the New-Englanders exceeded, the new scenes they had just entered upon, may in some measure account for it. They had an ocean, a thousand leagues in extent, between them and all the delights of life which they had once enjoyed. On their backs they had a wilderness without limits. As soon as it was dark, their ears were filled with the roaring of wolves and other savage beasts, or which was much worse, the yells of savage men. Where there was any gloom upon the mind, such a scene must tend to increase it.

* P. 283.

† This appears from a list of the several grants made to La Tour, communicated to governor Pownall by Monsieur D'Entremont a very ancient French inhabitant of Acadie descended from La Tour, and who was removed to Boston in 1756, and died in a few years after.

‡ *Hubbard.* It is probable the case was not just as represented. King Charles in 1625 confirmed Alexander's grant, under whom La Tour settled.

§ The French commissaries speak of this grant as made to Razilly.

|| *Hubbard.*

---

[1] Charles Saint Etienne de la Tour. This episode in the history of Acadia is well told by Francis Parkman in his *The Old Régime in Canada*, chapters I–III.

treaty of St. Germains, the same year, Acadie was relinquished by
the English, and La Tour became dependant upon the French alone.
In 1634, he obtained a grant of the isle of Sables; another of ten
leagues upon the sea and ten into the land at La Have; another of
Port Royal the same extent; and the like at Menis, with all adjacent
islands included in each grant. Razilly had the general command,
who appointed Monsieur D'Aulney de Charnisy his Lieutenant of
that part of Acadie west of St. Croix, and La Tour of that east. In
consequence of this division, D'Aulney came, as has been related,
and dispossessed the English at Penobscot in the year 1635. Razilly
died soon after, and D'Aulney and La Tour both claimed a general
command of Acadie and made war upon one another. D'Aulney, by
the French King's letter to him in 1638, was ordered to confine himself to the coast of the Etechemins, which in all his writings he makes
to be a part of Acadie. La Tour's principal fort was at St. John's.
As their chief views were the trade with the natives, being so near
together, there was a constant clashing of interest. In November
1641, La Tour sent Rochet, a protestant of Rochel, to Boston from
St. John's, with proposals for a free trade between the two colonies,
and desiring assistance against D'Aulney; but not having sufficient
credentials, the governor and council declined any treaty, and he
returned. The next year, October 6, there came to Boston a shallop
from La Tour, with his Lieutenant and 14 men, with letters full of
compliment, desiring aid to remove D'Aulney from Penobscot, and
renewing the proposal of a free trade. They returned without any
assurance of what was principally desired, but some merchants of
Boston sent a pinnace after them to trade with La Tour at the river
St. John. They met with good encouragement, and brought letters
to the governor, containing a large state of the controversy between
D'Aulney and La Tour; but stopping at Pemaquid in their way
home, they found D'Aulney upon a visit there, who wrote to the
governor and sent him a printed copy of an arrêt he had obtained
from France against La Tour, and threatned, that if any vessels
came to La Tour he would make prize of them. The next summer
(June 12) La Tour himself came to Boston, in a ship with 140 persons
aboard, the master and crew being protestants of Rochel. They took
a pilot out of a Boston vessel at sea, and coming into the harbour saw
a boat with Mr. Gibbon's lady and family, who were going to his
farm. One of the Frenchmen, who had been entertained at the house,
knew her, and a boat being manned to invite her aboard, she fled to
Governor's Island and the Frenchmen after her, where they found
the governor and his family, who were all greatly surprized, as was

the whole colony when they heard the news; * for had it been an enemy, he might not only have secured the governor's person, but taken possession of the castle opposite to the island, there not being a single man at that time to defend the place.† La Tour acquainted the governor, that coming from France, [in this ship] with supplies for his fort, [he] found it blocked up by D'Aulney his old enemy, and he was now come to Boston to pray aid to remove him. La Tour had cleared up his conduct, so as to obtain a permission under the hands of the Vice Admiral and Grand Prior, &c. for this ship to bring supplies to him, and in the permission he was stiled the King's Lieutenant General in Acadie. He produced also letters from the agent of the company in France, advising him to look to himself and to guard against the designs of D'Aulney. The governor called together such of the magistrates and deputies as were near the town, and laid before them La Tour's request. They could not, consistent with the articles they had just agreed to with the other governments, grant aid without their advice; but they did not think it necessary to hinder any, who were willing to be hired, from aiding him, which he took very thankfully; but some being displeased with these concessions, the governor called a second meeting, where, upon a more full debate, the first opinion was adhered to.‡ La Tour hired four ships of force, and took 70 or 80 volunteers into his pay, with which assistance he was safely landed at his fort, and D'Aulney fled to Penobscot, where he ran his vessels ashore; and although the commander of the ships refused to attack him, yet some of the soldiers joined with La Tour's men in an assault upon some of D'Aulney's men, who had intrenched themselves; but were obliged to betake themselves to flight, having three of their number slain. The ships returned in about two months, without any loss. The governor ex-

* The town was so surprized, that they were all immediately in arms, and three shallops filled with armed men were sent to guard the governor home.

† This occasioned new regulations for the better security of the place. The castle was rebuilt in 1644, at the charge of the six neighbouring towns. *Johnson.*

‡ Some of the magistrates, deputies and elders, were much grieved at this proceeding. A remonstrance to the governor was drawn up and signed by Mr. Saltonstall, Mr. Bradstreet, and Mr. Symonds of the magistrates, and Mr. Nath. Ward, Ezekiel Rogers, Nathanael Rogers and John Norton of the elders; wherein they condemn the proceeding, as impolitic and unjust, and set forth "that they should expose their trade to the ravages of D'Aulney, and perhaps the whole colony to the resentment of the French King, who would not be imposed upon by the distinction of permitting and commanding force to assist La Tour; that they had no sufficient evidence of the justice of his cause, and *in causa dubiâ bellum non est suscipiendum*; that La Tour was a papist attended by priests, friars, &c. and that they were in the case of Jehoshaphat who joined with Ahab an idolater, which act was expressly condemned in scripture." Manuscript etters and original papers.

cused the proceeding to D'Aulney, as not having interested himself in the quarrel between them, but only permitted La Tour, in his distress, as the laws of christianity and humanity required, to hire ships and men for his money, without any commission or authority derived from the government of the colony. D'Aulney went to France, and, being expected to return the next summer 1644, with a great force, La Tour came again to Boston, and went from thence to Mr. Endicot, who was then governor and lived at Salem, and who appointed a meeting of magistrates and ministers to consider his request. Most of the magistrates were of opinion that he ought to be relieved as a distressed neighbour, and in point of prudence, to prevent so dangerous an enemy as D'Aulney from strengthening himself in their neighbourhood; but it was finally agreed, that a letter should be wrote to D'Aulney, to enquire the reason of his having granted commissions to take their people, and to demand satisfaction for the wrong he had done to them and their confederates, in taking Penobscot, and in making prize of their men and goods at the Isle of Sables; at the same time intimating, that altho' these people who went the last year with La Tour, had no commission, yet if D'Aulney could make it appear they had done him any wrong (which they knew nothing of) satisfaction should be made; and they expected he should call in all his commissions, and required his answer by the bearer. They likewise acquainted him, that their merchants had entered into a trade with La Tour, which they were resolved to support them in. La Tour being able to obtain nothing further, returned to his fort.

SOME of the province of Maine going this summer (1644) from Saco to trade with La Tour, or to get in their debts, put in at Penobscot in their way, and were detained prisoners a few days; but for the sake of Mr. Shurt of Pemaquid, one of the company, who was well known to D'Aulney, they were released. La Tour afterwards prevailed upon Mr. Wanneston,[1] another of the company, to attempt, with about twenty of La Tour's men, to take Penobscot, for they heard the fort was weakly manned and in want of victuals. They went first to a farm house of D'Aulney's about six miles from the fort. They burned the house and killed the cattle, but Wanneston being killed at the door, the rest of them came to Boston.

IN September, letters were received from D'Aulney, informing that his master the King of France understanding that the aid al-

[1] "Wanneston." The third edition gives this name as "Wannerton," which is probably correct. Savage identifies Thomas Wannerton as being of "Portsmouth, Kittery, and anywhere along shore where drink was easily got."

lowed to La Tour, the last year, by the Massachusets, was procured
by means of a commission which he shewed from the Vice-Admiral
of France, had given in charge that they should not be molested, but
good correspondence should be kept with them and all the English;
and that, as soon as he had settled some affairs, he intended to let
them know what further commission he had, &c. Soon after, he sent
a commissioner, supposed to be a friar, but dressed in lay habit, with
ten men to attend him, with credentials and a commission under the
great seal of France, and copy of some late proceedings against La
Tour, who was proscribed as a rebel and traitor, having fled out of
France against special order. The governor and magistrates urged
much a reconciliation with La Tour, but to no purpose. La Tour
pretended to be a Huguenot, or at least to think favourably of that
religion, and this gave him a preference in the esteem of the colony
to D'Aulney; but as D'Aulney seemed to be established in his authority, upon proposals being made by him of peace and friendship,
the following articles were concluded upon, viz.

> THE agreement between John Endicot, Esq; governor of New-Eng-
> land, and the rest of the magistrates there, and Monsieur Marie
> commissioner of Monsieur D'Aulney, Knt. governor and lieut.
> general for his Majesty the King of France in Acadie, a province
> of New France, made and ratified at Boston in the Massachusets
> aforesaid, October 8, 1644.

THE Governor and all the rest of the magistrates do promise to Mr.
Marie, that they, and all the rest of the English within the jurisdiction of
the Massachusets, shall observe and keep firm peace with Monsieur
D'Aulney, &c. and all the French under his command in Acadie. And
likewise, the said M. Marie doth promise in the behalf of Mons. D'Aulney,
that he and all his people shall also keep firm peace with the governor and
magistrates aforesaid, and with all the inhabitants of the jurisdiction of
the Massachusets aforesaid; and that it shall be lawful for all men, both
the French and English, to trade with each other, so that if any occasion
of offence should happen, neither part shall attempt any thing against the
other in any hostile manner, until the wrong be first declared and complained of, and due satisfaction not given. Provided always, the governor
and magistrates aforesaid be not bound to restrain their merchants from
trading with their ships with any persons, whether French or others,
wheresoever they dwell. Provided also, that the full ratification and conclusion of this agreement be referred to the next meeting of the commissioners of the united colonies of New-England, for the continuation or
abrogation, and in the mean time to remain firm and inviolable.

THIS agreement freed the people from the fears they were under
of ravages upon their small vessels and out plantations. La Tour

was suffered to hire a vessel to carry a supply of provisions to his fort; which vessel he took under his convoy and returned home.*

* The agreement made with D'Aulney was afterwards ratified by the commissioners of the united colonies, but he proved a very troublesome neighbour notwithstanding. In 1645 he made prize of a vessel, belonging to the merchants of Boston going to La Tour with provisions, and sent the men home (after he had stripped them of their cloaths and kept them ten days upon an island) in a small old boat, without either compass to steer by or gun to defend themselves. The governor and council dispatched away a vessel with letters to expostulate with him upon this action, complaining of it as a breach of the articles, and requiring satisfaction; but he wrote back in very high and lofty language, and threatned them with the effects of his master's displeasure. They replied to D'Aulney, that they were not afraid of any thing he could do to them; and as for his master, they knew he was a mighty prince, but they hoped he was just as well as mighty, and that he would not fall upon them without hearing their cause, and if he should do it, they had a God in whom to trust when all other help failed. With this ship D'Aulney made an attempt the same year upon La Tour's fort while he was absent, having left only 50 men in it; but his lady bravely defended it, and D'Aulney returned disappointed, and charged the Massachusets with breach of covenant in entertaining La Tour and sending home his lady. They excused themselves in a letter, by replying, that La Tour had hired three London ships which lay in the harbour. To this letter D'Aulney refused at first to return any answer, and refused to suffer the messenger, Capt. Allen, to come within his fort; but, at length, wrote in a high strain, demanding satisfaction for his mill which had been burnt, and threatning revenge. When the commissioners met in September, they agreed to send Capt. Bridges to him, with the articles of peace ratified by them, and demanding a ratification from him under his own hand. D'Aulney entertained their messenger with courtesy and all the state he could, but refused to sign the articles, until the differences between them were composed; and wrote back, that he perceived their drift was to gain time, whereas if their messengers had been furnished with power to have treated with him and concluded about their differences, he doubted not all might have been composed, for he stood more upon his honour than his interest, and he would sit still until the spring expecting their answer. The general court, upon considering this answer, resolved to send the deputy governor Mr. Dudley, Major Denison and Capt. Hawthorn, with full powers to treat and determine, and wrote to D'Aulney, acquainting him with their resolution, and that they had agreed to the place he desired, viz. Penobscot or Pentagoet, and referred the time to him, provided it should be in the month of September. This was opposed by some, as too great a condescension, and they would have had him come to the English settlement at Pemaquid; but his commission of lieutenant-general for the King of France was thought by others to carry so much dignity with it, that it would be no dishonour to the colony to go to his own house; but it seems he was too good a husband to put himself to the expence of entertaining the messengers, and wrote in answer that he perceived they were now in earnest, and desired peace, as he did also for his part, and that he thought himself highly honoured by their vote to send so many of their principal men to him; but desired he might spare them the labour, and he would send two or three of his to Boston, in August following (1646) to hear and determine, &c. On the 20th of September, Messrs. Marie, Lewis, and D'Aulney's secretary, arrived at Boston in a small pinnace, and it being Lord's day, two officers were sent to receive them at the water side and to conduct them to their lodgings without any noise, and after the public worship was over, the governor sent Major Gibbons, with other gentlemen and a guard of musketeers, to attend them to his house, where they were entertained. The next morning they began upon business, and every day dined in public, and were conducted morning and evening to and from the place of treaty with great ceremony. Great injuries were alledged on both sides, and after several days spent, an amnesty was agreed upon. One Capt. Cromwell had taken in the West Indies a rich sedan made for the Vice Roy of Mexico, which he gave to Mr. Winthrop: This was sent

MR. Endicot was this year (1644) chosen governor, and Mr. Winthrop deputy governor. Mr. Pynchon, who, living very remote at Springfield, had been left out of the number of assistants, was again restored.* The general court shewed a prudent compliance with the powers prevailing in England, and passed the following order.

WHEREAS the civil wars and dissentions in our native country, through the seditious words and carriages of many evil affected persons, cause divisions in many places of government in America, some professing themselves for the King, and others for the parliament, not considering that the parliament themselves profess that they stand for the King and parliament against the malignant papists and delinquents in that kingdom. It is therefore ordered, that what person soever shall by word, writing, or action endeavour to disturb our peace, directly or indirectly, by drawing a party under pretence that he is for the King of England and such as join with him against the parliament, shall be accounted as an offender of a high nature against this commonwealth, and to be proceeded with, either capitally or otherwise, according to the quality and degree of his offence. Provided always, that this shall not be extended against any merchant strangers and shipmen that come hither merely for matter of trade or merchandize, albeit they should come from any of those parts that are in the hands of the King and such as adhere to him against the parliament, carrying themselves here quietly and free from railing or nourishing any faction, mutiny or sedition amongst us as aforesaid.

---

as a present to D'Aulney, and well accepted by his commissioners, the treaty renewed, and all matters amicably settled. In the mean time, D'Aulney effectually answered his main purpose, for by his high language he kept the colony from assisting La Tour, took his fort from him, with ten thousand pounds sterling in furs and other merchandise, ordnance stores, plate, jewels, &c. to the great loss of the Massachusets merchants, to one only of whom (Major Gibbons) La Tour was indebted 2500 l. which was wholly lost. La Tour went to Newfoundland, where he hoped to be aided by Sir David Kirk, but was disappointed, and came from thence to Boston, where he prevailed upon some merchants to send him with four or five hundred pounds sterling in goods to trade with the Indians in the bay of Fundy. He dismissed the English, who were sent in the vessel, and never thought proper to return himself or render any account of his consignments. D'Aulney died before the year 1652, and La Tour married his widow, and repossessed himself, in whole or in part, of his former estate in Nova Scotia; and in 1691, a daughter of D'Aulney and a canoness at St. Omers dying, made her brothers and sisters La Tours her general legatees. Under them, and by force of divers confirmations of former grants made by Lewis the 14th, between the peace of Ryswick and that of Utrecht, D'Entremont aforementioned claimed a great part of the province of Nova Scotia and of the country of Acadie. Of part of those in Nova Scotia he was possessed, when all the French inhabitants were removed by order of admiral Boscawen and general Lawrence.

* Feb. 26, 1644, the country's ammunition, for greater security, having been sent to Roxbury to be lodged in the house of the surveyor-general, J. Johnson, the house took fire by accident, at noon day, and was soon blown up, there being 17 barrels of powder in it, but no other damage was done. Every one was ready to make their observations, one was pretty obvious, viz. that there had not been due care taken to pay for the powder. *Hubbard.*

WE shall find the authority here, acquiescing under every change of government in England. When we consider the dependance of a colony upon its mother country, nothing less is ordinarily to be expected.*

THE Indians, this year, were at war among themselves. Miantinomo, the great sachem of Naraganset, not being able to unite them all against the English, shewed his resentment against Uncas, sachem of the Mohegins, and the two petty sachems, Pomham and Sachonoco, near Providence; but in an action between the Naragansets and Mohegins, Miantinomo was, unfortunately for him, taken prisoner. The court ordered ten men to serve as a garrison in the country of the two petty sachems, and a strong palisadoed house to be built there.

THE commissioners of the united colonies interposed between the Naragansets and Mohegins, and by messengers recommended peace to both of them; offering, as mediators and umpires, to settle and determine their differences. Yoncho, sachem of Munhanset on Long-Island, came to the commissioners at Hartford, and desired that he and his people might be preserved from all injuries, professing himself a friend both to the English and Dutch, having been a tributary to the former ever since the Pequod war, and he and his people were received into protection.† Cutshamach, sachem of the Massachusets in the neighbourhood of Boston, having subjected himself formerly to the English; Passaconaway and his sons, from Merrimack, now came voluntarily and desired that they also might be received upon the same articles. The Indians more and more acquiring the use of fire-arms, the commissioners, this year, passed an act, that no person within any of the united colonies should directly or indirectly sell any kind of arms or ammunition to an Indian, under penalty of twenty for one; nor any smith or other person mend any gun or other weapon for an Indian, under the like penalty.‡ There was a proposal likewise made, among the commissioners, for an ex-

* Capt. Daniel Gookins, who came to New-England from Virginia, was made free the 29th of the 3d month 1644. He was afterwards an assistant and major-general of the colony, a zealous active man, but rigid in his principles in church and state beyond most of those who came first from England. I find a person of his name, in Purchase, among the principal persons in Virginia.

† By an act of the commissioners this year, Southampton upon Long Island was annexed to the jurisdiction of Connecticut, and Martha's Vineyard to the jurisdiction of the Massachusets.

‡ Some of the people of Rhode Island applied to the commissioners this year, that their colony might be united to some one of the other colonies. The commissioners approved of the proposal, provided the major part of the inhabitants should join in the application, and recommended to Massachusets or Plimouth in such case to receive them.

clusive trade with the Indians, to be carried on by a company to consist of subscribers from the several governments; each government
to have a distinct committee to receive subscriptions, take in stock,
&c. the whole to be under the regulation of the commissioners. This
proposal was recommended to the several general courts, but never
agreed to. The Massachusets was more considerable than all the
other colonies together, and this alone was enough to have prevented
them from approving of such a motion.*

THE next year, 1645, a meeting extraordinary of the commissioners was held at Boston; when it was thought necessary to send messengers to the sachems of Naraganset and Mohegin to require their
appearance at Boston, and in the mean time to suspend the wars between the two nations. It seems to have been good policy not to
have interposed in this quarrel, but the English were afraid of the
success of the Naragansets, who, although they had, by an accident,
lost their chief sachem yet were much more numerous than the Mohegins, and had divers other stout sachems, Pessicus, Canonicus,
and others, to head their armies; and as the English had generally
espoused the cause of the Mohegins, it was feared that as soon as
they were subdued, if not in the course of the war, the Naragansets
and their allies would fall upon the plantations of the English,
against whom they were then in a peculiar manner enraged for the
death of Miantinomo their sachem; for after Uncas had taken him
prisoner, being at a loss how to dispose of him, he carried him to
Hartford and left him with the English there, who kept him under a
guard. Uncas applied to the commissioners for advice. They gave
it as their opinion, that Miantinomo ought to be put to death for
having procured a Pequod to shoot Uncas, and for having been at
the head of a conspiracy against the English; but they ordered Uncas
to carry him out of their jurisdiction, and to slay him without that
torture and cruelty usually practised by the Indians upon their prisoners. This sentence was executed accordingly, some of the English
inhabitants accompanying the Indians to see it performed.

AT first, the Naragansets gave kind words to the messengers from
the English governments, but they soon changed their tone and determined to have no peace without Uncas's head. Mr. Williams,
from Providence, gave notice to the commissioners, that the Naragansets would suddenly break out against the English. He himself
had always been their favourite, and they had settled a neutrality
with the people of his colony. The commissioners drew up a declaration, containing the foregoing with other facts, which they appre-

* Records of united colonies.

hended sufficient to justify them in making war against the Naragansets, and determined to raise 300 men * with all convenient
speed, and that 40 should be dispatched immediately from the Massachusets without waiting for the assembling of the general court,
which the governor consented to. The two commissioners from the
Massachusets † sent to the majors of Suffolk and Middlesex for their
assistance in raising the 40 men, and at the same time, lest there
should not be a voluntary inlistment, they sent warrants to the constables of the six nearest towns, intimating the necessity, and requiring them to impress the 40 men and a number of horses to be ready
in two days, which was done accordingly. An attempt having been
made for volunteers without success, the third day the whole number were impressed and sent away under Humphry Atherton [1] their
leader, with some horses and two of the Massachusets Indians for
their guides, to wait at Mohegin for the Connecticut and New-
Haven forces. The general court of the Massachusets met before the
forces were out of the jurisdiction. The deputies took no exception
to the impress of men upon an emergency, although they had no
voice in it, but thought it necessary that a commission from the
whole court should be sent after the men; but the magistrates refused
their consent, and the commissioners opposed the proceeding, lest it
should weaken their authority if any forces should be afterwards
sent out by them. A commission was likewise given to Major Gibbons to be general of the forces of the united colonies for this expedition, and instructions were given him, and vessels were preparing
to transport provisions and other necessaries. The news of an army
of English preparing to march, intimidated the Naragansets, and
brought them to submit to peace upon the terms proposed to them.
Soon after the death of Miantinomo, the Naragansets had sent a
present of wampom to Mr. Winthrop, desiring to keep peace with
the English, and to revenge their sachem's death upon Uncas and the
Mohegins. Mr. Winthrop refused to receive it upon those terms, but
the messengers desired they might leave it, until they had further
advised with their sachems, which was allowed to be done. The

* Massachusets 190, Plimouth 40, Connecticut 40, New-Haven 30.
† Mr. Winthrop and Mr. Pelham.[2]

---

[1] Humphry Atherton (d. 1661), of Dorchester, was frequently a deputy, and during
the last five years of his life an Assistant. In 1656 he became Major-General of the
Colony. Upon returning from a military review on Boston Common in September
1661, he encountered a cow, was thrown from his horse, and died within a few hours.
[2] Herbert Pelham (1600–1673). See Hutchinson's footnote on p. 123. Pelham was
the first treasurer of Harvard College.

commissioners being informed hereof, thought it proper, by messengers of their own, to return the wampom. To return a belt received from the Indians, is looked upon by them as the highest evidence of a refusal to comply with the proposals made at sending it. The messengers however departed from their instructions; for finding the Naragansets disposed to submit, and that the sachem and others were coming to Boston, they brought back the wampom, and wrote to the commander of the Connecticut forces and to the commander of the men sent from Massachusets, acquainting them with the prospect of peace, &c. This action offended the commissioners, who did not intend the proceeding of the forces should be retarded.

PESSACUS, with two other chief men of the Naragansets, and Awasequan in behalf of the Nianticks, Janemo the sachem being sick, within a few days after came to Boston, with a large number of Indians in their train. The commissioners assured them, that however the treaty should end, they should receive no injury, but should stay and return in safety; and then reminded them of their former treaty, by which they engaged not to enter into war with Uncas or any other Indians without first acquainting the English with the cause thereof; notwithstanding which, they had this summer several times invaded Uncas, and had slain, wounded and taken prisoners several of his people and done him much damage, and forced the English according to their engagements to send forces at different times to defend him; that when they were sent to by the Massachusets, and had fair offer made, they abused the messengers, threatned the colonies, and declared "let who will have begun the war we will continue it until we have Uncas his head."

THE sachems at first charged Uncas with injuries, that he had taken a ransom for Miantinomo's life and then slew him, and they were loth to acknowledge any breach of covenant with the English. They offered to make peace with Uncas for a year, or some short time, but this not being satisfactory, they desired to know what was expected from them. Whereupon the commissioners told them, that their breach of covenant was the cause of all the expence which the English had been at in preparing for war, and it was reasonable that they should reimburse it; but the commissioners, to shew their moderation, demanded only 2000 fathoms of wampum (which was a sum far short of their charges) to be paid at different periods, and that they should restore to Uncas, his captives and canoes, and make satisfaction for destroying his corn, &c. keep perpetual peace with the English and all their allies and subjects, and give hostages for the performance of their engagements. These were hard terms, and it was with great reluctance that they finally submitted to them; but they knew that part of the English forces was gone into their country, and they were afraid that, even whilst the treaty was depending, hostilities would be begun; and finally, the 30th of August 1645, they signed to the agreement as the commissioners had prepared it, and left some of their number * hostages as a security for the performance of it.† The small English army, which was ready to march, was disbanded, and the 4th of September, which had been appointed for a fast, was now ordered to be observed as a day of thanksgiving.‡

ABOUT this time there was another struggle for power between the assistants or magistrates, and the deputies. The latter could not bear their votes should lose their effect by the non-concurrence of

* Pessacus's child, and a child of his brother, and two other children of persons of note. They attempted to substitute three or four children of the meanest of the people, but were discovered. *Rec. &c.*

† They tried every way to avoid complying with the agreement. Soon after, they reported that the Mohawks had sent their advice to them to pay no peag, they would discharge them from the fine. When this would not do, they laid a scheme for carrying off a number of English children in order to redeem their own, but they were afraid to execute it. *Benedict Arnold's letter to Gov. Winthrop,* May 29, 1646.

‡ Uncas, the sachem of the Mohegins, was hated and envied by the Naragansets for his attachment to the English and the distinguishing favours shewn him in return. In 1638, having entertained some of the Pequods after the war with them, and fearing he had given offence, he came to the governor at Boston and brought a present which was at first refused; but afterwards, the governor being satisfied that he had no designs against the English, it was accepted, and he promised to submit to such orders as he should receive from the English concerning the Pequods, and also concerning the Naragansets and his behaviour towards them, and concluded his speech with these words: "This heart (laying his hand upon his breast) is not mine but your's. Command me any difficult service and I will do it; I have no men but they are all yours. I will never believe any Indian against the English any more." He was dismissed with a present, went home joyful, carrying a letter of protection for himself and men through the English plantations, and never was engaged in hostilities against any of the colonies, although he survived Philip's war, and died a very old man after the year 1680.

The Naragansets failed in the payment of the wampum; and in 1646, messengers were sent to them from the commissioners, but Pessacus their chief sachem not attending, in 1647 the message was repeated, and he then pretended sickness and sent Ninigrate, a sachem of the Nianticks, to act in his behalf, and told the messenger that it was true he had not kept his covenant, but added, that he entred into it for fear of the army which he saw, and that he was told that if he did not set his hand to such and such things, the army should go against the Naragansets. When Ninigrate appeared, he asked how the Naragansets became indebted to the English in so large a sum, and being told that it was for the expence the Naragansets had put them to by their breach of covenant, he then pleaded poverty; but the commissioners insisting on the demand, he sent some of his people back to procure what he could, but brought 200 fathom only. They gave him leave to go home and allowed him further time. The whole was not paid until 1650, when Capt. Atherton, with twenty men, was sent to demand the arrears, which was then about 300 fathoms. Pessacus put him off some time with dilatory answers, not suffering him to come into his presence. In the mean while his people were gathering together, but the Captain carrying his twenty soldiers to the door of the wigwam, entered himself with his pistol in his hand, leaving his men without, and seizing Pessacus

the former who were so much fewer in number; but by the firmness of Mr. Winthrop, the assistants maintained their right at this time, and (March 25, 1644) the deputies, not being able to prevail, moved that the two houses might sit apart, and from that time votes were sent in a parliamentary way from one house to the other, and the consent of both was necessary to an act of the court. This continued a short time, without any further provision, but finally, the magistrates consented, that in appeals from the lower courts and all judicial proceedings, if the two houses differed, the major vote of the whole should determine. The deputies also looked with envy upon the powers exercised by the magistrates in the recess of the general court, and sent up a vote or bill to join some of their number with the magistrates, who should receive a commission from the court, but this was refused as an innovation upon the charter. The house then desired the magistrates would suspend the exercise of their executive power until the next session. They answered, that they must act as occasion required, according to the trust reposed in them. The speaker told them they would not be obeyed. The court broke up in this temper. But, disturbances happening with the Indians, it was called together again in a short time, and the deputies voted that (*salvo jure*) for the peace and safety of the colony the governor and assistants should take order for the welfare of the people, in all sudden cases which may happen within the jurisdiction, until the next session of the court. By agreement, all the ministers were called in at the next session, in order to give their opinion upon the point in difference. They determined, that the governor, deputy governor, and assistants were invested with the magistratical power, (the nature and extent of this power is left in the dark,) and that they do not derive it from the people, who were only to design such persons as they thought fit for the exercise of those powers. Several

by the hair of his head, drew him from the midst of a great number of his attendants, threatning, that if one of them offered to stir he would dispatch him. Pessacus presently paid down what was demanded, and the English returned in safety. Ninigrate, after this, began to stir up new troubles from the Nianticks, but, upon sending Capt. Davis [1] with a troop of horse into the Indian country, he was struck with a panick and would not be seen by the English, until he had assurance of his life, and then he readily complied with their demands; and they and the other Indians continued quiet many years, until by familiar intercourse and the use of fire-arms they became more emboldened, and engaged in the war in 1675, which issued in their total destruction. *Records of united colonies.*

---

[1] Capt. Davis. This was Captain William Davis (*d.* 1676) of Boston, "a man of wealth, enterprise, and discretion." He married a daughter of William Pynchon of Springfield. By profession Davis was an apothecary.

other points were referred to the ministers at the same time, and all agreed to by both houses with some small amendment.*

THE controversy between the two houses [which caused this struggle was about] the identity of a swine, which was claimed by a poor woman as having strayed from her some years before, and her title being disputed by a person of more consequence, divided, not the court only, but the whole country. The identity of Martin Guerre was not more controverted in France. Pity and compassion for the poor woman prevailed with the common people against right. At last, those magistrates who had been in favour of the other side, for the magistrates were divided too Dudley on one side and Bellingham the other, persuaded the person who they supposed had a good title, and who had recovered below, to relinquish it, that the public peace might be restored.†

MR. Dudley had the place of governor for 1645, and Mr. Winthrop deputy governor. Herbert Pelham, Esq; ‡ who arrived not long before, was added to the assistants in the room of Mr. Stoughton, who I suppose died this year. Mr. Pelham being a gentleman distinguished by his family, estate, and the qualities of his mind, was also, this first year of his arrival, chosen commissioner for the united colonies, Mr. Winthrop being the other. [The magistrates and executive courts were vigilant in suppressing all offences against the authority of Government. Persons were tried and punished every term for disrespectful words of particular magistrates as well as of the legislative and executive courts. The Town of Hingham had chosen Bozoune Allen for their Captain and presented him to the General Court for confirmation, which it seems was not obtained during the session. Some of the inhabitants of Hingham were offended at the delay and used some expressions concerning the liberty of an English free born subject which were judged derogatory to the authority of the General Court for which they were convened before a magistrate & required to give bond to appear before a quarter court, which they refused to do and were committed to prison. They then petitioned the general court for a hearing before them as being a matter which concerned the liberty of the people, the peace of the churches and the glory of God which would be made to appear, but

* Mass. Records.
† MS.
‡ Mr. Pelham was of the same family with his Grace the Duke of Newcastle. He tarried but a few years in New-England. It appears by letters from England, that in 1650 he lived upon his estate in the country there. He was intrusted by the colony in their affairs in England, relative to an encouragement for propagating the gospel among the Indians, and was a great promoter of that work.

the petition was dismissed and the petitioners fined 100 *f*. When the Marshall came to Hingham to levy the fines Mr. Peter Hubbard the minister of the town desired to see his warrant and pronounced it insufficient, not being in his Majesty's name to whom he had been sworn, and added that they had sent to England for advice and expected an answer, that he looked upon the government as no more than a corporation in England without power to put men to death by virtue of the patent or to do some other things they did. For this he was tried and found guilty of uttering divers speeches tending to sedition and contempt of the government contrary to the law of God and peace and welfare of the country and the Court fined him Twenty pounds and required him to enter into bonds with sureties for keeping the peace etc. This looks like severity, though it seems necessary and that they could not otherwise have supported their authority.]

IN 1646, Mr. Winthrop was chosen governor, and Mr. Dudley deputy governor; Mr. Endicot and Mr. Pelham commissioners.*

A GREAT disturbance was caused in the colony, this year, by a number of persons of figure, but of different sentiments, both as to civil and ecclesiastical government, from the people in general. William Vassal, as we have observed, came over with the first patentees and was one of the assistants in 1630, but soon after returned to England, and in the year 1635 came back to New-England and settled at Scituate in the colony of New-Plimouth. He was a gentleman of a pleasant affable disposition, but always opposite to the government both in the Massachusets and Plimouth. Scituate in Plimouth is contiguous to Hingham in the Massachusets, and Mr. Vassal had much influence in the latter colony as well as the former, and had laid a scheme for petitions of such as were non-freemen to the courts of both colonies, and upon the petitions being refused, to apply to the parliament, pretending they were subjected to an arbitrary power, extrajudicial proceedings, &c. The two first of the Massachusets petitioners were Samuel Maverick and Robert Child.[1] Mr.

---

* The commissioners hitherto had been chosen by the assembly, but, they being general officers, the freemen challenged a right of chusing them, and the rather, because some of the deputies had some times been chosen, which was not agreeable to the commissioners of the other governments nor to the freemen themselves.

---

[1] Robert Child (1613–1654) is usually referred to as Dr. Robert Child. There is a sympathetic chapter on Child in Samuel Eliot Morison's *Builders of the Bay Colony*, pp. 244–268. The recognized authority is George Lyman Kittredge, whose paper on Child is in the *Publications* of the Colonial Society of Massachusetts, XXI, 1–146. Child's "Remonstrance and Petition" is printed at length in Thomas Hutchinson's *Collection of Original Papers*, pp. 188–196.

Maverick, being in the colony at the arrival of the charter, was made a freeman before the law confining freedom to such only as were members of churches was in force, but, being an episcopalian, had never been in any office. Child was a young gentleman, just before come from Padua, where he studied physic, and as was reputed, had taken the degree of doctor. The principal things complained of by the petitioners were,

1st. THAT the fundamental laws of England were not owned by the colony as the basis of their government according to patent.

2d. THE denial of those civil privileges, which the freemen of the jurisdiction enjoyed, to such as were not members of churches and did not take an oath of fidelity devised by the authority here,* although they were freeborn Englishmen of sober lives and conversation, &c.

3d. THAT they were debarred from christian privileges, viz. the Lord's supper for themselves, and baptism for their children, unless they were members of some of the particular churches in the country, though otherwise sober, righteous and godly, and eminent for knowledge, not scandalous in life and conversation, and members of churches in England.

AND they prayed, that civil liberty and freedom might be forthwith granted to all truly English, and that all members of the church of England or Scotland, not scandalous, might be admitted to the privileges of the churches of New-England; or, if these civil and religious liberties were refused, that they might be freed from the heavy taxes imposed upon them, and from the impresses made of them or their children or servants into the war; and if they failed of redress there, they should be under a necessity of making application to England to the honourable houses of parliament, who they hoped would take their sad condition into consideration, provide able ministers for them, New-England having none such to spare, or else transport them to some other place, their estates being wasted, where they may live like christians, &c. But if their prayer should be granted, they hoped to see the then contemned ordinances of God highly prized; the gospel, then dark, break forth as the sun; christian charity, then frozen, wax warm; jealousy of arbitrary government banished; strike and contention abated; and all business in church and state, which for many years had gone backward, successfully thriving, &c.

* A motion was made in the court, in the year 1645, that all freemen should be required to take the national covenant in conformity to the practice in England; but it was thought convenient to refer the consideration of this motion. *MS.* I do not find it to have been reassumed.

THE court, and great part of the country, were much offended at this petition. A declaration was drawn up and published by order of court, in answer to the petition, and in vindication of the government; a proceeding which at this day would not appear for the honour of the supreme authority. A parallel was attempted between the fundamental laws of England and those of the colony, which in some parts of it is liable to exception. The petitioners were required to attend the court. They urged their right of petitioning. They were told, they were not accused of petitioning but of contemptuous and seditious expressions, and were required to find sureties for their good behaviour, &c. A charge was drawn up against them in form; notwithstanding which, it was intimated to them, that if they would ingeniously acknowledge their offence they should be forgiven; but they refused, and were fined some in larger, some in lesser sums, two or three of the magistrates dissenting, Mr. Bellingham * in particular desiring his dissent might be entred. The petitioners claimed an appeal to the commissioners for plantations in England, but it was not allowed. Some of them resolved to go home with a complaint. Their papers were seized, and among them was found a petition to the right honourable the Earl of Warwick, &c. commissioners, from about five and twenty non-freemen, for themselves and many thousands more, in which they represent, that from the pulpits † they had been reproached and branded with the names of destroyers of churches and commonwealths, called Hamans, Judases, sons of Korah, &c. and the Lord intreated to confound them, and the people and magistrates stirred up against them by those who were too forward to step out of their callings, so that they had been sent for to the court, and some of them committed for refusing to give two hundred pounds bond to stand to the sentence of the court, when all

* Mr. Winthrop, who was then deputy governor, was active in the prosecution of the petitioners, and the party in favour of them had so much interest as to obtain a vote to require him to answer in publick to the complaints against him. Doctor Mather says, he was most irregularly called forth to an ignominious hearing before a vast assembly, to which, "with a sagacious humility" he consented, although he shewed how he might have refused it. The result of the hearing was that he was honourably acquitted, &c.

† This refers to a sermon preached by Mr. Cotton on a fast day, an extract from which is published in the Magnalia, B. III. p. 29. wherein he denounces the judgments of God upon such of his hearers as were then going to England with evil intentions against the country, which judgments the author observes they did not escape. One of the petitioners hath observed on the other side, that Mr. Winslow's horse died in his journey to Boston, in order to take passage to London, &c. It may be of service to the world to record signal instances of divine judgments upon heinous offenders against religion and morality. When party spirit or bigotry prevails, common accidents are often construed extraordinary interpositions of Providence.

their crime was a petition to the court, and they had been publickly used as malefactors, &c. They then proceed to pray,

1st. FOR settled churches in New-England, according to the reformation of England.

2d. THAT the laws of England may be established, &c.

3d. THAT all English freeholders may enjoy such privileges there, as in England and the other plantations.

4th. THAT a general governor, or some honourable commissioners may be appointed, &c.

5th. THAT the oath of allegiance may be taken by all, and other covenants which the parliament shall think most convenient — and [they further pray], that their petition, for which they had been punished, may be considered, and that certain queries may be resolved, as,

WHETHER the patent of the Massachusets was confirmed by parliament, and whether it was not necessary it should be,

WHETHER the court may forfeit their charter, &c.

WHETHER if treason be uttered in the pulpit or in the court and not questioned, the court do not consent, &c.

WHETHER it be not high treason, as well in New-England as in Ireland, to endeavour to subvert the fundamental laws of England, to take away the liberties of the English nation, to say the Massachusets is a free state, &c.

WHETHER the oath of allegiance and the covenant be not binding there.

WHETHER all English inhabitants, having lands, are not freemen.

WHETHER the court hath power to confine in prison, banish, impose censures, impress persons and goods for an offensive war, &c.

WHETHER the ministers may publickly vilify the English nation, laws, &c. and not be questioned.

WHETHER the petitioners ought to be hindered from settling in a church way, according to the churches in England, &c.

MR. Winslow,* who had been chosen agent for the colony to answer to Gorton's complaint, was now instructed to make defence against these petitioners; and by his prudent management, and the credit and esteem he was in with many of the members of parliament and principal persons then in power, he prevented any prejudice to the colony from either of these applications. [Massachusets bay was a favorite colony. The like complaints against Virginia would have met with a different reception. The decision in that day of several of these queries might have been of use to posterity.]

* Mr. Peters and Mr. Weld were dismissed from the agency and desired to return home, but both of them chose to remain in England.

IN 1647 and 1648, the same governor and deputy governor were continued, and the first of these years Robert Bridges * [1] was added to the assistants. The number of males, in each of the four colonies, being carried in to the commissioners in the year 1647, in order to proportion the sum of 1043 l. 10 s. 1 d. expended for the general service, it appeared that the Massachusets part or proportion of the sum was 670 l. 3 s. 4 d. Plimouth's 128 l. 13 s. 4 d. Connecticut's 140 l. 2 s. 5 d. and New-Haven's 104 l. 11 s.[†].

MR. Coddington and Mr. Partridge,[2] in behalf of the colony of Rhode island, presented a request to the commissioner's at Plimouth in the year 1648, to be received into the confederacy with the other united colonies of New-England. The commissioners returned an answer as follows.

In as much as your present state and condition is full of confusion and danger, having much disturbance among yourselves, and no security from the Indians, the commissioners desire therefore in several respects to afford both advice and help; but upon perusal of the ancient patent granted to New-Plimouth, they find Rhode island, upon which your plantations are settled, to fall within their line and bounds, which the honourable committee of parliament do not think fit to straiten or infringe, nor may we. If therefore yourselves and the inhabitants of the most considerable part of them, upon a due consideration of Plimouth patent and right, acknowledge yourselves within that jurisdiction, we shall consider and advise how you may be accepted upon just terms,[‡] and with tender respects to your convenience, and shall after afford you the same advice, protection and help which other plantations within the united colonies enjoy, which we hope in sundry respects may tend to your comfort and safety.[§]

* All I find of Bridges is, "that he was an inhabitant of Lyn, a magistrate of able parts, and forward to improve them for the glory of God and the good of his people." *Johnson.*

† Rec. unit. col.

‡ Plimouth would have been soon swallowed up in Rhode island, from the great superiority of the latter. Besides, the principles of the people of the two colonies were so different, that a junction must have rendered both miserable.

§ An epidemical sickness passed through the continent in the year 1647. English, French, Dutch and Indians were seized with it. It began with a cold accompanied with a light fever. Such as bled or used coolling drinks generally died; those who used

[1] Robert Bridges (*d.* 1656) came to New England in or about 1641 and became a leading spirit in the iron works established at Saugus. See a paper by Charles E. Mann in the *Lynn Historical Society Register*, XIV, 85–89. Politically he sympathized more or less with Dr. Robert Child.

[2] Alexander Partridge came to Boston in 1645, but because of his opinions was not allowed to stay. He removed to Rhode Island within a few months, and became chief of the military forces in that colony in 1648.

THE first instance, I find, of any person executed for witchcraft was in June 1648. Margaret Jones of Charlestown was indicted for a witch, found guilty and executed. She was charged with having such a malignant touch, that if she laid her hands upon man, woman or child in anger, they were seized presently with deafness, vomiting or other sickness or some violent pains. The husband of the woman, after she was executed, had taken his passage in a ship, which lay in Charles river bound to Barbados, well ballasted, but with 80 horses aboard, and being observed to rowl on a sudden, as if she would have overset, an officer was sent with a warrant to apprehend the man, and after he was committed to prison the ship ceased her rowling, which it is said was never renewed afterwards.* Such was the credulity and infatuation of that day. Happy would it have been, if this had been the only instance of it. Shall we wonder at the New-England magistrates, when we find such characters as Lord Chief Justice Hale, &c. soon after chargeable with as great delusion?

IN the beginning of 1649 † (March) died Mr. Winthrop, the father of the country, in the 63d year of his age. His death caused a general grief through the colony. He spent his estate and his bodily strength in the public service, although he was remarkable for his temperance, frugality and œconomy. His virtues were many, his errors few, and yet he could not escape calumny and detraction, which would sometimes make too great an impression upon him. He was of a more catholic spirit than some of his brethren, before he left England, but afterwards he grew more contracted, and was disposed to lay too great stress upon indifferent matters. He first proposed leaving off the custom of drinking one to another, and then procured a law to prohibit it. He pursued, with great vehemence, Mr. Vane's adherents. He might have some political views mixed with this instance of his zeal. Some writers say, that upon his death-bed, when Mr. Dudly pressed him to sign an order of banishment of an heterodox person, he refused, saying, "he had done too much of that work already." Mr. Endicot succeeded him in the place of governor, and Mr. Dudley took the place of deputy governor.

---

cordials and strengthening things generally recovered. It extended to the West-Indies. In Barbados and St. Christophers each, five or six thousand died. It was accompanied there with a great drought, which caused an extreme scarcity of all kinds, and occasioned a demand for New-England produce greater than had ever been known before. *Hubbard.* A general disorder of this kind has, at several different periods since, prevailed and passed through the continent, and in some instances about the same time it has extended as far as Europe.

* *Hubbard.*

† Mr. Thomas Shepard, minister of Cambridge, died the 25th of August 1649. He was of Emanuel College Cambridge.

I fancy that about this time the scrupulosity of the good people of the colony was at the height. Soon after Mr. Winthrop's death, Mr. Endicot, the most rigid of any of the magistrates, being governor, he joined with the other assistants in an association against long hair.*

IN every age, indifferent things have been condemned as sinful, and placed among the greatest immoralities. The text against long hair, in Corinthians, as contrary to the custom in the apostle's day, induced our ancestors to think it criminal in all ages and all nations, and to look upon it as one of the barbarisms of the Indians. I have wondered that the text in Leviticus, "Ye shall not round the corners of your heads," was never brought against short hair. The rule in New-England was, that none should wear their hair below their ears. In a clergyman it was said to be the greater offence; they were in an especial manner required to go *patentibus auribus*. A few years before, tobacco was prohibited under a penalty, and the smoak of it, in some manuscripts is compared to the smoak of the bottomless pit. Some of the clergy fell into the practice of smoaking, and tobacco by an act of government "was set at liberty." In England, perriwigs came into use soon after the restoration. In New-England, they were an eye-sore for thirty years after, and did not generally obtain until about the time of the revolution; and, even then, the example and authority of Dr. Owen, Dr. Bates, Mr. Alsop, Mr. Mede and other non-conforming ministers in England, besides Spanhemius and other foreign protestant divines, who wore wigs, were necessary to

* "Forasmuch as the wearing of long-hair, after the manner of Ruffians and barbarous Indians, has begun to invade New-England, contrary to the rule of God's word, which says it is a shame for a man to wear long hair, as also the commendable custom generally of all the godly of our nation, until within this few years.

We the magistrates who have subscribed this paper (for the shewing of our own innocency in this behalf) do declare and manifest our dislike and detestation against the wearing of such long hair, as against a thing uncivil and unmanly, whereby men doe deforme themselves, and offend sober and modest men, and doe corrupt good manners. We doe therefore earnestly entreat all the elders of this jurisdiction (as often as they shall see cause to manifest their zeal against it in their publike administrations, and to take care that the members of their respective churches be not defiled therewith; that so, such as shall prove obstinate and will not reforme themselves, may have God and man to witness against them. The third month 10th day 1649.

Jo. Endicott, governor
Tho. Dudley, dep. gov.
Rich. Bellingham
Richard Saltonstall
Increase Nowell
William Hibbins
Thomas Flint
Rob. Bridges

(*Harvard College Records.*)   Simon Bradstreet."

remove all scruples concerning them. Beards were left off early in New-England, and about the same time they were in Old. Leveret is the first governor who is painted without a beard. He laid it aside in Cromwell's court.

A DISPUTE between the colonies of the Massachusets and Connecticut, which began several years before, was this year brought to an end. A duty * had been laid by Connecticut, upon all goods which were carried out of the river, for the maintaining Saybrook fort at the mouth of it. The inhabitants of Springfield, being within the Massachusets province, refused to submit to the payment of this duty. Connecticut, in 1646, laid the case before the commissioners of the united colonies, or rather those of Plimouth and New-Haven, the other two being parties, the consideration whereof was referred to the next meeting in 1647, when the Massachusets urged, "That Connecticut had no authority to lay a tax upon the inhabitants of another colony; that the fort was of no use to them; that a demand of this tax had hindred the union for several years; that the Massachusets first took possession of the river and planted there, and had been at great expence, never expecting this tax; that the Massachusets people had as good right to lay the same tax for all goods imported from Connecticut, to maintain the fort at Boston." The Connecticut commissioners urged "the practice of many places in Europe; that the fort was a security to the whole river, and that the reason of this case was the same, as if Connecticut should be at any expence to make the river more navigable, Springfield surely would not in that case refuse to pay any part of the charge." The Massachusets denied, "that the fort was a security against any vessel of force, and admitted that any expence, which might make the river more useful to Springfield, ought in proportion to be borne by the inhabitants thereof." The commissioners of Plimouth and New-Haven determined, that the tax should be paid until the next meeting, but they would then hear any further objections from the Massachusets against it. In 1648, among other things, the Massachusets insisted upon Connecticut's producing their patent to shew their authority. Connecticut urged that the line had never been run by persons in behalf of the two governments, to ascertain whether Springfield was within the Massachusets jurisdiction or not. The commissioners, at this meeting, recommended the running the line, and ordered that, in the mean time, the tax should continue. The Massachusets represented, that Mr. Fenwick was to have joined with them in running the line but failed them, and thereupon it was

* 2 d. per bushel on corn, and 10 s. per cwt. on beaver.

run at their own charge; by which it appeared, that Weronoke (Westfield) was within their patent, and had been so adjudged by the commissioners; notwithstanding this, they were ready to join with their brethren of Connecticut in another survey if they would be at the charge, as the Massachusets had been before, and would also produce their patent, as the Massachusets had produced their patent. Connecticut commissioners denied that Mr. Fenwick had promised to join in running the line, having only in general terms promised to endeavour to clear Springfield from being within the Massachusets patent; and alledged, that the running the line referred to, was a year before this promise, and therefore proposed, that the southerly extent of the Massachusets patent should be first agreed upon and settled, and then at a mutual charge the line be run by some skilful man chosen by each colony, &c. that as for their patent, the Massachusets knew the original could not then be obtained, but they were ready to produce an authentic copy, &c.

UPON this, the Massachusets commissioners, to the dishonour of the colony, produced a law of their general court imposing a custom or duty upon the other colonies, of the tenor following:

WHEREAS the commissioners for the united colonies have thought it but just and equal, that Springfield a member of this jurisdiction should pay custom or contribution to the erecting and maintaining of Seabrooke [1] fort, being of no force against an enemy of any strength (before it was burnt *) in the commissioners own judgment expressed in their own order; which determination they have also continued by an order at their last meeting at Plimouth (though the said fort was then demolished by fire and the passage not secured) contrary to a clause provided on Springfield behalf. And forasmuch as this jurisdiction hath expended many thousand pounds in erecting and maintaining several forts, which others as well as ourselves have received the benefit of, and hath at present one principal fort or castle, of good force against an enemy of considerable strength and well garrisoned and otherwise furnished with sufficient ammunition, besides several other forts and batteries whereby vessels and goods of all sorts are secured: It is therefore ordered by this court and the authority thereof, that all goods, belonging or any way appertaining to any inhabitants of the jurisdiction of Plimouth, Connecticut or New-Haven, that shall be imported within the castle, or exported from any part of the bay, shall pay such custom as hereafter is expressed, viz. all skins of beaver,

* In the midst of winter 1647, the fort took fire, no body knew by what means, and all the buildings and goods were destroyed, the damage being a thousand pounds or more. Capt. Mason, the commander, witn his wife and child, narrowly escaping with their lives. *Hubbard.*

[1] Saybrook, at the mouth of the Connecticut River, is intended, of course.

otter, moose, &c. two pence per skin, and all goods packed in hogsheads or otherwise ten shillings a ton, corn and meal two pence a bushel, biscuit six pence per hundred, on pain of forfeiture, &c.*

HAD the Massachusets laid a duty on goods from Connecticut only, they might have had at least a colour, perhaps more than a colour, to justify them; but to extend their resentment to the other two colonies for giving judgment against them, no excuse can be framed for it. It was a mere exertion of power, and a proof of their great superiority, which enabled them, in effect, to depart from the union or combination whensoever they found it for their interest; and if done by a single magistrate would have been pronounced tyrannical and oppressive: But in all ages and countries, by bodies or communities of men such deeds have been done, as most of the individuals of which such communities consisted, acting separately, would have been ashamed of. [It looks as if men imagined the guilt of each person to be diminished in proportion to the number concerned in an unjust act.]

THE union or confederacy had rendered the colonies formidable to French and Dutch, as well as to the natives, and a breach at this time would have given great advantage to the enemies of New-England; the commissioners of Plimouth and New-Haven therefore agreed upon a final result of the following tenor, viz. "That they were in hopes, according to the advice given at Plimouth, this controversy might have been happily issued, but they find that the Massachusets line had not been since run, nor was the place where it should begin, agreed upon; that the original patent or an exemplification thereof is required from Connecticut, altho' Mr. Hopkins had offered to swear to the truth of a copy by him presented; and that the Massachusets had imposed a burthensome custom as a return or retaliation, not upon Connecticut only, the party interested, but upon Plimouth and New-Haven, whose commissioners according to an article of the union and at the request of the Massachusets had impartially considered the matter in controversy, and given their opinion therein; therefore the commissioners recommend it to the general court of the Massachusets, seriously to consider whether such proceedings agree with the law of love and the tenor and import of the articles of confederation; but in the mean time desire to be spared in all further agitations concerning Springfield." †

* Records of united colonies.
† Records of united colonies.
It is probable the fort at Saybrooke was soon after slighted and the garrison discontinued, as we meet with no further controversy concerning it. The Massachusets law was suspended in 1650.

THE confusions, at this time in England, were matter of concern
and grief to many people in the colonies. There is no doubt that
they concurred in sentiment, in point of religion, with the prevailing party in England; but I find scarce any marks of approbation
of the tragical scene of which this year they received intelligence.
Mr. Eaton, the worthy governor of New-Haven, in a letter to
Mr. Winthrop in 1648, writes thus,

I thank you for your love and pains in that sad but weighty relation
you have made concerning the state of England. The ten considerations
you mention, are very observable, and call for our compassion and prayers
for them that seem not enough sensible of their own danger.

From Virginia, Mr. Harrison,[1] pastor of a congregational church,*
writes,

that by their later letters they conceive the whole heavens are overshad-
owed, the Scots hang like a black cloud (45000 in number) upon the borders, the King fled from the army to the Isle of Wight, the agitators
turned levellers, intending to bring in a kind of parity among all conditions, none to have above 300, none under 10 l. per annum, &c.

A controversy which had long subsisted, between the colony of
New-Haven and the Dutch at the Manhados, was settled by the
commissioners of the united colonies in 1650. The Dutch, who had
built a small trading house at Hudson's river, soon after the English
began the settlement of New-Plimouth, courted a correspondence
and friendship with them; and, as a writer of that day observes,
"gave them a mess of pottage for their birthright," which they had

---

* This was a church, founded by ministers sent from Massachusets.[2] Mr. Harrison
came the latter end of 1648 to Boston. He, and Mr. Durand [3] the elder, were both required to depart the country, by Sir William Berkley, the governor of Virginia, who was
a persecutor of this small church, consisting of 118 persons only. Harrison went to
England, and was made a doctor. The church is supposed to have been dissolved or
scattered, as there never was any further account of it. *Hubbard.*

---

[1] Thomas Harrison (1619–1682) was originally Governor Berkeley's chaplain, but
he turned Puritan and began to preach to a congregation in Nansemond County, Virginia. Banished by Berkeley, he came to Boston, where he married Dorothy Symonds,
a cousin of John Winthrop. Later he went to London, where he won great distinction
as a preacher. See John H. Latané, *The Early Relations between Maryland and Virginia.*
[2] In the summer of 1642 the inhabitants of Upper Norfolk, or Nansemond, Virginia,
sent an appeal to New England for "faithful ministers." Three consented to go —
John Knowles of Watertown, William Thompson of Braintree, and Thomas James of
New Haven. In the following spring they were silenced by the government of the Old
Dominion and compelled to leave the colony.
[3] William Durand took refuge in Maryland. About a thousand other Puritans from
Nansemond did likewise. John Fiske, *Old Virginia and her Neighbours,* I, 365–366.

craftily before deprived them of.* They undoubtedly had a design to have possessed themselves of Connecticut river, and to have prevented the English from obtaining any footing there. Those of New-Plimouth had pitched upon a place for a house in 1632,† when it was vacant, and in 1633, erected it, although they were threatned by a party of Dutch whom they then found there. Those from the Massachusets, in the years 1635 and 1636, made their principal settlement upon that part of the river where the Dutch had their house,‡ and for many years made no attempts to remove them, allowing them free liberty of trade with English and Indians. The Dutch also admitted any English to settle among them at the Manhadoes.§ When Mr. Eaton and his company sat down at New-Haven, the Dutch, from the rapid increase of the English colonies, were alarmed, and charged them with encroachments, although they themselves had no pretence to any certain boundary, and would sometimes challenge the country from Cape Henlopen to Connecticut river, and at other times as far as Cape Cod. The English, regardless of this claim, went on extending their settlements to Milford, Stamford, and other places, until they were within a few miles of Hudson's river. Whether the Dutch had any pretence of title or not, no doubt can be made that they would have extirpated the English if it had been in their power, but they were few in number. Once indeed, being possessed of a ship of some force, they sent her to New-Haven and seized a Dutch vessel which lay in the harbour and carried her away, the English having no naval force nor fortifications on land to prevent it. At another time, they set up the arms of the States at or near Stamford, and threatned to do the like at New-Haven; and there were altercations for many years, first between Kieft the first Dutch governor, and afterwards Stuyvesant his successor, and Mr. Eaton the governor of New-Haven. The Dutch had always restrained the English, not settled among them, from trading with their Indians upon Hudson's river. In 1648, the commissioners passed an order, prohibiting any French or Dutch or other foreigners trading with the Indians within the jurisdiction of the united colonies. This law, if carried into execution, must have put an end to the Dutch trade at Hartford. In 1650, while the commissioners were sitting at Hartford, the Dutch governor (Stuyvesant) came thither in order to treat, and presented his proposals in writing, dated "New-Netherlands the 23d of September, N. S." being the day they were delivered. He complained

---

* Idem.
† Mr. Winslow's manuscript letter to governor Winthrop, Sept. 1633.
‡ Hartford.   § Mr. Willet, Baxter, and divers other families.

of the encroachments at Connecticut river as well as towards Hudson's river; of the reception of fugitives; of the law debarring them from trade with the Indians; and of the English, for selling goods too cheap to the Indians, and so spoiling the trade, &c. The commissioners took notice, that his proposals were dated at New-Netherlands, and refused to treat, until he altered the name of the place where they were dated. He offered, that if the English would forbear stiling the place Hartford, he would forbear stiling it New-Netherlands, and date his proposals at Connecticut. They consented that he should date at Connecticut, but would not give up their own right to date at Hartford. After several days spent in messages from one to the other, the matters in difference were submitted to Mr. Bradstreet and Mr. Prince,[1] appointed by the commissioners, and to Thomas Willet [2] and George Baxter,[3] appointed by the Dutch governor. Their result was to be binding to both parties. The line, which was settled, ran northerly only 20 miles in length from the sea, and afterwards as the Dutch and New-Haven should agree, so as not to come within 10 miles of Hudson's river.[4] This must be understood so far as New-Haven had jurisdiction.*

* Accordingly we find that the Massachusets, in the year 1659, so understood it, and made a grant of land opposite to fort Aurania (Albany) upon Hudson's river; and

---

[1] Thomas Prince (1601?–1673) was for many years an Assistant in the Plymouth Colony, and from 1657 to 1672 its Governor. He spelled his name Prence. He came to Plymouth in 1621; later he was one of the first settlers of Eastham, but returned to Plymouth when elected Governor.

[2] Thomas Willet (1610–1674) was a very useful member of the Plymouth Colony. At one time he commanded its trading-post at Penobscot (Castine); at another, 1639, he was in charge of its interests on the Kennebec. Later he engaged in the carrying trade between New England and New Amsterdam, where he acquired some land interests. In the 1650's he more than once notified the Dutch of the designs of the English; yet in 1664 he joined Col. Nicolls's expedition against them, and after the surrender of New Amsterdam he was appointed the first mayor of New York! From 1651 to 1664 he had been an Assistant in the Plymouth Colony, to which jurisdiction he returned for the decline of his days. See *Documents relative to the Colonial History of New York*, I, 496, note 2, and X (General Index, under Willett, Thomas).

[3] George Baxter may have been of Providence Plantation, as stated by Savage; but his career was in New Netherland, where at first Stuyvesant deemed him a "worthy friend." Early in the 1650's he was a magistrate of Gravesend, and according to John Fiske "Stuyvesant's English secretary of state." Later he turned against the Dutch, flew the English flag, and was locked up for his behavior. When the time came (1663) for formulating plans for ousting the Dutch from New Netherland, he, with others, was called upon to produce grievances against them. See *Documents relative to the Colonial History of New York*, using the General Index in vol. X; and John Fiske, *The Dutch and Quaker Colonies in America*, I, 297, 299, 310, 311, 313.

In 1663 a "Captayne George Baxter" brought over the new charter of Rhode Island and presented it to the Court of Commissioners at Newport. It is possible that this was the same George Baxter. See *Records of the Colony of Rhode Island*, I, 509, 511.

[4] See Appendix, No. VII.

THE same governor and deputy governor were re-elected for the year 1650.* A corporation in England, constituted for propagating the gospel among the Indians, began this year their correspondence with the commissioners of the united colonies, who were employed as agents for the corporation, as long as the union of the colonies continued. One professed design of the colony charter was the gospelizing the natives. The long neglect of any attempts this way cannot be excused. The Indians themselves asked, how it happened, if christianity was of such importance, that for six and twenty years together the English had said nothing to them about it. The answer by the English was, that they repented they had not done it long ago, telling the Indians withal, they were not willing to hear, &c. Some of the Indians, who were taken as servants into English families, attained to some acquaintance with the principles of religion, and seemed to have been affected with what they had been taught,

---

a number of the principal merchants in the colony were enterprizing a settlement and a trade with the Indians, which probably was laid aside upon the change of affairs in England. The country itself, a few years after, was recovered from the Dutch and granted to the Duke of York, too powerful a proprietor to contend with about bounds. As this settlement is the only piece of evidence of any certain boundary to the New-Netherlands, while in possession of the Dutch, it is difficult to assign any sufficient reason, why the colony of New-York should extend further upon the colonies of Connecticut or Massachusets than this agreement would carry it. When the Massachusets charter was granted, the Dutch had no possessions at any distance from Hudson's river. Any grants or patents of vast tracts or manors, made by the Dutch without possession or improvement, seem to be void both in law and equity, and would have been as good if they had extended 200 miles from the river as when they extended 20. Notwithstanding this settlement, after the English were possessed of New-Netherlands, Connecticut was disturbed in their possessions, and finally obliged to give up their claim to Long Island, and to submit to a line of about 20 miles distant from Hudson's river, giving an equivalent for their settled towns upon the Sound, the jurisdiction as well as property whereof they retained, which Douglass[1] says, but without any authority, did not originally belong to Connecticut. The line between the Massachusets and New-York still remains controverted.

* Mr. Willoughby, a gentleman from England, Capt. Wiggins, who lived in New-Hampshire, and Edward Gibbons were this year added to the assistants. Wm. Hawthorn, the first speaker upon record. Edward Gibbons was one of Mr. Wollaston's plantation, and a very gay young gentleman when the Massachusets people first came to Salem, and happened to be there at Mr. Higginson's and Mr. Skelton's ordination and forming the church. He was so much affected with the solemnity of the proceeding, that he desired to be received into their number. They had not sufficient knowledge of him, but encouraged him in his good intentions, and he afterwards joined to the church in Boston. *Mather.*

---

[1] The reference is to *A Summary, Historical and Political, of the First Planting, Progressive Improvements and Present State of the British Settlements in North America,* 2 vols. (London, 1760), by William Douglass, M.D. (1691?–1752). Dr. Douglass was a physician in Boston, Massachusetts. The town of Douglas, Massachusetts, was named for him. His historical effort is marred by prejudice and inaccuracy.

concerning their existence after death and with the fears of the divine displeasure. John, the sagamore of the Massachusets, would sometimes praise the English and their God, "much good men, much good God," and when he was struck with death sent for Mr. Wilson, and desired him to teach his son to know the God of the English after he was dead. Mention has also been made of Wequash the Pequod; but the first instance of an Indian, who gave any hopes of becoming a real christian, was that of Hiacoomes, in the year 1643, at Martha's-Vineyard.* Under the instruction of Mr. Mayhew, he was induced to forsake the Indian Pawaws, to attend the English assemblies, and, after some years, became himself a preacher to his own people. It was in the year 1646, that the general court of the Massachusets passed the first act or order to encourage the carrying the gospel to the Indians, and it was then recommended to the elders to consider how it might best be done. On the 28th of October, four persons, who are not named, made the first visit to the Indian wigwams. Wabun, the sachem,† had notice given him, and many Indians were gathered together. None of the English were sufficiently skilled in the Indian language to make a prayer in it, and the meeting was opened with a prayer in English; but one of the company, in a discourse in the Indian tongue, began with the moral law and a brief explication of it, and the wrath and curse of God the just portion of the breakers of this law, and then informed them of the coming of Christ into the world to recover mankind from sin, and the punishment of it, his sufferings and death, resurrection and ascension, and that he would come again at the end of the world to be the judge of all men. They then entred into a free conversation with the Indians, and desired them, upon any point which they did not understand, to ask such questions as they thought proper, which was done accordingly; and it became the constant practice, after a sermon, for as many of the Indians, as desired it, to stand up and pro-

---

* Martha's Vineyard and Nantucket were not included in either of the four New-England governments. The Earl of Stirling laid claim to all the islands, between Cape Cod and Hudson's river. James Forett, agent for his Lordship, on the 10th of October 1641, grants, to Thomas Mayhew of Watertown and Thomas Mayhew his son, Nantucket and two small islands adjacent, and the 23d day of the same month, Martha's Vineyard and Elizabeth islands; and agreeable to the opinion of that day, of which we have given so many instances, grants the same powers of government which the Massachusets people enjoyed by their charter. Mr. Mayhew was called the governor of the islands. The Duke of York, after his second grant in 1673, included them in his commission to his governors of New-York. The grants of the soil of these islands could not vacate the right of the Indian sachems and proprietors; and, I suppose, most of the present inhabitants and proprietors derive their titles from Indian grants posterior to the grant to Lord Stirling, or to that made by his agent to Mr. Mayhew and his son.

† I take it, of those who were afterwards called Natick Indians.

pose questions * to the preacher. This meeting gave so much encouragement, that, on the 11th of November, they paid the Indians another visit at the same place, and found a greater number than were present before. Two other meetings were held the same fall, and a particular account was transmitted to England, and published there with the title of "The day breaking, if not the sun rising of the gospel with the Indians in New-England." [1] Mr. Winslow being in England, sought to obtain subscriptions for encouraging the work. Mr. Eliot, a minister in New-England, at the same time applied himself with zeal, equal to that of the missionaries of the Romish church; but instead of adopting a favourite maxim of some of that church, that ignorance is the mother of devotion, he endeavoured to enlighten the understandings of the Indians, to draw them from their savage, barbarous, and wandering way of life, to civility, government and cohabitation; and it was a noted saying of his, "that the Indians must be civilized as well as (if not in order to their being) christianized." He obtained from the court the grant of a tract of land, to which he gave the Indian name of Noonanetum,[2] (Rejoicing;) drew as many families there as he could, with design to make a fortified town; instructed them in their husbandry, and excited them to industry and a prudent management of their affairs; caused some of them to learn such trades, as were most necessary for them, so as that they compleatly built a house for publick worship, 50 feet

* In Col. Goffe's journal, one of King Charles's judges, who attended an Indian lecture in 1660, after 13 or 14 years instruction, he takes notice of the following questions.

1st. In your text are these words, Save yourselves from this untoward generation; in other scriptures it stands, We can do nothing of ourselves: how can this be reconciled?

2d. You say the word is the sword of the spirit by which their hearts were pricked. How shall I take and use the sword of the spirit to prick my heart?

3d. What was the sin of Judas, or how did he sin in betraying Christ, seeing it was what God had appointed?

4th. The answer to these converts was, Repent and be baptized, &c. But ye do not suffer us to be baptized; therefore I fear none of the Indians sins are forgiven, and my heart is weary with that fear, for it's said in Matthew, Whose sins ye bind on earth are bound in heaven.

[1] This was written by the Rev. John Wilson, "probably with Shepard's aid," says Morison. It was reprinted in the *Collections* of the Massachusetts Historical Society, Third Series, IV, 1–23.

[2] Not the site of the present village of Nonantum in Newton, but land near the eastern boundary of the city, comprising Nonantum Hill and Waban Hill, was called Noonanetum by Eliot. Hutchinson appears to have confused the Indian community at Noonanetum with that at Natick which was established in 1651. As far as I have been able to discover, there was no grant of land to the aborigines in Noonanetum, nor was there any well-built meeting-house for the Indians there.

in length and 25 in breadth, which Mr. Wilson, in one of his letters, says, "appeared like the workmanship of an English housewright." Besides this settlement at Noonanetum, he visited and preached to the Indians at Dorchester mills,[1] Watertown, Concord, and as far as Pantucket falls [2] on Merrimack river; to the Indians also in the colony of Plimouth, although Massasoiet or Ousamequin, and his son, discountenanced the bringing the gospel to their tribe. The Naraganset sachem treated with contempt, a message he sent to them, but the Nipnets desired some might be sent to teach them to pray to God. Besides Mr. Winslow, Mr. Pelham and others forwarded the collections in England, and July the 27th 1649, the parliament passed an act or ordinance for the advancement of this good work; the following breviate whereof was printed:

WHEREAS the commons of England, assembled in parliament, have received certain intelligence from divers godly ministers and others in New-England, that divers of the heathen natives, through the pious care of some godly English who preach the gospel to them in their own Indian language, not only of barbarous are become civil, but many of them forsake their accustomed charms and sorceries and other satanical delusions, do now call upon the name of the Lord, and give great testimony of the power of God drawing them, from death and darkness, to the life and light of the glorious gospel of Jesus Christ, which appeareth, by their lamenting with tears their mispent lives; teaching their children what they are instructed themselves; being careful to place them in godly families and English schools; betaking themselves to one wife, putting away the rest; and by their constant prayers to almighty God, morning and evening in their families, expressed in all appearance with much devotion and zeal of heart. All which considered, we cannot but, in behalf of the nation we represent, rejoice and give glory to God for the beginning of so glorious a propagation of the gospel amongst those poor heathen; which cannot be prosecuted with that expedition as is desired, unless fit instruments be encouraged and maintained to pursue it, schools and cloathing be provided, and many other necessaries. Be it therefore enacted by this present parliament, that, for the furthering so good a work, there shall be a corporation in England consisting of sixteen, viz. a president,* treasurer and fourteen assistants, and that William Steel, Esq; *Herbert Pelham, Esq*; James Sherley, Abraham Babington, Robert Houghton, *Richard Hutchinson*,[3] George Dun, *Robert Tomson*, William Mullins, John Hodgson, Ed-

---

* William Steel, Esq; was the first president, and continued until the restoration.

[1] Dorchester mills — now known as Milton Lower Mills.
[2] Near Lowell, Massachusetts.
[3] Savage believes that this name should not be in italics, for he is convinced that Richard Hutchinson, brother of William, never came to Boston. *Genealogical Dictionary*, II, 512. But why might it not represent Richard Hutchinson, a younger son of William and Anne, who returned to England about 1640 and grew rich?

ward Parks, Edward Clud, *Richard Lloyd*,* Thomas Aires, John Stone, and *Edward Winslow*, citizens of London, be the first sixteen persons, out of whom, the said sixteen persons or the greater number of them shall chuse one of the said sixteen to be president, another to be treasurer. — They, or any nine of them, to appoint a common seal. And be it enacted, that a general collection be made for the purposes aforesaid through all England and Wales; and that the ministers read this act, and exhort the people to a chearful contribution to so pious a work.

Hen. Scobell, cleric. parlia.

LETTERS at the same time were published from the two universities of Oxford and Cambridge, calling upon the ministers of England and Wales, to stir up their congregations to a liberal contribution for the promotion of so glorious an undertaking.

THE purport of the first letter to the commissioners, from the corporation, was to acquaint them with Mr. Winslow's determination to return to New-England, which would be greatly prejudicial to the work, and to intimate to them that he ought to be no sufferer by his continuance in England. The commissioners of the Massachusets proposed to make Mr. Winslow the agent for the united colonies, but as he had gone over in the service of the Massachusets only, the rest of the colonies declined the proposal; and all that could be obtained, was a letter, from the commissioners to the corporation, approving of Mr. Winslow's stay in England, and desiring that one hundred pounds sterling might be paid him out of the collections,† with a promise, that if it was not approved of as a proper charge, it should be replaced by the colonies.‡

---

* I suppose this should be Richard Floyd, who was chosen treasurer then or soon after. Those in Italicks had been in New-England. James Sherley was a great friend to Plimouth colony.

† I cannot find that either of the colonies have ever advanced any considerable sums for this service.

‡ Great opposition was made to the collection in England; and the conversion of the Indians was represented as a mere pretence to draw money from men of pious minds. It went on so slowly, that an attempt was made to raise a sum out of the army. Hugh Peters was one of the collectors, but the corporation wrote to the commissioners that he not only refused to pay a penny himself, but discouraged others, because, as they supposed, he had no hand in laying the plan. However such favourable accounts were, from time to time, published of the success of the mission, that, when King Charles came in, the corporation was possessed of six or seven hundred pounds per annum, which was in danger of being all lost, being derived from the establishment of the parliament; but by the interest of some good men, of whom the celebrated Robert Boyle was one, a new charter was obtained, by which the estate was secured. Mr. Boyle was chosen and continued many years the governor, and the commissioners of the united colonies were the correspondents in New-England, until the charter was vacated. After that, commissioners were specially appointed by the corporation, consisting of the principal gentlemen of the civil order, and of the clergy in New-England, and vacancies by death or otherwise have from time to time been filled up until the present time.

PROPOSALS had been made in the year 1648 to Monsieur D'Aille-bout, the governor of Canada, for a free commerce between the Massachusets and that colony. The French professed to be greatly

---

Perhaps no fund of this nature has ever been more faithfully applied to the purposes for which it was raised. If we compare the requisites, to determine any one to be a convert in Mr. Eliot's esteem, with those of the popish missionaries, it is not strange that their number hath exceeded his. Before the converts in New-England were admitted to the ordinances, they were examined by some of the magistrates as well as ministers. The confessions of many of them, as taken from their own mouths, were sent to England and printed, and there approved of: And although the mission began in 1646, it was the year 1651 before the first church was gathered, viz. at Natick. Whereas, with the Romish priests, the repetition of a Pater Noster or Ave Maria, or perhaps the telling over a few beads, made them fit subjects of baptism. Mr. Eliot, as has been observed, always insisted upon their being civilized and becoming men, at the same time they became christians. This was *naturam expellere*, and it was with great reluctance they forsook any of their savage customs. The French Coureurs de Bois, and others, married among the Indians, and became savages themselves, and the priests went into their country and dwelt among them, suffered them to retain their old customs and conformed to them themselves. However, the number of Indians in New-England, which have from time to time made profession of Christianity, is far from inconsiderable. In 1660 there were ten Indian towns, of such as were called Praying Indians. (*Goffe's journal.*) Mr. Eliot mentions a visitation he made in 1670. He went down to the Indians at Maktepos, I suppose what we now call Mashpee, where Richard Bourne, a godly man, on the 17th of August was ordained pastor to an Indian church which was gathered upon that day, and the Indians, and such of their children as were present, were baptized. From thence he passed over to the Vineyard, where many were received into the church, men and women, and they and their children baptized, the sacrament of the Lord's supper was administred in the Indian church, and many of the English church desiring to join with them, it was celebrated in both languages. Two teaching and two ruling elders were ordained, and a foundation was laid for two churches more. The teacher of the praying Indians at Nantucket came to the Vineyard, and made report that there were about ninety families that prayed unto God in that island; and advice was given, that some of the most godly among them should join to the church at the Vineyard, and after some experience of their orderly walk, should issue forth into church state among themselves, and have officers ordained. The Indians were very desirous of having Mr. Mayhew for their pastor, but he declined it, conceiving that he could serve them better in the capacity he was in, of advising and instructing in the management of their church affairs, and was willing to die in the service of Jesus Christ. Advice was given for the settling of schools, and that all, who neglected sending their children, should be liable to censure. Mr. Eliot then takes notice of the state of the Indians in the Bay. Natick was the chief town, where most of the Indian rulers dwelt, and where their courts were held. There were two teachers, John and Anthony, and betwixt forty and fifty communicants, and sundry more proposed to join to the church. Punkapog (now Stoughton) was the second town where the sachems of the blood, as they term the chief royal line, had their residence and rights; which (in other parts) as Mr. Elliot says, were mostly alienated to the English towns. I suppose the Indians of Naponset or Milton before this time had removed, and were settled with those of Punkapog, beyond or about the blue hills. Their chief ruler and teacher was Ahauton. A family or two of his descendants remain to this day.

Hassunimesut, or as it is now pronounced Hassanemisco, were the Indians next in order of dignity and antiquity; from thence came some of the chief friends to praying to God. They lay upon Nichmug river, and were strict observers of the sabbath, and were judged by all travellers, especially such who had occasion to lodge among them,

pleased, and a correspondence was kept up upon the subject until
the year 1650, when the French governor sent an agent to Boston in
order to settle, not meerly trade, but a league or alliance, defensive

---

to be sincere in their religious professions. They had two teachers, Annuweekin and
Tuppukkoowelin, characterized sound and godly men. I suppose those who are called
Grafton Indians, about eight or ten families, are all the remains of Hassanemisco.

Ogguonikongquamesut was the next praying town which bordered upon Marlborough. The English meeting-house being placed within the line of the Indian town,
caused great disputes and discouragements. Solomon, judged to be a serious and sound
christian, was their teacher. I suppose they are all dispersed, if not extinct.

Nashope [1] was the next. Tahattawans was called a Sachem of the blood, a faithful
zealous Christian was their ruler. Their minister, John Thomas, a godly understanding
Christian, was their teacher. Their town lay in that part of the country where the
Maquas or Mohawks hunted, and had been much molested and for a time was deserted,
but in 1670 the Indians returned and dwelt there, but are now extinct.

Wamesut was another praying town upon Merrimack river where Concord river
falls into it. Their Sachem was Nomphon, a man of a noble spirit. This place had been
so much molested by the Mohawks, that, the year before, they joined with a body of
northern Indians and some of Punkapog in an expedition against them, which proved
unsuccessful. George was their teacher. They were not in general much noted for their
esteem for religion.

Pantucket, at the falls in Merrimack river, was the place of another set of praying
Indians. The Pennicook Indians had come down the river, and built a fort at Pantucket, and were great opposers, and obstinately refused to pray to God; but being
concerned in the expedition against the Mohawks, they were most of them cut off, and
since that time the Pantucket Indians were, at least several of them, become praying
Indians, and Jethro was sent to preach Christ to them.

Magunhukquok,[2] where Simon was teacher, on the west of Natick, and Quana-
tusset,[3] which was under the care of the Hassanamisco teachers, are the two other towns
mentioned. By this account, of Mr. Eliot, we see the state of the christianized Indians
in 1670. The greatest body of Indians, viz. Massasoiets or Woosamequins, and afterwards his son Philip's or Metacom's subjects, were ever averse to Christianity, so were
the Naragansets. These two nations engaging in war against the English in 1675, had
drawn off some of the Indians of the praying towns to join with them, and occasioned
fears and jealousies of all the rest, which caused a great discouragement; but the war
being at an end in 1676, and the two other nations, the Wamponoags and Narangansets,
the great enemies of christianity, being wholly extirpated, the Indians which remained
in the Massachusets and Plimouth have in general ever since professed to be Christians.
In 1687, as appears by a letter of Dr. Increase Mather to Dr. Leusden at Utrecht, there
were four Indian assemblies in Massachusets, besides the principal church at Natick.
In Plimouth, besides the principal church at Mashapee, there were five assemblies in
that vicinity, and a large congregation at Saconet. There were also six different societies, probably but small, with an Indian teacher to each, between the last mentioned
and Cape Cod, all under the care of Mr. Treat, minister of Eastham; one church at
Nantucket, and three at Martha's Vineyard. There were in all six assemblies formed
into a church state, having officers and the ordinances duly administred, and sixteen
assemblies which met together for the worship of God. It does not appear that the
number of christians have since decreased by the return of the Indians to paganism.
The Indians themselves are wasted, and their tribes or nations every where in Massa-

---

[1] Nashope — now a part of Littleton, Massachusetts.
[2] Now a part of Hopkinton, Massachusetts.
[3] Now a part of Woodstock, Connecticut.

and offensive, between the government of Canada and the colonies of Massachusets and Plimouth; but being informed that all matters of that nature were left to the commissioners of the united colonies, he returned to Canada, and the next year two gentlemen were sent with letters to the commissioners, praying in behalf of the French of Canada, and of the christianized Indians in Acadie, the aid of the English against the Indians of the Six Nations, urging, "That it was a just war, the Mohawks being breakers of the most solemn leagues, perfidious and cruel; that it was a holy war, the eastern Indians being persecuted and cruelly handled, because of their professing the christian religion; that it was of common concern, the Mohawks disturbing and interrupting the trade, both of English and French, with other Indians." They promised a due consideration and allowance for the expence of the war. If the English would not join in the war, it was then desired that the French might have leave to inlist volunteers, and that they might be victualled for the service; and if that could not be obtained, that, at least, the French might be allowed to pass through the colonies, by water and land, as occasion should require. Until these points were settled, they could not proceed upon the treaty of commerce. The commissioners having duly weighed the proposals, returned an answer, in substance as follows, viz.

THAT they were willing to admit that the French and eastern Indians might have just grounds, to their own satisfaction, for war against the Mohawks. That they looked upon all such Indians, as received the yoke of Christ, with another eye than upon others who worship the Devil.* That they desired, by all just means, to keep peace, if it may be, with all men, even with these barbarians. That the Mohawks living at a distance from the sea, have little intercourse with these parts, but in the war the

---

chusets and Plimouth extinct, except at Mashapee, Martha's Vineyard, and Nantucket. At Mashapee, and near it, are about eighty families; at the Vineyard about eighty; and at Nantucket, where the last year were ninety families, there are now but fifteen remaining. There is besides, a town of Indians in the western part of the province called Houssatonick Indians, who removed about thirty years ago from Hudson's river, who have a settled English minister or missionary supported by the corporation; perhaps seventy or eighty families generally reside there. They waste away, as all other Indians have done, and there would have been a more sensible diminution of their numbers, if they had not from time to time received additions from abroad of other nations, or of such of their own nation as did not at first incline to remove with them. These with a few families at Natick and Grafton, and a family or two together scattered here and there about the province, are all the Indians at present within the province of Massachusets-Bay.

* But such Indians have generally been taught to treat the English, as heretics, with greater cruelty, and it has been made more meritorious to extirpate them than if they had been infidels or the worst of idolaters.

English had with the Pequods, 14 or 16 years before, the Mohawks shewed a real respect and had offered no hostilities since. That the English engaged in no war before they had full and satisfying evidence that it was just, nor before peace, upon just terms, had been offered and refused. That the Mohawks, not being subject to them, nor in league with them, they could not require an account of their proceedings, and had no means of information what they had to say for themselves. That to make war with the Mohawks, would expose the Indians who were neighbours to the English, some of whom professed christianity, &c. That although they were ready to perform all neighbourly offices of righteousness and peace to the French colony, yet they could neither permit volunteers to be taken up, nor the French and eastern Indians to pass thro' the English jurisdiction to invade the Mohawks, lest they should expose, not the Indians only, but the smaller English plantations to danger. That the English were much dissatisfied with that mischievous trade the French and Dutch have had and still continue, by selling guns, powder and shot to all the Indians, which rendered them insolent, &c. That if all other difficulties were removed, yet they had no such short and convenient passage, either by land or water, as might be had by Hudson's river, to and beyond Aurania fort possessed by the Dutch. That the commissioners conceived the French deputies might proceed to settle a trade; but if they thought proper to limit it under such restrictions, a fitter season for these treaties must be attended, which the commissioners would readily improve whensoever it presented.

THE college at Cambridge became more and more an object of attention, and in the year 1650 was made a body corporate, by act of the general court, and received a charter under the seal of the colony.*

* Under this charter the college was governed until the year 1685, when the colony charter was vacated; saving that in 1673, by an order of the general court, some addition was made to the number of the corporation. Mr. Dudley [1] (who was a son of the college) when he received a commission for President of the colony, altered the title of the President of the college for that of Rector; but no attempts were made to take away the estate or stock of the college, or to impose officers disagreeable to the country in general, but the government continued, in name at least, under the former corporation, who were Increase Mather, rector; John Sherman, Nehemiah Hubbard, John Cotton, John Leveret and William Brattle, as fellows, (the two last were tutors also) and John Richards, treasurer. When Mr. Mather, the rector, went to England in 1688, in his minutes of an intended petition to the King, he says, "that when the civil government was changed, the college was under the inspection of these persons, and he supposed it continued so, except that Mr. Sherman was dead, in whose room he prayed Mr. Samuel Sewall might be appointed, and that the King would confirm the government in

[1] Joseph Dudley (1647–1720), of whom much more anon. He was a son of Governor Thomas Dudley. He became President of the Colony in 1686; and at a later time, Governor of the Province. There is a good biography of Joseph Dudley by Everett Kimball.

their hands; but although these were in name the governors, they were not always so in fact." I find the following original order, dated December the 9th, 1686.

"WHEREAS the monies, and other estate, belonging to Harvard-College in Cambridge, has been by us committed to the care and management of John Richards, Esq; for the benefit of the said college, it is ordered, that the produce thereof shall, for this year 1686, be disposed of as followeth:

"1st. There shall be allowed to the present rector of the college, as some acknowledgment of the services which he has done for that society, the remainder of the income not disposed underneath.

"2d. The present tutors, Mr. John Leveret and Mr. William Brattle, shall for this year, beginning the last commencement, be allowed each of them 40 l. beside what shall be due to them from their several pupils.

"3d. The scholars of the house (for this year) shall be Sir Gibbs, Rogers, Mitchel and Dudley, who shall be allowed each of them at least 5 l. Sir Gibbs's pension to be paid out of Mr. Webb's legacy, and Rogers's out of Capt. Keyn's legacy.

"4th. Major Richards shall be allowed for his care, in improving the college stock, after the proportion of 1 l. for 100 l.

"J. Dudley,
"William Stoughton."

The president of the colony, and afterwards the governor, assumed the whole authority when they thought fit. The rights of Magdalen college Oxford invaded, justly might alarm the whole nation, but Harvard college was too inconsiderable, had the proceedings been ever so arbitrary and oppressive, to occasion any great notice. Mr. Mather, the rector, went to England in 1688. No person was appointed in his stead. Sir E. Andros, the governor, wrote to Mr. Samuel Lee, the minister of Bristol in New Plimouth colony, to desire him to officiate at the commencement; but not receiving an answer in proper season (it seems the letter was delayed) Mr. William Hubbard was appointed, and officiated accordingly. In 1692, upon the arrival of the province charter, although by a clause in the charter with a special view to the college, it was provided, that no grants, &c. to any towns, colleges, schools of learning, &c. should be prejudiced through defect of form, &c. but should remain in force as at the time of vacating the colony charter; yet the president, and many others with him, were desirous of a new charter, with additional powers and privileges. An act, of the general court, passed for that purpose in 1692, incorporating the college on a larger foundation than the former charter. Among other things, the college was enabled to confer such degrees as are conferred by the universities in Europe, whereas under the former charter no higher degrees had been given than those of batchelors and masters of arts. This privilege was exercised in one instance only, a diploma for a doctorate, under the college seal, being presented to Mr. Mather the president. Before the expiration of three years the act of incorporation was disallowed. Those who interested themselves for the college were resolved upon further attempts; another provincial act passed in 1697, with some variations, which before 1700 was likewise disapproved; for at a session of the court, that year, a vote passed the council and house of representatives approving the form of a charter which they were willing the college should accept from the King, and I make no doubt the agents were instructed to endeavour to obtain a charter in such form. By this charter, the corporation was to consist of a president, vice-president and fifteen fellows. It may not be unacceptable to some to have their names preserved. Increase Mather president, Samuel Willard vice president, James Allen, Michael Wigglesworth, Samuel Torrey, Nehemiah Hobart, Peter Thacher, Samuel Angier, John Danforth, Cotton Mather, Nehemiah Walter, Henry Gibbs, John White, Jonathan Pierpoint, and Benjamin Wadsworth, together with the two senior tutors resident at college, were the first corporation named in the charter. The college was impowered to hold real estate to the amount of three thousand pounds per annum. The governor and the council were made the visitors. This application proved as ineffectual as the former.

The true reason, of the several failures, appears from a letter of Mr. Blaithwait to the president, dated 1st June 1704, which says, "that the only obstruction to the passing the charter was Sir Henry Ashurst's refusing to allow of a clause for a visitation by the King or his governor." A letter from Lord Bellamont to Mr. Stoughton upon this subject deserves notice.

"New-York, 31st May 98.

Sir, I received a letter from the reverend president of Harvard college, by Mr. White, fellow of the said college, together with a copy of an act of the assembly for incorporating the college. And I am of opinion, that his Majesty will not give his royal approbation to that act as it stands worded, because it differs very materially from the terms of incorporation proposed by their excellencies the Lords Justices of England, viz. that the king and his governors should be the visitors, whereas the act of assembly vests the power of visitation of that college as well in the council as governor, which his Majesty may probably think derogatory to his prerogative. And I am apprehensive also, that those noble Lords who, under the title of Lords Justices of England, lately exercised the royal authority, will confirm his Majesty that it will be a diminution to the prerogative of the crown, to make the council co-ordinate in the power of visitation with the King's governor. —— For my own part I have a very great respect for the King's prerogative, but I could wish a way were found to secure the statutes or privileges of Harvard college against the capricious humour of future governors, who, out of prejudice to the way of worship used there, or for some sinister ends, may be vexatious to the college. There is great difference between the exercise of the prerogative in England and in these remote parts of his Majesty's dominions. There, the subject, whenever that exercise is abused, has the King, the fountain of justice, near at hand to recur to for redress. In these provinces, governors, I fear by what I have discovered since my being in America, are made bold and presumptuous in breaking the laws and governing arbitrarily, out of conceit that their being so far from under the eye of the government of England will be a sure cause of impunity to them. Therefore upon the whole matter, I must in judgment and conscience declare for a qualification of the power of a governor in the case of the visitation of Harvard college, but what that qualification should be, I must leave to his Majesty's wisdom and goodness to determine.

I am,

Sir, your most humble servant,

BELLAMONT."

To the Honourable
Wm. Stoughton, Esq; &c.

During these attempts, until advice of the respective acts being disallowed, the college was governed conformable to them. While no acts were in force, temporary orders passed the general court from time to time, impowering such persons to act as a corporation as were therein named. But in 1707, all prospect of a new foundation being gone, it was thought proper to resort to the old, and the charter of 1650 hath been conformed to ever since. The several heads of the college, from its first establishment to this day, have been as follows. Mr. Eaton, appointed in 1638, continued until 1640, when Mr. Henry Dunstar was appointed, who was succeeded by Mr. Charles Chauncy in 1654, who continued until 1671. Doctor Leonard Hoar succeeded Mr. Chauncy. Douglass says, Mr. Hoar was a doctor of physick from Cambridge in Old England. He was educated at Cambridge in New England, and took his bachelor's degree in 1650, went over to England in November 1653, was made a doctor at Cambridge, and returned not long before he was elected July 30, 1672. The students were too much indulged in their prejudices against him, and he was obliged to resign March 15, 1674-5. His wife was daughter to Lord Lisle. Mr. Urian Oakes, minister of Cambridge, was his successor, and continued from April 7, 1675, until his death in 1681. Mr. Mather was chosen by the corporation and confirmed by the overseers, and moderated at the masters disputations, and conferred the degrees at the commencement in 1681; but his

MR. Endicot was chosen governor in the years 1651, 1652 and 1653, Mr. Dudley deputy governor.*

AT a sessions of the general court in October 1651, an act or order was passed, impowering the town of Boston to chuse seven commissioners to be presented to the court of assistants, and being authorized by them and sworn before them, or before the governor, they or any five of them, or any three, together with one magistrate, might hear and determine all civil actions, not exceeding ten pounds in value, and all criminal actions where the penalty or fine should not exceed forty shillings, the parties being such as were inhabitants of Boston neck or Noddle's island, or such as did not belong to the jurisdiction; and the county court was not to take cognizance of any such actions. This law was made for one year, for trial. I do not find that it was revived.†

[The Colony, upon the sollicitation of Mr. Winslow the Agent in

---

church in Boston being unwilling to part with him, on April 20th 1682, Mr. John Rogers was chosen and confirmed, but died in 1684, being suddenly seized the morning of commencement, July 1st, and dying the next day. Mr. William Hubbard of Ipswick moderated at the publick exercises. Mr. Mather succeeded Mr. Rogers, and continued at the head of the college until Sept. 6, 1701. Mr. Samuel Willard, by order of court, officiated several years as vice-president, no president being appointed instead of Mr. Mather, until Mr. John Leveret was by the governor, at the head of the overseers, declared president January 14, 1707, and the college was put under his care, "agreeable to the choice of the fellows of the house, approbation of the overseers, and votes of the council and assembly in their last preceding session. The governor directing him to govern that house and the scholars there with duty and allegiance to our Sovereign Lady the Queen and obedience to her Majesty's laws." Mr. Leveret continued in the presidentship until his death in 1724. Mr. Benjamin Wadsworth, a minister of one of the churches in Boston succeeded him. He died in 1737, and was succeeded by Mr. Holyoke, who continues in the presidentship at this time.

* In 1652, John Glover and Daniel Gookin were chosen assistants.

† Not only the town of Boston, but every town in the old colony, were to many purposes a corporate body; they might sue and be sued, might chuse their own officers for managing what was called the prudential affairs of the town, and the selectmen were judges of the breach of the by-laws of the town, the penalty of which could not exceed twenty shillings. Under the new charter, the selectmen have no judiciary power. They still are said to manage the prudential affairs. What is intended by the word prudential, when thus appropriated, is not very easy to determine. Be it what it may, all other town affairs are determined in a general town meeting of all the inhabitants. The inconveniency that must arise from such a constitution, where a town consists of a thousand or fifteen hundred voters, are too many to be enumerated, and too obvious to need it. There was a disposition, fifty years ago, in most of the principal inhabitants of Boston to be made a corporation. A plan was formed in order to be laid before the general court of the province, which by the charter is impowered to make corporations. When the heads of it were presented at a town-meeting, a demagogue called out, "It is a whelp now, it will be a lion by and by, knock it in the head. Mr. Moderator put the question." The people were prepared, and it was rejected by a great majority. Some of the best men in the town, despairing of doing any service, would never be present in a town-meeting afterwards.

England, had obtained the privilege of a trade to Barbados and Virginia notwithstanding their adherence to the Royal party, but the Act which passed this year making all ships and their lading prize which, after the first of January, should be found trading there, put an end to this privilege, and it brought on some suspicion in England of Mr. Winslow's fidelity to the State, because those places had been furnished from New England with large quantities of provisions, and ammunition; but he defended himself as being only the Petitioner, and if any ill consequence had hapned it must be attributed to the Committee of the State who had granted the licence. Sir Henry Mildmay, one of the Committee, then took occasion to observe, that notwithstanding all the priviledges and favours granted to the New England Colonies, yet they had never owned the Parliament or declared for it to that day. Mr. Winslow answered that they had owned it and adhered to it all along from the beginning of the troubles; they had suffered the loss of many ships and their ladings, taken by the King's party whenever they could master them; they fasted and prayed for it, and whenever they had notice of God's mercy and goodness towards it, they had their publick days of thanksgiving; they had espoused it's cause, and engaged in it's quarrel, and had proved faithful to any trust committed to them: If this was not owning it, he did not know what was. Besides, what business had he there at that time, or wherefore was he sent over to the Parliament: did he not own it by his so often applying to the Committee of Lords and Commons, and procuring so many orders which no other plantation had ever done? The New Englanders were hated of their neighbours in Virginia and Barbados, and had been imprisoned by them for refusing the oaths of allegiance and supremacy, the ground of which was an adherence to Parliament, and yet it was now said they did not own it, whereas, indeed, their outward weal, or woe, was bound up in it, and they must stand or fall as that did. Sir Henry Vane, who was too sagacious not to see Mr. Winslow's caution, observed that all he had said was true, but nevertheless they kept their Courts in their own names, and they had done so in the time of the late King. Mr. Winslow answered, that though this was the case as to one Colony (he meant Massachusets bay) it was not so as to the others. This, Sir Henry Vane admitted, but he and all the rest of the Committee enjoined Mr. Winslow to write to all the Governors of New England to keep their Courts, and issue their warrants, in the name of the Keepers of the Liberties of England, and in due time to send their answers; and he having signified to the Committee that the Colony of New Plimouth purposed to renew their patent under the powers then in being, answer was made that all the rest would do well in following the example.

Mr. Winslow urged the Colony to a compliance, there being a vast difference between the former and the present times, and if the Republick held it would grow better rather than worse for all the people of the nation both at home and abroad. But neither of his proposals were complied with.

The uncertainty of the continuance of the Republick probably had some weight, but there are most evident marks of an aim at Independency which originated, or were more apparent, upon the confusions in England, until the first charter was vacated. In their petition to the Parliament which was answer to the demands by Mr. Winslow, they pray governors may not be imposed upon them against their will, which though they must bear patiently, yet it would make them repent their going to America from whence many were grown too old to remove.]

SIR Ferdinando Gorges had made attempts, for many years, to settle the province of Main, but to little purpose. He was a zealous royalist, and neither he nor his descendants, who were in the same interest, could expect any favour from the parliament. The colony seems to have been deserted by the proprietors, and in the year 1651 the people were in confusion, and the authority of the government was at an end. In 1641, a charter had been granted by Sir Ferdinando to Acamenticus (York) making it a corporation, consisting of a mayor, eight aldermen and a recorder. His cousin Thomas Gorges was the first mayor. He lived about half a mile above what is called Trafton's ferry near Gorges point. The cellar of the house he dwelt in remains to this day. He went to England in 1643. The people of York say, that he returned [to the Province of Main] and died there. If so, it must have been before 1651, or some mention would have been made of him. The Massachusets, who, as hath been observed, claimed the province of Main as within the bounds of their charter, took the opportunity of the confusions there, and encouraged the disposition which prevailed in many of the inhabitants to submit to their jurisdiction, and in 1651 they appointed Mr. Bradstreet, Major Denison [1] and Capt. Hawthorn to treat with the gentlemen of that

[1] Daniel Denison (1612?-1682) was a son of William Denison of Roxbury, who was disarmed in 1637 because he sympathized with Wheelwright. Daniel married a daughter of Governor Dudley and was one of the early settlers of Ipswich. He was Speaker of the House of Deputies in 1649, 1651, and 1652; an Assistant, 1654-1682; and head of the military establishment in 1660. See a biographical sketch by Dr. Daniel Denison Slade in *New England Historical and Genealogical Register*, XXIII, 312-335.

province about the surrender thereof as in their best judgment and discretion should seem meet. The next year, 1652, Mr. Bradstreet and others were sent commissioners to summon the inhabitants of Kittery to come in and own their subjection to the Massachusets, as of right belonging to them. The inhabitants accordingly assembled Nov. 16, and agreed to submit, and about forty inhabitants subscribed an instrument of submission. The like was done at Acamenticus the 22d of the same month, and soon after at Wells, Saco, and Cape Porpoise. To the inhabitants of all these plantations larger privileges were granted than to those of the other parts of the Massachusets government, for they were all freemen upon taking the oath, whereas every where else none could be made free unless he was a church member. The province was made a county, by the name of Yorkshire. The towns from that time sent their deputies to the general court at Boston.*

THE trade of the province increasing, especially with the West-Indies, where the bucaneers or pirates at this time were numerous; and part of the wealth which they took from the Spaniards, as well as what was produced by the trade, being brought to New-England in bullion, it was thought necessary for preventing fraud in money to erect a mint for coining shillings, six-pences and three-pences, with no other impression at first than N E on the one side, and XII. VI. or III. on the other; but in October 1651, the court ordered, that all pieces of money should have a double ring with this inscription, MASSACHUSETS, and a tree in the centre on one side, and NEW-ENGLAND and the year of our Lord on the other side.† [1] At the same

---

* This regulation of the province of Main, although the major part of the inhabitants were brought to consent to it, yet it appears by the records, which are still preserved in the registry of the county of York, that great opposition was made to it by some of the principal persons; and the government of the Massachusets was severely reproached by them, for using violent compulsory means in order to reduce the province. They continued united to the Massachusets until 1665, when by King Charles's commissioners they were separated for a short time, as will hereafter be observed.

† The first money being struck in 1652, the same date was continued upon all that was struck for 30 years after, and although there are a great variety of dies, it cannot now be determined in what years the pieces were coined. No other colony ever presumed to coin any metal into money. It must be considered, that at this time there was no King in Israel. No notice was taken of it by the parliament, nor by Cromwell, and having been thus indulged, there was a tacit allowance of it afterwards even by King Charles the second, for more than twenty years; and although it was made one of the charges against the colony, when the charter was called in question, yet no great stress was laid upon it. It appeared to have been so beneficial, that, during Sir Edmund

---

[1] For a more detailed account of the coinage of Massachusetts see John Gorham Palfrey, *History of New England*, II, 403–405; or Edward Everett Hale in *Archaeologica Americana*, III, 281–306, 315.

sessions, a committee or council of trade was appointed after the example, as expressed in the order of the parliament of Great Britain, who were to meet at Boston or Charlestown to receive proposals for promoting trade, but nothing came from this attempt.*

In October 1651, hostilities began between the English and Dutch in Europe. The Dutch colony at Manhados was in too feeble a state,

---

Andross's administration, endeavours were used to obtain leave for continuing it, and the objections against it seem not to have proceeded from its being an encroachment upon the prerogative, for the motion was referred to the master of the mint, and the report against it was upon mere prudential considerations. It is certain that great care was taken to preserve the purity of the coin. I don't find, notwithstanding, that it obtained a currency any where, otherwise than as bullion, except in the New-England colonies. A very large sum was coined. The mint master, John Hull,[1] raised a large fortune from it. He was to coin the money, of the just allay of the then new sterling English money, and for all charges which should attend melting, refining and coining, he was to be allowed to take fifteen pence out of every twenty shillings. The court were afterwards sensible, that this was too advantageous a contract, and Mr. Hull was offered a sum of money by the court to release them from it, but he refused to do it. He left a large personal estate and one of the best real estates in the country. Samuel Sewall, who married his only daughter, received with her as commonly reported, thirty thousand pounds in New-England shillings.[2] "He was the son of a poor woman, but dutiful to and tender of his mother, which Mr. Wilson, his minister, observing, pronounced that God would bless him, and although he was then poor, yet he should raise a great estate." (*Magnalia*.)

* *Massa. Records.*

One Hugh Parsons of Springfield, was tried in 1652 for witchcraft, and found guilty by the jury. The magistrates refused to consent to the verdict, and the case as the law provided, came to the general court, who determined that he was not legally guilty of witchcraft.

Mr. Cotton, the celebrated minister of the church of Boston and the patriarch of New-England, died Dec. 23d 1652, in the 68th year of his age. Mr. Hubbard gives this character of him. "His excellent learning and profound judgment, eminent gravity, christian candour and sweet temper of spirit, whereby he could very placidly bear those who differed from him in their apprehensions, made him most desired whilst he was amongst them, and the more lamented when he was removed from hence. So equal a contention between learning and meekness, magnanimity and humility, is seldom seen in any one person." Upon his death-bed he ordered his son to burn all his papers relative to the religious disputes began in the time of Sir Henry Vane's year. He had bundled them all up, with an intention to do it himself, but death prevented his going into his study for that purpose. His son, loth to destroy what appeared to him valuable, made a case of conscience to Mr. Norton whether he was bound to comply. Mr. Norton determined against the papers. (*MS Letters.*) Mr. Cotton's life was published by his successor Mr. Norton, and afterwards by his grandson Dr. Cotton Mather.

---

[1] John Hull (1624–1683) was a man of many interests and activities. He learned the trade of a goldsmith and practised it with success. He was also a man of business and Treasurer of the Colony during King Philip's War. Samuel Eliot Morison includes an admirable sketch of Hull's life and achievements in his *Builders of the Bay Colony*, chapter V.

[2] "The fact is, her dowry was five hundred pounds, of which Sewall received, 11 February, thirty pounds, and 13 March, thirty-five pounds; the balance, four hundred and thirty-five pounds, being passed to a new account." John Langdon Sibley, *Biographical Sketches of Graduates of Harvard University*, II, 358.

openly to annoy the English colonies their neighbours, and therefore desired to preserve peace in America. The English colonies carried on an advantageous trade with the Dutch, and were for that reason willing to continue friendship, and a correspondence was kept up between the subjects of the two nations. In an address from the general court to Cromwell, they consider themselves as at liberty to continue in peace with the Dutch, and suppose their own act to be necessary to bring them into a state of war, notwithstanding the two nations were at war in Europe.* But in 1653, information was given by the Indians from several quarters, that the Dutch governor was privately soliciting them to a general confederacy, in order totally to extirpate the English. The massacre at Amboyna was then but a late affair. A general alarm was spread through the colonies. An extraordinary meeting of the commissioners was called at Boston, April 19,

to consider of several rumours and reports gathered from the Indians and others, that the Dutch had plotted with the Indians, and stirred them up to cut off the English.

The result of this first meeting was, that although the evidence was so strong, as that some of the commissioners looked upon it to be full proof, yet they thought it most expedient the Dutch governor should have opportunity of making answer; but before any message could be sent, letters were received from him, denying all which the Indians or any others had charged him with, wondering the English would give credit to Indian testimonies, and offering to come or send, or to make answer to any deputies which might be sent thither. It was thought proper to send agents to him, viz. Francis Newman,[1] an assistant of New-Haven, John Leveret [2] (afterwards governor of

* *Appendix.*

---

[1] Francis Newman (*d.* 1660) was Governor of New Haven from 1658 until his death in 1660. He settled at New Haven in 1638, was an Assistant in 1653, and a Commissioner of the United Colonies in 1654 and 1658.

[2] John Leverett (1616–1679) came to New England in 1633 with his father, Thomas Leverett. Thomas was an alderman of Boston, England, and became a ruling elder and selectman in Boston, Massachusetts. John Leverett was chosen a representative in 1651, Speaker of the House in 1663, Assistant in 1665, Deputy-Governor in 1671, and Governor in 1673. Says Savage, "No man in our country ever filled more important offices, nor with happier repute." He was the Colony's agent in England, 1655–1661, a critical time. His grandson John Leverett was President of Harvard College for sixteen years. See Charles Edward Leverett's *Memoir of Sir John Leverett* (1856), and Nathaniel B. Shurtleff's paper in *New England Historical and Genealogical Register*, IV, 121–136.

the Massachusets) and William Davis; and in a letter, sent by them from the commissioners, the governor was told,

that he had made use of Indian testimonies against New-Haven in a case of land, that Keift his predecessor had done it in a case of life, and that a Dutch governor and council at Amboyna had made a bloody use of the Japoneses confession (though extorted by torture) against Capt. Towerson and the English Christians there.

The commissioners demanded satisfaction for past injuries and security for the future. Whilst their agents were gone, they determined what number of men should be raised, if God should call them to war against the Dutch, viz. 500,* and appointed Capt. Leveret the commanding officer, unless the Massachusets should have some weighty objection against him. Notwithstanding the offers made by the Dutch governor in his letter, he refused to submit to any examination into the affair by the agents or commissioners, any further than a committee of his own council should concur with them. They took the testimony of divers Indians and others, and returned to Boston. But however strong proofs there were, the commissioners were divided in opinion, and a conference was had before the Massachusets general court and many of the elders. A state of the case was drawn by Mr. Eaton on the one side, and another by Mr. Denison on the other, and the elders † were desired to draw up their opinion, which was,

That the proofs and presumptions of the execrable plot, tending to destruction of so many of the dear saints of God, imputed to the Dutch governor and the fiscal, were of such weight as to induce them to believe the reality of it; yet they were not so fully conclusive, as to clear up a present proceeding to war before the world, and to bear up their hearts with that fulness of persuasion, which was meet, in commending the case to God in prayer and to the people in exhortations, and that it would be safest for the colonies to forbear the use of the sword; but advised to be in a posture of defence and readiness for action, until the mind of God should be more clearly known, either for a settled peace or more manifest grounds of war.

The deputies, by their vote, expressed a concurrence in sentiments with the elders. On the 26th of May, letters were received from Hartford and New-Haven, advising that the Dutch governor was endeavouring, by presents and other methods, to engage the Mo-

---

* Massachusets 333, Plimouth 60, Connecticut 65, New-Haven 42.

† The elders continued to be consulted in every affair of importance as long as the charter continued. The share they had in temporal affairs added to the weight they had acquired from their spiritual employments, and they were in high esteem.

hawks and the Indians between Hudson's river and Delaware to fall upon the English. A messenger arrived the same day from Manhados, with a long letter from the Dutch governor, complaining of encroachments and other grievances from the English, and exculpating himself in general terms from any plots or designs against them. The commissioners required further satisfaction and security from him. Mr. Norice,[1] teacher of the church at Salem, "in the name of many pensive hearts there," presented their sense to the commissioners in favour of a war, and the commissioners themselves were all of the same mind, except Mr. Bradstreet, one of the Massachusets commissioners; Mr. Hawthorne, the other, joining with those of the three other colonies; but their proceedings were interrupted by a declaration sent in by the general court of the Massachusets, "that no determination of the commissioners though they should all agree, should bind the general court to join in an offensive war which should appear to such general court to be unjust." This declaration occasioned such altercations between the Massachusets general court and the commissioners of the three other colonies at the next meeting, as threatned a dissolution of the confederacy, which seems, upon this occasion also, to have been prevented only by the inferiority of the rest to the Massachusets and their inability to stand alone. Where states in alliance are greatly disproportioned in strength and importance, power often prevails over right. The government of New-Haven were so sensible of their danger, that they sent their agents to England, to make a representation of it to Cromwell, who ordered three or four ships with a small number of forces for the reduction of the Dutch, and recommended to the Massachusets colony to afford their assistance. The ships were delayed, and did not arrive at Boston until the latter end of May or beginning of June 1654. The governor called the assembly, which met the 9th of June, and immediately came into the following resolution:

The general court having received and perused a letter from his Highness the Lord Protector of the Commonwealth of England, Scotland and Ireland, full of great and favourable respect to this colony, which they desire to keep in grateful remembrance, and shall be ready at all times, wherein they may with safety to the liberty of their consciences, publick peace and welfare, to their utmost to attend to his Highness's pleasure. This court therefore declares, that though they understand that the colony is not in such a capacity as may be apprehended to send forth such numbers of men as might vigorously assist in that undertaking, yet do freely consent and give liberty to his Highness's commissioners, Major

---

[1] "Mr. Norice" was Edward Norris (d. 1659), the fourth minister of Salem.

Robert Sedgewick * [1] and Capt. John Leveret, to raise within our jurisdiction the number of five hundred volunteers to assist them in their enterprize against the Dutch, provided the persons might be free from legal†
engagements.

The ships had a very long passage, so that the news of the peace with
the Dutch, which was signed the 5th of April, prevented their proceeding. This occasioned the commander in chief to turn his forces,
together with those raised in the Massachusets, another way, and to
dislodge the French from Penobscot, St. John's, &c. where they met
with no great resistance. It cannot be supposed that this was done
without instructions from Cromwell.‡ It was a time of peace between the two nations, but the English had good right to the country, and the complaints of the French in Europe could not prevail
upon Cromwell to give it up again.§ The peace with the Dutch, together with "the hopeful establishment of government in England,"
occasioned a publick thanksgiving in the Massachusets (Sept. 20th)
and an order, passed the last year, prohibiting trade with the Dutch,
was repealed. Stuyvesant, the Dutch governor, in these negocia-
tions conducted himself very artfully. New-Haven and Connecticut
were the two colonies with which he was immediately engaged in
controversy. He might have been a match for one, if not both those
colonies, but they were in alliance with the Massachusets. His all
depended upon preserving the friendship of that colony. He there-

* Sedgewick had been of the artillery company in London, afterwards lived at
Charlestown in New-England, and was the first military officer there, and in great
repute. I suppose he died in England. There were several persons descended from him,
living in England a few years ago.

† By legal engagements must be intended apprenticeship and other servitude, as
well as processes from courts, &c.

‡ The report in New-England was, that Sedgewick had only verbal instructions
from some of Oliver's sea commanders, and that this was the reason the country was so
easily given up at the treaty of Breda. *Hubbard*.

§ Mr. Dudley deputy governor, died July 31st 1653, in the 77th year of his age,
greatly lamented, being a principal founder of the colony, and having recommended
himself by great firmness and fidelity in the discharge of his trust; having never been
out of the magistracy, and generally either governor or deputy governor. He was
zealous, beyond measure, against all sorts of hereticks. At the next election for 1654,
Mr. Endicot was chosen deputy governor in Mr. Dudley's stead, Mr. Bellingham being
chosen governor.

———

[1] Robert Sedgwick (*d.* 1656) was an early settler of Charlestown, Massachusetts, and
was the founder of a distinguished American family. Though primarily a merchant, he
was one of the organizers of the Ancient and Honourable Artillery Company and its
captain in 1640. After the expedition of 1654, here described by Hutchinson, Cromwell
appointed Sedgwick one of the civil commissioners for the government of Jamaica.
While on this very difficult mission he died. There is a paper on Sedgwick by Henry
Dwight Sedgwick in the *Publications* of the Colonial Society of Massachusetts, III, 156.

fore kept up a constant [friendly] correspondence with Mr. Winthrop, and although he would not concede to proposals for a joint trade with the Six Nations, yet he encouraged trade between the Massachusets and Manhados, and, what was more, he, as well as his predecessor Kieft, made great pretences to religion. Kieft was a serious man. Plimouth fell in with Connecticut and New-Haven, and the Massachusets must have done so too, if the Dutch had committed any hostilities. Stuyvesant restrained his own people, but at the same time secretly encouraged the Indians to fall upon the English. The Naragansets were numerous, the Maquas, or Six Nations were more so. A general union of the Indians, which it was supposed he was endeavouring, must have been the ruin of the English colonies; and although it might be expected, that when they had rid themselves of the English, the Dutch would be in danger of the same fate, yet this was the least and most remote danger of the two. They were constantly in fear of the English. Their right to any part of the country had never been allowed in England. They were often threatened by the colonists in America, as the Dutch governors mention in their letters. Kieft complains to Winthrop, that 'some of the English had said publickly,' "that their countrymen were fools to suffer the Dutch to live there in the centre." [Their agent, Mr. Winslow, informed them by his letters that the powers in England were dissatisfied, that they might easily have gained the Dutch plantation and, after that, the French. After endeavouring in their answers to give a satisfactory account of their conduct to those who had been misled in England, they acknowledged that they inclined to the opinion of Cineas counsellor to Pirhus; their errand to New England was not to enlarge their territories or estate, hitherto (through the blessing of God) they had enjoyed their liberties in peace, and unless necessity enforced them they accounted it bad husbandry to put all to hazard; the reasons of their backwardness to war were serious and conscientious, but if political considerations only were to be weighed, the scales would turn on their side. They labour'd also in an address to Cromwell to exculpate themselves to him: In compliance with their nation they had debarred themselves from all commerce ever since they heard of the war and had been exercised with serious and conscientious thoughts of their duty the result whereof was that it was most agreeable to the gospel of peace and safest for those colonies at that season to forbear the use of the sword — if their understandings had mislead them, they humbly craved pardon.]

THE Massachusets [soon after] complied with Cromwell's proposal to extirpate the Dutch, notwithstanding their former scruples of the lawfulness of it. There must have been some other reasons, no doubt those I have mentioned, which caused them to be so backward in joining with the other colonies. They did not forsee what has since happened, that the neighbourhood of the colonies of different nations would one time or other engage the powers in Europe in their respective defence and annoyance. Without this, they had nothing to fear from either Dutch or French. They were ten times as numerous as both, and continually increasing in much greater proportion than either of the other, whose present or future interior force could cause no great apprehensions.

WHILST these disputes with the Dutch were depending, the Naraganset Indians made attacks upon the Indians of Long-Island who were under the protection of the English. This, together with the conspiracy which Ninigrate the Naraganset sachem was supposed to be in with the Dutch governor, the commissioners of the English colonies (all but Mr. Bradstreet) thought to be a sufficient ground for making war against the Indians, and came to a resolution in 1653, that 250 men should be forthwith raised in the several colonies, but the Massachusets general court refused to raise their quota. The hostilities between the Indians continuing until 1654, and many upland Indians, as they were called, viz. Wampanoags, Pocanoticks,* &c. being collected together, the commissioners sent a messenger to Ninigrate, who soon returned with the following answer, which is here inserted to shew the authority the English assumed at that time over the Indians, and the sense they still retained of their independancy.

JONATHAN GILBERT [1] returned 18 Sept. 1654, and brought Ninigrate's answer in the words following: Having acquainted him that the commissioners were met at Hartford, and that they had perused the letter sent to the governor of the Massachusets, he answered, he knew nothing of any such letter, and made strange of it.

CONCERNING his invading the Long-Islanders, he answered; Wherefore should he acquaint the commissioners, when as the Long-Islanders had begun with him and had slain a sachem's son and sixty others of his men, and therefore he will not make peace with the Long-Islanders, but doth desire that the English will let him alone, and that the commissioners would not request him to go to Hartford, for he hath done no hurt. What should he do there? If your governor's son was slain, and several other

---

* Afterwards called Philip's Indians.

---

[1] Jonathan Gilbert (d. 1682) was a man of distinction in Hartford. He kept an inn and was for many years marshal of the Colony. One of his grandchildren was Governor Jonathan Belcher of Massachusetts.

men, would you ask counsel of another nation how and when to right yourselves? and added, that he would neither go nor send to Hartford.

CONCERNING the upland Indians, his answer was, That they were his friends and came to help him against the Long-Islanders, which had killed several of his men. Wherefore should he acquaint the commissioners with it, he did but right his own quarrel, which the Long-Islanders began with him.*

UPON the receipt of this answer, the commissioners agreed to raise forthwith 270 foot and 40 horse out of the several colonies, and gave a commission to Major Simon Willard [1] to command them, with instructions

to take as many of the said forces as should be at the place of rendezvous by the 13th of October, and to march with them to Ninigrate, and to require his compliance with the demands made upon him; and, if he refused, to compel him to it; and, if it should be necessary, to send immediately for the remainder of the forces, and a greater number if necessary.

Willard marched with his men into the Naraganset country. Ninigrate with his men had secured themselves in a swamp, where it was not thought adviseable to attack them, and the forces returned with no other success than the bringing off a number of the Pequods, who had been left with the Naragansets by the English, ever since the Pequod war, upon the promise of an annual payment for each head. The commander made it a part of his excuse, that the instructions to him were equivocal. But the commissioners were offended at this proceeding, and charged him with neglecting an opportunity of humbling the pride of Ninigrate, which since the return of the forces was greatly increased; and left him to consider what satisfaction was to be expected from him, and those of his council who joined with him.† It is to be observed, that Major Willard was a Massachusets man, and although that colony had so far complied with the rest as to join in sending out the forces, yet they still were desirous of avoid-

* [This answer of Ninigret the Massachusets Assembly say was rather incult like himself than insolent or provoking.]
    † Records of united colonies.

---

[1] Simon Willard (1605–1674) came to New England in 1634 and soon settled in Concord, which town he represented in the General Court 1636–49. In 1657 he was chosen an Assistant and served in that capacity until he died. He was prominent also as a military man. At this time he was major-general of the colonial establishment. Willard's second wife was a sister of President Dunster of Harvard College; and his third wife, a niece of Dunster. Curiously enough, Willard's son Samuel was Vice President of the College, 1700–1707, and his great-grandson Joseph was President, 1781–1804. See Joseph Willard's *Willard Memoir; or Life and Times of Major Simon Willard.*

ing an open war. This was the second time of their preventing a general war, contrary to the minds of six of the commissioners of the other colonies.* [The commissioners charged the Massachusets colony with breach of covenant, for by one of the articles of the confederacy, all matters wherein six should agree was to be binding upon the whole. The Massachusets endeavour'd to justify themselves, by urging that they were not not bound to assist each other save only upon just occasions, and as the determination was unjust they did well not to promote it. This doctrine made their confederacy a rope of sand, a body without sinews, a supreme power the laws of which are to be obeyed or disobeyed by the subjects of it as they approve or disapprove of them; for it will always be in the power of any part of a society to determine a measure to be unjust, which is not according to it's mind.]

THE most remarkable occurrence in the colony, in the year 1655, was the trial and condemnation of Mrs. Ann Hibbins for witchcraft. Her husband,[1] who died in the year 1654, was an agent for the colony in England, several years one of the assistants, and a merchant of note in the town of Boston; but losses in the latter part of his life had reduced his estate, and increased the natural crabbedness of his wife's temper, which made her turbulent and quarrelsome, and brought her under church censures, and at length rendered her so odious to her neighbours as to cause some of them to accuse her of witchcraft. The jury brought her in guilty, but the magistrates refused to accept the verdict; so the cause came to the general court, where the popular clamour prevailed against her, and the miserable old woman was condemned and executed. Search was made upon her body for tetts, and in her chests and boxes, for puppets, images, &c. but there is no record of any thing of that sort being found. Mr.

---

* Mr. Edward Winslow, who had been several years governor of Plimouth colony, died May 8, 1655, on board the fleet which was sent against Hispaniola. He was sent to England agent for the Massachusets. He attained to such favour, as to be made one of Cromwell's grand commissioners in the expedition. He was a gentleman of the best family of any of the Plimouth planters, his father Edward Winslow, Esq; being a person of some figure at Draughtwich in Worcestershire. An elegy, occasioned by his death, has much of the spirit of Thomas Saffin's epitaph, which I remember to have read in Stepney church yard.

> The eighth of May, west from 'Spaniola's shore
> God took from us our grand commissioner,
> Winslow by name, a man in chiefest trust,
> Whose life was sweet and conversation just,
> Whose parts and wisdom most men's did excell,
> An honour to his place, as all can tell.

---

[1] William Hibbins.

Beach, a minister in Jamaica, in a letter to Doctor Increase Mather in the year 1684, says,

You may remember what I have sometimes told you your famous Mr. Norton once said at his own table before Mr. Wilson the pastor, elder Penn, and myself, and wife, &c. who had the honour to be his guests. That one of your magistrates wives, as I remember, was hanged for a witch, only for having more wit than her neighbours. It was his very expression, she having, as he explained it, unhappily guessed that two of her persecutors, whom she saw talking in the street, were talking of her; which, proving true, cost her her life, notwithstanding all he could do to the contrary, as he himself told us.

It fared with her as it did with Joan of Arc in France. Some counted her a saint and some a witch, and some observed solemn marks of Providence set upon those who were very forward to condemn her, and to brand others upon the like ground with the like reproach.* This was the second instance upon record, of any person's being executed for witchcraft in New-England.†

About this time, however inconsistent it may seem with the professed ecclesiastical constitution and the freedom of every church, the general court, in several instances, interposed their authority. They laid a large fine upon the church at Malden, for chusing a minister without the consent and approbation of the neighbouring churches and allowance of the magistrates, and soon after, viz. in 1653, they restrained the north church in Boston from calling Mr. Powell [1] to be their minister, who had the character of a well gifted, tho' illiterate man, and went so far, as to recommend to them Mr. Reyner [2] who had been a minister at New-Plimouth.

---

* *Hubbard.*

† She was not executed until June 1656. She disposed of her estate by will, executed May 27, 1656, and a codicil June 16. She appointed several of the principal gentlemen overseers, and hoped they would shew her so much respect, as to see her decently interred. There was no forfeiture of goods for felony.

---

[1] Michael Powell (*d.* 1673) of Dedham. In May 1646 the Court allowed him to keep an ordinary and sell wine in Dedham, but to allow him to be the minister of the Second Church in Boston was a different matter. See George Edward Ellis, *The Puritan Age in Massachusetts*, pp. 221–223.

[2] John Reyner (*d.* 1669) was bred at Magdalene College, Cambridge, where he received his bachelor's degree in 1625. He was minister of the Plymouth church from 1636 to 1654 and was accounted "an able and a Godly man; and of a Meek and humble sperite, sound in truth and every way unreprovable in his life and Conversation." Nevertheless, the Second Church in Boston did not see fit to call him, but chose John Mayo instead. Reyner went from Plymouth to Dover, N. H. See "Plymouth Church Records," I, 73, 107–108, in *Publications of the Colonial Society of Massachusetts*, vol. XXII.

IT was observed upon this occasion, that

let the experience of all reformed churches be consulted, and it will appear, that disorder and confusion in the church will not be avoided by all the determinations, advice and counsel of synods or other messengers of churches, unless they be a little acuated [1] by the civil authority; All men are naturally so wedded to their own apprehensions, that, unless there be a coercive power to restrain, the order and rule of the gospel will not be attended.*

MR. Endicot was governor in 1655, and was annually chosen until 1660, and Mr. Bellingham deputy governor each year.† During this period, the trade of the colony was in a flourishing state, free admission being allowed to all nations, and the vessels of the colony trading to and from France, Holland, and other parts of Europe; the importation of no commodities whatsoever being prohibited, or under any clog or restraint. Notwithstanding the great variety of sectaries in England, there had been no divisions of any consequence in the Massachusets; but from 1637 to 1656, they enjoyed, in general, great quietness in their ecclesiastical affairs, discords in particular churches being healed and made up by a submission to the arbitrament of neighbouring churches, and sometimes the interposition of the civil power. The reputation, not only of the constitution of the churches, but also of the New-England clergy had been for some time very great in England, and the opinions of Mr. Cotton, Hooker, Davenport, and others, are cited as authorities by many English divines. The persecution of the episcopalians by the prevailing powers in England, was evidently from revenge for the persecution they had suffered themselves, and from political considerations and the prevalence of a party, seeing all other opinions and professions, however absurd, were tolerated, but in New-England, it must be confessed, that bigotry and cruel zeal prevailed, and to that degree, that no opinions but their own could be tolerated. They were sincere, but mistaken in their principles; and absurd as it is, it is too evident, they believed it to be for the glory of God to take away the lives of his creatures for maintaining tenets contrary to what they professed

---

* *Hubbard.*

† Richard Russel and Thomas Danforth were chosen assistants in 1659, the former of Charlestown; his son, grandson, and two of his great grandsons have been since of the council. The latter was of Cambridge, and had a great share in managing the public affairs in the most difficult times. He left no male children.

---

[1] This misprint for "actuated" is carried over from the first edition; it is corrected in the third.

themselves. This occasioned complaints against the colony to the parliament and to Cromwell, but without success.*

Mr. Winslow, the agent for the colony in England, being dead, Mr. Leveret, one of Cromwell's commissioners in the expedition to Acadie, was appointed in his stead. Cromwell had been very desirous of drawing off the New-Englanders to people Ireland after his successes there, and the inhabitants of New-Haven had serious thoughts of removing but did not carry their design into execution. Jamaica being conquered, Cromwell renewed his invitation to the colony of the Massachusets to remove, and to go and people that island; and it appears, by Mr. Leveret's letters and a letter from the general court to Cromwell, that he had it much at heart.† Cromwell

---

* In 1655, a distemper went through the plantations in New-England like to that in 1647. It was so epidemical, that few were able to visit their friends at any distance to perform the last offices to them. It was attended with a faint cough. Mr. Nathaniel Rogers, minister of Ipswich, died of it July 2d. He was son of Mr. John Rogers, a celebrated puritan preacher at Dedham in England, descended from the protomartyr in Queen Mary's reign. *Hubbard.*

† "At my presenting your letter, of the first of December 1656, to his Highness, he was pleased to enquire of New-England's condition, and what news as to the business of Jamaica, to which I gave answer according to the advice received. By his resent thereof, together with what I had from him the 18th of November, he manifesteth a very strong desire in him for some leading and considerable company of New-England men to go thither; for at that time he was pleased to express, that he did apprehend the people of New-England had as clear a call to transport themselves from thence to Jamaica, as they had from England to New-England, in order to their bettering their outward condition, God having promised his people should be the head and not the tail; besides, that design hath its tendency to the overthrow of the man of sin: and withal was pleased to add, that though the people had been sickly, yet it was said to be a climacterical year, that others had been to view the place, as Mevis people, who upon liking were gone down, and Christophers people were upon motion, and he hoped by what intelligence he had from Capt. Gookin, that some considerable numbers would go from New-England. His Highness was pleased to hear me in what I objected. As to the bettering our outward condition, though we had not any among us that had to boast, as some particulars in other plantations, of raising themselves to great estates, yet take the body of the people and all things considered, they lived more comfortably like Englishmen than any of the rest of the plantations; to which his Highness replied, that they were more industrious, what then would they be in a better country; to which I added, that there were more in New-England produced to bespeak us a commonwealth than in all the English plantations besides, the which his Highness granted. I objecting the contrariety of spirits, principles, manners, and customs of the people of New-England to them that were at the island or in any other plantations that could remove thither, so not like to cement, his Highness replied, that were there considerable persons that would remove from thence, they should have the government in their hands and be strengthened with the authority of England, who might be capable of giving check to the ill and vicious manners of all. Whilst his Highness was pleased to entertain me with these discourses, an honourable gentlemen of his council came in, who hearing his Highness upon New-England, was pleased to express himself concerning New-England's rigidness and persecution; to which his Highness was pleased to answer very much in the favour of them, that they acted like wise men, and God had broken the designs of evil instruments, bearing witness with them against evil seducers which had

foresaw that the West-India planters would raise estates, far superior to those of the inhabitants of the northern colonies, and though a mere worldly consideration was not proper for him to urge, yet accompanied with the fulfilment of a divine promise, that God's people should be the head and not the tail, it was in character, and he artfully enough joined it with the other consideration. But all was insufficient to induce the people of New-England to quit a country where they could live tolerably, and were indulged with all the privileges they desired, and we have no account of many families having removed. A few accepted the invitation. Complaints were

---

risen up among them, mentioning one or two; to which that honourable gentleman replied, the miscarriage of particular persons proved not God's bearing witness against the body of them that withdrew and departed from them for their rigidness; to which, with their favour, I replied, that if Rhode Island and those parts were intended, that then God had born witness against them in general as well as against particulars, which would appear by that looseness and profaneness they were left to, so that they had not only declined christian religion but moral observations; to which the honourable gentleman was pleased to wave the credit thereof, and express, that if it were so, he thought his Highness ought to animadvert upon one and the other. Much more passed in discourse, and his Highness broke off with this, that he would not impose any particular injunction upon me." Extract from J. Leveret's letter to governor Endicot, London 20 Dec. 1656. [There are very strong lines of Cromwell's character [in] this letter.]

The Court's letter to Oliver Cromwell.

"SIR,

WE received by Capt. Gookin your Highness's proposals for the removal of some of our's to the island of Jamaica, which, by our order, were communicated to the people of this jurisdiction, in compliance with your Highness's good and pious intentions of planting the place with such as through the blessing of God may hopefully promote a design so religious. But if, by the intelligence from thence of the mortality of the English there, the motion here answereth not expectation, may it please your Highness not to impute it to us as declining your service, much less as disaccepting your favour and endeavours of promoting what may conduce to our welfare, wherein we have always found your Highness ready upon all occasions to testify the same; and in particular by your gracious acceptance of our last by Capt. Leveret, by whom we found ourselves necessitated to make our addresses to your Highness, that by your just favour we might be supported, without which, we have cause to fear, we cannot be secure from the clamours and calumnies of some whose endeavours may be to render us obnoxious to your displeasure. — We account it our duty, to our utmost power, to advance your Highness's service, and if all other opportunities shall be wanting, yet never to cease to present our requests to him that is able abundantly to recompence all your labours of love to his, to preserve your Highness, long to continue you a happy instrument to carry on his work, overthrow the enemies of his truth, and to enlarge the kingdom of his dear son, in whom we are

Your Highness's most obliged servants,
Jo. Endicot, gov.
Rich. Bellingham, dep. gov.
Edward Rawson, secr.
In the name and with the consent
of the general court."

Boston, in New England,
the 24th October, 1656.

carried to Cromwell from Rhode Island against the Massachusets, by Clark, Holmes and others, but Mr. Leveret, who was a captain of horse under Cromwell, during some part of the war, had much of his favour, and though he could not prevent the Rhode Islanders [also] from being favourably received, for no sect could fail of an advocate in Cromwell's court, yet he prevented so much as an enquiry into the conduct of the Massachusets. Nay, Cromwell applauded the colony for banishing the evil seducers which had risen up among them, of which Mr. Wheelwright and Mrs. Hutchinson were the chief, and probably he had a view to them in particular. This same Mr. Wheelwright had been several years in England, and lived in the neighbourhood of Sir Henry Vane, who had been his patron in New-England and now took great notice of him. Vane being disaffected to Cromwell, it is not likely that Cromwell had any great esteem for Wheelwright, yet he sent for him by one of his guard,* and after a very orthodox discourse, according to Mr. Wheelwright's apprehensions of orthodoxy, "and without shewing countenance to sectaries," † he [even] exhorted him to perseverance against his opposers, and assured him their notions would vanish into nothing. This meeting, effectually engaged Mr. Wheelwright in Cromwell's favour. Leveret's and Wheelwright's letters, compared, confirm a distinguishing part of Cromwell's character. Besides the complaints from Rhode Island, Rigby, Gorges, and Godfrey, who claimed lands by patents in the eastern parts of New-England, made complaints to Cromwell against the colony for usurpation; and there were others who envied the flourishing state of the colony; but by means of Mr. Leveret's discreet management, and the favourable opinion Cromwell had conceived, all

* "I have lately been at London about five weeks. My Lord Protector was pleased to send one of his guard for me, with whom I had discourse, in private, about the space of an hour. All his speeches seemed to me very orthodox and gracious, no way favouring sectaries. He spake very experimentally to my apprehension of the work of God's grace, and knowing what opposition I met withal from some whom I shall not name, exhorted me to perseverance, in these very words as I remember, 'Mr. Wheelwright stand fast in the Lord, and you shall see that these notions will vanish into nothing,' or to that effect. Many men, especially the sectaries, exclaim against him with open mouths, but I hope he is a gracious man. I saw the lord mayor and sheriff with their officers carry sundry of the fifth monarchy men to prison, as Mr. Can, Mr. Day with others who used to meet together in Colman street to preach and pray against the Lord protector and the present power, &c." *Mr. Wheelwright's letter to the church at Hampton, Ap. 20. 1658.*

† All that do not think as we do in religion, are sectaries. There would be some difficulty in determining who, upon this occasion, were referred to as sectaries, if the fifth monarchy men had not been mentioned presently after.

attempts to its prejudice were to no purpose.* He did not shew like favour to the other colonies.

CROMWELL seems to have been the first who had a true sense of the importance of the colonies to their mother country. The expedition to Hispaniola was by him well intended, though by his servants badly executed, and his plan for enlarging the national interest in America no doubt extended further than the conquest of that island. Let us take a view of the state of the colonies at that time. Barbados was then more populous than it is at present. That island and the Caribbees were under the same government. These with Virginia, Maryland and Bermudas refused to acknowledge the parliament whilst the King lived, and it occasioned some trouble to reduce them after his death. They were all the colonies, except New-England, which were settled when Cromwell took the government upon him. There were no less than three different governors over Virginia during his short rule, Digby, Bennet and Matthews. Barbados surrendered to Sir George Ayscough, upon condition that the government should be by governor, council and assembly, and Daniel Searl being appointed their governor continued until the restoration. It was a rash thing to resist the supreme authority in England and gave great offence. Until then, all the colonies had been indulged in a free open trade to and from all parts of the world, unless the privileges granted to the East-India company made an exception; but Cromwell obtained an act or ordinance of the parliament, prohibiting the plantations from receiving or exporting any European commodities, except in English built ships navigated by Englishmen, and all correspondence was forbidden with any nation or colony not subject to England, and no alien was allowed to set up a factory or carry on a trade in the plantations. Virginia made heavy complaints, that they were not allowed to send off their produce to, nor to import necessaries from, any foreign countries, whilst England alone (they said) could not take off their produce, nor could they at that time be supplied from thence with all things necessary for them. But, however grievous this act might prove to the other colonies, it is certain that those of New-England, whether it was designed to extend there or not, suffered nothing by it. In a letter to Cromwell,[1]

---

* "Although his Highness and divers of the council are very cordial friends to New-England, yet there are not wanting those who wait an opportunity of complaints coming against you to usher in something else; the great privileges belonging to New-England being matter of envy, as of some in other plantations, so of divers in England who trade to those places." *Leveret's letter to Endicot.*

---

[1] This letter is printed in Appendix, No. X.

in 1654, the Massachusets seem to be under fears least they should be deprived of the privileges which had been indulged to them by his predecessors, and hope his Highness will be no less propitious, and will not be displeased with them for asserting their just privileges, to the prejudice whereof some attempts had been made by the commanders of ships, especially by some armed with commission, which though for fear of offending they had patiently endured, yet they thought it not safe to approve of such actings, &c. If this letter had respect to any attempts to regulate the trade, they were attempts which were soon given over and caused little or no interruption, and they were not only indulged in their trade to all parts, but that extraordinary privilege of having their goods imported into England, free from all custom which other subjects were liable to pay, seems to have been continued until the restoration. No wonder if they were envied by the other colonies, and if the merchants in England were dissatisfied also with the continuance of the last mentioned extraordinary favour.

In the year 1656, began what has been generally, and not improperly, called the persecution of the Quakers.* Two years before, an order had been made, that every inhabitant who had in their custody any of the books of John Reeves and Lodowick Muggleton, "who pretend to be the two last witnesses and prophets of Jesus Christ," which books were said to be full of blasphemies, should bring or send them in to the next magistrate, within one month, on pain of ten pounds for each book remaining in any person's hands after that time. [I do not mention these persons as being Quakers.] No person appeared professing the opinions of the Quakers until July 1656, when Mary Fisher † and Ann Austin arrived from Barbados. A few weeks after arrived in the ship Speedwell of London, Rober Lock master, nine more of these itinerants, whose names "after the flesh," the language they used to the officers sent to make enquiry, were William Brend, Thomas Thurston, Christopher Holder, John Copeland, Richard Smith, Mary Prince, Dorothy Waugh, Sarah Gibbons, and Mary Witherhead.‡ On the 8th of Sep-

---

* This sect made its first appearance in England, in the year 1652. They soon spread themselves into America.

† Mary Fisher travelled as far as Adrianople, and coming near the grand vizier's camp, she procured a man to inform him that there was an English woman had something to declare from the great God to the great Turk. She was introduced, and delivered her message, &c. *New-England judged, by G. Bishop.* She fared better among the Turks than among christians.

‡ Mr. Neale says they came from Rhode Island. I take this account from the records of the superior court. See a letter from the president, &c. of Rhode Island in the appendix, shewing the sense they had of the quakers at that time.

tember, they were brought before the court of assistants, and being examined, and each of them questioned how they could make it appear that God sent them, after a pause they answered, that they had the same call which Abraham had to go out of his country; to other questions they gave rude and contemptuous answers, which is the reason assigned for committing them to prison. A great number of their books which they had brought over, with intent to scatter them about the country, were seized and reserved for the fire. Soon after this, as the governor was going from the public worship on the Lord's day to his own house, several gentlemen accompanying him, Mary Prince called to him from a window of the prison, railing at and reviling him, saying, Woe unto thee, thou art an oppressor; and denouncing the judgments of God upon him. Not content with this she wrote a letter, to the governor and magistrates, filled with opprobrious stuff. The governor sent for her twice from the prison to his house, and took much pains to persuade her to desist from such extravagancies. Two of the ministers were present, and with much moderation and tenderness endeavoured to convince her of her errors, to which she returned the grossest railings, reproaching them as hirelings, deceivers of the people, Baal's priests, the seed of the serpent, of the brood of Ishmael and the like.

THE court passed sentence of banishment against them all, and required the master of the ship in which they came, to become bound with sureties, to the value of five hundred pounds, to carry them all away,* and caused them to be committed to prison until the ship should be ready to sail. At this time there was no special provision by law for the punishment of quakers; they came within a colony law against hereticks in general. At the next sessions of the general court, the 14th of October following, an act passed, laying a penalty of one hundred pounds upon the master of any vessel who should bring a known quaker into any part of the colony, and requiring him to give security to carry him back again; that the quaker should be immediately sent to the house of correction and whipped twenty stripes, and afterwards kept to hard labour until transportation. They also laid a penalty, of five pounds, for importing, and the like for dispersing quakers books, and severe penalties for defending their heretical opinions. And the next year, an additional law was made, by which all persons were subjected to the penalty of forty shillings for every hour's entertainment given to any known quaker, and any quaker, after the first conviction, if a man was to lose one ear, and a second time the other; a woman, each time to be severely whipped;

* I cannot find what law they had for this.

and the third time, man or woman, to have their tongues bored through with a red hot iron; and every quaker, who should become such in the colony, [was] subjected to the like punishments. In May 1658, a penalty of ten shillings was laid on every person present at a quaker's meeting, and five pounds upon every one speaking at such meeting. Notwithstanding all this severity, the number of quaker's as might well have been expected, increasing rather than diminishing,* in October following, a further law was made for punishing with death all quakers who should return into the jurisdiction after banishment.† That some provision was necessary against these people, so far as they were disturbers of civil peace and order, every one will allow; but such sanguinary laws against particular doctrines or tenets in religion are not to be defended. The most that can be said for our ancestors is, that they tried gentler means at first, which they found utterly ineffectual, and that they followed the example of the authorities in most other states and in most ages of the world, who, with the like absurdity, have supposed every person could and ought to think as they did, and [with] the like cruelty have punished such as appeared to differ from them. We may add, that it was with reluctance that these unnatural laws were carried into execution, as we shall see by a further account of proceedings. Nicholas Upshall was apprehended in October 1656, fined twenty pounds, and banished for reproaching the magistrates and speaking against the law made against quakers, and returning in 1659 was imprisoned.‡ At

* This is the ordinary consequence of pity and compassion for the sufferers. And although it has been observed that persecution tends to frighten men from coming into a country, yet it was a characteristick of this sect, at the beginning of it, to court persecution, and to submit to death, with an infatuation equal to that of some roman catholic priests carrying their religion into China or Tartary.

† Great opposition was made to this law, the magistrates were the most zealous, and in general for it; but it was rejected at first by the deputies, afterwards, upon reconsideration, concurred by 12 against 11, with an amendment that the trial should be by a special jury. Capt. Edward Hutchinson [1] and Capt. Thomas Clark,[2] two of the court, desired leave to enter their dissent against this law. *New-England judged*.

‡ Nicholas Upshall was a member of Boston church, a very old man. When he was banished, he went first to Plimouth, where people were forbad entertaining him; but some that were more compassionate, prevailed upon the authority to suffer him to tarry until the spring. *New-England judged*.

[1] Edward Hutchinson (1613?–1675) of Boston was the eldest son of William and Anne Hutchinson; he was a very useful citizen. He lost his life in King Philip's War. The fact that his daughter Anne married "a Dyer, of Newport," may account for his feeling on this subject. He was a great-grandfather of Governor Thomas Hutchinson. See *The Diary and Letters of Thomas Hutchinson* (edited by Peter Orlando Hutchinson), II, 464–465.

[2] Thomas Clark (d. 1678) was a Boston merchant. In 1662 he became Speaker of the House, and in 1673 an Assistant.

the same court, William Robinson, Marmaduke Stephenson, Mary Dyer and Nicholas Davis were brought to trial. The first gave no particular account of himself. Stephenson had made a public disturbance in the congregation at Boston the 15th of June before. He acknowledged himself to be one of those the world called quakers, and declared that in the year 1656, at Shipton in Yorkshire, as he was at plough he saw nothing but heard an audible voice saying, "I have ordained thee to be a prophet to the nations," &c.

DYER declared that she came from Rhode Island * to visit the quakers, that she was of their religion, which she affirmed was the truth, and that the light within her was the rule, &c.

DAVIS came from Barnstaple,[1] he came into court with his hat on, confessed he had forsaken the ordinances and resorted to the quakers. The jury found, "that they were all quakers." Robinson was whipped 20 stripes for abusing the court, and they were all banished on pain of death.

PATIENCE SCOT, a girl of about 11 years of age, came I suppose from Providence, her friends lived there, and professing herself to be one of those whom the world in scorn calls quakers, was committed to prison, and afterwards brought to court. The record stands thus. "The court duly considering the malice of Satan and his instruments by all means and ways to propagate error and disturb the truth, and bring in confusion among us, that Satan is put to his shifts to make use of such a child, not being of the years of discretion, nor understanding the principles of religion, judge meet so far to slight her as a quaker, as only to admonish and instruct her according to her capacity, and so discharge her, Capt. Hutchinson undertaking to send her home." Strange, such a child should be imprisoned! it would have been horrible if there had been any further severity.†

* Her husband or son, William Dyer, was secretary of that colony.[2]

† Bishop says, that they cut off the right ear of Holder, Copeland, and Rous in the prison, and that Catherine Scott, mother of Patience Scott, reproving them for a deed

[1] Spelled correctly "Barnstable" in the first edition. The third edition follows the first.

[2] William Dyer, the Secretary of Rhode Island, was the husband of Mary Dyer. He spelt his name "Dyre" as Hutchinson does in this instance. He was a milliner in London before coming to New England. In Massachusetts he became a follower of Wheelwright and accordingly was disarmed, disfranchised, and virtually driven out. He took refuge at Newport, R. I. Mrs. Dyer, who had distinguished herself by walking out of the meeting with Mrs. Hutchinson when the latter was excommunicated, accompanied him. Between 1650 and 1657 she was in England, where she became a Quaker. There is a life of Mary Dyer by Horatio Rogers. For a contemporary account of the sufferings of this group see *A Call from Death to Life* (1660). For a modern account, written from the Quaker point of view, see Richard Price Hallowell, *The Quaker Invasion of Massachusetts*, or Rufus M. Jones, *The Quakers in the American Colonies*.

ROBINSON, Stephenson and Dyer, at the next general court, were brought upon trial, and "for their rebellion, sedition, and presumptuous obtruding themselves after banishment upon pain of death," were sentenced to die; the two first were executed the 27th of October.* Dyer, upon the petition of William Dyer her son, was reprieved, on condition that she departed the jurisdiction in 48 hours; and if she returned, to suffer the sentence. She was carried to the gallows, and stood with a rope about her neck until the others were executed. She was so infatuated as afterwards to return, and was executed June 1st, 1660.† The court thought it advisable to publish a vindication of their proceedings; they urge the example of England in the provision made against jesuits, which might have some weight against a charge brought from thence, but in every other part of their vindication, as may well be supposed from the nature of the thing, there is but the bare shadow of reason. Christopher Holder, who had found the way into the jurisdiction again, was, at this court, banished upon pain of death. At the same court, seven or eight persons were fined, some as high as ten pounds, for entertaining quakers; and Edward Wharton,[1] for piloting them from one place to another, was ordered to be whipped twenty stripes and bound to his good behaviour. Divers others were then brought upon trial, "for adhering to the cursed sect of quakers, not disowning themselves to be such, refusing to give civil respect, leaving their families and relations, and running from place to place vagabonds like," and Daniel Gold was sentenced to be whipped thirty stripes, Robert Harper [2]

of darkness, they whipped her ten stripes; though they allowed her to be otherwise of blameless conversation and well bred, being a minister's daughter in England. *New-England judged.*

* Mr. Winthrop, the governor of Connecticut, laboured to prevent their execution, and Col. Temple went to the court and told them, "that if according to their declaration, they desired their lives absent, rather than their deaths present, he would carry them away and provide for them at his own charge; and if any of them should return, he would fetch them away again." This motion was well liked by all the magistrates except two or three, and they proposed it to the deputies the next day, but those two or three magistrates, with the deputies, prevailed to have execution done. *New-England judged.*

† Being asked what she had to say, why sentence should not be executed. She answered, that she denied their law, came to bear witness against it, and could not chuse but come and do as formerly. This is the same Mary Dyer, who in the year 1637 was banished for her familistical tenets.

[1] Edward Wharton of Salem (*d.* 1678) was a long-suffering Quaker. In 1658 he was whipped for expressing sympathy for Robinson and Stephenson, and again later on for piloting some Quakers from Lynn to Salem. In spite of these and other punishments he continued to reside in Salem until his death. Whittier, in "The King's Missive" rightly calls him "much scourged Wharton."

[2] Robert Harper was of Sandwich, in the Plymouth Colony.

fifteen, and they, with Alice Courland, Mary Scott and Hope Clifton, banished upon pain of death; William Kingsmill whipped fifteen stripes, Margaret Smith, Mary Trask [1] and Provided Southwick [2] ten stripes each, and Hannah Phelps admonished.

THE compassion of the people was moved, and many resorted to the prison day and night, and upon a representation of the keeper, a constant watch was kept round the prison to keep people off.*

JOSEPH NICHOLSON and Jane his wife were also tried and found quakers, as also Wendlock Christopherson,[3] who declared in court, that the scripture is not the word of God; and Mary Standley, and all sentenced to banishment, &c. as was soon after Benjamin Bellflower; but John Chamberlain,[4] though he came with his hat on, yet, refusing directly to answer, the jury found him, "much inclining to the cursed opinions of the quakers," and he escaped with an admonition.†

NICHOLSON and his wife returned, and were apprehended, but upon their petition, had liberty with several others then in prison, to go for England. Christopherson returned also, and was sentenced to die. It is said he desired the court to consider what they had gained by their cruel proceedings.

For the last man (says he) that was put to death here, are five come in his room, and if you have power to take my life from me, God can raise up the said [5] principle of life in ten of his servants, and send them among you in my room, that you may have torment upon torment.‡

He was ordered to be executed the fifth day sevennight after the 14th of March 1660, afterwards reprieved till the 13th of June; but

---

* The pillory served for a pulpit to George Fox. He preached to the populace, and made so many converts that they delivered him in a tumultuous manner, and set a clergyman, who had been instrumental in Fox's punishment, upon the same pillory. *Volt. letters.*

† [Their forms in law proceedings were loose and irregular.]

‡ *New-England judged.*

---

[1] Mary Trask was the wife of Henry Trask of Salem. She was a sister of Provided Southwick, another Quaker.

[2] Provided Southwick of Salem and her brother Daniel were also fined for persistent Quakerism. When the fines were not paid, the General Court ordered them sold "to any of the English nation at Virginia or Barbadoes." Happily the sentence was not carried out.

[3] Wendlock Christopherson is usually called Wenlock Christison in New England history. Banished from Massachusetts, he went to Plymouth where he was imprisoned for fourteen weeks, "tied neck and heels together," in cold winter weather, and flogged. He returned to Boston and was sentenced to be hanged. The sentence was not carried into execution, however. For his career in Massachusetts and elsewhere see Samuel A. Harrison, *Wenlock Christison and the Early Friends in Talbot County, Maryland.*

[4] John Chamberlain was a currier in Boston.

[5] The first edition gives "same" instead of "said"; the third edition follows the first.

he was set at liberty upon his request to the court, and went out of the jurisdiction.

BELLFLOWER [1] afterwards, in court, renounced his opinions, as also William King (Kingsmill I suppose) the only instances upon record. Chamberlain was afterwards apprehended again, and found a quaker, and committed to close prison; but no further sentence appears.

IN September 1660, William Ledea [2] was tried and convicted of being a quaker, and sentenced to banishment, &c. but returning and being apprehended, the general court gave him liberty, notwithstanding, to go to England with Nicholson and others; but he refused to leave the country, and was brought upon trial for returning into the jurisdiction after sentence of banishment, acknowledged himself to be the person, but denied their authority, and told the court, that, "with the spirit they called the devil, he worshipped God; that their ministers were deluders, and they themselves murderers." He was told that he might have his life and be at liberty if he would. He answered, I am willing to die, I speak the truth. The court took great pains to persuade him to leave the country, but to no purpose. The jury brought him in guilty, and he was sentenced to die, and suffered accordingly March 14th, 1660.

MARY WRIGHT, of Oyster-bay, was tried at the court in September 1660. She said she came to do the will of the Lord, and to warn them to lay by their carnal weapons and laws against the people of God, told the court they thirsted for blood. The court asked her what she would have them do, she said, "repent of your bloodshed and cruelty and shedding the blood of the innocent Wm. Robinson, Marmaduke Stephenson, and Mary Dyer." She said, her tears were her meat many days and nights before she gave up herself to this work of the Lord, but added, that if she had her liberty, she would be gone quickly. Being found a quaker, she was banished.

EDWARD WHARTON, who had been whipped before, was now indicted for being a quaker, convicted and sentenced to imprisonment and afterwards to banishment. Judah Brown and Peter Pierson stood mute. They were sentenced to be whipped at the cart's tail in Boston, Roxbury and Dedham.

---

[1] Benjamin Bellflower lived in Reading, Mass. He "came into Court with his hat cockt: remaineing on his head. & refusing to pull it of w comanded. & said he could justifie his accon by ye Scripture." Hallowell's *Quaker Invasion*, p. 160, quoting from Massachusetts Archives.

[2] William Ledea is identified by Savage as William Leddra of Boston. His appealing letter to his friends, written the day before he was hanged, is printed in William Sewel, *History of the Quakers* (1844), I, 338–340.

JOHN SMITH, of Salem, for making disturbance at the ordination of Mr. Higginson, crying out, "What you are going about to set up, our God is pulling down," was committed to prison by order of the court.

PHILIP VERIN [1] was also tried and imprisoned, Josias Southwick,[2] first banished and returning, whipped at the cart's tail, and John Burstowe bound to his good behaviour. These are all * who were tried by the court of assistants, or by the general court. Some at Salem, Hampton, Newbury and other places, for disorderly behaviour, putting people in terror, coming into the congregations and calling to the minister in the time of public worship, declaring their preaching, &c. to be an abomination to the Lord, and other breaches of the peace, were ordered to be whipped by the authority of the county courts, or particular magistrates. At Boston, one George Wilson, and at Cambridge, Elizabeth Horton,[3] went crying through the streets, that the Lord was coming with fire and sword to plead with them. Thomas Newhouse went into the meeting-house at Boston with a couple of glass bottles, and broke them before the congregation, and threatened, "Thus will the Lord break you in pieces." Another time, M. Brewster [4] came in with her face smeared and as black as a coal. Deborah Wilson went through the streets of Salem, naked as she came into the world,† for which she was well whipped. For these and such like disturbances, they might be deemed proper subjects either of a mad-house or house of correction, and it is to be lamented that any greater severities were made use of.

* George Bishop [5] mentions several who suffered corporal punishment by order of particular magistrates or the county courts, of whom I find no notice any where else. *New-England judged.*

† One of the sect apologizing for this behaviour said, "If the Lord did stir up any of his daughters to be a sign of the nakedness of others, he believed it to be a great cross to a modest woman's spirit, but the Lord must be obeyed." Another quoted the command in Isaiah, cap. 20. R. Williams. One Faubord, of Grindleton, carried his enthusiasm still higher, and was sacrificing his son in imitation of Abraham, but the neighbours hearing the lad cry, broke open the house and happily prevented it.

---

[1] Philip Verin came to New England in 1635 from New Sarum (Salisbury), England. He settled at Salem.

[2] Josias or Josiah was another member of the Southwick family of Salem. He was "constrained to take an opportunity that presented four days after to pass to England by Barbadoes." *An Abstract of the Sufferings of the Quakers* (1733), I, 386.

[3] Elizabeth Horton is called Hooten by William Sewel, who describes her sufferings in detail in his *History of the Quakers* (1844), I, 412–413.

[4] Margaret Brewster. Her trial, in 1677, is quoted by Richard Price Hallowell in his *Quaker Invasion of Massachusetts*, pp. 193–202.

[5] George Bishop (d. 1668) was the author of *New England Judged not by Man's but the Spirit of the Lord* (London, 1661), a strong narrative of the sufferings of the Quakers in New England, 1650–1660.

After all that may be said against these measures, it evidently appears, that they proceeded not from personal hatred and malice against such disordered persons, nor from any private sinister views, as is generally the case with unjust punishments inflicted in times of party rage and discord, whether civil or religious, but merely from a false zeal and an erroneous judgment. In support of their proceedings, they brought several texts of the Old Testament. "Come out of her my people," &c. "If thy brother entice thee to serve other gods, thou shalt surely put him to death," and "for speaking lies in the name of the Lord, his father shall thrust him through when he prophecieth"; and the example of Solomon, who first laid Shimei under restraint, and then for his breach put him to death; as also many passages of the New Testament requiring subjection to magistrates, &c. and thus from a zeal to defend the holy religion they professed, they went into measures directly opposite to its true spirit, and the great design of publishing it to the world.

THAT I may finish what relates to the quakers, it must be further observed, that their friends in England solicited and at length obtained an order from the King, Sept. 9th, 1661, requiring that a stop should be put to all capital or corporal punishment of those of his subjects called quakers, and that such as were obnoxious should be sent to England. Whatever opinion they might have, of the force of orders from the crown controuling the laws of the colony, they prudently complied with this instruction, and suspended the execution of the laws against quakers, so far as respected corporal punishment, until further order. Indeed, before the receipt of this letter, but probably when they were in expectation of it, all that were in prison were discharged and sent out of the colony. The laws were afterwards revived so far as respected vagabond quakers, whose punishment was limited to whipping, and, as a further favour, through three towns only. But there was little or no room for carrying the laws into execution; for after these first excursions they became in general an orderly people, submitting to the laws, except such as relate to the militia and the support of the ministry, and in their scruples as to those, they have, from time to time, been indulged. At present they are esteemed as being of good morals, friendly and benevolent in their disposition, and I hope will never meet with any further persecution on account of their peculiar tenets or customs. May the time never come again, when the government shall think that by killing men for their religion they do God good service.*

* The author of the account of the European settlements in North-America, who is very erroneous in some historical facts which concern the Massachusets colony, but

FROM 1656 to 1660, I find but very few facts relative to the public affairs of the colony worth transmitting to posterity. After the peace with the Dutch in Europe, the trade between the English and Dutch colonies was revived, and Stuyvesant, the Dutch governor, in 1657, wrote to the commissioners of the English colonies, that the limits agreed and settled in 1650, both upon the main and upon Long-Island, were ratified and confirmed by the States General of the United Provinces, and desired, that the confirmation of the Lord Protector being ready, time and place might be appointed for the exchange. The commissioners in their answer, let him know, that they had ever conformed to that settlement, altho' he had not; but they said nothing of the Protector's confirmation. It does not appear that ever they sought for it. Towards the end of this period, the changes in England were so frequent that it was prudence in the colonies to take as little notice of them as might be, until there appeared a prospect of a lasting establishment. An express acknowledgement of Richard Cromwell was expected from the Massachusets, but they declined it. An original letter [1] from him to the governor, recommending the case of Mr. Sewall [2] a minister, is all that appears upon the records relative to him.*

THE rapid increase of the Massachusets colony, together with the figure which many of the first settlers made in England before their removal, and the correspondence which they maintained with their friends of great distinction there, many years after, eclipsed the colony of New-Plimouth,† whose growth and progress would other-

---

has many judicious observations which run through his whole performance, says upon the subject of the New-England persecutions, "Such is the manner of proceeding of religious parties towards each other; and in this respect, the New-England people are not worse than the rest of mankind, nor was their severity any just matter of reflection upon that mode of religion which they profess. No religion whatsoever, true or false, can excuse its own members, or accuse those of any other upon the score of persecution." *Vol.* II. *p.* 185. It is a doctrine of Calvin, *In hæreticos gladio vindicandum est*, and the death of Servetus is generally laid to his charge.

* Sir Thomas Temple came first to New-England in 1657, having, with others, obtained from Oliver a grant of lands in Acadie or Nova-Scotia, of which he was made governor. He was recommended by Nathaniel Fiennes, son to Lord Say. Mr. Fiennes calls him his near kinsman.

† Mr. William Bradford, who had been many years governor of Plimouth colony,

---

[1] See Appendix, No. XII.

[2] Henry Sewall (*c.* 1614–1700) came to New England in 1634 and settled at Newbury. About 1648 he returned to England, where most of his children were born. During the next decade Sewall crossed the ocean a number of times, and in 1661 he sent for his wife and children to come to Massachusetts. Upon their arrival they went to Newbury, where henceforth they made their home. Chief-Justice Samuel Sewall (1652–1730) was the eldest son of Henry Sewall.

wise have been thought considerable. The southern part of the colony in general, being of a light sandy soil, would have been incapable of supporting its inhabitants, were it not for the large bodies of salt meadow, the hay of which serves for fodder for their cattle in the winter, and the dung from it, being an excellent manure, produces good crops of grain, with little labour in the summer, light land being easily tilled. The northern parts, bordering upon the Massachusets, afford many good farms, particularly the town of Bridgewater, which hath been famous for the quality of the land and for good husbandry. They were few at first, and but little additions were made after the Massachusets was planted, except from their natural increase; and yet before the year 1643, besides the town of Plimouth, they had settled Duxbury, Scituate, Taunton, Rehoboth, Sandwich, Barnstable, Yarmouth, and Eastham. Upon the death of Mr. Carver, their first governor, soon after their arrival, they chose in his stead Mr. Bradford, being a grave discreet man. They were so well satisfied with his administration, that they continued to chuse him annually, until his death in 1657, except two years when they chose Mr. Winslow, and one year Mr. Prince.

THEIR ecclesiastical affairs were for divers years in discouraging circumstances. They had expectations that Mr. Robinson their pastor, whom they had left with one half his church in Holland, would follow them, but his death, in 1624, put an end to their hopes. They were unsuccessful in their attempts to settle a minister, the principles of one and the manners of another were exceptionable, and having several brethren among themselves well gifted, they chose to continue without a minister for some time, rather than to settle one who was not exemplary in his life, or who differed from them in points of doctrine or church government. But in 1643, they had a set of pious learned ministers; * one of which, Mr. Chauncey,[1] some years after, was chosen to the presidentship of the college in the Massachusets, and removed to Cambridge.

---

died the 9th May 1657. He was in great esteem. Having taken notice of Mr. Winslow's elegy, for the same reason we cannot well omit three or four of the first lines of Mr. Bradford's.

"The ninth of May about nine of the clock,
A precious one God out of Plimouth took;
Governor Bradford then expired his breath,
Was call'd away by force of cruel death," &c.

These will be sufficient, for a specimen of New-England poetry in that age.
* Mr. Hubbard gives the list of their names. Charles Chauncey, Ralph Partridge,

---

[1] Charles Chauncy (1592–1672) was at that time the minister at Scituate. See William Chauncey Fowler's *Memorials of the Chaunceys*.

THEY had many local laws. In criminal cases they took the Massachusets for their pattern, but in civil matters they professed to take the common law for their rule, more than was practised in the Massachusets.

AN exemplary piece of justice is recorded to their honour in the year 1638, when they caused three Englishmen to be executed for the murder of an Indian near Providence.

PLIMOUTH colony adjoining to the Massachusets, some short disputes subsisted between them concerning bounds. In order to settle the controversy, commissioners were appointed in the year 1640, viz. John Endicot and Israel Stoughton for the Massachusets, and William Bradford and Edward Winslow for Plimouth. It was not then effected. An observation had been taken by Nathanael Woodward, in the year 1638, upon part of Charles river, 41 degrees 59 minutes north latitude, the river still running southward; the persons employed not being able to proceed farther for want of provisions. In 1642, the northern bounds of the Massachusets were ascertained by the same Woodward, with Solomon Saffery,* and a station fixed, which has since been allowed to be the Massachusets corner 3 miles south of Charles river; and from this corner, the lines between the Massachusets and the governments of Plimouth, Rhode-Island, and Connecticut have been run and confirmed by acts of the several governments.†

William Hooke, Nicholas Street, John Lothrop, John Mayo, Edward Bulkley, William Leveridge, Richard Blinman, John Miller, and Marmaduke Matthews.[1]

* Douglass says, they were two obscure sailors who assisted in the survey, but they are called, in the record, two able mathematicians.

† There has been a pretence started or revived of late years, that the Massachusets had extended the southerly part of Charles river to a brook too small to be accounted a branch of it; but such pretences, after so many years acquiescence, can have little weight; especially if it be considered, that what is now a small brook, after the country has been opened and cleared of wood for an hundred years, may probably have been a navigable stream for canoes and boats at the time of fixing the station.

---

[1] The towns to which they ministered were as follows:

Chauncy	Scituate
Partridge	Duxbury
Hooke	Taunton
Street	Taunton
Lothrop	Barnstable
Mayo	Barnstable and Eastham
Bulkley	Marshfield
Leveridge	Sandwich
Blinman	Marshfield
Miller	Yarmouth
Matthews	Yarmouth

CHAP. II.

Historical Occurrences, from the Restoration of King Charles the Second, to the year 1686, when the Charter was vacated.

SINCE the year 1640, the people had been without any apprehensions of danger to their religious or civil privileges. They
prudently acknowledged subjection to the parliament, and afterwards to Cromwell, so far as was necessary to keep upon terms, and
avoid exception, and no farther. The addresses to the parliament
and Cromwell shew this to have been the case. [I would not be understood that they denied the restoration of the former government,
there is sufficient evidence to the contrary.] After Cromwell's death,
during the frequent changes in the supreme authority in England,
they seem to have taken part with none, but to have waited until
some settlement was made, which should have a prospect of stabil-
ity.* I have no where met with any marks of disrespect to the memory of the late King, and there is no room to suppose they were under
disaffection to his son, and if they feared his restoration it was because they expected a change in religion, and that a persecution of
all non-conformists would follow it.† At the election in May, they
could have received no intelligence from England, to enable them to
make any certain judgment of affairs. Mr. Endicot was then chosen

---

* I find this remark in an ancient manuscript, wrote about the year 1665, "When a
packet of letters was sent by Mr. John Thurloe, containing an express order of the council, signed by Henry Lawrence president, requiring and enjoining the governor and
magistrates of the Massachusets colony to proclaim Richard in these following terms,
that is to say, Lord Protector of the common-wealth of England, Scotland and Ireland,
and the territories thereunto belonging, they did not obey the said order. And since his
Majesty King Charles the second was proclaimed in the Massachusets, at Boston and
other places, they have not failed, in all their courts and judicial proceedings throughout
the colony, to give that tribute of honour to his Majesty, which in such like cases is commonly rendered by the courts of law at Westminster."

† They had undoubtedly a good opinion of the persons in whose hands the administration then was; but the uncertainty of their continuance in power was reason enough
for caution.

governor, and Mr. Bellingham deputy governor, both of them as fixed in their principles as any of their brethren. The business of this session of the general court went over, and nothing passed relative to affairs in England. On the 27th of July, Capt. Pierce, a noted shipmaster in the trade between England and the colony, arrived and brought the news of the King's being proclaimed. If they received at the same time the King's declaration from Breda, and depended that a royal promise would be, as it always ought to be, religiously complied with, they need not have been under great concern about their public affairs either in church or state. No advices were received from authority, and the King was not proclaimed in the colony; * nor was any alteration made in the forms of their public acts and proceedings. There was a session of the general court in October, and a motion was made for an address to the King, but it did not succeed. Mr. Norton, one of the ministers of Boston, was very earnest for it; but rumours came by the way of Barbados, that the government in England was in a very unsettled state, the body of the people dissatisfied; that the Scotch had demanded Monk to be delivered up to them, that Lord Fairfax was at the head of a great army, &c. and they had seen so many changes in the course of a few months, that they thought it was not very certain that an address to the King would not fall into the hands of the committee of safety, council of state, or a junto with some other title. On the 30th of November, a ship arrived from Bristol, which brought advices of the proceedings of parliament, and that all matters were fully settled. They were also informed by letters from Mr. Leveret their agent, and others, that petitions and complaints were preferred against the colony to the King in council, and to the parliament (a citation being posted upon the exchange in London) by Mason, Gorges and others. The governor and assistants met forthwith; called the general court to convene the 19th of December; a very loyal address to the King was presently agreed upon; and another to the two houses of parliament. Letters were sent by Sir Thomas Temple,[1] who was a constant

---

* This was the first instance of the accession of a Prince to the throne since this colony had been planted, and perhaps the propriety and necessity of this ceremony in the plantations were not fully understood and considered. I find nothing said about it, until notice taken in England of the neglect.

---

[1] Sir Thomas Temple (1614–1674), Col. William Crowne, and Charles Etienne de la Tour obtained from Cromwell a grant of Acadia, which had been captured by the English under Sedgwick in 1654. La Tour sold his interest to Temple, whom Cromwell appointed governor of Acadia in 1657. Temple came over from England and took possession of his domain at once. The Restoration made him feel insecure and he then returned to England to defend his claim. In this he was entirely successful, and was

friend to the colony, to Lord Manchester, Lord Say and Seal, and other persons of note, to pray them to intercede in behalf of the colony. A most gracious answer was given to the address, by the King's letter dated Feb. 15, 1660, which was the first public act or order concerning them after the restoration, except a few lines, the 23d of January before, from secretary Morice, to inclose an order for the apprehending two of the late King's Judges; both letters it is probable by the same ship, which arrived in May following.

BEFORE the receipt of this letter, the governor and council, March 18th, took public notice of a book published by Mr. Eliot not long before, intitled, The Christian Commonwealth, &c. which they declare they find, on perusal, full of seditious principles and notions in relation to all established governments in the christian world; especially against the government established in their native country. Upon consultation with the elders, their censure was deferred until the general court met, "that Mr. Eliot might have the opportunity, in the mean time, of making a public recantation."

AT the next sessions, in May, Mr. Eliot gave into the court the following acknowledgment under his hand.

UNDERSTANDING by an act of the honoured council, that there is offence taken at a book published in England by others, the copy whereof was sent over by myself about nine or ten years since, and that the further consideration thereof is commended to this honoured general court now sitting at Boston: Upon perusal thereof, I do judge myself to have offended, and in way of satisfaction, not only to the authority of this jurisdiction, but also to any others that shall take notice thereof, I do hereby acknowledge to this honoured court, that such expressions as do too manifestly scandalize the government of England by King, Lords, and Commons, as antichristian, and justify the late innovators, I do sincerely bear testimony against, and acknowledge it to be, not only a lawful, but eminent form of government.

2d. ALL form of civil government, deduced from scripture, I acknowledge to be of God, and to be subjected to, for conscience sake. — And whatsoever is in the whole epistle or book inconsistent herewith, I do at once most cordially disown.   John Eliot.

THE books were ordered by the court to be called in, and this acknowledgment to be posted up in the principal towns in the colony. When the times change, men generally suffer their opinions to change with them; so far, at least, as is necessary to avoid danger. [As no

---

created a baronet besides. Later, under the Treaty of Breda, his Acadian holdings were given back to the French. Temple then made his home in Boston for a few years before returning to England. He was a friend of Harvard College and a member of Cotton Mather's church.

one form of civil government can be said, peculiarly to be of divine authority or moral obligation more than another Mr. Eliot's recantation affords no matter for reproach. His book was ill judged.] Between the reigns of Henry the seventh and James the first, how many times did the whole body of the clergy of England change or shift their opinions in matters of greater importance?

A DAY of public thanksgiving was appointed by authority, to acknowledge the favour of heaven, in inclining the King graciously to accept and answer the address made to him.

THEY were, notwithstanding, under no small degree of fear, lest the revolution of government in England should produce as great a change in the form of their government, both in church and state. They were alarmed from all quarters. Reports were spread, that Virginia and the islands were forbid trading with them, that three frigates would soon be sent from England, and that a general governor over all the colonies was to come in one of them.* At the same sessions, in May, they passed the following vote.

FORASMUCH as the present condition of our affairs, of the highest concernment, call for diligent and speedy use of the best means, seriously to discuss and rightly to understand our liberty and duty, thereby to beget unity amongst ourselves, in the due observance of obedience and fidelity to the authority of England and our own just privileges: For the effecting whereof, it is ordered, that Mr. Simon Bradstreet, Mr. Samuel Symonds,[1] Major-General Denison, Mr. Danforth,[2] Major William Hawthorn, Capt. Thomas Savage, Capt. Edward Johnson,[3] Capt. Eleazer

---

* "The general vogue of people is, that a governor will be sent over; other rumours there are concerning you. I made bold to address myself to Lord Say and desired his favour. His lordship professed his great respect for the plantations, and thanked God he prayed for you daily, promising to improve his interest, &c. — Episcopacy, common prayer, bowing at the name of Jesus, sign of the cross in baptism, the altar and organs are in use, and like to be more. The Lord keep and preserve his churches, that there may not be fainting in a day of trial." *Leveret's letter to Massa. Lond. 13th Feb.* 1660.

---

[1] Samuel Symonds (*d.* 1678) was an Assistant 1643–73, and Deputy-Governor from 1673 until he died. He was one of the aristocracy of Ipswich. His first wife, Deborah Harlakenden, was probably a sister of Roger Harlakenden, the friend of Thomas Shepard.

[2] Thomas Danforth (1623–1699) of Cambridge was an Assistant 1659–78, Deputy-Governor 1679–86 and 1689–92, and one of the judges of the court that conducted the trials of the witches in 1692. He was also Treasurer of Harvard College, 1650–69, and Steward, 1669–82. *Danforth Genealogy*, pp. 18–19.

[3] Edward Johnson (1598–1672) of Woburn was the author of a history of New England best known by its running title *Wonder-working Providence of Sions Saviour in New England* (1654). He was a representative in the General Court 1643–71, 1648 excepted, and Speaker of the House in 1655. He was also town clerk for thirty-two years. See Alfred Johnson, *History and Genealogy of One Line of Descent from Captain Edward Johnson.*

Lusher,[1] Mr. Mather, Mr. Norton, Mr. Corbett, and Mr. Mitchell,* be and hereby are a committee, immediately after the dissolution or adjournment of the court, to meet together in Boston, on second day next, at 12 of the clock, to consider and debate such matter or thing of publick concernment, touching our patent, laws, privileges, and duty to his Majesty, as they in their wisdom shall judge most expedient, and draw up the result of their apprehensions, and present the same to the next session for consideration and approbation, that so (if the will of God be) we may speak and act the same thing, becoming prudent, honest, conscientious and faithful men.†

An answer was drawn up, and accepted by the court, at a session specially appointed to receive the same.‡

In the ship which arrived from London the 27th of July, there came passengers Col. Whaley and Col. Goffe, two of the late King's judges. Col. Goffe brought testimonials from Mr. John Rowe, and Mr. Seth Wood, two ministers of a church in Westminster. Col. Whaley had been a member of Mr. Thomas Goodwin's church. Goffe kept a journal or diary, from the day he left Westminster, May 4, until the year 1667; which, together with several other papers belonging to him, I have in my possession. Almost the whole is in characters or short hand, not very difficult to decypher. The story of these persons has never yet been published to the world. It has never been known in New-England. Their papers, after their death, were collected, and have remained near an hundred years in a library in Boston. It must give some entertainment to the curious. They left London, before the King was proclaimed. It does not appear, that they were among the most obnoxious of the judges; but as it was expected vengeance would be taken of some of them, and a great many had fled, they did not think it safe to remain. They did not attempt to conceal their persons or characters when they arrived at Boston, but immediately went to the governor, Mr. Endicot, who received them very courteously. They were visited by the principal persons of the town; and among others, they take notice of Col.

* The four last named were ministers.[2]
† *Massachusets Records.*
‡ *Appendix.* [No. XIII]

---

[1] Capt. Eleazer Lusher (*d.* 1672) of Dedham was a representative in the General Court in 1640 and many years thereafter; and an Assistant from 1662 until his death.

[2] The four ministers' churches were as follows:

Increase Mather	Second Church, Boston
John Norton	First Church, Boston
Thomas Cobbett	Ipswich
Jonathan Mitchell	Cambridge

Crown's coming to see them. He was a noted royalist.[1] Although they did not disguise themselves, yet they chose to reside at Cambridge, a village about four miles distant from the town, where they went the first day they arrived. They went publickly to meetings on the Lord's days, and to occasional lectures, fasts, and thanksgivings, and were admitted to the sacrament, and attended private meetings for devotion, visited many of the principal towns, and were frequently at Boston, and once, when insulted there, the person insulting them was bound to his good behaviour. They appeared grave, serious and devout, and the rank they had sustained commanded respect. Whaley had been one of Cromwell's Lieut. Generals, and Goffe a Major-General. It is not strange that they should meet with this favourable reception, nor was this reception any contempt of the authority in England. They were known to have been two of the King's judges; but King Charles the second was not proclaimed, when the ship that brought them left London. They had the news of it in the channel. The reports afterwards, by way of Barbados, were, that all the judges would be pardoned but seven. The act of indemnity was not brought over until the last of November. When it appeared that they were not excepted, some of the principal persons in the government were alarmed; pity and compassion prevailed with others. They had assurances, from some that belonged to the general court, that they would stand by them, but were advised, by others, to think of removing. The 22d of February, the governor summoned a court of assistants to consult about securing them, but the court did not agree to it. Finding it unsafe to remain any longer, they left Cambridge, the 26th following, and arrived at New-Haven the 7th of March. One Capt. Breedan,[2] who had seen them at Boston, gave information thereof upon his arrival in England. A few days after their removal, an hue and cry, as they term it in their diary, was brought by the way of Barbados, and

[1] It is not easy to understand why Hutchinson calls William Crowne (1617?–1683) "a noted royalist." Crowne fought on Parliament's side in the Civil Wars and in one way or another amassed a considerable fortune before coming to America in 1657. From Charles de la Tour he and Col. Thomas Temple acquired Nova Scotia, which extended well into the present State of Maine. Their title to this domain was jeopardized by the accession of Charles II, and ultimately was lost by the Treaty of Breda, 1667. Still Crowne appears to have been on good terms with the King, and thus he was able to help Massachusetts at court. Massachusetts rewarded him with a grant of five hundred acres. He spent the decline of his days in Mendon, Mass., in Rhode Island, and finally in Boston. *Dictionary of American Biography.* He was the father of John Crowne, the Restoration dramatist.

[2] Capt. Thomas Breeden, or Breedan, was a merchant of large property who came and went between New England and Old England. Thomas Temple made him his deputy-governor of Acadia.

thereupon a warrant to secure them issued, the 8th of March, from the governor and assistants, which was sent to Springfield and the other towns in the western parts of the colony, but they were beyond the reach of it.*

* They were well treated at New-Haven, by the ministers and some of the magistrates, and for some days seem'd to apprehend themselves out of danger. But the news of the King's proclamation being brought to New-Haven, they were obliged to abscond. The 27th of March, they removed to Milford, and appeared there in the day time, and made themselves known; but at night, returned privately to New-Haven, and lay concealed in Mr. Davenport the minister's house until the 30th of April. About that time, news came to Boston that ten of the judges were executed, and the governor received a royal mandate, dated March 5, 1660, to cause Whaley and Goffe to be secured. This greatly alarmed the country, and there is no doubt that the court were now in earnest in their endeavours to apprehend them; and to avoid all suspicion, they gave commission and instruction to two young merchants from England, Thomas Kellond and Thomas Kirk, zealous royalists, to go through the colonies, as far as Manhados, in search of them. They had friends who informed them what was doing, and they removed from Mr. Davenport's to the house of one Jones,[1] where they lay hid until the 11th of May, and then removed to a mill, and from thence, on the 13th, into the woods, where they met Jones and two of his companions, Sperry [2] and Burril,[3] who first conducted them to a place called hatchet-harbour, where they lay two nights, until a cave or hole in the side of a hill was prepared to conceal them. This hill they called Providence hill; and there they continued, from the 15th of May to the 11th of June, sometimes in the cave, and, in very tempestuous weather, in a house near to it. During this time, the messengers went through New-Haven to the Dutch settlement, from whence they returned to Boston by water. They made diligent search, and had full proof that the regicides had been seen at Mr. Davenport's, and offered great rewards to English and Indians who should give information that they might be taken, but, by the fidelity of their three friends, they remained undiscovered. Mr. Davenport was threatned with being called to an account, for concealing and comforting traitors, and might well be alarmed. They had engaged to surrender, rather than the country or any particular persons should suffer upon their account; and upon intimation of Mr. Davenport's danger, they generously resolved to go to New-Haven, and deliver themselves up to the authority there. The miseries they had suffered and were still exposed to, and the little chance they had of finally escaping, in a country where every stranger is immediately known to be such, would not have been sufficient to have induced them. They let the deputy governor, Mr. Leete, know where they were, but he took no measures to secure them; and the next day, some persons came to them, to advise them not to surrender. Having publickly shewn themselves at New-Haven, they had cleared Mr. Davenport from the suspicion of still concealing them, and, the 24th of June, went into the woods again to their cave. They continued there, sometimes venturing to a house near the cave until the 19th of August, when the search for them being pretty well over, they ventured to the house of one Tomkins, near Milford, where they remained two years, without so much as going into the orchard. After that, they took a little more liberty, and made themselves known to several persons in whom they could confide, and each of them frequently prayed, and also exercised, as they term it, or preached at private meetings in their chamber. In 1664, the commissioners from King Charles arrived at

---

[1] "William Jones is said to have been the son of the regicide John Jones, executed the preceding October." Lemuel A. Welles, *The History of the Regicides in New England.*

[2] Richard Sperry.

[3] William Burrill.

THE proclaiming the King having been deferred until August 1661, the governor, upon intelligence from England of what was doing there to the prejudice of the colony, did not think proper to delay

Boston. Upon the news of it, they retired to their cave, where they tarried 8 or 10 days. Soon after, some Indians, in their hunting, discovered the cave with the bed, &c. and the report being spread abroad, it was not safe to remain near it. On the 13th of October 1664, they removed to Hadley, near an hundred miles distant, travelling only by night, where Mr. Russel, the minister of the place, had previously agreed to receive them. Here they remained concealed fifteen or sixteen years, very few persons in the colony being privy to it. The last account of Goffe, is from a letter, dated Ebenezer, the name they gave their several places of abode, April 2d, 1679. Whaley had been dead some time before.[1] The tradition at Hadley is, that two persons, unknown, were buried in the minister's cellar. The minister was no sufferer by his boarders. They received more or less remittances every year, for many years together, from their wives in England. Those few persons who knew where they were, made them frequent presents. Richard Saltonstall, Esq; who was in the secret, when he left the country and went to England in 1672, made them a present of fifty pounds at his departure; and they take notice of donations from several other friends. They were in constant terror; though they had reason to hope, after some years, that the enquiry for them was over. They read, with pleasure, the news of their being killed, with other judges in Switzerland. Their diary, for six or seven years, contains every little occurrent in the town, church, and particular families in the neighbourhood. These were small affairs. They had indeed, for a few years of their lives, been among the principal actors in the great affairs of the nation; Goffe especially, who turned the members of the little parliament out of the house, and who was attached to Oliver and to Richard to the last; but they were both of low birth and education. They had very constant and exact intelligence of every thing which passed in England, and were unwilling to give up all hopes of deliverance. Their greatest expectations were from the fulfilment of the prophecies. They had no doubt, that the execution of the judges was the slaying of the witnesses. They were much disappointed, when the year 1666 had passed without any remarkable event, but flattered themselves that the christian æra might be erroneous. Their lives were miserable and constant burdens. They complain of being banished from all human society. A letter from Goffe's wife, who was Whaley's daughter, I think worth preserving. (*Appendix.*)[2] After the second year, Goffe writes, by the name of Walter Goldsmith, and she of Frances Goldsmith. and the correspondence is carried on, as between a mother and son. There is too much religion in their letters for the taste of the present day; but the distresses of two persons, under these peculiar circumstances, who appear to have lived very happily together, are very strongly described.

Whilst they were at Hadley (Feb. 10, 1664) Dixwell, another of the judges, came to them, but from whence, or in what part of America he first landed, is not known. The first mention of him in their journal, is by the name of Col. Dixwell; but ever after, they call him Mr. Davids. He continued some years at Hadley, and then removed to New-Haven. He was generally supposed to have been one of those who were obnoxious in England, but he never discovered who he was, until he was on his death-bed. I have one of his letters, signed James Davids, dated March 23d 1683. He married at New-Haven, and left several children. After his death, his son, who before had been called Davids, took the name of Dixwell, came to Boston, and lived in good repute; was a ruling elder of one of the churches there. Some of his grandchildren are now living. Col. Dixwell

[1] For some more or less interesting correspondence between Hutchinson and Dr. Ezra Stiles in regard to the date of Whalley's death, see *Extracts from the Itineraries and Other Miscellanies of Ezra Stiles* (New Haven, 1916), pp. 520–521.

[2] Appendix, No. XIV.

it any longer, and called the general court together the 7th of August, when, after a great variety of forms for a proclamation had been proposed, the following was agreed to.

FORASMUCH as Charles the second is undoubted King of Great-Britain and all other his Majesty's territories and dominions thereunto belonging, and hath been some time since lawfully proclaimed and crowned accordingly: We therefore do, as in duty we are bound, own and acknowledge him to be our Sovereign Lord and King, and do therefore hereby proclaim and declare his sacred Majesty Charles the second, to be lawful King of Great-Britain, France and Ireland, and all other the territories thereunto belonging.   God save the King.

AN order passed the court the same day, and was posted up in Boston, forbidding all disorderly behaviour on the occasion; declaring that no person might expect indulgence for the breach of any

---

was buried at New-Haven. His grave stone still remains with this inscription. "J. D. Esq; deceased March 18th, in the 82d year of his age, 1688." [Sir Edmund Andros, not long before Col? Dixwell's death travelling from New York to Boston stop'd at New haven and attended the publick worship there, and observing something in Dixwell which distinguished him from the rest of the auditory, after service he asked the name of the old gentleman and being answered that it was Mr. Davids who came many years ago from England he replied that he had a very suspicious appearance. But death soon after secured Dixwell from all danger of further enquiry.]

It cannot be denied, that many of the principal persons in the colony greatly esteemed these persons for their professions of piety and their grave deportment, who did not approve of their political conduct. Mr. Mitchell, the minister of Cambridge, who shewed them great friendship upon their first arrival, says in a manuscript which he wrote in his own vindication, "Since I have had opportunity, by reading and discourse, to look a little into that action for which these men suffer, I could never see that it was justifiable." After they were declared traitors, they certainly would have been sent to England if they could have been taken. It was generally thought they had left the country; and even the consequence of their escape was dreaded, least when they were taken, those who had harboured them should suffer for it. Mr. Endicot, the governor, writes to the Earl of Manchester, that he supposes they went towards the Dutch at Manhadoes, and took shipping for Holland; and Mr. Bradstreet, the then governor, in December 1684, writes to Edward Randolph, "that after their being at New-Haven, he could never hear what became of them." Randolph, who was sent to search into the secrets of the government, could obtain no more knowledge of them, than that they had been in the country, and respect had been shewn them by some of the magistrates. I am loth to omit an anecdote handed down through governor Leveret's family. I find Goffe takes notice in his journal of Leveret's being at Hadley. The town of Hadley was alarmed by the Indians in 1675, in the time of publick worship, and the people were in the utmost confusion. Suddenly, a grave elderly person appeared in the midst of them. In his mien and dress he differed from the rest of the people. He not only encouraged them to defend themselves; but put himself at their head, rallied, instructed and led them on to encounter the enemy, who by this means were repulsed. As suddenly, the deliverer of Hadley disappeared. The people were left in consternation, utterly unable to account for this strange phœnomenon. It is not probable, that they were ever able to explain it. If Goffe had been then discovered, it must have come to the knowledge of those persons, who declare by their letters that they never knew what became of him.

law, and "in a particular manner, that no man should presume to drink his Majesty's health," * which the order says, "he hath in an especial manner forbid."

AN address to the King was likewise agreed to and ordered to be sent to England.

INTELLIGENCE arriving of further complaints against the colony, and orders being received from the King, that persons should be sent over to make answer, the governor called the court together again, the 31st of December, and Simon Bradstreet, one of the magistrates, and John Norton, one of the ministers of Boston church, were chosen agents for the colony, and instructions given them; the sum of which was, to represent the colony as his Majesty's loyal and obedient subjects, to endeavour to take off all scandal and objections, and to understand his Majesty's apprehensions concerning them, to do nothing which might be prejudicial to the charter, and to keep the court advised of these transactions and all occurrences.†

THESE gentlemen engaged in the service with great reluctance, Mr. Norton particularly. A ship was stopped for them upon demurrage, and then discharged, and then stopped again. At length the committee, appointed to do every thing necessary for their dispatch in the recess of the court, engaged "to make good all damages they might sustain by the detention of their persons in England or otherwise." They departed the 10th of February.

THEIR reception in England was much more favourable than was expected, their stay short, returning the next fall with the King's most gracious letter, some parts of which cheared the hearts of the country; and they then looked upon, and often afterwards recurred to them, as a confirmation of their charter privileges, and an amnesty of all past errors. The letter was ordered to be published, and, in an order for a public thanksgiving, particular notice is taken of "the return of their messengers, and the continuance of the mercies of peace, liberties, and the gospel." ‡

---

* "Hoc est ad nostros non leve crimen avos." *Ovid.*

† Mr. Pynchon writes to Mr. Davenport at New-Haven, March 26, 1662, "Our general court, after much agitation and opposition, have at last sent two messengers to England, Mr. N. and Mr. B. who went from Boston 10th Feb. I pray God it may be for the best. The event is doubtful to me, seeing we have so many false friends and open enemies." The fears of the people, while they were absent, appear from many passages in private letters, mentioning reports that Mr. Bradstreet and Norton were detained in England, that Mr. Norton was in the Tower, &c.

‡ Lord Say, who, upon the restoration, which he had been instrumental in promoting, was made Lord Privy Seal, retained his friendship for the colony, as appears by the following letter.

THERE were some things however in the King's letter hard to comply with; and although it was ordered to be published, yet it was with this caution, that

inasmuch as the letter hath influence upon the churches as well as civil state, all manner of actings, in relation thereto, shall be suspended until the next general court, that so all persons concerned may have time and opportunity to consider what is necessary to be done, in order to his Majesty's pleasure therein.

The King expressly declares,

We will preserve, and do hereby confirm the patent and charter heretofore granted unto them by our royal father of blessed memory, and they shall fully enjoy all the privileges and liberties granted unto them in and by the same, and we will be ready to renew the same charter to them, under our great seal of England, whensoever they shall desire it.

His majesty's gracious pardon to all his subjects was likewise declared, for all treasons, &c. during the late troubles, except to such as stood attainted by act of parliament, if any such should have transported themselves thither; but then it was required, that all their laws should be reviewed, and such as were contrary or derogatory to the King's authority and government should be annulled and repealed; that the oath of allegiance should be duly administred; that the administration of justice should be in the King's name, that free-

---

"London 10th July 1661.

Gentlemen and honoured friends,

HAVING so safe a hand and so true a friend to convey a line to you, as the bearer Mr. Crowne, I was loth to omit writing, because it may be my last, my glass being almost run out, and I retiring home. — You have had several appeared here against you, and have been examined against you, as Captain Breedan and others, of whom, and about what, this bearer can more particularly inform you than I will at this time write; and I must say for Mr. Crowne, he hath appeared, both here in the council and to the Lord Chamberlain and others, as really and cordially for you as any could do, and hath allaied the ill opinion of your cruelty against the quakers, willingly neglected his passage to stay here to serve you, and by his means and information of the state of your government, as now it is, I hope you will have no governor put upon you but of your own liking; wherefore I must request you will really own and accordingly requite Mr. Crowne his love, care and pains for you, of which I have been an eye witness. I have brought him to the Lord Chamberlain and others, and have requested their Lordships to assist him in your behalf. I have not been wanting, both to the King and council, to advance your interest; more I cannot do, but earnestly to pray the Lord to stand with you and for you. I remain your assured loving friend to serve you,   W. SAY & SEALE.

For his ever honoured friends, the governor of the Massachusets colony in New-England, for the time being, to be communicated to the rest of the magistrates and deputies there.

dom and liberty should be given to all such as desired to use the book of Common Prayer, and perform their devotions in the manner established in England; and that they might not undergo any prejudice thereby, that all persons of good and honest lives and conversations should be admitted to the sacrament of the Lord's supper, according to the book of Common Prayer, and their children to baptism; that, in the choice of governor and assistants, the only consideration to be had, should be of the wisdom, virtue and integrity of the persons to be chosen, and not of any faction with reference to opinions and outward profession; that all freeholders of competent estates, not vicious, &c. though of different persuasions concerning church government, should have their votes in the election of all officers civil and military, and finally, that this letter should be published, &c.

HOWEVER reasonable the several things required by the King appear to us at this day,* yet many of them were grievous to our ancestors. The agents met with the fate of most agents ever since.† The favours they had obtained, were supposed to be no more than might well have been expected, and their merits were soon forgot; the evils which they had it not in their power to prevent, were attributed to their neglect or unnecessary concessions. Mr. Bradstreet was a man of more phlegm, and not so sensibly touched; but Mr. Norton was so affected that he grew melancholy. He died suddenly,

* When the legislator has believed it a duty to permit the exercise of many religions, it is necessary that he should enforce also a toleration amongst these religions themselves. *Spir. Laws.*

† Mr. Davis, a merchant in Boston, lately arrived from England, writes to Mr. Davenport at New-Haven as follows, "Mr. Norton hath lost himself much in the esteem of the generality, and will do more. — I was told that he declared to the court, if they complied not with the King's letter, the blood that should be spilt would lie at their door. — Yesterday, half a dozen of the great church went to him, and Mr. Wilson, and elder Penn, in the name of themselves and others, desiring that an assistant might be chosen (intending Mr. Allen, I suppose, whom the Lord appears much with, having given him large room in the hearts of the people) but some, I hear, have gone on the other side and opposed it."

Doctor Mather says upon this occasion, "Such has been the jealous disposition of our New-Englanders about their dearly bought privileges, and such also has been the various understanding of the people about the extent of those privileges, that of all the agents which they have sent over unto the court of England for now 40 years together, I know not any one who did not, at his return, meet with some very froward entertainment among his countrymen. And there may be the wisdom of the holy and righteous God as well as the malice of the evil one acknowledged in the ordering of such temptations. Of these temptations, a considerable share fell to Mr. Norton, concerning whom there were many who would not stick to say, that 'he had laid the foundation of ruin to all our liberties,' and his melancholy mind imagined, that his best friends began therefore to look awry upon him." *Magnalia.*

very soon after his return (April 5, 1663*). [Mr. Norton was one of the first characters among the Clergy. He made himself famous in Europe, as well as in America, by a controversy with one of the dutch Divines, and by his other writings. The elegancy of his Latin was exceeded by very few of his contemporaries, and Foreigners, as well as those of his own Nation, spoke of him with great applause. But the most valuable part of his character, was his integrity and firmness of mind, in resisting the temptation to popular applause, when it could be obtained only by approving of popular prejudices. I have given two instances, one when the people were under delusion in their opinions of Witchcraft, the other, which required more fortitude, when they generally favoured political measures, which did not appear to him to tend to the true interest of the Country. Count d'Estrades, Ambassador from the French King, in a letter dated at London Feb. 27th 1662, speaks of the arrival of two deputies from New England, accompanied by two French Protestant ministers, who presented a petition to the King and Parliament, full of many and strong reasons, not to consent that Acadie should be restored to France. These deputies, I, at first, supposed to be Bradstreet and Norton, but this letter is in the New Stile, was wrote only seven days after their sailing from Boston. Sir Thomas Temple and Col? Crowne, to whom Cromwell granted part of Acadie and Nova Scotia, must therefore be the deputies D'Estrades intends, though there is nothing appears in the Records or Files of the Massachusets Colony, to shew they had authority to make such engagements in behalf of the Colony, as D'Estrades says they offered to make. After this petition was presented, D'Estrades not only laid claim to Acadie as part of his Master's dominions, but also to the whole of New England, however, he thought fit to wave enforcing the title to the latter, until there should be a more convenient opportunity.] The only thing done at this session, in compliance with his Majesty's orders, besides making the letter public, was the giving directions, that all writs, processes, &c. should be in his Majesty's name. A committee was afterwards appointed, to consider what was proper to be done as to the other parts, who were to report the next session;

---

* Upon his sudden death, the Quakers remarked, "John Norton, chief priest in Boston, by the immediate power of the Lord, was smitten; and as he was sinking down by the fire-side, being under just judgment, he confessed the hand of the Lord was upon him, and so he died." *Represent. to King and Parliament.*

A drunken justice, who had been a great persecutor of the Quakers in England, was threatned by Fox with divine punishment. The justice died of an apoplexy two days after. His death was not ascribed to his intemperance, but to Fox's predictions. *Volt. Lett.*

Subito mori piis pariter atque impiis commune est. *Eras. Epist.*

and liberty was given to any of the reverend elders, to any freemen, and to any other the inhabitants, to send in their thoughts, that so, after serious consideration, something might be agreed upon, "satisfactory and safe, conducing to the glory of God and the felicity of his people."

THE year 1662 was remarkable for a synod or general council of all the churches, held at Boston in the month of September, by order of the general court.

THE two questions referred to their decision, and concerning which the country was much divided in sentiment, were these,

1st, WHO are the subjects of Baptism?

2d, WHETHER, according to the word of God, there ought to be a consociation of churches, and what should be the manner of it?

THE result of this synod was printed, by order of the general court, and is particularly mentioned by Doctor Mather, Mr. Neal, and other writers.*

JOHN TOUTON, a French doctor and inhabitant of Rochel in France, made application to the court, in behalf of himself and other protestants expelled from their habitations, on account of their religion, that they might have liberty to inhabit here, which was readily granted to them.

CAPTAIN Breedan, who, as we have before mentioned, had been in England, and had complained of the government for harbouring

---

* It being part of the result of this synod, that the children of such, as made a public profession of their faith, &c. although not in full communion, might be admitted to baptism, several of the members dissented. Mr. Chauncey, the president of the college, and Mr. Davenport of New-Haven, opposed it in print. Mr. Allen answered the first, and Mr. Richard Mather the other. His son, Mr. Increase Mather, a young gentleman about three and twenty, was with the dissenters. He writes Mr. Davenport, October 21, 1662, "I have your writings still in my hands. I offered the synod to read them, but Mr. Norton advised them not to suffer me; whereupon, I let them have a copy of them, which was generally transcribed. I have given in your's and Mr. Street's testimony, unto the general court, with a preface subscribed by Mr. Chauncey, Mr. Mayo, my brother, and myself, in the name of others of the dissenting brethren in the synod, wherein we declare, that we fully concur with what is inserted by yourself in those papers. Some of the court would fain have thrown them out without reading, but the major part were not so violent. It was moved they might be printed. All the answer we could get, was, that we might do as we would. We count it a favour we were not commanded to be silent. — You may see which way things are like to be carried."

Mr. Eleazer Mather, of Northampton, writes to Mr. Davenport of New-Haven, 4th of 5th month 1662, "There was scarce any of the congregational principles, but what were layen at, by some or other of the assembly; as relations of the work of grace, power of voting of the fraternity in admission, profession of faith and repentance not to be required of such as were baptized in the church, in reference to the baptism of their children. Mr. Parker, of Newbury, was one of the great antagonists of the congregational way and order, though it not being the work of the present synod, his many motions, to consider whether we were in the right ecclesiastical order, were not attended."

regicides, and had laid divers other things to its charge to render it obnoxious, returned to New-England this year, and behaved with great insolence in the face of the court, usurping authority and laying his commands on them, but he soon found they had not lost their spirit. They committed him to prison for his contemptuous carriage, and afterwards fined him two hundred pounds,* and ordered that he become bound in two hundred pounds with sureties, to be of good behaviour, standing committed until sentence be performed. On the other hand, Isaac Cole, the constable of Woburn, being charged with having refused to publish the King's letter, and Edward Converse, one of the selectmen of that town, with having spoken disrespectfully of it, as tending to popery, process was ordered against them, and they were held to answer for a high misdemeanor; but the facts charged against them not being proved, they were acquitted.

THE severe acts of parliament against nonconformists caused some of them again to think of a place of refuge. Several ministers came over, and more intended to follow; but New-England was threatned with a loss of their privileges, and if the threat had been executed, they would not not have been secure in these remote parts.†

THE inhabitants upon Connecticut river being increased to three townships, Springfield, Northampton, and Hadley, at the sessions of the general court, in May 1662, they were made a county by the name of Hampshire.

A LETTER was sent, signed by the governor, in the name of the general court, dated Oct. 20, 1663, to Doctor John Owen, desiring him to come over, and to accept the call or invitation which the first church in Boston had given him, to become their teacher, in the room of Mr. Norton; but he could not be prevailed upon.‡ [Many

---

* Afterwards, upon application from Sir Thomas Temple, seconded by governor Winthrop of Connecticut, the fine was remitted or granted to Sir Thomas Temple, to be disposed of at his pleasure.

† "Here is come, with Woodgreene, one Mr. Davies, a rich merchant, and there came with him one Mr. Allen, a young man, a very able teacher, recommended by Mr. Goodwin. He hath taught here divers times since he came. Many are expected this summer. Mr. Bartlett, of Biddeford, and his son, were shipped for New-England; but an oath being required of them before they could get out of the harbour, they chose to die in prison rather than take it." E. Mather's letter to Davenport, July 1662. Another MS. in 1662, says, "There is great talk of many ministers, with their congregations, coming over the next year, if room can be found for them. There was a general governor, and a major general chosen, and a bishop with a suffragan; but Mr. Norton writes, that they are not yet out of hopes to prevent it; the governor's name is Sir Robert Carr, a rank papist."

‡ Capt. Gookin, one of the assistants, in a letter dated July 1666, says, "Doctor Owen, and some choice ones who intended to come with him in Mr. Pierce, are diverted,

others were discouraged from removing, by a rumor that a General Governor would be sent over, and that a reform or change would be made in the New England Governments, ecclesiastical as well as civil. It was, therefore, represented to Lord Clarendon, that if His Majesty should think it for his service to have his English subjects, of differing judgments from Episcopacy, to remove to his own Plantations, rather than to those of other Nations, it might be advisable to issue a proclamation, declaring that the governments of the several Colonies should remain as they were, which would encourage many to remove, some to one Colony, and some to another, as suited their principles, some of the Colonies being more strait, others more large; but Mr. Mavericke, one of the Commissioners afterwards appointed, was continually complaining to his Lordship of the Massachusets Colony. So early as the year 1662 he obtained testimonials from some of the principal Merchants and others of the episcopal persuasion, in and near Boston, which testimonials were left among Lord Clarendon's papers, together with several letters urging the appointment and dispatch of Commissioners, complaining of Massachusets, as disaffected to the King, as paying no regard to the Acts of Navigation, as refusing to comply with the requisites in the King's Letter brought by their Agents, denying his authority to make such requisitions without the Parliament; and a charge was made against the Governor of New-Haven Colony for neglect of duty, in not apprehending Whaley and Goffe when they were in his power, and when he was desired to do it by messenger from Boston. To all this it was added that the Dutch were continually increasing at the Manhadoes, were extending their bounds, and inviting the English to live among them, and that many families had complied with the invitation.]

In 1664, the people of New-England were surprized with the appearance of a very large comet, which continued from the 17th of November, until the 4th of February following. At first, it appeared in the east bearded, afterwards, in the west with a tail. They were not alone in their opinion, that comets were omens of great evils. So judicious a writer as Sleidan observes, that a comet was seen all the month of August preceding the October when Zuinglius was slain; he adds, that the Queen-Mother of France died about the same time. One had appeared just before Mr. Cotton's death. The death of

---

and that, not from hopes of better times there, but from fears of worse here; which some new counsels, there acting, gave them occasion for, so that in all probability, a new cloud is gathering, and a storm preparing for us."

their aged governor, and the troubles the colony met with the next year, from the King's commissioners, tended to confirm people in their opinion. The aurora borealis, and even eclipses, in former ages have been deemed prodigies and of ill omen.*

In the year 1664, the line between the Massachusets and Plimouth was fully and amicably settled and ran, by a committee from each colony, their return being accepted by the general court of the Massachusets, and ordered to be recorded; and there is no doubt the general court of Plimouth colony accepted it likewise.†

The first prosecution, I find upon record, of any of the people called anabaptists, was in the year 1665.[1] William Turner,[2] Thomas Gold,[3] Edward Drinker,[4] John George,[5] and Thomas Osborne,[6] were charged before the governor and other magistrates, with "gathering

* Cœlum visum est ardere plurimo igni, portentaque alia aut obversata oculis, aut vana exterritis ostentavere species. *Liv.*

† Although there have been disputes concerning this line since the present charter, between the proprietors of the towns in the county of Plimouth and Suffolk which were bounded by the colony lines, yet the station from whence they then began to run, has never been doubted. The committee say in their return, "We all mutually agreed upon the first station, having measured three miles southerly of the southernmost part of the said river." Charles river being just before mentioned.

---

[1] Apparently Hutchinson overlooked the sufferings of John Clarke, Obadiah Holmes, and John Crandal in Boston in 1651. They are well recounted by Isaac Backus in his *History of New England. With Particular Reference to the Denomination of Christians called Baptists*, chap. IV.
Backus is also the best authority on the later "prosecutions" here related by Hutchinson. *Ibid.*, chap. VI.

[2] William Turner, of Boston, was originally of Dorchester. Early in King Philip's War he offered to form a company of volunteers, but as he and most of his associates were Baptists the authorities were not interested. When the war became more dangerous, the government changed its attitude and Turner was placed in command on the upper waters of the Connecticut. On May 18, 1676, he defeated the Indians at the falls which have since been called Turner's Falls, but was surrounded and killed by the savages on the following day. See papers by the Rev. George M. Bodge in *New England Historic and Genealogical Register*, XLI, 70–80, 201–218.

[3] Thomas Gold or Gould (d. 1674), of Charlestown and East Boston, was imprisoned in the summer of 1668 and not released until the spring of 1669. Turner received even harsher treatment. By retiring to Noddle's Island, Gold, who was pastor of the First Baptist Church, kept out of trouble. See Nathan E. Wood's *History of the First Baptist Church of Boston*.

[4] Edward Drinker (d. 1700) was a potter by trade, and had been constable in Charlestown. He was imprisoned (1669–1670), but apparently forgave the Colony and fought in King Philip's War as a lieutenant in Capt. William Turner's company. See Nathan E. Wood's *History of the First Baptist Church of Boston*.

[5] John George (d. 1666), of Charlestown, was a chimney cleaner, according to Nathan E. Wood, *History of the First Baptist Church of Boston*, p. 58.

[6] Thomas Osborne had sympathized with the Quakers and felt less and less response to the teachings of the orthodox church. He lived in Charlestown. See Richard Frothingham's *History of Charlestown*, p. 196.

themselves into a pretended church state,* in opposition to the order of the churches in Christ in the colony, and intermedling with those holy appointments of the Lord Jesus, which are proper only to office trust." They confessed they had joined in a church society, that they had been rebaptized, and that one of them administred the Lord's supper. They were admonished, and threatned that if they continued to meet and practise contrary to the order of the gospel, the court would proceed against them according to their demerits. They persevered notwithstanding, and were sentenced by the court to be disfranchised, if they were freemen; and if they still continued their practice, to be committed to prison, upon conviction before one magistrate, until the general court should take further order; and some time after, they were imprisoned and banished. *Nitimur in vetitum* was verified in this proceeding, as it usually is in the like cases. Severity made converts, and then it was thought adviseable to cease from further prosecutions.† The baptists in England were distinguished at this time into three divisions.

---

* This severity was disagreeable to many. A petition to the court was signed by Capt. Hutchinson,[1] Capt. Oliver,[2] and others in 1668, for favour to Thomas Gold and the rest, but it gave offence, and some of the petitioners were obliged to acknowledge their fault; some expressions in the petition being construed reproachful, and the chief promoters were fined. Mr. Increase Mather writes to his brother at Northampton, July 3d 1665, "In this town is lately congregated a church of anabaptists. They take advantage from the commissioners, who declared that they would have liberty given to all sorts and sects of men."

† This was not the first appearance of antipædobaptism in the colony. Mr. Dunstar, the president of the college, made profession of it, and was forced to quit his presidentship. Mr. Chauncey, his successor, held immersion necessary, but was content that the ordinance should be administred to infants, provided it was done in that way. In Mr. Hooker's time, soon after the year 1640, it appears by his letters, that many were inclined that way, and he expresses his apprehensions that the number would increase. "In 1644, one Painter,[3] for refusing to let his child be baptized, (his wife desiring it) was brought before the court, where he declared their baptism to be antichristian. He was sentenced to be whipped, which he bore without flinching, and boasted that God had assisted him. His neighbours gave him the character of an idle lying fellow." (*Hubbard*.)

Mr. Westgate,[4] who had been in New-England, writes from Harlestone, 5th 2d month 1653, to Mr. Thomas Lake,[5] a merchant of note in Boston, "Pray inform me, in your

---

[1] Edward Hutchinson, (1613?–1675), who had already distinguished himself by dissenting from the death penalty for returning Quakers. See p. 169.

[2] James Oliver (*d.* 1682) was a prominent merchant of Boston and captain of the Artillery Company. He served in King Philip's War and took part in the Great Swamp fight.

[3] This was Thomas Painter of Hingham. He appears to have been somewhat of a rover, for Savage finds him, first and last, in Hingham, Providence, Boston, Charlestown, New Haven, Rowley, Newport, and Westerly.

[4] John Westgate, of Boston, was dismissed from the church in 1647 "on desire of the church of Pulham Mary in Norfolk, England." Harlestone is in Norfolk.

[5] See editor's note 3 to p. 293.

Such as look upon all who had not been baptized, after they came to adult age, as little better than heathens, and will not join in prayer with the most eminent congregational ministers, if they were providentially in a family together. Others are sober, moderate men, and manifest the power of godliness in their conversations, and these, upon our occasional meetings we join hand in heart with,[1] and call some of them out to pray with us, and we would not have this difference in judgment between us make the least breach in affection, for many of those, we look upon to be eminent precious holy men. We have a third sort, but they are not many (and most of them at London) that take into fellowship those that are godly, and desire to join with them, though they come not up to be baptized, and walk lovingly together.*

The first baptists of the Massachusets are represented, by the writers of that day, to have been of the same principles with those first described. Some of them were not so. I have seen a letter, dated not many years after this time, from Mr. Miles,[2] the baptist minister at Swanzy, to one of the congregational ministers at Boston, which breathes the true spirit of the gospel, and urges christian concord, charity and love, although they did not agree in every point.

FROM the restoration until the vacating the charter, the colony never stood well in England; the principal persons, both in church and state, were never without fearful expectations of being deprived of their privileges. The years 1664 and 1665 afforded them greater occasion for fears than they had met with at any time before.† In

---

next, whether Mr. Cotton be alive, and if he be dead, what supply the church have in his stead, and how the state of it stands; and also the state of the other church in Boston, of which I can hear nothing. Inform me whether the number of those that oppose baptizing of infants increase, and how it is taken by the magistrates and churches, and who of Boston church declare themselves that way."

When the proceedings against the congregationalists in England were complained of, they were told by Dr. Stillingfleet, that they were justified by the proceedings of their brethren in New-England, against dissenters from the established worship there. *Still. misch. of separation.*

* Mr. Westgate's letter to Mr. Increase Mather.

---

[1] The third edition changes this phrase to "hand and heart." The second edition follows the first. "Hand and heart" agrees with the original document as printed in Massachusetts Historical Society *Collections*, Fourth Series, VIII, 580.

[2] John Miles, or Myles (*d.* 1683), was the founder and first pastor of the Baptist church at Swansea, Mass., which was in the Plymouth colony. The church was established in 1663. "He and some of his flock, weary of the persecution in Wales which ensued under the Act of Uniformity passed when Charles II came to the throne sought in the New World freedom of opinion and worship. This church in Swansea was in some sense a reorganization of the original church in Swansea, Wales, but added to itself members who were already residents of the region, and who had held Baptist doctrines." Nathan E. Wood, *History of the First Baptist Church of Boston*, p. 13.

† In the year 1664, the wheat through the colony was spoiled by blast or mildew. This is represented as a new or unusual thing, but continued more or less for divers

the spring of 1664, intelligence was brought that several men of war were coming from England, and several gentlemen of distinction aboard them. As soon as the general court met in May, they ordered the captain of the castle to give the speediest notice, upon sight of the ships, to the governor and deputy governor, appointed a committee to repair on board to present the respects of the court to the gentlemen, and to acquaint them, that it was the desire of the authority of the place, that strict orders should be given to the under officers and soldiers, in their coming ashore to refresh themselves, at no time to exceed a convenient number, and those without arms, and to behave themselves orderly, and to give no offence to the people and laws of the place. This was no more than a prudent precaution, considering how strict the laws were against all immoralities, the sense the magistrates had of their obligations to execute them upon all offenders without distinction, the certainty that the crews of men of war would offend, and the danger of tumults, quarrels and bloodshed, when they should be brought to punishment. Preparation was likewise made, for receiving and entertaining the gentlemen in the best manner.

A DAY of fasting and prayer * was appointed to be observed throughout the jurisdiction, to implore the mercy of God to them under their many distractions and troubles, according as they should stand in need. And apprehending it to be of great concernment, that the patent or charter should be kept safe and secret, they ordered the secretary to bring it into court and to deliver it, together with a duplicate, to four of the court,† who were directed to dispose of them as might be most safe for the country.

THE ships arrived, Saturday the 23d of July, with Col. Richard Nichols [1] and George Cartwright,[2] Esq; ‡ who, together with Sir

---

years together, until the people were discouraged from sowing, but little wheat having been raised since, except in the towns upon Connecticut river.

* This was their practice, upon every important occasion. Their dependance upon these days, however, was not such as caused them to neglect any other means in their power for promoting the public weal. Modern historians censure this conduct as weakness. Cato only censured the ancient Romans for not joining their endeavours to their prayers. "Ubi socordiæ tete atque ignaviæ tradideris, nequicquam deos implores, irati infestique sunt." *Cato apud Salust.*

† Mr. Bellingham, Maj. Gen. Leveret, Capt. Clark, and Capt. Johnson.

‡ Sir Robert Carr and Mr. Maverick arrived at Piscataqua about the same time.

---

[1] Richard Nichols, or Nicolls (1624–1672), a consistent royalist, was groom of the bedchamber to the Duke of York. He was virtually chairman of the commissioners appointed to regulate New England affairs, but after he captured New Netherland the organizing of that government engaged most of his attention.

[2] George Cartwright was a colonel. Can he have been the dramatist whose solitary

Robert Carr [1] and Samuel Maverick, Esq; [2] had received a commission * from the King for reducing the Dutch at the Manhados, visiting the colonies in New-England, hearing and determining all matters of complaint, and settling the peace and security of the country, any three or two of them to be a quorum, Col. Nichols during his life being one. At their desire, the governor ordered a meeting of the council on Tuesday the 26th. The commissioners laid their commission before the council, with the King's letter of the 23d of April, and part of an instruction referring to the reducing the Manhados, and proposed the raising such a number of men as the country could spare, to begin their march on the 20th of August, promising, that if in the mean time they could prevail by treaty or any nearer assistance, they would stop the progress of raising or marching the men.

THE council gave their answer, that they would cause the general court to assemble the 3d of August and communicate the proposal to them. The commissioners then acquainted the council, that there were many more things to signify to them at their return from Manhados, and the council was desired, in the mean time, further to consider of his Majesty's letter to the colony, June 28, 1662, and to give a more satisfactory answer than formerly. The commissioners then proceeded to the Manhados.

THE court assembled at the time appointed. They first resolved, "that they would bear faith and true allegiance to his Majesty, and

* *Appendix.* [No. XV]

tragedy, *The Heroick Lover, or the Infanta of Spain* (London, 1661), was dedicated to Charles II?

[1] Sir Robert Carr was a baronet of Sleeford in Lincolnshire. Palfrey (*History of New England*, II, 580) quotes from Pepys (*Diary*, III, 314), "Sir Robert Carr's, where it seems people do drink high." Carr had married a sister of Henry Bennet, one of the Secretaries of State.

[2] Samuel Maverick (*c.* 1602–*c.* 1670) was on Noddle's Island when Winthrop and his fleet arrived in 1630. He had been in New England since 1624, but no one knows whence or how he came. (See editor's note to p. 21.) His position in the Colony was anomalous: though an avowed Episcopalian he was admitted a freeman (see *ante*, p. 145). But his ways were not the ways of the Puritans. In 1641 he extended hospitality to two individuals who had escaped from their custody, and was fined accordingly. Later, as we have seen, he joined with Dr. Robert Child in his attempt to liberalize the local government. For this offense he spent some time in jail and was fined heavily. All things considered, it is not surprising that he thought that the government of Massachusetts-Bay should be investigated and reformed.

For the best account of Maverick's career, see William H. Sumner, *History of East Boston*, pp. 60–177. Maverick's "Description of New England," an interesting document, is in *New England Historical and Genealogical Register*, XXXIX, 34–48.

adhere to their patent, so dearly obtained, and so long enjoyed by undoubted right, in the sight of God and men": And then resolved to raise a number, not exceeding two hundred men, at the charge of the colony, for his Majesty's service against the Dutch. The men were raised, but the place surrendring upon articles, no orders were given for them to march.* The court, in the next place, considered of his Majesty's letter of 1662, and repealed the law relating to the admission of freemen, and, instead of it, provided another that allowed English subjects, being freeholders, rateable to a certain value, certified by the minister of the place to be orthodox, and not vicious in their lives, to be made freemen, although not members of the church. The other parts of the letter were referred until the commissioners return.

THEY agreed upon an address to the King,[3] setting forth the purchase of the soil from the council of Plimouth; the charter from King Charles the first; the great charge they had been at in transporting themselves and families; in purchasing lands of the natives, and settling the colony; his Majesty's explicit confirmation of their privileges, &c. they then express their grief, in having four persons sent over, one of them their known and professed enemy,† with such extraordinary powers, by means whereof they were like to be subjected to the arbitrary power of strangers, proceeding not by any established law but their own discretion; and being thus subjected to complaints, appeals, and the determinations of new judges, the government and administration would be made void and of no effect; and although they had but tasted of the words and actions of the gentlemen, yet they had enough to satisfy them, that the powers, given by the commission, would be improved to the subversion of their all;

---

* Thomas Clark and John Pynchon,[1] as commissioners from the Massachusets, attended the King's commissioners to Manhados. The Manhados surrendered the 27th Aug. 1664; the inhabitants becoming English subjects, and being left in the enjoyment of their estates and many of their privileges. Stuyesant,[2] the Dutch governor, also becoming subject to the English government. I have the copy of a letter sent to him from the Dutch West India company, requiring him to come home and give a more satisfactory account, by word, of mouth, than he had done by his letters.

† Maverick.

---

[1] John Pynchon (1625-1703), of Springfield, was the only son of William Pynchon, one-time Treasurer of the Bay Colony and founder of Springfield. He was an Assistant from 1665 till the old form of government was abolished in 1686; also under the new charter. Savage calls him "the chief man in all the West."

[2] Stuyvesant is spelled correctly in the third edition. "Stuyesant" is obviously a printer's slip.

[3] See Appendix, No. XVI.

that if things went on according to the present appearance, they must either seek new dwellings or sink under intolerable burdens; the inhabitants would be driven to they knew not what extremities, and a hopeful plantation ruined; that if any profit was expected by the King, or by new rulers imposed upon them, they would be disappointed, the country being poor and but just affording subsistence; that if the people should be drove out of the country (for to a coalition they would never come) it would be hard to find another people that would stay long in it; that the body of the people was satisfied with the present government; that there was no government under heaven, where there were no discontented persons; that there were but few among them, and fewer that had cause to be so. They appeal to God, that they came not into this wilderness to seek great things for themselves, but for the sake of a quiet life. They profess their subjection to his Majesty, and willingness to testify their dutiful affection in any righteous way; but it was a great unhappiness to be reduced to the hard case of having no other way of doing it, but by destroying their own being, which nature taught them to preserve, or yielding up their liberties, far dearer to them than their lives; which if they had had any reason to expect, they would not have wandered from their fathers' houses to the ends of the earth; a royal donation from so great a Prince being the greatest security in human affairs. They sent letters, humbly to sue for favour, to several of the nobility, and among others, to the Lord Clarendon, from whom they had an unfavourable answer.*

THE Dutch being reduced, Nichols remained at New-York, the other commissioners returned to Boston the 15th of February, and acquainted the governor and council, that the next day they should go to Plimouth, to deliver the King's letter to that government, and desired orders might be given to all the inhabitants to assemble together the next election day; to which it was answered, that all were at their liberty, but the reason of such a motion they could not see into, nor should they encourage it, not only on account of the business of the season, but because the wives and children of a considerable part of the people, together with many aged persons, must be left exposed to the rage of the natives. To which Cartwright replied, "that the motion was so reasonable, that he that would not attend to it was a traitor." This was rough usage, and could have no good consequences. The commissioners sent letters, in their own name, about the country, to invite the people to assemble.

* *Appendix.* [No. XVII]

HAVING dispatched their business at Plimouth,* they went to the Naraganset country, and at Warwick, held their court, made enquiry into the titles of lands there, and made divers determinations, which had no long effect, and came privately and separately to Boston, the latter end of April, and so prevented, designedly as was supposed, that respect which was intended to have been shewn them

* His Majesties commissioners propositions to Plimouth jurisdiction.
  WE were comaunded, particularly to recomend these thinges to you from his Majestye.

1. That all householders, inhabitinge in your colonye, take the oath of allegiance. And that your administrations of justice be in his Majestyes name.

2. That all men of competent estates and civill conversation, though of different judgment, may be admitted to be freemen, and haue liberty to choose and be choosen officers, both civill and military.

3. That all men and woemen, of orthodoxe opinions, competent estates, knowledge, civill liues and not scandalous, may be admitted to the sacrament of the Lord's supper, and their children to baptisme [if they desire it] either by admittinge them into the congregation already gathered, or permittinge them to gather themselves into such congregations, where they may enjoy the benefit of the sacrament, and that difference in opinion may not breake the bonds of peace and charity.

4. That all lawes and expressions in lawes, derogatory to his Majesty, if any such haue beene made in these parts, in the laite troublesome tymes, may be repealed, altered and taken off from the file.

The Courts answer.

1. To the first we consent; it haueing been the practise of this court, in the first place to insert in the oath of fidelity, required of every householder, to be true and loyall to our soveraigne Lord the King, his heires and successors: alsoe to administer all actes of justice in his Majestyes name.

2. To the second we alsoe consent; it haueing beene our constant practise, to admitt men of competent estates, and civill conversation, though of different judgments, yet beinge otherwise orthodoxe, to be freemen, and to haue liberty to choose and to be choosen officers, both civill and military.

4. To the 4th we consent; that all lawes and expressions of lawes, derogatory to his Majestye, [if any such be found amongst us, which at present we are not conscious of] shall be repealed, altered and taken off the file.

3. To the 3d; we cannot but acknowledge it to be a high favour from God and from our Soveraigne, that we may enjoy our consciences in point of God's worship, the main end of transplanting ourselves into these remote corners of the earth; and should most heartily rejoice, that all our neighbours, so qualified as in that proposition, would adjoine themselves to our societies according to the order of the gospel, for the enjoyment of the sacraments to themselves and theirs; but if thro' different perswasions, respecting church government, it cannot be obtained, we would not deny a liberty to any, according to the proposition, that are truly conscientious, altho' differing from us (especially where his Majestye commands it) they maintaining an able preaching ministry for carrying on of publick sabbath worship, which, we doubt not, is his Majestyes intent, and withdraw not from paying their due proportions of maintenance to such ministers as are orderly settled in the places where they live, until they have one of their owne, and that in such places, as are capable of maintaining the worship of God in two distinct congregations. We being greatly incouraged by his Majestyes gracious expressions, in his letter to us, and your honours further assurance of his royal purpose to continue our liberties, that where places, by reason of our paucity and poverty are uncapable of two, it is not intended, that such congregations as are already in being should be rooted out,

at their arrival. Mr. Endicot, the governor, died the 15th of March 1665. Mr. Bellingham, the deputy governor, with some of the magistrates assembled, as usual, the 2d of May, the day before the election, to prepare for the business of the next day. The commissioners desired to speak with them, which though at first they refused, being no court, yet when it was urged by the commissioners, it was submitted to. Five writings were delivered, as part of their instructions. The first, expressing "the great kindness of the King for the colony, and his desire to advance a plantation, which had given so good an example of sobriety and industry to all others."

THE second, declaring, "that the King was so far from any thought of abridging, that he was very ready to enlarge all the concessions made by his royal father in the charter, or to make any alterations for the prosperity of the colony."

THE third, "that the principal end of their journey, was, to remove all jealousies the King might have of the loyalty and affections of his good subjects towards him, or which they might have of his good opinion and confidence in them, and his protection over them."

THE fourth, "that, by this means, the designs of wicked and seditious persons would be disappointed, and a foundation laid for mutual confidence and satisfaction; the King would look upon his colony of the Massachusets within the same limits of affection, duty and obedience to his person and government as Kent or Yorkshire, and they again would have the same confidence of his care and protection as the others had, and all have great reason to acknowledge the good effects, which by God's blessing would proceed from this commission." These were given as from his Majesty.

THE fifth, was a message of their own, "assuring the council, in his Majesty's name, that whatever had been granted by his royal predecessor, or promised by himself, should to the utmost be made good; and desiring, they might have no just cause to represent to his Majesty any thing which might seem to come short of that just duty and allegiance, which might merit his Majesty's favour." They then acquainted the council with the favourable representation they had

---

but their liberties preserved, there being other places to accommodate men of different perswasions, in societies by themselves, which, by our knowne experience, tends most to the preservation of peace and charity.

The league, between the 4 colonies, was not with any intent (that ever we heard of) to cast off our dependance upon England, a thing which we utterly abhorre; intreating your honours to believe us, for we speak as in the presence of God.

New-Plimouth,
May 4, 1665.

By order of the general court for the jurisdiction of New-Plimouth, per me Nathanael Morton, secr.

made to his Majesty, of the readiness of the colony to have assisted in the expedition against the Dutch, if it had been necessary.*

BEFORE there was an opportunity for an answer, they acquainted the deputy governor, and the rest, with two other instructions; one "for publishing the letters which had been sent to the King, with the answers to them"; the other, "for laying before the commissioners a map or plan of the colony, that they might hear and determine all claims made by such as bordered upon it." They also complained of slanderous reports about the country, that they were come to raise a revenue of 5000 *l.* a year for the King, to lay 12 *d.* per acre annual rent on all improved lands, &c.

As soon as the election was over, viz. on the 4th of May, these matters were laid, by the governor, before the general court. The commissioners were immediately desired to communicate, to the court, the whole which his Majesty had given in command to declare to them, that so they might have their whole work before them; but they replied, that they would not observe that method, but when they had an answer to what they had given in, they would then present them with more work. The refusal itself was not so displeasing as the terms and manner in which it was expressed and delivered.

THE 5th, the court gave their answer in substance as follows; reserving liberty to enlarge afterwards if there should be cause, viz.

THAT they acknowledged, with all humble thanks, his Majesty's grace and favour, in his letters and messages, and they would lay hold of every opportunity to shew their duty and loyalty to him.

THAT what relates to the Dutch being fully accomplished, no further answer could be expected, only an acknowledgment of the favourable representation which the commissioners had made of the conduct of the court.

As to a map of the colony, it was preparing, and they should soon have satisfaction therein.

THAT his Majesty's letters had been laid before the court, and so had the papers received from the commissioners, and copies were spread about

---

* Mr. Smith,[1] in his history of New-York, says, that Col. Nicolls and Sir George Carterett, in their letter to the secretary of state, complain much of the backwardness of the Massachusets. Two hundred men, its certain, were raised and ready to march with great expedition.

---

[1] William Smith (1728–1793) graduated from Yale in 1745 and became an eminent lawyer. In 1763 he was appointed chief justice of New York. During the Revolution he was neutral for a while, but finally chose the British side. After the war he was made chief justice of Canada and continued in that office until his death. His *History of the Province of New York* was first printed in London in 1757.

the country, and if the commissioners desired any further publication, they would endeavour their satisfaction.

THAT they were willing to advise with the commissioners upon the best way of putting a stop to all false rumours, and finally, that their confidence of his Majesty's grace and favour and royal intentions to them, being further cherished by the commissioners, would undoubtedly draw from them more ample expressions and demonstrations of duty, loyalty and good affection to his Majesty, according as by their patent they were bound.

To this answer, the commissioners replied,

THAT to the preface, "they desired the court to improve the liberty reserved of enlarging, &c."

To the first head, "That the opportunity, they seemed so willing to lay hold of, was now brought to their hands."

To the second, "That nothing further was necessary."

To the third, "That many things of great moment could not be issued, until a perfect map was had."

To the fourth, "That they would not aggravate any neglect, but they hoped, the general court, by practical assertions of duty, would give his Majesty satisfaction upon the points contained in the letter of 1662, which had so long slept in some hands."

To the fifth, "They were fully persuaded, the printing the results and conclusions which should be made on his Majesty's part, and the part of the colony, would silence all those false and malicious reports which they expected should be enquired into."

To the conclusion, "That although their parent laid them under peculiar obligation, yet it did not circumscribe all that duty and allegiance which was due to his Majesty from natural born subjects, and which they themselves, in former papers, had more fully expressed."

THE same day, the commissioners communicated other parts of their instructions, viz.

THAT they should inform themselves of the state of the neighbouring Indian Princes, and enquire what treaties had been made between them and any of the King's subjects, and if there had been any failure, on the part of any of his Majesty's subjects, the commissioners should take effectual course, that reparation and satisfaction be made for any injury sustained thereby, and use all ways and means to let those Princes, and other Indians, know of his Majesty's charge, &c.

THE commissioners informed the court of great complaints received from the Naraganset Indians, and desired to be advised how they should atttain a true information, that they might do justice, and give the King a just account, &c.

THAT they should make due inquiry, what progress had been towards the foundation and maintenance of any college or schools, for the education of youth and conversion of infidels, the King having taken abundant satisfaction in the accounts he had received, of the designs of the colony herein, which he hoped would draw a blessing upon all their other undertakings.

THAT they should not give too easy an ear to clamours or accusations against such as then were, or had been, in places of government, except from men of equal condition; and then they should proceed to examine and determine, according to the rules of justice, without respect of persons or opinions.

THAT they should not receive any complaints against a magistrate, except for something done against equity or against the charter; nor interrupt the course of justice between party and party, except the proceedings should be expresly contrary to the rules prescribed by the charter; or the matter, in difference, arose from some expression or clause in some grant under the great seal. In those cases, to examine and proceed according to justice.

UPON the subject of this instruction, the commissioners acquainted the court,

they had received many complaints from the English of hard measure in several kinds, one more especially, which they offered to communicate, and dared not refuse to examine it, but had so much respect to the authority in the several colonies, that they would leave it to the choice of the court, whether it should be heard at Providence in Rhode Island, or at Boston, either at that time, or after the commissioners return from the eastward, where they were going.

This referred to a criminal prosecution against one John Porter, jun.[1] to whom they had granted a warrant of protection as it was termed.

"THAT, in due season, they should inquire how far the particulars, required by the King's letter of 1662, had been complied with," as first,

"THAT all persons take the oath of allegiance."

2d, "THAT all process, and administration of justice, be performed in our name."

---

[1] John Porter, Jr. (d. 1684), was the eldest son of John Porter of Salem, formerly of Hingham. He had been locked up for gross misconduct, chiefly abusing his parents; but he escaped from prison and complained to the Commissioners, whom he found at Warwick, R. I. The unpleasant story of his case may be found in *Records of Massachusetts Bay*, IV (Part II), 216–218.

3d, "THAT such as desire to use the book of Common prayer, be be permitted so to do, without incurring any penalty, reproach, or disadvantage, it being very scandalous, that any persons should be debarred the exercise of their religion according to the laws and customs of England, by those who were indulged with the liberty of being of what profession or religion they pleased."

4th, "THAT persons of good and honest conversation might enjoy the privilege, of chusing and being chose into places of government and the like."

The commissioners desired they might be enabled to give the King such information, as should be fully satisfactory.

THE 8th of May they delivered three other writings, as parts of their instructions, viz.

THAT they should duly inquire, whether any persons attainted of high treason, now reside there, or have been entertained there, and by whom, and what is become of them, and endeavour to cause them to be apprehended and sent to England.

THAT they should take care that such orders be established, as that the act of navigation be punctually observed, it being of infinite concernment, and what the hearts of the whole nation were set upon, but had been evaded, under pretence that acts made in the assembly there, during the late rebellion, were in force, notwithstanding the act of parliament; an assertion the King would not suffer to be made, but that all such acts of assembly should be repealed, taken off the files, and no more remain upon record; and that they should cause justice to be done to Thomas Dean,[1] who had been denied it, in a prosecution upon the act of parliament.

THE commissioners desired a book of the colony laws, that they might examine, &c. and that any laws, contrary to this act, might be declared null.

THAT they should inform themselves of the whole frame and constitution of government, civil and ecclesiastical, the yearly taxes and impositions, the shipping, the militia, horse and foot, fortified towns and forts, &c.

THEY desired some persons might be appointed to draw up an information of all those particulars, to satisfy his Majesty's desires.

BEFORE the court gave answer to these papers, they sent a message, May 9th, to the commissioners, to acquaint them, that the

---

[1] Thomas Dean (1640?–1686) was a Boston merchant. He returned to England about 1678 and died there. His grievance is not entirely clear to the editor, but the official narrative of it may be read and pondered in *Records of Massachusetts Bay*, IV (Part II), 218.

court apprehended their patent to be greatly infringed by the warrant granted to John Porter; upon which, the commissioners desired a conference with a committee, that the court might have better information, which was agreed to, and held the 11th.

THE commissioners asserted, that they were to be justified by their commission in what they did, and that the charter was not infringed. The committee urged,

that the general court had full power and authority to make laws, and provide for the execution of them; they were very ready to give an account, to his Majesty, of all their proceedings, whensoever he required it; but it would be an insuperable burden, if the colony must be brought upon a level, and stand with every criminal upon whom sentence had been passed, at the bar of another tribunal, which their charter knew nothing of.

The commissioners being asked, "whether they proposed a jury should pass upon these and the like cases?" they replied No, theirs was a commission of oyer and terminer. "Whether they would admit of new evidence?" Yea. The committee then further urged, "That they esteemed it their greatest unhappiness, to be held to give up their privileges by charter, and the rights of Englishmen, or else be accounted among such as denied his Majesty's authority." The commissioners nevertheless insisted upon their own authority, and required a submission to it. The court then proceeded to give answer to the other instructions, which had been communicated.

To that which relates to the Indians, called the 5th instruction, they say,

that they have been too long acquainted with the falsehood of the Naraganset and other Indians, to wonder that they should complain of injuries, when they themselves were the aggressors; that all matters, relating to the Indians, had been managed by the commissioners of the united colonies, and their records might be examined.

To the next or sixth instruction,

That there is a small college at Cambridge, from which, they might say without boasting, more than an hundred able preachers, physicians, and other useful persons had issued; for the particulars of the foundation and benefactions, they referred to the president and fellows; that the country was well provided with schools, that there was also at Cambridge a small fabrick of brick for the use of the Indians, built by the corporation in England, in which there were then eight Indian scholars, one of which had been admitted into college, that there were six towns of Indians in the jurisdiction professing the christian religion, that they had schools to teach the youth to read and write, and persons appointed to instruct them in civility and religion, who had orders to wait upon the commissioners and shew them the towns and manner of life of the Indians, if it should be desired.

To the proposition upon the 7th and 8th instructions, by which an offer is made of the choice of a place for hearing and determining complaints, they say,

That hearing and determining appeals from their judgments is inconsistent with their charter; nevertheless as they desired to be doers of truth and righteousness, and not to shun the light, if the commissioners would be pleased to impart the complaints that had been brought against the government, they hoped to be able to give such answer as should satisfy his Majesty that their actions had been consonant to reason and equity, and not such as evil minded men had represented them.

To the ninth, touching his Majesty's letter of June 1662, they say,

That they had endeavoured formerly to satisfy his Majesty's expectations, &c. and now further say, touching the oath of allegiance, that, in August last, the court by a publick declaration expressed their resolution, God assisting, to bear faith and true allegiance to his Majesty, and to adhere to their patent the duties and privileges thereof; that many now in authority and also many of the common people had taken the oath of allegiance before they left their native country, and they had ordered that the oath in the form prescribed by the colony law should be taken by all freemen and all other householders.*

AND touching civil liberties, they observed the qualifications mentioned in his Majesty's letter,† orderly evidenced to them,‡ as appeared by their late law and practice thereupon.

AND as to ecclesiastical privileges, they had commended to the ministry and people here the word of the Lord for their rule.

To the next or tenth instruction,

That they knew of no persons attainted of high treason, who had arrived here, except Mr. Whaley and Mr. Goffe, and they before the act of parliament, and they departed this jurisdiction the February following, and a proclamation against them coming soon after by way of Barbados,

---

* The oath was in this form. "Whereas I A. B. am an inhabitant within this jurisdiction, considering how I stand obliged to the King's Majesty, his heirs and successors, by our charter and the government established thereby, do swear accordingly, by the great and dreadful name of the ever-living God, that I will bear faith and true allegiance to our sovereign Lord the King, his heirs and successors.

So help me God."

† Orthodox in religion and not vicious in their lives.
‡ By certificate from the minister.

the court sent two gentlemen, Mr. Kellond and Mr. Kirke, after them to Connecticut and New-Haven to apprehend them.

To the eleventh instruction they say,

The act for trade had been for some years observed here, that they had been misrepresented to his Majesty, the act not having in any instances that they knew of been greatly violated, and such laws as appeared to be against it were repealed, and that justice had been done in the case of Thomas Dean, as they would find upon enquiry.

To the twelfth,

For the form of their constitution they refer to their patent, the annual ordinary charges of government were about 1200 *l.* for their ecclesiastical constitution, they had none imposed by civil authority; all that was enjoined by that, was attendance on publick worship on Lord's days and other occasional days. The people who maintained, also chose their ministers, whose administrations were known, and they hoped consonant to the word of God, and if any deviated, in such case, they made use of a synod and the civil authority. The militia consisted of about four thousand foot and four hundred horse, more might be in the lists, but aged and infirm were excused. They had a fort or keep, at the entrance of Boston harbour, with five or six guns; two batteries in the harbour, and one at Charlestown. The number of their ships and vessels as follows; about eighty from 20 to 40 tons, about forty from 40 to 100 tons, and about a dozen ships above 100 tons.

THESE papers were delivered to the commissioners on the 16th of May, and on the 18th they made their reply.

THEY were sorry to find, by the court's answer to the 7th and 8th instruction, that they put more value upon their own conceptions, than the wisdom of the King in interpreting the charter. The commissioners would reduce all the discourses upon this head to one question. Do you acknowledge his Majesty's commission wherein we are nominated commissioners, to be of full force to all the purposes therein contained?

To their answer to the 9th instruction the commissioners reply,

That the court had been so far from endeavouring to give his Majesty satisfaction, by observing what he required, that they had even complained of his Majesty for enjoining them, and for the commission given to enquire whether they had observed them or not; that they professed highly to prize the King's favour, and yet in the same paper refuse to do what the King required, viz. that all who came into the colony should take the oath of allegiance, making provisoes not expressed in their charter, and so curtailing the oath. That the end of the first planters coming over, as the court expressed in their address 1660, was liberty of conscience, and yet it was denied to those for whom the King required it. That they had tentered the King's qualifications for freemen, by suffering none to be made such who were not church members, unless they paid ten shillings to a single rate, which not one church member in a hundred did pay, and, although they commend the word of the Lord to the ministry and people for their rule, yet it was with a proviso that they have the approbation of the court. The commissioners supposed, the King and his council and the church of England understood the word of God as well as the Massachusets corporation. They feared these answers would highly offend the King, and advised to an ingenuous and free consent to what he desired.

ON the 19th of May, the court, by a message to the commissioners, desired to be excused from a direct answer to the question, "whether they acknowledged his Majesty's commission," &c. and chose rather to plead his Majesty's charter, and his special charge to the commissioners not to disturb them in the enjoyment of it; they were ready to give such an account of their proceedings, as that the commissioners might be able to represent their persons and actions to his Majesty.

THE commissioners, by a message on the 20th, insisted on a direct answer to their question, and on the 22d, the court declared, that it was enough for them to give their sense of the powers granted to them by charter, and that it was beyond their line to determine the power, intent or purpose of his Majesty's commission.

ON the 23d the commissioners informed the court, that since they had been pleased to send them a more dubious answer than the former, that they might discharge their duty to his Majesty, they intended to sit to-morrow morning at the house of Capt. Thomas Breading,[1] as his Majesty's commissioners, to hear and determine the cause of Mr. Thomas Dean and others, against the governor and company and Joshua Scottow[2] merchant, defendants, and that they thought proper to give this notice, and expected that they would appear, by their attorney, to answer to the complaint. They sent at the same time a summons to Joshua Scottow. The court thereupon drew up a declaration, which they sent to the commissioners, but they not receding from their purpose, when the time appointed for

---

[1] "Breading" is a curious variation of "Breeden" or, as Hutchinson spells it on p. 184, "Breedan."

[2] Joshua Scottow, or Scottaway (d. 1698), was a merchant of Boston who had grown up with the Colony. He had been confidential agent for La Tour in his negotiations with Massachusetts in 1654–57. Apparently Dean believed that foreign goods which he would have liked to import but could not were smuggled in and found their way into the warehouse of Scottow. See Records of Massachusetts Bay, IV (Part II), 218. For his services in King Philip's War, see George Madison Bodge, Soldiers in King Philip's War, chapter XXIII.

their meeting was come, the court ordered the declaration to be published by sound of trumpet, in the following words:

WHEREAS in the debate and conference, had between this court and Col. Richard Nichols, Sir Robert Carr knight, George Cartwright and Samuel Maverick esquires, his Majesty's honourable commissioners, we have pleaded only the maintenance of his Majesty's authority, in the government of the people of this colony according to the rules and prescriptions of his charter under the great seal of England, the full and peaceable enjoyment whereof his Majesty hath given good assurance of to all his loyal subjects of this place, giving special charge to the above-named gentlemen not to disturb us therein, yet accounting it our duty to God and his Majesty, by all lawful ways and means to give full satisfaction unto his Majesty, touching all such cases and complaints against us, as in his wisdom and prudence he shall see reason to take cognizance of; we have sundry times, in our conferences both by word and writing, tendered unto the abovesaid gentlemen our readiness to present unto them a full and clear account of the grounds of our proceedings in any case, matter, or complaint that themselves shall see meet to inquire into, whereby they may be enabled to represent the matter truly to his Majesty, his Majesty's letters to this colony of April 23d 1664 expressly declaring this to be his principal end in sending hither the abovesaid gentlemen in such a capacity, and that, for such pious and good intentions as is therein more particularly declared, and not in the least to infringe our charter or any the privileges thereof.

ALL this notwithstanding, the abovesaid gentlemen, not resting satisfied with these our tenders and proposals made unto them, (wherein we have endeavoured to answer his Majesty's just expectation) contrary to the express charge of his Majesty unto them, they have, by warrant under three of their hands, given protection to John Porter junior, an high offender against God, his Majesty's authority, laws, and the peace of his good subjects here, (who breaking prison made his escape out of the hands of justice) and that before any signification to the government of this place of any complaint made against them, their sentence, or proceedings against the said Porter, and requiring all officers, as well military as civil, to be observant to them therein. And although this court have expressed their sense of this act, in conjunction with some other of their proposals, to be an infringement of our privileges granted us by his Majesty's royal charter, yet they have not withdrawn their protection of the said Porter, but have proceeded to summon, as well the governor and company of this his Majesty's colony, as also particular persons, to appear before them to answer to the complaint of Thomas Dean and others for injustice done unto them. The submission unto which proceedings of theirs being, as we apprehend, inconsistent with the maintenance of the laws and authority here, so long enjoyed and orderly established under the warrant of his Majesty's royal charter, the upholding whereof being absolutely necessary

for the peace and well being of his Majesty's good subjects here —— This
court doth therefore in his Majesty's name, and by his authority to us
committed by his royal charter, declare to all the people of this colony,
that in observance of their duty to God and to his Majesty, and to the
trust committed unto us by his Majesty's good subjects in this colony,
we cannot consent unto, or give our approbation of, the proceedings of
the abovesaid gentlemen, neither can it consist with our allegiance that
we owe to his Majesty, to countenance any who shall in so high a manner
go across to his Majesty's direct charge, or shall be their abettors or con-
sentors thereunto. God save the King.

By the court,   Edward Rawson, secr.

AFTER the publishing of this declaration, the commissioners sent
the following writing to the court.

Gentlemen,

WE thought, when we received our commission and instructions, that
the King and his council knew what was granted to you in your charter,
and what right his Majesty had to give us such commission and commands. And we thought the King, his Chancellor,* and his Secretary, had
sufficiently convinced you that this commission did not infringe your
charter. But since you will needs misconstrue all these letters and endeavours, and that you will make use of that authority, which he hath
given you, to oppose that sovereignty, which he hath over you, we shall
not lose more of our labours upon you, but refer it to his Majesty's wisdom, who is of power enough to make himself to be obeyed in all his dominions; and do assure you that we shall not represent your denying his
commission in any other words than yourselves have expressed it in your
several papers, under your secretary's hand. But for the better manifestation of the transactions between us, and for the satisfaction of all concerned in these parts, we desire that you will cause his Majesty's commission to us, his Majesty's letters of June 28th 1662, of April 23d 1664, of
February 25th 1664, by Mr. Secretary Morrice, and all those papers we
have given into the court, and your's also, may be printed and published.

Richard Nichols,   Robert Carr,
May 24, 1665.   Geo. Cartwright,   Sam. Maverick.
To the general court of his Majesty's
    colony of the Massachusets.

THE commissioners, at the same time, laid before the court proposals for amendments or alterations of the laws, to the number of
twenty six.

THE court, the same day, acquainted the commissioners that they
should be ready, by writing or conference, whenever the commissioners pleased to lay before them the grounds and reasons of their

* This refers to the Chancellor's letter.

claim and exercise of jurisdiction in the eastern country, that so his Majesty might be satisfied of the true state of the controversy; and that as his Majesty had directed his commissioners to examine into the proceedings in the case of Thomas Dean and cause justice to be done, the court had summoned the said Dean before them, at nine of the clock the next day, to make out the truth of his complaint to his Majesty, and the commissioners were desired to be present, that they might understand the grounds of the said complaint and that justice may be done.

THE commissioners replied the 26th,

that they could not have imagined that the court, after interruption of the authority committed by his Majesty to the commissioners, would have assumed to themselves the hearing of the same case wherein the governor and company are impleaded, it being unheard of and contrary to all the laws of Christendom that the same persons should be judges and parties; and declared it contrary to his Majesty's will and pleasure that the cause should be examined by any other persons than themselves.

THE commissioners broke off from any further conference, and all, except Colonel Nichols, went to New-Hampshire and the province of Main, where they appointed justices of the peace and exercised divers acts of government, and then returned to Boston. The court declared that their proceedings, at the eastward, tended to the disturbance of the public peace, and desired a conference with them concerning their doings there, but received such an answer from Sir Robert Carr, as determined them to put a stop to all further treaty. He told them, amongst other things, that the King's pardon to them, for all their deeds during the late rebellion, was conditional, and depended upon their future good behaviour, and threatened the leaders or contrivers of their measures with the punishment which so many concerned in the rebellion had met with in England.

They had no better success at Connecticut, than in the Massachusets colony. At Plimouth [1] and Rhode-Island, they met with less opposition. They sat as a court at Providence and Warwick, in the colony of Rhode-Island, and spent divers months in the colony, examining into purchases and titles of lands from the Indians, hearing the complaints of Gorton and his company against the Massachusets, enquiring into the proceedings of the executive powers of that colony, and receiving all complaints which discontented persons were ready to offer.

COL. NICHOLS, by his discreet behaviour, gained the esteem of the

[1] See Appendix, No. XVIII.

people, and afterwards, whilst he was governor of New-York, kept up a friendly correspondence with the governor and company of the Massachusets. Carr and Cartwright were men very unfit for such a trust, and by their violent proceedings rendered themselves odious. Maverick seems to have been appointed, only to increase the number and to be subservient to the others. He had lived in the colony from its beginning. He was always in opposition to the authority. Upon the restoration, he went home to complain to the King, was two or three years soliciting that commissioners might be appointed; at length, the measures against the Dutch at New-York being agreed upon, the conduct of that affair and this extraordinary power was [1] committed to the same persons. He was in the colony again in 1667 with a message from Col. Nichols, which is the last account given of him. Sir Robert Carr went first to Delaware and soon after home to England, and died at Bristol June 1st 1667, the day after he landed.* Cartwright in his passage was taken by the Dutch, stripped and very ill used. He had taken the minutes of all their proceedings, and went home the most enraged; but the enemy took all his papers from him, and he never could recover them. The principal persons in the colony were afraid of further proceedings. Capt. Gookins,[2] one of the assistants, writes to his friend in 1666, "In all probability a new cloud is gathering and a new storm preparing for us, which we expect every day."

THE government of the colony, I imagine, will not be thought culpable for refusing entirely to submit to the absolute authority of the commissioners, which must have superseded their charter; and if this authority had been once admitted, they would have found it very difficult ever after to have ejected it. Some part of their conduct may appear extraordinary; particularly their refusing to make

* Morton's Memorial.[3]

---

[1] In the third edition "were" is substituted for "was," thus making the grammatical construction correct.

[2] Daniel Gookins, or Gookin (1612–1687), came to New England by the way of Virginia. He lived in the Old Dominion from 1621 to 1644, and was so impressed with the New England ministers who preached for a while in his vicinity that he followed them to Boston when they were banished. Having settled at Cambridge, he was soon elected a deputy to the General Court, and in 1652 became an Assistant. His chief work was superintending Indian affairs. He executed it with fidelity and was the friend and protector of the friendly Indians during the dark days of King Philip's War.

In 1674 he wrote a treatise on the Indians of New England. It remained in manuscript for over a hundred years and was then published by the Massachusetts Historical Society in the first volume of its *Collections* (1792). There is a biography — privately printed in Chicago in 1912 — by Frederick William Gookin.

[3] Nathaniel Morton, *New-England's Memorial.*

the oath of allegiance necessary, unless with restrictions and limitations; and to cause all proceedings at law to be more expressly in his Majesty's name and by his authority. From some original manuscripts, which discover the sentiments of some persons of influence amongst them upon the nature of civil subjection, their conduct in this and some former instances may be pretty well accounted for.

THEY distinguished civil subjection, into necessary and voluntary. From actual residence within any government, necessarily arose subjection, or an obligation to submit to the laws and authority thereof. But birth, was no necessary cause of subjection. The subjects of any prince or state had a natural right to remove to any other state, or to another quarter of the world, unless the state was weakned and exposed by such remove, and even in that case, if they were deprived of the right of all mankind, liberty of conscience, it would justify a separation, and upon their removal, their subjection determined and ceased. The country to which they themselves had removed, was claimed and possessed by independent princes, whose right to the lordship and sovereignty thereof had been acknowledged by the Kings of England.* They therefore looked upon themselves obliged, and accordingly, as appeared by their records, actually had purchased,† for valuable considerations, not only the soil, but the dominion, the lordship, and sovereignty of those princes, and without such purchase in the sight of God and men, they had no right or title to what they possessed. The King, indeed, in imitation of other Princes of Europe who laid claim to countries meerly from the discovery of them, had granted this country to certain of his subjects, and the first planters thought it proper to purchase the title of such grantees, to prevent molestation from them or from other states, and they had also received a charter of incorporation from the King, containing a mutual compact, from whence arose a new kind of subjection, to which they were held, and from which they would never depart.

THIS was what they called voluntary civil subjection, arising meerly from compact, and from thence it followed, that whatsoever could be brought into question relative to their subjection must be determined by their charter. The compact between the King and

* Bartholomew Sharp the buccaneer was tried in England for robbery and piracy upon the Spaniards in South-America, and acquitted because he had a commission from the Indian Princes of Darien. *Det. of Scots Settlement.*

† Mr. Josias Winslow the governor of Plimouth in a letter dated May 1st 1676, says "I think I can truly say that before these present troubles broke out, the English did not possess one foot of land in this colony but what was fairly obtained by honest purchase of the Indian proprietors."

the city of London, as contained in it's charter, was not the constituting cause of subjection in the inhabitants there, because they
were resident, and from thence necessary subjection remained, but
when residence, the sole grounds of this necessary subjection, ceases,
then it becomes voluntary and depends upon compact alone. By
this compact they acknowledged they were so bound, that they were
not at liberty to subject themselves to, or to seek protection from,
any other prince, they were to pay a fifth part of all silver and gold
mines, they were to make no laws repugnant to the laws of England;
&c. but on the other hand, they were to be governed by laws made
by themselves, and by officers elected by themselves, &c. But however pleasing these principles were in speculation, or whatever foundation they may have in nature, yet they could not continue to practise upon them, nor would they bear the test when adopted by
English subjects. In a short time, as we shall see hereafter, they
were content fully to comply with the oath of allegiance without
qualifying it, and to give up other points, which they had before
insisted upon; and their posterity, who claim by birthright as well as
charter, the peculiar privileges of Englishmen, and who enjoy the
protection, are very sensible that they likewise owe the allegiance of
English subjects, which by a general rule of law is not considered as
local, but perpetual and unalienable.*

THE King's letter to New-Plimouth dated April 10, 1666, highly
approving their behaviour, may be seen in the appendix. Mr. Maverick, who had been one of the commissioners, delivered to the governor a writing of the same date, said to be copy of a letter to the
Massachusets from the King,† wherein he requires five persons to be
sent to England to answer for the conduct of the colony, and that
Mr. Bellingham and Mr. Hawthorne be two of the number. A special court was called by the governor, September 11th, to consider
of this letter, and those of the elders who were in town were desired
to be present to give their advice. A letter was agreed upon to Mr.
Secretary Morice,[1] wherein the court seem willing to doubt of the

---

* July 15, 1665, Capt. Richard Davenport commander of the castle, being fatigued
with labour, laid down upon his bed to rest, and was struck dead with lightning. Three
or four of the people were hurt, a dog was killed at the gate. There was only a wainscot
partition, between the room where the captain was killed and the magazine of powder.
Hubbard.

† Maverick delivered it to the governor, when he was sitting in a court of assistants
for the trial of causes, affirming it came under cover with a letter from the King to Sir
Robert Carr and the rest of the commissioners. *Sup. Court Records.*

---

[1] Sir William Morice (1602–1676) was one of the Secretaries of State of Charles II.

genuineness of the King's letter, and excuse themselves from sending any persons over, supposing the ablest among them could not declare their cause more fully than it had been already done.*

I WILL finish what relates to these commissioners, with a short account of a prosecution commenced by one of them against Arthur Mason [1] a constable.

THE commissioners, with other gentlemen, meeting sometimes at a public house called the Ship† tavern, the constable expected to find them there upon a Saturday evening, which would have been a breach of law, but before he came, they had adjourned to Mr. Kellond's a merchant, who lived opposite to the tavern. Another constable, who had been at the tavern before, had been beaten by them. Mason, who had more courage and zeal, went into the company with his staff, and told them he was glad to see them there, for if he had found them on the other side the street he would have carried them all away, and added, that he wondered they should be so uncivil as to beat a constable and abuse authority. Sir Robert Carr said, it was he that beat him, and that he would do it again. Mason replied, that he thought his Majesty's commissioners would not have beaten his Majesty's officers, and that it was well for them that he was not the constable who found them there, for he would have carried them before authority. Sir Robert asked, if he dare meddle with the King's commissioners? Yes, says Mason, and if the King himself had been there I would have carried him away; upon which Maverick cried out, treason! Mason, thou shalt be hanged within a twelvemonth. Sir Robert Carr spake to Sir Thomas Temple and some

* Several persons of Boston, with John Appleton [2] of Ipswich, petitioned the general court, praying them to comply with the King's order, but they were censured for intermeddling; and some of the elders inclined that the two magistrates should be sent, and thought they ought to obey for conscience sake, but Mr. Mitchel opposed it, urging that if two might be sent for ten might, that the civil magistrate was the minister of God for the good of the people, and so far as his commands tended to their good they ought to obey, but none would say it was for the good of the colony to send away their rulers. *Mr. Cobbet's letter & MS. papers.*

† The opposite corner to what is called Clark's ship-yard at the north part of the town.

[1] Arthur Mason (*d.* 1708) married Joanna Parker in 1655 and became the father of a large family.

[2] John Appleton (1622–1699) was a deputy to the General Court 1656–1665 and much of the time thereafter till 1679. Later he distinguished himself as a local leader in the opposition to Governor Andros; in consequence he was fined £50, disqualified for holding office, and required to give a thousand pound bond for good behavior for one year. See *Memorial of Samuel Appleton*, by Isaac Appleton Jewett, pp. 13–15.

others of the company, to take notice of what passed, and the next day Maverick sent a note to Mr. Bellingham the governor, charging Mason with high treason for the words spoken, and requiring the governor to secure him. The governor appointed a time for Maverick to come to his house and to oblige himself to prosecute the constable, at the next court of assistants, but Maverick, instead of appearing, thought proper only to send another note, promising to appear against the constable and charge him home, and therefore required his person should be secured. The governor thought it adviseable to cause Mason to recognize, as principal, in five hundred pounds, with two sufficient sureties in two hundred and fifty each, for his appearance; but the day before the court, Maverick sent another note to the governor, desiring to withdraw his charge, being "satisfied that although the words were rash and inconsiderate, yet there was no premeditated design in Mason to offer any injury to the King or his government." The governor returned for answer, "that the affair was of too high a nature for him to interpose in, Mason being bound over to answer." Upon his appearance, a bill was laid before the grand jury, wherein he was charged with maliciously and treasonably uttering the treasonable words mentioned. Accordingly to the liberty taken by grand juries at that day, they only found "that the words charged were spoken," and Mason being brought upon trial and the words fully proved, the court of assistants suspended judgment, and referred the cause to the next general court, where it was resolved, that although the words were rash, insolent, and highly offensive, yet, as his accusers and witnesses all cleared him from any overt act, or evil intended against the King, the court did not see cause to adjudge him a capital offender, but sentenced him to be admonished in solemn manner by the governor.* However trivial this anecdote may appear, yet there are circumstances which throw some light upon the character of the commissioners, as well as that of the governor and the judiciary and ministerial powers of the government at that time.

THE commissioners had prevailed on some of the inhabitants of the towns in New-Hampshire † to sign a petition and complaint to his Majesty of the wrongs they had sustained from the Massachusets, "who had usurped the government over them," but the inhabitants of Dover, in town meeting, and Portsmouth and Exeter, by writings under the hands of the town officers, declared their dissent, and all the towns desired to be considered as part of the Massachu-

* Sup. Court Rec.
† Portsmouth, Dover and Exeter.

sets colony, as they had been for many years before.* Three persons † were also appointed to repair to the province of Main, to settle the peace of the towns there, by bringing them to an orderly submission, which was not immediately effected.‡

I HAVE endeavoured impartially to relate the proceedings between the commissioners and the colony. On the one hand, I think it appears that the government had not sufficient excuse for not complying more fully with what the King required of them by his letter in 1662. Mr. Norton their agent, who knew the resolutions of the King and his ministers, saw the necessity of it. This would, probably, have prevented such a commission from issuing. On the other hand, it cannot be denied that the commission was a stretch of power, superseding in many respects the authority and powers granted by the charter, and there appears in the conduct of the general court, upon this occasion, not an obstinate perverse spirit, but a modest steady adherence to what they imagined, at least, to be their just rights and privileges.§ At the same time they endeavoured, not only by repeated humble addresses, and professions of loyalty, to appease his Majesty, but they purchased a ship-load of masts (the freight whereof cost them sixteen hundred pounds sterling) and presented

* The secretary was ordered to issue an attachment directed to the constables of Dover and Portsmouth to apprehend one Abraham Corbet,[1] and to bring him before the governor or magistrates at Boston, to answer for his tumultuous behaviour against the government, who fined him 20 l. and bound him to his good behaviour.

† Thomas Danforth, Eleazer Lusher, and John Leveret, Esqrs.

‡ Ferdinando Gorges, grandson to Sir Ferdinando, attempted a settlement in the province of Main under himself as Lord Proprietor, soon after the restoration. He obtained a letter from King Charles dated the 11th of January 1664, directed to the governor of the Massachusets colony, and council of New-England, requiring restitution to be forthwith made and quiet possession delivered, or otherwise, without delay, reason be shewn for the contrary. By their humble address they excused themselves from the delivery, and attempted to give reasons for their conduct, but Mr. Gorges appointed officers in several parts of the province, whose authority was of short continuance.

§ The King having recommended, by a letter Feb. 22d 1665, to the governor and council, an expedition against Canada, the court in their answer to Lord Arlington, July 17th 1666, say that "having consulted with Sir Thomas Temple, governor of Nova-Scotia, and with the governor of Connecticut (Mr. Winthrop, who had lately been in England) they concluded it was not feazable at present, as well in respect of the difficulty, if not impossibility of a land march over the rocky mountains, and howling desarts, about four hundred miles, as the strength of the French there, according to reports."

1 Abraham Corbet, or Corbett, "since the arrival of the commissioners at Boston, and probably by authority derived from them, had taken upon him to issue warrants in the king's name on several occasions, which was construed a high misdemeanor, as he had never been commissioned by the authority of the colony." Jeremy Belknap, History of New Hampshire (1784), I, 107. After being disciplined for this, he tried to organize an anti-Massachusetts party in Portsmouth and Dover, but apparently with little success. Ibid., I, 108–111.

to the King, which he graciously accepted; and the fleet in the West-Indies being in want of provisions, a subscription and contribution was recommended through the colony, for bringing in provisions to be sent to the fleet for his Majesty's service.* It appears, by the record, that several towns had liberally subscribed, and it was recommended to the rest not to fall short of what had been done by those who had gone before them, but I find no record of the whole amount. About two hundred and fifty of the inhabitants of St. Christophers, which had been taken by the French, arriving in the spring of 1666, and more being daily expected, provision was made by the court for the relief and support of such as were in necessity. Upon the news of the great fire in London, a collection was made through the colony for the relief of sufferers. The amount of it cannot be ascertained. I have a letter from Mr. Seaman and other dissenting ministers in London, to Mr. Syms [1] and Mr. Shephard [2] ministers of Charlestown, advising the receipt of 105l. sterling collected in that church. If others contributed in proportion, a large sum must have been raised.

THERE had been a press for printing at Cambridge for near twenty years. The court appointed two persons,† in October 1662, licencers of the press, and prohibited the publishing any books or papers which should not be supervised by them, and in 1668 the supervisors having allowed of the printing "Thomas a Kempis de imitatione Christi," the court interposed, "it being wrote by a popish minister, and containing some things less safe to be infused among the people," and therefore they commended to the licencers a more full revisal, and ordered the press to stop in the mean time. In a constitution less popular this would have been thought too great an abridgment of the subject's liberty.

FROM 1666 to 1670 Mr. Bellingham was annually chosen governor,

* This was so well received that a letter was sent to the general court under the King's sign manual, dated the 21st of April 1669, signifying how well taken it was by his Majesty. So the letter expresses it.

† Capt. Daniel Gookins and Mr. Jonathan Mitchell the minister of Cambridge.

---

[1] Zechariah Syms, or Symmes (1599–1672), was a graduate of Emmanuel College, Cambridge. He came to New England in 1634, in the same ship with Mrs. Anne Hutchinson, whom he found it necessary to reprove vehemently for "the corruptness and narrowness of her views." From December 1634 he was either teacher or pastor of the Charlestown church for the rest of his life. John Harvard was one of his parishioners. See Richard Frothingham, *History of Charlestown*, pp. 71–74.

[2] Thomas Shephard, or Shepard (1635–1677), was the eldest son of the Rev. Thomas Shepard of Cambridge. He graduated from Harvard in 1653, and was ordained in April 1659 as colleague of Mr. Symmes at Charlestown. His death evoked from President Urian Oakes of Harvard College "the best New England elegiac poem of the century." See Samuel Eliot Morison, *Builders of the Bay Colony*, p. 210.

and Mr. Willoughby[1] deputy governor. Nova-Scotia and the rest of Acadie, which had been rescued from the French by Cromwell, were restored by the treaty of Breda. The French made little progress in settling this country. The only inconvenience the Massachusets complained of, until after the revolution, was the encouragement given to the Indians to make their inroads upon the frontiers. Sir Thomas Temple who, with others had a grant of the country first from Cromwell, and afterwards from King Charles, thought he had reason to complain, and the King's order was repeated to him, to give up his forts to the French, some pretence being made for not complying with the first order.

AFTER forty years, the greatest part of our first emigrants had finished their pilgrimage, and were arrived at the place of their everlasting abode. Some of them lamented their being born too soon, to see New-England in its most flourishing state. This will be the case with their posterity for many generations yet to come. Mr. Wilson, the first minister of Boston church, died August 7th 1667, in the 79th year of his age. He left an amiable character, and is represented by his contemporaries, as one of the most humble, pious and benevolent men of the age. He was son of Doctor Wilson, a prebend of St. Paul's, Rochester and Windsor, and rector of Cliff, in the reign of Queen Elizabeth. He married a daughter of Lady Mansfield, and a near kinswoman of Sir William Bird. It was with much difficulty, that he persuaded her to go to New-England. After having spent one winter there without her, he returned to England to fetch her. His life has been published by Dr. Mather. I have it in manuscript by another hand. In both are related many instances to shew his prophetick spirit. We may very well remark upon those sort of prophecies, *Qui bene conjiciet, hunc vatem.* Richard Mather, a learned grave divine, and a minister of Dorchester died the 22d of April 1669, aged 73. Charles Chauncy batchelor of divinity, the venerable learned president of the college, died the 19th of February 1671, in his 80th year.* Besides these, we are not to omit Jona-

* This is the Charles Chauncy of whom Rushworth [2] in his collections for the year 1629 takes this notice, "Mr. Charles Chauncy, minister of Ware, using some expressions in his sermon, that idolatry was admitted into the church, that the preaching of the gospel would be suppressed, that there is much atheism, popery, arminianism and heresy crept into the church; and this being looked upon to raise a fear among the people that some alteration in religion would ensue, he was questioned in the high commission, and by order of that court the cause was referred to the bishop of London, being his

[1] Francis Willoughby (*d.* 1671), of Charlestown, had been a deputy now and then in the 1640's, and was elected Assistant in 1650. He came to New England from Portsmouth, England, in 1638.

[2] John Rushworth, *Historical Collections of Private Passages of State. Weighty Matters in Law. Remarkable Proceedings in Five Parliaments* (London, 1659–1701).

MASSACHUSETS-BAY 223

than Mitchell, the minister of Cambridge, who died the 9th of July 1668, in his 43d year, and is always spoken of as one of the most learned men and best preachers in his day. Mr. Davenport, who had been minister of New-Haven from the first settlement of that colony, removed to Boston about the year 1667, to the great grief of his people, and against the mind of many of the principal persons of the church in Boston, which caused them, some time after, to separate from their brethren, and to form a new society ever since known by the name of the south church.* He died of the palsie March 16th 1670, in the 73d year of his age.†

ordinary, who ordered him to make a submission in Latin." A letter which he wrote two years before to Mr. Cotton will be thought by some worthy of being preserved.

"Salutem in fonte salutis.

Good Sir,

My kindest respects and most loving salutations to yourself and your wife. The present convenience of a messenger from Ware makes me bold to trouble you with these few lines. I am now (by God's good hand) vickar of Ware, and desire your best direction how I may, with most profit and edification of my charge, proceed in the Lord's work. I have a very large parish and a dissolute town to deal with (as you may well guess) and which is worse, we have little government in the place to assist us. The people have wanted instruction for many years (such I mean as might build them up in the faith and make them wise unto salvation) besides, the places round about me are a barren wilderness, and so must undergo much opposition. I have already sustained *aliqua gravamina conscientiæ*, to go thus far in regard to the government and discipline of our church, and am likely to undergo more in the book of articles, which we are bound to read publicly and to yield our assent unto; the article concerning the ordination of bishops and ministers doth somewhat trouble me, as also the ceremonies which we are bound unto, which though I forbear myself, yet I know not how to avoid but that my curate must use if I will stand here. I pray afford your wisest advice herein. *Hæc sub sigillo.*

I shall be glad to see you at my poor vickarage, *in transitu*, and for my part (if God permit) I will not fail to see you once a year. I pray salute Mr. Johnson and Mr. Bellingham with their wives in my name, and the rest of my christian friends in your town or family, and I beseech you remember me unto the Lord in your prayers, and the Lord give a blessing to your person and labours.

Your's in the Lord with all hearty affection,

Ware, March 15, 1627. Charles Chauncy."

* Mr. Thomas Thacher[1] was the first minister of this church, and Mr. Rainsford,[2] brother to Lord Chief Justice Rainsford, was the first ruling elder.

† In 1667 the people at Cape Fear, being under distressing circumstances, a general contribution, by order of court, was made through the colony for their relief. Although

[1] Thomas Thacher (1620–1678) came to New England in 1635. Shortly after his arrival he became an intimate in the family of the Rev. Charles Chauncy, afterwards president of Harvard College. Before being called to the South Church, Thacher had been minister at Weymouth for twenty years. But lately he had resided in Boston, where he practised medicine and occasionally preached.

The name of Thacher's Island, off Cape Ann, commemorates an historic shipwreck in 1635 of which Thomas Thacher's parents were the sole survivors. See "Biographical Sketches of the Thacher Family" in *New-England Magazine*, July, 1834; also Hamilton Andrews Hill, *History of the Old South Church*, I, 122–125.

[2] Edward Rainsford. See editor's note 1 to p. 65.

MR. Gorges's claim to the province of Main, supported by the acts of the commissioners, had encouraged the people to withdraw from their subjection to the Massachusets; but the province, according to some accounts, was in the utmost confusion, and, in 1668, some of the principal persons applied to the general court of the Massachusets to reassume the jurisdiction over them. The court always thought it the part of good governors, as well as of good judges, to amplify their jurisdiction; and "from a sense of their duty to God and their King" published a declaration, requiring the inhabitants of the county of York to yield obedience to the laws of the colony, and to chuse officers, within the several towns, as they had done before the late interruption. As this proceeding was made one of the grounds of complaint against the colony, a more particular account of it may not be improper.

THE declaration of the court was of the form following.

WHEREAS this colony of the Massachusets, in observance of the trust to them committed by his Majesty's royal charter, with the full and free consent and submission of the inhabitants of the county of York, for sundry years, did exercise government over the people of that county; and whereas, about three years now past, some interruption hath been made to the peace of that place, and order there established, by the imposition of some who, pretending to serve his Majesty's interest with unjust aspersions and reflections upon this government here established by his royal charter, have unwarrantably drawn the inhabitants of that county to submission unto offices that have no royal warranty, thereby infringing the liberty of our charter, and depriving the people now settled of their just privileges; the effect whereof doth now appear to be, not only a disservice to his Majesty, but also reducing a people that were found under an orderly establishment to a confused anarchy: The premises being duly considered, this court doth judge meet, as in duty they stand bound to God and his Majesty, to declare their resolution, again to exert their power of jurisdiction over the inhabitants of the said county of York, and do hereby accordingly, in his Majesty's name, require all and every of the inhabitants there settled, to yield obedience to the laws of this colony as they have been orderly published, and to all such officers as shall be there legally established by authority of his Majesty's royal charter and the order of our commissioners, whom this court hath nominated and impowered to settle all affairs necessary for the government of the people there, and to keep a court this present summer the first Tuesday in July,

---

this was a colony subject to the proprietary government of Lord Clarendon and others, yet the foundation was laid, about the time of the restoration, by adventurers from New-England, who supposed they had a right to the soil as first occupants and purchasers from the natives, and, issuing from the Massachusets, to the same civil privileges, but they were disappointed as to both. *MS.*

at York town, as hath been formerly accustomed, and, for that end, we have commanded our secretary to issue out warrants to the inhabitants there, in their respective towns to meet to chuse jurors, both grand and petit, constables and other officers for the service of that county as the law requireth; the said warrant to be directed unto Nathanael Masterson, who is by this court appointed marshal of that court as formerly, and by him the said warrants are to be delivered to the several constables to be accordingly executed, a due observance whereof, with an orderly return to be made to the court to be held as aforesaid, is hereby required of all persons respectively concerned, as they will answer the contrary at their peril.

By the court,   Edward Rawson, secr'y.

THE commissioners appointed were Major General Leveret, Mr. Edward Tyng,* Capt. Waldron,† and Capt. Pike.‡ They made return to the general court, who gave them thanks for their good services, allowed and approved of what they had done, and ordered their proceedings to be entered upon their records as followeth.

UPON receipt of this court's commission which is recorded in the last session, we presently appointed Peter Wyer [1] clerk of the writs, and hearing Masterson,[2] appointed by the court, was imprisoned, we appointed another marshal, by warrant under our hands, but the former marshal being set at liberty the other did not act. The court being by law to be kept in York the first Tuesday of July 1668, being the 7th day of the month, we repaired to York upon Monday the 6th day. Mr. Jocelin [3] and several others, stiled justices of the peace, coming nigh to the ordinary where we were before the door, after salutes passed, they told us they desired to speak with us in the morning. To their desires we complied and gave them a meeting, where we acquainted them we were ready to hear what they had to say, but not as sent to treat with them about what we had to do by virtue of the general court's commission. They acquainted us that they had lately received, in a pacquet from Col. Nichols, his letter to the governor and magistrates of the Massachusets colony, which they desired

* Edward Tyng was afterwards an assistant.
† Richard Waldron was speaker of the deputies and represented Dover.
‡ Robert Pike was of Salisbury. He was afterwards one of the council named in the province charter.

---

[1] Peter Wyer, or Weare, had been a resident of York since 1640.

[2] Nathaniel Masterson of York, formerly of Salem and Boston, had been imprisoned by the royal Commissioners because he stood up for the right of Massachusetts to govern the inhabitants of Maine.

[3] Henry Jocelin, or Josselyn (d. 1683), had been appointed a justice of the peace by the royal Commissioners. He was a faithful lieutenant of the Gorges family and became the most important man in Maine. Originally (1634) he was in the employ of John Mason at Piscataqua. See New England Historical and Genealogical Register, II, 204–206; and XI, 31–34.

us to read, and first their commission, the which we read, and having read
them, we told them that those concerned the general court and had been
under their consideration, all but the letter from Col. Nichols, and that
they had sent their declaration into the county, so that we had nothing to
say, only that we did not understand that the commissioners had power
to make any such temporary settlement, his Majesty having before him
the case, for that the Massachusets had, in obedience, sent their reasons
why they did not deliver up the government of that country to Mr.
Gorges, which was according to his Majesty's command. Then Mr.
Jocelin told us there was not above five or six of a town for us; to which
we replied, we should see by the returns made to the court's warrants or
appearances, and further told them we must attend to our commission,
in prosecution whereof we should attend to his Majesty's and the country's service, not our own, and if we met with opposition we should advice
what to do. Many other things passed, but with mutual respect. They
said they must attend their commission. We parted and repaired to the
meeting-house, and there opened the court by reading our commission
publicly and declaring to the people wherefore we came, whereto there
was great silence and attention. Then, by the marshal, we called for the
town returns to be brought in for the election of associates,* and returns
were made from five towns, the other two being hindred (as they said) by
the justices, yet, in one of them, above half the electors sent in their votes.
Whilst the court was busy in opening, sorting and telling the votes, the
justices came, and without doors, by some instrument, made proclamation that all should attend to hear his Majesty's commands; upon which
orders were given to the marshal, and accordingly he made proclamation,
that if any had any command from his Majesty, they coming and shewing
it to the court, the court was open and ready to hear the same. Thereupon
these gentlemen came in, and manifested their desire, that what they had
shewn to us in private might be read in court to the people; to whom we
replied, that the court was in the midst of their business in opening the
returns of the county from the several towns of election, and so soon as
that was over, and after dinner, they should have their desire granted; so
they left us, and we proceeded to see who were chosen associates, had the
returns of the jurymen and their names entred, both the grand jury and
that of trials, also of the constables, but did not swear any one, but adjourned the court and went to dinner; in which time we heard that the
gentlemen were going to the meeting-house to sit as an assembly, they
having before issued out their warrants for the towns to send their deputies, whereupon we sent to speak with them after dinner. They returned
they would, provided we would not proceed any further till we spake with
them. We sent them word we did engage it. They sent us word they
would meet with us at the meeting-house, and presently after their mar-

* The associates seem to be intended in the room of magistrates, and being joined
with persons appointed by the general court had the same power as the court of magistrates or assistants had in the colony.

shal and Nathaniel Phillips[1] went up and down, and at all public places published a paper or writing, whom meeting upon their return, it was demanded what, and upon what authority, they had published to the people to make a disturbance, they answered, they published what they had in the King's name; they were demanded to shew their order or authority; they answered, that was for their security; so refusing to shew it they were committed to the marshal. Then we went to court, where we found the house full and the gentlemen to have taken up our seats, so room being made, we went up to them and told them we expected other things than that they would have put such an affront upon the court, nor should motions hinder us from prosecuting our commission; we could keep the court elsewhere. Some of the people began to speak, but we commanded silence, and the officer was commanded by us to clear the court, whereupon Mr. Jocelin spoke to some nigh him to depart; so they coming from their seat we came to private discourse, and they insisted to have their commission and the King's mandamus of 1666 to be read; we told them we would perform what we had promised when the court was set, so we repaired to our seat, and they being set by us desired that their commission might be read, which was done, and the grounds of it expressed to be from the people's petitioning, who were told that they could best give answer thereto, but said nothing; then that part of the mandamus of 1666, which they desired might be read, was read. After which they desired that Colonel Nichols's letter to the governor and magistrates of the Massachusets might be read, but, that not being concernment to them there, save only for information of the justices of what had passed from him to the governor and magistrates to whom it was directed, it was refused; some short account being publicly given, that that which had been read, for the matter, having been before under the consideration of the general court, they had the declaration of their intendments, in prosecution whereof we were commissionated to keep court and settle the country, which work we had begun, and, God willing, would prosecute, to perform the trust committed to us, and have declared to the people that we were not insensible how that, at the time of the interruption of the government, in the year 1665, by such of the gentlemen of the King's commissioners as were then upon the place, they had manifested their displeasure, by telling the people that the Massachusets were traitors, rebels, and disobedient to his Majesty, the reward whereof, within one year, they said, should be retributed, yet we told them, that, through the good hand of God and the King's favour, the Massachusets were an authority to assert their right of government there, by virtue of the royal charter derived to them from his Majesty's royal predecessors, and that we did not doubt but that the Massachusets colony's actings for the forwarding his Majesty's service, would outspeak

---

[1] Nathaniel Phillips was a son of William Phillips (d. 1683), a distinguished man in Maine who had moved from Boston to Saco in 1660. The Phillipses were convinced of the rightfulness of Gorges's claim and were in high favor with the royal Commissioners in 1665. William Durkee Williamson, *History of the State of Maine*, I, 688.

other [1] words, where there was nothing but words for themselves or against us. Which done, the gentlemen left us, and we proceeded to the work of the court, to impannel the grand jury, gave them their oaths and charge, and then, the associates present, we called to take their oaths, one of them, viz. Mr. Roger Plaisted,[2] expressed publicly that he was sent by the town he lived in, accordingly he had applied himself to the major-general more privately, to know how we reassumed the government, and how they were to submit to it, which he now mentioned in public that he might render himself faithful to them that sent him; to which he was answered in public as he had been in private, that we reassumed the government by virtue of the charter, and that they were to have the like privileges with ourselves in the other counties. We had also from Scarborough a paper presented, which we herewith present to the court. Then having sworn the constables present, impannelled the jury for trials, sworn them, and committed what actions were entred and prosecuted to them, in which time the gentlemen sent to desire that at our leisure time they might speak with us; they were sent for and presented us with a paper. After we had received it, we attended to settle the business of the military officers and trained bands, and commissionated for York, Job Alcock lieutenant, Arthur Bragdon ensign; for Wells, John Littlefield lieutenant, Francis Littlefield jun. ensign; for Scarborough, Andrew Augur lieutenant; for Falmouth, George Ingerfield lieutenant; for Kittery, Charles Frost captain, Roger Plaisted lieutenant, John Gaffingsley ensign; for Saco, Bryan Pendleton major; and he to settle Black-point. Mr. Knight of Wells, the morning before we came away, being Thursday the 9th of July, came and took his oath in court to serve as an associate. The court made an order for a county court to be held the 15th of September there at York, and for that end continued the commission to Capt. Waldron, Capt. Pike, and others, for the better strengthening the authority upon the place, as by their commission may appear. The associates that are now in place are Major Pendleton, Mr. Francis Cotterell, Mr. Knight of Wells, Mr. Raynes of York, Mr. Roger Plaisted of Kittery. Which is humbly submitted to the honourable general court as the return of

	Your servants	John Leveret
The 23d of October 1668.		Edward Tyng
		Richard Waldron.

THIS proceeding of the Massachusets was reported and published by Jocelyn * in a more unfavourable light, and as an act of greater

* "The province of Main or the country of the Troquois (Iroquois) heretofore called Laconia or New Somersetshire, is a colony belonging to the grandson of Sir Ferdinando

[1] The first edition gives "others words"; the third "others' words."

[2] Roger Plaisted (d. 1675), of Kittery, had been a representative in the General Court in 1663 and 1664, and was to serve again in 1673. He was killed by the Indians in 1675. His brother John became Chief Justice of New Hampshire in 1716.

force and violence. Indeed, he does not pretend that there was any opposition made by the inhabitants, but only by the particular persons appointed by the commissioners to govern there, and it always appeared to be the desire of a great part of the people to live under the government of the Massachusets.

THE people of New-Hampshire had continued in a quiet and orderly state ever since the year 1641. There was no person who had any pretence to the powers of government, Mason having only a grant of the soil from the council of Plimouth. Sir Ferdinando Gorges received a royal charter [for the province of Main], granting the same royalties, privileges and franchises as are of right or ought to be enjoyed by the bishop of Durham, in the county palatine of Durham, with power to constitute a deputy governor, a chancellor, a treasurer, a marshal, a judge of admiralty, officers of admiralty for ordering maritime affairs, master of ordnance, a secretary, &c. and by repeatedly nominating some such officers and attempting to establish a form of government consisting of different persons from those appointed by the Massachusets, there were always two different parties and interests kept alive in that province, but New-Hampshire had been so long united to the Massachusets that the people of both colonies were of one heart and mind in civil and religious affairs. The town of Portsmouth shewed an instance of their great regard to the public interest, and in 1669 made a collection, as it is termed in the instrument presented to the general court, more

---

Gorges of Ashton Phillips in the county of Somerset. The said Sir Ferdinando Gorges did expend in planting several parts of New-England above twenty thousand pounds sterling, and when he was between three and fourscore years of age, did personally engage in our royal master's service, and particularly in the siege of Bristol, and was plundered and imprisoned several times, by reason whereof he was discountenanced by the pretended commissioners for foreign plantations, and his province encroached upon by the Massachusets colony who assumed the government thereof. His Majesty, that now reigneth, sent over his commissioners to reduce them within their bounds, and to put Mr. Gorges again into possession. But there falling out a contest about it, the commissioners settled it in the King's name (until the business should be determined before his Majesty) and gave commissions to the judge of their courts, and the justices to govern and act according to the laws of England, and by such laws of their own as were not repugnant to them. But, as soon as the commissioners were returned for England, the Massachusets enter the province in a hostile manner with a troop of horse and foot, and turned the judge and his assistants off the bench, imprisoned the major or commander of the militia, threatned the judges and some others that were faithful to Mr. Gorges interests. I could discover many other foul proceedings, but, for some reasons which might be given, I conceive it not convenient to make report thereof to vulgar ears," &c. *Josselyn's voyage to New-England, p. 199.*

This Mr. Josselyn I take to be brother to the justice of peace mentioned in the report of the Massachusets commissioners. He writes with acrimony, and in this account, as well as several other parts of his voyages to New-England, discovers a strong prejudice against the people of the colony.

probably a subscription, of sixty pounds per annum for the term of seven years, for the use of Harvard college, to be paid into the hands of the overseers, and they say they hoped to make it more.*

THE colony, about this time, made a greater figure than it ever did at any other time. The report made by the commissioners to the King had produced no further troubles from England. The plague, the fire of London, the discontents among the people of England, caused by their jealousies of a design to subvert the constitution there, may well enough be supposed to have been the cause of a respite in favour of the people here. The Massachusets governed, without opposition, the province of New-Hampshire and province of Main, and were beginning settlements even further eastward. The French were removed from their neighbourhood on the one side, and the Dutch and Swedes on the other. Their trade was as extensive as they could wish. No custom-house was established. The acts of parliament of the 12th and 15th of King Charles the second, for regulating the plantation trade, were in force, but the governor, whose business it was to carry them into execution, was annually to be elected by the people, whose interest it was that they should not be observed. Some of the magistrates and principal merchants grew very rich,† and a spirit of industry and œconomy prevailed through the colony. But a change of affairs came on soon after.

MR. Bellingham continued governor in 1671 and 1672.‡ Mr. Leveret was chosen deputy governor both those years, and in 1673, he succeeded Mr. Bellingham in the place of governor, when Mr. Samuel Symonds was chosen deputy governor.

THE strict union, which had been from the beginning, between the civil and ecclesiastical parts of the constitution, was about this time

---

* Boniface Burton, aged 113 years, died the 13th June 1669. *Almanack for* 1673.

April 4th 1671, Mr. Willoughby the deputy governor died. He was a great opposer of the persecutions against the Baptists. Elder Penn died the 30th of September the same year. He was a leading man in church and town affairs. He is the same person who was chosen beadle in 1630.

† Josselyn, p. 180.

‡ Mr. Bellingham died December 7th, 1672. He lived to be the only surviving patentee named in the charter. It is always mentioned as a part of his character, that he hated a bribe. He was bred a lawyer, but, like some much greater lawyers, made his last will and testament in such a manner, that after some years dispute, the general court thought it necessary to supply the defects of it, by making a disposition of his estate themselves. Mr. Leveret was among the junior assistants, but he had been long employed in public affairs and places of great trust. Oliver Cromwell had made him one of his commissioners in 1654, for the reduction of the Manhadoes. He was in England at the restoration, and appeared an advocate for the colony. Upon his return to New-England, soon after, he was chosen a member for Boston. In 1664 was chosen major-general, and in 1665 an assistant.

in danger of being broke, or greatly weakned. After Mr. Wilson's death, the first church in Boston invited Mr. Davenport, the minister of New-Haven, to succeed him. He was then about 70, had gone into the wilderness with persons closely attached to him, and remained with them about 30 years, and they were extremely averse to his leaving them; and besides, he was at the head of a party more strict and rigid than the body of the people of the country, for he had always opposed the admitting to baptism the children of any who were not in full communion with one or other of the churches.* It is not strange that there should have been a party of Boston church which opposed his settlement. The two parties in this church, the first in rank (although the church of Salem was the oldest) in the country, produced two parties, not in the other churches only, but in the state also. A considerable part of the church, both for number and estate, formed themselves, as has been observed, into a separate society. Seventeen ministers † bore a public testimony against the proceedings of the three elders ‡ of the first church in Boston, viz. against Mr. Davenport for leaving his church at New-Haven, contrary to his professed principles, and against all of them for communicating parcels only of letters from the church of New-Haven to the church in Boston, by which artifice the church was deceived, and made to believe the church of New-Haven consented to his dismission, when if the whole had been read, it would have appeared they did not. This testimony was sent to the elders the day before a public fast. An answer was given, in which the elders deny, that the letters concealed would have been evidence of the refusal of the church of New-Haven to consent to Mr. Davenport's leaving them and settling at Boston; the church was only unwilling to make his dismission their immediate act. Neither the church of New-Haven, nor the elders of the church of Boston can be wholly justified. There does not seem to have been that fairness and simplicity in their proceedings which the gospel requires. The first church refused the invitation of the new society to join with other churches in ordaining their officers, &c. The ministers and members of churches in the colony were engaged, some on one side and some on the other,

* [The church in Boston adhered to this principle of Mr. Davenport their minister, and for many years after, admitted no children to Baptism whose parents were not in full communion.]

† John Allin, John Higginson, John Ward, John Wilson, Edmund Browne, Samuel Whiting senior, Thomas Cobbet, John Sherman, Samuel Phillips, Thomas Shepard, Increase Mather, Samuel Torrey, Zechary Symmes, John Brocke, Edward Bulkley, Samuel Whiting junior, John Hale.

‡ Mr. John Davenport, Mr. James Allen, and the ruling elder James Penn.

and the contentions were sharp; * at length the house of deputies espoused the cause of the first church, and having at their session in May 1670 appointed a committee to enquire into the prevailing evils which had procured or been the cause of the displeasure of God against the land, they reported among other causes, these that follow, viz.

Declension from the primitive foundation work, innovation in doctrine and worship, opinion and practice, an invasion of the rights, liberties and privileges of churches, an usurpation of a lordly and prelatical power over God's heritage, a subversion of gospel order, and all this with a dangerous tendency to the utter devastation of these churches, turning the pleasant gardens of Christ into a wilderness, and the inevitable and total extirpation of the principles and pillars of the congregational way; these are the leaven, the corrupting gangrene, the infecting spreading plague, the provoking image of jealousy set up before the Lord, the accursed thing which hath provoked divine wrath, and doth further threaten destruction.

They then take notice of the late transaction of churches and elders in constituting the third church in Boston, as irregular, illegal, and disorderly.†

SEVERAL of the ministers, at the next session of the general court, presented a petition or address, acknowledging the great goodness of God in favouring the land for so long a time with a godly and able magistracy, and desiring, that it might also be remembered that the people were led forth into this wilderness not only "by the hands of Moses, but also of Aaron, viz. that reverend ministry which had transported the ark of the covenant, the presence of God in his

---

* Before this, viz. in July 1669, a council had been called by Mr. Bellingham the governor, fearing, as he says in the order, "a sudden tumult, some persons attempting to set up an edifice for public worship, which was apprehended by authority to be detrimental to the public peace." Mr. Bellingham, it is evident, was warmly engaged against the seceders, but the council thought it best not to interpose, and if any person had offended against the laws they advised to proceed against them in a due course of law. They judged it meet to declare, "that it was the duty of those who were about to erect a new meeting-house to observe the laws and orders of the general court for regulating prudential affairs, &c. and if they did not, they should have no countenance of authority in their proceedings."

† Mr. Flint,[1] the minister of Dorchester, in his diary, whilst this court was sitting, has this observation: "A spirit of division, persecuting and oppressing God's ministers and precious saints, is the sin which is unseen and none bears witness against. It is a great sin and threatens a sword of divine wrath. God's seers fear it, and their bowels and compassions are moved at it."

---

[1] Josiah Flint, or Flynt (1645–1680), was the father of Henry Flynt (H. C. 1693), who was a fellow of Harvard College for sixty years and a tutor for fifty-five years. See John Langdon Sibley's *Biographical Sketches of Graduates of Harvard University*, II, 150.

ordinances, settled in gospel order." This being premised, they solemnly professed that they still adhered to the safe and sober principles of the congregational way, in opposition to separation, morellian or anarchical confusion and licentious toleration. This profession they made, to vindicate their integrity and innocency from the unjust charge of innovation and loud cry of apostacy laid upon the generality of the ministry, heightened by the reports of the committee chosen by the house of deputies in their last session, and the votes of the major part of the house. They go on and say, that

this charge evidently appears to be the transports of a party, by instancing the business of the third church, and so designing to hinder the consummation of that work of God, in the peaceable settlement thereof in actual and full communion with other churches, and by misrepresenting that weighty and worthy transaction, before inquiry had been made into the state of the case. These things were matters of great grievance, inasmuch as an antiministerial spirit had thereby been strengthened and emboldened, the hearts and hands of those who laboured in the ministry weakened, the spirits of many being filled with groundless jealousies and suspicions against the ministrations of the elders. They made this humble representation in hopes of redress, either by being called upon publicly to vindicate themselves, or by the court's moving for a general convention of churches by their elders and messengers, for the decision of questions and accommodation of differences, or by such other means and measures as to the wisdom of the court should seem meet.*

[Separations, and divisions, in churches and religious societies, are liable to subdivisions *ad infinitum*, and it argues the perverseness of human nature, that the fiercest disputes, and the strongest alienations, are often caused by a difference of sentiment upon a single, and perhaps an immaterial, tenet only; and, if the separatist renounces the tenet, he oftener joins to a Society from which he has differed in many other and more material points than to that from which he separated. Thus, in New England, a Baptist who separated from the Congregational churches on the point of Infant Baptism only, if he renounces the tenet, generally goes over to the Episcopal church, rather than to the Congregational from which he had separated.]

THE court took this address into their immediate consideration, and having first asserted their own authority, and that the acts of

---

* Signed by John Allin, Thomas Cobbet, William Hubbard, Samuel Whiting, Samuel Whiting junior, John Sherman, Samuel Phillips, Samuel Torrey, John Ward, John Higginson, Thomas Shepard, Antipas Newman, Edmund Browne, Thomas Thacher, Seaborn Cotton.

the court were not liable to question by any, and that free debates were the indubitable right of the court, they then acknowledged, that in an hour of temptation such acts may pass in one court, as may, according to principles of religion, prudence and state interest, be reviewed, and upon mature deliberation be rectified in another; and in the case then under consideration, the court thought it their duty to declare, that several expressions in the votes referred to in the petition appeared exceptionable; and, that the court might remove all just grounds of grievance in the hearts of the reverend elders, and that their ministry might not be made ineffectual by that antiministerial spirit that too much ran through the country, it was ordered, that all papers referring to the case should be accounted useless, and not be improved against the reverend elders, as having been the cause of God's displeasure against the country; and whereas many had taken upon them to publish the secrets of the court in that case, the court further declared, that they knew no just cause of those scandalizing reflections indefinitely cast upon magistrates, elders and churches, either in reference to the new church in Boston or otherwise, and therefore, until they were further informed, they judged them to be innocent, calumniated and misrepresented. The court then profess, that they will adhere to the primitive ends of their coming over, and retain the sober principles of the congregational way and the practice of their churches, "in their purest and most athletick constitution." *

I HAVE been more particular in relating this transaction, because it gives us a pretty good idea of the connection between the civil and ecclesiastical power, the churches, notwithstanding their claim to independency, being liable to controul as oft as their proceedings were disapproved by the civil magistrate, and on the other hand, the magistrates, who were annually elected, being sometimes liable to be displaced by the influence of the clergy in elections, when their proceedings were supposed to bear hard upon the liberties of the churches, for the clergy still retained a great proportion of the weight they had at the beginning. Indeed parishes were multiplied in the colony, many of them small, and in new settlements. The stipends to the ministers were lessened, and, soon after this time, some of them complained, as many curates do in England, "that they prophecied in sackcloth." Notwithstanding this, as long as the charter

---

* This change of sentiments in the court was owing to the change of persons in the house of deputies, there being of fifty members, the number of the house this year, twenty only who were of the house the year before; and this is an evidence of the whole colony's being engaged in this dispute.

continued, their influence in the affairs of government continued, as we shall have further occasion to observe.

THE war with the Indians, commonly called Philip's war, endangered the very being of the colony, and it was a question with some, whether the Indians would not prevail to a total extirpation of the English inhabitants. At the first arrival of the English the Indians were treated with kindness, to obtain their friendship and favour; but they having no acquaintance with fire-arms, the English grew by degrees less apprehensive of danger, finding by means of corslets or armour, that they were not much exposed to danger from bows and arrows of so simple construction as those of the Indians. The quarrels which the Indians had always been engaged in amongst themselves were a further security to the English, who on the one hand endeavoured to restrain them from an open war with one another, and on the other to keep up so much contention as to prevent a combination, and to make an appeal to the English, as umpires, necessary from time to time. The English, before their arrival, had such ideas of the sachems, that at the first meetings respect was shewn them, in some proportion to what would have been required by the Prince of a petty state in Europe; but the base sordid minds of the best of them, and the little authority they had over their own subjects, soon rendered them contemptible. At New-Plimouth, the governor in the first treaty with Massasoiet, in 1620, acquainted him that King James considered him as his good friend and ally. This was too great an honour for Massasoiet, he was content to acknowledge the King to be his sovereign. The next year, the governor caused the petty sachems to sign an instrument, in which they owned themselves to be subject to King James.* Subjects [and sovereigns] were words of which they had no precise ideas. For near forty † years together, they were under no great concern, or of no long continuance, in that colony, from the neighbouring Indians, Massasoiet

---

* "Sept. 13. A. D. 1621. Know all men by these presents, that we whose names are underwritten, do acknowledge ourselves to be the loyal subjects of King James, King of Great Britain, France and Ireland, defender of the faith, &c. In witness whereof, and as a testimonial of the same, we have subscribed our names or marks as followeth,

Ohquamehud	Nattawahunt	Quadaquina
Conwacomet	Caunbatant	Huttamoiden
Obbatinnua	Chickatawbut	Apannow."

† Alexander eldest son of Massasoiet, soon after his father's death, about 1656, was suspected of plotting with the Naragansets against the English. Mr. Josias Winslow with eight or ten stout men armed, took him by surprize at a hunting house about six miles distant from the English towns, and carried him to the governor. This raised his indignation to that degree as to bring a fever upon him which put an end to his life and plots together. Philip his brother a young lad succeeded him. *MS.*

or Ousamequin always courting the friendship of the English. After his death * and the death of his eldest son Wamsutta or Alexander, Metacom or Philip † his second son, a man of great spirit, by his behaviour raised suspicions of a design against the English, but, appearing before the court in Plimouth in 1662, he expressed his desire to continue in friendship, and promised, that he and his successors would always remain faithful subjects to the Kings of England, and that he would never alienate his lands, and never make war with any other Indians without the privity and allowance of the government of New-Plimouth.‡ The Indians within the Massachusets bounds, were not under one general sachem, but divided into smaller cantons. These, one after another, were brought to acknowledge their subjection to the Massachusets government, particularly in 1643, when danger was apprehended from the Naragansets, five sachems subjected themselves by the same instrument.§ Besides rules and orders which they were encouraged to make for their own government, for any offence against the English they were punished by the English laws, and so likewise for any capital or heinous offence among themselves. The case of a squaw convicted of adultery was referred to

* Massasoiet just before his death when he was treating for the sale of some of his lands at Swansey, insisted upon it as a condition that the English should never attempt to draw off any of his people from their religion to christianity, and would not recede until he found the treaty would break off if he urged it any further. *Hubbard.*

† In 1662, when Massasoiet's two sons were at Plimouth, the governor gave them their English names. The Indians in general were fond of having names given to them. Their father never took an English name. Philip was charged by the English with being not only haughty but perfidious and impious. They charged him with pride and ambition, in aspiring to the sovereignty of a country which he would have enjoyed as his inheritance if they had not prevented; with perfidy in breaking promises made whilst under restraint and in the power of those to whom they were made; and with impiety in refusing to receive his religion from his enemies.

‡ However it may be questioned whether this was a reasonable requisition, some of the terms ¹ of it were plain and well understood.

§ We have and by these presents do, voluntarily and without any constraint or persuasion, but of our own free motion, put ourselves, our subjects, lands, and estates under the government and jurisdiction of the Massachusets, to be governed and protected by them according to their just laws and orders so far as we shall be made capable of understanding them; and we do promise for ourselves and all our subjects and all our posterity, to be true and faithful to the said government and aiding to the maintenance thereof to our best ability, and from time to time to give speedy notice of any conspiracy, attempt or evil intention of any, of which we shall know or hear of against the same, and we do promise to be willing, from time to time, to be instructed in the knowledge and worship of God. In witness whereof we have hereunto put our hands the 8th of the first month 1643–4.

Cutchamacke   Nashowanon   Wossamegon.
Maskanomet   Squaw Sachem

¹ The first edition gives "the terms" instead of "some of the terms."

the elders, for advice whether she should die or not. They were merciful to her, and she escaped with a smart whipping. Notwithstanding the laws to restrain all persons from selling guns or ammunition to the Indians, they were generally furnished with both, and were become good marksmen.

IN 1670 the Pokanoket or Philip's Indians were again suspected by their frequent assembling together, by fixing up their guns, grinding their hatchets, and other preparations, and by insults offered to the English in different places, to be meditating a general war. The government of Plimouth, in March, sent messengers to them to inquire into the reason of this behaviour, and at the same time wrote to the Massachusets, acquainting them therewith. The governor and magistrates, always averse to an open breach, immediately dispatched their own messengers * to Taunton, to prevent a war if possible, which Plimouth had intimated that they should be obliged to begin, if they could not otherwise bring the Indians to reason. They met at Taunton, the 13th of April, where the governor † and two other of Plimouth gentlemen ‡ met with them, and whilst they were in conference and examining witnesses concerning the behaviour of the Indians, the governor received a message from Philip, signifying that he was at three mile river, and that he desired the governor to come up thither to speak with him. The governor returned answer § that he was at Taunton ready for a treaty, and expected Philip to come to him, promising security. Philip refused to move, until two of the governor's messengers ‖ offered to remain as hostages, and then he declined coming into the town, and resolved to go on as far as the mill, with all his men in arms, desiring the governor to come to him there. This return was made to the governor, with further intelligence that Philip was on the march with all his men in arms, and soon after he appeared at the mill, placing centinels round a hill near to it, but sent no message into the town. Some within the town were for attacking him, but the Massachusets commissioners were afraid of the event and would not consent to it. All agreed, that the governor should not condescend to go out to him. At length the Massachusets commissioners offered to go out and try to persuade him to come in. At first he was unwilling, and his counsellors declared he should not go, but finally he consented, provided his men might go with him, they to be on one side of the meeting-

---

* William Davis, William Hudson, and Thomas Brattle.
† Mr. Prince.
‡ Mr. Josias Winslow, and Constant Southworth.
§ By old Roger Williams and some others.
‖ Mr. Williams and Mr. Brown.

house, and the English on the other. Philip denied that he had any further purpose in bringing his men together and arming them, than to defend himself from any attacks which might be made by the Naraganset Indians, some of whom had been engaged in quarrels with some of his people; but, upon enquiry, it appeared, that he was on better terms with the Naragansets than ever before, and plentiful evidence being produced of his preparations both of ammunition and provisions, and of parties of his men being destined for the attack of Taunton, Seaconk, and other places, he was confounded and made a full confession. Such improvement was made of it by the commissioners that they required of him satisfaction for past damages and security against future injuries. The first was not long insisted on, but with respect to the latter, he was prevailed on to deliver up what English arms he then had with him, being about 70 guns, and to promise to send in the remainder in a few days. A writing was also drawn up, which he consented to sign, acknowledging his past breach of faith, and promising future fidelity.*

THE loss of so many guns must have been grievous to Philip, at a time when he only waited a good opportunity of falling upon the English. His submitting to the acknowledgment in writing was of no consequence. The Indians, in general, will promise any thing required of them to remove an impending danger, or to procure an immediate benefit, and they regard such promises not a minute longer than it is for their advantage to do it. When Philip was at liberty he thought no more of his engagements, the guns were not brought in, and he himself refused to come to Plimouth, when required. Many strange Indians resorted to him. On the 23d of August Mr. Morton,

---

* "Taunton, 12th April 1671. Whereas my father, my brother, and myself, have formerly submitted ourselves, our country, and our people unto the King's Majesty of England and colony of New Plimouth, by solemn covenant under our hands, but I having of late, through my indiscretion and the naughtiness of my heart, violated and broken this my covenant with my friends, by taking up arms with evil intent against them, and that groundlessly, and being now deeply sensible of my unfaithfulness and folly, desire at this time solemnly to renew my covenant with my ancient friends and my father's friends above-mentioned, and do desire this may testify to the world against me, if ever I shall again fail in my faithfulness towards them (that I have now and at all times found so kind to me) or any other of the English colonies. And as a real pledge of my true intention, for the future to be faithful and friendly, I do freely engage to resign up to the government of New-Plimouth all my English arms, to be kept by them for their security, so long as they shall see reason. For the true performance of the premises I have hereunto set my hand, together with the rest of my council.

In the presence of   The mark of Philip chief sachem P
  Wm. Davis   The mark of Tacasoe V
  Wm. Hudson   The mark of Capt. Wispash T
  Tho. Brattle.   The mark of Woukaponkanet T
                                                  The mark of Nimrod L.

secretary, in the name of the court of Plimouth, wrote to the Massachusets governor, to be communicated to the council, acquainting him that they had summoned Philip to appear on the 13th of September, that, if he did not do it, they had determined, on the 20th to send out forces to reduce him to reason, unless better reason should seasonably appear to them, by the Massachusets advice, to prevent it; that it was a common cause, and they should well accept of assistance; but it was plainly intimated, that if aid should be refused they would engage alone. Philip happened to come to Boston, with his counsellors, the same day the letter was received, and represented his case so favourably to the governor and council, that, in their answer to Plimouth, they urged that government to refer the difference between Philip and them to commissioners from the Massachusets and Connecticut.* Plimouth declined this proposal, and insisted on Philip's appearance at the time proposed,† but finally the Massachusets declaring that there did not appear sufficient grounds for commencing hostilities, Plimouth consented to give Philip fur-

* At this time there was a breach in the union between the colonies from some misunderstandings, but the next year 1672 it was healed, and some alterations made in the articles.

† The nature of Philip's subjection to the government of Plimouth was enquired into, upon this occasion, by the Massachusets. They say in their letter of the 8th of September, "We do not understand how far he hath subjected himself to you, but the treatment you have given him and proceedings towards him do not render him such a subject, as that, if there be not a present answering to summons, there should presently be a proceeding to hostilities; and the sword once drawn and dipped in blood may make him as independent upon you, as you are upon him." Notwithstanding, that in the treaties from time to time, the Indians have acknowledged themselves subjects to the Kings of England, yet they still retained, in their idea of subjection, a degree of independency which English subjects have no pretence to. The Six Nations go no farther than to call the great King their father. They never call themselves subjects. When Philip was at Boston, in 1671, and the letters, which had been received from Plimouth, were read to him, he expressed himself before the governor and council as follows: "That his predecessors had been friendly with Plimouth governors, and an engagement of that nature was made by his father and renewed by his brother, and (when he took the government) by himself, but they were only agreements, for amity and not for subjection any further, as he apprehends; he desired to see a copy of the engagement they speak of, and that the governor of the Massachusets would procure it for him. He knew not that they were subjects. Praying Indians were subjects to Massachusets and had officers and magistrates appointed, they had no such thing with them, and therefore were not subject." (*Massachusets files.*) In the several treaties between the Massachusets and the Eastern Indians, from Sir William Phips's treaty in 1693 down to the last treaty of peace in 1749, the Indians have always acknowledged subjection to the crown of England; notwithstanding such agreements, they have remained as independent of the Massachusets government as they were before any treaty was made with them. When they call the King their Sovereign, perhaps they have no other idea than the Six Nations have when they call him Father. It is indeed at this day of no other importance than a matter of meer speculation, the eastern Indians, the subject of these treaties, if the remains of all their tribes were collected into one, not deserving the name of a nation, and in a few years more they will be extinct.

ther time until the 26th, promised him safe conduct, and desired commissioners from Massachusets and Connecticut to be present and give advice. Whilst Philip was at Boston he engaged that he would not enter into a quarrel with Plimouth, until he had first addressed himself to the Massachusets for advice and approbation.

THE mediators met at Plimouth, and matters seemed to be accommodated; Philip signed to such articles as it was thought reasonable he should do, which were as follows:

WE Philip and my council, and my subjects, do acknowledge ourselves subject to his Majesty the King of England and the government of New-Plimouth, and to their laws.

2dly. I am willing, and do promise, to pay unto the government of Plimouth one hundred pounds in such things as I have, but I would intreat the favour that I might have three years to pay it in, forasmuch as I cannot do it at present.

3dly. I do promise to send unto the governor, or whom he shall appoint, five wolves heads, if I can get them, or as many as I can procure, until they come to five wolves yearly.

4thly. If any difference fall between the English and myself and people, then I do promise to repair to the governor of Plimouth, to rectify the difference amongst us.

5thly. I do promise not to make war with any, but with the governor's approbation of Plimouth.

6thly. I promise not to dispose of any of the lands that I have at present, but by the approbation of the governor of Plimouth.

For the true performance of the premises, I the said Sachem, Philip of Pawkamauket, do hereby bind myself and such of my council as are present, ourselves, our heirs, our successors, faithfully. In witness whereof we have hereunto subscribed our hands, the day and year above written.*

In the presence of	The mark *P* of Philip the
the court and divers	Sachem of Pawkamauket
of the gentlemen of	The mark ⸎ of Uncompan
the Massachusets	The mark ⌊ of Wotokom
and Connecticut.	The mark ⁊ of Samkana.

THE English have been charged, by some writers, with acts of injustice to the Indians, which have provoked them and occasioned the frequent wars. There have been many instances of abuses offered to particular persons among the Indians, by evil minded Englishmen, and the inhabitants of some parts of the province which

---

* There is no date to the printed articles in Mr. Hubbard's history of the war.

An Englishman was found dead, having been shot through the body, in Dedham woods, in the spring of the year 1671; an Indian, the supposed murderer, was taken and imprisoned, whether executed or not I do not find, but it kept the colony in an alarm for some time.

have suffered most by Indian cruelties, may have been under too strong prejudices, and, by this means, offenders, when brought upon trial, may have been acquitted by too favourable juries. We are too apt to consider the Indians as a race of beings by nature inferior to us, and born to servitude. Philip was a man of high spirit, and could not bear to see the English of New-Plimouth extending their settlements over the dominions of his ancestors; and although his father had, at one time or other, conveyed to them all that they were possessed of, yet he had sense enough, to distinguish a free voluntary covenant from one made under a sort of duresse, and he could never rest until he brought on the war which ended in his destruction. The eastern wars have been caused by the attachment of those Indians to the French, who have taken all opportunities of exciting them to hostilities against the English.

FROM 1671 to 1674 * we meet with no transaction of moment relating to the Indians, but it is affirmed that Philip was all this time using measures to engage the Indians in all parts of New-England to unite against the English. The Indians about Hadley confessed such

* In May 1672, the union between the three colonies, being renewed by commissioners, was ratified by the general court at Boston. They were to meet now but once in three years, unless upon extraordinary occasions. The proportion of men for any general service was settled for 15 years to come as follows, viz. Massachusets 100, Plimouth 30, Connecticut 60.

May 28th 1672 War was proclaimed against the Dutch in Boston, in consequence of the King's declaration of war published in England. This was the first instance of any public declaration of war in the colony. In the Dutch wars, in the time of the parliament and Cromwell, and in the former war after the restoration, until forces came to reduce the Manhados, correspondence and commerce continued between the colonies, notwithstanding the war in Europe.

March 21st 1673, the castle at the entrance of Boston harbour, being of timber, was burnt down by accident. A new fortress of stone was erected, said then to be a strong work.

In August the same year advice came to Boston that the Dutch, after taking several ships at Virginia, had possessed themselves of New-York, whilst Col. Lovelace the governor was at New-Haven, and that the Dutch force was bound further northward. This intelligence caused a great alarm in the colony. The castle having been destroyed not long before, Boston was less capable of defence. The best preparations were made which could be made. The Dutch fleet returned to Europe.

This acquisition was accidental, according to the account given by the Dutch at New-York. Four Hollanders and three Zealanders met off Martinico, one side with French the other English colours, and prepared to fight, until by hoisting their proper colours they better understood one another. They then joined together and agreed upon an expedition to Virginia and New-York. The Dutch Guinea fleet was intended for the same service, but these other ships saved them the trouble. *MS. Account of a message from Hartford to New-York.*

A collection was made in 1672 for rebuilding Harvard-college, amounting to 1895 l. 2 s. 9 d. The town of Boston gathered 800 l. of which 100 l. was given by Sir Thomas Temple, as true a gentleman, says Doctor Mather, as ever sat foot on the American strand.

a plot. The Naragansets had engaged to bring four thousand men. This could not be done immediately. The English were upon the watch. Some fire-arms had been taken from the Indians. To provide sufficient arms, ammunition and provisions, whilst under suspicion, was a work of time. They did not expect to be prepared before the spring of 1676, but Philip precipitated his own nation and his allies into a war, before they were prepared. This was evident from the distraction of the Indians in all parts of New-England, upon the first news of the disturbance from Philip. They were amazed, not knowing which way to turn, sometimes ready to declare for the English, as they had been used to do in the former contests with Philip, at other times inclining to join with Philip, as first or last most of them did. The war was hurried on by a piece of revenge, which Philip caused to be taken upon John Sausaman, a praying Indian. He had been bred up in the profession of the Christian religion, was some time at the college, and afterwards employed as a schoolmaster at Natick, but, upon some misdemeanor, fled to Philip, who made him his secretary and chief counsellor and confident. After remaining some years with Philip, Mr. Eliot the Indian evangelist, who had been his spiritual father, prevailed with him to return to the christian Indians at Natick, where he manifested public repentance for his apostasy and became a preacher, and conformed more to the English manners than any other Indian. In the year 1674, Sausaman upon some occasion went to Namasket, (Middleborough) where he fell into company with some of Philip's Indians, and with Philip himself. There, he discovered, by several circumstances, that the Indians were plotting against the English. He informed the governor what he had discovered, and told him, that if he should be known to be the informer it would cost him his life. It was not long after that Sausaman was met by three or four Indians upon a frozen pond, who knocked him down and put him under the ice, leaving his gun and hat upon the ice to make the world believe that he accidentally fell in and was drowned. When the body was found and taken up, the wounds appeared upon his head. An Indian happened to be upon an hill at a distance, and saw the murder committed. He concealed it for some time, but at length discovered it. The murderers were apprehended, tried upon the Indian's testimony and other circumstances, convicted and executed, two of them denying the fact to the last, the third, when he came to die, confessing he was a spectator of the murder committed by the other two. This trial was at Plimouth in June 1675.* Philip, enraged to see the immediate actors brought

* Mr. Winslow, governor of Plimouth, writes to Mr. Leveret, the Massachusets governor, July 4, 1675. — "I do solemnly profess we know not any thing, from us, that

to punishment by the English laws, and expecting that it would be his own turn next, being conscious that the murderers were employed by him, took no pains to exculpate himself, but gathered what strangers he could, and, together with his own men, marched them up and down the country in arms. The English of Plimouth ordered a military watch in every town, but took no other notice of the Indians behaviour, hoping, that when Philip saw no measures were used for apprehending him, the threatened storm would blow over, as it had done several times before. But the Indians coming in to him from several quarters, gave him fresh courage, and he behaved with insolence, first threatening the English at Swanzey, then killing some of their cattle, and at length rifling their houses.* An Englishman was so provoked, that he fired upon an Indian and wounded him.† June 24th, in the morning, one of the inhabitants of Rehoboth was fired upon by a party of Indians, and the hilt of his sword shot off.‡ The same day in the afternoon, being a fast, as Swanzey people were coming from publick worship, the Indians attacked them, killed one and wounded others, and killed two men who were going for a surgeon, beset a house, in another part of the town, and there murdered six more. The Massachusets, before this, had determined to raise 100 men for the assistance of Plimouth; but, before they marched, it was thought best to send messengers to Philip at Mount Hope,§ to divert him from his design if possible; but the

---

might put Philip upon these motions, nor have heard that he pretends to have suffered any wrong from us, save only, that we had killed some Indians, and intended to send for himself for the murder of John Sausaman. The last that was executed this week confessed that he saw the other two do the murder. Neither had we any thoughts to command him in about it." This action of Philip, in procuring the death of Sausaman, has always been pronounced to be a most heinous crime. Philip no doubt considered him as a traitor and renegade, who had justly forfeited his life. The Indians left murderers to the revenge of relations and friends, but punished traitors by public execution.

* In 1671, he confessed that he intended to provoke the English to begin with him first. At this time, a whimsical opinion prevailed, that the side which did the first execution would finally be conquered.

† This is said to be the first gun. (*Hubbard.*)

‡ Governor Winslow's letter 24th of June.

§ Philip's chief seat of government was at Mount Hope;[1] but he removed to other places for hunting and fishing, particularly to Namasket or Middleborough; and he had a hunting house in Taunton, near a swamp or pond called the Fowling Pond, which has been since set off from Taunton, and with other lands made a town by the name of Raynham. In 1763, a jury which went to view some controverted bounds, were satisfied that they had discovered the ruins of Philip's house, and the hearth where he used to cook, covered over with earth, the coals remaining intire to that time.

---

[1] Mount Hope was near Bristol, Rhode Island, and not far from Swansea, Massachusetts.

messengers seeing some of the Swanzey men lying murdered in the road, did not think it safe to go any further, and returned as fast as they could with this intelligence to Boston. On the 26th, a foot company under Capt. Henchman,[1] and a troop under Capt. Prentice,[2] marched from Boston towards Mount Hope, and were overtaken by another company of 110 volunteers under Capt. Mosely,*[3] and all arrived at Swanzey the 28th, where they found Plimouth forces under Capt. Cudworth.[4] They made the minister's house, (Mr. Miles †) near the bridge, their head-quarters. About a dozen of the troop went immediately over the bridge, where they were fired upon from out of the bushes, one killed and one wounded. This action drew the body of the English forces after the enemy, whom they pursued a mile or two until they took to a swamp, killing about half a dozen of them. Philip thought it best to quit his station at Mount Hope. A day or two after, Major Savage ‡[5] being arrived with more forces from Boston, and a general command, marched into the Indian towns § which they found deserted, with marks of great haste. They discovered Philip's wigwam amongst the rest. They met with none of the enemy. The next day, they returned to their head-quarters at Swanzey. It is not my design to enter into every minute circum-

---

* Mosely had been an old privateerer at Jamaica, probably of such as were called Bucaneers.

† This was the Baptist minister mentioned page 197.

‡ Mr. Joseph Dudley, then member for Roxbury, afterwards governor of the province, accompanied him.

§ They passed through many fields of corn. *Hubbard.*

---

[1] Daniel Henchman, or Hinchman (*d.* 1685), was at one time an usher in the South Grammar School in Boston. He was also a proprietor of Worcester, in which town he died. See Massachusetts Historical Society *Proceedings,* Second Series, VIII, 64–67, and George Madison Bodge, *Soldiers in King Philip's War,* chapter II.

[2] Thomas Prentice (*d.* 1710) lived in Cambridge, but on the south side of the river in what later became Newton. He had represented Cambridge in the General Court, 1672–74. Later he was influential in bringing about the separation of Newton from Cambridge. See Francis Jackson, *History of Newton,* pp. 469–475.

[3] Samuel Mosely (1641–1680), of Dorchester and Boston, was a cooper. On one of his trips to the West Indies he captured "two prizes from some unmentioned enemy," and brought them home with him. The vessels were commanded by Dutchmen and may have been engaged in irregular commerce. See Edward Strong Moseley, *Genealogical Sketch of One Branch of the Moseley Family,* pp. 14–19.

[4] James Cudworth (*d.* 1682), of Scituate, had represented his town at Plymouth for a number of years and had been an Assistant 1656–58. After King Philip's War, in 1681, he was elected Deputy-Governor of the Plymouth Colony. Sent to London as the Colony's agent, he died there of smallpox. See Francis Baylies, *Historical Memoir of New Plymouth,* Part III, 13–15.

[5] Thomas Savage (1608?–1682). See editor's note 3 to p. 65.

stance of the war.* The Massachusets government sent Capt. Hutchinson [1] as their commissioner to treat with the Naragansets.† It was thought convenient to do it sword in hand, therefore all the forces marched into the Naraganset country. Connecticut, afterwards, sent two gentlemen in behalf of that government, and on the 15th of July, they came to an agreement with the Naraganset Indians, who favoured Philip in their hearts, and waited only a convenient opportunity to declare openly for him; but, whilst the army was in their country, were obliged to submit to the terms imposed upon them.‡

* A letter to London mentions an instance of heroism in a maid servant of one Mr. Minot [2] of Dorchester. She was left at home, upon a Lord's day in July, when an Indian came to the door, and finding it shut, attempted the window. When she perceived it, she hid two young children she had with her under two brass kettles, and ran up stairs and charged a musket; but the Indian was quicker than she was, and fired first, and missed her. She fired, and shot him in the shoulder. He was not so disabled as to give over his design; but she had resolution enough, as he was entering the window, to clap a shovel full of live coals to his face, which caused him to flee, and marked him so, that he was known when found dead in the woods at five miles distance. The same letter takes notice of Cornellis, a Dutchman, under sentence of death for piracy, but pardoned on condition of enlisting. "He pursued Philip so hard, that he got his cap, and now wears it. The general finding him a brave man, sent him with a command of twelve men to scout, with orders to return in three hours on pain of death. He met 60 Indians haling their canoes ashore: he killed 13, and took 8 alive, and pursued the rest as far as he could go for swamps, and, on his return, burnt all the canoes. The exploit took up eight hours. A council of war was called, and Cornellis was again sentenced to die for breach of orders, but a second time received his pardon; and a short time after was sent out on the like design, and brought in 12 Indians alive, and two scalps."

† "We do judge that it will be of absolute necessity to put all the Indians, that are neighbouring to the English, to the test of their fidelity. — If they desire our friendship, they must not harbour or nourish any that are our declared enemies; but in case that Philip or any of his men, women, or children be fled to them, that they forthwith deliver them up, and also that they send hostages for our security, and do join with us in the pursuit and conquest of their and our enemy; this we judge to be just and equal, as well as necessary. — We have commissioned Capt. Hutchinson to repair to Naraganset Indians, who will bring a small party with him and will have a view to the forces with you for his assistance." *General court's letter to Maj. Savage. July 4, 1675.*

‡ "Articles, covenant, and agreement had, made, and concluded by and between Maj. Thomas Savage, Capt. Edward Hutchinson, and Mr. Joseph Dudley, in behalf of the government of the Massachusets colony, and Major Wait Winthrop and Mr. Richard Smith in behalf of Connecticut colony, on the one party, and Agamaug, Wampsh alias Corman, Taitson, Tawageson, counsellors and attornies to Canonicus, Ninigret, Mattatoag, old Queen Quaiapen, Quananshit, and Pomham, the six present sachems of the whole Naraganset country, on the other party, referring to several dif-

---

[1] Edward Hutchinson. See editor's note 1 to p. 169; also George Madison Bodge, *Soldiers in King Philip's War*, pp. 88, 106–112.

[2] Lemuel Shattuck, in *New England Historical and Genealogical Register*, I, 172, thinks this was Capt. John Minot (1626–1669); but it seems more probable that it was John Minot (1647–1690), his son, for the Captain died in 1669.

As soon as the treaty was finished, the forces left the Naraganset country, and came to Taunton the 17th in the evening. Hearing that Philip was in a swamp at Pocasset, the Massachusets and Plimouth forces joined, and arrived at the swamp the 18th, which they resolutely entered. They found about one hundred wigwams empty.

---

ferences and troubles lately arisen between them, and for a final conclusion of settled peace and amity between the said sachems, their heirs and successors for ever, and the governors of the said Massachusets and their successors in the said government for ever.

1st, That all and every of the said sachems shall from time to time carefully seize, and living or dead, deliver unto one or other of the abovesaid governments all and every of sachem Philip's subjects whatsoever, that shall come or be found within the precinct of any of their lands, and that with greatest diligence and faithfulness.

2d. That they shall, with their utmost ability, use all acts of hostility against the said Philip and his subjects entering his lands, or any other lands of the English, to kill and destroy the said enemy, until a cessation from war with the said enemy be concluded by both the abovesaid colonies.

3d. That the said sachems, by themselves and their agents, shall carefully search out and deliver all stolen goods whatsoever taken by any of their subjects from the English, whether formerly or lately, and shall make full satisfaction for all wrongs or injuries done to the estate of any of the subjects of the several colonies, according to the judgment of indifferent men, in case of dissatisfaction between the offenders and the offended parties, or deliver the offenders.

4th. That all preparations for war, or acts of hostility against any of the English subjects, shall for ever for the future cease, together with all manner of thefts, pilferings, killing of cattle, or any manner of breach of peace whatsoever, shall with utmost care be prevented, and, instead thereof, their strength to be used, as a guard round about the Naraganset country, for the English inhabitants safety and security.

5th. In token of the abovesaid sachems reality, in this treaty and conclusion, and for the security of the several English governments and subjects, they do freely deliver unto the abovesaid Gentlemen, in behalf of the abovesaid colonies, John Wobequob, Weowchin, Pewkes, Wenew, four of their near kinsmen and choice friends, to be and remain as hostages in several places of the English jurisdiction, at the appointment of the honourable governors of the abovesaid colonies, there to be civilly treated, not as prisoners, but otherwise at their honours discretion, until the abovesaid articles are fully accomplished to the satisfaction of the several governors, the departure of any of them in the mean time to be accounted a breach of the peace of these present articles.

6th. The said gentlemen, in behalf of the governments to which they do belong, do engage to every of the said sachems and their subjects, that if they or any of them shall seize and bring into either of the abovesaid English governments, or to Mr. Smith, inhabitant of Naraganset, Philip sachem alive, he or they so delivering shall receive for their pains forty trucking cloth coats; in case they bring his head, they shall have twenty like good coats paid them; for every living subject of said Philip, so delivered, the deliverer shall receive two coats, and for every head one coat, as a gratuity for their service herein, making it appear to satisfaction that the heads or persons are belonging to the enemy, and that they are of their seizure.

7th. The said sachems do renew and confirm unto the English inhabitants or others, all former grants, sales, bargains, or conveyances of lands, meadow, timber, grass, stones, or whatever else the English may have heretofore bought, or quietly possessed and enjoyed, to be unto them and their heirs and assigns for ever, as also all former articles made with the confederate colonies.

Lastly. The said counsellors and attornies do premeditately, seriously, and with good advice, covenant, conclude, and agree all abovesaid solemnly, and call God to

The enemy had deserted them, and retired deeper into the swamp. The English followed, but in disorder, which was inevitable, penetrating a thick swamp. They found they were in danger one from another, every man firing at every bush he saw shake. Night coming on, it was necessary to retreat. They lost fifteen men. How many they killed of the enemy is uncertain. It was an unsuccessful attempt, and the more unfortunate because, as they were afterwards informed, Philip was in such distress, that if they had followed him half an hour longer, he would have surrendered himself and his men, which would have put an end to the war.* This disappointment encouraged the Indians, in other parts of New-England, to follow Philip's example, and begin their hostilities against the English. Some few had begun before. The Nipnet or Nipmuck Indians had killed four or five people at Mendon, in the Massachusets colony, the 14th of July. The governor and council, in hopes of reclaiming the Nipnets, sent Capt. Hutchinson with 20 horsemen to Quabaog (Brookfield) near which place there was to be a great rendezvous of those Indians. The Inhabitants of Quabaog had been deluded with the promise of a treaty, at a place agreed upon, the 2d of August. Some of the principal of them accompanied Capt. Hutchinson thither. Not finding the Indians there, they rode forward four or five miles, towards the Nipnets chief town. When they came to a place called Meminimisset, a narrow passage between a steep hill and a thick swamp, they were ambushed by two or three hundred Indians, who shot down eight of the company, and mortally wounded three more,

---

witness, they are and shall remain true friends to the English governments, and perform the abovesaid articles punctually, using their utmost endeavour, care, and faithfulness therein. In witness whereof they have set their hands and seals.

Petaquamscot, July 15, 1675.

Signed, sealed, and delivered in the presence of us under-written, being carefully interpreted to the said Indians before sealing,		
Daniel Henchman		
Thomas Prentice		
Nicholas Page		
Joseph Stanton interpreter		
Henry Hawlaws		
Pecoq Bukow		
Job Neff."		

Tawageson his mark   C

Taytson his mark   O

Agamaug his mark   T

Wampsh alias Corman   X
his mark

* Mather's history of the war.[1]

A letter from Boston to London, Nov. 10, 1675, says, that a brother of Philip's, a privy-counsellor and chief captain, who had been educated at Harvard college, was killed in this fight.

---

[1] Increase Mather, *A Brief History of the War with the Indians in New-England.*

Capt. Hutchinson * being one of the number. The rest escaped through a by-path to Quabaog. The Indians flocked into the town; but the inhabitants being alarmed, had all gathered together in the principal house. They had the mortification to see all their dwelling-houses, about twenty, with their barns and outhouses burnt. The house, where they had assembled, was then surrounded, and a variety of attempts made to set fire to it. At length, the Indians filled a cart with hemp and other combustible matter, which they kindled, and, whilst they were thrusting it towards the house, a violent shower of rain fell suddenly and extinguished the fire.† August 4th, Major Willard, who had been sent after some other Indians westward, heard of the distress of Brookfield, when he was about 4 or 5 miles from Lancaster, which caused him, with 48 men, to alter his course, and the same night he reached Brookfield, after 30 miles march; and though the Indian scouts discovered him, and fired their alarm guns, yet the main body, from their high joy, always accompanied with a horrid noise, heard nothing of them. Willard joined the besieged,‡ and the Indians immediately poured in all the shot they could, but without execution, and then quitted the siege, and destroyed all the horses and cattle they could find and withdrew to their dens. They were not pursued, being much superior in numbers. The English were not yet used to fighting. A party likewise were sent from Springfield to the relief of Brookfield. Finding it effected, they returned, meeting none of the enemy. Philip, and his people, continued in the swamp at Pocasset until the last of July. After several skirmishes with captain Church and other parties, they escaped from the swamp, notwithstanding the Massachusets forces kept their guards round it, and went away to the westward, without being very closely pursued, the reason of which Mr. Hubbard says, it is better to suspend than too critically to inquire into. The 5th

* Capt. Hutchinson was carried to Quabaog, and afterwards to Marlborough, where he died the 19th of August.

"Capt. Hutchinson had a very considerable farm thereabouts, and had occasion to employ several of the Nipmug sachem's men in tilling and ploughing the ground, and thereby he was known by face to many of them. The sachems sent word they would speak with none but Capt. Hutchinson himself, and appointed a meeting at such a tree, and such a time. — The guide that conducted him, and those that were with him, through the woods, brought them to a swamp, not far off the appointed place, out of which those Indians ran all at once, and killed 16 men, and wounded several others, of which wounds Capt. Hutchinson afterwards died, whose death is the more lamented in that his mother and several others of his relations died by the hands of the Indians, now above 30 years since." *Letter to London, Nov. 10, 1675.*

† Hubbard. Mr. Mather takes no notice of the rain, but says Willard came upon the Indians and prevented the execution.

‡ Mr. Mather says, he set upon the Indians, and caused them to turn their backs.

of August, Philip with about forty men, besides women and children, joined the Nipmuck Indians in a swamp ten or twelve miles from Brookfield.* The Indians upon Connecticut river near Hadley, Hatfield, and Deerfield, began their hostilities about the same time, as also those at Penicook and other places upon Merrimack river, so that, before the end of August, the whole Massachusets colony was in the utmost terror. Philip having left Plimouth, and the Naragansets not having engaged, that colony was less affected. There were several skirmishes about Hatfield, viz. at Sugarloaf-hill, at Deerfield, and Squakeag, (Northfield) the latter end of August and beginning of September, in which the English, upon the whole, were losers. September the 1st, Hadley was attacked upon a fast day, while the people were at church, which broke up the service, and obliged them to spend the day in a very different exercise.† The commanders in that part of the country, not being able to do much service by sending out parties, determined to garrison the towns, and to collect a magazine of provisions at Hadley. There being about 3000 bushels of corn at Deerfield in stacks, Capt. Lothrop [1] with

---

* "Upon Friday being the 5th of this instant (August) Philip and his company came to us at this swamp, six miles from the swamp where they killed our men. Philip brought with him about forty men, but women and children many more, the number I cannot tell. Philip's men were, about 30 of them, armed with guns, the rest had bows and arrows. He observed there were about ten of Philip's men wounded. Philip was conducted to the swamp by two Indians, one of them Caleb of Tatumasket, beyond Mendon. The Indians told Philip, at his first coming, what they had done to the English at Quabaog; then he presented and gave to three sagamores, viz. John alias Apequinash, Quanansit, and Mawtamps, to each of them about a peck of unstrung wampom, which they accepted. Philip, as I understood, told Quabaog and Nipmuck Indians, that when he first came towards the Nipmuck country, and left his own, he had in his company about 250 men, besides women and children, including the Squaw sachem and her company; but now they had left him, and some of them were killed, and he was reduced to 40 men, besides women and children. I heard also that Philip said, if the English had charged upon him and his people at the swamp in his own country one or two days more, they had been all taken, for their powder was almost spent; he also said, that if the English had pursued him closely, as he travelled up to them, he must needs have been taken." *MS. narrative of George, a christian Indian, taken prisoner in the ambushment of Capt. Hutchinson, &c.*

"Sept. 23d, an alarm was made in the town of Boston, about ten in the morning, 1200 men were in arms before eleven, and all dismissed before twelve. One that was upon guard at Mendon, 30 miles off, got drunk and fired his gun, the noise of which alarmed the next neighbours, and soon spread to Boston." *Letter to London.*

"October 7th was observed as a solemn fast throughout the colony with a very great shew of outward penitence, and no question with much inward affection by very many; the governor himself beginning the duty of the day with a most heavenly prayer." *Letter to London.* † P. 187.

---

[1] Thomas Lothrop (*d.* 1675), of Salem and Beverly, had been a deputy to the General Court in various years since 1647. He was admitted a freeman in 1634. See George Madison Bodge, *Soldiers in King Philip's War*, pp. 133-141.

80 men was sent to guard it down in carts, and were set upon by seven or eight hundred Indians, and all the English but seven or eight were cut off. Capt. Lothrop and his men fought bravely, but in the Indian manner, betaking themselves to trees, which, in so great a disproportion of numbers, must be inevitable destruction, for many of the lesser party must be unguarded and exposed. Capt. Moseley, who was quartered at Deerfield, came out with his company too late to rescue Lothrop; but, keeping his men together in a body, fought the whole number of Indians for several hours, with the loss of two men only, until Major Treat,[1] with about 160 Mohegin Indians, came to his aid, and put the enemy to flight. This was a heavy stroke to the county of Essex, to which most of Capt. Lothrop's company, being young men, belonged. A body of Indians, who had a fort about a mile from Springfield, had hitherto professed great friendship to the English; but Philip's Indians prevailed with them to join in a plot for the destruction of the town, and to receive in the night three hundred of those Indians into the fort. It was discovered the night before by Top, a Windsor Indian, which, although it saved the lives of many of the inhabitants, yet was no security for their dwellings, thirty odd houses, besides barnes, &c. being burnt before forces came from Westfield, Hadley, and other parts, to repel the Indians.* The 19th of October, they came, with all the force and

* They burned a farm house of Mr. Pynchon's, and another of Mr. Purchas's,[2] the latter end of September; their loss was esteemed at a thousand pounds sterling each. *Letter to London.*

The Springfield Indians had lived in so good correspondence with the English for 40 years, that more dependance was placed upon them than upon any other Indians. This instance of perfidy seems to have increased the jealousies and suspicions, which had before begun, of the Indians round Boston, viz. Punkapog, Natick, &c. although many of them actually went out with the English forces against the enemy.

At the sessions in October, the general court ordered, "that no person shall entertain, own, or countenance any Indian, under the penalty of being a betrayer of the government." (This I suppose was capital.)

"That a guard be set at the entrance of the town of Boston, and that no Indian be suffered to enter, upon any pretence, without a guard of two musketeers, and not to lodge in town.

"That any person may apprehend an Indian, finding him in town, or approaching the town, and that none be suffered to come in by water."

The Natick Indians, and most of the other Indians who had subjected themselves to

[1] Robert Treat (*c.* 1622–1710), of Milford, Connecticut, had been an Assistant in the New Haven government and also in the Connecticut government which supplanted it. He was commander-in-chief of the Connecticut forces in the present war, and later was governor of the colony for many years.

[2] Thomas Purchas (*d.* 1678) was an old settler at Pejepscot, now Brunswick, Maine. He came to this country about 1628. After the plundering of his house in 1675, he removed to Lynn, Massachusetts.

fury they cauld raise, upon Hatfield, but were repulsed, the Connecticut and Massachusets forces being, by good providence, at hand, so as to prevent any great loss. This discouraged them from continuing any longer in that part of the country, and they withdrew to the Naragansets, their general rendezvous. Some stragglers remained until the end of November, and a few lurked in the swamps all winter, doing now and then some mischief, enough to keep the inhabitants upon constant watch and guard. In November a party was sent out under Capt. Henchman to Hassanimisco, (Grafton) Mendon, and the towns thereabout. They returned without any remarkable exploit. [The war thus far had proved very unsuccessful to the New English and private letters from Boston to London about this time express the fears of the writers that the Colony would be extirpated.]

THE Naragansets,* contrary to their engagements, had received

---

the English government (Punkapog excepted) were hurried down to Deer island, where they remained the winter. They complained of their sufferings there. All of the colour were thought by many of the people worthy of death, and although their rage did not carry them that length, as to murder any of them without the authority of government, as some persons have lately done the Conestogoe Indians in Pensylvania, yet their clamour seems to have prevailed on the authority to use greater severity than otherwise they would have done. "On the 10th of September, at nine o'clock at night, there gathered together about forty men, some of note, and came to the house of Capt. James Oliver; two or three of them went into his entry to desire to speak with him, which was to desire him to be their leader, and they should join together and go and break open the prison, and take one Indian out thence and hang him. Capt. Oliver, hearing their request, took his cane and cudgelled them stoutly, and so for that time dismissed the company, which had he but in the least countenanced, it might have been accompanied with ill events in the end." (*Letter to London*) In a short time after, the same poor Indian was executed, and died protesting his innocence. Mr. Eliot the minister, and some others, who had firmness enough to stem the popular current, interceding for him to no purpose. A circumstance, at the execution of this Indian, shews the great propriety of distinguishing them from all the rest of the human race by the name of savages. "Being half alive and half dead, there came an Indian, a friend of his, and with his knife made a hole in his breast to his heart, and sucked out his heart's blood. Being asked his reason therefore, his answer was, Umh Umh nu, me be stronger as I was before, me be so strong as he and me too, he be ver strong man before he die." *Letter to London.*

* Before the Naraganset expedition articles of war were agreed upon by the general court, and were as follows:

"Laws and ordinances of war passed by the general court of the Massachusets, for the better regulating their forces, and keeping their soldiers to their duty, and to prevent profaneness, that iniquity may be kept out of the land.

1st. Let no man presume to blaspheme the holy and blessed trinity, God the Father, God the Son, and God the Holy Ghost, upon pain to have his tongue bored with a hot iron.

2d. Unlawful oaths and execrations, and scandalous acts in derogation of God's honour, shall be punished with loss of pay and other punishment at discretion.

and comforted Philip's Indians and others, the enemies of the English. It was not doubted that some of that nation had mixed with the others in their hostilities. If they should all openly engage in the spring, there would be no resisting them; scattered in every part of the country, all the forces the English could raise would not be a match for them. One company of soldiers after another had wasted away in the year past. There was no great room to hope for better success in the year to come. The commissioners of the united colonies therefore agreed, to raise one thousand men, and to march, in the winter, into the Naraganset country. The Massachusets were to

---

3d. All those who often and wilfully absent themselves from the public worship of God and prayers, shall be proceeded against at discretion.

4th. Whosoever shall be convicted to do his duty negligently and carelesly, shall be punished at discretion.

5th. No person shall presume to quarrel with his superior officer, upon pain of cashiering and arbitrary punishment; not to strike any such upon pain of death.

6th. No commander or soldier shall depart from his charge or captain without licence, upon pain of death.

7th. Every private soldier, upon pain of imprisonment, shall keep silence when the army is to take lodging, or when it is marching, or in battle, so as the officers may be heard, and their commands executed.

8th. No man shall resist, draw, lift, offer to draw or lift his weapon against his officer, correcting him orderly for his offence, upon pain of death.

9th. No man shall resist the provost marshal, or any other officer, in the executing his office, upon pain of death.

10th. No man shall utter any words of sedition or mutiny, upon pain of death.

11th. They that shall hear mutinous speeches, and not acquaint their commander with them, shall be punished with some grievous punishment.

12th. Drunkenness in an officer shall be punished with loss of place, and in a private foot soldier, with such punishment as a court martial shall think fit.

13th. Rapes, ravishments and unnatural abuses, and adultery, shall be punished with death.

14th. Fornication and other dissolute lasciviousness, shall be punished with discretion, according to the quality of the offence.

15th. Theft or robbery, shall be punished with restitution, and otherwise with discretion.

16th. Murder, shall be expiated with the death of the murderer.

17th. All soldiers coming to their colours to watch or be exercised, or to service, shall come completely armed and them fixed, upon pain of punishment.

18th. If any shall negligently lose, or sinfully play away their arms at dice or cards, or otherwise, they shall be kept as pioneers or scavengers, till they furnish themselves with as good arms.

19th. None shall presume to spoil, sell, or carry away any ammunition committed unto him, upon pain of death.

20th. No soldier shall outstay his pass, without a certificate of the occasion under the hand of a magistrate, upon pain of losing his pay.

By grievous punishment is meant disgracefully cashiering, the strapado, or riding the wooden horse to fetch blood.

Arbitrary punishment, or punishment at discretion, is meant not to extend to life or limb."

raise 527, the other two colonies the remainder. Mr. Winslow,* the governor of Plimouth, was pitched upon for the general. The 8th of December, the Massachusets forces marched from Boston, and were soon after joined by Plimouth men. Connecticut men joined them, the 18th, at Pettyquamscot.[1] The evening and night were stormy and the men had no covering. At break of day, the 19th, they marched through the snow fourteen or fifteen miles, until one o'clock afternoon, when they came to the edge of the swamp where the enemy lay.[2] They had met with an Indian, who was disgusted with the rest, and offered himself as a pilot. The Indians knew of the armament coming against them, and had fortified themselves with all the art and strength they were capable of. The English fell in, suddenly and unexpectedly, upon this seat of the enemy, and neither drew up in any order of battle, nor consulted where or how to assault. Some Indians appearing at the edge of the swamp, they that were in the front of the army, in the march, fired upon them. The Indians returned the fire and fled. The whole army entered the swamp, following the Indians to their fortress, which was upon a piece of upland in the midst of the swamp, pallisadoed all round, and within a hedge of near a rod thick. At one corner only, was a gap the length of one log, where the breastwork was not above four or five feet high; but they had placed a block-house over-against this passage. At this passage, and no where else, the English must enter. As it pleased God to order it, they fell in upon that part of the fort where the passage was. The captains entered, at the head of their companies. The two first, Johnson [3] and Davenport,[4] were shot dead at the en-

---

* Mr. Winslow had always shewn great readiness to expose himself in the service. "Some resolute attempt for Philip's surprisal must be put in execution. Would to God I was with our men, so as I might not in the mean time be missed at home. I should hope, by the blessing of God, to give a good account in a short time." *Winslow to Leveret*, July 26, 1675. "My person, I hear, has been much threatened — I have about 20 men at my house, have sent away my wife and children to Salem, that I may be less incumbered, have flankered my house, and resolve to maintain it as long as a man will stand by me." *Id. July* 4.

---

[1] The Tower Hill region of South Kingston, Rhode Island.

[2] The scene of the Great Swamp Fight was in the township of South Kingston, Rhode Island. The Shore Line of the New York, New Haven and Hartford Railroad now traverses the swamp and passes just south of the site of the Indians' fort.

The most satisfactory modern treatise on this critical time in New England history is George W. Ellis and John E. Morris, *King Philip's War* (New York, 1906).

[3] Isaac Johnson, of Roxbury (d. 1675), had been a deputy to the General Court in 1671. See George Madison Bodge, *Soldiers in King Philip's War*, chapter IX.

[4] Nathaniel Davenport, of Boston (d. 1675), was a son of Richard Davenport of Salem, who came over with John Endicott in 1628. Nathaniel married Elizabeth Thacher, a daughter of Thomas Thacher, first minister of the Old South Church. See George Madison Bodge, *Soldiers in King Philip's War*, chapter XI.

trance, as were many of their men. Four other captains, Gardner,[1] Gallop,[2] Siely,[3] and Marshal[4] also lost their lives. As soon as the forces were entered, they attacked the Indians in their places of shelter, who fought desperately, and beat the English out of the fort; but, after two or three hours, the advantage of the English was such, that they began to fire the wigwams, which were five or six hundred, and in many of them the Indian women and children perished, the men which were left alive fled into a cedar swamp at some small distance, without any necessaries of life, or any shelter from the cold and storms, except the boughs of trees. The day being near spent, the English thought it high time to retire to their quarters, 15 or 16 miles distant, carrying dead as well as wounded men with them. Many of the wounded men perished, by being exposed to this long march in a cold night, who might otherwise have been saved. The number of killed and wounded amounted to 170.* Some of the enemy confessed they lost 700 fighting men that day, besides 300 more who died of their wounds and the hardships to which they were exposed. The number of old men, women and children, which perished by the fire, cold, and famine, they could not tell.† The Indians took possession of the fort, the next day.‡ The English made no further attack.§ They were scant of provisions, the weather being

---

* "Happy it was for them that Capt. Andrew Belcher (father of the late governor Belcher) arrived that very evening at Mr. Smith's with a vessel load of provisions, otherwise many must have perished for want." *Church.*[5]

† This is Mr. Hubbard's account. Mr. Mather supposes 1000 to have perished in the whole; that of the English 85 were killed, and 145 wounded. When the Narraganset Indians came to the Quabaug Indians, and gave them an account of the fight, they said they had lost but 40 fighting men, and about 300 old men, women, and children burnt in the wigwams. *MS. letter.*

‡ Mather.

§ The following letter dated Naraganset 26th 11th month 1675, which, though not

---

[1] Joseph Gardner, of Salem (*d.* 1675), was a son of Thomas Gardner, one of the Old Planters of Cape Ann. Joseph married Ann Downing, who was a daughter of Emanuel Downing and so a niece of Governor John Winthrop. See George Madison Bodge, *Soldiers in King Philip's War,* chapter X.

[2] John Gallop, of Stonington, Connecticut (*d.* 1675), had served in the Pequot War, for which Connecticut had made him a grant of one hundred acres. First he was of Boston; later of Taunton, New London, and Stonington. See Richard Anson Wheeler, *History of Stonington,* pp. 382–383.

[3] Nathaniel Siely, or Seeley, of Fairfield, Connecticut. See Elizabeth Hubbell Schenck, *History of Fairfield,* I, 405.

[4] Samuel Marshall of Windsor, Connecticut. See Henry R. Stiles, *History of Ancient Windsor,* II, 465–466.

[5] Benjamin Church, *The Entertaining History of King Philip's War.*

extreme cold, delayed the vessels which had it on board. Some weeks were spent doing nothing, except that some proposals of peace were made on both sides, which came to nothing. February the 5th, the

---

signed, I take to be from Major Bradford [1] of the Plimouth forces, has never been published. It is less favourable than the printed aaccounts.

"After a tedious march in a bitter cold night that followed Dec. 12th, we hoped our pilot would have led us to Pomham by break of day; but, so it came to pass, we were misled, and so missed a good opportunity. Dec. 13th, we came to Mr. Smith's, and that day took 35 prisoners. Dec. 14th, our general went out with horse and foot, I with my company was left to keep garrison. I sent out 30 of my men to scout abroad, who killed two Indians, and brought in 4 prisoners, one of which was beheaded. Our army came home at night, killed 7, and brought in 9 more, young and old. Dec. 15th, came in John, a rogue, with pretence of peace, and was dismissed with this errand, that we might speak with Sachems. That evening, he not being gone a quarter of an hour, his company, that lay hid behind a hill, killed two Salem men within a mile of our quarters, and wounded a third that he is dead. And at a house, three miles off, where I had ten men, they killed two of them. Instantly, Capt. Mosely, myself and Capt. Gardner were sent to fetch in Major Appleton's [2] company, that kept three miles and an half off, and coming, they lay behind a stone wall and fired on us in sight of the garrison. We killed the Captain that killed one of the Salem men, and had his cap on. That night they burned Jerry Bull's house, and killed 17. Dec. 16th, came that news. Dec. 17th came news that Connecticut forces were at Petaquamscot and had killed 4 Indians, and took 6 prisoners. That day, we sold Capt. Davenport 47 Indians, young and old, for 8ol. in money. Dec. 18th, we marched to Petaquamscot with all our forces, only a garrison left; that night was very stormy, we lay, one thousand, in the open field that long night. In the morning Dec. 19th, Lord's day at five o'clock, we marched. Between twelve and one we came up with the enemy, and had a sore fight three hours. We lost, that are now dead, about 68, and had 150 wounded, many of which are recovered. That long snowy cold night, we had about 18 miles to our quarters, with about 210 dead and wounded. We left 8 dead in the fort. We had but twelve dead when we came from the swamp, besides the eight we left. Many died by the way, and as soon as they were brought in, so that Dec. 20th, we buried in a grave 34, next day 4, next day 2, and none since here. Eight died at Rhode-Island, 1 at Petaquamscot, 2 lost in the woods and killed, Dec. 20, as we heard since; some say two more died. By the best intelligence, we killed 300 fighting men, prisoners we took, say 350, and above 300 women and children. We burnt above 500 houses, left but 9, burnt all their corn, that was in baskets, great store. One signal mercy that night, not [to] be forgotten, viz. that when we drew off, with so many dead and wounded, they did not pursue us, which the young men would have done, but the sachems would not consent; they had but ten pounds of powder left. Our general, with about forty, lost our way, and wandered till seven o'clock in the morning, before we came to our quarters. We thought we were within two miles of the enemy again, but God kept us; to him be the glory. We have killed now and then one since,

---

[1] Major William Bradford (1624–1704) was the son of Governor Bradford of the Plymouth Colony. In 1658 he was elected an Assistant, and in 1682 Deputy-Governor. In the Great Swamp Fight he was wounded, and carried the bullet in his body the rest of his life.

[2] Samuel Appleton (1624–1696), of Ipswich. He had been a deputy to the General Court, and was chosen an Assistant in 1681. He was imprisoned by Andros from October 1687 till March 1688. See Isaac Appleton Jewett, *Memorial of Samuel Appleton*, pp. 16–21.

army returned to Boston. There was a remarkable thaw in January, which melted the snow and opened the earth, so that the Indians could come at the ground-nuts, which seems to have been all their

and burnt 200 wigwams more; we killed nine last Tuesday. We fetch in their corn daily, and that undoes them. This is, as near as I can, a true relation. I read the narrative to my officers in my tent, who all assent to the truth of it. Monhegins and Pequods proved very false, fired into the air, and sent word, before they came, they would do so, but got much plunder, guns and kettles. A great part of what is written was attested by Joshua Teffe, who married an Indian woman, a Wampanoag. He shot 20 times at us in the swamp, was taken at Providence, Jan. 14, brought to us the 16th, executed the 18th. A sad wretch, he never heard a sermon but once these 14 years. His father, going to recall him, lost his head, and lies unburied."

This being so important an expedition, I will add another letter, from Mr. Dudley, afterwards governor, to governor Leveret.

Mr. Smith's, 21, 10. 1675.

May it please your honor,

The coming in of Connecticut force to Petaquamscot, and surprisal of six and slaughter of 5 on Friday night, Saturday we marched towards Petaquamscot, though in the snow, and in conjunction, about midnight or later, we advanced; Capt. Mosely in the van, after him Massachusets, and Plimouth and Connecticut in the rear; a tedious march in the snow, without intermission, brought us about two of the clock in the afternoon, to the entrance of the swamp, by the help of Indian Peter, who dealt faithfully with us; our men, with great courage, entered the swamp about 20 rods; within the cedar swamp we found some hundreds of wigwams, forted in with a breastwork and flankered, and many small blockhouses up and down, round about; they entertained us with a fierce fight, and many thousand shot, for about an hour, when our men valiantly scaled the fort, beat them thence, and from the blockhouses. In which action we lost Capt. Johnson, Capt. Danforth,[1] and Capt. Gardiner, and their lieutenants disabled, Capt. Marshall also slain, Capt. Seely, Capt. Mason,[2] disabled, and many other of our officers, insomuch that, by a fresh assault and recruit of powder from their store, the Indians fell on again, recarried, and beat us out of the fort, but by the great resolution and courage of the General and Major, we reinforced, and very hardly entered the fort again, and fired the wigwams, with many living and dead persons in them; great piles of meal and heaps of corn, the ground not admitting burial of their store, were consumed; the number of their dead, we generally suppose the enemy lost at least two hundred men; Capt. Mosely counted in one corner of the fort sixty-four men, Capt. Goram[3] reckoned 150 at least: But, O! Sir, mine heart bleeds to give your honor an account of our lost men, but especially our resolute Captains, as by account inclosed, and yet not so many, but we admire there remained any to return, a captive woman, well known to Mr. Smith, informing that there were three thousand five hundred men engaging us, and about a mile distant a thousand in reserve, to whom, if God had so pleased, we had been but a morsel, after so much disablement: she informeth, that one of their sagamores was slain, and their powder spent, causing their retreat, and that they are in a distressed condition for food and houses, that one Joshua Tift, an English-

---

[1] Dudley intended "Davenport" instead of "Danforth." Capt. Nathaniel Davenport was killed just inside the fort. See George Madison Bodge, *Soldiers in King Philip's War*, p. 187.

[2] John Mason (1646–1676), of Norwich, Connecticut. He was a son of the redoubtable John Mason who fought in the Pequot War.

[3] John Gorham, of Barnstable. He died of a fever, while in the service of his colony, February 5, 1676, at Swansea, Massachusetts.

provisions, some from among themselves, reporting that corn was sold for two shillings the pint. They took this opportunity to leave the Naraganset country. A general junction of the Indians was thereupon expected, and every part of the English colonies was in terror. The 10th of February several hundred of the enemy assaulted Lancaster, burnt the houses, and killed and captivated 40 persons, the minister's wife and children among the rest, he himself (Mr. Rowlandson) being absent. Mischief was done about the same time at Marlborough, Sudbury, and Chelmsford. The 21st they fell upon Medfield, where there were two or three hundred soldiers, and yet they burned half the town down and killed eighteen of the inhabitants. The 25th, they burned seven or eight houses at Weymouth. This seems to be their nearest approach to Boston, between

---

man, is their encourager and conductor. Philip was seen, by one credibly informing us, under a strong guard. After our wounds dressed, we drew up for a march, not able to abide the field in the storm, and weary, about two of the clock, obtained our quarters, with our dead and wounded, only the General, Ministers, and some other persons of the guard, going to head a small swamp, lost our way, and returned again to the enemy's quarters, a wonder we were not a prey to them, and, after at least thirty miles marching up and down, in the morning recovered our quarters, and had it not been for the arrival of Goodale [1] next morning, the whole camp had perished; the whole army, especially Connecticut, is much disabled and unwilling to march, with tedious storms, and no lodgings, and frozen and swollen limbs. Major Treat importunate to return, at least, to Stonington; our dead and wounded are about two hundred, disabled as many; the want of officers, the consideration whereof the General commends to your honor, forbids any action at present, and we fear whether Connecticut will comply, at last, to any action. We are endeavouring, by good keeping and billetting our men at several quarters, and, if possible, removal of our wounded to Rhode-Island, to recover the spirit of our soldiers, and shall be diligent to find and understand the removals or other action of the enemy, if God please to give us advantage against them.

As we compleat the account of our dead, now in doing, the council is of the mind, without recruit of men, we shall not be able to engage the main body.

I am Sir, your honor's

I give your honor hearty thanks	humble servant,
for your kind lines, of which	humble servant,
I am not worthy.	Joseph Dudley."

Since the writing of these lines, the General and Council have jointly concluded to abide on the place, notwithstanding the desire of Connecticut, only entreat that a supply of 200 may be sent us, with supply of commanders; and, whereas we are forced to garrison our quarters with at least one hundred, three hundred men, upon joint account of the colonies, will serve, and no less, to effect the design.   This is by order of the council.

Blunderbusses and hand granadoes, and armour, if it may be, and at least two armourers to amend arms."

---

[1] This was probably Richard Goodale or Goodall, mariner, who was one of the founders of the First Baptist Church of Boston. There is an entry of a disbursement of £22 on June 24, 1676, to "Richard Goodall for frait." George Madison Bodge, *Soldiers in King Philip's War*, p. 197.

fifteen and twenty miles distant; at least they did no mischief nearer.*

MARCH was a troublesome month, the Indians attacking North-Hampton and Springfield, upon Connecticut river, Groton, Sudbury, and Marlborough, in the Massachusets, Warwick and Providence in Rhode-Island colony, burning their houses and barns, and destroying the cattle, and many of the inhabitants. They killed also eleven persons of one family in Plimouth, (Mr. Clark's) [1] and on the 26th of March Capt. Pierce,[2] of Scituate in that colony, with 50 English, and 20 Indians of Cape Cod, being drawn into an ambushment by a small number of the enemy, found themselves surrounded by a great body of Indians, who killed every Englishman and great part of the friend Indians.† The 28th of the month, they burned 40 houses, besides barns, at Rehoboth. Where Philip spent the winter was never certainly known. Some conjectured that he went to the Mohawks, others that he went to Canada, which his friends said was his intention in the fall. He knew the premium set upon his head, disguised and concealed himself, so that we hear but little of him until he was killed.‡ His affairs were now at the highest flow, and those of the English never at so low an ebb. But presently after, a sudden turn came on.

The beginning of April, the Connecticut men under George Denison of Stonington, with some friend Indians, killed, and took prisoners, forty-four of the enemy.§ Before the end of the month, the same commander, with sixty-six volunteers English, and one hundred and twelve Pequod Indians, took and slew seventy-six more of the enemy, without the loss of one man in either of these exploits. Between these two successful actions, happened a very unfortunate

* The 23d of February, being a fast day with the first Church in Boston, they were disturbed by an alarm, from a report that the Indians were within ten miles of Boston.

† The captives afterwards reported that the English fought so valiantly that they slew 140 of the enemy. *MS.*

‡ The first account of him I have met with, is in a MS. letter of Mr. Cotton, of Plimouth, upon the return of an Indian spy, who reported that Philip was with the Hadley Indians, &c. within half a day's march of Albany.

§ [Among the prisoners was Canonchet son of Miantinamo and chief Sachem of Naraganset who was cruelly put to death for breach of Treaty.]

[1] William Clark was elected a deputy in 1680. His house was about three miles southeast of the village of Plymouth, on the west bank of Eel River.

[2] Michael Pierce (*d.* 1676) was originally of Hingham, Massachusetts. See Samuel Deane's *History of Scituate, Massachusetts* (1831), pp. 121–124, 325–326; and Frederick Clifton Pierce, *Pierce Genealogy*, pp. 17–36. The battle in which he lost his life was fought on the west bank of the Pawtucket River just north of Central Falls, Rhode Island.

one for the Massachusets. April 20th, news came to Boston of the loss of Capt. Wadsworth [1] and 50 of his men, who going to relieve Sudbury [were] attacked by the enemy. In May and June, the enemy appeared in various parts of the colonies, but their vigor abated, their distresses, for want of provisions and ammunition, increased, and at the same time the Mohawks fell upon them and killed 50 of them. It was commonly said, that Philip fell upon a party of Mohawks and killed them, and reported that they were killed by the English, expecting by this means to engage that nation in the war, but one that was left for dead revived and escaped to his countrymen, and informed that, not the English, but Philip and his Indians had been the murderers, which brought that revenge upon the guilty, which, without this discovery, would have been taken of those who were innocent. The beginning of July, the Connecticut forces met with a party of Indians in the Naraganset country, pursued them into a swamp, and killed and took eighty of them, without any loss except one or two friend Indians, and in their march back 60 more of the enemy fell into their hands.* The Massachusets and Plimouth men in several parts of the country, were likewise very successful from time to time, killing and taking small parties of Indians scattered about the country, and no commander was more fortunate than Captain, afterwards Colonel, Church,[2] of Plimouth colony. He has published an account of his exploits. But Philip was the object. Upon his life, or death, war or peace depended. News was brought, that, after a year's absence, he had returned to Mount-Hope, his old quarters, and that great numbers of Indians were flocking to him, with intent to fall upon the neighbouring towns. The Massachusets and Plimouth, both, ordered their forces after Philip. The former returned to Boston, having missed Philip, but they killed and

* The brave actions of the Connecticut volunteers have not been enough applauded. Denison's name ought to be perpetuated. The Naraganset fight had enraged the Indians and made them desperate, and the English plantations, after that, were in greater terror than before, but this successful hunting them, and ferreting them out of their burrows, sunk and broke their spirits, and seems to have determined the fate of English and Indians, which until then was doubtful and uncertain.

---

[1] Samuel Wadsworth (c. 1630–1676), of Milton. He was the father of President Wadsworth of Harvard College. See a sketch of his life in Horace Andrew Wadsworth's *Two Hundred and Fifty Years of the Wadsworth Family in America*, pp. 57–63.

[2] Benjamin Church (1639–1718), of Duxbury, Massachusetts, and Little Compton, Rhode Island. The "account of his exploits," mentioned by Hutchinson, was written by his son Thomas Church. It appeared in 1716 under the title *Entertaining Passages Relating to Philip's War*. The best edition to use is that prepared by Henry Martyn Dexter and published in 1865. The "Introductory Memoir" is an adequate outline of Church's life.

took 150 of the enemy, who were now so reduced that they were continually coming in, and surrendering themselves upon promise of mercy. Two hundred, in one week, came in to Plimouth. Philip fled from one swamp to another, divers times very narrowly escaping, losing one chief counsellor after another; his uncle and sister, and at last his wife and son were taken prisoners. Being reduced to this miserable condition, he was killed the 12th of August, as he was flying from a party under Capt. Church, out of a swamp near Mount-Hope. One of his own men, whom he had offended, and who had deserted to the English, shot him through the heart. Instead of his scalp, he cut off his right hand, which had a remarkable scar, well known to the English, and it produced a handsome penny, many having the curiosity to see it. This was a finishing stroke, the parties of Indians that remained being drove from one hole or swamp to another, so that before winter they were all killed, captivated, or forced to surrender themselves, except some few, who were supposed to have fled to the French, and others, to nations of foreign Indians. The cruelties which had been exercised upon the English, were urged in excuse for the treatment which the Indians received, who were made prisoners or surrendered themselves. In all the promises of mercy, those, who had been principal actors in any murders of the English, were excepted, and none had any promise made of any thing more than their lives. A great many, therefore, of the chiefs were executed at Boston and Plimouth, and most of the rest were sold, and shipped off for slaves to Bermudas and other parts. Every person, almost, in the two colonies, had lost a relation or near friend, and the people in general were exasperated; * but all does not sufficiently excuse this great severity. [They are called Rebels and Murderers and treated as such. They knew not what was intended by Subjects and at most supposed they had broken their promise to live in peace with the English.]

THE same time that Philip began his hostilities in Plimouth colony, the Tarenteens, or Eastern Indians, were insulting the English settled in New Hampshire and the Province of Main. They began

---

* Mr. Increase Mather, in a letter to Mr. Cotton, 23d 5 mo. 1677, mentions an instance of rage against two prisoners of the Eastern Indians, then at Marblehead, a fishing town which goes beyond any other I have heard of. "Sabbath day was se'nnight the women at Marblehead, as they came out of the meeting-house, fell upon two Indians that were brought in as captives, and in a tumultuous way, very barbarously murdered them. Doubtless, if the Indians hear of it, the captives among them will be served accordingly." The Indians had murdered some of the fishermen in the Eastern harbours of the province.

with robbing the English, as they passed in their boats and canoes, and plundering their houses of liquors, ammunition, and such moveables as they could easily carry off. In September (1675) they came to the house of one Wakely,[1] an old man, in Casco bay, and murdered him, his wife, and four children and grand-children, and carried four more of his grand-children away captives. They then fell upon Saco, and killed thirteen men, and burned the houses, killed six men and a woman at Black-point (Scarborough) and burned 20 houses. They next fell upon Kittery, and killed two men. Mr. Plaisted,[2] lieutenant of the town, with 20 English, went out to bury the dead, and was set upon by the Indians. He fought bravely, with seven of his men (the rest flying) until he and his son, and one more, were killed. The other four escaped to the garrison. They then came towards Piscataqua, making spoil upon the inhabitants on the branches of that river, viz. at Oyster river, Salmon-falls, Dover, Exeter, &c. burning their houses and barns, and a mill belonging to Mr. Hutchinson, a merchant in Boston, and killing more or less of the people in every place, to the number of about fifty, in the whole. The government's hands were full, from the attempts of Philip and his accomplices, and during the summer, nothing more was done, than to commit the care of the Eastern plantations to the chief officers of the respective regiments, to defend them against the enemy; but in the fall, forces were drawn from the other counties, in order to have marched into the Eastern country, but were prevented by the severity of the weather, which sat in sooner than usual. The Indians in those parts, at the same time, sued for peace, and there was a good prospect of its being settled; but the endeavours of Major Waldron to effect it were next year frustrated. However, during the winter, and the next spring, and the greatest part of the summer, those plantations were at rest.

THE accounts which were transmitted to England of the distresses of the colony, during the war, although they might excite compassion in the breasts of some, yet they were improved, by others, to render the colony more obnoxious. A fine country, it was said, was in danger of being lost to England, by the penuriousness of those who were at the head of affairs, in not raising monies for the defence of it, and by their obstinacy in refusing to apply to the King for relief. This appears as well by other letters, as by one from Lord Anglesey

---

[1] Thomas Wakely, formerly of Hingham, Massachusetts.

[2] Roger Plaisted, "a brave and trustworthy officer, made a lieutenant under authority of Massachusetts in 1668." See editor's note 2 to p. 228.

to Mr. Leveret,* between whom there was a friendly correspondence kept up. In Cromwell's court Mr. Leveret had been, perhaps, upon a level with Mr. Annesly.† There seems to have been no ground for the charge; neither men nor money were wanting for the service. An application to England, for men, was [not] necessary, and I meet with no papers which intimate that there was any thought of it in any persons in the colony. Fighting made soldiers. As soon as the inhabitants had a little experience of the Indian way of fighting, they

---

* Sir,   "London, May 16, 1676.

I received your letter, intimating the troubles of that country, unexpectedly brought upon you by the Indians, and as I thank you for it, so I wish the continuance of your correspondence and informations, as often as occasion offers, having as great a sympathy as any for your sufferings, and as warm inclinations, both to advise and assist you, to my power, against your barbarous and ungrateful enemies. But when I have said this (as the best proof of it) I must chide you and that whole people of New-England, that (as if you were independent of our master's crown, needed not his protection, or had deserved ill of him, as some have not been wanting to suggest and urge testimony thereof) from the first hour of God's stretching out his hand against you to this time (though we have successive and frequent tidings (like Job's messengers) of the great devastations and spoils that are made by fire and sword upon those plantations, which God hath so signally blessed, and made to flourish till now) you have not yet (as certainly became you) made your addresses to the King's Majesty, or some of his ministers, for his perusal, that he might be authentically informed both of your enemies and your condition, by what means you are brought low, and what are the most proper and hopeful remedies for your recovery.

I can write but by guess, yet it is not altogether groundlessly reported, that the French do underhand assist and supply your enemies, that you are divided among yourselves, that you have not used ordinary providence, that you are too tenacious of what is necessary for your preservation, as if you kept your goods for your enemies, and wanted hearts to make use of them yourselves, that you are poor and yet proud. This was not the spirit that carried you into that wilderness and led you on there ever since, building and planting for yourselves and God. But these calamities may come upon you to bring you to your first post, and to do your first works, tho' I would not willingly judge you therein.

It may not be fit for me to advise you what to do, till better informed, but I know his Majesty hath a tender and compassionate heart for all his subjects that are industrious and orderly, and hath power sufficient, as well as will, to help his colonies in distress, as others have experienced, and you may, in good time. He knows how to deal with the French, either by the interposition of their own King, or by authorizing and assisting you to right yourselves against them. He can send ships or men to help you, or furnish you with ammunition, as the case requires, or, by a general collection, open the bowels and purses of his people here towards you, where there are many that mourn for your distress, and will not only be intercessors to the throne of grace, but to God's vicegerent also, for your relief, if you are not wanting to yourselves and failing in that dutiful application which subjects ought to make to their sovereigns in such case.

If these hints may work any thoughts of heart in you, that may produce speedy and effectual councils for your re-establishment, I shall rejoice that I have been your remembrancer, and shall promote in the best manner I can your requests to that end, being to you, and the good people of that colony, an affectionate friend and hearty well-wisher,

To my most esteemed friend   ANGLESEY.

    John Leverett, Esq; governor, &c.

† Afterwards Earl of Anglesey.

became a match for them. An addition to their numbers they did not want. Be that as it may, this is certain, that as the colony was at first settled, so it was now preserved from ruin without any charge to the mother country. Nay, as far as I can judge from the materials I have, the collections made in the colony, after the fire of London, for the relief of the sufferers there, and, upon other occasions, for the relief of divers of the plantations, with other public donations, from the first settlement until the charter was vacated, will not fall much, if any thing, short of the whole sum that was bestowed upon the colony, from abroad, during that time.

In the height of the distress of the war, and whilst the authority of the colony was contending with the natives for the possession of the soil, complaints were making in England, which struck at the powers of government, and an enquiry was set on foot, which was continued from time to time, until it finally issued in a quo warranto, and judgment thereupon against the charter. In the summer of 1676* Edward Randolph[1] was sent to the Massachusets with his Majesty's letter of March 10th, 1675-6, and copies of the petitions and complaints of Mason[2] and Gorges.†[3] The King commanded that agents should be sent over, to appear before him in six months after the receipt of the letter, fully instructed and impowered to

* In the spring of the year 1676, the Dutch took the fort at Penobscot from the French. Some vessels from New-England went and drove off the Dutch, but kept no possession.
† The letter was directed "To the governor and Magistrates of the town of Boston." Randolph was, besides, directed by the Lords committee for trade, &c. to enquire into the state of the colony. The several queries and his answers may be seen in the appendix.[4]

---

[1] Edward Randolph (1632-1703). "Little is known of Randolph's early life. He was connected with the family of John Mason, grantee of New Hampshire, and was a personal correspondent of several high-placed men, among them William Blathwayt. He may be described, indeed, as being hand in glove with the latter gentleman from 1676 until his death in 1703. Randolph had already been employed in Scotland to look after the estates which had come into the hands of the king in 1672 upon the death of Charles Stuart, Duke of Richmond and Lennox." Edward Channing, *History of the United States*, II, 159. There is a lengthy Memoir of Randolph by Robert Noxon Toppan in volumes I and II of *Edward Randolph* published by the Prince Society in 1898.

[2] This was Robert Tufton Mason (*d.* 1688), a grandson of Capt. John Mason the founder of New Hampshire. Capt. Mason died in 1635. His daughter married Joseph Tufton; but their son Robert, in order to meet the terms of his grandfather's will, took the name of Mason in 1655.

[3] This was Ferdinando Gorges (1630-1718), a grandson of Sir Ferdinando and heir to his territory in the Province of Maine. Sir Ferdinando had died in 1647.

[4] They are not in the Appendix, but were published by Hutchinson in his *Collection of Original Papers* (1769), pp. 477-503.

answer. The governor summoned a special court, to meet the 9th of August. The elders which were then in town were desired to attend, and to consider of this question proposed to them by the court, viz.

WHETHER the most expedient manner of making answer to the complaints of Mr. Gorges and Mr. Mason, about the extent of our patent line, be, by sending agents or attornies to answer the same, or to answer by writing only?

THEY soon agreed upon the following answer. ――

It seems unto us the most expedient way of making answer unto the complaints of Mr. Gorges and Mr. Mason, about the extent of our patent line, to do it by appointment of agents, to appear and make answer for us, by way of information at this time, and in this case, provided they be, with utmost care and caution, qualified as to their instructions, by and according to which they may negotiate that affair, with safety unto the country, and with all duty and loyalty unto his Majesty, in the preservation of our patent liberties.

The reasons for their opinion were subjoined. The court determined according to this advice. William Stoughton * and Peter Bulkley † were chosen for the purpose. Soon after their arrival in England, a hearing was had before the Lords of the committee of the council, upon the principal points of their agency, the claims of Gorges and Mason, in both which they were unsuccessful. The province of Main was confirmed to Gorges and his heirs, both as to soil and government. To put an end to all future disputes, as well as to gratify many of the inhabitants of that province, John Usher [1] was employed by the Massachusets to purchase the right and interest of Gorges's heirs, which he did for twelve hundred pounds sterling, and assigned it over to the governor and company. This, instead of con-

---

* Mr. Stoughton was second son of Mr. Israel Stoughton, one of the first magistrates of the colony. He was educated at Harvard college, some years a preacher, but never settled in any parish. A sermon of his at the election is in print. He came early into the magistracy (in 1671).

† Mr. Bulkley was speaker of the house of deputies, son, I suppose, of the celebrated minister of Concord, of the same name. They sailed October 30, 1676.

---

[1] John Usher (1648–1726) was primarily a successful bookseller in Boston, as was his father before him. But with the acquisition of wealth, he mounted from glory to glory until he was Lieutenant-Governor of New Hampshire. During the Andros régime Usher was treasurer of the province of New England and a member of the Council. After Usher's death his estate at Medford was purchased by Col. Isaac Royall. See *Medford Historical Register*, III, 136 *et seq.*

ciliating matters, gave further offence to the crown.* With respect
to Mason's claim, it was determined, that the Massachusets had a
right to three miles North of Merrimack river, to follow the course
of the river, so far as it extended, and that the expressions in the
charter do not warrant the over-reaching those bounds by imaginary
lines or bounds.†

THE controversy between the Massachusets and Mr. Mason having subsisted so many years, it may not be amiss to set his claim or
pretence in its true light. A copy of a grant, made by the council of
Plimouth, to Capt. John Mason, of all the lands between Naumkeak
and Merrimack, dated March 9th, 1621, is the first, in order of time,
that has been produced. This grant was said to be only sealed, unwitnessed, no seisin endorsed, nor possession ever given with the
grant, and no entry upon any record.

ANOTHER copy of a grant, August 10th 1622, of all the lands from

---

* The colony supposed they acquired, by the purchase, a right to the jurisdiction,
and considered themselves, in their corporate capacity, Lords proprietors of the province of Main, as Lord Baltimore and the Penns do of Maryland and Pennsylvania. It
was made a question by some, whether the right of jurisdiction, in the heirs of Gorges,
was such an interest as could legally be sold or devised. [It was said they made the
purchase at a time when it was designed to purchase Gorges's title for the Crown and
this was afterwards charged against them.] Since the incorporation by the new charter,
it is of no great consequence which way it be determined.

† The Massachusets thought themselves aggrieved by the determination of his late
Majesty in council, settling the boundary less favorably for them than they ever expected. The river Merrimack, which runs upon a Western course as far as Dunstable,
afterwards turns to the Northward. It is not certain, that at the time of the grant to
the Massachusets colony, in 1628, this alteration of the course was known to the grant-
ors, or to any European. It is certain, that a few years after our ancestors came over,
evidence was taken and preserved, that this river retained the same name among the
natives from the mouth to the crotch, and there seemed to be no intention in 1677, that
Massachusets line should cross the river. [I have seen a map published in 1635 wherein
the course of it is well described to Winipasioky.] However, in 1738, it was thought
an equitable construction of the province charter that so far as the river kept a western
course, and no farther, the province line should run the same course, keeping the distance of three miles north of the river, but after that to run due west. There was,
besides, a mistake made to the prejudice of the province; for, instead of running as far
as the river kept a western course (the real intention of the royal determination) it stops
several miles short, at Patucket, where the river inclines to the south. Whereas if the
line had been continued to the bend, and then crossed the river, or if the due west line
had begun a few miles short of Patucket, in either case, several miles in breadth, the
whole length of the line would have belonged to the Massachusets, which now falls to
New-Hampshire. This, my Lord Wilmington, who was then president of the council,
assured me in the year 1741, proceeded from a misapprehension of the course of the
river. He did not conceive that at Patucket the river inclined to the southward, or that
any loss was occasioned to the Massachusets. The New Hampshire agent was better
able to manage the controversy than the agents for the Massachusets. [There is room
from the words of the determination in 1677 to question whether the river was understood farther than it kept its western course, but a conformity immediately after to
other constructions seems to remove the doubt.]

Merrimack to Sagadehoc, which, it was said, did not appear to have been signed, sealed, or witnessed, by any order of the council.

ANOTHER grant, or copy of a grant, of part of the same lands, viz. all between the rivers Merrimack and Piscataqua, to Captain John Mason alone, dated Nov. 7, 1629.

ANOTHER grant in 1635, April 22d, of all the lands between Naumkeag and Piscataqua river.*

IN all this confusion of grants, or copies of grants, the greatest stress is laid upon that of November 7th, 1629. It is a strange thing that the council of Plimouth, unless all those grants, prior to the Massachusets grant, had been either deemed imperfect and invalid from the beginning, or else resigned and thrown up, should grant the same lands to the Massachusets, Mason and Gorges both being members, and the most active members of the council. It is not easy to account for a grant of all the lands between Merrimack and Piscataqua to Mason in 1629, when three miles between those two rivers had been granted the year before to the Massachusets. The grants which were made, or pretended to be made, in 1635, were the efforts of a number of the members of the council, to secure some part of the dying interest to themselves and posterity, in which they all failed.†

SIR William Jones, the attorney general, gave his opinion upon the whole case, which was transmitted to the Massachusets, and is as follows.

THE case of the governor and company of Massachusets Bay, in New-England, in America.

3d Nov. 14 Jac. The whole tract of New-England was granted to 40 persons, Lords and others, by the name of the council of New-England,

* Douglass says, v. 2. p. 26. That Mason in 1635, and Gorges in 1639, obtained royal patents, with powers of jurisdiction; but Douglass was under a mistake as to Mason. About that time, as has been before observed, it was intended a general governor should be sent over, and Mason was appointed, and received a commission as governor over that part of the continent from Naumkeag to Piscataqua, but subject to the general governor. The design of a general governor was laid aside, and we hear no more of the commission to Mason, which he never came to America to publish. *Ancient MS.*

† An action was brought in Feb. 1682, at Portsmouth, against one Wadley of Exeter, in which this grant of 1635 was principally relied on, and Mr. Chamberlayne, secretary of the province, and one Mr. Reynes made oath, that they had compared the copy with the original, which did not appear to have been either signed, sealed, or witnessed. The lands in question had been many years occupied, and the plaintiff failed in his suit. It was observed, on the trial, that the council of Plimouth was to consist of forty persons, who had power of granting lands in New-England, provided it was done by the major part of them, or the major part of a lawful assembly of the said council, and under their common seal. Nothing of this appeared. The original grant could not be found in 1691, when Allen entered a caveat against the Massachusets charter. He pretended it was in New-England. *Hubbard MS.*

established at Plimouth, whereby power is given them to set out lands and hereditaments to adventurers and planters, as should, by a commission of survey, and distribution executed, be named.

19 Mar. 1628. The said council grant the Massachusets colony to Roswell and others.

4 Mar. 4 Car. 1. The grant to Roswell, &c. was, by letters patent, confirmed to the said proprietors and others, their associates, who were then incorporated, with power of government granted to them, and of making laws, not repugnant to the laws of England.

The company, in pursuance of this grant of the council of Plimouth and charter from the King, transport themselves and make a settlement upon the said lands, distributing the same, from time to time, freely to adventurers and planters, without any rent reserved to the company; yet so that, where the said lands were possessed by the natives, the planters did also purchase from them.

May 1657.[1] It is enacted by the laws of the place, That any person, who had, by himself, his grantees or assigns, before the law about inheritance 14 Octo. 1652, possessed and occupied, as his or their proper right in fee simple, any houses or lands there, and should so continue without disturbance, lett, suits, or denial, legally made by having the claims of any person thereto entered with the recorder of the county, and such claim prosecuted to effect within 5 years next after the 20th of that present May 1657, every such proprietor, their heirs and assigns, shall for ever after enjoy the same, without any lawful lett, suit, disturbance, or denial, by any other claim of any person or persons whatsoever, any law or custom to the contrary notwithstanding.

No claims made of the lands in question, within the Time limited.

In 1635, the patent of 3d [2] Nov. 14 Jac. surrendered.

Mr. Mason's title.

2 Mar. 1621. Mr. Mason, by grant from the council at Plimouth, under their common seal, to his ancestor John Mason, claims some ten towns within the Massachusets bounds of their patent, to be called Mariana, to hold to him and his heirs, in fee and common socage, &c. subject to the exceptions in the grant to the grand council, yielding a fifth part of all ore found to his Majesty, and another fifth part to the council, with a letter of attorney to the chief officer there for the time being, for delivery of possession and seisin to the grantee Mason, or his attorney.

Note, the grant only sealed with the council seal, unwitnessed, no seisin endorsed, nor possession ever given with the grant.

---

[1] The first edition gives "1637" instead of "1657." The context sustains the second edition, as does Shurtleff's *Records of Massachusetts Bay*, IV (Part I), 288.

[2] The first edition gives "30" instead of "3d" November; "3d" is correct. The number of the year of James's reign in which the grant of New England was made should be "18" instead of "14," both here and on p. 266. But all three editions give "14."

10 Aug. 1622. The said council grant, aliene, sell, and confirm to Sir Ferdinando Gorges and Capt. John Mason, their heirs and assigns, all the lands lying between the rivers Merrimack and Sagadehoc.

Note as in the Grant of 1621.

7 Nov. 1629. The said council grant part of the premises to Capt. John Mason, single, and his heirs, extending between the rivers of Merrimack and Piscataqua.

Note as above.

1631. The same council did again grant a small parcel of the premises granted to Sir Ferdinando Gorges and Capt. John Mason, unto the said Sir Ferdinando and Capt. Mason, with about six or seven others, their associates, lying on both sides the river Piscataqua, upon which lands some settlements were made, and some part thereof divided between the said grantees and adventurers after 1631.*

April 1635. Capt. John Mason obtains a new grant from the said great council, of all the lands from Naumkeag river to Piscataqua river, by the name of New Hampshire, at which time all that part of the lands, so granted, which are now contained within the bounds of the Massachusets, were actually distributed to and planted by the inhabitants of that colony, by virtue of their grant from the said council.

The whole matter in difference was referred to the two Lord Chief Justices, by his Majesty in council.

They, after a solemn hearing of counsel on both sides, reported unto his Majesty:

That as to the right of the soil of the province of New-Hampshire and Main, they could give no opinion, not having proper parties before them, it appearing, that not the Massachusets, but the ter-tenants, had the right of soil and whole benefit thereof, and yet were not summoned to defend their titles.

As to Mr. Mason's right of government within the soil he claimed, their Lordships, and indeed his own counsel, agreed he had none,† the great council of Plimouth, under whom he claimed, having no power to transfer government to any.

As to the bounds of the Massachusets colony, their Lordships have, by their said report, excluded thereout the four towns of Dover, Portsmouth, Exeter and Hampton, parcel of Mr. Mason's claim, "but determined the remainder of his claim to be within their bounds." Which report was confirmed by his Majesty in council.

---

* If Mason supposed any of the preceding grants to be in any force, why should he take a grant of part of the lands only contained in those former grants, and take in associates, and come to a division with them?

† Although Douglass, as has been observed, goes further, and says, that "Aug. 19, 1635, King Charles, by patent, confirms the grant called New-Hampshire, with power of government and jurisdiction (as in the palatinate or bishoprick of Durham) with power of conferring honours," yet this is not probable. His heirs were certainly unacquainted with it, or they would have made mention of it before the King in council in 1691.

1st Query. Whether Mr. Mason's grants, being only under the council of Plimouth's seal, unwitnessed, and without any entry or record of them any where, without seisin endorsed, and no possession having ever gone along with them, be valid in law to oust about 50 years possession, a title under the government of the Massachusets, and a purchase from the natives?

I think it not good according to the law of England, and New-England having no particular law of their own (to my knowledge) which differs from the law of England, as to the manner of passing lands, I do not see how any of these grants can be good.

Or, admitting they be good in law,

2d Quer. Whether Mr. Mason be not stopped by the law of the place, as above, having not made his claim thereto within the time prescribed?

If Mr. Mason's estate do lie within the jurisdiction of the assembly which made this law, and that this assembly were rightly constituted according to the powers given by charter, I think Mr. Mason was bound by this law, which I look upon to be a reasonable law, and agreeing in reason with the law of England.

And if Mr. Mason have right thereto,

3d Quer. Whether ought not that right to be tried on the place, ten of the towns claimed by him remaining within the Massachusets by the chief justices report?

I think his right ought to be tried upon the place, for so much thereof as lies within the Massachusets jurisdiction, liable to such appeal as the charter allows, if it allows any.

4th Quer. Or, if triable here, by what court can it properly be so, whether in one of the four courts at Westminster, or upon a special Commission, and how, in your judgment, whether by jury or otherwise?

It cannot properly be tried here by any of the four courts, but according to the law of the place, if it lie within any jurisdiction, and if within none, the King may erect courts, to proceed according to the law of England, unless altered by the legislative power of the place.*

18 Sept. 1679. W. JONES.

A commission was issued by the crown for the government of New-Hampshire. The Massachusets, thereupon, forbore any further

---

* Before 1691 Mason's heirs had sold their title to Samuel Allen, and nothing more was heard of it until 1737, after the determination of the controversy between the Massachusets and New-Hampshire. A large tract of country, which always before was supposed to be within the Massachusets province, being left out of it, John Tufton, now a lieutenant colonel in the army, a descendant from Mason, and who then took the name of Tufton Mason agreeable to the last will of his ancestor, laid claim to it, as heir in tail to the first grantee, and having suffered a recovery, sold his interest to divers persons, who now call themselves proprietors, &c. Capt. Mason was a generous adventurer in a noble design, the peopling a new country, which has a tendency to multiply the human race. Many of the first adventurers failed. Those who came after saw their errors, avoided them, and succeeded. This has often been the case with other great undertakings. The first undertakers ought not to be forgotten.

exercise of jurisdiction. The towns of Salisbury, Amesbury and Haverhill, by their original grants from the Massachusets colony, extending more than three miles from Merrimack, the Massachusets continued to exercise jurisdiction over the whole of those towns, although, according to the determination, part of them lay without the patent.

BESIDES this controversy about bounds, the agents had other complaints to answer. Randolph, who, the people of New-England said, "went up and down seeking to devour them," returned to England, and represented the colony as refusing any obedience to the acts for regulating the trade of the plantations. A ship, belonging to Mr. Usher, put the owner ashore at some English port, and went over to Holland. Mr. Stoughton writes (1st Dec. 1677)

Randolph upon this news was full of business, being employed, as he said, by my Lord treasurer, to make enquiry about it, in order to further proceedings, but now we have intelligence as if that vessel were again put into Plimouth, and had not been in Holland. If she either make her market here, or pay her duties before she go elsewhere, it may help to allay matters. The country's not taking notice of these acts of navigation to observe them, hath been the most unhappy neglect that we could have fallen into, for, more and more every day, we find it most certain, that without a fair compliance in that matter, there can be nothing expected but a total breach, and the storms [1] of displeasure that may be.

THE Quakers also renewed their complaints against the colony. In the distress of the colony by the Indian war, among other sins, which were the cause of it, the toleration shown to Quakers was thought to be one; the court therefore made a law,

That every person, found at a Quaker Meeting, shall be apprehended ex officio, by the constable, and, by warrant from a magistrate or commissioner, shall be committed to the house of correction, and there have the discipline of the house applied to them, and be kept to work, with bread and water, for three days; and then released, or else shall pay five pounds in money, as a fine to the country, for such offence, and all constables neglecting their duty, in not faithfully executing this order, shall incur the penalty of five pounds, upon conviction, one third whereof to the informer.

I know of nothing which can be urged, in any wise tending to excuse the severity of this law, unless it be human infirmity, and the many instances in history of persons, of every religion, being fully persuaded that the indulgence of any other was a toleration of impiety,

---

[1] The first edition gives "and all the storms" instead of "and the storms."

and brought down the judgments of heaven, and therefore justified persecution.* This law lost the colony many friends. [The agents then in England complain of it and know not what answer to give when inquired of nor how to quiet the clamour raised against the Colony for so unreasonable an act of persecution.]

SEVERAL addresses were made to the King, from the general court, whilst the agents were in England, and the court made several laws to remove some of the exceptions which were taken in England, particularly an act to punish high treason with death; another, requiring all persons, above 16 years of age, to take the oaths of allegiance, on pain of fine and imprisonment; "the governor, deputy governor and magistrates having first taken the same, without any reservation, in the words sent to them by his Majesty's orders." † The King's arms were ordered to be carved and put up in the court-house. But it was

* At the same time that this punishment was provided for quakers, other provoking evils were enumerated; in the order following, viz.

1. Neglect of care of the children of church members. A reformation recommended to the elders and brethren.

2. Pride, in mens wearing long hair like womens hair, others wearing borders of hair, and cutting, curling, and immodest laying out their hair, principally in the younger sort. Grandjurors to present, and the court to punish all offenders, by admonition, fine, or correction, at discretion.

3. Excess in apparel, strange new fashions, naked breasts and arms, and pinioned, superfluous ribbands on hair and apparel. The court to fine offenders at discretion.

4. Quakers meetings.

5. Prophaneness, in persons, turning their backs upon the public worship before the blessing is pronounced. Officers of churches and selectmen, to appoint persons to shut the meeting-house doors, or to take any other meet way to attain the end.

6. Prophane cursing or swearing. If any person heard another curse or swear, and did not inform, he was made liable to the same penalty with the prophane person.

7. Tipling-houses. Inspectors to be appointed, and if they did not do their duty, they were to incur the penalty of the law against tipling-houses.

8. Breach of the fifth commandment. All inferiors in families absent at night, in corrupt company, without leave, admonished, and fined, not exceeding 10s. for the first offence, whipped, not exceeding five stripes, for all after offences.

9. Idleness. All idle persons to be taken notice of by the constable, their names to be returned to the selectmen, who had power, in case of obstinacy, to send them to the house of correction.

10. Oppression in shopkeepers and merchants, by taking too much for their goods, and in mechanicks, who required too much for their labour. Every person who had been oppressed in this way, might apply to the grand-jury, or to the county court, who had power to cause the offender to make twofold restitution, and to fine at discretion.

11. A loose and sinful custom of riding from town to town, men and women together, under pretence of going to lectures, but, really, to drink and revel in taverns, tending to debauchery and unchastity. All single persons, being offenders, to be bound to their good behavior, with sureties in 20l. fine, or suffer fine and imprisonment.

For most of these offences I have not seen any instances of prosecution. Excessive penalties, or penalties not adapted to the nature of the offence, prevent prosecutions. The multiplying laws, with such penalties, in any government, tends to lessen the weight and authority of the penal laws in general.

† Mass. Records.

a more difficult thing to conform to the acts of trade.* They acknowledge in their letter to the agents they had not [observed them.] They

apprehended them to be an invasion of the rights, liberties, and properties of the subjects of his Majesty in the colony, they not being represented in parliament, and according to the usual sayings of the learned in the law, the laws of England were bounded within the four seas, and did not reach America; however, as his Majesty had signified his pleasure that those acts should be observed in the Massachusets, they had made provision, by a law of the colony, that they should be strictly attended from time to time, although it greatly discouraged trade, and was a great damage to his Majesty's plantation.

The passing this law, plainly shews the wrong sense they had of the relation they stood in to England.† The people of Ireland, about the same time, were under the same mistake. Perhaps they had not greater colour for an exemption from English acts of parliament, than a colony of natural born subjects, departing the kingdom with the leave of their Prince. Particular persons in Ireland, did penance for advancing and adhering to these principles. The whole colony of the Massachusets, suffered the loss of their charter, this being one great article of charge against it. I am glad I have this instance of Ireland, and that so sensible a gentleman as Mr. Molineux,[1] the friend of Mr. Locke,[2] engaged in the cause; for it may serve as some excuse for our ancestors, that they were not alone in their mistaken

* [Their Agents wrote to them from England that the country's not taking notice of the Acts of navigation, to observe them, was the most unhappy neglect they could have fallen into, for they found it, every day, to be more and more certain that without a fair compliance in that matter, there could be nothing expected, but a total breach, and all the storms of displeasure that may be.]

† "This court being informed, by letters received this day from our messengers, of his Majesty's expectation that the acts of trade and navigation be exactly and punctually observed by this his Majesty's colony, his pleasure therein not having been, before now, signified unto us, either by express from his Majesty, or any of his ministers of state:

"It is therefore hereby ordered, and by the authority of this court enacted, That henceforth, all masters of ships, ketches, or other vessels, of greater or lesser burthen, arriving in or sailing from any of the ports in this jurisdiction, do, without coven or fraud, yield faithful and constant obedience unto, and observation of, all the said acts of navigation and trade, on penalty of suffering such forfeitures, loss, and damage, as in the said acts are particularly expressed, and the governor and council, and all officers commissioned and authorized by them, are hereby ordered and required to see to the strict observation of the said acts."

[1] William Molineux or Molyneux (1656–1698). In 1698 he published *The Case of Ireland's being bound by Acts of Parliament in England stated.*

[2] John Locke (1632–1704), the philosopher.

apprehensions of the nature of their subjection. No prejudice can be caused, by this mistake, against their posterity. They have indeed as high notions of the value of English liberties [1] as their ancestors had, and, as a British-colony, they humbly hope for all that tenderness and indulgence from a British parliament which the Roman Senate, while Rome remained free, shewed to Roman colonies, but they are sensible that they are colonists, and therefore subject to the controul of the parent state.*

MR. Leveret continued governor, by annual election, from his being first chosen in 1673, until his death, March 16th 1678. The weighty affairs of the war, and the agency, during his administration, conducted with prudence and steadiness, caused him to be greatly respected.† He was succeeded by Simon Bradstreet (May 1679) who was one of the first assistants, and had continued to be annually chosen an assistant fifty years together, being about seventy-six years of age when he first entered upon the office of governor. A few months before, upon the death of Mr. Symonds, Mr. Bradstreet succeeded him as deputy governor. Upon Mr. Bradstreet's being chosen governor, Thomas Danforth came into the deputy governor's place, and they were continued in their respective places, from year to year, until the dissolution of the government.

WHILST the agents were in England, days of fasting and prayer, some by the court, some by the whole people, were repeatedly appointed by authority, to implore the divine blessing upon their endeavours for obtaining favor with the King, and the continuance of charter privileges, and November 21st 1678 was observed as a fast by all the churches in the three colonies. A council or synod of the

* [This observation was made before the unhappy disputes occasioned by the Stamp Act. From the Revolution down to the date of that Act there does not appear any doubt of the authority of Parliament to bind the Plantations by it's Acts, and when the doubt was first started some, who then appeared to be of the party in opposition to government, and who afterwards were among the most active, pronounced the denial of this authority to be highly criminal; nor has it yet been shewn that there is any bond, which can keep the Kingdom and its Plantations together as one state, except the authority of Parliament over the whole. The distinction between Taxation and Legislation in general does not seem to have been known under the first charter.]

† He died of the stone. His only son maintained but an indifferent character. His grandson, John Leveret, after sustaining, in the civil order, several honorable posts, speaker of the assembly, justice of the superior court, member of the council, one of the three commissioners with power of controlling the army sent against Port Royal, was, in 1707, chosen president of Harvard college, in which post he continued until his death, having the character of a gentleman and scholar, and also of a man of virtue and religion.

[1] The first edition gives "notions of English liberties" instead of "notions of the value of English liberties."

churches in the colony of Massachusets, being convened by order of court in May 1679, these two questions were referred for their consideration and answer.

QUEST. 1st. What are the reasons that have provoked the Lord to bring his judgments upon New-England?

QUEST. 2d. What is to be done, that so those evils may be removed?

I do not censure the authority of the colony for their great anxiety on this occasion, or for using every proper measure to obtain the smiles of heaven, as well as the favor of their earthly sovereign, and only remark, that we have no evidence of any extraordinary degeneracy.* At this time, Great-Britain, Scotland especially, was suffering under a prince inimical to civil and religious liberty. New-England therefore, without a miraculous interposition, must have expected to share the same judgments, and, perhaps, had not greater reason to make the two inquiries, than either of the two kingdoms.

THE complaint of Gorges and Mason, and the uncertainty of the event, restrained the general court from any attempt to hold possession of the country Eastward of Main. Upon the exchange of Surinam for New-York, that country, and the islands and countries contained in the former grant to the Duke of York, were granted anew, and Major Andros, governor under the Duke, erected a fort, and established a custom-house at Pemaquid, part of the territory between Kenebeck and St. Croix. Whilst the Dutch were in possession of New-York, this territory had been neglected, and the inhabitants being without any powers of government, the Massachusets (in 1672) had sent their commissioners, who appointed and held courts, and established civil and military officers from Pemaquid to Gorges, the sea-coast being well inhabited, and the fishery in a flour-

* Mr. Neale says, "the people began to grow intolerably licentious in their morals, that devout people observed the judgments of God seemed to follow them, blasting epidemical diseases, uncommon losses by sea, &c." The small-pox, which is always travelling about the world, then prevailed. There had been wars with French and Dutch, and captures by the enemy might well have been expected. [But the judgment to which they had special reference was the hazardous state of their charter. It would have been well, if they had considered whether the charges against them which caused this hazard were not well grounded, and whether they had done what was incumbent on them to remove it. The only charges which their agents were concerned about, as appears by their letters, were the extension of the bounds of the charter so as to comprehend the two Provinces of New Hampshire and Main, and their neglect or refusal to conform to the Acts of Parliament for regulating the Plantation trade. The construction of the words in the Charter which define the bounds, was strained and unnatural and would comprehend New Plimouth as well as the other two colonies. They had declared their conformity to the acts or orders of the Parliament or House of Commons before the Restoration, what reason could be assigned for not conforming to Acts of the King, Lords and Commons after the Restoration?]

ishing state, but upon the Duke's taking possession, by his governor, they laid aside their pretences to jurisdiction.

THE agents were detained in England until the fall of 1679. They thought themselves not at liberty to return, without the King's express leave. The popish plot prevented an attention to plantation affairs, and it was thought too great a hardship to detain them any longer. Upon their repeated application they were dismissed, and arrived at Boston, December 23d. They had obtained nothing but time, a further opportunity for the colony to comply with the requisitions made by the crown. Assurances seem to have been given by the agents that other persons should be sent over to supply their places, and although, upon their return, no mark of disapprobation of their conduct was shewn by the general court, but a vote passed thanking them for their pains, yet many were dissatisfied, especially with Mr. Stoughton, who they thought to have been too compliant.* They brought with them the King's letter of July 24, 1679, containing the following requisitions.

1. THAT agents be sent over in six months, fully instructed to answer and transact what was undetermined at that time.

2. THAT freedom and liberty of conscience be given to such persons as desire to serve God in the way of the church of England, so as not to be thereby made obnoxious, or discountenanced from their sharing in the government, much less that they, or any other his Majesty's subjects (not being papists) who do not agree in the congregational way, be by law subjected to fines or forfeitures, or other incapacities.

3. That no other distinction be observed in making of freemen, than that they be men of competent estates, rateable at 10s. according to the rules of the place, and that such, in their turns, be capable of the magistracy, and all laws made void that obstruct the same.

4. THAT the ancient number of eighteen assistants be henceforth observed, as by charter.†

* Mr. Stoughton, perhaps, ever had the interest of his country at heart, but in the pursuit of it governed himself by the rules which Cicero, in one of his epistles, prescribes for a wise magistrate. "Nunquam enim, præstantibus in republica gubernanda viris, laudata est in una sententia perpetua permansio; sed ut in navigando tempestati obsequi aetis est, etiamsi portum tenere non queas; cum vero id possis mutata velificatione assequi, stultum est eum tenere, cum periculo, cursum, quem ceperis, potius quam, eo commutato, quo velis tandem pervenire." *Ad Lentul.*

† They continued to limit themselves to eight or ten assistants. At first, as has been observed, it was done to leave room for persons of quality expected from England. Those expectations had long ceased. In a popular government, and where the magistrates were annually chosen, increasing the number would give a better chance to aspiring men. On the other hand, the greater the number of assistants the less the

5. THAT all persons coming to any privilege, trust or office, take the oath of allegiance.

6. THAT all military commissions, as well as the proceedings of justice, run in his Majesty's name.

7. THAT all laws repugnant to, and inconsistent with, the laws of England for trade, be abolished.

8. WHILE Mr. Gorges's complaint was before the council, the agents, without his Majesty's permission, who was some time in treaty for the same, bought Mr. Gorges's interest in the province of Main, for 1200l. His Majesty had heard of some effects, of a severe hand upon his subjects there, and therefore required an assignment of the said province, on repayment of the said 1200l.

9. THAT, as for that part of New-Hampshire province three miles North of Merrimack river, granted to Mr. Mason, the government whereof remained vested in his Majesty, designing to settle the same to the satisfaction of his subjects there, the Massachusets recall all commissions granted by them for governing there.

A compliance with the first of these instructions was delayed. The reasons assigned were, the danger of the seas (Connecticut agent having been taken by the Algerines) and the heavy debt of the colony,* which made it almost incapable of the expence.

As to the second and third, they had no laws to restrain the inhabitants from chusing church of England men into the magistracy, or other office, that law, confining the privilege to church members, being long since repealed, and all protestants of 10s. rateable estate were capable of being made freemen.

THE fourth, they complied with at the next election, in 1680.

AND also with the fifth, sixth, and seventh, in manner as has been mentioned.

THEY justified their purchase of the province of Main, at the desire of the inhabitants, and in favor to them; and denied their having ever used any acts of severity, and were silent as to the re-conveying it.

THE 9th and last they had complied with, as we have just mentioned. [While the agents were in England the Lords of the Committee for Trade and Plantations required their answer to certain heads which I do not find any notice of in their publick report on their return.]

---

weight of the house of deputies, the election of all officers depending upon the major vote of the whole court. This last reason might cause the deputies to refuse their consent to an increase.

* Caused by the late war.

THE first commission for the government of New-Hampshire, was to Mr. Cutt, as president of the province. The following letter was voted, by the new assembly, at their first meeting, and sent to the governor of the Massachusets, to be communicated to the assembly there.

PORTSMOUTH, in the province of New-Hampshire, March 25th, 1680.
    Much honored ——
THE late turn of Providence made amongst us by the all ordering hand, hath given occasion for this present application, wherein we crave leave, as we are in duty bound, first thankfully to acknowledge your great care of us, and kindness towards us, while we dwelt under your shadow, owning ourselves deeply obliged, that you were pleased, upon our earnest request and supplication, to take us under your government, and ruled us well, while we so remained, so that we cannot give the least countenance to those reflections that have been cast upon you, as if you had dealt injuriously with us. Secondly, that no dissatisfaction with your government, but merely our submission to divine providence, to his Majesty's commands, to whom we owe allegiance, without any seeking of our own, or desires of change, was the only cause of our complying with that present separation from you that we are now under, but should have heartily rejoiced, if it had seemed good to the Lord and his Majesty to have settled us in the same capacity as formerly. Thirdly, and withal we hold ourselves bound to signify, that it is our most unfeigned desire, that such a mutual correspondence betwixt us may be settled, as may tend to the glory of God, the honor of his Majesty, whose subjects we all are, and the promoting the common interest, and defence against the common enemy, that thereby our hands may be strengthened, being of ourselves weak, and few in number, and that if there be opportunity to be any ways serviceable unto you, we may shew how ready we are thankfully to embrace the same. Thus wishing the presence of God to be with you in all administrations, and craving the benefit of your prayers and endeavours for a blessing upon the heads and hearts of us who are separated from our brethren, we subscribe   JOHN CUTT, President, at
                                                    the consent of the council
                                                    and general assembly.

Directed, to the honourable governor and council of the Massachusets-
    Bay, to be communicated to the general court in Boston.

This letter was read in general court, May 22d 1680, and ordered to be recorded. [Instances of gratitude in a multitude, or in the body of a people are so rare that without being uncharitable, we may well suppose the weak state of this new Province and a view to protection from Massachusets had no small share in the motives to this letter.]

THE province of Main continued to be protected by the Massachusets. After the purchase from Gorges, the major part of the court
were of opinion, that it should be sold again to the highest bidder,
towards reimbursing the expence of defending it, which they computed at eight thousand pounds, and a committee was appointed for
this purpose, but this vote was reconsidered. However, there was a
necessity of a different administration, from what there had been
formerly. Whilst the province was supposed to be included in the
bounds of the Massachusets charter, the towns were represented in
the general court, and it was to all intents and purposes considered
as a county, but the determination of 1677 had confined the Massachusets to three miles north or north east of Merrimack river. The
colony must consider itself therefore in the place of Gorges, invested
with the powers granted to him by charter or patent. Accordingly,
they appointed their deputy governor Thomas Danforth, president
of the province of Main, to govern under the Massachusets, the lords
proprietaries, and to be accountable to them, and thither he repaired
towards the end of 1679, together with Mr. Nowell, &c. and there
appointed officers, held courts, and made provision for administring
government in the form prescribed by the patent to Sir Ferdinando
Gorges.*

RANDOLPH kept a continual watch upon the colony, and went
divers times to England with complaints, and returned with fresh
orders and powers.† In 1676, he brought over the complaint of
Mason and Gorges. In 1678, he came over with power from the commissioners of the customs, as an inspector and to make seizures and
bring informations for breaches of the acts of trade, but he was generally if not always condemned in costs, and it appears by a representation, he afterwards made to the commissioners, that he had
been a great sufferer. He brought with him also a commission to
divers persons, himself at the head of them, to administer an oath to
the governor faithfully to execute the oath [1] required by the act of

---

* The people of the province of Main were well contented, whilst they enjoyed the
privileges of the Massachusets colony. To become a province of that colony was disagreeable, and they never cordially submitted. Although the Massachusets accounted
themselves a free state, yet this was no security to the others that they should be less
arbitrarily governed than when a single person was the proprietor. "In August 1680,
the deputy governor, Mr. Saltonstall, Nowell, &c. sailed from Boston with 60 soldiers,
in a ship and sloop, to still the people at Casco-bay, and prevent governor Andros's
usurpation." *MS. letter.*

† In a representation of his services to the committee of council, he says he had made
eight voyages to New-England in nine years.

---

[1] The first edition gives "duty" instead of "oath." The third edition follows the
first.

trade.* The governor, Mr. Leveret, did not take the oath in consequence of that commission. Randolph was in England again in 1679 † and returned the latter part of the same year.

THE governor, at the first session after the receipt of new orders from the King, took the oath, which was administred by the deputy governor in open court, not as one of the commissioners. Randolph went home again, the next winter, to renew his complaints, and upon his return to Boston, in 1681, brought with him a commission from the crown for collector and surveyor and searcher of the customs in New-England.‡ He laid his commission before the general court and desired he might be aided in the execution of his office with their countenance and authority, but, no notice being taken of his application, he set up an advertisement in the town-house, to acquaint all persons concerned that an office was erected, &c. This, he said, was taken down by the marshal, by order of the general court or some of the members, he therefore, in a letter to the governor, demands the final resolution of the court, whether they will admit the said patent to be in force or not, that he might know how to govern himself. There is no record of any resolution of the court herein. During these distresses of the colony there were two parties subsisting in the government, both of them agreed in the importance of the charter privileges, but differing in opinion upon the extent of them, and upon the proper measures to preserve them. The governor, Mr. Bradstreet, was at the head of the moderate party. Randolph, in all his letters, takes notice of it. The governor's son in a letter from New-London, April 1681, writes,

* Edward Randolph, Thomas Savage, William Taylor, George Curwin the elder, Thomas Brattle, Thomas Deane, James Whetcomb, Richard Wharton, John Richards, Humphrey Warren, Thomas Kellond, John Hubbard, Humphrey Davy, and Samuel Mosely, together with the members of the council, for the time being, were the commissioners.

† "Mr. Randolph yet waits to get the country better qualified for his reception. By a letter which he wrote to one of Boston, in the west, who was so ingenuous as to send the very original to us, we perceive great things are upon the wheel, relating to us, in his airy fancy. They were such as not to be committed to paper, but to be communicated in the safer way of private discourse." *Bulkley's letter to Bradford,* 1679.

‡ William Dyre,[1] at the same time, called himself surveyor and searcher-general. I suppose this was the beginning of the office of surveyor-general, his commission extending to New-York, but the powers and duties of these offices were not then fully settled. Randolph did not chuse to acknowledge himself Dyre's inferior, or subject to his controul.

---

[1] William Dyre may have been the son of Mary Dyer, who was hanged on Boston Common in 1660. See *Edward Randolph* (published by the Prince Society), VI, 166.

As to what you say about the change some people expect this election, so far as it concerns yourself it may be an advantage. Better the ruin, if it must be so, under other hands than yours. Time will make it appear who have been the faithful and wise conservators of New-England's liberties, and that the adored saviours of our interests, many of them, have consulted very ill the interest espoused by them.

Mr. Stoughton, Mr. Dudley, and William Brown [1] of Salem, fell in with the governor. The deputy governor, Mr. Danforth, was at the head of the other party, the principal members of the court with him were Major Gookins of Cambridge, Peter Tilton [2] of Hadley, Elisha Cooke [3] and Elisha Hutchinson [4] of Boston. This party opposed the sending over agents, the submitting to acts of trade, &c. and were for adhering to their charter according to their construction of it, and leaving the event. Gookins, being aged, desired a paper he drew up as his dying testimony might be lodged with the court, containing the reasons of his opinion. He was a very zealous but an upright man, and acted from principle. He seems to have been the only magistrate who a few years before opposed the people in their rage against the Indians, friends and enemies without distinction, and exposed himself to the reproaches of his brethren in the magistracy upon the bench, as well as to hootings and offensive language from the populace as he passed the streets. Tilton was one of the most rigid, and was concerned in a paper, published about that time, representing the great apostasy both of magistrates and ministers.

IN 1680 * a letter had been received under the King's sign manual,

---

* Lord Culpeper governor of Virginia came to Boston the 24th of August this year, in his return to England.

It appears by the records that the Hon. George Russell (I suppose a younger brother to the celebrated Lord Russell) was in New-England in 1680, and presented with the

---

[1] William Brown (1639–1716) later became a member of Andros's Council, and of the Council of Safety which followed it. He was left out in the new charter but was chosen to the Council in 1693.

[2] Peter Tilton (d. 1696) came to Hadley from Windsor, Connecticut, and was recorder of the town from 1661 to 1693. Lucius Manlius Boltwood, *Genealogies of Hadley Families* (included in Sylvester Judd, *History of Hadley*, Springfield, 1905), p. 143.

[3] Elisha Cooke (1637–1715), physician and politician, was graduated from Harvard College in 1657, married a daughter of Governor Leverett, and advanced rapidly. He was elected to the House of Deputies in 1681, became its Speaker, and in 1684 was chosen an Assistant. His subsequent career is narrated in the text. See John Langdon Sibley, *Biographical Sketches of Graduates of Harvard University*, I, 520–525.

[4] Elisha Hutchinson (1641–1717) was the son of Capt. Edward Hutchinson, and so the grandson of Anne Hutchinson. Also he was the grandfather of Governor Thomas Hutchinson. He was a Deputy in 1680–83 and a member of the Council from 1684 until his death. He was a strong, active man and made many visits to England, but he was not successful in business. Peter Orlando Hutchinson, Editor, *Diary and Letters of Thomas Hutchinson*, II, 466–467.

charging the colony with neglecting to send over other agents in the room of those who had obtained leave to return, and requiring that they be sent in three months after the receipt of the letter, and that they come prepared to answer the claim which Mason had made to the lands between Naumkeag and Merrimack. Immediately upon the receipt of this letter, the court chose two agents, Mr. Stoughton and Mr. Nowell, and instructions were drawn up, but both of them peremptorily refused to engage in the affair; Mr. Stoughton, notwithstanding the exceptions some had taken to his former conduct, being strongly urged to it. As for Mason's claim, it was looked upon as groundless and extravagant, and the court gave themselves but little concern about it further than to observe, that if he had any pretence to the lands, his title would be fairly tried upon the spot, where by law and according to the opinion of the attorney and solicitor general in 1677, it ought to be tried. After this, Randolph * brought to Boston the King's letter of October the 21st 1681,† complaining

freedom of the colony. Mr. Richard Saltonstall, son of Sir Richard, returned this year after many years absence, and was again chosen first assistant, and so the two succeeding years. He went back to England, before 1683, and died at Hulme, April 29th 1694. *MS. letter.* He left an estate in Yorkshire. Mr. Saltonstall was related to Mr. Hamden,[1] who like his ancestors was a true friend to New-England. In a letter from Mr. Saltonstall's daughter, dated May 1694, I find this little piece of English history, "The court is altered as well as other places, Mr. H——n was to wait on master, and all looked very smooth. He asked him concerning the report he heard, (this was a second time, not that mentioned in my other letter) he said no, no, there was nothing in it, he did not intend to remove him. He kissed hands, and, that night, a new commission was granted to a young person under 30 years of age, who they say must go before all the grave judges. His virtues may be wrote in a little room, but not his vices. A few days after, the archbishop was sent to tell him how well he was esteemed, but he growing into years might like his ease. If he would be Lord or Earl, he should be either, or have any pension. To the first he answered, that he would die a country gentleman of an ancient family, as his was, and honor enough for him. For the second, he said, he should not take the King's money, and the King's servants want bread; he always spake against giving pensions to others, and at such a time as this it was a great oppression. While he had a roll and can of beer he would not take the King's money. It is wondered at by many, considering how useful he was in the year 88 and following — but enough of this."

I hope the friendship shewn by the family of Hamden to New-England will excuse my inserting this anecdote, although it has no relation to the affairs of the colony.

* In April 1681, Randolph set up a protest on the exchange in Boston, against the acts of the court.

† "As for the large and particular account you are pleased to give me of the con-

1 John Hampden, the younger (1653–1696) was a grandson of John Hampden, the opposer of ship-money. His interesting career is recounted by Charles Harding Firth in the *Dictionary of Biography.* Anne Waller, the wife of Sir Peter Saltonstall, was a cousin of the elder Hampden. Sir Peter and Sir Richard (1586–*c.* 1658) were first cousins. Leverett Saltonstall, *Ancestry and Descendants of Sir Richard Saltonstall,* p. 10.

that the collector had not been able to execute his office to any effect, that attachments had been brought against him and his officers for doing their duty, that he had been obliged to deposit money before he could bring an action against offenders, that appeals, in matters relating to the revenue, had been refused, and that they had seized into their hands the moiety of forfeitures belonging to his Majesty by law.

It was therefore required,

that fit persons be sent over, without delay, to answer these complaints, with powers to submit to such regulations of government as his Majesty should think fit, that restitution be made of all monies levied from the officers, that they be encouraged in putting the acts of trade in execution, without charge, as in England, that an account be given of forfeitures received, and that appeals be allowed.

The court denied the charge, and said in their answer,

that Mr. Randolph was acknowledged collector, and his commission enrolled, that no suits had been countenanced against any officers, except where the subject had been unjustly vexed, that they knew of no forfeitures, except a fine upon a master of a ship for abusing the government, that they would encourage his officers, and require no deposit for the future; but as to admitting appeals, they hoped it would be further considered.

However, the sending over agents could be no longer delayed. At a court called in Feb. 1681, when his Majesty's letter by Randolph was read, they determined to come to the choice of agents. Mr. Stoughton and Mr. Dudley were chosen, the court being much divided. Mr. Stoughton again utterly refused, and Mr. Richards * 1 was chosen in his stead. The design of taking away the charter became every day more and more evident. Agents impowered to submit to regulations of government, were, in other words, agents impowered

---

cerns of the country in general, your's was sent hither to me to my house here, by Mr. Randolph, where I have been for some weeks, and do intend to stay some weeks longer, so that I doubt Mr. Randolph, by whom I send this, will be gone e'er I come to London, but, when I shall be there, I shall endeavour to inform myself, the best I can, how matters do stand as to your colony, and shall do them the best service and friendly offices I can, and it will be very well and adviseable, that, upon Mr. Randolph's arrival, matters relating to trade be so settled, as that there be no further just complaints upon that account." *Sir George Downing's letter to Governor Bradstreet, East-Hadley, Sept.* 28. 1681.
    * Mr. Richards was a wealthy merchant, of a fair character, and one of the assistants, [but seems to have been to Mr. Dudley as Bibulus was to Caesar.]

---

    1 John Richards (d. 1694), who had been Speaker of the House in 1680, was elected an Assistant in 1681. His first wife was the widow of Adam Winthrop; his second, a daughter of Governor John Winthrop of Connecticut.

to surrender their charter. However, the general court would have been glad to put a more favorable construction upon it, [as] being inconsistent with his Majesty's repeated declarations, and therefore they directed their agents not to do, or consent to any thing that should violate or infringe the liberties and privileges granted by charter, or the government established thereby. A new matter of charge had been brought against them in England, viz. the coining money. This they excused,

it having began in the times of the late confusions, to prevent frauds in the pieces of eight current among them, and if they had trespassed upon his Majesty's prerogative, it was through ignorance, and they humbly begged his pardon.

The other points of exception were answered as before mentioned. The agents sailed May 31st. A public fast was appointed to be observed June 22d, through the colony, to pray for the preservation of their charter and success to the agency. Randolph was in England not long after them, ready to disclose every thing the agents desired to conceal. The governor had desired him to do nothing to the prejudice of the colony. He promised, in his answer, that if they would make a full submission to his Majesty, he would endeavour to procure his Majesty's royal pardon, and the continuance of their privileges, so far as that they should have liberty of conscience and the free exercise of their religion, and that no money should be raised without the consent of the people: for other matters, their agents were most proper to solicit.* The agents, in their first letters to the general court, acquainted them,

that his Majesty was greatly provoked by their so long neglecting to send agents, and they desired the court to consider whether it was best to hazard all, rather than satisfy his Majesty as to the mode of submission to the laws for regulating trade, since they seriously intended to submit to the substance.

[By the mode of submission to which the Agents advise must be understood a conformity to Acts of Parliament without a Law of the Colony to give force to them.] They had not then been heard before the council, but soon after, upon presenting the court's address, they were commanded to shew their powers and all their in-

---

* In Feb. 1681, Randolph exhibited to the Lords of the council articles of high misdemeanor against a faction of the general court sitting in Boston, viz, Thomas Danforth, Daniel Gookin, Nathaniel Saltonstall, Samuel Nowell, Richards, Davy, Gedney, and Appleton, magistrates, and Fisher, Cooke, Brattle, Stoddard, Bathurst, Hathorn, Wait, Johnson, Hutchinson, Sprague, Oakes, Holbrook, Cushing, Hammond, and Pike, deputies.

structions, not publicly, but to Sir Lionel Jenkins, secretary of state, and it appearing, upon perusal, that they did not contain such powers as had been required, they were informed by Lord Radnor,[1] that the council, nem. con. had agreed to report to his Majesty, that unless the agents speedily obtained such powers as might make them capable to satisfy in all points, a quo warranto should proceed. The agents represented the case of the colony as desperate, and left it to the court to determine whether it was most adviseable to submit to his Majesty's pleasure, or to suffer a quo warranto to issue. Many cities had submitted. Bermudas * in the plantations, and the city of London had refused, and quo warranto's had gone out, the determination of which might enable the Massachusets to judge what would be prudent for them to do.†

* Bermudas was the second colony, for many years scarce deserving the name, Virginia being the first. The charter bears date the "29th June in the 13th year of King James 1614, by the name of the governor and company of the city of London for the plantation of the Somer Islands." This charter never was removed to the colony as that of the Massachusets had been. The company continued to meet as a propriety in London. A governor deputed by the company, with a council and assembly, exercised some degree of legislative power in the islands, but the governor and company in London had the power of making laws not repugnant, &c. In 1663 a law was made by the company that every vessel, above five tons, built in the island without express leave of the company first had and obtained, should be forfeited and sold for the use of the company. The inhabitants made complaint of great oppression, and prayed for a dissolution of their charter, that a governor might be appointed by the crown and the subjects governed as they were in Virginia and Barbados. *True relation of the illegal proceedings of the Somer islands company, &c.* 1678.

† Randolph was incessant. June 14th 1682 he writes to the Earl of Clarendon, "His Majesty's quo warranto against their charter and sending for Thomas Danforth and for Samuel Nowell,[2] a late fanatick preacher and now a magistrate, and Daniel Fisher [3] Elisha Cooke, deputies, to attend and answer the articles of high misdemeanors, I have now exhibited against them in my papers sent Mr. Blaithwait,[4] will make the

[1] John Robartes (1606–1685), first Earl of Radnor, was lord president of the Council, 1679–1684.

[2] Samuel Nowell (1634–1688) was a preacher but never a settled minister. He was the son of Increase Nowell, one of the original Assistants. Samuel graduated from Harvard in 1653, became an Assistant in 1680, and was elected Treasurer of the College in 1685. He died in London, whither he had gone to defend New England.

[3] Daniel Fisher (d. 1683) had represented Dedham in the General Court almost continuously since 1658, and was Speaker of the House in 1680–82.

[4] William Blaithwait, or Blathwayt (1649?–1717) was a successful politician who held many lucrative offices under Charles II, James II, and William III. In 1680 he had been appointed "Surveyor and Auditor General of all our revenues arising in America." For many years he was also Secretary at War; and William, who thought well of him because he could speak many languages, made him one of the Commissioners of Trade and Plantations in 1696. "He was a good example of the influential, permanent under official who has always exercised great power in the actual operation of the English constitution, sometimes unhappily." See Edward Channing, *History of the United States*, II, 158, 218, 230, 283.

Upon receipt of these advices, it was made a question, not in the general court only, but amongst all the inhabitants, whether to surrender or not. The opinions of many of the ministers, and their arguments in support of them, were given in writing, and, in general, it was thought better to die by the hands of others, than by their own.* An address was agreed upon by the general court, another was prepared and sent through the colony to be signed by the several inhabitants, which the agents were to present or not, as they thought proper, and they were instructed to deliver up the deeds for the province of Main, if required, and it would tend to preserve their charter, otherwise not; and they were to make no concessions of any privileges conferred upon the colony by the charter.

Cranfield,[1] governor of New-Hampshire, being on a visit at Boston, advised to the agents waiting upon Lord Hide,[2] and tendering him an acknowledgment of 2000 guineas for his Majesty's private service, and, at the same time, promised to represent the colony in a favorable light. The court agreed to the proposal, and shewed him the letter they wrote to the agents thereupon, but he, infamously, represented the colony as rogues and rebels, and made his game of them for making such an offer, and the agents complained of their being ridiculed for the sham put upon the country.† Upon the agents receiving [the before-mentioned] final resolution of the court, their business was at an end. It was immediately determined a quo warranto should go against the charter, and that Randolph should be the messenger of death. The agents [as appears by their letters were greatly distressed in England. They had orders to offer the Two thousand pounds, but had not credit to obtain it. The court had

---

whole faction tremble. If the party were considerable enough to revolt upon his Majesty's resolution to settle the plantation, their first work would be to call me to account for endeavouring openly the alteration of their constitution, which by their law is death."

* The clergy turned the scale for the last time. The balance which they had held from the beginning they were allowed to retain no longer.

† "Truly Sir if you was here to see how we are ridiculed by our best friends at court for the sham Cranfield hath put upon you, it would grieve you. I will assure you, whatever letters he hath shewn you, his Majesty last night told my friend that he had represented us as disloyal rogues." *Dudley to Bradstreet, Feb. 1682.*

---

[1] Edward Cranfield was Lieutenant-Governor of New Hampshire 1682-85. His term was marked by oppression, and it was a happy day for the people of the province when he embarked for Jamaica. See Jeremy Belknap, *History of New Hampshire*, I (1784), 188-221.

[2] Laurence Hyde (1641-1711), second son of Edward Hyde, first Earl of Clarendon, became Viscount Hyde of Kenilworth in 1681 and later Earl of Rochester. At this time he was "the great favourite" of Charles II.

wrote to Lord Hide, afterwards Earl of Rochester, to which letter Cranfield was prior, they were therefore obliged to deliver it, otherwise they would have endeavoured to stifle the whole affair. An offer of money which, it was known they could not procure though authorized to borrow on the credit of a government just expiring, procured no thanks to the agents, nor to their principals. They] arrived at Boston the 23d of October 1683, and the same week Randolph arrived * with the quo warranto, and a declaration from the King, that if the colony, before prosecution, would make full submission and entire resignation to his pleasure, he would regulate their charter for his service and their good, and with no further alterations than should be necessary for the support of his government there. Two hundred copies of the proceedings against the charter of London were sent at the same time, by advice of the privy council, to be dispersed through the province. The governor and major part of the assistants, despairing of any success from a defence, passed the following vote:

The magistrates have voted, that an humble address be sent to his Majesty by this ship, declaring that, upon a serious consideration of his Majesty's gracious intimations, in his former letters, and more particularly in his late declaration, that his pleasure and purpose is only to regulate our charter, in such a manner as shall be for his service and the good of this his colony, and without any other alteration than what is necessary for the support of his government here, we will not presume to contend with his Majesty in a course of law, but humbly lay ourselves at his Majesty's feet, in a submission to his pleasure so declared, and that we have resolved, by the next opportunity, to send our agents, impowered to receive his Majesty's commands accordingly. And, for saving a default for non-appearance upon the return of the writ of quo warranto, that some meet person or persons be appointed and impowered, by letter of attorney, to appear and make defence, until our agents may make their appearance and submission, as above. The magistrates have passed this with reference to the consent of their brethren the deputies hereto.

Edward Rawson,

15th Nov. 1683.   Secretary.

This lay in the house, under consideration, a fortnight, and was then passed upon as follows:

Nov. 30, 1683. The deputies consent not, but adhere to their former bills.   Wm. Torrey, Cler.

* The next day after Randolph arrived, a terrible fire happened in Boston, in the richest part of the town. Some of the people, in their rage and jealousy, supposed the town to be set on fire by his procurement. I find this insinuated in an interleaved almanack, and other manuscripts.

HAD this been made an act of the general court, it is doubtful whether the consequent administration of government would have been less arbitrary than it was, upon the judgment against the charter; but, upon the revolution,[1] they might have reassumed their charter, as Rhode-Island * and Connecticut did their respective charters, there having been no judgment against them.† [Whilst the foregoing vote lay before the deputies, the governor and assistants passed a further vote in the form following —

Upon consideration of the present dissent between the two houses and the impossibility of coming to a good issue in this session, the magistrates judge it to be most expedient and the only way at present best, that a power of attorneyship be sent to a meete person in England to appear and answer in the case of the quo warranto there depending, and that the governor and council by their letter to Sir Lyonel Jenkins do forthwith make an humble signification of the substance of the magistrates vote for a submission to his Majesty according to what in his gracious declaration is contained, unto which they have not yet been able to obtain the consent of the representatives of the freemen, but shall still use their best endeavours that they may, praying his honours favorable representation thereof to his Majesty, and that their interest, by this their present appearance by their attorney, is not to maintain a suit with his Majesty, but only to save a default and contempt until they have further tried to give his Majesty a more full satisfaction. The magistrates have passed this their brethren the deputies consenting.

21 Nov. 1683   Edward Rawson, Secry

* Rhode Island made a full surrender of their charter as appears by the following advertisement in the London gazette, Windsor Sept. 13, 1684. "His Majesty has graciously received the address of the colony of Rhode Island and Providence plantations in New-England, humbly representing, that upon the signification of a writ of quo warranto against their charter, they had resolved in a general assembly not to stand suit with his Majesty, but wholly to submit to his royal pleasure themselves and their charter, whereof his Majesty has thought fit to accept the surrender." The order in council to the attorney general to bring writs of quo warranto against Connecticut and Rhode Island was dated July 15, 1685.

Connecticut had the offer of being annexed to Massachusets or New York. They prayed the continuance of their privileges, but if they must lose their charter they chose to be annexed to Massachusets. This was construed a surrender.

† However agreeable to law this distinction might be, yet equity does not seem to favour it. The charter of London was adjudged forfeited upon a long argument of the greatest lawyers in the nation. The Massachusets was decreed forfeited upon default of appearance. Not only the charter of London but all the charters in the King's dominions I suppose (unless Bermudas is an exception) whether surrendered or whether there had been judgment against them, were re-assumed except that of the Massachusets.

[1] The Glorious Revolution of 1688.

But the deputies sent this back at the same time with the first vote, with their refusal of concurrence. The magistrates, notwithstanding, wrote to Sir L. Jenkins that they had done everything in their power to give his Majesty satisfaction, being fully assured that he would regulate their Charter in such manner as would be for his own service and the good of the colony; and to this they had been also persuaded by their late agents, but they could by no means obtain the consent of the deputies, or representatives of the people: They would earnestly labour to give the people a better understanding before the next ship sailed, and should be glad to give him an account of their success.]

A letter of attorney was sent to Mr. Humphrys,[1] to appear and answer for the province. Addresses were sent, one after another, but to no purpose. In September, a scire facias was received by Mr. Dudley and communicated to the governor, who called a special court. The time for their appearance at Westminster was past before it was received in Boston.* No other answer, than another humble address, was attempted. The case was desperate, and judgment

---

* The proceedings were in this form and order.

The first scire facias, directed to the sheriff of Middlesex, bore test 16th Ap. 36 Car. 2d. whereon a nichil returned.

Trin. 36 Car. 2d. an al. scir. fac. directed to the same sheriff, returned 2d June 1683, whereon another nichill returned.

12th June 36 Car. 2d. the agent for the company moved by his council for time, to send to New-England for a letter of attorney under the corporation seal, to appear and plead to those scire facias's, until Michaelmas term then next, when the court ordered Mr. Attorney should be attended therein, to shew cause the last day of that term why the defendants should not have time to appear.

Mr. Attorney moved against that order, and had it in some part set aside, but waved it, and on hearing council of both sides it was ordered.

18th June 84, That judgment be entered up for his Majesty as of this term, but if defendants appear first day of next term and plead to issue, so as to take notice of a trial to be had the same term, then the said judgment by Mr. Attorney's consent to be set aside, otherwise the same to stand recorded.

On the first day of Michaelmas term following, the company's agent retained counsel to move, and brought several merchants to testify, in the court of chancery, that in the time given it was impossible to have a letter of attorney returned from New-England, so, as they had not given time long enough to perform a matter, it was, in effect, giving no time at all; for a time not sufficient was equally fatal to no time given.

To which the then Lord Keeper replied, that no time ought at all to have been given, in regard that all corporations ought to have attorneys in court at all times to appear for them upon all occasions. And so set aside the order for time to appear and plead, and judgment was entred as in the copy.

---

[1] Humphrys was agent for Massachusetts at London. At this time letters were directed to him thus: "Robert Humfreys, Esq. at his chamber in ye Kings Bench Buildings, in ye Inner Temple." Shurtleff's *Records of Massachusetts Bay*, V, 425.

was entered up, [June 18, 1684,] copy of which was received by Mr. Rawson, July 2d 1685.

BEFORE any new government was settled, K. Charles died. Mr. Blaithwait wrote to the governor,* and recommended the proclaiming K. James, without delay. This was done, with great ceremony, in the high street in Boston (April 20th.)

THERE were all the symptoms, notwithstanding, of an expiring constitution. Several of the towns neglected to send their deputies in the year 1684. Little business was done at the court [except the passing of an act or law to establish and confirm all grants of land made by the General Court, or by any Town or Towns in the jurisdiction as conveying an estate in fee simple, unless otherwise expressly declared in the grant; and to enable the Secretary to affix the Colony seal to the exemplification of any such grant when desired, and to insist that such grant was confirmed by this law]. The people, indeed, shewed some resentment against the magistrates, who had been forward for surrendering. Mr. Dudley, Richards and Brown were dropped, Cooke, Johnson and Hutchinson chose in their stead. Mr. Bradstreet, the governor,† Mr. Stoughton, Bulkeley, Saltonstall and Gidney ¹ had fewer votes than usual. There seems to have been as much indifference in the legislature about public affairs in 1685, expecting every day to be superseded.

THE election for 1686 was the 12th of May. Mr. Dudley being left out, Mr. Stoughton, from complaisance to him, refused to serve.‡

THE 15th, the Rose frigate arrived from England, with a commission to Mr. Dudley,§ as president, and divers others, gentlemen of the council, to take upon them the administration of government.

* He said he did not write as to a government the charter being vacated.

† The governor had 690 votes, Danforth had 631 for governor. *MS.*

‡ One Joseph Redknap died at Boston at the age of 110. He came over at 60, had been a wine cooper in London.

§ Mr. Dudley, when he found he could do his country no service in his agency, that he might not wholly lose his labour, took measures to serve himself, and had recommended himself to the court when he was in London. After his return he kept up a friendly correspondence with Randolph, who warmly espoused his interest, and writes, July 18th, 84, to Col. Shrimpton — "No better news could have come to me, than to hear Mr. Dudley, principally, was left out of the election, the fitter man to serve his King and country, in an honourable station, for they have declared him so," — and again the 26th. "I am extremely solicitous that Mr. Dudley might have the sole government of New-England, for no man better understands the constitution of your country, and hath more loyalty and respect to his Majesty's affairs, but I dare not

¹ Bartholomew Gedney, or Gidney (1640–1698), of Salem, like Elisha Cooke, was both physician and politician. He was destined to be both a member of Andros's Council and a member of the Council appointed in the new charter. Later he was one of the judges at the witchcraft trials.

A copy of the commission was presented [May 17th] and the following answer resolved upon by the court, nemine contradicente.

GENTLEMEN,

WE have perused what you left with us, as a true copy of his Majesty's commission, shewed to us the 17th instant, impowering you for the governing of his Majesty's subjects inhabiting this colony, and other places therein mentioned. You then applied to us, not as a governor and company, but (as you were pleased to term us) some of the principal gentlemen and chief inhabitants of the several towns of the Massachusets, amongst other discourse, saying, it concerned us to consider what therein might be thought hard and uneasy; upon perusal whereof, we find, as we conceive, First, That there is no certain determinate rule for your administration of justice, and that which is, seems to be too arbitrary. Secondly, That the subjects are abridged of their liberty, as Englishmen, both in the matters of legislation and in laying of taxes, and indeed the whole unquestioned privilege of the subject, transferred upon yourselves, there not being the least mention of an assembly in the commission, and therefore we think it highly concerns you to consider whether such a commission be safe for you or us; but if you are so satisfied therein, as that you hold yourselves obliged thereby, and do take upon you the government of this people, although we cannot give our assent thereto, yet we hope we shall demean ourselves as true and loyal subjects to his Majesty, and humbly make our addresses unto God, and in due time to our gracious prince, for our relief.

May 20th 1686.   By order, EDW. RAWSON, Sec'y.

THESE for Joseph Dudley, Esq; and the rest of the gentlemen named in his Majesty's commission.

THE court appointed a committee to take into their custody such papers as referred to the charter, and titles of land, by purchase from

---

openly appear in it, lest it be thought there is some private design in it, but I am, upon all occasions, hinting his merit to his friends." — But, however obnoxious Mr. Dudley had rendered himself, yet he was, with less reluctance, received as their chief ruler, at this time, from a general expectation, which had obtained, of Kirk's [1] being sent over to take the government. Their agent (Humphries) had advised them of the danger of it, and they expected something of the same tragedy he had been acting in the west of England. Mr. Rawson, in a letter to Hinkley, July 1685, writes, that "Colonel Kirke, whom his late Majesty appointed and designed to be our governor, is confirmed by his present Majesty, and is preparing to sail with two frigates, and may be expected in 4 or 5 weeks." This was before his and Jeffries's campaign, as King James called it, in the west; but after the news of the tragedies there, Rawson writes — "Our condition is awful."

---

[1] Col. Percy Kirke (1646?-1691), whose "Lambs" — his regiment — have gone down in history as the harshest of English soldiers because of their behavior in the west of England after the battle of Sedgmoor in 1685.

the Indians or otherwise, and ordered the secretary to deliver the same, and adjourned to the second Wednesday in October.

THE 25th of May the president and council met, and his Majesty's commission was published.

NEW Plimouth, Connecticut, and Rhode-Island, who were less obnoxious, and had been more pliant than the Massachusets, were all to be in like degree sufferers, although not included in Mr. Dudley's commission,* the execution was only respited a few months.

WE have taken no notice of the affairs of New-Plimouth since the year 1676. Having conquered Philip's country of Mount-Hope, now Bristol, it was confirmed to that colony by K. Charles. The Massachusets had applied for it. Mr. Winslow, the governor of Plimouth, died in 1680, Dec. 18th, and was succeeded by Thomas Hinkley, who continued until that colony was included in the same commission with the Massachusets, &c. It was agreed, that the grand council of Plimouth could confer no powers of government. They had nothing therefore to support them at New-Plimouth, but the King's approbation, from time to time, of their proceedings. It might then well be expected that they should act with great caution, to avoid giving offence. They had been amused, from year to year, with assurances that the King would grant them a charter. Such an one as Connecticut had received they prayed for. The name of the Massachusets was odious. The governor kept upon good terms with Randolph, who engaged to do every thing in his power to obtain the charter.† They had orders to send over a copy of their patent, in order to form a new one, in which the Naraganset country was to be included; but, upon the quo warranto coming over to Massachusets, Mr. Blaithwait wrote to the governor, Sept. 27th 1683, —

I must deal plainly with you. It is not probable any thing will be determined, in that behalf, until his Majesty do see an issue of proceedings in relation to the Massachusets colony, and that, upon regulating their charter, that colony be brought under such an actual dependance upon the crown as becomes his Majesty's subjects. From hence it will be, that your patent will receive it's model; and although you may be assured of all you desire, yet it will be expected that, in acknowledgment of so great

* I find the following passage in a letter from Ireland, March 26th 1684. "Our last packet from England brings us news of two very loyal addresses to his Majesty, one from New-Plimouth and the other from Connecticut, which were both very graciously received, by which I suspect you, of the Massachusets, are more whiggish, and your neighbours more toryish, to express it in the language of late in use."

† They sent over Mr. James Cudworth, as their agent, in 1681, to sollicit their patent, but he died soon after his arrival.

favors, such provisions may be inserted as are necessary for the maintenance of his Majesty's authority.

After this, they could have no great reason to hope for success. However, they continued their pursuit, and in Nov. 1683, they forwarded
another address, wherein they congratulated his Majesty upon his
deliverance, in answer to their prayers they hoped, from the late
horrid conspiracy,* and they had appointed the 15th instant for a
day of solemn thanksgiving, for the salvation of his Majesty's royal
person from that and other hellish conspiracies. They go on to pray
his Majesty's favor, in granting them a charter, having sent over a
true copy of their patent from the council of Plimouth. Randolph
writes to the governor of Plimouth the 4th of March following, that
he had presented the address, with the necessary amendments, to his
Majesty in council, that it would be printed, was graciously received,
and that they would find the benefit of it, in dispatch, and settlement
of their colony. Upon the death of King Charles, they were distinguished by King James from the other colonies, by a letter under his
sign manual,† acquainting them with his accession to the throne, the
great things the parliament had done, the defeat of Argyle, and the
landing of Monmouth, and the care taken to prevent his success, all
to prevent any false and malicious rumours that might be spread
among his Majesty's subjects at that distance. An address was sent
to the King, upon his accession, taking notice of the assurances they
had received from his royal brother, and praying that his Majesty
would fulfil them. This was the last effort.‡ Connecticut kept more

---

* This must be the protestant plot.
† June 26th 1685.
‡ King Charles's grant, under his sign manual, of Philip's country, is in these words,
"We have taken into our royal consideration, how that, by your loyalty and good conduct in that war, you have been the happy instruments to enlarge our dominions, and
to bring that new territory of Mount-Hope into a more immediate dependence upon us.
We are therefore graciously pleased to give and grant, and do hereby give and grant
unto you, the full and entire property of the said territory or scope of land, commonly
called Mount-Hope, containing, by common estimation, seven thousand acres, be the
same more or less, for the sole and proper use and behoof of yourselves and the rest of
our said colony of New-Plimouth, to be holden of us, our heirs and successors, as of our
castle of Windsor in the county of Berks, yielding and paying, &c. seven beaver skins
each and every year, &c."
This country of Mount-Hope, with several townships and parts of townships, always
reputed part of the colony of New-Plimouth, by a new line, never, until then, conceived
by any person whatsoever, was, in the year 1741, by commissioners from New-York, &c.
determined to be within the bounds of Rhode-Island charter, and this determination,
perhaps, for want of proper evidence, which might have been produced on the part of
the Massachusets, was afterwards confirmed by his late Majesty in council.
In this and other controversies about boundaries, it has been the misfortune of the
Massachusets province to have been represented as too great and powerful a province,

silent, inactive and reserved, submitting when compelled to it, and reassuming their rights as soon as they had opportunity for it.*

To avoid any interruption in relating the several steps taken for vacating the charter, we have passed over some events, the remembrance of which should be preserved.

THE Indians, at the eastward, continued their hostilities, after those, at the westward, were subdued and dispersed. In August 1676, they surprized the house of Mr. Hammond,[1] an ancient trader at Kenebeck, and, from thence, crossed over to Arowsick island, [where] there was a large house, with, what was there esteemed, a strong fort, built round it, belonging to Major Clark[2] and Capt. Lake,†[3] two merchants of Boston, who owned the island and great part of the main land near to it. The Indians hid themselves in the night under the walls of the fort. When the centinel left his station at day-light, some of the Indians followed him in at the fort gate, whilst the rest ran to the port holes, and shot down every person

that his Majesty's small province of New-Hampshire, the small colony of Rhode-Island, were oppressed and born down, &c.

* The condition of the dissenters in England, in the latter part of the reign of King Charles the 2d, had caused many of them to turn their thoughts again towards New-England. "Divers persons in England and Ireland, gentlemen, citizens and others, being inclined to remove themselves into foreign parts, where they may enjoy, without interruption, the public exercise of christian religion, according to what they apprehend of divine institution, have prevailed with Mr. Blackwell to make your country a visit, and enquire whether they may be there welcome, and whether they may reasonably expect that liberty they promise themselves, and others, who will attend their motion." *Letter from Dan. Coxe to Gov. Bradstreet, London Oct.* 10. 1684. The alteration which happened presently after, in the public affairs of the colony, was alone sufficient to discourage this emigration. At the same time, some of the protestants in France, after a relation of their miserable state in France, conclude a letter from Rochel 1st October 1684 — "New-England, the country where you live, is in great esteem, I, and a great many other protestants, intend to go there. Tell us, if you please, what advantage we can have, and particularly the peasants, who are used to the plough. If somebody at your country would send a ship here to fetch over French protestants, he would make great gain."

† Capt. Lake was the ancestor of the late Sir Bibie Lake.

[1] "Richard Hammond at Stinson's point (Woolwich). He had been for a long time a trader with the Indians." Hammond was killed, his house was set on fire, and sixteen persons were taken prisoners. William Durkee Williamson, *History of the State of Maine*, I, 535.

[2] Thomas Clark (d. 1678). He was Speaker of the House of Deputies in 1662 and was chosen an Assistant in 1673. He is the Thomas Clark who voted against the death penalty for returning Quakers.

[3] Thomas Lake (d. 1676) had bought half of Arowsick island from John Richards in 1654 and had kept a trading post there for many years. He was a prominent merchant and had come to Boston *via* New Haven. His daughter Ann became the second wife of Increase Mather.

they saw. Capt Lake, finding the Indians had possessed themselves of the fort, escaped with Capt. Davis * [1] and two others, at a back door, to the waterside, intending to pass to another island near to Arowsick. Capt. Lake was killed just as he landed. His bones were, after some time, found and brought to Boston. Davis was wounded, but made his escape, as did the other two. At these two houses, fifty three English were killed and taken. The news of this stroke broke up all the plantations at and near Kenebeck, the inhabitants transporting themselves to Piscataqua and Boston, or some other place of security. This brought the Indians further westward, to Casco, Spurwinck, Black-point, Wells, and Cape Nidduck, within the bounds of York, at all which places they did more or less mischief. Mugg, a noted Indian, well known to the English,† was at the head of the enemy. The prisoners, by his means, were treated with more humanity and courtesy than had been known, and he sent one or two of them to Piscataqua, in order to ransom their friends; but the goods sent for their ransom were seized by other Indians. Mugg himself came to Piscataqua, and afterwards to Boston, where, in behalf of Madockawando and Cheberrina, sachems of Penobscot, he entered into treaty with the governor and council, Nov. 13th 1676. This was the first treaty with any of the Tarrateens, or eastern Indians. "They promised to cease all acts of hostility, to return the captives, to do their utmost to repair the damage sustained by the English, to buy no powder or ammunition of any other than persons deputed by the governor, provided they could have a supply in that way, and to account all other eastern Indians in the number of their enemies, who did not assent to the same covenant and agreement." No mention is made of any subjection to the government of the colony, or to the King of England, but they are considered as a free independent people. The treaty is at large in Mr. Hubbard's history of the war.[2] The Indians continued, notwithstanding, to do mischief on the eastern frontier in 1677, when Major Andros, by virtue of his

---

* Davis was afterwards of the council for Massachusets province.

† He had lived, from a child, in English families.

---

[1] Sylvanus Davis (*d.* 1704), of Sheepscot, removed to Falmouth in 1680. There he commanded the fort, but was captured by the French and Indians in 1690 and taken to Canada. He was put into the Council by the Charter of 1691 and spent his later days at Hull. An account of the war, written by him, is printed in Massachusetts Historical Society *Collections*, Third Series, I, 101.

[2] William Hubbard, *A Narrative of the Troubles with the Indians in New England from the First Planting thereof in the Year 1607 to this Present Year 1677* (Boston, 1677). It has been reprinted many times.

commission from the Duke of York, having placed forces at Pemaquid, the Indians made overtures of peace and friendship, and, as a
proof of their sincerity, brought in 15 English captives, and they
continued for some time quiet. An attack was made upon the western frontiers, by 40 or 50 Indians said to be river Indians,* but
whether Connecticut or Hudson's river is not mentioned. This was
the 19th of September 1677. They surprized many of Hatfield, as
they were raising a house and unarmed, and killed and carried away
about twenty, and the next day took three or four more from Deerfield.

By the advice of the governor of New-York, commissioners were
sent, about this time, from the Massachusets and Connecticut, to
the Maqua's, to secure their friendship to the English interest in
general and to engage them against the Tarrateens, or eastern Indians, who had been their ancient enemies. I suppose this was the
first treaty † between the Mohawks, or Five Nations, and the Massachusets colony.‡

* The Indians which originally belonged to Connecticut river, after Philip's war,
removed to a place called Scatacook, and were known by the name of Scatacook Indians, and when there have been treaties with the Six Nations, more or less of these
Indians have generally been present. They proved a heavy scourge to the county of
Hampshire, joining with the French and Canada Indians, and sufficiently revenged
themselves of the English. Being well acquainted with most of the houses upon Connecticut river for 40 years, before their removal, they served as pilots in the frequent
invasions during King William's and Queen Ann's wars.

† Pynchon and Richards were sent to Albany in 1677, in order to demand the delivery of some eastern Indians among the Mohawks, but governor Andros persuaded
them to desist.

‡ In 1680, the people were greatly surprized with the appearance of a comet, first
discovered the 18th of November, and visible the 10th of February, after which, for a
few days it could be discerned by telescopes. "Dec. 16th, its appearance is very terrible,
for, though the head be small, yet the tail is near 30° in length, and ascends almost to
our zenith, growing continually broader, and is brightest on the sides, especially the
south, the middle being considerably darker than the sides." Interleav'd Almanack.

Aug. 17th 1682, another comet appeared, and continued until the 15th of September, "The head or star much bigger than that of 1680, and of a dim colour, though the
coma, or blaze, was much smaller, not even extending above 15° in length." Idem. It
was the general opinion, that any unusual appearances in the heavens were presages of
calamities coming upon the world.

Nov. 27, 1676, "A fire broke out in Boston about 5 in the morning, at one Wake-
field's house, by the Red Lion, by a candle carelesly set, which so prevailed, that it
burnt down about 45 dwelling-houses, the north meeting-house, and several warehouses;
the wind was at south-east when it began, and blew hard; soon after it veered south,
and brought so much rain, as much prevented further mischief, without which, all that
end of the town had probably been laid in ashes, and Charlestown also endangered, by
the flakes of fire which were carried over the river." Id.

"Aug. 8, 1679, about midnight a terrible fire began at one Gross's house, the sign of
the three mariners, near the dock in Boston. All the warehouses, and a great number
of dwelling houses, with vessels then in the dock, were consumed. It continued till near
noon the next day; the most woeful desolation that Boston ever saw; eighty odd dwell-

In the year 1685, Mr. Hinkley, governor of Plimouth, sent, to the corporation in England, an account of the praying Indians then in that colony. They amounted to 1439, besides boys and girls under 12 years old, which were supposed to be more than three times that number.*

---

ing-houses, and seventy odd warehouses, with several vessels and their lading consumed to ashes. The whole loss computed to be two hundred thousand pounds." *Id.*

* The particular places where these Indians then lived were,

At Pawmet Billingsgate and Eastham or Nauset - - -	264
At Manamoyet - - - - - - - - -	115
At Sackatucket and Nobscusset - - - - -	121
At Matakeesee - - - - - - - - -	70
At Skarnton or Scanton - - - - - - - -	51
At Mashpee - - - - - - - - -	141
At Suckanesset - - - - - - - - -	72
At Monamet - - - - - - - - -	110
At Saltwater Pond - - - - - - - -	90
At Namasket and Titicut - - - - - - -	70
At Namatakeeset - - - - - - - - -	40
At Moxisset - - - - - - - - -	85
At Cooxit - - - - - - - - - -	120
At Seconet - - - - - - - - - -	90

1439

From the dissolution of the charter in 1686, until the arrival of the province charter in 1692.

MR. Dudley's short administration was not very grievous.* The house of deputies, indeed, was intirely laid aside; but the people, the time being short, felt little or no effect from the change.

* "I have forbore writing to your grace, until I have been some time in the place, to see how the people here would demean themselves under this new government. At my first arrival, I met with outward expressions of joy and satisfaction, and many seemed well pleased at the change, having been struck with a panick fear, upon the apprehensions of Col. Kirk's coming hither to be their governor; but finding a commission directed to a gentleman amongst themselves, the then governor and company, growing hardy, began, by their ministers, to tempt Mr. Dudley not to accept of his Majesty's commission to be president, hoping thereby to continue the government amongst themselves; but that failing them, they adjourned the meeting of their general assembly to the 2d of October next, and broke up with hopes, that, either by some unhappy accidents in the affairs of state at home, or some dissention, raised by their artifices among the members in this new government, they might prevail so far as to dissolve this constitution, and reassume the government, which to accomplish, they are very solicitous. — Of a president and 18 members of the council, there is only myself, since Mr. Mason's departure for England, that is of the church of England. It was never intended, that the charge should be supported by myself and some few others of our communion. I humbly represent to your grace, that the three meeting-houses in Boston might pay twenty shillings a week each, out of their contributions, towards defraying of our church charges, that sum being less per annum than each of their ministers receive. Thus much relating to the affairs of our church. That of our state little differs. Most part of our chief officers, as justices of peace, &c. are congregational men, not above three church of England men are officers in the militia, so that, in the main, I can only assure your Grace, that the persons only, and not the government, is changed." *Rand. letter to Abp. of Cant.*[1]

Mr. Dudley's commission made him president of the council for Massachusets Bay, New-Hampshire and Main, and the Naraganset country, or King's province, William Stoughton was named deputy president, Simon Bradstreet, Robert Mason, John Fitz-Winthrop, John Pynchon, Peter Bulkley, Edward Randolph, Wait Winthrop, Richard

[1] This letter, undated, is printed in Hutchinson's *Collection of Original Papers* (1769), pp. 550–552.

MR. Dudley, having made Randolph trumpeter of his attachment
to the prerogative and answered his ends, soon after grew cool
towards him. Randolph, in return, vilified Dudley, in a great number of letters he wrote to London about a month after his arrival;
which letters, or the copies, are preserved.* Mr. Stoughton was Mr.
Dudley's chief confident. He was not suspected, by the body of the
people, of being unfriendly, or of want of strong attachment to the
religious principles and to the ecclesiastical constitution of the country, and his compliance, in taking a share in the administration, was
charitably supposed to be, at least in part, for the sake of keeping out
oppressors and tyrants. Mr. Dudley professed as great an attachment to the interest of the colony as Mr. Stoughton, and was very
desirous of retaining their favour. A letter, the day he demanded
the government, to Mr. Mather,[1] then the minister of the greatest

---

Wharton, John Usher, Nathanael Saltonstall, Bartholomew Gidney, Jonathan Tyng,
Dudley Bradstreet, John Hinks, and Edward Tyng were named of the council, not by
separate warrants, or by mandamus, but all in one commission.

Besides the president, Stoughton, Bulkley, Pynchon, Gidney, and Tyng had been of
the assistants before. N. Saltonstall, who was also in the commission, appeared once to
excuse himself, having a few days before taken the oath of assistant. The governor,
Mr. Bradstreet, was also named, and the president, with the council, waited upon him
at his house, the 14th of May, immediately upon opening the commission; but he made
several excuses, and did not accept. His son, Dudley Bradstreet, also refused.

* Randolph writes to one of the nobility, by Mr. Dudley when he went to England
agent for the colony, "Major Dudley is a great opposer of the faction, against which I
have now articled to his Majesty." October 27, 1686, he writes to the Archbishop of
Canterbury. "I have taken care to inform myself how the money sent over here for
evangelizing the Indians is disposed of. Here are seven persons, called commissioners,
or trustees, who have the sole management of it, the chief of which are, Mr. Dudley our
president, a man of a base, servile, and antimonarchical principle, Mr. Stoughton of the
old leaven, Mr. Richards, a man not to be trusted in public business, Mr. Hinkley, a
rigid independent, and others like to these." &c.[2]

[In a letter to the Lord High Treasurer Aug. 23ᵈ 1686 he writes "Unless his Majesty
please in a very short time to send us over a Governor from England all that is already
done will be of little advantage to his Majesty's interest. The independent faction still
prevails and persons of dangerous principles from England, Ireland and other places
are here received and highly encouraged. They have lately put Cap Blackwell, Oliver's
treasurer in London, and son in law to Lambert excepted by the Act of indemnity, and
a violent Commonwealth's man, to be of the commission of the peace and he is a man
consulted with in all publick affairs. The independent minister and others make an ill
use of his Majesties indulgence and liberty of conscience. Some of them have spoken

---

[1] Increase Mather (1639–1723), son of Richard Mather and father of Cotton Mather.
Increase was the pastor of the Second Church in Boston, and also President of Harvard
College 1685–1701. There is an excellent biography of Increase Mather by Kenneth
Ballard Murdock.

[2] Printed in Hutchinson's *Collection of Original Papers* (1769), pp. 552–554.

influence in the colony, is a proof of it.* The people were not so charitable as to believe him sincere. However, there was no molestation to the churches of the colony, but they continued both worship and discipline as before. The affairs of the towns were likewise managed in the same manner as formerly. Their courts of justice were continued upon the former plan, Mr. Stoughton being at the head of them. Trials were by juries as usual. Even in the court of admiralty, the trials were by juries; but, as the jurors were returned by the marshal, very different verdicts were given, from what would have been given, under the former administration. The president, as ordinary, took all matters of wills and administrations into his own hand. In general, the former laws and established customs, so far as related to judicial proceedings, seem to have been their rule, although the government which framed them was dissolved. Mr. Dudley considered himself, as appointed to preserve the affairs of the colony from confusion until a governor arrived, and a rule of administration should be more fully settled. [It is not improbable that if Dudley had been left to prosecute his plan and a house of representatives had been made part of the constitution the people would have been reconciled to it, for except Randolph and Mason all the council were such men as had friends and commissions to support them, and when Bradstreet, Saltonstall, Dudley Bradstreet, and Champernoon declined serving Mr. Dudley nominated eight persons, out of which he proposed four should be selected to supply the vacancies, all of them persons of note and who had been assistants or in other places of trust. These were Samuel Shrimpton, W. Wm Browne, jnr., James Russell, Samuel Sewall, Symond Lynde, Thomas Greaves, Nicholas Page and Richard Smith. But this recommendation had no effect, the commission to Dudley being

---

treasonable words in their pulpits which, to no purpose, I have complained of to the President and Council, so that I am humbly of opinion that liberty of conscience will much obstruct the settlement unless duly regulated by the authority of a prudent Governor."]

* "Reverend and dear Sir,
"I rose this morning with full intention to wait on you by eight of the clock, before I had your letter to put me forward, and am sorry to find you from home. I am very solicitous, whatsoever be the issue of the present hurry, for my dear mother at Cambridge, and cannot be happy if it do not flourish. I never wanted your favour and advice so much as now, and would pray an opportunity with you this evening if possible. Sir, for the things of my soul I have these many years hung upon your lips, and ever shall; and in civil things am desirous you may know with all plainness my reasons of procedure, and that they may be satisfactory to you. I am,
"From your own house,   Sir, your Servant,
   "May 17th, 86.   J. DUDLEY."

superseded.] The necessity of the thing justified the former magistrates in continuing, so long as they did, to exercise authority, although the judgment against the charter had been declared in form; otherwise, under the same administration in England, which had caused their charter to be vacated, they would undoubtedly have been called to answer. But their authority was weak. Mr. Dudley writes to his friend Randolph, Sept. 1685. "I suppose it cannot be thought expedient or safe to let the government here be at such strange uncertainties, as it must needs be, until his Majesty's pleasure be known."

CONNECTICUT, Plimouth, and Rhode Island continued their former administration. Mr. Dudley had some dispute with Plimouth governor concerning the admiralty jurisdiction, which he claimed as vice-admiral of New-England; but it remained undetermined.

DECEMBER 19, 1686, Sir Edmund Andros arrived at Nantasket, in the Kingfisher, a 50 gun ship, with commission from king James for the government of New-England. He was less dreaded than Kirk, but he was known to be of an arbitrary disposition. He kept a correspondence with the colony, whilst he was governor of New-York. His letters, then, discovered much of the dictator. The depressed state of the colony prevented a proper return. He landed at Boston the 20th, and his commission was published the same day.

THE beginning of his administration gave great encouragement. He made high professions of regard to the public good and the welfare of the people, both of merchants and planters, directed the judges to administer justice according to the custom of the place, ordered the former established rules to be observed, as to rates and taxes, and that all the colony laws not inconsistent with his commission should be in force.

THE major part of his council were men, who although they had been of the moderate party, yet they wished the public interest, and would have been glad to have continued under the old form of government. With a good share of firmness of mind they might have been serviceable so long as they were permitted to hold their places in council. But their behavior under the old charter discovered they had more of the willow than of the oak in their constitutions. Perhaps, if they had been less pliable, they would have soon been displaced, and others more inclined to oppression appointed in their stead.* Sir Edmund had no affection for them. Palmer, Brockholt,

* There are no public records from the dissolution of the old charter government in 1686, until the restoration of it in 1689. If there was any book of records, it was secreted or destroyed. I cannot find, upon any of the files, a list of Sir Edmund's council.

Mason, Usher, and Randolph of the council, together with West,[1] Bullivant,[2] Graham,* [3] and others, who were not of the council, were his confidents and advisers. Soon after his arrival there appears, by some loose minutes, to have been a pretty full meeting of the council. Many of them returned home, and a few only who lived at or near Boston attended constantly, and some of those complained, that the governor had always three or four of his creatures to say yes to every thing he proposed, after which no opposition was allowed.† Nero concealed his tyrannical disposition more years than Sir Edmund and his creatures did months. It was not long before the case of some who apprehended themselves oppressed came under consideration: one of the council told them, that they must not think

By accident, I met with a list of their names upon a defensive leaf of an old colony law book, which list I suppose to be genuine, viz.

Mas. Joseph Dudley	M. Richard Wharton	P. Nath. Clark
M. Wm. Stoughton	N. Y. Henry Courtland	John Cothill
N. Ham. Robert Mason	M. John Usher	R. Walter Newberry
N. Y. Anth. Brockholt	M. Barth. Gidney	R. John Greene
Plim. Tho. Hinkley	M. Jona. Tyng	R. Richard Arnold
R. Isl. Walter Clark	N. H. John Hinks	R. John Alborow
Con. Robert Treat	M. Edward Tyng	M. Samuel Shrimpton
C. John Fitz Winthrop	P. Barnabas Lothrop	N. Y. John Young
N. Y. Francis Nicholson	P. Wm. Bradford	N. Y. Nich. Bayard
N. Y. Frederick Philipse	P. Daniel Smith	N. Y. John Palmer
N. Y. Anthony Baxter	Edw. Randolph	M. Wm. Brown
M. John Pinchon	P. John Sprague	R. Richard Smith
C. Wait Winthrop	P. John Walley	C. John Allin.

* Jacob Leisler writes to Mr. Bradstreet, after the revolution, that "Col. Dongan, in his time, had erected a Jesuit's college at New-York, under colour of a grammar school, and that Palmer and Graham sent their sons thither for education." Douglass says, that "Sir Edmund Andros was a bigotted papist." I have met with no evidence of it, [except that when he entered Casteen's house and carried away his goods, he left the furniture of a Romish Chapel untouched. The like conduct would have been justifiable in a good Protestant].

† Randolph to Blaithwait, May 21, 1687, "His Excellency has to do with a perverse people. Here is none of the council at hand, except Mr. Mason and myself, Mr. Brockholt and Mr. Usher, who appear lively for his Majesty's interest."

[1] John West was appointed Secretary by Andros. Apparently he was a non-New Englander, for he was sent home with Andros in 1690.

[2] Benjamin Bullivant was an apothecary and physician from London. Andros made him a justice of the peace. Although imprisoned in 1689, he was allowed to remain in Massachusetts after the deportation of his chief. He was one of the first wardens of King's Chapel, Boston. See *John Dunton's Letters from New-England* (Prince Society, 1867), pp. 94–96. A journal kept by Bullivant in 1690 is printed in Massachusetts Historical Society *Proceedings*, XVI (1878), 103–108.

[3] James Graham had been a merchant in New York. He came to Boston with Andros, became his Attorney-General, and was shipped to England with him in 1690. See John Gorham Palfrey, *History of New England*, III, 553–554.

the privileges of Englishmen would follow them to the end of the world. This gave an alarm through the government, and it was never forgotten. [Such imprudent irritating expressions from persons in whom the Governor placed his confidence confirmed the opinion which had been conceived of his own intention to enslave them.]

ONE of the first acts of power, after the change of government, was the restraint of the press. Randolph was the licenser. There was not so much room to complain of this proceeding as if the press had been at liberty before. It only changed its keeper, having been long under restraint during the former administration. A restraint upon marriages was more grievous. None were allowed to marry except they entered into bonds with sureties to the governor, to be forfeited in case there should afterwards appear to have been any lawful impediment. Magistrates still continued to join people in matrimony. Other provision could not immediately be made. There was but one episcopal minister in the country. His name was Ratcliffe. Sir Edmund considered the congregational ministers as mere laymen. Randolph wrote to the bishop of London,

I press for able and sober ministers, and we will contribute largely to their maintenance; but one thing will mainly help, when no marriages shall hereafter be allowed lawful but such as are made by the ministers of the church of England.

THERE had been very few instances of even occasional assemblies for religious worship according to the rites and ceremonies of the church of England for more than fifty years. When the commissioners for [1] King Charles were at Boston in 1665, they had a chaplain with them; but there was no house for public worship. Most of the inhabitants who were upon the stage in 1686 had never seen a church of England assembly. About that time, a small number of persons formed themselves into a society which [consisted of] near 400 persons.* The agents in England, and the general court in their an-

* "I have some time since humbly represented unto your Grace a necessity of having a church built in Boston, to receive those of the church of England. We have at present near 400 persons who are daily frequenters of our church, and as many more would come over to us; but some being tradesmen, and others of mechanick professions, are threatened by the congregational men to be arrested by their creditors, or to be turned out of their work, if they offer to come to our church." *Rand. letter to Abp. of Cant.* Oct. 27, 1686.[2]

---

[1] The first edition gives "from King Charles" instead of "for King Charles." The third edition follows the first.

[2] This letter is printed in Hutchinson's *Collection of Original Papers* (1769), pp. 552–554.

swers to the complaints against them in 1677, had declared that no persons should be hindered from performing divine service according to the church of England.* This was enough to prevent any open discouragement even whilst the charter government continued. When the governor and many of the council were members of the church of England, it might well be expected, that they would countenance and encourage the establishment and growth of that church. They did not stop there. The people were menaced, that their meeting-houses should be taken from them, and that public worship in the congregational way should not be tolerated.† Randolph had the insolence to reprove and threaten the governor of Plimouth for exacting taxes from the quakers for the support of the ministry in that colony before the authority was superseded.‡ But

* "A dispute happened at the grave of one Lilly.[1] He left the ordering of his funeral to his executors. They forbad Mr. Ratcliffe,[2] the episcopal minister, performing the service for burial. Nevertheless he began. Deacon Frairey[3] interrupted him, and a stop was put to his proceeding. Frairey was complained of, and besides being bound to his good behaviour for twelve months, it was thought the process would cost him 100 marks." *J. Moodey's letter to Mather,* 8 Feb. 88.

† Among other complaints against Sir Edmund, this was one, "That the service of the church of England had been forced into their meeting-houses." This was an equivocal expression. Sir Edmund had made use of a meeting-house for the church service, against the wills of the proprietors, but after their service was over, and compelled no congregationalist to join with him. Indeed he threatened to shut up the doors if he was refused, and to punish any man who gave two pence towards the support of a nonconformist minister. *Narrative, &c.*[4]

‡ "Perhaps it will be as reasonable to move that your colony should be rated to pay our minister of the church of England, who now preaches in Boston, and you hear him not, as to make the quakers pay in your colony." *Rand. letter to Hinkley, June* 22, 1686. The late governor of Plimouth, Mr. Hinkley, complained of this, as one great grievance, that not being allowed to make rates for the support of the ministry, the people would sink into barbarism. Sir Edmund writes to him, March 5, 1687, "I am very much surprized you should issue forth so extraordinary a warrant as is now brought to me, under your hand and seal, dated the 12th of December past, so much mistaken and assuming (for payment of your minister) extrajudicially to command distress to be made on the

[1] Samuel Lilly, a Boston merchant. This paragraph should not be enclosed in quotation marks. It is based on, but does not actually quote from, Moodey's letter — which is printed in full in Massachusetts Historical Society *Collections,* Fourth Series, VIII, 369–371.

[2] Robert Ratcliffe (*d.* 1708) was the first Episcopal minister settled in New England. He came in the frigate *Rose* in May 1686, remained three years, and departed for England in July 1689. See Henry Wilder Foote, *Annals of King's Chapel,* I, 42–45, 49–51, 86–88, 96.

[3] Theophilus Frairey, or Frary (*d.* 1700), was one of the sons of John Frary of Dedham. He was a deacon of the Old South Church. Elsewhere in this letter Moodey speaks of him as Captain Frary.

[4] Increase Mather, *A Narrative of the Miseries of New-England.*

it was not long before the people were freed from their fears of persecution, by King James's proclamation for a general toleration. The
design was seen by some, but the greater part swallowed the bait.
Several churches had agreed to set apart days of thanksgiving for his
Majesty's gracious declaration for liberty of conscience. The governor forbad them. The reason is not mentioned. It must be supposed
to have been this, that he looked upon it to be the royal prerogative
to appoint such days. He told them they should meet at their peril,
and that he would send soldiers to guard their meeting-houses.
Many congregations agreed to address the King. Some persons, who
supposed popery to be at the bottom, strongly opposed the addresses. The late deputy governor was at the head of them.*

SWEARING by the book, which had never been practised, was now
introduced, and such as scrupled it were fined and imprisoned.

THE fees to all officers, under the charter, had been very low.
They are generally so where they are established by the people.
Under the new administration, they were exorbitant. Fifty shillings
was the common fee for probate of a will. The governor was the
supreme ordinary, and acted by himself,† except a few months
whilst he was at New-York and in the eastern country, when Mr.
Dudley was his deputy.‡ It was a great burden upon widows and
children who lived remote, to be obliged to come to Boston for every
part of business relative to the settlements of estates. The fees of all

---

goods of his Majesty's subjects. Out of regard to you, I have put a stop to the execution thereof, that neither the constable nor you may be exposed. Hoping you will be
mindful of the station you are in, for his Majesty's service, and the quiet of his subjects,
that they be not amused or troubled by mistaken notions, or clandestine illegal practices." &c. Mr. Willard writes to Mr. Mather, July 10, 1688, "Discouragements upon
the hearts of the ministers increase, by reason that a licentious people take the advantage of a liberty to with-hold maintenance from them."

* "Referring to an address to his Majesty, I do humbly propound and desire, that
no mention be made of the proclamation for a general toleration. There will be no need
of touching upon it in the least, and I am assured many dangerous rocks will be shunned
thereby. For my own part, I do more dread the consequences thereof than the execution of those penal laws, the only wall against popery. We may, without breach of
charity, conclude the popish counsels are laid deep. Time will shew more. God Almighty bring them to nought." *Danforth to Mather, 8 Nov. 87.*

Douglass says, "they were not politicians sufficient to penetrate into the wicked and
pernicious contrivance of that toleration." V. I p. 440.

† He introduced the forms used in the spiritual courts, in proving wills, granting
administrations, &c. which forms have been retained in the several counties ever since.
Before his time, both probates of wills and granting administrations, in point of form,
were very loose and uncertain.

‡ There was a commission or deputation to Mr. Hinkley, to be judge of the prerogative court for Plimouth colony, and I suppose others to Connecticut, Rhode-Island, and
New-Hampshire, but wills were sent to Boston for final probate, and in like manner
administrations, if the estate exceeded 50 l. *Hinkley to Blaithwait.*

other officers were complained of as oppressive. The harpies themselves quarrelled about their share of the prey. Randolph, who from his commission of secretary, expected all the clerkships in the country, complains that West, who seems at first to have been a deputy only, ran away with a thousand a year of his dues.*

But the greatest profit arose from patents for lands. The charter being vacated, the people were told that their titles to their estates were of no value. The expression in vogue was that "the calf died in the cow's belly." Besides, the general court had not made their grants under the seal of the colony. This was represented as a notable defect, which possession and improvement could not heal. However, it was made public that all who would acknowledge the insufficiency of their title derived from the former government, by petitioning for new patents, should be quieted upon reasonable terms. The fees for the patents varied according to circumstances both of persons and estates. In the complaint to King James it is alledged, that the fees of some amounted to fifty pounds. Prudence was used. Mens titles were not questioned all at once. Had this been the case, according to the computation then made, all the personal estate in the colony would not have paid the charge of the new patents. Some that had been most attached to the old administration were among the first who were threatened. I find a petition of Samuel Sewall, who had been a magistrate (afterwards chief justice) for confirmation of his title to a valuable island in Boston harbour (Hog island.) In a letter to a friend, a short time after, he laments his compliance. There are many hundred petitions of the same kind upon the files. Some favorites looked with an envious eye upon some of the best

---

* Randolph farmed his office to West, which caused the last mentioned to exact much greater fees than the former had done. *Hinkley's letter to Blaithwait, June 28, 1687.*

Randolph's own letters shew this to have been the case. "West extorts what fees he pleases, to the great oppression of the people, and renders the present government grievous. I have wrote you the want we have of two or three honest attornies, if any such thing in nature. We have but two, one is Mr. West's creature, came with him from New-York, and drives all before him; he also takes extravagant fees, and for want of more the country cannot avoid coming to him. I have wrote Mr. Blaithwait the great necessity of judges from England. I know there are some loyal gentlemen and able lawyers who have not practice. The judges with us, being now three, have three hundred and ninety pounds a year between them all, besides their fees, which they make very considerable to them. Now two will serve our occasions. They ought to be of the council, and their salaries made up four hundred pounds a year apiece, they well deserve it." *Randolph to Povey, Jan. 24, 1687.*[1]

---

[1] This letter is printed in Hutchinson's *Collection of Original Papers* (1769), pp. 556–558.

estates, especially where the property was in a town or company. A petition of Capt. Hutchinson and others labored, [because] their title was originally derived from the Indian sachems and proprietors, and the lands had been long possessed and improved. One of the best islands in New-England, in Plimouth harbour, called Clark's island, from the name of the person who first landed there, had been appropriated for the benefit of the poor of the town. This was granted to Nathaniel Clark, who had been secretary of that colony, and was afterwards of Sir Edmund's council, and one of his greatest tools.* Randolph petitioned for half an acre of land, to be taken out of the common in Boston, for a house lot. The answer given to it does not appear. In the latter part of the administration, petitions multiplied greatly, and property became every day more and more precarious.† This was not the only invasion of their property. The

* "Awful and considerable changes have attended poor Plimouth since your departure from the Gurnet,¹ by reason of the motions about Clark's island. The committee chosen about that affair were at so much charge as necessitated our people to engage, by free and voluntary subscriptions, to reimburse them, and to vote the securing some lands till the money was paid to them. For this, Lorkin tetches the committee with a writ, charging that they had resolved and raised money upon his Majesty's subjects contrary to law, and the town-clerk, godly deacon Fance, for calling for the vote, and Mr. Wiswall, for writing the paper, paid three pounds seven shillings each, besides expences, and all nine are bound over to the superior court at Boston, where they are like to be considerably fined, besides all costs of court," &c. *J. Cotton's letter to Mather, Plimouth, July* 9, 1688.

† I find the following letter on this subject, from the late governor to a person of note.

"Honoured Sir,

"I have been so interrupted since you was here, that I have not begun any matter of argument to prove our right and title to our lands, nor can it well be done, until all their objections be known, nor do I think I can add any thing which is not in your own thoughts. The brief heads that are in my present thoughts are as followeth. 1st. The grant of the council of Plimouth to the six gentlemen and their associates. 2dly. The King's confirmation to them and twenty more, and their assigns, impowering them, in general court, to dispose of the lands to the best advantage of the people and plantation, which we have done, and know not how to do it better, if it was to be done again. A second right and title is our purchase from the Indians of their right, which certainly was something. 3dly. Our possession and improvement for almost sixty years. If this will not give right to land in a wilderness, where neither the King nor any Christian had ever any property, I know not what will. The only objection insisted upon, that I hear of, is that our lands were not granted under the seal of the company. Ans. Nor was it necessary that so it should be. 1st. Our patent doth not require it, but leaves the manner of disposing to our liberty; nor is there any law of England that requires us here, in this case, to grant lands under the seal of the company, nor is it necessary for proprietors of lands in England so to do. It is true, where land is conveyed by deed, a seal is essential; but it may be done as well by livery and seisin, without deed or other writing, as the

¹ The Gurnet, or Gurnet Point, is the last bit of Plymouth a traveller bound for England would pass on his way out of the harbor. It is exposed to the open ocean northeastward of the town.

governor, with four or five of his council, laid what taxes they thought proper. This the people complained of as their greatest grievance. They thought themselves intitled to the liberties and immunities of free and natural born English subjects, and that consequently no monies ought to be raised from them but by their representatives. They had no hopes of a restitution of their charter privileges in general; but they hoped that, even under so arbitrary a prince, they should be allowed a house of representatives.* This was among the first things they applied for. King James assured their agent, he would take as much care of New as of Old England, and no doubt he intended to bring his subjects, in both, under the same regulation. The charges of government, over and above the fees of the several officers, were not excessive. Under the charter, the salaries were below the dignity of the offices, the highest allowance to the governor not exceeding one hundred pounds per annum. What salary Sir Edmund received does not appear.† The second year of his administration, the public charge was greatly increased by a war with the Indians. There was a general submission to the taxes, and the assessments were proportioned upon the inhabitants of the towns by officers chosen by themselves. It is probable, this was the reason of continuing to the towns some of their privileges. Every

---

law books tell us; and copyholders in England have no other evidence for their lands but the court roll, or a copy of it. When William the conqueror made himself master of the land, he gave a great part of it to his nobles and followers, but without any seal, for there was none used in England many scores if not hundreds of years after, which shews it is no strange thing to convey land without seal. And if there should have been an error or omission, yet seeing the grantor and grantees judged it good, and rested satisfied therein, who shall question it, or hath any thing to do with it?   I am,
Sir, your willing servant in what may,
S. B."

"In point of equity. Our great sufferings, first and last, and loss of so many lives to maintain our own right and the King's interest, and the vast charge we have been at in private and public buildings and improvements, ought to have a just consideration. Would it not seem a strange thing, that a piece of ground in the wilderness, not worth five shillings, but by buildings, &c. worth five hundred pounds, should become the King's, I know not how. We may be sure so just a prince will never allow it."

* "Let me advise not to represent any thing by way of complaint to his Majesty; for that, I fear, will do us more hurt than good. My letter by Belcher may be of use, to shew our friends why we supplicate his Majesty to confirm us in our possessions, and to grant us the same privileges which other of his plantations are not denied, viz. a general assembly, without which our condition is little inferior to absolute slavery." *Danforth to Nowell, 22d Oct.* 88.[1]

† [After New York was included in his commission his salary was fixed by the King at £1000 per annum.]

---

[1] This letter is printed in Hutchinson's *Collection of Original Papers* (1769), pp. 565–567.

town was suffered to meet once a year to choose their officers; but all meetings at other times, or for other purposes, were strictly forbidden. An intire new model of government was intended, but there was not time to perfect it. There are minutes of a great number of bills, passed the council and approved by the governor, but the bills themselves are lost. The old laws of the colony seem to have continued the rule for the administration of justice, except where they were superseded by any new edicts. Mr. Dudley and Mr. Stoughton were two of the judges of the superior court, and neither of them disposed to go to the extremes which some others of the council wished for.* The law proceedings were more formal than they had been.

THE monies, applied for the propagation of the gospel among the Indians, amounted to six or seven hundred pounds sterling per annum, which continued to be intrusted with some of the old magistrates and ministers. Mr. Boyle,† who had been long governor of the corporation in England, was a very moderate churchman, and most of the members were dissenters, or favourers of the cause. The archbishop of Canterbury promised Randolph ‡ that a commission should be directed to some persons to audit and report the accounts of that money. The legality of such a commission, it being contrary to the charter of the corporation, might have been questioned, perhaps, with as good reason as the legality of the royal order, which his grace and the six bishops soon after very justly refused to obey. One would think, that merely a difference of place should not make the

---

* "His excellency tries all ways to bring the people to quit rents. — A little time will try what our new judges, Dudley and Stoughton, will say, when either Indian purchases, or grants from the general court are questioned before them." *Randolph's letter to Povey, May* 21, 1687.[1]

† Mr. Boyle died in 1692, and was succeeded by Mr. Thompson.

‡ "The poor Indians (those who are called ministers) come and complain to Mr. Radcliffe, our minister, that they have nothing allowed them. We have spoken to the commissioners to have some allowance for them. All we can get is the promise of a coarse coat against winter; and they would not suffer Aaron, an Indian preacher, who can read English very well, to have a bible with the common prayer in it, but took it away from him. I humbly presume to remind your grace of your promise to me when in England, that a commission should be directed to some persons here, unconcerned, to audit and report their accounts of that money. We want good schoolmasters, none here being allowed of but of ill principles. The money now converted unto private or worse uses, will be sufficient to set up good and public schools, and provide a maintenance for our minister, who now lives upon a small contribution. We are yet forced to meet in his own house." *Rand. Octob.* 28, 1686. *to Archbishop of Canterbury.*[2]

---

[1] This letter is printed in Hutchinson's *Collection of Original Papers* (1769), pp. 554–557.

[2] This letter is printed in Hutchinson's *Collection of Original Papers* (1769), pp. 552–554.

same measure, towards English subjects, appear reasonable in the one case, and arbitrary and oppressive in the other. The archbishop either altered his sentiments, or was diverted by greater affairs from pursuing his design.

THE Indians upon the frontiers, in the summer of 1688, renewed their hostilities. A garrison had been kept at Pemaquid, but it was no security to the scattered settlements upon the frontiers. The governor, from a prejudice against the late administration, by whom, without sufficient grounds for it, he supposed the Indians had been treated with too great severity, if not injustice, resolved to try mild measures, and endeavour to win them by good words and small courtesies. Randolph, writes to William Penn, Nov. 9, 1688,

This barbarous people, the Indians, were never civilly treated by the late government, who made it their business to encroach upon their lands, and by degrees to drive them out of all. That was the grounds and the beginning of the last war. His excellency has all along taken other measures with them. I hope the proclamation and the Indians confidence in the governor's favor to such as shall submit, may put a stop to their present rage.

Castine, a Frenchman, who lived among the Indians at Penobscot, made profession of friendship to the English; but was suspected to be a false friend, and to stir up the Indians against them. His trading-house was plundered this year, whilst he was absent from it, which he rightly charged upon the English. The Indians informed some of their captives that Castine furnished every Indian who engaged against the English with a pound of powder, two pounds of lead, and a quantity of tobacco. Some cattle, belonging to the inhabitants of North Yarmouth, having been killed by the Indians, a justice of peace, —— Blackman, seized a party of 18 or 20 Indians at or near Saco. Reprisals were made the 5th Sept. and one Henry Smith and his family taken at New Dartmouth; and the next day Edward Taylor and his family were taken from the same place, and all carried to Taconnett, up Kenebeck river, where they found nine captives taken from the lower parts of the river. The Indians killed divers of these captives in their frolicks, as appears by Smith's examination, who made his escape from them.* Sir Edmund was then at New-York.† Upon his return to Boston, he ordered the Indians, which Blackman had seized, to be released. The Indians returned several

* Mr. Neale supposes the first blood to be shed, afterwards, at North-Yarmouth.

† Mason, one of his council, died, in the journey to York with Sir Edmund, at Esopus.

English captives in exchange. The 20th of October he published a proclamation commanding the Indians to set at liberty his Majesty's subjects, lately taken by them, and that such Indians, as had been actually concerned in the murder of any of his Majesty's subjects, should surrender themselves by the 11th of November, to answer for their crimes, or otherwise be pursued and proceeded against with the utmost severity; and all that were innocent were allowed to live near the English towns if they desired it, and all persons were to take notice and conform themselves accordingly. The Indians treated the proclamation with contempt. The English, being laid under restraint, were more unsafe than if war had been publicly declared.

THE people in general, as has been observed, were patient under the new government. There are a few instances of prosecution for contempt of, or opposition to, the authority. One John Gold of Topsfield was tried and convicted, by verdict of a jury, of treasonable words, what they were is not mentioned, and fined fifty pounds, &c. Mr. Appleton [1] of Ipswich, who had been an assistant, and Mr. Wise [2] the minister of that town, were imprisoned.* Mr. Wise, after the revolution, brought an action against Mr. Dudley, chief judge, for denying him the benefit of the habeas corpus act. Mr. Mather, one of the ministers of Boston, had been a very active person in dissuading from the surrender of the charter, and published reasons against it. Randolph frequently mentions him, in his letters, as a factious person. He behaved with so much prudence, as to give no room to take hold of any part of his conduct. A forged letter was therefore forwarded, in his name, by way of Barbados, directed to a person in Amsterdam, but intercepted and shewn by Randolph to

* This was the punishment for remonstrating, in an address, against the taxes as a heavy grievance, such an address being preferred about this time. The selectmen of Ipswich voted, "That inasmuch as it is against the privilege of English subjects to have money raised, without their own consent in an assembly on parliament, therefore they will petition the King, for liberty of an assembly, before they make any rates." Sir Edmund caused them to be imprisoned and fined, some 20, some 30, and some 50l. as the judges, by him instructed, should see meet to determine. *Narrative of New-England miseries, &c.*

[1] Samuel Appleton (1624–1696). See editor's note 2 to p. 255.
[2] John Wise (1652–1725). He was graduated from Harvard in 1673, and had been the minister at Ipswich since 1683. He had a keen and vigorous mind, and did not hesitate to express his convictions. See John Langdon Sibley, *Biographical Sketches of Graduates of Harvard University*, II, 428–441; also Henry Martyn Dexter, "Address on Rev. John Wise," in *Celebration of the Two Hundreth Anniversary of the Organization of the Congregational Church and Parish in Essex, Mass.*, pp. 113–137. Wise's *Vindication of the Government of New England Churches* (Boston, 1717) is a landmark in the history of American political theory.

Sir Lionel Jenkins,[1] who was reflected upon in the letter. There were many passages in favor of Ferguson, Lord Shaftsbury, Oates, &c. all which must have made the writer obnoxious to the King and his ministers, and raised a prejudice against the country. Sir Lionel either suspected the forgery, or treated the thing with contempt, asking whether it was that star-gazer * wrote it, so that Randolph missed his aim. Mr. Mather, two or three years after, being informed of the danger he had been in, exculpated himself in a letter to a friend, and charged the forgery upon Randolph or his brother. This letter coming to Randolph's knowledge, he brought an action of defamation against Mr. Mather, and laid his damage at five hundred pounds. The jury gave the defendant costs. But Randolph, I know not how, was bringing a new action for the same defamation. Mr. Mather's friends advising him of it, he kept concealed to avoid the service of the writ. About this time, some of the principal men of the colony flattered themselves, that they might obtain a partial relief, by a representation of their grievances to the King, and Mr. Mather was thought a proper person to be their agent or messenger, and he embarked in the night and in disguise. The service of Randolph's writ would have prevented his voyage.†

THERE seems to have been but little room to hope for success. King James was making daily advances towards despotism in England. It was not likely that he should consent to any degree of liberty in the colonies. Sir Edmund knew too well the disposition of his master, to give himself any concern about the complaints preferred against him. There were two persons in London at that time, who had been assistants under the charter, Samuel Nowel and Elisha Hutchinson. They joined with Mr. Mather in a remonstrance to the King. One of the new council, Richard Wharton,[2] sensible of the distresses of the country, concurred with the others also, as appears by his letters, but all was to no purpose. At first indeed a report was agreed upon, by the committee for foreign plantations, in which an

---

* Mr. Mather had just before published a discourse upon comets.

† Mr. Mather sailed in April 1688. Some of his church carried him aboard in the night in disguise.

---

[1] Sir Leoline Jenkins (1623–1685) was Secretary of State 1680–1684. His name Leoline appears to be a corruption of Llewellyn rather than a variant of Lionel. But it is given as Lionel in all three editions of Hutchinson.

[2] Richard Wharton (d. c. 1690), of Salem, was interested on a large scale in lands in Maine. He went to England in July 1687 to complain of Andros and his schemes, and died in London.

assembly was mentioned, but Lord Sunderland [1] struck out that clause, with his own hand, before the report was presented.* The inhabitants of Cambridge made a particular application,† and Mr. Hinkley, the late governor of Plimouth petitioned in behalf of that colony. The sum of the application made by the agents was contained in the following heads, viz.

THAT his Majesty's subjects in New-England may be quieted in the possession of all property both in houses and lands, as they enjoyed them, before the government was changed, on the 24th May 1686, and that the ancient records there settled for title of lands may be confirmed.

THAT there be liberty of conscience in matters of religion, that their former methods of swearing in giving evidence may be allowed, and that all their meeting-houses may be left free to them, according to the intention of the builders thereof.

THAT no laws may be made nor monies raised there without the consent of a general assembly, as it is in the other plantations.

* Narrative of miseries, &c.[2]
† Cambridge address was in the following words.
"To the King's most excellent Majesty,
"The petition and address of John Gibson, aged about 87, and George Willow, aged 86 years, as also on behalf of their neighbours the inhabitants of Cambridge in New-England, in most humble wise sheweth,
"That your Majesty's good subjects, with much hard labour and great disbursements, have subdued a wilderness, built our houses, and planted orchards, being encouraged by our indubitable right to the soil, by the royal charter granted unto the first planters, together with our first purchase of the natives, as also, by sundry letters and declarations sent to the late governor and company, from his late Majesty your royal brother, assuring us of the full enjoyment of our properties and possessions, as is, more especially, contained in the declaration sent when the quo warranto was issued out against our charter. But we are necessitated to make this our moan and complaint to your excellent Majesty, for that our title is now questioned to our lands, by us quietly possessed for near 60 years, and without which we cannot subsist. Our humble address to our governor Sir Edmund Andros, shewing our just title, long and peaceable possession, together with our claim of the benefit of your Majesty's letters and declarations assuring all your good subjects that they shall not be molested in their properties and possessions, not availing.
"Royal Sir. We are a poor people, and have no way to procure money to defend our cause in the law, nor know we of friends at court, and therefore unto your royal Majesty, as the publick father of all your subjects, do we make this our humble address for relief, beseeching your Majesty graciously to pass your royal act, for the confirmation of your Majesty's subjects here in our possessions, to us derived from our late governor and company of this your Majesty's colony. We now humbly cast ourselves and the distressed condition of our wives and children at your Majesty's feet, and conclude with that saying of Queen Esther, if we perish, we perish." *Narrative of N. E. miseries.*

[1] Robert Spencer (1640–1702), second Earl of Sunderland, was Lord President of the Privy Council and principal Secretary of State. His tact and ability made Sunderland one of the chief advisers of James II and of William III.

[2] Increase Mather, *A Narrative of the Miseries of New-England* (Boston, 1689). It is reprinted in *Andros Tracts* (Prince Society), II, 3–14.

THAT all townships may have liberty to assemble and manage the business of their several precincts, as under the former government, and have power to receive and dispose of all voluntary contributions.

THAT the college at Cambridge in New-England the revenues thereunto belonging, be confirmed in the hands of a president and fellows as formerly.

This application meeting with no success, the agents preferred the following petition.

To the right honorable the Lords Committee for trade and plantations.

THE humble petition of Increase Mather, Samuel Nowell, and Elisha Hutchinson, sheweth,

THAT since your Lordships seem to be of opinion, that his Majesty will not at present grant an assembly to be held within his dominion of New-England, for the making of laws or raising of money, the petitioners humbly conceive, that it will be much for his Majesty's service and the peaceable government of his subjects there, that, until his Majesty shall be graciously pleased to grant an assembly, the council should consist of such persons as shall be considerable proprietors of lands within his Majesty's dominions, and that, the counties being continued as at present, each county may have one, at least, of such of the inhabitants of the same to be members thereof. And that no acts may pass for law but such as have or shall be voted by the manifest consent of the major part of the council. And that all laws so made may, by printing, be published for the general instruction of all the inhabitants.

Your petitioners therefore most humbly pray, that your Lordships would be pleased favorably to report the same to his Majesty for his gracious direction and order therein, and your petitioners as in duty bound shall pray, &c.

HOWEVER modest these desires may appear to us, at this day, who are in the possession of such ample privileges, yet they could not prevail in the reign of King James. The solicitations in England had not the least influence upon measures in New-England.*

WRITS of intrusion were brought against some of the principal persons in the colony, who refused to petition for patents. Col. Shrimpton [1] hired Deer-island of the town of Boston, the rent was

---

* June 21, 1688, Randolph writes, with an air of triumph, that they were as abitrary as the great Turk.

[1] Samuel Shrimpton (1643–1698) was a Bostonian of large estate. In 1694 he was captain of the Artillery Company. A portrait of him, and useful references, are in Justin Winsor, *Memorial History of Boston*, I, 584. For a contemporary account of the Deer Island episode, see *Andros Tracts* (Prince Society, 1868), I, 94. Shrimpton was a patriotic member of Andros's Council, and became a member of the Council of Safety after the governor's downfall.

appropriated to the support of a school. An action was commenced for recovering possession.* Besides the real oppressions from this arbitrary administration, many groundless jealousies were raised, which increased the terror of the people. Castine, it was intimated, was robbed with the privity of the authority, in order to incense the French and Indians.† Upon the first insurrection of the Indians, the inhabitants began to fortify and garrison their houses. Sir Edmund ordered them to desist. An Indian who came in to Sudbury, affirmed to the people there, that the Indians understood, from the governor, that the French and Irish would take possession of Boston in the spring. A Penicook Indian affirmed, that the Maquas or Mohawks had sent a messenger to inform the Penicook tribe, that Sir Edmund had hired them to fight against the English. These idle stories were spread about the country. The Mohawks, it is true, made peace with the French, under the influence of Sir Edmund. The close connection between the courts of England and France at this time well accounts for it.

THE Indians neglected to comply with the governor's order to deliver up the murderers. They continued their hostilities, he, thereupon, raised a small army of seven or eight hundred men,‡ and, in the beginning of November, marched at the head of them, through frost and snow, into the eastern country. This measure was universally condemned, the men were [1] exposed to extreme hardships, without any prospect of service, the Indians taking care to keep out of their reach. Some of his enemies charged him with a design to starve or freeze the men, but other persons, who were more candid, acknowledged that he readily took to himself his full share of the hardships of the campaign, and that he was a kind and good general to the men under his command. Notwithstanding his care, many died with

* Besides the general exception to all titles, that they were derived from a grantor which had no title, in the case of towns there was this further, that they were not capable of taking any estate.

† Sir Edmund had given orders to Pipon, commander of the fort at Pemaquid, to range the coast as far as St. Croix. This appears by a letter from Pipon to the governor, and the whole was included in Sir Edmund's commission. But Dr. Mather gives this reason for doing it at this time. "A parcel of French wines had been seized at the eastward, and at the instance of the French ambassador, an order had been obtained to restore them. A new line was supposed to be then made for the province to evade the order. This line took in Castine's country. He thereupon fled, and his arms and goods were brought to Pemaquid. And this brought on the war.

‡ These men were impressed into the service. Under the charter, this had been the usual way of raising men. This is the reason we do not meet with it among the grievances.

---

[1] The first edition gives "being" instead of "were."

hardships, more, it was thought, than the whole number of Indians at that time in hostility. Not one Indian was killed. They all fled into their more remote dens, where they remained the whole winter. Besides the fort at Pemaquid, Sir Edmund built a fort at Pejypscot falls, and another at Sheepscote, and placed garrisons in them, and, upon his return to Boston, left the command of the country with Anthony Brockholt,[1] one of his council and favorites. [Whilst the Governor was absent the Indians, a small party of 11 Indians from Canada, killed 6 Indians in friendship with the English and belonging to Springfield on Connecticut river and six of the English Inhabitants of Northfield on the same river. Complaints were made at the same time by the English at and near Casco bay in the Eastern parts of New England of the insolent behaviour of the Indians there and the Council judged it necessary to raise a number of men for the defence of the Country. The Governor, on his return, was displeased with this act of the Council in his absence and talked of calling the council to account for a high misdemeanor and would not give any orders or concern himself about the forces sent to Casco. He was anxious to prevent a war, if possible. He had a more favorable opinion of the Indians than the Inhabitants who had suffered so much by them and imagined he should be able to preserve peace with them. This disposition occasioned many idle and incredible reports which seem to have been all the foundation of a charge made against him for supplying the Indians with ammunition and encouraging them to make war against the English. He went however in person to the frontiers and took the command of the forces that he might encourage his men patiently to submit to what fell to their share and he was beloved by the soldiers whilst among them notwithstanding he was so much hated by the people in general.]

In the summer of 1688,* the governor received a new commission, which was published, with great parade, from the balcony of the town-house.† And soon after, [he went to N. York to publish his

* Several letters mention the arrival from England, about this time, of John Palmer, who had been of Sir Edmund's council, both in New-England and New-York, with a commission or appointment for chief judge of the supreme court.

† New-York was included in this commission [and the East and West Jerseys which are said to be annexed to His Majesty's territory of New England]. He went thither soon after. Mr. Smith supposes Dongan to have continued until the revolution. His commission was undoubtedly superseded by this new commission to Andros; who took the administration upon him in the summer of 1688. Mr. Blaithwait writes to Ran-

1 Anthony Brockholt, or Brockholes, or Brockholst, was a member of the Council of Governor Dongan of New York in 1687. *Documentary History of the State of New York* (edited by E. B. O'Callaghan), I, 188.

commission where] he received the joyful news of the birth of a prince, and ordered a general thanksgiving through his government. The suspicions concerning this birth, were transmitted with the news, and very easily received by the people in general.*

DURING the winter of 88, there was no account received in New-England of the landing of the Prince of Orange. Something transpired by way of Virginia, as the spring opened. The rumour brought the governor from Pemaquid to Boston. Soon after his arrival, viz. April 16th, he writes to Brockholt.

There's a general buzzing among the people, great with expectation of their old charter, or they know not what; hope, that all magistrates and officers will be careful not to be wanting in their duty, and particularly

---

dolph, March 11, 1687–8, "Sir, I am to thank you for your's of the 23d of November, and would not fail to answer the chief particulars. If the union of all New-England under one governor be acceptable on your side the water, what will the joining and annexing to the same governmenment be, of all the English territories in America, from Delaware-bay to Nova-Scotia. This is already determined by his Majesty, and a commission is in hand, constituting Sir Edmund Andros governor also of New-York, as united to New-England. And for the two Jerseys, scire facias's are expediting towards their union. This, besides other advantages, will be terrible to the French, and make them proceed with more caution than they have lately done."

* There was special command given to the ministers. The proclamation and order were as follows.

"By his Excellency,

"A proclamation for a general thanksgiving for her Majesty's being safely delivered of a Prince.

"WHEREAS I have received certain information of her Majesty's being safely delivered of a Prince, which being a great blessing bestowed on their Majesties and all his Majesty's dominions, I have therefore thought fit, and do, with the advice of the council, order that there be a general thanksgiving for the same, to be observed within the city of New-York and dependencies on Sunday the second day of September next coming, and fourteen days after in all other parts of this dominion. Of which, all ministers, officers, and persons, are to take notice and conform themselves accordingly. Given at New-York, the four and twentieth day of August, in the fourth year of his Majesty's reign, annoq; Dom. 1688.

"By his Excellency's command,   E. ANDROS.
    JOHN WEST, D. secr'y.   God save the King.
"Vera copia, Benj. Bullivant."

    "Suffolk, ss. }
    New-England } To Mr. Cotton Mather, minister in Boston.

"IN his Majesty's name, you are hereby required to cause the above-written proclamation to be publickly read in the congregation, on the next Lord's day after you shall receive it, and that you do then and there publickly stir up your hearers to the solemn work of the day, as is required by the same, and hereof you are not to fail. Given under my hand and seal at Boston, the first day of September, in the fourth year of his Majesty's reign, King James the second, of England, &c. and in the year of our Lord 1688.

                                                    BENJ. BULLIVANT."

trust, that the soldiers be in good order, and diligent to avoid surprize, and see they have provisions fitting duly served out, and, if occasion, more than the ordinary allowance,

&c. — A few days before, one Mr. Winslow [1] came from Virginia, and brought a printed copy of the Prince of Orange's declaration. Upon his arrival he was imprisoned by Justice Foxcroft [2] and others, "for bringing a traiterous and treasonable libel into the country," as the mittimus expressed it. Winslow offered two thousand pounds bail, but it could not be accepted. A proclamation was issued, charging all officers and people to be in readiness to hinder the landing of any forces which the Prince of Orange might send into those parts of the world. [This was in consequence of orders he had received dated when the invasion from Holland was expected but which its probable were not received until the news or report of the Prince's being landed in England.] The old magistrates and heads of the people silently wished, and secretly prayed, for success to the glorious undertaking, and determined quietly to wait the event. The body of the people were more impatient. The flame, which had been long smothered in their breasts, burst forth with violence, Thursday the 18th of April, when the governor and such of the council as had been most active, and other obnoxious persons, about fifty in the whole, were seized and confined, and the old magistrates were reinstated. This was certainly a rash precipitate proceeding. Little or no inconvenience could arise from a few days delay. The revolution in England could not, at any time, have been effected without risque to all persons there who moved in it. Their lives depended on the success of the attempt. But the fate of New-England depended upon that of Old. If the Prince succeeded, they might have assumed the government without any hazard. If he failed, had they remained quiet, they would have been in no worse state than before; but the consequence of an insurrection would have been death to the principal actors, and a still harder slavery than before to all the rest of the inhabitants. An anonymous letter, directed to the governor of Plimouth, gives a more circumstantial account of this revolution, than any that has yet been printed.

[1] John Winslow (b. 1669) was the son of John Winslow, a merchant of Boston. He was a grandson of John Winslow, of Plymouth, and Mary (Chilton) Winslow. Palfrey indicates that Winslow brought the news from Nevis in the West Indies, not from Virginia, and Winslow's affidavit sustains him. It is barely possible that the vessel touched at Virginia on her way to Boston. See John Gorham Palfrey, *History of New England*, III, 574.

[2] Francis Foxcroft (d. 1727) married a daughter of Thomas Danforth. Though imprisoned in 1689, he was allowed to remain in the colony after the Glorious Revolution.

Boston, April 22d, 89.

Hon^d Sir,

The consideration of my sending you a blank, wherein only the declaration was inclosed, seems to deserve a check, and constrains me to an apology, not having so much as liberty granted me by the messenger to write two or three lines, whereby you might have understood the present state of things, which, by this time, you are doubtless acquainted with; but lest it should prove otherwise, I have taken the pains to give a brief account. — I knew not any thing of what was intended, until it was begun, yet being at the north end of the town, where I saw boys running along the streets, with clubs in their hands, encouraging one another to fight, I began to mistrust what was intended, and, hasting towards the town-dock, I soon saw men running for their arms, but before I got to the red lion, I was told that Capt. George and the master of the frigate * were seized and secured in Mr. Colman's [1] house, at the north end, and when I came to the town-dock, I understood that Bullivant and some others of them were laid hold of, and then, immediately, the drums began to beat, and the people hastened and ran, some with, and some for arms. Young Dudley † [2] and Colonel Lidget,[3] with some difficulty, attained to the fort. The governor immediately sent Dudley on an errand, to request the four ministers,‡ Mr. Joyliffe § [4] and one or two more, to come to him at the fort, pretending that, by them, he might still the people, not thinking it safe for him to go to them. They returned for answer, that they did not think it safe for them to go to him. Now, by this time, all the persons whom they concluded not to be for their side, were seized and secured, except some few who had hid themselves, who afterwards were found, and dealtby as the rest. The governor, with Palmer, Randolph, Lidget, West, and one or two more, were in the fort. All the companies were soon

---

* The Rose.

† Mr. Dudley, his father, was absent, holding court in the Naraganset country. Some of Providence went out and seized him. He was brought to Roxbury and a guard placed round his house, to secure him, as the order expresses it, against violence. He was afterwards committed to prison.

‡ Mr. Allen, Moody, Willard, and Cotton Mather.

§ A person who had been many years a leading man in town affairs in Boston.

---

[1] Presumably this was William Colman, whose son Benjamin became the first minister of the Brattle Street Church.

[2] Presumably this was Thomas Dudley (1670–1697), who had graduated from Harvard College in 1685. See Sibley's *Harvard Graduates*, III, 318.

[3] Charles Lidget (*d.* 1698) was the son of Peter Lidget, a rich merchant of Boston. He was a justice of the peace under Andros.

[4] John Joyliffe (*d.* 1702) was for many years a selectman of Boston; and in 1691, town recorder. He was placed in the Council by the Charter of 1691, but was not continued in that office by the next election.

rallied together at the town-house, where assembled Capt. Winthrop,*[1] Shrimpton,* Page,†[2] and many other substantial men, to consult matters; in which time the old governor ‡[3] came among them, at whose appearance there was a great shout by the soldiers. Soon after, the jack was set up at the fort, and a pair of colours at beacon-hill, which gave notice to some thousand soldiers on Charlestown side that the controversy was now to be ended, and multitudes would have been there, but that there was no need. The frigate, upon the news, put out all her flags and pendants, and opened all her ports, and with all speed made ready for fight, under the command of the lieutenant, he swearing that he would die before she should be taken, although the captain sent to him, that if he fired one shot, or did any hurt, they would kill him, whom they had seized already; but the lieutenant, not regarding, kept those resolutions all that day. Now, about four of the clock in the afternoon, orders were given to go and demand the fort, which hour the soldiers longed for, and had it not been just at the nick, the governor and all the crew had made their escape on board the frigate, a barge being sent for them, but the soldiers, being so near, got the barge. The army divided and part came up on the back side of the fort, part went underneath the hill to the lower battery or sconce, where the red coats were, who immediately upon their approach retired up to the fort to their master, who rebuked them for not firing on our soldiers, and, as I am informed, beat some of them. When the soldiers came to the battery or sconce, they presently turned the great guns about and pointed them against the fort, which did much daunt those within, and the soldiers were so void of fear, that, I presume, had those within the fort been resolute to have lost their lives in fight, they might have killed an hundred of us at once, being so thick together before the mouths of the cannon of the fort, all laden with small shot, but God prevented it. Then they demanded a surrender, which was denied, until Mr. West and another should first go to the council, and, after their return, we should have an answer, whether to fight or no. Upon their return, they came forth from the fort,§ and went disarmed to the town-house, and from thence,

* They were both of them of Sir Edmund's council.

† He married president Dudley's sister.

‡ Other accounts say, that he and the old magistrates were guarded by the militia with great formality.

§ Mr. John Nelson, a young gentleman of Boston, at the head of the soldiers, demanded the fort the second time, and then the governor came down and surrendered himself and the fort. *Neale.*

[1] Waitstill Winthrop (1642–1717), a son of Governor John Winthrop of Connecticut. He was placed in the Council by the Charter of 1691, and continued therein by election. Later he was chief justice of the province.

[2] Nicholas Page, or Paige (d. 1717). Savage disagrees with Hutchinson and points out that Paige's wife was not a sister of Joseph Dudley, but a niece. *Genealogical Dictionary*, III, 332.

[3] Simon Bradstreet (1603–1697) had been governor 1679–86, just prior to the revocation of the Charter.

some to the close gaol, and the governor, under a guard, to Mr. Usher's house. The next day they sent the two colonels to demand of him the surrender of the castle, which he resolved not to give, but they told him, if he would not give it presently, under his hand and seal, he would be exposed to the rage of the people, and so left him; but he sent and told them that he would, and did so, and they went down, and it was surrendered to them with cursings, and they brought the men away and made Capt. Fairweather [1] commander in it. Now, by the time that the men came back from the castle, all the guns, both in ships and batteries, were brought to bear against the frigate, which were enough to have shattered her in pieces at once, resolving to have her. It is incident to corrupt nature to lay the blame of our evil deeds any where rather than on ourselves, so Capt. George cast all the blame now upon that devil Randolph, for had it not been for him he had never troubled this good people, earnestly solliciting that he might not be constrained to surrender the ship, for by so doing both himself and all his men would lose their wages, which otherwise would be recovered in England, giving leave to go on board and strike the topmasts and bring the sails on shore, and so he did. The country people came armed into the town, in the afternoon, in such rage and heat, that it made us all tremble to think what would follow, for nothing would satisfy them, but that the governor must be bound in chains or cords, and put in a more secure place, and that they would see done before they went away; and, to satisfy them, he was guarded by them to the fort. —— *

The former governor, Mr. Bradstreet,† with several of the magistrates chosen in 1686, and some of the principal merchants and other principal inhabitants, being convened at the town-house, signed the following message to Sir Edmund Andros, which was the first public act done by them

At the town-house in Boston, April 18, 1689.

SIR, Ourselves and many others, the inhabitants of this town and places adjacent, being surprized with the people's sudden taking arms, in the

---

* [Since the former edition I have met with a narrative of this Revolution given by Mr. Riggs to the Privy Council by order.

The following is a list of the persons committed to prison: Mr. Dudley, Palmer, Randolph, Lydgatt, M Gregory, George, Brackett, Graham, West, Trefry, Sherlock, Manning, Jouadain, Bullivant, Foxcroft, White, Ravencroft, Pipon, Roberts, Farewell, Jameson, Kane, Leakin, Broadstreet and Cutler.]

† Mr. Bradstreet was eighty-seven years of age, had been sixty years a magistrate. His venerable presence was necessary, but his time for business was over. Mr. Foster, [2] a wealthy merchant, who had not been many years from London, was among the most active, and there are more original papers of his hand writing than of any other person's.

---

[1] John Fairweather (1634–1712) was a constable in 1673, and captain and representative in 1684.

[2] John Foster (d. 1711), of Boston. He was put in the Council by the Charter of 1691.

first motion whereof we were wholly ignorant, being driven to it by the present accident, are necessitated to acquaint your excellency, that, for the quieting and securing the people inhabiting this country from the imminent danger they many ways lie open and exposed to, and tendering your own safety, we judge it necessary, that you forthwith deliver up the government and fortifications, to be preserved and disposed according to order and direction of the crown of England, which suddenly is expected may arrive,* promising all security from violence to yourself, or any of your gentlemen or soldiers, in person or estate, otherwise, we are assured, they will endeavour the taking of the fortifications by storm, if any opposition be made.

　　To Sir Edmund Andros, Knight.

William Stoughton	S. Bradstreet	Wait Winthrop
Thomas Danforth,	John Richards	Sam. Shrimpton
	Elisha Cooke,	Wm. Browne
	Is. Addington	Barth. Gedney
	John Foster	
	Peter Serjeant	
	David Waterhouse	
	Adam Winthrop	
	† J. Nelson.	

* A circular letter was drawn up, to have been sent, in the name of the Prince of Orange, to confirm all governors in their places. That to New-England was stopped, by a representation from Mr. Mather, the agent, to Mr. Jephson, secretary to the Prince.

† Mr. Nelson was a gentleman of good family and a near relation to Sir Thomas Temple, an enemy to the tyrannical government of Andros, but an Episcopalian in principle, and of a gay free temper, which prevented his being allowed any share in the administration after it was settled, although he was at the head of the party that demanded the surrender of the fort. He went not long after upon a trading voyage to Nova Scotia, where he was taken by a party of French or Indians and carried to Quebec. Notwithstanding the slight put upon him, yet such was his regard for his country that he ran very great risque of his life in an attempt to give intelligence of the designs of the French. The following letter, remaining upon the Massachusets files, ought to be made public to do honor to his memory.

　　　　　　　　　　　　　　　　　　　　"August 26, 1692.

"About 14 days ago arrived two men of war and six merchant ships from France, which came furnished with recruits of provision, ammunition, 30 more great guns, 24 pateraroes, one mortar and 30 shells. — A little before the arrival of these ships, Madockawando, the Penobscot sachem, came here, who made and received divers compliments, presented the governor with five English captives, and received from him presents encouraging him and the rest to continue the war, but all gave but little satisfaction to the Indians, who expected greater recompence. They would often discourse their discontent, to some of us who understand their language. I was in hopes to make some improvement of their discontent, by proposing the settlement of a trading house up Penobscot river at Negas. They were glad of the proposal, and it is the only means of recovering our interest with these eastern Indians. I promised to send my thoughts thereon to yourselves, of which I would have you to consider, &c. — Madockawando gave daily advice of all their results, he is certainly well affected towards us. Two days ago he was dispatched from hence, with orders to get together all the Indians he can, they make account of two or three hundred, they are to remain at Penobscot until the

HOWEVER exceptionable the first rising of the people might be, yet this measure of the magistrates and other gentlemen seems to have been necessary. It is difficult to conceive in what other way the

---

two men of war join them, who are preparing themselves as well as they can, adding to their number 200 Canadians, so that, in all, they will have above 400, who, with the Indians, are to assault Wells, Isles of Shoals and Piscataqua. The design is dangerous if you should be unprovided, I have therefore improved my utmost endeavours to give you this intelligence. By money, and a promise of good reward from yourselves, I have corrupted two Frenchmen, viz. Arnaud Du Vignon and Francis Albert to be bearers of this letter, and also to be guides to two Dutchmen and two Englishmen, who promise to be with you in 22 days. I pray that they may be contented. I have furnished them with 13 French crowns which it is just should be allowed to my wife. My charge is, otherwise, great here, there being so many of my poor countrymen to relieve, &c. The two men of war, which come from hence, are, the one a great Dutch square stern ship of about 500 tons, takes in six guns from hence, so that she will have in all 38 guns, &c. the other is a French frigate of 34 guns, who is the admiral. They take at Port Royal and along the coast, all the small vessels, shallops, boats, &c. to land their men. You will do well to prepare, for their reception, a good fireship, and other means necessary, according as your prudence shall direct. — I recommend myself unto your prayer, and remain gentlemen your humble servant,

J. NELSON.

August 27th, The ships of war go from hence in 12 or 15 days, their voyage probably to St. John's and Penobscot will cost them a month's time more, so that you may expect them in about 6 or 7 weeks hence. After their attempt upon your coast, they are to cruize for about a month, &c. so that all concerned in shipping must take care to their affairs. Let no public talk be made of this letter, for, by the escape of some prisoners, the report will come hither greatly to my damage. — Excuse my broken manner of writing. I am forced to do it as I can get opportunity, and that is in my bed because of the often coming in and out of the man that attends me who once surprized me and took from me my inkhorn, but in all things else I am well treated. So are all the rest according as the country affords, &c.

The letters came to Springfield the 23d of September, and a day or two after to Boston. The Frenchmen, not long after, by some means or other were retaken and carried to Canada, where they were punished as deserters. Before their execution they confessed the whole. Mr. Nelson was carried out with them, in expectation of the same fate. They were shot before his eyes. He was sent back to prison and soon after to France, but, on his passage, prevailed with a fellow passenger to convey intelligence of a second design, of 12 men of war and 2000 troops, which were every day expected at Canada, to make a descent upon the English colonies from Piscataqua to Carolina. He was confined in France, in a small hole, for two years, without opportunity of seeing any person but a servant who brought his victuals to a grate. A gentleman, who had taken notice of the person who carried the victuals from day to day, had the curiosity to enquire what prisoner was there, and to speak to him at the grate, and to ask if he could do him any service. Mr. Nelson desired no other favor than to have a letter sent to England, to inform Sir Purbeck Temple of his condition, which was done, and, soon after, a demand was made of his release or exchange. He was then looked upon as a person of some importance. He was sent to the Bastile and, just before the peace of Ryswick, was allowed to go to England, upon his parole, and security given by a French gentleman for his return. The peace being concluded and he intending to return, was forbad to do it by King William, but, to prevent any trouble to his friend, he went contrary to order, and surrendered himself. Being discharged, upon his return to England he was brought into trouble there for going back to France contrary to the King's order, but at length returned to his family after ten or eleven years absence.

people could have been quieted. Had they been left to themselves, the consequences must have been terrible. Some who had been the most firm in support of the charter were afraid, however, of being called to account for their concern in this action.*

A long declaration was read from the balcony or gallery of the town-house. This is printed at large in Neale and other writers. There would be room to doubt whether this declaration was not a work of time, and prepared beforehand, if it did not appear, by the stile and language, to have been the performance of one of the ministers of the town of Boston,† who had a remarkable talent for very quick and sudden composures; besides, it was not printed until several days after, and perhaps was corrected and enlarged. Indeed, it fully appears from many private letters, still preserved, one of the best sorts of evidence of the truth of historical facts of this nature, that none of the magistrates were privy to the rising of the people, and, in the people themselves, it seems to have been sudden, and without any previously concerted plan.

THE next day, April 19th, an order was signed by most of the persons who subscribed the advice to Sir Edmund, and also by Wm. Johnson [1] of Woburn, and James Russell [2] of Charlestown, directed to John Pipon, commander of the castle, and accompanied with an order from the late governor, to deliver the fort and stores to Capt. Fairweather, which was complied with. The 20th, the tumult being

---

* Mr. Danforth the deputy governor, writes to Plimouth April 20th, "Their enterprize herein was without the privity of those who, when begun, judged themselves obliged to endeavour the prevention of bloodshed, and, thereupon, did give their sense and advice to the governor, Sir Edmund, as they apprehended very necessary. —— I yet fear what the consequences will be, and heartily pray that no bitter fruit may spring forth from this root. We have need of God's pity and pardon, and some do apprehend it will be wisdom to hasten our address, to those that are now supreme in England, for pardon of so great an irruption, and for a favourable settlement under the sanction of royal authority." And in a letter to Increase Mather, July 30th, "The antient magistrates and elders, although they had strenuously advised to further waiting for orders from England, and discouraged any attempts of that nature, so far as they had opportunity, yet were they now compelled to assist with their presence and councils for the preventing of bloodshed, which had most certainly been the issue, if prudent councils had not been given to both parties."

† Mr. Mather.

---

[1] William Johnson (d. 1704) was the son of Capt. Edward Johnson, the author of *Wonder-working Providence of Sions Saviour in New England*. He had been an Assistant, 1684–86.

[2] James Russell (1640–1709) was a son of Richard Russell, who was prominent in the earlier history of the Colony. James's first wife was a daughter of Governor Haynes of Connecticut. Before the revocation of the Charter he was an Assistant and Treasurer of the Colony. After the overthrow of Andros he was placed in the Council by the Charter of 1691.

abated, the new council began to consider what form of government they should establish, in the room of that which was dissolved. They first invited divers other persons to join with them, who were required to sign an approbation of the advice given to Sir Edmund, and, being thus strengthened, they took the title of "A council for the safety of the people, and conservation of the peace." Those who thus associated with the first mentioned, were James Russell, John Phillips, Penn Townsend, Joseph Lynde, John Joyliffe, Eliakim Hutchinson, Nath. Oliver, John Eyre, Jeremiah Dummer, Wm. Johnson, John Hawthorne, Andrew Belcher, Richard Sprague, James Parker, Dudley Bradstreet, Nath. Saltonstall, Richard Dummer, Robert Pike, John Smith, Edmund Quincy, William Bond, and Daniel Pierce. They chose Mr. Bradstreet their president, Isaac Addington [1] clerk of the council, and Wait Winthrop commander in chief of the militia, and appointed officers in the several ports for entering and clearing vessels, and John Foster and Adam Winthrop,[2] two of their number, stewards or treasurers.

THEY continued to pass orders, from time to time, for the regulation of the inhabitants; but the authority was weak, and there was a necessity of a further settlement. They were careful to avoid reassuming their charter. Besides the exceptions that might be taken whilst the decree against it stood in full force, there were many who were desirous of a settlement from England, sensible of the defects in the charter; and when the governor and assembly, afterwards addressed, for the restitution of it, they desired such further privileges as were necessary. They had, no doubt, received advice of the convention called by the Prince of Orange, and in imitation of it, on the second of May, they recommended to the several towns in the colony to meet, and depute persons, not exceeding two for each town, except Boston four, to form an assembly, to sit the ninth of the same month. Sixty-six persons met, and presented a declaration to the president and former magistrates in particular,* taking no notice of such as had associated with them; but upon receiving an answer in writing, they desired the whole council to continue in their station

* They declare the governor, deputy governor, and assistants chosen and sworn in 1686, according to charter rights, and the deputies then sent by the freemen of the several towns, to be the government now settled in the colony. *Records.*

---

[1] Isaac Addington (1645–1715) was a nephew of Governor John Leverett. Increase Mather had him appointed Councillor and Secretary in the Charter of 1691, in which offices he was continued by popular election.

[2] Adam Winthrop (1647–1700) was a son of Adam Winthrop and a grandson of John Winthrop. He graduated from Harvard College in 1668. He was made a member of the Council by the Charter of 1691, but he was left out by the election of 1693.

until the 22d instant, at which time it was agreed there should be a meeting of the representatives of all the towns in the colony, at Boston, who were to be specially instructed by their towns. Letters had been sent to Plimouth and to Connecticut,* to acquaint the principal gentlemen there, with what had been done at Boston. Both those colonies were content the governor should be confined at Boston, and both reassumed their old form of government. Nothing passed relative to New-Hampshire or Rhode-Island. As soon as the news reached New-York, Nicholson, the lieutenant-governor, dispatched the following letter, directed to Simon Bradstreet and Wait Winthrop, Esquires, and others.

Gentlemen, NEW-YORK, 1689, 1st May.

IT was an extraordinary surprize to us to hear of the confusions the inhabitants at Boston have occasioned, by taking that part of the government to themselves, and that they have seized upon the person of his excellency and several of the officers. We cannot imagine, that any such

---

* Plimouth imitated the Massachusets in securing one of the council who was within that colony, as appears by the following declaration.

A declaration of sundry of the inhabitants of Plimouth, Ap. 22, 1689. "Whereas we have not only just ground to suspect, but are well assured that Nath. Clark [1] hath been a real enemy to the peace and prosperity of this people, and hath, by lying and false information to the late governor, caused much trouble and damage to this place, endeavouring to deprive us of our lands, and exposing us to the unjust severity of persons ill affected to us, whereby a considerable part of our estates is unrighteously extorted from us, to the great prejudice of our families, and the loss of many necessary comforts; and he persisting, from time to time, in his malicious forging complaints against one or other of us, whereby we are in continual hazard of many further great inconveniences and mischiefs. We do therefore seize upon his person, resolving to secure him for the hands of justice to deal with him according to his demerit.' MS. [The General Court also agreed on an Address to K. William and Q. Mary, June 6, 1689, which was presented praying for a Grant or Confirmation of all their former Liberties, either by a Charter or Act of Parliament as should seem meet.]

Mr. Treat, the governor of Connecticut, gives this account of their proceedings, in his letter to their agent, Jan. 6, 1689. "In the beginning of May last, upon the amazing reports and tidings of the revolution of the government in the Massachusets, and seizing of the governor and so many of his council, and that part of the country up in arms before we knew any thing of it, but the news did soon fly like lightning, and soon after, our men in most places gave out, that they would no longer obey us, or submit to Sir Edmund's government; at the same time, the eastern Indians went on in their barbarous cruelties in murdering our countrymen at the eastward; and we had, by letters from New York and Long-Island, caution given us of several pickaroons that were on the coast to alarm us on the sea board; the true and real grounds of the procedure of the colony in assuming the government was, salus populi est suprema lex."

---

[1] Nathaniel Clark (d. 1717), of Plymouth, had been Secretary under Andros. "Clark's Island in Plymouth harbor, which had been appropriated by the town of Plymouth for the support of the town's poor, was granted [by Andros] without color of claim to Nathaniel Clarke, one of his creatures." Francis Baylies, *Historical Memoir of New Plymouth* (1866), Part IV, p. 44.

actions can proceed from any person of quality amongst them, but rather promoted by the rabble, and that for the safety of his excellency's person those measures have been taken; but hope, and doubt not, before this time, the fury of those persons may be allayed, and that his excellency and the rest of the officers may be restored to their former stations, or at least have liberty to come hither. For this part of the government, we find the people in general inclined to peace and quietness,* and doubt not the people will remain in their duties. We do not question but you will send us a speedy answer, the matter being of so great consequence, tending to the peace and quietness of us all, which if you do, we remain your friends and servants,

Fra. Nicholson
Frederick Flypse
N. Bayard
S. Courtland.

* The inhabitants of New York, having never experienced any great degree of liberty, there would have been no grounds of fears of a revolt, if it had not been for the example of New-England. From their first subjection to England, the government had been the same, and the Dutch governors who preceded were not less absolute than the English. Upon the news from Boston, Capt. Nicholson, the lieutenant governor, proposed to admit part of the trained bands to watch and ward by turns within the fort, under their own officers, and offered to apply the money arising from the customs, to the fortifying the city, and making it defensible against a foreign enemy. Jacob Leisler, a captain of the trained bands, happened to have a ship just arrived with wines, the duties whereof would have amounted to one hundred pounds, which he refused to pay, "the collector being a papist, and there being no legal authority to receive it." Soon after he excited the people upon the east end of Long Island to march to New York, in order to take possession of the fort, to prevent its being delivered up to foreigners. When they came within twelve miles of the city, being about eighty in number, they sent three of their leaders to the lieutenant governor, who, having convened his council, gave them such answers as induced them and the rest of the company to return home. A rumor was soon after spread, of a design to massacre the inhabitants, during the public worship in the Dutch church, upon a Sunday. The Friday before the day for the supposed execution, the people rose, and seemingly compelled Leisler to head them. One Hall went as their leader to the fort. The guard, consisting of the trained bands, readily admitted them. Leisler followed, and took the command of the men. This was the 31st of May. The same evening they sent for the keys from the lieutenant governor, who was obliged to deliver them. The trained band consisting of six companies, the captain of each company was to command his day according to their order. When it came to Leisler's turn, the 3d of June, he caused an alarm, and the people being all brought together, a declaration was prepared in writing ready to be signed, "that with their lives and fortunes they would defend the protestant religion, and keep the fort for King William and Queen Mary, until their Majesties further order." The people then chose a committee, who assumed the name of a "committee of safety." They appointed Leisler captain of the fort. The lieutenant governor withdrew. In his absence, Leisler takes upon him the administration, and, after some time, calls himself lieutenant governor, and chooses a council. The province continued in great confusion, until the arrival of governor Slaughter with a commission from King William and Queen Mary. Leisler held the possession of the fort against the governor, longer than he could justify himself in so doing. His enemies took the advantage of it, and he was tried, condemned, and executed as a traitor. The party rage which was raised on this occasion, was kept up many years after in New-York, and descended to the posterity of each side.

The following answer was returned.

Gentlemen,   BOSTON, 11th May, 1689.

IN answer to yours of the first of May instant, giving an account of your having received the general intelligence of the revolution occurring here, expressing your hopes that before this time the fury of the people may be allayed, and that Sir Edmund Andros and the rest of the officers may be restored to their former stations, or at least may have liberty to come to you. We perceive you have not a particular account how things are at present circumstanced with us, there being no other form of government than a committee for safety of the people and conservation of the peace, the soldiers still continuing in arms. And the people are so well satisfied in the justifiableness of their late action, that they continue their spirit and resolution, to pursue what they have put forth in their public declaration printed, which is here inclosed, as also a printed copy of the advice given by ourselves and others unto Sir Edmund, which will shew the necessity of our then interposing. And we have no other station than to intend the common safety and conservation of the peace, and it is not in our power to set any persons at liberty who are confined and kept by the soldiers. This being all the present answer we can make to you, if accepted, we remain,

Gentlemen, your friends and servants,
To Capt. Fran. Nicholson,   S. Bradstreet
   Fred. Phillips, Nich. Bayard,   Wait Winthrop.
   and Steph. Cortland, Esqrs.

THE representatives of 54 towns met at Boston, on the 22d of May.* They soon discovered a desire to re-assume the charter. The major part of the council were against it. Two days were spent in disputes. The people without doors were also much divided in sentiments. On the 24th, the governor and magistrates, chosen in 1686, signed a paper, declaring their acceptance of the care and government of the people, according to the rules of the charter, for the conservation of the peace and safety of the people, until, by direction from England, there be an orderly settlement of government, provided an addition should be made of fit persons to assist them, as was desired, and that what had been before done be allowed, and the stewards be reimbursed: This they did for the satisfaction of the people, and from the present necessity, but they did not intend, nor would be understood to intend, an assumption of the charter government. Their declaration was accepted by the representatives, notwithstanding its being qualified in the conclusion of it.† The next

* Each town gave instructions to their members whether to re-assume or not. Forty of the fifty-four were for re-assumption of the charter.

† By this declaration all the gentlemen who had joined the governor and assistants chosen in 1686 were excluded from the new council.

day, Mr. Winthrop, and most of the other gentlemen who had acted as members of the council, and who had a strong party in favour of their continuing so to act, generously quitted all claim to it, in confidence, as they express it, that the people will be inviolably preserved in their obedience to the directions expected from England, and that the persons of all the gentlemen confined should be well treated, and promised to endeavour to pacify the people, who were dissatisfied on their account, and to promote the public tranquility, as far as should be in their power.

THE 26th (being Sunday) a ship arrived from England, with advice of the proclaiming King William and Queen Mary. This was the most joyful news ever received in New-England. The fears of the people of any very bad consequences from their late actions, were now over. On the 29th, the proclamation was published in Boston, with greater ceremony than had been known, the governor and council, civil and military officers, merchants of the town, and principal gentlemen of the town and country being on horseback, the regiment of the town, and many companies of horse and foot from the country, appearing in arms; a grand entertainment was prepared in the town-house, and wine was served out to the soldiers.

THE 5th of June, the representatives of the several towns, upon a new choice, assembled at Boston. The council immediately proposed to them to exhibit articles against the gentlemen seized by the people, or else to consent to their inlargement, upon security given; but this was not agreed to.* The next day, the representatives urged to the council, to take upon them the part they ought to bear in the government, according to the charter, until orders should be received from England, and declared "they could not proceed to act in any thing of public concerns, until this was conceded." An acceptance was voted, this declaration being given as the reason of the

* Some days after, Sir Edmund, by letter, demanded an immediate release of himself and the other persons concerned in government, or under his charge, then in custody, or under restraint. The 27th June the representatives resolved that Mr. Joseph Dudley, Sir Edmund Andros, Mr. Edward Randolph, Mr. John Palmer,[1] Mr. John West, Mr. James Graham, Mr. George Farwell,[2] and Mr. James Sherlock,[3] were not bailable, and sent up several heads of charges against them.

[1] John Palmer was perhaps the most unendurable of Andros's judges. For the colonists' grievances against him see *Andros Tracts* (Prince Society), I, 165–166.

[2] George Farwell was one of Andros's attorneys. "Lawyer, Attourney, Attourney General, and Clerk of all Courts at times." *Andros Tracts* (Prince Society), I, 167–168.

[3] James Sherlock was the High Sheriff of Suffolk County under Andros. Savage says he was formerly of Portsmouth, New Hampshire, and had been appointed a member of the New Hampshire Council in 1684.

vote. By these steps, the change was made from the unlimited power of Sir Edmund and four of his council, to the old government, which had continued above fifty years; but the weight and authority did not return with the form. They were scrupulous of their power themselves, and made an apology, in an address to the crown, for causing certain pirates to be executed. They found it very difficult to raise men, and continue them in service, for the defence of the province. Several contemptuous pamphlets against them were published with impunity. Thirty years before, the authors of the like would have been guilty of a capital offence. And although the first advices, received afterwards from England, gave them some grounds to expect a re-establishment of government in the old form, yet these advices were soon succeeded by others which caused them to despair of it.* Mr. Mather, the agent in England, waited the event of the prince of Orange's expedition. Soon after the withdraw of King James, Mr. Mather was introduced to the Prince of Orange, by Lord Wharton,[1] and prevented the circular letter before mentioned, for confirming governors, being sent to New-England.† The 14th of March, Lord Wharton introduced him again to the King,‡ when, after humbly congratulating his Majesty's accession, Mr. Mather implored his Majesty's favour to New-England. The King promised all the favour in his power; but hinted what had been irregular in

* "We are far from willingly doing any thing arbitrary; but the long want of directions from England for settlement of government doth weaken our hands." *Gov. Bradstreet's letter to Sir H. Ashurst, Oct.* 26, 89.

"The long delay of orders from England referring to the persons confined upon the revolution, and want of confirmation of the government, hath given occasion to divers ill designing men, who were taken off from their employment and ways of unjust gain, studiously to employ themselves in opposing and undervaluing authority, which hath emboldened others to those practices which hath rendered them criminals of the highest nature, by committing felonies, piracies, and murders, and thereby common enemies to mankind, and necessitated us to draw the sword of justice against them, and bring them to trial and condemnation, and to execute some, to deter others, &c. which we trust will not be offensive to his Majesty. *Bradstreet's letter to Ashurst, Jan.* 29, 1689-90.

† [There is a minute in the Records of the Board of Trade that this letter was stopped on application from Sʳ W. Phips and Mʳ Mather.

An Order was also passed in Council appointing two Commissioners to proceed to N. England and take on them the Government there and cause K. William and Q. Mary to be proclaimed.

The Merchants and Planters in London were to recommend one of the Commissioners. The Lords Committee for Trade and Plantations were to prepare and consider of a Charter in the meantime; but nothing was done upon this Order.]

‡ King William and Queen Mary were proclaimed 13th Feb.

[1] Philip Wharton (1613–96), fourth Baron Wharton, who "conducted him to William, at the palace, and introduced him." For interesting glimpses of Lord Wharton, see Kenneth Ballard Murdock, *Increase Mather*, pp. 202, 211, 214, 216, 219, 236.

their former government. Whereupon Mr. Mather undertook that, upon the first word, they should reform any irregularities they should be advised of, and Lord Wharton offered to be their guarantee. The King then said, that he would give orders that Sir Edmund Andros should be removed, and called to account for his mal-administration, and that the King and Queen should be proclaimed by the former magistrates. Mr. Mather was a faithful agent, and was unwearied in securing friends for his country. Besides several of the nobility and principal commoners, he had engaged the whole body of the dissenting ministers, whose weight, at that time, was far from inconsiderable.

THE family of Ashurst had always been friendly to New-England. The first addresses after the restoration, were sent to Mr. Ashurst, Mr. Leveret, and Mr. Richard Hutchinson,[1] to be delivered to the King. Sir Henry Ashurst, a member of parliament, was more particularly engaged at this time by Mr. Mather, who desired that he might be impowered by the colony to appear as their agent. Mr. Hampden, another member, also shewed great friendship. The house of commons voted the taking away the charters of the plantations to be a grievance,* and a bill passed the house for restoring charters, and the New-England charters were expresly mentioned; but whilst the bill lay in the house of Lords, the parliament, sooner than expected, was prorogued, the King going to Ireland. The King, from the beginning, discovered a design to reserve the appointment of the governor to himself. It was in vain, after losing this chance in parliament, to try for the restoration of the old charter. A new charter, with as many of the old privileges as could be obtained, was all that

---

* At a committee of grievances, Martis 5° Martii 1688, resolved nem. con. that it is the opinion of this committee, that the late prosecutions of quo warrantos against the cities, two universities, the towns corporate, boroughs and cinq ports, and the plantations, and the judgment thereupon, and the surrenders of charters to the violation of their ancient rights, are illegal and grievances. By the house. "Resolved, that this house doth agree with the said committee in said resolve, and that [2] the late prosecution of quo warrantos against the cities, two universities, the towns corporate, boroughs and cinq ports, and plantations, and judgment thereupon, and the surrenders of charters to the violation of their ancient rights, are illegal and a grievance." MS.

---

[1] Richard Hutchinson (b. 1615) was a younger son of William Hutchinson and his wife Anne. If Savage is correct, this Richard returned to England, after a few years spent in New England, and grew rich. Genealogical Dictionary, II, 511. Hutchinson, the historian, held that the rich Richard of England was a brother of William Hutchinson. See Peter Orlando Hutchinson, editor, Diary and Letters of Thomas Hutchinson, II, 457.

[2] The first edition gives "that" instead of "and that" at this point. The third edition follows the first.

could be hoped for. In the mean time, application was made, for express power and authority to be granted to the colony to exercise government according to the old charter, until a new could be settled. This was obtained.* At the same time an order was sent, commanding the delivery of the sails taken from the Rose frigate, and another order for Sir Edmund Andros, and the other persons, to be sent to England.† Mr. Mather intended to have returned to New-

---

* WILLIAM R.

Trusty and well-beloved, we greet you well. Whereas we are informed by several addresses from the colony of the Massachusets bay, and particularly by the address coming to us in the name of the governor and council and convention of the representatives of the people of the said colony, that they had joyfully received the notice of our happy accession to the throne of these kingdoms, and caused the proclamation thereof to be issued throughout the said territory: We have therefore thought fit hereby to signify our royal approbation of the same, and gracious acceptance of your readiness in performing that which was necessary, on your parts, for the preservation of the peace and quiet of our said colony. And whereas you give us to understand, that you have taken upon you the present care of the government, until you should receive our order therein; we do hereby authorize and impower you to continue, in our name, your care in the administration thereof and preservation of the peace, until we shall have taken such resolutions and given such directions for the more orderly settlement of the said government, as shall most conduce to our service, and the security and satisfaction of our subjects within that our colony. And so we bid you farewell. Given at our court in Whitehall, the 12th day of August, 1689, in the first year of our reign.

By his Majesty's Command,

Colony of Massachusets.   SHREWSBURY.

† WILLIAM R.

Whereas Sir Edmund Andros, knt. late governor of our dominion of New-England, has been seized by some people in Boston, and is under close confinement there, together with Edward Randolph, John Trefry,[1] and divers other subjects, who have humbly requested us, that they be either set at liberty, or sent in safe custody into England, to answer before us what may be objected against them: We do hereby will and require that the said Sir Edmund Andros, Edward Randolph, John Trefry, and others our subjects that have been in like mannar seized by the said people of Boston, and shall be at the receipt of these our commands detained there under confinement, be forthwith sent on board the first ship bound hither, to answer before us what may be objected against them, and that you take care that they be civilly used in their passages from New-England, and safely conveyed to our royal presence. Given at our court at Whitehall this 30th day of July, 1689, in the first year of our reign.

By his Majesty's command,

NOTTINGHAM.

To such as, for the time being, take care for preserving the peace and administring the laws in our colony of the Massachusets-bay in New-England, in America.

Of all that were concerned in the late government, Mr. Dudley felt most of the people's resentment. Oppression is less grievous from a stranger, than one of our own country. Danforth writes to I. Mather, "Mr. Dudley is in a peculiar manner the object of the people's displeasure, even throughout all the colonies where he hath sat judge; they deeply resent his correspondence with that wicked man Randolph for overturning

---

[1] "John" Trefry was probably Capt. Thomas Trefry, a cousin of William Blathwayt. See *Edward Randolph* (Prince Society), VI, 208. He appears to have been Andros's right-hand man in military affairs. *Ibid.*, VI, 257.

England with these orders; but his son being taken with the small-pox at Deal, prevented his embarking. Letters arrived in England, presently after the King's order to the old magistrates, from Sir Edmund Andros, Mr. Dudley, &c. complaining of their usage. Nicholson and Usher came to London also with their complaints, and the Indians falling upon Piscataqua about the same time, it was imputed to the revolution in the Massachusets, and the friends of New-England were afraid the powers would be recalled,* and a governor sent over without delay.

THE letters did not arrive in New-England until very late in the year, but came very opportunely to calm the commotions which had very much increased there. Sir Edmund, his servant having enticed the centinel to drink, and then to suffer him to be upon guard in his stead, escaped from the castle, and went to Rhode-Island, where Major Sanford [1] stopped him, and sent him back to the castle again.†

the government. —— The governor and council, though they have done their utmost to procure his enlargement, yet can't prevail, but the people will have him in the jayl, and when he hath been by order turned out, by force and tumult they fetch him in again," &c. Mr. Dudley to C. Mather, June 1st. "I am told, that this morning is the last opportunity for rolling away the stone from the mouth of this sepulchre, where I am buried alive, in which I yet trouble you for your assistance." To governor Bradstreet, Sept. 12th, "After twenty weeks unaccountable imprisonment, and many barbarous usages offered me therein, the last seven weeks whereof are upon account of your letters to me, I have now to complain, that on Monday, the whole day, I could be allowed no victuals till nine of the clock at night, when the keeper's wife offered to kindle her own fire to warm something for me, and the corporal expresly commanded the fire to be put out. — I may be easily oppressed to death. — God will hear them that complain to him. — I pray your directions for your oppressed kinsman,   J. D."

* Nath. Mather's letter to Increase Mather, &c.

† Leisler, at New-York, was greatly alarmed at Sir Edmund's escape. He writes to the Massachusets governor from New-York, Sept. 3d. "The escape of Sir Edmund, and his arrival at Rhode-Island, where Col. Dongan did, the same day, land some of his people, and himself not far off, caused a jealousy in us of a bad design. In this interim of time arrived here Mr. John Emerson, John Leverett, William Brattle, Thomas Maccarty, and John Perry, from the ferry, after watch set in the night well armed, and, as reported, went into a tavern, where doors and windows were shut, a man on horseback was dispatched post out of the town, made us all believe them of Sir Edmund's people, and he himself not far off. I sent for the strangers of whom I demanded a pass; they said they had one, but lost it; they knew no body but Major Brockholt and Capt. Locker, two known papists, whereby I suspected them to be really of Sir Edmund's people, and beat the drum. I sent twelve soldiers to search the house for their portmanteaus, two were brought and owned to be theirs. I found about forty letters, most of them directed to disapprovers of our actions, which caused me to alarm the town, by which arlarm I got immediately about five hundred men courageously armed, and,

[1] Peleg Sanford, or Sandford, of Newport, Rhode Island, had been governor of Rhode Island 1680–82. His granddaughter, Margaret Sanford, became the wife of Governor Thomas Hutchinson. *New England Historical and Genealogical Register,* XXVII, 81.

The first opportunity after the arrival of the King's order, he, with Mr. Dudley and several others, embarked for England.* The general court thought it adviseable to send over two of their members to join with Sir Henry Ashhurst and Mr. Mather in maintaining their charges against their oppressors, as well as in soliciting the restoration of the charter, with such additional privileges as should be thought proper, viz. Elisha Cooke, and Thomas Oakes,† both of them assistants. Mr. Cooke was a gentleman of good understanding, and had been well educated, had always adhered stiffly to the old charter, and when all the rest of the assistants declined reassuming it, he alone was in favour of it.‡ Mr. Oakes [1] was a man of less consequence, but attached to the same side, having been some time a representative of the town of Boston, and not of the assistants when they refused to reassume. They were instructed, among other things, to sollicit in parliament, or elsewhere, the confirmation of their ancient charter, and all its rights and privileges, civil and sacred, and, if there should be opportunity, to endeavour the obtaining such farther privileges as might be of benefit to the colony. The agents disagreed, and by this means, certain articles intended against Sir Edmund were never signed by them.§ He obtained, some time after, the govern-

---

while the committee read the letters, I sent out parties to search for strangers, and for the men of the house where they arrived, being persons who never joined with us to watch and fortify, nor armed in any alarm. The letters being read, and nothing found, we suspected that those of consequence were gone, and so remained upon our guard. In the morning Mr. Lawrence perused a letter from his grand-child, wherein the characters of the said gentlemen were discovered; upon which slender proof and my charity, I ventured to release the said gentlemen, who confessed we had just cause to suspect them, all things falling out as they did."

The four persons first named belonged to the college at Cambridge.

* The beginning of February.

† Mr. Oakes was not chosen assistant until May, after they embarked.

‡ This appears from the files of the court.

§ Mr. Mather said, that the Earl of Monmouth told him they had cut the throat of their country in not doing it; but Mr. Cooke's excuse was, Sir John Somers's [2] advice, which he said was against doing it. An enquiry into the conduct of Sir Edmund and the rest it was designed should be avoided, and this was the reason of Sir John Somers's advice to Mr. Cooke. "When the agents first appeared before the council, Sir Edmund, Dudley, Randolph, &c. had notice to be present also, and came prepared with a charge

---

[1] Thomas Oakes (1644–1719) was a brother of Urian Oakes, the president of Harvard College. Thomas graduated from Harvard in 1662 and became a physician. In 1689 he was Speaker of the House, and in 1690 an Assistant.

[2] Sir John Somers (1651–1716) presided over the committee that framed the Declaration of Rights, and later became successively Attorney-General and Lord Chancellor. In 1690 he appears to have been the chief adviser to the Massachusetts agents. For this incident in their negotiations see Kenneth Ballard Murdock, *Increase Mather*, pp. 230–231.

ment of Virginia, [and died in London in the year 1713]. Mr. Dudley was appointed chief justice of New-York, and the latter end of the year 1690, was at Boston, in his way to his post.   Nicholson en-

---

against the colony, for rebellion against lawful authority, for imprisoning the King's governor, &c. Sir John Somers thereupon said, that the agents were upon the defensive part, and were ready to answer any complaints. Sir Robert Sawyer, who had brought the quo warranto then declaimed largely against the colony for those deeds by which he supposed the charter forfeited; but, in the close, to prevent an answer, acknowledged that what he said was foreign to the present case, and one of the lords said, let us keep to the matter before us. The agents were then required to give the reasons of the opposition to Sir Edmund and his authority. They began with his proclamation, and other endeavours to stifle the news of the prince's landing, and the imprisonment of the person who brought over the declaration. Lord president (Marquis of Carmarthen) asked who imprisoned Sir Edmund and the rest? Sir John Somers replied, The country, my Lord, oppressed by an arbitrary government, did there as we did here, rose as one man, took the opportunity of the news of the revolution in England to free themselves from the yoke they were under. Lord president. You say it was the country and the people, that is no body, let us see A B and C, the persons that will make it their case. Here is a charge against the King's governor, but no body has signed the paper. Sir J. Somers. My Lord, we are here, in behalf of the country, to manage their concerns, and not in the behalf of any particular persons. One of the agents then whispered Sir John, that if that was a stick, they would sign the paper immediately; but he replied no, we are in our way, and have followed the direction of the board, and if they will bring us off thus they may. One of the Lords said, I perceive the revolution was there as it was here, by the unanimous agreement of the people; for who seized and imprisoned the late lord chancellor? Who seized and imprisoned the lord such and such, naming several, and secured the garrison of Hull? &c. I think we understand the matter well enough, and see no reason why we may not go forward with the proof. Another lord spake to the same purpose, and said the people were to be commended for what they had done; but lord president applied himself to the agents, and said, gentlemen, here has been a pretty deal of time spent, my lords will give his Majesty a true and impartial account of what has been said on both sides, and wait his Majesty's further pleasure, and you may withdraw for the present. The next day Sir Edmund and the rest were discharged from any further attendance, and a report being made to his Majesty in council, the same was approved, and the matter was ordered to be dismissed on both sides." (*Mr. Cooke's letter.*) Thus the agents were diverted, by their own council, from pursuing their instructions, and supporting a charge which had been prepared and offered to the Lords of the council. It was well known, that it would be most agreeable to have no enquiry made. Lord president's own arbitrary actions, whilst Earl of Danby, for which no satisfaction had been given, would have stared him in the face, and it would not have well consisted with the oblivion intended for what had past at home, to have been very strict in enquiring into tyranny in the colonies. [But the articles themselves after all the cry against Sir Edmund Andros and near one hundred depositions carried over by Mr. Cooke against him, were reduced to these two viz. First. It is objected against Sir Edmund Andros that he being Governor of the Massachusets Colony, after notice of his present Majesty's intention to land in England, issued out a proclamation requiring all persons to oppose any descent of such as might be authorized by him, endeavoured to stifle the news of his landing, and caused him that brought the King's declaration there to be imprisoned as being a seditious and treasonable paper.

Secondly. That in the time of his government, he without form or colour of legal authority, made laws destructive of the liberty of the people, imposed and levied taxes, threatened and imprisoned them who would not be assisting to the illegal levies, denied that they had any property in their lands without patents from him, and during the

deavoured for the government of New-York, but had not interest to carry it, and was appointed lieutenant governor of Virginia, under Lord Howard of Effingham.*

THE war with the Indians, which began before the revolution of government, continued all the year after. Madockawando, sachem of the Penobscots, who came into Pemaquid, was sent to Boston, where he arrived just about the time the governor was confined. The authority treated him kindly, and sent him home, and at the same time wrote to St. Castine, and desired him to use his influence over the Indians, and offered him safe conduct, if he inclined to come to Boston. Madockawando had promised his interest for redemption of the captives which had been taken, and for putting an end to the war; but both he and Castine deceived the government. Madockawando proved a most virulent enemy.

THE Indians of Penicook, upon Merrimack river, in the spring of the year 1689, professing great friendship to Major Waldron, of Quochecho,† [1] were civilly treated by him, and one of their chiefs were lodged in his garrison. The Indian, in the night, opened the gate to a great number of Saco and Penicook Indians, who lay hovering round it. They killed the major and twenty two others, and carried away twenty-nine captives, and plundered and burnt the neighbouring houses. The authority at Boston were equally anxious for the protection and defence of the people, as if they had been within the colony, and sent out forces for their relief. Intelligence arrived, soon after, of mischief done in several parts of the county of York, or province of Main, and, on the 22d of August, the fort at Pemaquid, the command of which (being garrisoned by 14 men only)

---

time of actual war with the Indians, he did supply them with ammunition, and several Indians declared that they were encouraged by him to make war upon the English, and he discountenanced making defence against the Indians.

The Council for the Agents must be sensible that the Governor would avail himself of his Commission under the great seal, and his Instructions from the King, which however unconstitutional was one only of an infinite number of like acts in the late reigns; and as for hearsay of Indians, that he would deny what they charged upon him, and call the charge a base aspersion. He urged to be heard, but as nobody would own the articles and they were not allowed to be read, the answers which he and Dudley and the rest had prepared were rejected of course.]

* He wrote to the Massachusets authority, to enquire into the state of the Indian war, and with an air of boasting concludes his letter, "From him who has the honour to be their Majesties lieutenant governor and commander in chief of the colony of Virginia, F. Nicholson."

† In New-Hampshire.

---

[1] Quochecho, or Cocheco, has developed into the present Dover, New Hampshire.

was given to one Weemes,[1] an officer Sir Edmund had left there, was besieged by the Indians. It was so situated as to be overlooked from a rock near to it.* From thence the Indians galled the garrison to such degree, that the next day they capitulated upon terms, which were kept with Indian [fidelity], some of the men being butchered, and the others carried captive. There were no hopes of security by sea or land, the French from Quebec instigating the Indians, and joining parties with them, and the French from Acadie, by their small privateers, infesting the coasts, and taking many vessels. In the winter, therefore, the general court were meditating an attempt both upon Port-Royal and Quebec. Sir William Phips † came to New-England in the summer of 1689. He was thought the fittest person for the command of the forces. Eight small vessels, with seven or eight hundred men, was thought a sufficient force for Port-Royal.

The fleet sailed the 28th of April, and returned the 30th of May. The fort at Port-Royal being in no capacity to stand a siege, surrendered with little or no resistance. Sir William took possession (as appears by his journal) of the whole sea coast from Port-Royal to Penobscot and the New-England settlements. The plunder was thought equal to the whole expence. But this was conjecture. The

---

* Both English and French have fell into the like mistake, in the situation of several forts, built since that time.

† Sir William Phips was a New-England man, born at Pemaquid in 1650, where he kept sheep until he was eighteen years old, then was an apprentice to a ship carpenter. When he was free, he set up his trade, and built a ship at Sheepscote. After that, he followed the sea, and hearing of a Spanish wreck near the Bahamas, he gave such an account of it in England, that in 1683, he was appointed commander of one of the King's frigates, the Algier Rose of 18 guns, and went in search of it, but failed. Soon after, being fitted out by the Duke of Albemarle upon a second voyage, he was more successful, and brought home a treasure of near three hundred thousand pounds, his own share being about sixteen thousand pounds only. The King knighted him. He was soon after appointed high sheriff of New-England, which he [professed to accept] with a view to serve his country, under a tyrannical government, but he could do no service, and was in England again in 1688. King James, about the time of his abdication, offered him the government of New-England. It was not a time to accept of it. Sir William had the character of an honest man. His education was very low. He was of a hasty temper, and being a stout man, he would use his cane and fist after he was governor. Some instances of this sort with a captain of a man of war and a collector occasioned complaints against him in England, which he was sent for to answer, and so far justified or excused his past conduct, that he was returning to his government, when he fell sick and died, and was buried in St. Mary Woolnoth church, London. By a series of fortunate incidents, rather than by any uncommon talents, he rose from the lowest condition in life to be the first man in his country.

---

[1] Lieutenant James Weems. For an instance of his manners and vocabulary when roused, see *Andros Tracts* (Prince Society), I, 25. His loyalty to Andros, as expressed in one of his letters (*ibid.*, III, 39), somehow commands respect.

acquisition was so easy that the court were confirmed in the prose-cution of their design upon Canada. Besides, the ravages began upon the frontiers by French and Indians, as soon as the spring opened, made it appear more necessary than ever. Casco fort, with above 100 persons, was besieged * and taken, whilst the forces were gone to Port-Royal. There was a still further inducement, they hoped to recommend themselves to the King's favour, and to obtain the establishment of their government. A small vessel had been sent to England express, the beginning of April, with a representation of the exposed state of the colony, and the necessity of the reduction of Canada, and praying for a supply of arms and ammunition, and a number of the King's frigates to attack the French by sea, whilst the colony forces should march by land and perform their parts.† But their hands were too full in England to give any attention to this proposal. The Massachusets, however, determined to proceed, and Connecticut and New-York engaged to furnish a body of men. Two thousand were expected to march by Lake Champlain and attack Montreal, at the same time that the forces by sea should be before Quebec. It was late in the season to undertake this great affair, but they tarried longer than otherwise they would have done, in expecta-

* May 17th.

† — "The consideration of the premises, hath put the government here upon send-ing a vessel on purpose to give their Majesties and most honorable privy council a true information of the present condition of these their Majesties colonies. Sundry planta-tions easterly, in the province of Maine, are utterly ruinated and depopulated. The war was begun there the summer 1688, and about 700 soldiers then levied in this colony by Sir Edmund, and sent thither, the charge whereof is not yet defrayed. — Last summer we had as great a number, or more, in constant pay; the whole of the rates already made amount to more than twenty thousand pounds. This people are now so very poor, that many profess they have not corn for their families, and those to whom wages are due, cry, that if they have them not, they and their families must starve. — There being now wars between Holland and France, some are fearful lest the Hollanders should essay the possessing themselves of Canada, and though it is hopeful they may prove better neigh-bours than the French, yet, considering the damage that will thereby be sustained by the crown of England, in loss of fishery, masting, furs, &c. it were better to expend two or three thousand pounds for the gaining that place, than that the French, or Dutch either, should have it. — This small vessel, coming upon this sole errand and business, to serve their Majesties interest, must not be permitted to return empty. We have con-fidence, that, may their Majesties have a true information, they will judge the present war made by the French and Indians upon their subjects here, to be more their Majes-ties concern than their subjects, and will not suffer them to sink and perish under so heavy a burden, but will order to be sent out of the King's store four or five hundred barrels of powder, with shot proportionable, and four or five thousand fuzees, our guns being many of them lost in the war. — You may assure their Majesties that it will en-courage their subjects here, with all alacrity of mind, to serve their Majesties therewith, for reducing the French in Canada to their Majesties obedience, if their Majesties shall give orders for a suitable number of frigates to attack them by sea. — *Dep. Gov. Dan-forth's letter to Sir H. Ashurst, April 1, 1690.*

tion of the stores they had sent for to England. None arriving, the 9th of August the fleet sailed from Nantasket.[1] There were between thirty and forty vessels, great and small, the largest of 44 guns and 200 men, perhaps not of superior strength to a sixth rate man of war, the whole number of men about two thousand. They did not arrive before Quebec until the 5th of October. Great dependence was had upon a division of the French force, but it happened, most unfortunately, that the forces designed against Montreal had [returned], and the news of it had reached Montreal before the fleet arrived at Quebec, so that Count Frontenac, the French general, was able to employ the whole strength of Canada against this little army.* This

* When a plan is thus formed, consisting of various parts, upon the due execution of every one of which the success of the whole depends, it must give great pain to men, who have not lost all feeling, not to have it in their power to perform the parts assigned them, and much greater to have been guilty of neglect or unfaithfulness. It is difficult, at this day, to ascertain the cause of the New-York and Connecticut forces failing. A letter from Boston to London, Nov. 24th 1690, says, "That the enemy had notice of our coming, very long before we could get at them, and whereas we had laid in beforehand, that the five nations of the western Indians, with a party of English from Connecticut and Albany, should, by land, alarm the French quarters about Montreal; it fell out that, when these were upon their march, some that therein served the French interests, by their wiles, decoyed them into a retreat that proved unlucky for us." The distracted state of the government of New-York, one party determined to ruin the public interest if the other had engaged in it, must have contributed to this disappointment. Leisler writes in a rage to governor Bradstreet, Sept. 15th 1690, "I have used all arguments and means possible to reinforce for Canada, but by Major Winthrop's[2] treachery and cowardice, with the rest of his tools, hath rendered the work altogether impracticable, his errand being so far effected as to leave us in a weaker state than he found us. Nevertheless, we despair not in the least so to maintain that post, that it shall defy him and all his assailants ever to dare attempting such lewd unaccountable practices in such a rebellious manner, as his keeping a garrison in Livingston's house, posting centinels to challenge the grand rounds, and other crimes, not only to stop our proceedings to pass the lake, but to answer the ambitious ends of the confederates united therein to divert our forces another way. —— Good God! how monstrous is it, under pretence of general assistance, to cover their particular interests and bring to pass such treacherous purposes. Mr. Livingston,[3] that betrayer of the province and arch confederate with yourselves, being willing to have exposed us to the remaining inhabitants; however, God be thanked, we had those that made early provision against these devices," &c.

Thus Winthrop's character seems to have been made a sacrifice to Leisler's vanity and madness.

---

[1] The Nantasket of our ancestors was the present Hull — at the southern entrance to Boston harbor.

[2] Fitz-John Winthrop (1638–1707) was the eldest son of Governor John Winthrop of Connecticut. He had spent a number of years in England and had held a commission in the British army. During the last few years of his life he was governor of Connecticut. His journal of the expedition of 1690 is printed in *Documents Relating to the Colonial History of New York*, IV, 193–196.

[3] Robert Livingston (1654–1725) was town clerk of Albany, and had been appointed Secretary of Indian Affairs by Andros. He was the founder of the Livingston family in America.

must have struck a damp upon the spirits of the English forces, and they could have but little hopes of succeeding. Le Hontan,[1] a French writer, says, the general was at Montreal when he heard the news of the fleet's being in the river, and that, if the English had made their descent before his arrival at Quebec, or two days after, they would have carried the place without striking a blow, there not being 200 French in the city, which lay open and exposed on all hands, but that they lost three days in consulting, before they came to a resolution. Success is wisdom with mankind in general. From the ill success of this undertaking, both English and French writers have treated it with ridicule and peculiar contempt. The next morning after the fleet arrived, Sir William sent a summons ashore. If it was too pompous, the answer was too insolent. The English were called hereticks and traytors, and told, that if it had not been for the revolution, New-England and Canada would have been all one. The French say the Major who carried the summons was threatned with a gibbet, and had like to have swooned. No notice is taken of this in the English journals. And it is not likely to be true. An attempt was made to land the next day (the 7th) but the violence of the wind prevented. The 8th, they landed all the effective men, amounting to between twelve and thirteen hundred.* They were fired upon from the woods by French and Indians, and marched in disorder, and did not attempt to cross Charles river, which lay between them and the town. Night overtook them. Upon examining a deserter, he gave them such an account of the strength of the French, as discouraged them from advancing any farther. The ships were drawn up the next evening before the town. They did little damage to the enemy, but were much shattered by the cannon from their batteries. The forces continued ashore until the 11th, rather upon the defensive, when they embarked with precipitation. A council of war was called the next day, and proposals were made for another attempt, after a few days refreshment for the men; but tempestuous weather came on, which drove some of the vessels from their anchors and scattered the whole fleet, and they made the best of their way back to Boston, where Sir William arrived the 19th of November. Some of the fleet

---

* Le Hontan makes them three times that number, and that they left 300 dead on the spot.

---

[1] "Le Hontan" should be Lahontan. Louis Armand de Lom d'Arce, baron de Lahontan (1666–1715), was a French soldier who came to Canada in 1683 and fought against the Iroquois and the English. The work referred to in the text is his *Nouveaux Voyages dans l'Amérique Septentrionale* (1703). An English translation was brought out in the same year.

were blown off to the West-Indies, one was lost upon Anticosta, and two or three were wrecked or never heard of. It appears by manuscript letters, that about two hundred men were lost by the enemy and sickness.* The small-pox, which prevailed in Boston before they sailed, had got into the army. Many died of the camp disease after their return, and spread the infection among the inhabitants of Boston. This was a humbling stroke to New-England. The return of the New-York and Connecticut forces was the most visible cause of the disappointment. Walley,[1] who had the command of the land forces, gave in a journal of his proceedings to the general court. His conduct was censured by particular persons, but there was no public enquiry.

THE government was utterly unprepared for the return of the forces. They seem to have presumed, not only upon success, but upon the enemy's treasure to bear the charge of the expedition. The soldiers were upon the point of mutiny for want of their wages.† It was utterly impracticable to raise, in a few days, such a sum of money as would be necessary. An act was passed for levying the sum, but the men could not stay until it should be brought into the treasury. The extreme difficulty, to which the government was thus reduced, was the occasion of the first bills of credit ever issued in the colonies, as a substitute in the place of money.‡ The debt was paid by paper notes from two shillings to ten pounds denomination, which

* Sir William says, in his representation to King William, that he did not lose above 30 men by the enemy.

† Arma tenenti, omnia dat, qui justa negat.

‡ Barbadoes was the first which followed the example. Mr. Woodbridge,[2] a New-England man, was the projector. Their bills sank so low, that the island was in confusion, and they soon abolished them. All the colonies upon the continent, Nova-Scotia excepted, have, first or last, with very different success, gone into the same substitute. It may be made a query, whether the project of a land bank in England in the reign of King William, which entirely failed, was not taken from this expedient of New England.

---

[1] John Walley (d. 1712), of Boston, and later of Plymouth Colony, was named a member of the Council in the Charter of 1691. He had been an Assistant in the Old Colony, and also a member of Andros's Council. His journal, mentioned in the text, is printed by Hutchinson as Appendix XXI of this volume of the History.

[2] Dudley Woodbridge (1677–1720). "To supply the want of cash, a Mr. Dudley Woodbridge suggested a scheme for the establishment of a bank, proposing himself to be the sole manager." John Poyer, History of Barbados (London, 1808), p. 193. Woodbridge was a great-grandson of Governor Thomas Dudley and a grandson of the Rev. John Woodbridge, the first minister of Andover, Massachusetts. He graduated from Harvard in 1696, and became Director General of the Royal Assiento Company of England and Agent of the South Sea Company in Barbados. He was also Judge Advocate of that island. Dean Dudley, History of the Dudley Family, p. 1065.

notes were to be received, for payment of the tax which was to be levied, and all other payments in the treasury. This was a new experiment. They had better credit than King James's leather money in Ireland, about the same time. But the notes would not command money, nor any commodities at money price. Sir William Phips, it is said, exchanged a large sum, at par, in order to give them credit. The soldiers, in general, were great sufferers, and could get no more than twelve or fourteen shillings in the pound. As the time of payment of the tax approached, the credit of the notes was raised, and the government allowing five per cent. to those who paid their taxes in notes, they became better than money. This was gain to the possessor, but it did not restore to the poor soldier what he had lost by the discount.* Sir William Phips, after a few weeks tarry in Boston, embarked for England, to sollicit an expedition from thence against Canada, the government, at the same time, sending their humble address to their Majesties, shewing the necessity of it.

Whilst the forces were gone to Canada, and the event [was] uncertain, the Indians pretended to be disposed to peace. Major

---

* The government, encouraged by the restoration of credit to their bills, afterwards issued others for charges of government. They obtained good credit at the time of their being issued. The charges of government were paid in this manner from year to year. Whilst the sum was small, silver continued the measure, and bills continued their value. When the charges of government encreased, after the second expedition to Canada in 1711, the bills likewise encreased, and in the same or greater proportion the silver and gold were sent out of the country. There being a cry of scarcity of money in 1714, the government caused 50,000l. to be issued, and in 1716, 100,000l. and lent to the inhabitants, to be paid in at a certain period, and in the mean time to pass as money. Lands were mortgaged for security. As soon as the silver and gold were gone and the bills were the sole instrument of commerce, pounds shillings and pence were altogether ideal, for no possible reason could be assigned why a bill of twenty shillings should bear a certain proportion to any one quantity of silver more than another: Sums in bills were drawing into the treasury from time to time by the taxes, or payment of the loans, but then other sums were continually issuing out, and all the bills were paid and received without any distinction either in public or private payments, so that, for near forty years together, the currency was in much the same state, as if an hundred thousand pounds sterling had been stamped in pieces of leather or paper of various denominations, and declared to be the money of the government, without any other sanction than this, that, when there should be taxes to pay, the treasury would receive this sort of money, and that every creditor should be obliged to receive it from his debtor. Can it be supposed that such a medium could retain its value? In 1702, 6s. 8d. was equal to an ounce of silver. In 1749, 50s. was judged equal to an ounce of silver. I saw a five shilling bill which had been issued in 1690 and was remaining in 1749, and was then equal to eight pence only in lawful money, and so retained but about one eighth of its original value. Such was the delusion, that not only the bills of the Massachusets government passed as money, but they received the bills of the government of Connecticut, New-Hampshire and Rhode Island also as a currency. The Massachusets bills passed also in those governments. In 1749 bills of credit were abolished, and unless the evils which they occasioned should be forgotten, the government, it must be presumed, will never issue any more.

Pike [1] and Major Hutchinson,* [2] two of the assistants, were appointed to treat with them at Wells, but nothing was done. On the 29th of November, six of the chiefs, viz. Edgeremet, Toqualmot, Watombamet, Naictumbuit, Walombee, and John Hawkins,† brought in ten captives, and in behalf of the Penicook, Winnapissiaukee, Ossapy, Pigwacket, Amascoggin, Pejepscot, Kenebeck Indians, and all adjacent places, within the territories of those Sagamores, agreed upon a truce until the first of May ensuing, upon which day they were to meet at the house of lieutenant Storer, [3] in Wells, and to bring in all the English captives, and to settle articles for a firm and lasting peace. This agreement was made at Sagadehoc, with Capt. John Alden, [4] appointed by the governor and council for that purpose. In consequence of this truce, the land enjoyed rest for the winter.

AT the day appointed, Mr. Danforth, the deputy governor, and several others, with a proper guard, repaired to Wells, but no Indians appeared. Capt. Converse [5] went out, and meeting with some of them, they came in, bringing two captives with them, and promised in twenty days to bring in all the rest. The deputy governor returned disappointed, and a fresh supply of 35 men were sent to Storer's house, where they were scarcely arrived, when, on June 9th, an attack was made upon the garrison by 200 Indians, with Moxus, a noted Sachem, at their head; but the fortunate arrival of these recruits prevented the enemy from succeeding. Divers were killed at

---

* Grandson to Mrs. Hutchinson.

† The last received his name from the English, his Indian name not mentioned. The others are names of dignity, it being their custom when one chief dies to give the name to his successor in office, though not of his family. There were an Edgeremet and Narctombuit at the treaty of Falmouth in 1749. Toxus has been the name of a Norridgewock chief for divers successions. Perhaps from the same cause that the Pharaohs and Ptolemies kept up those names in Egypt, a respect for them that first bore them.

---

[1] Robert Pike (d. 1706) of Salisbury.

[2] Elisha Hutchinson (1641–1717) was a son of Edward Hutchinson, who will be remembered because of his opposition to the death penalty for returning Quakers and because of his lamented death in King Philip's War. Elisha was the grandfather of Governor Thomas Hutchinson. See editor's note to p. 280.

[3] Joseph Storer (1648–1730). There is a sketch of his life in Edward Emerson Bourne, History of Wells and Kennebunk, pp. 331–333.

[4] John Alden (1622–1702) was the son of John and Priscilla Alden of Plymouth; he resided in Boston. During the witchcraft to-do he was put in jail, but he escaped and ultimately was cleared.

[5] James Converse (1645–1706) of Woburn. He frequently represented his town in the General Court, and in 1699 and later was Speaker of the House. He was a grandson of Edward Converse mentioned on p. 193.

Berwick, Exeter and Cape Nidduck.[1] A small army was sent into the eastern country by sea, which landed at Maquoit, and marched to Pejepscot, but met with none of the enemy. As the English were re-embarking, they were attacked by a great body of Indians. Their vessels were aground. English and Indians kept firing all night. The Indians were, by this army, diverted from going over to the Isles of Shoals, which they intended to have done. The frontiers were unmolested after this, until the 28th of September, when 7 people were killed and taken at Berwick, and the next day, between 20 and 30 at Sandy-beach; and in October, a family was destroyed at Rowley, and another at Haverhill. On the 25th of January, the town of York was destroyed. Most of the houses were unguarded. A gun, fired by the Indians, caused many of the inhabitants to run to their doors. They found themselves surrounded with Indians; about 50 of the English were killed upon the spot, and near an hundred captivated. The minister, Shubael Dummer, who was in great esteem, was shot dead, as he was mounting his horse at his door, and his wife and family made prisoners. They set fire to the houses, four fortified houses only holding out against them, viz. Alcock's, Prebles's, Harman's, and Norton's. A party of men were sent from Portsmouth, but too late to give relief.

WHILST the colony was thus distressed within themselves, their enemies in England took the advantage of their distresses, and used them as an argument against the restitution of the charter, imputing all to the bad administration of government. The difference between their agents also increased. Mr. Wiswall,[2] a minister of Plimouth colony, a gentleman of piety and learning, was in Boston when Mr. Cooke and Oakes were about to embark, and he was desired to go with them. He had no credentials. He joined in politicks with Mr. Cooke, rather than with Mr. Mather. The people of Plimouth were extremely desirous of continuing a separate government, but if that could not be obtained, they chose to be annexed to the Massachusets, rather than New-York. When Mr. Slaughter [3] was appointed governor of New-York, Plimouth was put into his commission, but by the industry and discreet application of Mr. Mather,

[1] Cape Nidduck, now usually spelled Neddick, is in York, Maine.

[2] Ichabod Wiswall (c. 1637–1700), of Duxbury, entered Harvard College but did not graduate. His poem on the comet of 1680, and useful biographical references, are printed in Colonial Society of Massachusetts *Publications*, XI, 403–408.

[3] Col. Henry Slaughter, or Sloughter (d. 1691). For this incident and his brief career as governor, see John Romeyn Brodhead, *History of the State of New York*, II, 594–595; and Edward Channing, *History of the United States*, II, 295.

the commission was altered.* An order, after this, was issued to the Lords chief justices, Holt and Pollexfen, and the attorney and sollicitor general,† to draw up a new charter for the Massachusets, and Plimouth was included in it. When Mr. Wiswall understood this, he opposed it, in hopes of obtaining a separate grant. This offended the sollicitor general, and he struck out Plimouth, and it was again intended they should be annexed to New-York. When this news reached the colony of Plimouth, many people were alarmed, yet their general court persisted in desiring Sir Henry Ashurst, their agent, to apply for a separate charter, without signifying, that they chose to be joined to the Massachusets, rather than to New-York, nor could they raise any money, the people about Bristol, Dartmouth, &c. pretending that there were no hopes of any charter for

* Connecticut, to remove all exception, obtained the opinion of three great lawyers upon the case of that colony, which was as follows.

"The corporation of Connecticut colony in New-England, not having under their public seal surrendered their charter, and there being no surrender upon record, only when it was proposed to them, by the late King James, that they should take their choice, whether they would be under the governor of New-York or of Boston, they humbly prayed, that they might still enjoy the privilege of chusing their own governor according to their charter, but, if the King was resolved otherwise they said they had rather be under Boston than under New-York. After which, Sir Edmund Andros did, by a commission from the late King James, invade the liberty of the people in that colony, and exercise a government over them contrary to their charter, which they most unwillingly submitted to. But since the late happy revolution in England, the people of Connecticut have chosen a governor and assistants according to their charter, and doubt not but that they have a legal right to their former privileges.

Qu. Whether the charter belonging to Connecticut in New-England is, by means of their involuntary submission to Sir Edmund Andros's government, void in law so as that the King may send a governor to them contrary to their charter privileges, when there has been no judgment entered against their charter nor any surrender thereof upon record.

I am of opinion, that such submission as is put in this case doth not invalidate the charter, or any of the powers therein which were granted under the great seal, and that the charter, not being surrendered under the common seal, and that surrender duly enrolled of record, nor any judgment entered of record against it, the same remains good and valid in law, and that the corporation may lawfully execute the powers and privileges thereby granted, notwithstanding such submission and appointment of a governor as aforesaid.

2d. Aug. 1690.   ED. WARD.

I am of the same opinion; as this matter is stated there is no ground of doubt.
                                                                              GEO. TREBY.
I am of the same opinion.   J. SOMERS."

† Treby and Somers.

The proceedings against Rhode Island having been very near the same with those against Connecticut, the same opinion would serve to justify them in reassuming their charter. The refusal of the Massachusets house of deputies to comply with the demands of an arbitrary Prince, and to make the like submission which the other two colonies had done, caused a judgment against their charter, and however equitable a re-assumption might have been, yet they were barred from a lawful claim to it.

them, nor the Massachusets neither. The sentiments of many of the best men in the colony were known to Mr. Mather, otherwise, it is not improbable, Plimouth would finally have been included in New-York commission, although near 300 miles distant.*

WHEN Mr. Mather found it impossible to obtain the restitution of the old charter, his next care was to preserve as many of the privileges contained in it as he could. Sir Henry Ashurst joined with him in all his measures. Mr. Cooke was for the old charter, or none at all. Mr. Oakes, the other agent, joined with Mr. Cooke.† It was doubtful whether they had authority, by their instructions, to sollicit for any other. In the first draught of a new charter, the governor only was reserved to the King, the deputy governor and council, and other officers, were to be chosen by the people, and the governor had no negative in any case. This draught was made by the attorney general, according to what he took to be the King's mind, as expressed in council. It was presented at the council board the 8th of June 1691,‡ when it was objected, that, "by such a charter as this, the

* Your service in keeping us from New-York, and all other intimations for the good of this colony is thankfully received, and it would have been well pleasing to myself and sundry others of the most thinking men, who are desirous of supporting the ministry and schools of learning, to have been annexed to Boston, yet the greatest part of the people, and of our deputies, are most desirous of obtaining a charter for themselves, if possible to be procured, though, so far as I can discern, they had much rather be annexed to the Massachusets than to New-York, yet are not willing to have it mentioned, lest it should divert any endeavours for obtaining a distinct charter for themselves. —— It was voted, that two hundred pounds should be raised by a voluntary contribution. On trial made, though some particular men and towns did contribute liberally, yet others, by reason of the great charge of the war, and partly being discouraged by some leading men, telling them that they would but throw away their money, that they would never be like to obtain a charter, nor you neither for the Massachusets, thereby, the sum proposed fell considerably short, and by the courts order, the whole sum not being raised, none was to be sent. —— Not being in a capacity to make rates for the equal defraying the charge, I see little or no likelihood of obtaining a charter for us, unless their Majesties out of their royal bounty and clemency graciously please to grant it, *sub forma pauperis*, to their poor but loyal subjects of this colony. *J. Hinkley to Mather, Octob.* 16. 1691. The charter was complete before this letter could arrive.

† Mr. Oakes, however, signed the petition for a new charter, although Mr. Cooke refused.

‡ Whilst the Massachusets agents were solliciting a charter for that colony, a project was set on foot, by Doctor Cox, for forming a grand colony or state, more extensive than all the other colonies together. The original draught of a charter has this entry upon it, "In the council chamber at Whitehall, the 22d of August 1690. The right honorable the lords of the committee for trade and foreign plantations, are pleased to refer the consideration of this draught of a grant, to Mr. Attorney general, who is desired to consider how far the same is consisting with law, and to report his opinion thereupon to the committee, William Blathwait." The report of the Attorney general runs thus, "May it please your lordships, in obedience to your order of reference, I have perused this draught, and I conceive their Majesties may erect such a corporation (as is here purported) and enable them to purchase such lands and exercise government in the same.

King's governor would be made a governor of clouts," * and an order passed for preparing the heads of another draught. When they were prepared, a copy was given to Mr. Mather, with an order from their Lordships, that "if the agents were not satisfied therewith, they should bring in their objections to the attorney general." Mr. Mather was so dissatisfied, that he declared he would sooner part with his life than consent to them. He was told "the consent of the agents was not desired; the agents of New-England were not pleni-potentiaries from a sovereign state; if they declared they would not

But the clause of confiscating the ships and goods of their Majesties subjects, who shall trade to such place without the company's permission, will not be good in law. Also some clauses, particularly about the oaths and courts and officers, need be more clearly and intelligibly penned. Geo. Treby, Aug. 25th 1690."

By this charter, certain persons were to be made a corporation, capable in law to plead and be impleaded, &c. and to acquire and purchase lands goods and chattels of the several natives and other inhabitants of that part of the continent of America, lying and being in breadth from 36 1-half degrees of north latitude, which is the northerly bounds of Carolina, to 46 1-half degrees of north latitude, and in length from the pacifick ocean, otherwise called the south sea, unto the westerly bounds of the English colonies of New-York, New-Jersey, Pensylvania, Maryland and the heads of the great rivers, in a certain ridge of mountains, separating the colony of Virginia from the rest of the continent, which runs into the bay of Chesipeak and from thence into the atlantic ocean, together with all islands, lakes, quarries, mines, &c. and all appurtenances whatsoever, to hold use and to give grant and dispose of the same, in as ample manner as any other corporation within the realm of England might or could do.

The governor, deputy-governor, and assistants, were to be annually chosen by the company in England.

They had power to cause to be transported subjects and strangers, also goods, chattels, and merchandize.

None were to inhabit or dwell within the bounds of the patent, or to trade with the natives, without leave of the corporation.

All who should go thither, or be born there, to have the liberty of free and natural born subjects.

Power to establish provinces, counties, cities, towns, districts and jurisdictions, as should be thought fit.

Under their common seal in the King's name, to appoint judges, justices, sheriffs, constables, and all other officers civil and military.

By such commanders, governors and officers as should be appointed by the corporation to erect forts, &c. to assemble and put in warlike posture the inhabitants, and to encounter by sea and land all persons invading, annoying, &c.

A general court established, each city or borough to send two members, with power to make laws, &c. for the royal approbation, to raise taxes for the support and defence of the colony.

Free liberty of conscience to all the inhabitants.

* Mather's Narrative.[1]

[1] Increase Mather, A Brief Account concerning Several of the Agents of New-England, their Negotiation at the Court of England (London, 1691), p. 11. It is reprinted in Andros Tracts (Prince Society), II, 271–296. Hutchinson's reference to Mather's Narrative of the Miseries of New England is obviously an error, since the incident described took place in 1691 and the Narrative was printed in 1688 or 1689.

submit to the King's pleasure, his Majesty would settle the country, and they might take what would follow." Sir Henry Ashurst, with Mr. Mather, drew up, notwithstanding, their objections against the minutes, insisting upon the King's promise, and that charters might as well be refused to be restored to any of the corporations in England, where they had been taken away, as to New-England.* The objections were presented to the attorney general and laid before the

---

* Mr. Hampden, upon this occasion, desired the opinion of Mr. Hooke,[1] a counsellor of note, which he gave as follows:

"There are two parties which sollicit the affairs of New-England.

1. Those who labour for an union of the whole territory under a captain-general, who should govern by commission from the King, without any respect to former charters.

Against this party, it is justly objected, that a people, who, some years since, left their native country for the sake of their consciences, and adventured to inhabit a wilderness, which had just before been swept of its inhabitants by a dreadful plague, who had added so many of the heathen to the inheritance of our blessed Savior, which no other christian planters have done, who have added so great a territory to the English empire, and are so useful to all other English plantations, who, rather than break with England, submitted to the Turkish commission of Sir Edmund Andros, and who have maintained civility beyond any other people on earth, I say, that such a people should have their whole constitution overturned by a new sort of government, would be hard and unreasonable. That for the present government to do all this, by taking advantage of the arbitrary and justly exploded proceedings of the last reign, would be scandalous and dishonorable.

2. The other party, labour to have the several charters of the respective colonies restored.

Against them, it is justly objected, that a bare restoration of their charters, and especially of the Massachusets, would be of no service at all, as appears both from the charter itself and the practice of that colony, who have hardly pursued the terms thereof in any one instance, which hath given colour to evil minded men to give them disturbance.

1. As to the charter itself, that colony, should they have their charter, would want,

1st. Power to call a parliament, or select assembly, for there, many thousand freemen have, thereby, an equal right to sit in their general assembly.

2. Power to lay taxes and raise money, especially on inhabitants not being of the company, and strangers coming to or trading thither.

4. They have not any admiralty.

5. Nor have they power to keep a prerogative court, prove wills, &c.

6. Nor to erect courts of judicature, especially chancery courts.

2. The deficiency of their charter appears from their practice, wherein they have not had any respect thereto, but, having used the aforesaid powers without any grant, they have exercised their charter powers, also, otherwise than the charter directed.

1. They have made laws contrary to the laws of England.

2. Their laws have not been under their seal.

3. They have not used their name of incorporation.

4. They have not used their seal in their grants.

5. They have not kept their general courts, nor,

6. Have they observed the number of assistants appointed by the charter.

A middle way, therefore, seems most desirable, viz. that new charters be granted to the respective colonies, wherein the former to be recited, and the proceedings against

---

[1] Possibly John Hooke (1655–1712), serjeant-at-law.

council, and a copy sent to the King in Flanders, but all had no effect. The King approved of the minutes, and disliked the objections made to them, and the charter was drawn up by Mr. Blaithwait * according to them. The only question with the agents was, whether to submit to this new settlement, or to signify to the ministers of state that they had rather have no charter at all. Mr. Cooke continued firm to his first principles, and as he would never take any one step towards obtaining the charter, so he utterly refused to accept of it, when granted, and he endeavoured to prevent the colony from accepting it also.† Mr. Wiswall's principles and conduct were the same with

---

them respectively, and a new grant made, in terminis, by the words grant and confirm, and reciting the deficiency in the former charter, all those powers may be vested in the government of the Massachusets for the time being; and the colonies which have no charters to be annexed to the Massachusets colony," &c.

* The charter has been said to have been drawn up by Sir John Somers, a mistake from his having drawn the first which was refused; others said it was done by Mr. Locke.[1] There are so many inaccuracies as are not to be accounted for, if done by either of those great men. It is more probable they should come from Mr. Blathwayt.

London, Nov. 4. 1691.

† Hon. Sir,

The foregoing went by Capt. Blower, soon after which, Mr. Blathwayt prepared the draught of the charter, which was agreed to by the lords of the committee, and afterwards by them referred to the Lords of the council and there also passed, so as the dedimus was signed by the lords of the great seal October the 7th, that so the seal might be affixed when they pleased, but a stop was put thereto for some time, and it was given out, that there would be no further proceeding therein till the King's return to court, who was then expected the first fair wind, which was not till the 19th day, but some being restless and impatient till that matter was made irretrievable, got it to pass the great seal about two days before, and the commission and instructions for the government were then said to be also prepared, though his Majesty has not yet declared who shall be the governor, and lieutenant or deputy governor, and I am informed, that it will be a week at least before he will, there being several that now move for it besides Sir William, and, it's said, there are no less than twenty that lay in for the government of New-York. I have, herewith, sent a copy of the charter, which, in some things, you will find comes short of the minutes, and the province of New-Hampshire left out, and notwithstanding the country of Nova-Scotia, &c. is therein granted, yet an after-clause thereby takes away all the right to the soil to the eastward of Sagadehock. Had any petition come from New-Hampshire, respecting their desire to be continued under the Massachusets, in all probability it had been granted them, but the contrary being affirmed, and that they desired to be distinct, gave the advantage to Mr. Allen [2] to gain

---

[1] Originally this sentence did not end here, but continued with the descriptive phrase "then one of the board of trade." These words have been blotted out in all the copies of the first edition that I have seen, and they were omitted when the second and third editions were printed. Apparently after the final proof had been read Hutchinson discovered that the Board of Trade did not exist at the time the charter was drawn. By inking over the phrase he did his best to correct the error before volume I went to the public.

[2] Samuel Allen, a merchant of London, who bought the claims of the Mason heirs to New Hampshire in April 1691. Jeremy Belknap, *History of New Hampshire* (1784), I, 239.

Mr. Cooke's, and he endeavoured to prejudice the colony of Plimouth against the charter, as [the] other did [as] that of the Massachusets.* The nomination of the officers reserved to the crown was left, for the first time, to the agents, or rather to Mr. Mather, who was considered as *instar omnium*.†

SIR WILLIAM PHIPS was the person recommended for governor. He had been chosen by the colony an assistant, the year before, and was acceptable to the people in general. Mr. Stoughton had been appointed deputy-president by King James, and although he had

his point, which doubtless will be much to their prejudice. —— When the court shall have the charter before them, they will then see how far it answers their desire and expectation, and know what they have to trust to, whom I pray God to direct for the best. It must be remembered, that you have no plenipotentiaries for you here, and if any thing said or done here, by any employed by you, should be construed as obliging of you, you know how far you have obliged yourselves by your commissions and instructions to them. I hope you have been careful not to perpetuate any public revenue, or any officers salary or stipend, nor large fees, &c. *Mr. Cooke's letter to Gov. Bradstreet.*

* — "I do believe Plimouth's silence, Humphries [1] neglect, and the rashness and imprudence of one at least who went from New-England in disguise by night,[2] hath not a little contributed to our general disappointment. — Plimouth, the Massachusets as far west as the Narraganset country, and northward 3 miles beyond Merrimack river, the province of Mayne, and the lands from Sagadehoc eastward, as far as the easternmost extent of Acadia or Nova-Scotia, are clapt into one province, under such restrictions as I believe will not be very acceptable to those inhabitants who must lose their ancient names. There are in the new charter 28 counsellors (of which 4 for Plimouth) a governor and deputy, all nominated by one, who acts as if he were a sole plenipotentiary, The governor, deputy and secretary are to be nominated and continued, only *durante bene placito*. Sir W. P. hath one that labours hard for his advancement. — I only reflect on New-England's condition, under this juncture of providence, much like that of the Jews, under Cyrus ascending the throne of their oppressor. At his first appearance, they were in hope to rebuild their city and sanctuary, but were deprived of their expected privileges all his days, by ill-minded counsellors. —— All the frame of heaven moves upon one axis, and the whole of New-England's interest seems designed to be loaden on one bottom, and her particular motions to be concentrick to the Massachusets tropick. You know who are wont to trot after the Bay horse. Your distance is your advantage, by which you may observe their motions. Yet let me mind you of that great statesman, Eccles. vii. 14. Few wise men rejoice at their chains. — Doubtless it would be accounted hypocrisy before God, and ground of despair among men, to see any person receive and entertain the present and undeniable evidences of his disappointment, with the usual testimonies and compliments attending the desire accomplished. *Wiswall to Hinkley, Nov.* 5. 1691.

† "Pray let me, by eight o'clock, have the names you would have for governor, deputy and assistants, that I may give them to my lord president," &c. *Sir H. Ashurst to I. Mather, Sept.* 3, 91.

[1] Robert Humphrys was agent for Massachusetts at London. See editor's note 1 to p. 288.
[2] Increase Mather, when about to leave Boston in 1688, donned a wig and a long white cloak and disappeared into the night. See Kenneth Ballard Murdock, *Increase Mather*, p. 187.

not recovered his interest so far, with the people, as to obtain a vote for an assistant, yet he stood well with many persons of influence, particularly with Mr. Mather, the son, who wrote to his father in favour of him.† Mr. Addington, the secretary, was at that time secretary to the colony. The emoluments of that office were small, compared with the duty, and so he was in less danger of a competitor. The 28 counsellors were persons of the best characters in the several parts of the colonies, of which, by the charter, they were to be inhabitants or proprietors. Several, who had been of the assistants chosen by the people, were left out of the number, Mr. Cooke in particular, also Thomas Danforth, William Browne, William Johnson, John Smith,[1] Thomas Oakes, and Jeremiah Swayne.[2] All these, except Mr. Browne, who was supposed to have been too compliant with Sir Edmund, were rigidly attached to the old charter, and Mr. Mather, no doubt, expected they would appear in opposition to the acceptance of the new; for, however extraordinary it may appear, the people of the country were far from being unanimous in submitting to it, expecting, that if it should be refused, they might maintain their right to their old privileges. They thought it would be a singular hard case, that the effects of the late despotism must be felt by them alone, of all their Majesties subjects; all other charters, whether there had been judgments against them, or whether there had been a surrender only, being, by one means or other, restored. But, it was said, there was this difference between the case of the Massachusets and most of the other charters. In general, there was no room for legal exception to the powers exercised by the corporations, but the Massachusets charter not being intended, when it was granted, for such government as is necessary to be exercised in a colony remote from its mother country, a reversion of the former judgment would have been of no service; and Sir George Treby declared to Mr. Mather, Sir John Somers and the two Lords chief justices being present and assenting to it, that "if the judgment against the charter should be reversed, and the government should exercise those powers which, before the quo warranto, they had done, a new

† "Mr. Stoughton is a real friend to New-England, and willing to make any amendment for the miscarriages of the late government. I wish that you might be able to do any thing to restore him to the favour of his country." *Cotton to Increase Mather.*

[1] John Smith (*d.* 1695), of Hingham, was elected a deputy in 1683, and continued to serve in that capacity until he became an Assistant in 1686.

[2] Jeremiah Swayne (1643–1710), of Reading, Massachusetts. As Major Swayne he fought against the Indians in Maine in 1689. See Cotton Mather's *Magnalia*, Book VII, p. 67; also *Historical Address and Poem, delivered at the Bi-Centennial Celebration of the Incorporation of the Old Town of Reading* (1844), p. 115.

writ would issue out against them in Westminster-hall, and there would be a judgment against them, and such an one, as that there would be no room for a writ of error." By the old charter, it was said, they had power to imprison or inflict punishment, in criminal cases, according to the course of corporations in England, but that, unless capital cases be expressly mentioned, the power would not reach them; that no power was given to erect judicatories or courts for probate of wills, or with admiralty jurisdiction, nor any power to constitute a house of deputies or representatives, nor to impose taxes on the inhabitants, nor to incorporate towns, colleges, schools, &c. which powers and privileges had been, notwithstanding, usurped. Whether many of the corporations in England had not deviated as much from their original constitution, and whether particular persons are not punishable for usurpations, and not the corporation itself extinguished or dissolved, as was urged in the case of the city of London, it is not necessary to determine. Seventy years practice under a new charter, in many respects to be preferred to the old, has taken away, not only all expectation, but all desire of ever returning to the old charter. We do not envy the neighbouring governments which retained, and have ever since practised upon, their ancient charters. Many of the most sensible men in those governments, would be glad to be under the same constitution that the Massachusets province happily enjoys.

SIR William Phips arrived at Boston, with the charter, the 14th of May 1692. He issued writs for a general assembly, which met the 8th of June following.

ALTHOUGH a party was formed which opposed a submission to the charter, yet a majority of the court wisely and thankfully accepted it, and appointed a day of solemn thanksgiving to Almighty God, for

granting a safe arrival to his excellency the governor and the Rev. Mr. Increase Mather, who have industriously endeavoured the service of this people, and have brought over with them a settlement of government, in which their Majesties have graciously given us distinguishing marks of their royal favour and goodness.

SIR William arrived just at the beginning of as strange an infatuation as any people were ever under. A considerable number of innocent persons were sacrificed to the distempered imagination, or perhaps wicked hearts, of such as pretended to be bewitched. But having proceeded as far as I proposed, I leave the relation of this unfortunate affair, and other transactions and occurrences since the present charter, to be communicated to the public by some abler pen.

CHAP. IV.

The Ecclesiastical Constitution of the Colony, and the special Religious Customs.

IT was one great design of the first planters of the Massachusets colony, to obtain, for themselves and their posterity, the liberty of worshipping God in such manner, as appeared to them to be most agreeable to the sacred scriptures. Whilst they remained in England, they continued in the communion of the church, such of them excepted as were excluded from it for non-conformity to some of the ceremonies. With some of the ceremonial parts of worship, they were all more or less dissatisfied. The canons or laws of the church, and the rigid execution of them, they accounted a grievous burden. The [episcopal] form of government in the church, was not a general subject of complaint. They were very careful to distinguish themselves, from the Brownists and other separatists. Had they remained in England, and the church been governed with the wisdom and moderation of the present day, they would have remained, to use their own expression, "in the bosom of that church where they had received their hopes of salvation." * They were of the same stamp with Doctor Preston, Doctor Sibbs, Mr. Hildersham, Rogers, Dod and other old puritans, who tho' called nonconformists, yet, I suppose, never separated, but refrained from such ceremonies and such parts of the liturgy only, as they scrupled to use.† However, they did not suppose the form of episcopal government to be enjoined by divine authority, so as to make it unlawful to submit to, or to estab-

* The son of one of the first ministers, in a preface to a sermon preached soon after the revolution, remarks "that if the bishops in the reign of King Charles the first had been of the same spirit with those in the reign of King William, there would have been no New-England."

† [Before his (Mr. Cotton's) departure from England, by conferences in London he had brought off Master Davenport and Master Goodwin from some of the English Ceremonies, but neither of these two nor himself at that time did mind the least degree of separation, yet so soon as he did taste of the New English air, he fell into so passionate an affection with the Religion he found there that incontinent he began to persuade it with a great deal more zeal and success than before he had opposed it. *Baylies' dissuasive etc.*]

lish any other form. They knew very well, that upon their arrival in America, they would be no longer subject to any diocesan in England, but they took no measures for the establishment of episcopacy, under any restrictions or limitations by royal or national authority. They must, however, have supposed some form or other of church government would be necessary, but they were far from being determined what it should be.* Mr. Hildersham [1] advised them to agree upon it before they left England, but it was neglected; perhaps it was impracticable. They knew [2] how far Mr. Endicot had proceeded in forming the first church, and how much it resembled the constitution of the separatists at [New] Plimouth, and soon after the news of it, one company who were designed for New-England, formed themselves into a church in the new hospital at Plimouth [in England], and John Warham and John Maverick were chosen and ordained their ministers. Both of them had before been ordained by bishops. The separatists used to boast, that "if the old puritans were secure of the magistrate's sword and might go on with his good licence, they would shake off the prelate's yoke, and draw no longer in spiritual communion with all the profane in the land, and though they then preached and wrote against the separatists, yet if they were in a place where they might have their liberty, they would do as they did." † The inconveniences we suffer under one extreme, it must be allowed, carry us insensibly into the other. The New-England puritans, when at full liberty, went the full length which the separatists did in England. It does not follow, that they would have done so if they had remained in England. Upon their removal, they supposed their relation both to the civil and ecclesiastical government, except so far as a special reserve was made by their charter, was at an end, and that they had right to form such new model of both as best pleased them. In the form of worship, they universally

* *Hubbard.*
† *Robinson — Bradford.*[3]

[1] Arthur Hildersham (1563–1632) was one of the most prominent Puritan divines of his time in England. He was an active promoter of the Millenary Petition, and was frequently suspended because of his non-conformity.

[2] The third edition inserts "not" at this point, though the context makes it clear that Hutchinson intended the affirmative. The first edition is like the second.

[3] As I do not find this interesting letter in Bradford's *History of Plymouth Plantation*, I am inclined to believe that Hutchinson read it in Bradford's Letter Book. The earlier part of the Letter Book was destroyed before the extant fragment was discovered in a grocer's shop at Halifax, Nova Scotia, after the American Revolution. See Massachusetts Historical Society *Collections*, First Series, III, 27–77; Jeremy Belknap, *American Biography*, II, 246.

followed the New-Plimouth church.* I find a common prayer book among the list of books presented by William Backhouse [1] for the use of the ministers, but it was never made use of in any church. The first notice, after the charter, of any step towards forming themselves into a church estate was, upon occasion of great sickness and mortality, about a month after their arrival, when the governor, at Charlestown, wrote to Mr. Johnson [2] at Salem, to set apart a day to humble themselves and seek God in his ordinances, and solemnly to enter into covenant with him, and as they lived in three † distinct places and had men of ability in each, they might become three distinct bodies. At Charlestown, the governor, deputy-governor, Mr Johnson, who had removed from Salem, and the minister, Mr. Wilson, on the 30th of July, the fast day, entred into a church covenant; two days after, they allowed five more to join them, and so others, from time to time, and at length, they, in form, chose Mr. Wilson for their minister and ordained him; ‡ but all joined in a protestation, that it was not a renouncing of the ministry he received in England, but that it was as a confirmation, in consequence of their election.§ In the other plantations, they formed themselves into distinct churches, one after another, but seem to have had no settled scheme or plan of church government, until Mr. Cotton || came over, in 1633.¶ His praise was in all the churches, as the principal projector of the plan of government of the New-England churches, which, from that time, took the name of congregational. This was called the middle way between brownism and presbyterianism,° and is said to be distinguished by four characteristicks, viz.

* [The church at New Plymouth was as I am informed one of the first churches that was settled in New England, having been a part of Master Robinson's church in Holland, that famous Brownist from whence they brought their church opinions and practices; and which they there still hold without any alteration, so far as ever I could learn. Master W. (Williams) an eminent man of the church at Plymouth told W. R. that the rest of the churches of New England came at first to them at Plymouth to crave their direction in church courses and made them their pattern. *Rathbone's Narrative.*]

† Mr. Prince supposes the three to be Dorchester, Charlestown and Salem. Salem had been in a church state a year before.

‡ August 30th.

§ Mr. Prince has taken no notice of this circumstance mentioned by Hubbard.

|| Whatever Mr. Cotton delivered was soon put into an order of court, if of a civil, or set up as a practice in the church, if of an ecclesiastical concernment. *Hubbard.*

¶ [In 1634 the Court recommended to the elders and brethren of every church to consult and advise on one uniform order of discipline in the church agreeable to the Scriptures; and how far the magistrates are bound to interpose for the preservation of the uniformity and peace of the church.]   ° Hubbard.

---

[1] William Backhouse (1593–1662) was a renowned alchemist of England.

[2] Isaac Johnson (*d.* 1630), who came in the *Arbella* with Winthrop.

1st. THE subject matter of the visible church, viz. saints by calling, such as are acquainted with the principles of religion, and who profess their faith, and the manner how they were brought to the knowledge of God by faith in Christ, either *vivâ voce*, or else by a publick declaration thereof made by the elders, as it has been delivered to them in private; although, if such profession be scandalized by an unchristian conversation, it is not to be regarded.

2d. THE constitutive part of a particular visible church ought to be, a restipulation or mutual covenanting, to walk together in their christian communion, according to the rule of the gospel.

3d. No church ought to be of larger extent or greater number than may ordinarily meet together in one place, for the enjoyment of all the same numerical ordinances and celebrating all divine worship, nor fewer, ordinarily, than conveniently may carry on church work.

4th. THAT there is no jurisdiction to which particular churches are or ought to be subject, by way of authoritative censure, nor any other church power, extrinsical to such churches, which they ought to depend upon any other sort of men for the exercise of.

THESE are said to be the principles, upon which a platform of church government was formed.

AN odious sense had been affixed to the name of independents, which seems to have been the reason why it was avoided, rather than any material distinction in the constitution of the churches, which appears, or can be inferred, from either of those characteristicks; but the platform, agreed upon and published in 1648, although it does not own that dependance which shall subject any one church to any other, or even to the whole united together, yet it professes a relation which one church hath to another,* and connects them to-

---

* We may see something of the relation the churches considered themselves in, one to another, before the platform in 1647, by the following letter from the church of Salem to the church of Dorchester.   "Salem, 1st 5th m°. 39.

"Reverend and dearly beloved in the Lord. We thought it our bounden duty to acquaint you with the names of such persons as have had the great censure past upon them in this our church, with the reasons thereof, beseeching you in the Lord, not only to read their names in public to your's, but also to give us the like notice of any dealt with in like manner by you, that so we may walk towards them accordingly, for some of us, here, have had communion ignorantly with some of other churches, 2 Thes. iii. 14. We can do no less than have such noted as disobey the truth.

Roger Williams and his wife,
 John Throgmorton and his wife,   These wholly refused to hear the church, denying
 Thomas Olney and his wife,   it, and all the churches in the Bay, to be true
 Stukeley Westcot and his wife,   churches, and (except two) are all re-baptized.
 Mary Holliman,
 Widow Reeves,
John Elford, for obstinacy, after divers sins he stood guilty of and proved by wit-

gether by certain rules to be observed as the terms or conditions upon which such connection is to continue, and, upon the irregular walk or demeanor of any one church, they are no longer to remain members of the same body, and the other churches are not to admit them to their fellowship or communion. And, although it was the business of a synod, or general council of all the churches, to debate and determine matters of religion, and to give directions relating to the worship of God and the good government of the church, "which were to be received with reverence and submission," yet the synod was to exercise no church censures by way of discipline, nor any act of church authority or jurisdiction, further than was done at the first council of the apostles, elders, and whole church, as recorded in the 15th chapter of Acts, which was declared to be a precedent. All this provision may appear but a weak band of society, and, one would think, that merely being rejected from a society, which, it is to be presumed, after sufficient cause given for such rejection, there would remain no great fondness for continuing with, would be no great punishment. But this constitution of church government was adapted to the constitution of civil government, both as popular as can well be conceived, and notwithstanding an acknowledgment or declaration from both, of separate and distinct rights, yet each was aiding and assisting to the other.* By the laws established in the

---

ness —— William James for pride, and divers other evils, in which he remained obstinate —— John Talby for much pride, and unnaturalness to his wife, who was lately executed for murdering her child —— William Walcot for refusing to bring his children to the ordinance, neglecting willingly family duties, &c.

Thus, wishing the continued enjoyment of both the staves, beauty and bands, and that your souls may flourish as watered gardens, rest

Your's in the Lord Jesus,

For the church of Christ   HUGH PETERS,
  in Dorchester.   by the church's order,
                                            and in their name."

"Of late divers of the ministry have had set meetings to order church matters, by which it is conceived they bend towards presbyterian rule." *Lechford*, 1641.

* A constant watch was kept over the churches by the magistrates, and when any contention or disorder arose in a church, it was recommended to some of the neighbouring churches, to enquire into the causes thereof. The following order of the civil government shews in what manner they proceeded.

"At a council held at Boston, the 5th of Sept. 1656.

"The council being informed of the uncomfortable differences that of late have fallen out in the church of Christ at Sudbury, notwithstanding several endeavours to compose the same, which yet have been fruitless, out of their tender care to preserve and procure peace and unity amongst them, lately wrote to the said church, in an amicable way, to advise and counsel them forthwith to call in to their help such council from the neighbouring churches as the rule prescribes, from whose labours, through the blessing of God, a blessing might have been expected, which too great a part of that church, as they understood by their letter, is far from inclining unto. The council, judging it to be

colony, no man could have a share in the administration of civil government, or give his voice in any election, unless he was a member of

---

their duty to take an effectual course for the healing of their breaches, do therefore desire and order, that the churches of Christ in Cambridge, Watertown and Concord, do each of them, respectively, send two messengers to meet at said Sudbury, on the 7th day of October next, by 8 of the clock in the morning, to consider and advise in the premises, viz. to endeavour to compose and settle the distractions at Sudbury, to give their judgments in the cases of differences there; and it is expected and desired that the church of Sudbury, and all persons concerned therein, give this council, at the time and place aforesaid, the opportunity of meeting with them, to declare what shall concern themselves, or the council shall see cause to enquire of them, in reference to this business; making their return to the council of this jurisdiction, what success their endeavours, through the blessing of Christ, hath procured, and whose the fault hath been, or is, that so, if necessity require, such further course may be taken therein, as may most conduce to the glory of God, the uniting their hearts in truth and peace, according to the rule of the gospel. And it is ordered, that Lieut. Goodenow, or such as he shall appoint, shall take care for the entertainment of the said council and all persons concerned therein. [*This was very agreeable to 'the procuration,' the canonical term for the provision made by a church for the archdeacon at his visitation.*][1] And it is ordered, that the said council shall have liberty to adjourn to some other place, if they shall see cause. By order of the council,

EDWARD RAWSON, Secr'y."

"Master Peters went from Salem, on foot, to Dover, to appease the difference between Master Larkham [2] and Master K——.[3] He went by the sending of the governor and assistants. Master Wilson went to Green's harbour, &c. and at another time, Master Wilson, Master Mather, and others, heard the difference between Master Hooke [4] and Master Doughty,[5] at New Taunton. ——

"It may be, it will be said they did these things by way of love and friendly advice. Grant this. But were not the counselled bound to receive good counsel? If they would not receive it, was not the magistrate ready to assist, and to enforce peace and obedience? *Lechford.*

"Every church hath power of government in and by itself, and no church or officer have power over one another, but by way of advice or counsel, saving that the general court now and then over-rule some church matters." *Id.*

---

[1] These brackets are the author's; they do not indicate new material added in this edition.

[2] Thomas Larkham (d. 1669) was a preacher, who enjoyed great popularity at Dover, New Hampshire, for a year or two about 1640. His disagreement with Hanserd Knollys, his predecessor in office, caused a disgraceful tempest in a teapot which is narrated by Jeremy Belknap in his *History of New Hampshire* (1784), I, 46–49.

[3] Hanserd Knollys (1598?–1691) renounced the Church of England in 1636 and came to New England soon afterward. At Boston he was suspected of Antinomianism, so he moved on to Dover, New Hampshire, where he became the settled minister. His dispute with Thomas Larkham and the discovery of his lack of chastity led to his dismissal. He returned to England. See Jeremy Belknap's *History of New Hampshire* (1784), I, 44–49.

[4] William Hooke (d. 1667) was minister at Exmouth, Devonshire, before he came to New England. From Taunton he went to New Haven, about 1644. In 1656 he returned to England, where he was in high favor with Cromwell. Hooke's sister married Edward Whalley, the regicide.

[5] Francis Doughty. "One master *Doughty*, a Minister, opposed the gathering of the Church there [Taunton], alleadging that according to the Covenant of *Abraham*, all

one of the churches.* No church could be gathered without the allowance of the magistrates, consisting of and elected by members of the churches; and a minister, for preaching to such a society, was liable to a penalty. Mr. Matthews,[1] a minister, about the year 1650, was fined ten pounds for this offence. A law was made in 1638, that if any person stood excommunicated six months, they should be liable to fine, imprisonment, or banishment, as the court of assistants should determine; but this law approached too nigh to the ecclesiastical laws in England, so much complained of, to continue long in force, and in 1639 it was repealed. But the first laws seem to deprive an excommunicated person, and also a whole church, if separated from the rest, of all civil privileges, although the platform does not suppose deprivation of civil rights and authority to be the necessary consequence, yet even by the platform, all others were to "forbear to eat and drink with excommunicated persons." Whilst they remained in this state, they would have very little chance for a public post where all the electors were church members.†

THE elders or ministers, although they were not considered as one of the estates, yet no matters of great weight or moment, whether of a religious or civil nature, were determined without their advice, and a formal reference to them; (in early times they were generally present in the courts) and they were thus naturally led to use their influence with their people, to acquiesce in and approve of the measures, which they themselves had been consulted upon and advised to.

BUT however defective this constitution may appear in theory, we

* This law was dispensed with in favour of Mr. Humphries, who lived at Lynn, where no church was gathered, nor was he a member of any other church, yet was an assistant several years. Mr. Cotton says they supposed he would have been a member if he had had opportunity for it.

† In 1637, when Mr. Winthrop the governor had been very active in the banishment of many of the members of Boston church, for adhering to Mrs Hutchinson, some of those which remained, pressed the elders very hard to call the governor to answer, as an offender against the church, for what he had done in the state, but the elders did not think proper to comply. *Magnalia.*

mens children that were of baptized parents, and so *Abrahams* children, ought to be baptized; and spake so in publique, or to that effect, which was held a disturbance, and the Ministers spake to the Magistrate to order him: the Magistrate commanded the Constable, who dragged master *Doughty* out of the Assembly. He was forced to goe away from thence, with his wife and children." Thomas Lechford, *Plain Dealing* (1867), p. 91. Doughty moved to Long Island.

[1] Marmaduke Matthews (1606?– c. 1683), of Malden. Before coming to Malden he preached at Yarmouth and at Hull. Charlestown and Roxbury objected to his ordination at Malden; and after he was settled, his unorthodox utterances got him into trouble with the General Court. About 1654 Matthews returned to the Old World, and was succeeded at Malden by Michael Wigglesworth. See Richard Frothingham, *History of Charlestown*, pp. 121–129.

shall seldom meet with an instance where there has been so steady and so general an adherence to the principles upon which it was founded, and so much harmony subsisting, not only in particular churches, but between one church and another, for fifty years together.

In general, the ordination of ministers was by imposition of the hands of their brethren in the ministry, but some churches, perhaps to preserve a more perfect independency, called for the aid of no ministers of any other churches, but ordained their ministers by the imposition of the hands of some of their own brethren.* The ordination at Salem, August 29th 1660, was performed in this manner, as I find minuted by a gentleman then just arrived from England, who was present.†

The church at Salem kept this day as a fast, for the ordaining a teacher and a ruling elder. Mr. Higginson [1] preached in the morning, continuing until one o'clock, then broke off for one hour, then, the congregation being assembled again, they went to the work of the ordination, which was thus — first Mr. Higginson, who was to be ordained teaching elder, prayed; after prayer, Major Hathorne a private member, being, it seems, desired by the church, stood up and spake to the brethren of the church that they should now, if they did continue in the mind they were in before as to the choice of Mr. Higginson for their pastor, declare their consent by silence; and then spake to Mr. Higginson to declare his acceptance, and then spake to the messengers of the churches that were sent to be present, and to all others, to speak if they knew any weighty reasons against their proceeding to ordination, and then, none speaking, Major Hathorne and two of the deacons of the church, laying their hands on Mr. Higginson's head, pronounced words of ordination and prayed over him, and then Major Hathorne exhorted the church in a few words to remember their duty, &c. towards him whom they had ordained to be their pastor. Then Mr. Higginson did after the same manner as is before expressed, proceed to the ordination of Mr. Brown for the ruling elder, which being done, they sung a psalm and concluded with prayer. After the exercise, I was invited to the elder's house, where was good company and good cheer.

* This is said by Bailey to be Brownism. *Doct. of Brownists*.[2]

† I have seen an account of an ordination about the year 1640, of Mr. Hooke, at Taunton, then Cohannet, in Plimouth colony, by the schoolmaster and one of the brethren, an husbandman, although Mr. Wilson and Mr. Mather, two ministers, were present, but the general practice was otherwise, and at this day an ordination by the lay brethren, although it might not be condemned as invalid, yet would be generally disapproved and discountenanced.

---

[1] John Higginson (1616–1708) was the eldest son of Francis Higginson, the first minister of Salem.

[2] Robert Baillie, *A Dissuasive from the Errours of the Time.*

Most of the churches, not all, had one or more ruling elder. In matters of offence, the ruling elder, after the hearing, asked the church if they were satisfied; if they were not, he left it to the pastor or teacher to denounce the sentence of excommunication, suspension or admonition, according as the church had determined. Matters of offence, regularly, were first brought to the ruling elder in private, and might not otherwise be told to the church. It was the practice, for the ruling elders to give public notice of such persons as desired to enter into church fellowship with them, and of the time proposed for admitting them, if no sufficient objection was offered; and when the time came, to require all persons who knew any just grounds of objection to signify them. Objections were frequently made, and until they were heard and determined, the ruling elder seems to have moderated in the church, but the churches consent to the admission was asked by the pastor or teacher, who also rehearsed and proposed the church covenant and declared them members. When a minister preached to any other than his own church, the ruling elder of the church, after the psalm sung, said publicly, "if this present brother hath any word of exhortation for the people at this time, in the name of God, let him say on." * The ruling elder always read the psalm. When the member of one church desired to receive the sacrament at another, he came to the ruling elder who proposed his name to the church for their consent. At the communion they sat with the minister. I find nothing further relating to this officer in their public assemblies. They were considered, without doors, as men for advice and counsel in religious matters, they visited the sick, and had a general inspection and oversight of the conduct of their brethren. Every thing which I have mentioned as the peculiar province of the ruling elder, so far as it is in itself necessary or proper, may with propriety enough be performed by the minister. It is not strange, therefore, that this office in a course of years sunk into almost an entire desuetude in the churches. Indeed the multiplying unnecessary and mere nominal officers, or officers whose duties and privileges are not with certainty agreed upon and determined, seems rather to have a natural tendency to discord and contention than to harmony and peace.

We meet with nothing peculiar, in the beginning of the churches, relative to the office of deacons. Mention is made of the duty of deaconesses or widows, who were "to shew mercy with chearfulness, and to minister to the sick and poor brethren," but I find no instance of any specially chosen or appointed to this service.

* Lechford.

THE ministers of the several churches, in the town of Boston, have ever been supported by a free weekly contribution. I have seen a letter from one of the principal ministers of the colony, expressing some doubts of the lawfulness of receiving a support in any other way. In the country towns, compulsory laws were found necessary; and in the year 1654 the county courts were impowered to assess upon the inhabitants of the several towns which neglected the support of the ministry, a sum sufficient to make up the defect.*

IN Boston, after prayer and before singing, it was the practice, for several years, for the minister to read and expound a chapter. Whether it was because this carried the service to too great a length, or any other reason could be given for it, in a few years it was laid aside, except when it came in place of a sermon.† Exceptions, may we not say cavils, have been made, by some learned serious ministers, against reading the scriptures, as part of the divine service, without an exposition. The other parts of religious public worship, and the manner of administring the sacraments, not differing from what is at this day the practice of the churches of New-England and of the church of Scotland, it is unnecessary to take any notice of them.

FROM a sacred regard to the religion of the christian sabbath, a scruple arose of the lawfulness of calling the first day of the week Sunday, and they always, upon any occasion, whether in a civil or religious relation to it, stiled it either the Lord's-day or the Sabbath. As the exception to the word Sunday was founded upon its superstitious idolatrous origin, the same scruple naturally followed, with respect to the names of all the other days of the week, and of most of the months, which had the same origin; accordingly, they changed Monday, Tuesday, &c. into the second and third days of the week, and instead of March and April, used the first and second months, and instead of the third Tuesday in May, the language was, the third third day of the third month, and so of the rest.‡ All their

---

* In 1644 one Briscoe a tanner of Watertown, published a book against the support of ministers by tithes or taxes, and reproached the ministers who took salaries in that way. The ministers thought him, who denied the authority of the civil magistrate to provide for the support of ministers, *fuste potius erudiendum quam argumento*, and therefore they left it to the magistrates to defend the cause, who convened the tanner before them and brought him to an acknowledgment, if not to a sense of his error. *Hubbard.*

† To preach a sermon which was not composed by the preacher himself, was looked upon, if not criminal, yet highly disreputable. One Mr. Bond [1] having taken this liberty, and being discovered, presently after removed to Barbados. *MS.*

‡ This was a scruple of the Brownists.

---

[1] Sampson Bond "was employed at the First Church [in Boston] as assistant to the Rev. James Allen for some time." Savage.

records and other writings are dated in the common form, which they brought from England with them, until the year 1636, when Mr. Vane was governor, but after that, the alteration seems to have been very strictly observed, in all public and private writings and discourse, for many years together. In the interregnum, it much obtained in England, but the scruple, there, went off at once, upon the restoration, here, it abated, and it continues scarce any where, at this day, except among the people called Quakers. Perhaps, the great dislike to some other peculiarities of that people caused the decline of that custom in the colony, and made them consider the singularity, in the same light with some others of the same nature, which they condemned.*

THAT every thing approaching to an acknowledgment of the authority of the pope, and his power of canonization, might be avoided, they never used the addition of saint when they spake of the apostles and the ancient fathers of the christian church, and even the usual names of places were made to conform. The Island of Saint Christophers was always wrote Christophers, and, by the same rule, all other places to which saint had been prefixed. If any exception was made, an answer was ready: Abraham, Isaac, and Jacob had as good right to this appellation as Peter, James, and John.

THEY laid aside the fasts and feasts of the church of England, and appointed frequently, as occasion required, days of fasting and thanksgiving; but, besides these occasional fasts and thanksgivings, they constantly, every spring, appointed a day for fasting and prayer to implore the divine blessings upon their affairs in the ensuing year; and in the fall, a day of thanksgiving and public acknowledgment of the favors conferred upon them in the year past. If they more readily fell into this practice from the example of the people of God of old, yet they might well have been justified without any example. It has continued without interruption, I suppose, in any one instance, down to this day. This is a custom to which no devout person of any sect will take exception. By a law of the colony, every person ab-

---

* They began the Sabbath the evening of the last day of the week. It was some time before this custom was settled. Mr. Hooker, in a letter without date, but wrote about the year 1640, says, "The question touching the beginning of the sabbath is now on foot among us, hath once been spoken to, and we are to give in our arguments each to the other, so that we may ripen our thoughts touching that truth, and if the Lord will it may more fully appear." And in another letter, March 1640, "Mr. Huit [1] hath not answered our arguments against the beginning the sabbath at morning."

---

[1] Ephraim Huit (d. 1644), of Windsor, Connecticut. He was the first teacher to the church there, and colleague of the Rev. John Warham. See Henry R. Stiles, *History and Genealogies of Ancient Windsor*, II, 415.

senting himself from the public worship, on these days, without sufficient excuse, was liable to five shillings fine. It would have been as well, perhaps, if this provision had been omitted.

THESE were the principal of the special ecclesiastical or religious customs. There were some attempts to introduce singularities into some of the churches, particularly, Mr. Davenport, of New-Haven, who afterwards removed to Boston, required all his congregation to stand up whilst the text was naming; the principal reason which was given for it being, that it was the word of God, and deserved peculiar honor; * and Mr. Williams, of Salem, required all the women of his congregation to wear veils; but neither of these customs spread, or were of any long continuance. It was observed, as to the latter, that so uncouth an appearance, contrary to the practice of the English nation, would probably draw more eyes than if they were dressed like other women. Mr. Cotton, of Boston, happening to preach at Salem, soon after this custom began, he convinced his hearers, that it had no sufficient foundation in the scriptures: The married women had no pretence to wear veils as virgins, neither married nor unmarried would chuse to do it from the example of Tamar the harlot, nor need they do it for such purposes as Ruth did in her widowhood. His sermon had so good an effect, that they were all ashamed of their veils, and never appeared covered with them afterwards.†

DURING the fifty years the charter continued, there were very few instances of any society of christians differing, professedly, in doctrine, discipline, or form of worship from the established churches. The number of baptists was small. The quakers came over in small parties; but notwithstanding the strange delusion they were under in courting persecution, and the imprudence of the authority in gratifying this humor, as far as their utmost wishes could carry them, as has been observed in the course of the history, yet they were never numerous enough to form a society of any consequence, except upon the borders of Rhode Island.‡ Nor was there any episcopal church in any part of the colony, until the charter was vacated.

THE test, which we have just mentioned, went a great way towards producing this general uniformity. He that did not conform, was deprived of more civil privileges than a nonconformist is

---

* "At Quinnipyack (New-Haven) Mr. Davenport preached in the forenoon, that men must be uncovered and stand up at the reading the text, and in the afternoon the assembly jointly practised it." *Mr. Hooker to Shepard, March* 20, 1640.

† *Hubbard.* Mr. Cotton, when he was in England, thought more favourably of this custom. He mentions the old countess of Lincoln her always coming to church veiled.

‡ The sanguinary laws were of short continuance, otherwise the number of quakers would have increased.

deprived of, by the test in England. Both the one and the other must have occasioned much formality and hypocrisy. The mysteries of our holy religion have been prostituted to mere secular views and advantages. Besides this test, another reason may be assigned. As good, if not better lands than any in the colony lay contiguous to it, and men, of different opinions, chose to remove where they might enjoy both civil and religious liberty, rather than remain and be deprived of either. In this way, birth and quick growth were given to a neighbouring colony, which admitted persons of all religions, and gave equal privileges to all, and as soon as what they called a sectary sprang up in the Massachusets colony, it was transplanted to Rhode-Island.

I SHALL finish what I have to say upon the ecclesiastical constitution of the colony with a short summary of the platform, as I find it prepared by a very sensible divine,* who made a figure in the colony soon after the platform was established.

1. ECCLESIASTICAL policy, church government, or church discipline, is nothing else but that form and order, which is to be observed in the church of Christ upon earth, both for the constitution of it, and all the administrations which therein are to be performed, the parts of which are all of them described in the word of God, and it is not left in the power of any to alter, add, or diminish any thing therein.

2. THERE is a catholic visible church, viz. the company of those who profess the christian faith, whether in church order or not; but there is no political catholic church, the state of the members of the visible church, since the coming of Christ, being only congregational.

3. A CONGREGATIONAL church, by the institution of Christ, is a part of the visible church, consisting of a company of saints by calling, united into one body by an holy covenant, for the publick worship of God, and the mutual edification one of another, in the fellowship of the Lord Jesus; the matter of which, as to its qualification, ought to consist of such persons as have attained the knowledge of the principles of religion, who are free from gross scandal, and, with the profession of their faith and repentance, walk in blameless obedience to the word of God; as to its quantity, it ought not to be of greater number than may ordinarily meet together conveniently in one place, nor fewer than may conveniently carry on church work. The form of such a church is an agreement, consent, or visible covenant, whereby they give themselves unto the Lord, to the observing the ordinances of Christ together in the same society.

4. THE fraternity or brotherhood of such a church is the first subject of all ordinary church power, which is either a power of office, or of privilege. But the power of privilege is in the brethren, formally and immedi-

* Mr. Hubbard.

ately, the other is in them no otherwise than that they design the persons unto office, who only are to act and exercise that power.

5. THE ordinary officers of the church are such as concern their spiritual and moral, or temporal and natural good. Of the first of which are pastors, teachers, ruling elders, 1 Tim. v. 17. In the last mentioned, most of the churches in New-England, as many of the congregational churches elsewhere, are not so well agreed, accounting ruling elders should be able to teach.

6. IT is in the power of the churches to call their own officers, and remove them from their office again, if there fall out just cause, yet so as the advice of neighbour churches, where it may conveniently be done, be first had. They who are to officiate ought to be tried and proved before they be elected. 1 Tim. v. 22.

7. ELDERS are to be ordained by imposition of hands, which is to be performed by the elders of the same church, if it be furnished with any, or those of neighbour churches, and it may be done by some of the brethren deputed thereunto, which latter is also disapproved by Dr. Hornbeck, the learned professor of divinity at Leyden, from Numb. viii. 10.

8. THE power of government, in a congregational church, ought to proceed after the manner of a mixed administration; for, in an organick church, no act can be consummate without the consent both of the elders and brethren, so as the power of government or rule in the elders prejudice not the power of privilege in the brethren, nor the power of privilege in them prejudice the power of rule seated in the elders, seeing both may sweetly agree together.

9. FOR the maintenance of the ministers of the church, all that are taught, are to communicate to him that teacheth, in all good things; and in case of neglect, the magistrate ought to see that the ministry be duly provided for.

10. FOR the admission of members, there ought to be either a personal relation in public, or by the elders, acquainting the church what satisfaction they have received from the persons in private. The things, wherein satisfaction is required, are faith and repentance, which ought to be found in all church members.

11. WHERE members of churches are called to remove from one church to another, it is convenient, for order sake, that it be done by letters of recommendation or of dismission.

12. THE censures of the church, which are for the preventing, removing, or healing offences, are excommunication or admonition, wherein the church ought to proceed according to the rule, Matt. xviii. 15, 16, 17. wherein the offence is to be brought to the church by the mouth of the elders.

13. PARTICULAR churches, although they are distinct, and have not one power over another, yet, because they are united unto Christ, not only as a mystical but as a political head, they ought to have communion one

with another, by way of mutual care, consultation, admonition, and participation in the same ordinances.

14. SYNODS, orderly assembled and rightly proceeding according to the pattern of Acts xv. are the ordinance of Christ, and, if not absolutely necessary to the being, yet necessary to the well-being of churches, for the establishment of peace and truth therein. And many churches may so assemble together by their messengers and elders. And their directions and determinations, so far as consonant to the word of God, are to be received with reverence and submission, not only for their agreement therewith, without which they bind not at all, but also for the power whereby they are made, as an ordinance of God appointed thereunto in his word.

15. CHURCH government and civil government may very well stand together, it being the duty of the magistrate to take care of matters of religion, and to improve his civil authority for observing the duties commanded in the first as well as the second table, seeing the end of their office is not only the quiet and peaceable life of the subject in matters of righteousness and honesty, but also in matters of godliness. 1 Tim. ii. 1, 2.

AFTER all that may be said in favor of the constitution, the strength of it lay in the union, declared in the last article, with the civil authority. The usual way of deciding differences and controversies in churches, it is true, was by a council, consisting of the elders and other messengers of neighbouring churches, and where there was a general agreement in such councils, the contending parties generally acquiesced; but if the council happened to differ in apprehensions among themselves, or if either of the contending parties were contumacious, it was a common thing for the civil magistrate to interpose and put an end to the dispute. [These were the first Independent Churches, for tho' Robinson was a Brownist, yet his church was upon a Presbyterian Constitution until Hugh Peters, instructed by letters from Mr. Cotton in New England, brought it into a new frame; and it was not until after Mr. Cotton's going to New England and his correspondence with Mr. Goodwin upon this Subject, that Independent Churches were known there.]

CHAP. V.

The System or Body of Laws established in the Colony.

AT the first meeting of the court of assistants, at Charlestown, Aug. 23d, 1630, they established rules of proceeding in all civil actions, and instituted subordinate powers for punishing offenders. The supreme authority being in the court of assistants, they resolved upon frequent meetings for the due execution of it. As it was necessary for every family to provide lodgings before winter, the first law proposed and passed was for the regulating the price of wages of workmen, under a penalty to him that gave, as well as to him who received, more than the limited price.* They proceeded to other laws for punishing idleness and encouraging industry; and, as they were in the midst of savages, much more numerous than themselves, they obliged every man to attend military exercises, and limited the bounds of their plantations that none might be more exposed than was necessary.

IN civil actions, equity, according to the circumstances of the case, seems to have been their rule of determining. The judges had recourse to no other authorities, than the reason and understanding which God had given them. In punishing offences, they professed to be governed by the judicial law of Moses, but no farther than those laws were of a moral nature.

WHILST they were thus without a code or body of laws, and the colony but just come to its birth, their sentences seem to be adapted to the circumstances of a large family of children and servants, as will appear from the following, which, from amongst many others of the same sort, I have taken out of the public records.

Josias Plaistowe, for stealing four baskets of corn from the Indians, is ordered to return them eight baskets, to be fined five

* Carpenters, joiners, bricklayers, sawyers, and thatchers not more than 2s. per day, &c.

pounds, and hereafter to be called by the name of Josias, and not *
Mr. as formerly he used to be.

Captain Stone,[1] for abusing Mr. Ludlow, and calling him justass,
is fined an hundred pounds, and prohibited coming within the patent
without the governor's leave, upon pain of death.

Serjeant Perkins, ordered to carry forty turfs to the fort, for being
drunk.

Edward Palmer, for his extortion, in taking two pounds thirteen
shillings and four pence for the wood work of Boston stocks, is fined
five pounds, and ordered to be set one hour in the stocks.

Captain Lovel, admonished to take heed of light carriage.

Thomas Petit, for suspicion of slander, idleness, and stubborn-
ness, is censured to be severely whipped, and to be kept in hold.

Catherine, the wife of Richard Cornish, was found suspicious of
incontinency, and seriously admonished to take heed.

Daniel Clarke, found to be an immoderate drinker, was fined forty
shillings.

John Wedgewood, for being in the company of drunkards, to be
set in the stocks.

John Kitchin, for shewing books which he was commanded to
bring to the governor, and forbidden to shew them to any other, and
yet shewed them, was fined ten shillings.

Robert Shorthose, for swearing by the blood of God, was sentenced to have his tongue put into a cleft stick, and to stand so for
the space of half an hour.

[Ordered that Philip Ratcliffe shall be whipped, have his ears cut
off, fined 40 s, and banished out of the limits of the jurisdiction, for
uttering malicious and scandalous speeches against the government
and the church of Salem.

Mr. John Hall bound himself in twenty pounds for his servant
John Burrowes, that he shall not seduce any man, nor move ques-

---

* They were very careful that no title or appellation should be given where it was
not due, not more than half a dozen of the principal gentlemen took the title of esquire,
and in a list of 100 freemen you will not find above 4 or 5 distinguished by Mr. although
they were generally men of some substance. Good-man and good-wife were common
appellations.

---

[1] Capt. John Stone (d. 1633) was the John Stone whose death was a contributing
cause of the Pequot War. See editor's note 1 to p. 42. His sentence, which was issued
by the Court of Assistants in September 1633, is printed in full in *Records of the Court
of Assistants*, II, 35.

tions to that end, nor question with any other, except with the magistrates or teaching elders.

George Palmer, having committed folly with Margery Ruggs through her allurement, because he confessed voluntarily, was only set in the stocks.

Margery Ruggs for inticing and alluring George Palmer was censured to be severely whipped.]

Great numbers of the like kind might be added.

IN the year 1634, the plantation was greatly increased, settlements were extended more than 30 miles from the capital town, and it was thought high time to have known established laws, that the inhabitants might no longer be subject to the varying uncertain judgments, which otherwise would be made concerning their actions. The ministers, and some of the principal laymen, were consulted with, about a body of laws, suited to the circumstances of the colony civil and religious. Committees, consisting of magistrates and elders, were appointed almost every year, for 12 or 14 years together; and whilst they were thus fitting a code, particular laws, which were of greatest necessity, from time to time, were enacted; and in the year 1648, the whole, collected together, were ratified by the court, and then first printed.

MR. Bellingham, of the magistrates, and Mr. Cotton, of the clergy, had the greatest share in this work.

LET us consider the character of our new planters, the state and condition they were in before they left England, and after their arrival in America, and we shall see the source of the peculiarities in their laws and customs. It has been observed, that they were dissatisfied not only with the ceremonies, but also with the rigid discipline, at that time, of the church of England: In this they were not singular; the principal commoners, great part of the clergy, and many of the nobility, were of the same sentiments. They must have had very tender and scrupulous minds, or they would not have banished themselves from their dear country, friends, and acquaintance, and launched into an unknown world, rather than submit to any thing against their judgments and consciences. They professed a sacred regard to the word of God, in the old and new testament, as a sufficient rule of conduct, and that they were obliged to follow it. They looked upon the observation of the first, as well as second table necessary to be enjoined; and, as the constitution of their churches would not admit of ecclesiastical courts, provision must be made for the punishment of many offences here, by the civil magistrate, which are not offences by the common law. Whether every breach of the laws of the first as well as second table has not such tendency, by mere example, to disturb the peace of civil society, as that provision for the punishment thereof is necessary, by some authority or other, I need not determine: They thought it had, and, upon this principle, they did not [enact] such punishments for crimes, as were merely in proportion to their affecting the safety or peace of society, a principle, upon which the nations of Europe have been more and more modelling their criminal laws for several ages past, but annexed greater penalties to some immoralities and impieties than had been known in the country they left, determined many others to deserve the notice of the civil magistrate, which would have escaped it in England, and perhaps judged some actions criminal, which to minds less scrupulous would have appeared indifferent.* The generality of the colony being very near upon a level, more than common provision was necessary to enforce a due obedience to the laws, and to establish and preserve the authority of the government, for, although some amongst them had handsome fortunes, yet in general their estates were small, barely sufficient to provide them houses and necessary accommodations; a contempt of authority was therefore next to a capital offence. The country being new and uncultivated, the utmost industry, oeconomy, and frugality were necessary to their subsistence, and laws, with heavy penalties, to enforce the observance of them. They were in the midst of savages, whose numbers were much greater than their own, and were under continual alarms and apprehensions of danger, and a strict discipline could not be dispensed with. If we add, that they were at their full liberty, the troubles in England taking off from the colonies, the attention of the several successions of supreme power there, for near thirty years together; from all these circumstances, we may pretty well account for all the peculiarities in the laws of the colony.

In that branch of law, more especially, which is distinguished by the name of crown law, they professed to have no regard to the rules of the common law of England. They intended to follow Moses's plan, as has been observed, but no farther than it was of a moral nature,† and obligatory upon all mankind, and perhaps they did not,

* The character, which the colony acquired by the strictness and severity of their laws, induced many persons of pious minds to come over themselves, and others to send their children for education, many of whom remained here. Pennsilvania, by a greater latitude in their system, have drawn inhabitants in much greater proportion. Our ancestors valued themselves upon being a colony for religion. Penn had no other motive to found his colony than human policy.

† They did not go the length of the Brownists, who are said to have held, "that no prince nor state on the earth hath any legislative power, that God alone is the lawgiver, that the greatest magistrate hath no other power but to execute the laws of God set

in many instances, err in judgment upon the morality of actions, but their grand mistake lay, in supposing certain natural punishments, in every state, alike proportioned to this or that particular kind of offence, and which Moses had observed; whereas such punishments are and ought to be governed by the particular constitutions and circumstances of the several kingdoms and states where they are applied; and although they were undoubtedly well fitted to the state of the ancient Israelites, and the great end of punishment, viz. the preventing the like offences, could not, it may be, have been otherwise so well effected, yet they were by no means obligatory upon other states whose constitutions or circumstances differed; and other states have, therefore, continually more or less varied from them. Idolatry, was the sin which easily beset the Israelites, and it was necessary to make it a capital offence. Perhaps, if it should be thought proper to prohibit idolatry in China, at this day, the same penalty might be necessary, and yet not so in New-England.

MURDER,* sodomy, witchcraft, arson, and rape of a child under ten years of age, were the only crimes made capital in the colony which were capital in England, and yet, from the mistaken principle I have just mentioned, their laws were more sanguinary than the English laws; for many offences were made capital here, which were not so there. The first in order, being a breach of the first command in the decalogue, was the worship of any other God besides the Lord God. Perhaps a roman catholic, for the adoration of the host, might have come within this law. After the miserable Indians submitted to the English laws, special provision was made, by another law, that if any of them should powow or perform outward worship to their false gods, the powower (who was their priest) should be fined five

---

down in scripture, that the judicial laws of Moses bind at this day all the nations of the world, as much as ever they did the Jews." *Baylie.*[1]

Roger Williams said, that "although they professed to be bound by such judicials only, as contained in them moral equity, yet they extended this moral equity to so many particulars, as to take in the whole judicial law, no less than the rigidest Brownists." *Idem.*

Although they did not go to this extreme, it must be allowed they did not keep within the limits they professed as their rule. They were charged with holding it to be the duty of the magistrate to kill all idolaters and hereticks, even whole cities, men, women, and children, from the command of the Israelites to root out the Canaan*ites. Idem.*

* Homicide was either murder, excusable homicide, or justifiable. They did not make the distinction of manslaughter from murder. The benefit of the clergy was of popish extract, and burning in the hand with a cold iron appeared to them a ridiculous ceremony.

---

[1] Robert Baillie, *A Dissuasive from the Errours of the Time.*

pounds, and others present twenty shillings each. The Indians have been punished, upon the latter law, but I never met with an instance of a prosecution of any Englishman, upon the former.

To blaspheme the holy name of God, Father, Son, or Holy Ghost, with direct, express, presumptuous, or high-handed blasphemy, either by wilful or obstinate denying the true God, or his creation or government of the world, cursing God, or reproaching the holy religion of God, as if it was a politic device to keep ignorant men in awe, or to utter any other kind of blasphemy of the like nature and degree, was also made capital.

MAN-stealing, from Exodus xxi. 16. was also capital.

So was adultery with a married woman, both to the man and woman, although the man was single, and several have suffered death upon this law.* Male adultery with an unmarried woman, was not capital.

HE who was convicted of wilful perjury, with intent to take away the life of another, was to suffer death, from Deut. xix. 16. This crime may well enough be denominated murder, and yet, a wilful perjury, by which a man's life is in fact taken away, was never made capital in England. Many offences are made so, which seem to be inferior in their guilt and consequences to the public. The difficulty of conviction may be one reason, and the discouragement, it would sometimes be, to witnesses to give their testimonies, another and stronger reason, in vindication of the common law. In this instance, the Massachusets law agreed, I take it, with the civil law, the laws of Scotland at this day, and of many other states in Europe.

A CHILD above sixteen years of age, that cursed or smote his father or mother, unless provoked by cruelty and in its own defence, or unchristianly neglected in its education, and also a stubborn and rebellious son, according to Deut. xxi. 20. upon conviction, were to suffer death. There have been several trials upon this law. I have

---

* Philo places the command against adultery before that against murder. —— There was a pretty extraordinary instance of a prosecution for adultery in the year 1663. Mr. N. P. a young merchant, had been intimate with a married lady of one of the first families in the country. After her husband's death he married her. After they had lived together three or four years, a prosecution was began against both of them, for adultery in the lifetime of the first husband. They were both committed to prison, and separately brought upon trial for their lives. The court and jury were favourable to the husband, and acquitted him of a capital offence, probably because he was not at the time charged a married man. The wife likewise met with a favourable jury, and they found her also not guilty; but the court, who thought otherwise, refused the verdict, and the cause was carried before the general court, where she very narrowly escaped, the whole court determining that there was proof of a crime which approached very near to adultery, but in favor of life she was discharged.

met with one conviction, but the offender was rescued from the gallows by order of the King's commissioners in 1665.*

HIGH treason is not mentioned.† Before they had agreed upon the body of laws, the King's authority, in England, was at an end. Conspiracy to invade their own commonwealth, or any treacherous perfidious attempt to alter and subvert, fundamentally, the frame of their polity and government was made a capital offence.

RAPE, it was left to the court to punish with death or other grievous punishment, at discretion.‡ No judge would desire to have a capital punishment left to his discretion, and it may be doubted whether, in any case, it can be of public utility.

SEVERAL offences were capital upon a second conviction, as the returning of a romish priest into the jurisdiction, after banishment upon the first conviction. The law was the same with respect to quakers also.

THE denial of either of the books of the old and new testament, which were all enumerated, to be the written and infallible word of God, was either banishment or death, for the second offence, at the discretion of the court, and, what is very extraordinary, an inhabitant who was guilty of this offence upon the high seas, [where they had no jurisdiction,] was made liable to the penalty.

BURGLARY and theft, in a house or fields, on the Lord's day, were capital upon a third conviction. These were all the offences which they made capital.

* In the first draught of the laws by Mr. Cotton, which I have seen corrected with Mr. Winthrop's hand, divers other offences were made capital, viz.

Prophaning the Lord's day in a careless or scornful neglect or contempt thereof. Numbers xv. 30 to 36.

Reviling the magistrates in highest rank, viz. the governor and council. Exod. xxii. 18. 1 Kings xxii. 8, 9, 44.

Defiling a woman espoused. Deut. xxii. 23 to 26.

Incest within the Levitical degrees.

The pollution mentioned in Levit. xx. 13 to 16.

Lying with a maid in her father's house, and keeping it secret until she was married to another. Exod. xxi. 16.

The punishment by death, is erased from all these offences by Mr. Winthrop, and they are left to the discretion of the court to inflict other punishment short of death.

From the same prejudice in favor of Israelitish customs, a fondness arose, or at least was increased, for significant names for children. The three first that were baptized in Boston church were, Joy, Recompence, and Pity. The humour spread. The town of Dorchester, in particular, was remarkable for such names, Faith, Hope, Charity, Deliverance, Dependance, Preserved, Content, Prudent, Patience, Thankful, Hate-evil, Holdfast, &c. Many of which at this day are retained in families, in remembrance of their ancestors.

† In 1678, when complaints were made against the colony, it was by law made capital.

‡ Rape was not capital by the Jewish law, and for that reason it was not so for many years by the colony law.

LARCENY or theft, was punishable by fine or whipping, and restitution of treble the value, and theft-boot, by a forfeiture of the value of the goods to the government.

THE penalty of drunkenness, was ten shillings, excessive drinking, three shillings and four pence, tippling above half an hour, half a crown, profane cursing and swearing, ten shillings, and if more than one oath at a time, twenty shillings.

I HAVE seen a letter, dated about the year 1660, wherein a gentleman writes to his friend in London, that "he had lived several years in the country, and never saw a person drunk, nor never heard a profane oath."

THE penalty of profanation of the sabbath, was ten shillings.*

FORNICATION, might be punished by enjoining marriage, by fine or corporal punishment; and a freeman, for this offence, might be disfranchised upon conviction.†

IDLENESS, was no small offence; common fowlers, tobacco-takers, and all other persons who could give no good account how they spent their time, the constables were required to present to the next magistrate, and the selectmen of every town were required to oversee the families, and to distribute the children into classes, and to take care that they were employed in spinning and other labour, according to their age and condition.

CONTEMPT of authority, was punished with great severity, by fine, imprisonment, or corporal punishment.

LESSER offences, as all breaches of the peace, and also every offence *contra bonos mores*, where there was no determinate penalty, the court, before which the offence was tried, punished at discretion.

THEY had a law against slavery, except prisoners taken in war. Negroes were brought in very early among them.‡ Some judicious persons are of opinion, that the permission of slavery has been a publick mischief.

---

* When exception was taken in England to the laws, that, relative to the Sabbath, restraining persons from walking in the streets or fields, was one; but although their charter was in danger, they refused to make any alteration in the law.

† Exodus xxii. 16, 17. caused some doubt whether fine or corporal punishment was to be inflicted for fornication. I have several manuscripts on both sides the question.

‡ Josselyn [1] mentions three or four blacks in Mr. Maverick's family at Noddle's-Island in 1638.

---

[1] John Josselyn (*ff.* 1630–1675), in *An Account of Two Voyages to New-England* (London, 1675). This work was reprinted by the Massachusetts Historical Society in its *Collections*, Third Series, III, 211–396; in this edition the reference to Maverick's negroes will be found on p. 231.

THEIR laws concerning marriage and divorce were somewhat singular. I suppose there had been no instance of a marriage, lawfully celebrated, by a layman in England, when they left it. I believe there was no instance of marriage by a clergyman after they arrived, during their charter, but it was always done by a magistrate, or by persons specially appointed for that purpose, who were confined to particular towns or districts. If a minister happened to be present, he was desired to pray. It is difficult to assign a reason for so sudden a change, especially as there was no established form of the marriage covenant, and it must have been administred, many times, in the new plantations, by persons not the most proper for that purpose, considering of what importance it is to society, that a sense of this ordinance, in some degree sacred, should be maintained and preserved.* At this day, marriages are solemnized by the clergy, and altho' the law admits of its being done by a justice of peace, yet not one in many hundred is performed by them.†

IN matters of divorce, they left the rules of the canon law out of the question; with respect to some of them prudently enough. I never heard of a separation, under the first charter, *a mensa et thoro.* Where it is practised, the innocent party often suffers more than the guilty. In general, what would have been cause for such a separation in the spiritual courts, was sufficient, with them, for a divorce *a vinculo.* Female adultery was never doubted to have been sufficient cause; but male adultery, after some debate and consultation with the elders, was judged not sufficient. Desertion a year or two, where there was evidence of a determined design not to return, was always good cause; so was cruel usage of the husband. Consanguinity, they settled in the same degrees as it is settled in England, and in the Levitical laws. It is said, a man may give his wife moderate cor-

* The Scotch writers tell us, that by their laws it is not necessary marriages should be celebrated by a clergyman, that the consent of parties, signified before a magistrate, or only before two witnesses, and without consummation, will make a marriage valid.

† The publication of the banns was very early required, and no magistrate, or other person specially authorized to join persons in marriage, had authority to do it before the parties had been published according to law. The same law was renewed under the province charter, and after more than an hundred years experience, has been found very beneficial; there have been instances, but they are rare, of young people going to New-Hampshire, where licences to marry are granted by the governor. As these instances have been, many of them, not for the most reputable causes, their example has had but little influence. Perhaps, in a few years, the people of England will be equally well satisfied with the provision made by the late marriage act, and no body will be at the pains of a journey to Scotland, to avoid conformity to it. Upon Mr. Dudley's being appointed president of the colony, &c. in 1686, he published an order of council, authorizing and impowering ministers and justices of the peace, the order says, "to consummate marriages," after three several times publication or licence from the president or deputy.

rection without exposing himself to any penalty in the law; our legislators had more tender sentiments of this happy state, and a man who struck his wife, was liable to a fine of ten pounds or corporal punishment: A woman who struck her husband, was liable to the same penalties.*

IN testamentary matters, the county courts had jurisdiction by law.† In the beginning, they so far followed the civil law, as to consider real estates as mere *bona*, and they did not confine themselves to any rules of distribution then in use in England, and which, afterwards, were more fully established by the statute of distributions. They considered the family and estate in all their circumstances, and sometimes assigned a greater portion to one branch than another; sometimes they settled all upon the widow; in other cases, assigned the whole estate to the administrators, or to any relation who would undertake to support or provide for the family, and pay certain sums to the children when they came to age or marriage. All this [may be excusable] in a new plantation, where most people soon spent what little personal estate they had, in improvement upon their lands. When they established a general rule, they conformed very near to the rules respecting personal estate in England, only they gave the eldest son a double portion,‡ and in the real estate, the widow generally was considered for her dower only, but still, according to the circumstances of the estate and family, the court would consider the widow, and allow her a greater or lesser part, and enjoin her to take care of the children unable to provide for themselves, in proportion to what she received. They had no law for the distribution of the estates of persons dying insolvent; however, as executors and administrators were not held to prefer in payment one debt to another, whether by judgment, bond, or simple contract; the usual way was, for a creditor of an insolvent person to apply to the general count, to appoint commissioners to examine the claims, and also to discover the estate by examining upon oath, &c. and each creditor was paid in proportion.§ The common law was altered with respect to fee-simple estates, and they descended to every child. It seems

---

* This seems to leave the wife to the mercy of the husband, who ordinarily must have paid the fine himself, or suffer her to be whipped.

† In the reign of Henry the seventh, it was said by Fineux, that the jurisdiction of the spiritual court in matters testamentary was but lately introduced by custom.

‡ From Deuteronomy xxi. 17. This law of Moses extended as well to real as personal estate, and perhaps had as great weight as either the civil law, or the peculiar circumstances of a new country.

§ About the year 1680, a law was made to enable the county courts to appoint commissioners to examine claims to the estates of persons dying insolvent, and to distribute in proportion to the creditors.

very natural to suppose, that estates in fee-tail would descend in like manner, except so far as the entail limited or cut the fee, as in gavelkind all the sons take as heir of the body. Notwithstanding this, the construction of a general tail was such, that the heir at common law took as heir of the body, to the exclusion of the other children. Traitors and felons might dispose of their estates, real and personal, by will, after sentence, and if they died intestate, distribution was made as in other cases, there being no forfeitures. They held their lands, as of the manor of East-Greenwich, in the county of Kent, in free and common socage, and not in capite, nor by knight service. They strangely supposed that socage-tenure included all the properties and customs of gavelkind, one of which is, "the father to the bough, the son to the plough." * God having forbad the alienation of lands from one tribe to another in the commonwealth of Israel, so among the first laws of the colony it was provided, "that no free inhabitant of any town should sell the lands allotted to him in the town, but to some one or other of the free inhabitants of that town, unless the town gave consent, or refused to give what others offered without fraud." This law could not continue long in force. All the valuable ends were answered by making lands liable to pay taxes upon them to the town where they lay, though the lands be not the property of the inhabitants.

THEY made provision, by temporary laws, for the charges of government. This was done for divers years in the most equitable way, by assessing every inhabitant in proportion to the profits of his whole estate real and personal, and his income by any ways and means whatsoever. This is practicable only in cases where the taxes are not very heavy. By imposts, excises, and other duties, taxes are insensibly paid, which if proportionally laid upon every individual, and paid in one sum out of an annual income, would be thought intolerable. The clergy, at all times, have been exempt from all taxes for their persons or estates under their own improvement, not merely because this was agreeable to the Levitical law,† but because they depended upon the people from year to year for their support, and whatever was added to their annual expence by a tax, so much must have been added by the people to enable their ministers to pay it.

---

* "As to what is objected against persons condemned making wills, &c. we conceive it to be according to our patent and its original, viz. that of East-Greenwich, according unto which, as we conceive, notwithstanding the father's crime, yet the children are to possess the estate." *Massa. Records.*

† Upon occasion of some disputes with the clergy at Rome, a memorial was presented, in which was this maxim, "That the clergy ought to contribute to the support of the state, let the old testament say what it will." *Spirit of Laws.*

After the year 1645, imposts and exercises were introduced. Where the officers are annually elected by the people, one great objection against such duties, viz. the influence such officers may have upon the peoples liberty, in other elections, can have no place.

THEIR military laws, at first, were more severe, every person being required to appear in arms, in order for military exercise, once every month. Some few persons in public office were, only, excepted. This was afterwards lessened to eight times in a year, and at length to four. Every inhabitant was to be furnished with arms and ammunition. A few months actual service against the Indian enemy in Philip's war, made better soldiers, than all their exercise at home had done in forty years.

UPON the division of the colony into regiments, colonels and lieut. colonels were appointed to each regiment. This lasted but a short time; ever after they had one field officer only to every regiment, a serjeant major; and a major general for the whole. He was chosen by the freemen. The officers of the several companies, ordinarily, were chosen by the companies respectively, and presented to the general court for their approbation.

IT may not be amiss to add a brief account of their legislative and judiciary forms, and some special customs.

THE magistrates or assistants, and the deputies or representatives of the people, at first, sat together in one room, and, for several years voted together, without any distinction, the major part of the whole number determining the vote, for in 1635, when the general court was ordered, for time to come, to be held twice a year only, it was at the same time resolved, that inasmuch as in those courts held by the magistrates and deputies, there might arise some difference of judgment in doubtful cases, therefore no law, order, or sentence should pass as an act of the court, without the consent of the greater part of the magistrates on the one part, and the greater number of the deputies on the other part, and for want of such accord, the cause or order was to be suspended, and if either party thought it sufficiently material, a committee was to be chosen, one half by the magistrates, and one half by the deputies, which committee might chuse an umpire, and by them the cause was to be determined. This was a prudent precaution on the part of the magistrates; for their number being limited, and the number of deputies increasing in proportion as new towns were planted, without such provision, the magistrates would, in a few years, have lost all their weight in the legislative part of the government. There is no record of the general court's sitting and acting, in distinct and separate houses, until the year 1644. In the charter, as has been observed, there was no mention of a house of representatives; a general court was to consist of the magistrates and freemen, and this occasioned the dispute whether there was a negative voice in each part of the legislative body, but at length it was agreed, that, in matters of legislation, they should act distinct and separate, and that no legislative act should be valid that was not approved by the major part of each house.

THE judicial power, both in civil and criminal matters, was at first exercised by the court of assistants, except in cases cognizable by a justice of peace. In divers cases of violent death, juries of inquest were impanelled by the governor, and a jury was also impanelled for trial of any persons charged by the jury of inquest. I find but one instance of trial by jury in any case, except murder, and that was in an action of assault and battery, until November 1633, when it was ordered that process should be directed by the secretary to the beadle, to warn 24 jurors, 14 days before the court, who were to be named by the secretary. In 1634, an order or law was made, that no trial should pass upon any for life or death, without a jury regularly chosen by the freemen. Grand juries were first established by law in September 1635. At the first court afterwards, an hundred offences were presented.

THE colony increasing, and the settlements extending remote from the capital, it was soon found necessary to make a division into shires or counties, and courts were held in each county, in some four in a year, in others two, in Yorkshire or the province of Main, but one. These courts were held by the magistrates who lived in each county, or any other magistrates who would attend, together with such other persons as the freemen of the county, from time to time, should nominate, and the general court approve of, so as to make five in all, any three to hold a court. They had power to determine all civil causes,* and all criminal, the penalty not extending to life, member, or banishment. Grand and petit juries were summoned to attend them. Appeals, from them, lay to the court of assistants and from thence to the general court. The higher offences against law were cognizable by the assistants only, except upon application, by appeal or petition, to the general court. In all actions, civil or criminal, in which any stranger was a party or interested, who could not stay, without damage, to attend the ordinary courts of justice, the governor or deputy governor, with any two magistrates, had power to call a special court, to hear and determine the cause, either civil or criminal, if triable in a county court; the record of the proceedings to

* At first in civil causes they were limited to ten pounds.

be transmitted to the records of the courts of assistants. In divers towns, a petty court was established for small debts and trespasses under twenty shillings: And in every town the selectmen, who were annually chosen by the town, had power to hear and determine all offences against the by-laws of the town, the penalty of which could not extend beyond twenty shillings, and the by-laws could not extend to matters criminal in their nature, but were limited to the regulation of their buildings, fences, streets, &c. to the preventing nusances, and to other matters tending to the convenience and accommodation of the inhabitants.

THE star-chamber, high-commission, as well as all the ecclesiastical courts, were in their zenith when our ancestors left England; but they brought away no affection for them. A discontented attorney,* who published in 1642, a little pamphlet relative to New-England, says, that "in their general courts and quarter-sessions, they exercised all the powers of parliament, king's-bench, common-pleas, chancery, high-commission, star-chamber, and all other the courts of England, and in divers instances put to death, banished, fined, cut off ears, whipt and imprisoned for ecclesiastical and civil offences." It will appear from their ecclesiastical constitution, and the professed independency of the churches, that there was no room for the exercise of great part of the powers of the spiritual courts.

ALL causes which, in England, would have fallen within the jurisdiction of the high court of admiralty, were likewise heard and determined in the courts of common law. There were divers instances of trials, condemnations, and executions for piracies, murders, and other felonies committed upon the high seas. The necessity of the thing, that justice might be done, must have been the plea for this extraordinary proceeding. To have sent such offenders to England, where they might have had a trial, to the legality of which no exception could have been made, would have been much more regular, and the expence attending it must have been matter of little weight,

---

* This was one Thomas Lechford, who left England about the year 1637, being dissatisfied, as he says, with the ecclesiastical government, and having made himself obnoxious by his opposition to episcopacy. When he came to New-England, he says, he found every church-member a bishop, and not inclining to become one himself, he could not be admitted a freeman among them, but was very active in censuring their proceedings in civil and ecclesiastical matters. The court took the advantage of an offence of another nature, his going to the jury, and pleading with them out of court, and debarred him from pleading any man's cause besides his own, and at the same time admonished him not to presume to meddle beyond what he should be called to by the court. Being deprived of the means of supporting himself, he returned to England in 1641, a zealous episcopalian. Episcopacy being declining there, he had room to indulge the ruling passion, by attacking Old-England and New in the same piece, to which he gave the title of Plain Dealing.

when compared with the putting men to death, where the authority for it was but doubtful, if even that may be said in favor of it.

THEIR judicial proceedings were in as summary a way, as could well consist with the preservation of any tolerable degree of method or order. They seem to have not much regarded forms in books of entries. Writs and processes were not in the King's name, and were very concise. I find a writ in 1650 in this form:

To the Marshal or his Deputy.

You are required to attach the goods or lands of William Stevens to the value of one hundred pounds, so as to bind the same to be responsible at the next court at Boston, 29th of the 5th month, to answer the complaint of Mr. James Astwood in an action of debt, to the value of fifty pounds, upon a bill of exchange, and so make a true return hereof under your hand. Dated 29th 2d mo. 1650.   per curiam,

Wm. Aspinwall.

THEY did not trouble themselves with pleas in abatement. They made no alteration [in forms] upon the several changes of government in England. There is no room to suppose, that the omission of his majesty's name proceeded from disaffection, or that they imagined themselves altogether independent. So far as their dependence was expressed in their charter, it could not be disputed. The reasonable and necessary connexion, between a colony and the state from which it springs, perhaps, was not fully understood. They were not long afraid of any checks or restraints from the powers at home. After a few years the authority of the king in England was at an end. The house of commons, in 1642, passed a resolve, which shews the colony to have been a favorite. Both Oliver and Richard Cromwell, during their protectorates, wrote to the government in a stile more proper for one ally to another, than for the head of a sovereign state to one of its branches or dependances.

FOR more than the ten first years, the parties spake for themselves, for the most part; sometimes, when it was thought the cause required it, they were assisted by a patron, or man of superior abilities, but without fee or reward.

WHERE there was so much of equality in the circumstances of the inhabitants, and once a year every office expired, it is not strange, that every order of men should be fond of acquiring and retaining their full share of power and authority; and although it had been a known rule in the constitution they came from, that matters of evidence were determinable by the jury, and points of law, ordinarily by the court, and the general court was so sensible of the expediency of this rule, that in 1642, they passed a temporary law or order,

that in all trials between party and party, the jury shall find matter of
fact, with damages and costs, according to their evidence, and the judges
are to declare the sentence upon it, or they may direct the jury to find
according to the law,

yet the jury seldom found a special verdict, which, a contemporary
writer says, was the cause of many inconveniencies.* I do not find
that this law was ever revived. It was a very common thing, for the
court to refuse to receive the verdict of the jury, and, in this case, the
cause was carried before the general court. The jury sometimes gave
their verdict, that there were strong grounds of suspicion, but not
sufficient evidence to convict. The court would give sentence upon
this verdict, and punish for many offences which, by the evidence
upon trial, the party appeared to them to have been guilty of, although he was not convicted of the particular crime he was charged
with. *Secundum allegata et probata* was a rule of proceeding to which
they did not confine themselves.†

IN criminal prosecutions, regularly, a bill was to be found by a
grand jury, in which they were not very formal. Sometimes the bill
would be indorsed, that the jury had strong grounds of suspicion,
but not sufficient evidence to put upon trial. I have met with instances of one of the court standing up, after a verdict of the petty
jury of not guilty, in a capital trial, and charging the prisoner, in
open court, with burglary and theft, which were not capital, and a
new trial ordered upon such charge. The court would sometimes ask
the party charged, whether they would be tried by bench or jury?

AN attorney-general was not an established officer. On some occasions, a person has been specially authorized to bring informations
for the king or government.‡ The treasurer, as receiver-general for
the colony, took care for the recovery of public dues. In criminal
matters, a spirit of virtue produced informers, without reproach to
their characters.

OATHS were administred, with no other ceremony than holding up
the hand. This was sufficient to distinguish a witness from the rest of
the court. Kissing, or laying the hand upon the book, was scrupled,

---

* Lechford, p. 28.

† Mr. Hinkley, governor of Plimouth, writing to Mr. Stoughton for advice, in 1681,
he answers him: "The testimony you mention against the prisoner, I think, is clear and
sufficient to convict him; but in case your jury should not be of that mind, then, if you
hold yourselves strictly obliged by the laws of England, no other verdict, but not guilty,
can be brought in; but, according to our practice in this jurisdiction, we should punish
him with some grievous punishment, according to the demerit of his crime, though not
found capital."

‡ Sup. court's records.

as an idolatrous ceremony, and it has never since been practised
in the government, nor the other governments in New-England,
except when special commissions from England, to take depositions to be used in some of the courts of law there, have made it
necessary. There is no law to enjoin this, or restrain any other mode.
Oaths are said to be, generally, administred according to the religion
he that swears holds to be true. The Christian is sworn upon the
gospels, the Jew upon the old testament,* and the Mahometan upon
the alcoran. To have the fear of God before our eyes is all that is
essential, and this is more likely to be produced by a due gravity and
solemnity, at the administration on his part who administers the
oath, as well as his who takes it, than by any particular ceremony.
Gentlemen who come among us, from other parts of the British dominions, approve of this form, and it is kept up now more from the
decency of it, than from any religious scruples.

FOR the first twenty years, they used too little formality in their
deeds and conveyances of the titles to lands; but in the year 1651, it
was thought necessary to order, that no estate of inheritance should
pass, unless it was expressed in the deed or conveyance "to have and
to hold to the grantee and his heirs for ever," or words to that effect;
and so no estate tail, except expressed "to the heirs male of the body
lawfully begotten for ever, or to the grantee for life, or term of
years," &c.

As early as the year 1640, they made provision for a public registry, and no mortgage, bargain, sale, or grant of any realty was good,
where the grantor remained in possession, against any persons, except the grantor and his heirs, unless the same was acknowledged
before a magistrate, and recorded; and all grants that had been before made were to be acknowledged and recorded, within one month
after the end of October that year, if the party was within the jurisdiction, if not, within three months after their return, otherwise to
be void, except as aforesaid.

EVERY marriage, birth, and death was likewise registred, first in
the town, and, at the end of the year, carried by the town clerk, or
clerk of the writs, as he was then called, to the county register; and
every neglect was punished with twenty shillings fine.

---

* It is said by some writers, that swearing by the book took its rise from the Jews,
who laid their hands upon the old testament; but our first planters, who were not ignorant of this custom among the Jews, attributed it to their proneness to idolatry.

"Cum, ut mos Græcorum est, jurandi causâ, ad aras accederet." *Cic. pro L. C.
Balbo.*

[In France, formerly, if not at this time, the person to whom an Oath was adminis-
tered was required to hold up his hand. [*Illegible*] *Itinerary, p. 3. p. 30.*]

CHAP. VI.

Of the original State of the Country, with respect to the Inhabitants and Soil.

THE Massachusets first planters distinguished the natives by four divisions, eastern, western, northern, and southern. The eastern people, had the general name of Tarrateens or Tarrenteens; they had their residence at Kennebeck, and the other rivers in the province of Main, and country east of it, and were part of the Indians called by the French Abenakis. The several subdivisions of these Tarrenteens or Abenakis, according to the rivers where they dwelt or generally resided, as St. John's, Penobscot, Norridgewock, Ameriscoggin, Saco, &c. were not known to the English until many years after.* There was great enmity between the Tarrenteens and Aberginians, or Indians of Massachusets Bay, who although they had been formerly a great people, yet were so reduced, that, upon alarms, they would fly to the English houses as to asylums, where the Tarrenteens durst not pursue them. The French traders were better known than the English to these Tarrenteens, and early planted prejudices against the English, which could never be eradicated. These were the Indians who first used fire arms, which, with ammunition, they obtained from the French. The second year after the Massachusets planters arrived, the Tarrenteens destroyed some of the English who went to trade with them, and pretended that they were drowned; but the truth being discovered, some of the Indians concerned in the murder were taken and hanged. Although they refrained from open hostilities for above forty years, yet they kept no great correspondence with, nor shewed any affection for, the English colonies, but at all times were attached to the French, who speak

---

* The Indians of the river St. François, viz. the Aresaguntacooks and Weweenocks, were a colony of the Abenakis, removed from the eastern parts of New-England for the sake of French neighbourhood. They fixed at first upon the falls of Chaudiere, but soon after removed to St. François. *Charlevoix.*[1]

---

[1] Pierre François Xavier de Charlevoix, *Histoire et Description de la Nouvelle France.*

of them as the most mild and docile of any of the Indian tribes. The western Indians went by the general name of Mohawks,* and under this name were included all the Indians westward of Quinnipiack (New-Haven) although the Indians of Hudson's river,† the Moheganders or Mackhanders, were people of a different nation and language. The name of Mohawks struck terror into the Indians who lived east of them.

THE southern Indians were divided into many distinct nations or tribes. Those upon Long-Island and the main land opposite upon the sea coast, were accounted among the most savage. The Massachusets Indians had but little knowledge of them. There was another subdivision, by the name of the River Indians, who had seated themselves in several commodious places upon the banks of Connecticut river. The next to them were called Mohegins, between Connecticut river and the Pequod river, and upon some of the higher branches of the last-mentioned river. Then came the Pequods, seated between and about New-London and Stonington, near to the sea coast. These were supposed to be among the most warlike, active, and daring, and made the Naragansets, though more numerous, stand in awe of them, and would have made the English do so likewise, if they had been owners of English arms, and understood how to use them. They were represented to have been under greater prejudices against the English, from the beginning, than any other tribe. Next to the Pequods were the Naragansets, who lived along the sea coast from Stonington round point Judith, and on what is called the Naraganset bay. They consisted of several lesser principalities, but all united under one general ruler, called the chief sachem,‡ to whom all the others owed some kind of fealty or subjection. The Nianticks were included, and considered as a branch of

---

* Mohawks they were called by the Indians of New-England, which signifies Canibals, from the Indian word *moho*, to eat. *R. Williams.*[1]

† The Indians called by the French Loups (Wolves) moved from Hudson's river. *Charlevoix.*

‡ Canonicus and Miantinomy were considered as having equal authority, until the latter was killed. *R. Williams.*

The ancient Indians among the Naragansets reported, when the English first arrived, that they had in former times a sachem called Tashtassuck, incomparably greater than any in the whole land in power and state, that he had only two children, a son and a daughter, and not being able to match them according to their dignity, he joined them together in matrimony, and that they had four sons, of which Canonicus, who was sachem when the English came, was the eldest. *MS.* This is the only piece of Indian history, or tradition of any sort from the ancestors of our first Indians, I have ever met with.

---

[1] Roger Williams, *A Key into the Language of America.*

the Naragansets. The Naragansets must have been very numerous. None of the Indians were supposed to increase, but to be continually decreasing, not in the English colonies only, but among the French in Canada also, and yet in 1675, at the beginning of Philip's war, it was generally agreed that the Naraganset tribe consisted of 2000 fighting men. They were the most curious coiners of the wampom-peag,* and supplied the other nations with money, pendants, and bracelets; also with tobacco-pipes of stone, some blue and some white; they furnished the earthen vessels and pots for cookery and other domestic uses. They were considered as a commercial people, and not only began a trade with the English for goods for their own consumption, but soon learned to supply other distant nations at an advanced price, and to receive bever and other furs in exchange, upon which they made a profit also. The Pequods jeered them for their indisposition to war, and called them a nation of women.

The Wamponoags were next to the Naragansets. Their sachem was Massasoiet or Woosamequin, whose chief seat was sometimes at Pokanocket † or Sowam, and at other times at Namasket, now Middleborough. The Nipnets, who were seated upon some lesser rivers and lakes or large ponds, more within the continent, where Oxford now is, and towns near it, were supposed to be tributaries to Massasoiet. The Indians upon Cape Cod, although not considered as part of the Wamponoags, yet were supposed to be also under some kind of subjection to Massasoiet. However, it is certain, that when Philip, the son of Massasoiet, had engaged almost all the other Indians of the country in war with the English, his solicitations could not prevail with those of Manamet to join him, but they adhered to the English, and were a defence to Sandwich, and the towns further upon the cape. There seems to have been two cantons or sachemdoms of the cape Indians, one extending from Eel river in Plimouth, to the south shore of the cape, and comprehended what are now called the Mashpee Indians,‡ and then extended upon the cape to

---

* The people of New-Plimouth, in the year 1627, began a trade with the Dutch at Manhados, and there they had the first knowledge of wampompeag, and their acquaintance therewith occasioned the Indians of these parts to learn to make it. *Hubbard.* It is not probable the New-England Indians had any instrument of commerce. The English could not have been seven years among them without discovering it. *Argentum & aurum pro pitii an irati dii negaverint dubito.* Tac.

† Bristol.

‡ I received this account of the Cape Indians from the Reverend Mr. Hawley, a worthy missionary to the Mashpee tribe, who are the principal body of Indians now remaining in New-England. The town of Mashpee consists of 65 wigwams, besides 9 wigwams at a place called Scanton, and 4 at Sockanosset, in the bounds of Falmouth, who are likewise under Mr. Hawley's charge. In 1648 Papmunnuck sold lands to the people of Barnstable, as being the chief of this tribe. They have not preserved a succession of

the eastern part of Barnstable, and as far westward as Wood's-hole, and divers petty sachems or sagamores were comprehended in this division, of which Mashpee was one; the eastern part of the cape from Nobskusset or Yarmouth made another sachemdom, the capital of which was Nausit, or Eastham: These were known to the people of New-Plimouth by the name of Nausit Indians. The Indians upon Nantucket, and those upon Martha's Vineyard, are supposed to have been distinct and separate tribes, having their own sachems and sagamores. The Nantucket Indians were a large body.

THE several scattered tribes from the Pockanockets to Piscataqua river, were called the Northern Indians, and by some Aberginians. There were many distinct settlements upon the lesser channels of Piscataqua or Newichewannock river. Merrimack also had its receptacles, from the mouth fifty miles or more, as Wainooset, Patucket, Amoskeag, Penicook, &c. and Newbury falls was a noted plantation, there being plenty of fish there at all seasons. And for the same reason, and because of the great plenty of shell-fish, at Agawam (Ipswich) there was a noted tribe with their sachem. Naumkeag (Salem and Marblehead) and Saugus (Lynn) made another division. Saugus Indians had a distinct sachem, known by the English name of George, who lived forty years or more after the English came there.

AT Massachusets, near the mouth of Charles river, there used to be a general rendezvous of Indians. That circle, which now makes the harbours of Boston and Charlestown, round by Malden, Chelsea, Nantasket, Hingham, Weymouth, Braintree, and Dorchester, was the capital of a great sachem,* much reverenced by all the plantations of Indians round about, and to him belonged Naponset (Dorchester Mills now Milton) Punkapog (Stoughton) Wessagusset

---

sachems, but for many years past have affected government in imitation of the form of government in the English townships. However, the great grandson of this Papmunnuck they considered as the chief speaker in 1761. He died that year. Another of his descendants is now a schoolmaster near fourscore years of age. But some deny that Papmunnuck was their chief, and make Tookenchosen the sachem. There are as many adult persons of this tribe as there were fourscore years ago, but not so many children and youth. Complaints are made of the practice of the parents, in binding out their children as servants in English families, and some late attempts have been made by the government to restrain or regulate this practice.

* The tradition is, that this sachem had his principal seat upon a small hill or rising upland, in the midst of a body of saltmarsh in the township of Dorchester, near to a place called Squantum, and it is known by the name of Massachusets hill, or mount Massachusets to this day. The blue hills, so called, in the township of Milton, &c. are called in Capt. Smith's map in 1614, Chevi hills, but they were called before Massachusets mount. Prince Charles changed the name, and also gave the name of Charles's river to what had been before called Massachusets river.

(Weymouth) and several places upon Charles river, where the natives were seated. At Mistick a Sagamore was seated, upon a creek which meets with the mouth of Charles river.

IT is not possible to make a just computation of the number of Indians within the limits of New-England. It is agreed that they looked with a jealous eye upon the English planters, and, when it was too late, repented that they had not, by a general union, discouraged and prevented the first attempts of settlements among them.

THE life of hunters and fishermen is said to be averse to human society, except among the members of single families. The accounts which have been transmitted of the natives, at the first arrival of the Europeans, represent them to have been as near to a state of nature as any people upon the globe * and destitute of most of the improvements which are the usual effects of civil society. Some writers † tell us, that husbands and wives, parents and children, lived always in one room or wigwam, without any apartments, and made no privacy of those actions which nature teaches even some irrational animals ‡ to be ashamed of in public. All agree, that a young woman was not less esteemed for having accompanied with a man, their usual practice being to live together upon trial, before they took one another for husband and wife.§ We hear of no instances of refined conjugal affection. The superior strength of the man to that of the woman, instead of being employed in the most laborious services

---

* Sallust's description of the Aborigines of Italy suits very well for our natives — "Genus hominum agreste, sine legibus, sine imperio, liberum atque solutum."

† *Mr. Shepard's clear Sun-shine of the Gospel*, 1648.

‡ The Elephant, the deer, &c. who never couple but in secret.

§ Champlain, who lived a whole winter, about 1615, among the Algonquins, says, "they have a sort of marriage; when a young girl arrived to eleven, twelve, thirteen, fourteen or fifteen years, she would have suitors in proportion to her charms, who would apply to her father and mother; although, often enough, except among the discreeter sort, the girls would not stay for their consent. The enamoured Indian tenders to his mistress a few belts, chains, or bracelets of wampom. If the girl likes him she will receive the present, and he comes and lodges with her three or four nights, without saying one word, where they enjoy the fruits of their affections. If, after a week or fortnight spent in this manner, they cannot agree, which is very often the case, she quits her lover, who leaves his wampon and other presents made her. Disappointed, he seeks another mistress, and she another humble servant, and continue so to do until two meet together who are agreeable each to the other. There are some who pass their youth thus with many such husbands, who have not the sole possession, for, as soon as it is night, the young women, although married, run from one wigwam to another and take what they like; but no violence is offered to the women, all depending on their consent. The husband takes the like liberty, without raising any jealousy, or but little, between them, nor is it any damage or loss of reputation to them, such being the custom of the country." Did ever any other people, in this respect, approach nearer to the brutal part of the creation?

necessary for their mutual support, was made use of to keep the wife in subjection, and oblige her to every kind of drudgery, not only to the carrying her children upon her back in all their removes, but to the carrying their provisions and packs of every kind, in their huntings and other marches. The women not only provided bark and stakes, the materials of their houses or cabins, but were the housewrights who built them, and as often as the family moved, for the sake of fishing or hunting, the women took down the houses and carried them on their backs. They planted, hoed and gathered the corn, and provided barns (holes in the ground cieled with the rind of trees) for the reception of it. Not to mention their employments in providing shell-fish and other fish for the family, bearing burdens, of wood and water, dressing their food, &c. The men commended themselves for keeping their wives employed, and condemned the English husbands for spoiling good working creatures. A family seems, necessarily, to carry an idea of government, but parents had no authority over their children. The Storgée in the parent might be observed towards their young. No return was made on the part of the child, but, assoon as it was capable, it was as ready to resist and oppose its parent as any other person.

EVERY nation or tribe had one whom they acknowledged as the head or chief. The son succeeded to the father. If no son, the Queen ruled; if no Queen, the next of kin of the blood royal.* They gave the title of Sachem to the chief, and sometimes that of Sagamore. Some suppose these two titles to be indifferently used, others that the Sagamores had a small territory,† and perhaps were, in some degree, dependant upon a Sachem. There were several Sagamores in the Massachusets bay, Sagamore George at Saugus or Lynn, John at Medford, Passaconaway at Merrimack, his son at Wechuset, Shawanon at Nashaway, and many others. Massasoiet, the chief of the Wompanoag Indians, was always called Sachem, so was Myantinomo, chief of the Naragansets, and Saccus of the Pequods.

WHAT power and authority the Sachems and Sagamores had it is more difficult to determine.‡ Murder, and a bare attempt upon the

---

* *Wood's Prospect.*

† "The inferior Sachems and subjects plant and remove at the pleasure of the highest and supreme Sachems, and I humbly conceive that it pleaseth the Most High to make use of such a bond of authority over them, without which they could not long subsist in human societies, in this wild condition wherein they are." *Rog. Williams's letter to Massa. Gov.* 12. 3*d mo.* 1656.

‡ The earliest writers represent the Sachem as ruled by the people, rather than a ruler of them, and that he held the reins no longer than he pleased the people, and, when they thought proper, resigned them to one that was more worthy, and as quietly betook himself to a private condition as if he had never known any other. Some tribute was

life of their chief, are said to have been capital offences. Such a malefactor, being apprehended, (an escape to another nation was not very difficult) the Sachem called some of his wisest men together, and the offender being pronounced guilty, his brains were beat out with a tomahawk. Other punishments they had not. We hear of no laws. Where they had no idea of property, but few laws were necessary. They had nothing to lose, worth even any corporal punishment, much less the life of a subject, where they were not over-stocked. Of personal injuries and affronts every man was his own avenger; they had no religion which forbad rendering evil for evil. Military authority they had none; every man fought and ran away at his pleasure; for this reason, they never could stand a body of English, and their wars between themselves were extremely precarious: Uncas, with an inferior number of Mohegins, and of no repute, beat Myantinomo at the head of the Naragansets, who held the Mohegins in contempt. Their arms were bows and arrows, their captains only carried a spear. Their bowstrings were made of Moose sinews. Their arrows were pointed with a small flat stone, of a triangular form, the basis of which they fastened with a leathern string into a cleft made in the end of a young stick of elder wood; and, simple as they were, they did execution upon naked bodies. Many of these stones, or heads of arrows, are found, to this day, in the earth, in places where the Indians used to resort. After the arrival of the English, they made the heads of their arrows of brass, fastened them to a small stick 6 or 8 inches long, formed to fix into the end of the pithy elder, which they bound round to strengthen it. They seldom missed their mark, when they aimed at a beast or bird, running or flying. In their wars they are said to have always engaged in a loose disorderly manner, and as soon as their artillery was spent, to have taken to their heels. The Mohawks secured their bodies against the arrows of other Indians by a covering of seahorse skins. Their principal weapon was the tomahawk, a club two or three feet long, with a knob at the end; since they knew the use of iron, improved by the addition of a sharp pointed hatchet opposite to the knob. Roger Williams says it was their constant practice to strike off the heads of their dead enemies, at which they were very expert.

THEY were remarkable for firm well compacted bodies, strong and active, capable of enduring the greatest hardships and fatigues, re-

---

paid to support the prince. Cutshamoquin, a Sachem, complained to Mr. Elliot, that some of his subjects, after they became christians, were more slack in their tribute of corn, &c. than they were before.

gardless of cold, whilst travelling in the severity of winter.* Having
made holes in the ice, they would sit round them, upon their naked
bottoms, catching pickrel, breams, pearch, and other freshwater fish.
A small pouch of parched corn, ground or rather pounded into meal,
and called Nuichicke, which is well enough translated Nocake,†
would support them several days in their travelling, when they
could get no other provisions; and sometimes they were destitute
even of this; but after abstinence they never failed of a proportionable indulgence, the first opportunity they had for it, and would
make up at one meal for all they had missed. Their cloathing was
of the skins of wild beasts; after the English came, they began to
use woollen, and in a few years wholly laid aside skins. One of their
old garments of skins would purchase a new one of woollen, and a
good quantity of strong water or sack into the bargain. The men
threw a light mantle or covering over them, and although they wore
a small flap, called Indian breeches, yet they were not over nice
in concealing their nudities.‡ The women were more modest, and
wore a coat of cloth of skins, wrapt like a blanket, about their loins,
and reaching down to their hams, which they never put off in company, and if the husband had a mind to sell the wife's beaver petti-
coat, he must have provided another of some other sort, before he
could prevail with her to part with it. In winter, [they wore the
hairy side of the skin next their bodies and] the old men sometimes
wore a sort of trousses of skins, fastened under their girdles with but-
tons. Their shoes without heels, which they called Mockassins,§
were cut out of a moose's hide. Their ornaments were pendants in
their ears, carved of bone, shells and stone, in the form of birds,

* "They were at a loss what could induce the English to leave England and come to
America. The most probable conjecture they could make was, that the English wanted
fewel at home and came over for the sake of the wood. When they had burnt up the
wood near the settlements, they removed to a new place for the sake of firing." *R. Williams.* The same author says, that he has known them run between eighty and an
hundred miles in a summer's day and back again within two days. "The inhabitants
of Formosa have been seen to out-run horses in their full speed. The Chinese alledge,
as the cause of their swiftness, that, till the age of 14 or 15, their knees and loins are
bound exceeding tight." *Du Halde.*[1] The Americans are bound in this manner the first
year or two only.

† The Indian corn boiled, after being a little broken, they called Nasaump. The
English call it Samp. Boiled with clams it makes a savory dish.

‡ Champlain says, the men in Canada generally threw aside all covering in the summer, and that the women and girls were no more moved at seeing them in that fashion
than if they had [seen] nothing strange. p. 273.

§ The Virginians had the same name for shoes.

---

[1] Jean Baptiste Du Halde, *A Description of the Empire of China and Chinese-Tartary
together with the Kingdoms of Korea and Tibet.*

beasts or fishes, belts of wampompeag upon their arms and hanging down over their shoulders. Their hair was cut into various forms and stuck with feathers. Upon their cheeks, and in many parts of their bodies, some of them, by incisions, into which they conveyed a black unchangeable ink, made the figures of bears, deer, moose, wolves, eagles, hawks, &c. which were indelible, and generally lasted as long as they lived.*

THEIR food, in winter, was birds and beasts of all sorts, fish from the ponds, and shell-fish. In summer, they had fish from the sea, but no way to save that or their meat from putrefaction; berries of all sorts, green corn, beans,† and squashes. They boiled their victuals in earthen pots; their spits were sticks fastened in the ground, cleft a-top, where they fixed their meat, and placed them round a fire, until they had sufficiently toasted it. The earth was their table; trenchers, napkins, or knives, they knew not the use of. Salt they had none, nor bread.‡ Indian corn boiled was the nearest akin to bread. They had no set meals, eat when they were hungry as long as victuals lasted, and being improvident, not caring for the morrow, they and their families would sometimes keep a fast of two or three days together. Water was their only drink.§ Their houshold furniture was very small. A skin or mat was their bed; they never used a chair or stool, always sitting on the ground.‖ A few earthen and wooden vessels answered all the purposes of a family. As they had no metals of any kind, what few tools they had were of stone, their hatchet and chizzel are kept as curiosities; the former somewhat in shape like an iron hatchet, saving that, instead of an eye for the handle, it had a neck, where they fastened a withe.¶ Their arts and manufactures lay in a very narrow compass. Their skins they

---

* Since they have been furnished with paints from Europe, they daub their faces with vermilion, and sometimes with blue, green, and other colours.

† Beans, called in Europe French beans, are, undoubtedly, natural to the country, as much as Indian corn. In Canada the French called them beans of Brazil, when they first found them amongst the natives.

‡ The Indians of Canada mixed up their Indian meal and water into a cake, which they dried by the fire. *Champ.*

§ Tobacco was in general use. This refreshed their spirits.

‖ At this day, when hundreds of them are at a conference with any of the English governments, they all sit upon the ground, with their elbows upon their knees.

¶ Roger Williams says he knew an old squaw, many years after all the rest of the Indians used iron hoes for their corn, who was superstitiously attached to the clam shell and would never use an English hoe, though three times more work might have been done with it in the same time.

"The Samogitians are so given to superstition, that whereas it was the old custom of that country to till the ground with wooden ploughs and coulters, and that the governor of one of their provinces brought them the use of iron plough shares for the ease of the labourer, and that some years after, by an unusual distemper of the air, they had a dear

dressed by scraping and rubbing, and sometimes stained or coloured them with odd sort of embroideries. They had a sort of cordage or lines, from the wild Indian hemp, with which they made nets 30 or 40 feet long, for taking Sturgeon. They had two sorts of canoos, one of pine or chesnut trees, which they burned hollow, and then scraped the inside with clam shells and oyster shells, and hewed the outside with stone hatchets. Those were generally two feet wide, and about 20 feet long; the other sort were made of the bark or rind of the birch tree, with knees or ribs, and though easily broken upon the rocks or shore, yet were tight and secure against the waves. Some of these were very neat, and the most ingenious of any part of their manufactures.*

THEY that speak most favorably, give but an indifferent idea of the qualities of their minds. Mr. Wilson speaks of them, but with compassion, as the most sordid and contemptible part of the human species. Mr. Hooker says, they are the veriest ruins of mankind upon the face of the earth. Perhaps, the Indians about the Massachusets bay were some of the lowest of the American nations. We hear nothing of that formality and order in their counsels, but little of those allegories and figures in their speeches and harangues, which the French observed among the Iroquois and other nations, at the beginning of their acquaintance with them. Indeed, in their discourses together upon any matter which they deemed important, they seldom used any short colloquiums, but each spake his mind at large without interruption, the rest of the company giving attention, and when he had finished some other gave as large an answer. They shewed courtesy to the English at their first arrival, were hospitable, and made such as could eat their food welcome to it, and readily instructed them in planting and cultivating the Indian corn, and some of the English who lost themselves in the woods, and must otherwise have perished by famine, they relieved and conducted home. Their manner was to come into the English houses without knocking, and

year or two, they threw away their iron plough shares and fell to the old wooden ones again, attributing a kind of Divinity to the one and unluckiness unto the other." *Howel.*[1]

* "I have seen a native go into the woods with his hatchet, carrying only a basket of corn with him, and stones to strike fire. When he had felled his tree (being a chesnut) he made him a little house or shed of the bark of it, he puts fire and follows the burning it with fire in many places, his corn he boils, and hath the brook by him, and sometimes angles for a little fish; but so he continues burning and hewing, until he hath, within ten or twelve days (lying there at his work alone) finished his boat." *R. Williams.*

[1] Presumably William Howel, *An Institution of General History.*

to sit down without ceremony. R. Williams compared the Quakers to them. There was no trading with them but for ready pay. He that trusted them lost his debt and his customer.

THE principle or persuasion that all things ought to be in common * might cause hospitality, where the like was expected in return, without any great degree of virtue. Some appearances there were of compassion, gratitude, and friendship, and of grief at the death or distress of their children or near relations. Some degree of these social affections is inseparable from human nature. [One of them being asked who was a good man answered, he that will not lye nor steal.] Vices they had many. They were false, malicious, and revengeful. The least injury caused in them a deadly hatred, which could never be allayed. They were infinitely cruel to their enemies, cutting and mangling their bodies, and then broiling them alive upon hot embers, and inflicting the most exquisite torments they could invent. They were not known to feed upon the flesh of their enemies after the English came among them.† The men were lazy and idle, never employing themselves about any other business than what was of absolute necessity for their support, and such as the women were not capable of. More dirty, foul, and sordid than swine, being never so clean and sweet as when they were well greased.‡ Drunkards they were not, but the only reason was they had nothing that would intoxicate them. Assoon as they had a taste of the English sack and strong waters, they were bewitched with them, and by this means more have been destroyed than have fell by the sword. The English women had nothing to fear, as to any attempt upon their honor. The same observation is made of the

* An Indian gift is a proverbial expression, signifying a present for which an equivalent return is expected.

† Champlain says the Algonquins took the heart of one of their enemies killed in battle, cut it into pieces, and gave it to his brother and several other prisoners to eat, who took it into their mouths, but would not swallow it.

A journal of a French officer in Canada, which was taken on board a small vessel in the West Indies, gives an account of a feast made by some of the Indians who were at the taking of Fort William Henry, at which they sacrificed some of the English prisoners, boiled their flesh, and forced the other prisoners to eat it.

‡ I have seen a great half-naked Indian sitting at a small distance from the governors and commissioners of several of the colonies, in the midst of a conference, picking lice from his body for half an hour together, and cracking them between his teeth. — One of the laws our Indians made, upon their first pretences to civility, laid a small penalty upon such as cracked lice with their teeth. The Hottentots had the same taste. "They plead in excuse the law of retaliation, and urge that it is no shame to eat those that would eat them." *Kolben's voya. &c.*[1]

[1] Peter Kolben (or Kolb), *The Present State of the Cape of Good Hope.*

Canada Indians, with respect to the French women. La Hontan, a French author, who has given a different account, is charged with a fondness for embellishing his memoirs, and being very credulous. They had their choice among their own women. We have but little reason to wonder that so few Englishmen incline to cohabit with Indian women.

THEY had some sports and games with which they sometimes diverted themselves. Football was the chief, and whole cantons would engage one against another. Their goals were upon the hard sands, as even and firm as a board, and a mile or more in length, their ball not much larger than a hand-ball, which they would mount in the air with their naked feet, and sometimes would be two days together before either side got a goal. They had two principal games of chance, one they called puim, this was much the same with a game Charlevoix mentions among the Miamis, which he calls jeu des pailles, or the game of straws. They took a number of packets of small sticks or straws, unequal in number, but near of a size, and shuffling them together, he, to whose lot the highest number fell, was the forwardest in the game. Another game they called hub bub, the same the French called jeu de plat, the game of the dish among the Hurons. They took five small pieces of bone, flatter than a die and longer, black on the one side and white on the other, these they put into a small wooden tray or platter, and giving it a stroke on the ground the bones all flew into the air, and the gamesters whisk their hands to and fro among the bones, and then smite themselves on the breast and thighs, crying out, hub, hub, hub, so as to be heard at a great distance. According as the bones happened to be more or less of one colour, so they won or lost. Whilst any one continued to win he held the tray, and upon his losing, gave it to the next. The Negroes in Guinea have a game of the same sort, which they call paw-paw. Shooting at marks was a diversion for their children, as soon as they were capable of drawing a bow. Swimming, running, and wrestling they were, as early, accustomed to. Their hunting and fishing, being all they did, which could be called labor, for their maintenance or support, served also as diversions. Deer, Moose, and Bears were their chief objects; Wolves, Wild Cats, Racoons, Otters, Musquashes,[1] and even Bevers, were not much regarded, until the English, from the value they set upon their skins or furs, encouraged the pursuit of them. [Their Dogs were generated by a Wolf and a Fox, which they tamed and used in hunting, but after the English

[1] Musquash is the Algonquin word for muskrat, and appears to have been the name used by our ancestors in the eighteenth century.

arrived they used English Dogs of which they were very fond.] Besides their bows, they had other devices to take their game, sometimes by double hedges a mile or two in length, and a mile wide at one end, and made narrow, by degrees, until they came to a gap of about six feet, against which they lay hid to shoot the Deer, as they came through in the day-time, and, at night, they set Deer-traps, being springs made of young trees. They had their traps also for Bevers and Otters. Their ordinary fishing was with hooks and lines. They made their hooks of bones, their lines of wild hemp, stronger and neater than the English lines.* They had a way of taking Sturgeon by lighting a torch made of birch bark, which waving [1] to and fro by the side of their canoe, would delight the Sturgeon, and cause them to come tumbling and playing, throwing up their white bellies, into which the Indians struck their spears or darts.† The Sturgeons backs were impenetrable. They had grand fishings at the several falls of the rivers, at most of which a canton or company of Indians had their chief residence, and at fixed seasons the several neighbouring cantons met by turns, partly for recreation, and partly to make provision for the year. During these meetings, all that came were at home, and had all things in common, and those who had entertained their neighbours expected the like kindness.

RELIGION they had as little as can well be imagined. Some notions they had of a future state. A Mahometan paradise, where they were to solace themselves in fruitful corn-fields and fine flowery meads, with pleasant rivers to bathe in; curious wigwams, provided for them without any labor of their own; hunting, fowling, and fishing without any weariness or pains to molest them; but at the door was a snarling animal, who denied a peaceful entrance to all unworthy of it.‡ This caused them to bury the bows and arrows of the deceased with their bodies,§ to affright or repel Cerberus, and good store of wampom-

---

* Douglas [2] says they had no threads of flax, hemp or any other herbs, but the earliest accounts of the Massachuset Indians assert the contrary, and Champlain says that it was part of the employment of the Indian women of Canada to twist the wild hemp and make it into nets for fishing.

† The natives of the Canary islands happened to hit upon the same way of taking fish.

‡ Wood's prospect.

§ [This was a practice among the Spartans before Lycurgus's time for he forbad to bury any thing with the dead in their Sepulchres.]

---

[1] The first edition gives "weaving" instead of "waving." The third edition follows the first, though it is fairly clear that "waving" is correct.

[2] William Douglass, *A Summary, Historical and Political.*

pag to purchase some peculiar favors or privileges.* Their enemies, and others unworthy the joys of elyzium, they consigned to an eternal habitation and place of torment. However warm some of their imaginations might be, it is agreed that in general no people had greater fears of death discovered by the distress and despair of the dying person, and the sighs and groans of the surviving parents or near friends, who mourned without hope. Idolatry † there were

* They supposed the souls of all great and good men and women went away to the south-west. A south-west wind ordinarily makes fair pleasant weather. In the spring and summer, near the sea, in the afternoon it frequently succeeds a raw wind from the south to the south-east, blowing from the sea all the forenoon. In the country from whence this pleasant wind came, they concluded the divinity would chuse to reside. *R. Williams.* This agrees exactly with the accounts the first East India voyagers give of the Japanese.

† Amongst Mr. Eliot's manuscripts I found the following story. "This spring time in the year 1653, being sundry days at Pautucket, and spending a sabbath among them, there was a woman at the meeting who had a small bright brass image of a man about her neck, hanging by a string fastened about the neck of the image, I observed it, but thought little of it; afterwards when I thought to have gone away, my horse had run and gone homeward, as they found by his footing, whereupon I sent some after my horse, and purposed to have gone on foot after till they met me with my horse. Many being gathered together to take leave of me, among the rest there was that woman with an image about her neck; I asked her why she wore it there, she roundly and readily answered me, I pray unto it. Why, says I, do you account that to be your God? She as readily answered me yes. At which I marvelled, having never seen the like before at any place I ever came to. I therefore declared to her and to the company about us the greatness of the sin of idolatry. I urged the second commandment. I shewed how much idols should be demolished. I desired her to give it to me that I might demolish it, but she refused. I offered her half a crown for it, but she was not willing. Perceiving it was tied with a riding knot, I slipped the knot and slipped off the image; then she swelled with anger and cried. I presently gave her half a crown, which she took but was not pacified. I told the company, the first pond I came to I would cast it in. When I departed, the woman girt up her loins and ran after me; when I perceived it, I asked her whither she went, she answered, whither I went, and she would not leave me so long as I had her God about me. It began to rain, which was some discouragement to my going forward; then I considered that this act of mine, in taking away and abolishing the idol, was neither so proper nor so valid as it would be if the rulers and sachems should do it. — I resolved to return, and did so and the woman after me. When I came to the wigwam, there being four sachems present which prayed to God, I desired them all to come together. Being come, I told them that seeing the rain had driven me back, God would not have me yet to go, but somewhat else is to be done about this idol and the sin of idolatry, and because the woman is not content with what I have done I do commit the matter and the idol unto you to judge. So I laid it upon the ground before them where they sat, and went to confer with the company. When they had sat about half an hour in consultation, they desired the company to come before them, which they did. They said they had agreed upon their judgments. 1st, That the act in taking away the idol was well done. 2dly, That one man should be appointed to demolish the idol, and three others for witnesses that it was done. 3dly, They adjudged the idolatress to be a great sinner, yet as it was the first time, and she had done it ignorantly, therefore they would spare her, yet they did all one after another reprove her very solemnly. After execution was done upon the idol, one declared that he understood there were some more idols like to that, in other houses. I requested the sachems to send for those also. The officer or constable went well guarded, and presently brought a bright brass image or seraphim

no signs of among them. They acknowledged a God, whom they mentioned by the word Ketan; he gave them rain in time of drought, and fair weather after great rains. Upon him they had their first dependence for recovery from sickness, but [how they expressed this dependance we are not told. Morton, who was among them so early as 1622, could not discover any kind of worship.] If he failed them they applied to their powows, which, it is most likely, brought upon them the charge of worshipping the Devil. The powows the English called their priests. We have many idle stories of the intercourse they had with the Devil. Their craft was in danger from the preachers of the gospel, who condemned their cheats and juggles as diabolical, and they were great opposers of the gospel, and threatned the new converts with death and destruction, and many were so intimidated that the powows were supposed to have fascinated or bewitched them. Passaconaway, a great sagamore upon Merrimack river, was the most celebrated powow in the country. He made the Indians believe strange things; that he could make water burn, rocks move and trees dance, and metamorphose himself into a flaming man; that in winter he could raise a green leaf out of the ashes of a dry one, and produce a living snake from the skin of a dead one.*

WHEN the powow was sent for in any malady, after a hideous bellowing and groaning, he made a stop, and all the auditors with one voice uttered a short note, and then the powow renewed his roaring, smiting his naked breast and thighs, and jumping about until he foamed at the mouth. The patients were frequently cured of imagi-

---

with his wings spread, to the sachems, who presently passed the same judgment they had done upon the former, and it was executed accordingly. — I asked, how it should come to pass that there should be such idolatry here, and in no place else that I had heard of. They rendered this reason. That being the most northerly place that I resort to, some of those Indians have commerce with the Indians that are yet more northerly, who have commerce with those whom the French teach to pray to such idols, therefore they think the idols and idolatry come from them.

The Oqui of the Algonquins, or French Indians, was the same with the powow of the English Indians. Champlain says, that what caused it to be supposed they intended the Devil, was that when they saw a man do any thing extraordinary, or have any extraordinary qualities, as a brave warrior, or a furious fellow to the degree of madness, they called him Oqui. That some of these Oqui's undertook to heal the sick, cure the wounded, and to foretell future events. The Oqui's persuaded the sick to cause feasts to be made that they might have a share in them, and to perform many ceremonies in hopes of a speedy cure. Sometimes the physician acquired reputation by the sudden restoration of the patient, but if they were very ill the horrid noise and disturbance the Oqui made, was much more likely to kill than cure.

* They had a tradition that a crow brought the first grain of Indian corn, and although this bird often robbed their fields, not one Indian in an hundred would kill them. *R. Williams.*

nary distempers, by these ridiculous pranks, and such instances of recovery worked upon the credulity of the Indians, so far as to make them to suppose the powows could heal them and poison them when they pleased. The latter was the easiest, and it is not unlikely that they had enough of the Devil in them to do it, in order to carry on the fraud and raise their characters. These poor deluded creatures were soon convinced that the English medicines had a healing virtue beyond all the charms of the powows.* There is a noted instance of Mr. Winslow, the governor of Plimouth, his reviving old Massasoiet, by the help of a dose of Mithridate, when given over by his own physicians. Mr. Mayhew visiting the son of Towanquattick, a Sagamore at Martha's Vineyard, who was ill of a fever, and whom the powows pronounced a dead man, let him blood, and he soon recovered.† Many of the powows became converts to Mr. Eliot and Mr. Mayhew,[1] among the rest, Passaconnaway, the Sagamore already mentioned. Some of the converts gave this account,

that when any of the Indians fell into a strange dream, wherein Chepian appeared unto them as a serpent, the next day they tell the other Indians of it, and, for two days after, the rest of the Indians dance and rejoice for what they tell them about this serpent, and so they become their powows.

Being asked what these powows do, and what use they are of, they said, "their principal employment was to cure the sick, by certain odd gestures and beating themselves, and then they shall pull out the sickness by applying their hands to the sick person, and so blow it away." This account was given to Mr. Eliot, who made this inference, "so that their powows are great witches, having fellowship with the old Serpent, to whom they pray, and by whose means

* "I find, by God's blessing on some means used in physick and chirurgery, they are already convinced of the folly of powowing, and are easily persuaded to give it over, as a sinful and diabolical practice." *Mr. Eliott's letter, Nov.* 12, 1648.

† Their sweatings in their hot houses was a more rational remedy than the powowing. By these they are said to have easily got rid of the French disease. The Six Nations make use of a plant, which they pretend is a specific for that distemper, but make a secret of it. I will mention an instance of their sagacity. Observing that the musquash fed freely upon the hemlock [2] without hurt, they took out the stomach of the animal, dried and pulverized it, and gave it to their children who had eaten of the plant, and found it to be an antidote for the poison.

[1] Thomas Mayhew (1621–1657), son of Governor Thomas Mayhew of Martha's Vineyard. See Hutchinson's footnote on the Mayhews on p. 136. Mayhew's own description of the incident may be found in Massachusetts Historical Society *Collections,* Third Series, IV, 78.

[2] Presumably Water Hemlock (*Cicuta maculata*) of the Parsley family. It grows in moist places in New England, and is notoriously poisonous if eaten by human beings.

they heal sick persons," &c. Some of them were jugglers, and without arriving to any great degree of perfection, they might raise the admiration of the generality of their blockish countrymen. However, the contemporaries of the aboriginals all say, that, besides the Ketan, or their good spirit, they had some notion of an evil spirit, which is sometimes called Chepian, but generally Abamocho,* lord of those infernal regions to which they consigned their enemies. Mr. Mayhew, in a letter dated in 1650, relates a conversation between Hiacoomes a christian Indian, and Myoxco, a chief man of a place at the Vineyard. Myoxco demanded how many Gods † the English worshipped, and being answered, one, he reckoned up about 37 principal gods he had; and shall I, said he, throw away these 37 gods for one? ‡

THE Indians of Canada, according to Charlevoix, had an infinite number of genii, or subaltern spirits, good and bad, who had their particular worship. Very circumstantial accounts have been published, by the French writers, of the religious rites and ceremonies of the northern Indians, their feasts and fasts, their priests, and even their nuns or vestal virgins; which accounts have either been too easily received, or else the northern differed much from the more southern Indians, who, at best, gave themselves but little concern upon any point of religion. A deep enquiry into futurity could not consist with that indolent state of mind, which they made the sum-

---

* "The Indians who had never seen any man blacker than themselves, happened to spy a Negro a top of a tree who had lost his way, ran to the next plantation to inform the English that they had seen Abamocho, and to intreat their assistance to conjure him down. The English went out and found the poor wandering black and conducted him to his master." *Wood.*

Query, Whether it was not as natural for them to have taken the first white man they saw for Abamocho, as the first black, their own colour being a medium between both.

† Mr. Eliot, in translating the bible, could find no Indian word for God. In the prayers and sermons made by the Indians in their own language, they have been taught to use the word Jehovah, or the English words God or Lord. R. Williams uses the Indian word *Manitoo*, by which word they seem rather to have expressed their admiration at any thing which excelled, whether animate or inanimate.

‡ Roger Williams says that when they saw one man excell others in wisdom, valour, strength, &c. they would cry out, he is a god. And when they heard of the English ships, houses, and manner of plowing their fields, they pronounced that they were gods. By their eastern, western, southern, and northern gods, which the same author speaks of, they probably intended no more than the chief sagamores of the several places to which souls went. This is very consistent with the gross notions they had of a future state.

I began to suspect, from this instance of plurality of gods, something like the mythology of the ancients. *Romulus in cœlo cum diis agit ævum.* CIC. But I have no where met with any evidence of their making any of their deceased heroes the objects of their religious worship, nor so much as preserving the remembrance of their names; and it is probable the Indian run over a number of names to impose upon Mr. Mayhew, or to get rid of his importunity, and that, from this authority only, other writers have mentioned a plurality of Gods.

mit of all happiness. An Indian convert discoursing with Woosama-quin, the great Sachem, he enquired of the convert, what worldly good things he had gained by his new religion; and not receiving a satisfactory answer, gave himself no further thought about it. Mr. Mayhew * says, that upon the first proposals of religion to them, they generally made these three enquiries. 1. What earthly riches they should get. 2. What approbation they should have from other sagamores and governors. 3. How they should come off from the powows.†

MANY people pleased themselves with a conjecture, that the Indians in America were the descendants of the ten tribes of Israel. There was as little affinity between the Indian and the Hebrew language, as between the languages of any two nations upon the earth, and the New-England Indians had no one custom peculiar to the Israelites, except that of the separation of the women on certain occasions. This custom obtained among most of the nations upon the continent. This French speak of others, viz. that, at certain repasts, they never make use of knives; it is not probable they ever had any to use, on any occasion, until they were brought to them from Europe; they called the first English knifemen. That they never break the bones of the beasts they eat, and that, in some of their songs, you may distinguish the word Hallelujah. One Capt. Cromwell,[1] a rich bucanier, who died at Boston about 1646, assured governor Dudley, that he had seen Indians to the southward circumcised. This increased the faith of many.‡ The authors of

* His letter to the corporation, 1650.

† R. Williams says that when he had discoursed of the creation, of the soul, of the danger of it, and the saving of it, they assented; but when he spake of the resurrection of the body, they cried out, we will never believe this.

‡ Their greasing their hair is called, by R. Williams, anointing their heads.

They are said to call the seven stars the Bear. This would be very strange, if there was any evidence of their calling them so, when the first European arrived. So remarkable a constellation must have been always distinguished by them. A Bear being so common an animal with them, they probably were acquainted with the name of the constellation being the same with that of the animal, from their most early converse with the English or French.[2]

[1] Thomas Cromwell, of Boston, made a large fortune by privateering. Returning from one of their voyages Cromwell and his men visited Plymouth, where they created more excitement than that colony had known, or was to know, in a long, long time. For a first-hand account of the episode, see William Bradford, *History of Plymouth Plantation* (Original Narratives edition), pp. 404–405.

[2] As originally printed this paragraph did not end here. In the first edition there was an additional sentence: "Aries or Taurus they had no word for, the animals being unknown to them." Apparently Hutchinson caught himself in error at the last minute, and obliterated the sentence before the volume went out. It was not printed in the second and third editions.

the universal history seem to have as little grounds for the conjecture, that the Indians are the posterity of the ancient Scythians, and that Massachusets, a compound Indian word, might be derived from Masagetes.

OUR ancestors attempted to account for the first peopling America, consistent with the sacred history of the creation, but were obliged to leave the matter in the same uncertainty, as all others have done who have since made the like attempt.

The language of the Indians, from Piscataqua to Connecticut, was so nearly the same, that they could tolerably well converse together. It was observed, that without the greatest difficulty, they could not be brought to pronounce the letters L or R. For Lobster, they said Nobstan. The Tarrenteens [, the Eastern tribes,] sounded the R easily. Labials they used with freedom. It is observed of the western Indians, particularly the six nations, that they have no labials in all their language, and they and the Nipnets, who lived little more than 100 miles from them, could not better understand one another than the English and Chinese.

AT the beginning, our planters promised themselves great things from the soil, and imagined they were rich, having the property of so great an extent of territory. The general court allowed no more than 200 acres of land, in the first dividend, for 50 pounds sterling advanced for the plantation. Mr. Johnson, in a will made in 1629, supposes his interest, as a proprietor, worth six hundred pounds sterling,* but many years had not passed, before an ingenious writer† observed, that the planters had found, by experience, that their improved lands were of no greater value (in many places not so great) than the labour and expence in subduing them. Several accounts of the opinions, which at first prevailed, both of the soil and climate, have been preserved. Wood,[1] a writer of a fertile imagination, who lived in the country four years, which, from some passages in his history, appear to have been before the year 1636, or the Pequod war, says,

The soil is, for the general, a warm kind of earth, there being little cold spewing land, no moorish fenns, no quagmires, the lowest grounds be the

---

* In 1716, several gentlemen joined in the purchase of about 500,000 acres of land in the eastern country, called the Pejepscot purchase. The whole consideration was no more than about one hundred pounds sterling, *Douglass.*

† Mr. Hubbard.

---

[1] William Wood (*d.* 1639) "probably came to Salem, 1629, and 15 Aug. 1633 left our country, as his book relates" (Savage). His book, *New England's Prospect*, was printed in London in 1634. It has been reprinted a number of times, notably by the Prince Society in 1865, with a preface by Charles Deane.

marshes, over which, every full and change, the sea flows; these marshes be rich ground and bring plenty of hay, of which the cattle feed, and like as if they were fed with the best up-land hay in New-England,* of which likewise there is great store, which grows commonly between the marshes and the woods. This meadow ground lies higher than the marshes, whereby it is freed from the overflowing of the seas, and besides this, in many places where the trees grow thin, there is good fodder to be got amongst the woods. There be likewise in divers places near the plantations great broad meadows, wherein grow neither shrub nor tree, lying low, in which places grows as much grass as may be thrown out with a scyth, thick and long, as high as a man's middle, some as high as the shoulders, so that a good mower may cut three load in a day. Many object this is but coarse fodder. True it is, that it is not so fine to the eye as English grass, but, being made into hay, the cattle eat it as well as lea hay, and like as well with it. The worst that can be said against the meadow grounds is, that there is but little edish or after pasture, which may proceed from the late mowing, more than any thing else.† For the more upland grounds, there be different kinds, in some places clay, some gravel,

* This account is much too favorable. Take the saltmarsh of the several parts of the country, one acre with another will not produce more than three quarters of a load of hay. Cattle, remote from the sea, must have salt, and a little salt hay would undoubtedly be grateful, and black cattle and horses and sheep may be kept alive through the winter with salt hay, but all creatures prefer English hay when they can have both. The natural upland grass of the country commonly called Indian grass, is poor fodder, perhaps not better, if so good as barley straw.

† I conclude, from this account, that they had then no hay of English grass. Land of a tolerable quality, where English grass, a name given to all imported grasses, has been mowed, we now find by experience, will afford after feed until the severe frosts burn the grass and cause it to wither. It has been made a question, whether the seed of the white clover is not in the earth in all parts of the country, and our farmers affirm, and there is no doubt of the fact, that if they break up new ground in the woods, where no dung has ever been spread, and lay it down the next or the same year, and give it a thin coat of ashes, the white honey suckle comes in as thick as if the seed had been sown. Some connoisseurs say, that the plant and flower differ from the English honey suckle. Ashes will, certainly, in some of our improved lands, bring in this sort of grass, when barn dung, or sea manure, will bring in other sorts of English grass in the same field. On the other hand, in travelling the woods where no cattle has been, and where the soil has been so good that the brakes and Indian grass have been four or five feet high, I have searched for English grass without being able to find a spire of any sort. Some have supposed that the pigeons, which come down to the plantations in infinite numbers, and other birds of passage, scatter the seeds in their dung through the continent. There is a tradition, that the grass called fowl meadow grass, which is superior to any other grass of the fresh water meadows, was first brought to the meadows in Dedham, by a large flight of wild fowls, and that from thence the grass and the meadows, where it was first discovered, and from whence it has been communicated to many parts of the country, took their names. I do not find the observation any where made that, at the beginning of the English settlements, the European grass came into ground which had been broke up, before any seed was sown. [It may have passed without notice for] on the other hand, it is not probable that the seeds of all that great variety of grasses, distinct from what is called wild or Indian grass with which our fields [now] abound, was ever imported or sown among us.

some a red sand, all which are covered with a black mould, in some places a foot deep, in others not so much. Such is the rankness * of the ground, that it must be sown the first year with Indian corn, which is a soaking grain, before it will be fit to receive English seed. For the natural soil, I prefer it before the counties of Surry or Middlesex, which, if they were not enriched with continual manurings, would be less fertile than the meanest grounds in New-England; wherefore, it is not impossible, nor much improbable, that, upon improvements, the soil may be as good in time, as England. If any man doubt of the goodness of the ground, let him comfort himself with the cheapness of it; such bad land in England, I am sure, will bring in store of good money. There hath as good English corn grown there as can be desired, especially rye, oats and barley; There hath been no great trial of wheat and beans, only thus much I affirm, that these two grains grow well in gardens.

THIS author's account of the country is not unfavorable. An anonymous manuscript which was sent to England in the beginning of the year 1637, gives us a different idea.

THE soil, it is, for the nature of it, mixed; the upland, rather participates of sand than clay, yet our rye likes it not, an argument it is both cold and barren, yet I find some of it manured to yield some increase but not to answer expectation; the low lands are, for the most part, covered with underwoods, the soil, which is a mixture of clay and sand, seems to have been fattened by the continual fall of leaves from the trees growing thereon. This soil is like your woodland in England, best at first, yet afterwards grows more barren. This raised the report of so rich a soil, but we † that came after found, by dear experience, that affection, not judgment, was the author of it; for, after five or six years, it grows barren beyond belief; and whereas, after the land in England proves fertile for grass, this yields none at all, but, like the land about Dunstable, puts on the face of winter in the time of summer. I do believe, that if we had marl, lime, or other manure, this barrenness might, in part, be cured, but, as yet, we are destitute of these supplies. The natural coldness confutes the opinion of those, who did conceive it to be originally fertile, and experience confirms this to be true, for beans, millet, and fitches and roots, which delight in a cold soil, prosper here alike. For the present, we make a shift to live, but hereafter, when our numbers increase, and the fertility of the soil doth decrease, if God discover not means to enrich the land, what shall become of us I will not determine, but, it is probable, we must

---

* Rather the roughness of the ground. The Indian corn requiring frequent plowings, what are now called horse hoeings, besides hoeing and hilling by hand, the land is pulverized, and there will be fine tilth necessary for English grain the next year. Indian corn is likewise gathered late, after the frosts set in, and, if the corn has been well tended, there will be no grass or weeds when the frosts break up in the spring, immediately after which it should be ploughed for the English grain.

† I suppose he means the Massachusets planters who came after Plimouth men.

either disband ourselves, like beasts streightened in their pasture, and so be liable to destruction from the natives (I mean the Pequods) or else, continuing together, be made the subject of some fearful famine and the misery that accompanieth it. Hay, we have here of the low lands, such as it is, which, in my opinion, is inferior in goodness to our reed and sedge in England, for it is so devoid of nutritive vertue, that our beasts grow lousy with feeding upon it, and are much out of heart and liking; besides, it breeds among them sundry diseases which we know not how to cure. Some have learned to make better provision, by burning the grass when it is near ripe, and so suffering a new crop to spring out of the ashes of the old. This they cut down, before it be half ripe, and make it into hay, but this proves like your after meath in Old England, not fit to labour with, yielding a faint nourishment, which brings our cattle so low, and many times to diseases of which they hardly ever recover.

A gentlewoman, a few years after, in another manuscript, sends the following account.

When I remember the high commendations some have given of the place, and find it inferior to the reports, I have thought the reason thereof to be this, that they wrote surely in strawberry time. — When I have thought again of the mean reports, and find it far better than those reports, I have fancied the eyes of the writers were so fixed on their old English chimney tops, that the smoke put them out. The air of the country is sharp, the rocks many, the trees innumerable, the grass little, the winter cold, the summer hot, the gnats in summer biting, the wolves at midnight howling, &c. Look upon it, as it hath the means of grace, and, if you please, you may call it a Canaan. —— I perceive some among you have imagined they might enlarge their estates by coming here, but I am taught that great men must look to be losers, unless they reckon that gain which, by the glorious means of life, comes down from heaven. Men (by what I hear) of your rank and worth, will be welcome on New-England's coasts; he only can advise you best, who can lead you to his place, &c.

Mr. Hubbard, whose manuscript history was wrote about 1680, could make a better judgment.

As for the soil, it is, for the general, more mountainous and hilly than otherwise, and, in many places, very rocky and full of stones, yet intermingled with many plains and valleys, some of which are sandy and inclinable to barrenness, especially those which abound with pitch pines, and there are many such, as likewise many swamps or boggy places, full of small bushes and underwoods. But here and there, are many rich and fruitful spots of land, such as they call interval land, in level and champain grounds, that oftentimes are overflown by the channels of water which run beside them, which is supposed to enrich the soil that is so watered.* The fatness of the earth washed by the rains, and melting of the snow from the surface of the higher parts of the country, being, by those floods, cast upon the levels which lie by the sides of those greater streams. In many such places, their land hath been known to be sown or planted full forty years together, without any considerable abatement of the crop, never failing of thirty or forty bushels per acre. But for the generality of the soil, it is of a lighter sort of earth, whose fruitfulness is more beholden to the influence of the heavens, advantage of the season, skill and industry of the tiller, than to the strength of its own temper. Such as came hither first upon discovery, chanced to be here in the first part of the summer, when the earth was newly adorned with its best attire of herbs and flowers, flourishing with such early fruits as weather beaten travellers are wont to refresh themselves with beholding; as strawberries, gooseberries, rasberries, cherries, and whorts, as they observed who first landed about Martha's Vineyard, from whence they promised themselves and their successors a very flourishing country, as they did who landed first upon the coast of Florida. All sorts of grain sown in the spring, are found to grow pretty naturally here. The cold ofttimes proves so extream, as to kill that which is committed to the ground before winter.†

From these several accounts, some judgment may be made of the opinion our forefathers had formed of the country. Experience convinced many of them, that the value of the land when cleared, would make but poor wages for their labor in clearing it. It is a happy thing, that a fondness for freeholds to transmit to posterity, with privileges annexed to them, excited so many of the first planters of America to hard labor, and supported them under hard fare. A great part of this vast continent, filled with wild beasts and savage men scarcely superior to them, now affords the necessaries and conven-

* The two great rivers, Connecticut and Hudson's river, are most remarkable for large tracts of this interval land, which are so often overflowed as to need no other manure, the waters in a freshet bringing down so much muck from the mountains, like the waters of the Nile, as to keep the ground in good heart to bear a crop of wheat every year. Sometimes, a great freshet, in the months of June and July, is prejudicial to the crops upon the mowing and pasture land, for that season, making the grass foul and disagreeable to the cattle.

† Our farmers, by sowing their seed early, the ground being prepared in ridges to throw off the rains and melting snows, raise winter wheat and rye with good success. The great discouragement has been the blast. An idle opinion obtained among the vulgar, that since the execution of the Quakers, about a century past, wheat has always blasted. Generally, between the first and the tenth of July, it has been observed, that the dew, called the honey dew, falling upon the wheat (the morning after being hot and calm) causes the rust or blast. Ordinarily, if the wheat be sown early, it will be so forward, by this time, that the grain will not suffer by it. The spring or summer grain, being later before it is ripe, is, in general, the most exposed. Sir Henry Frankland, several years ago, imported from Lisbon the seed of summer wheat, which ripens there in twelve weeks, and the flower of it is in great esteem. This sort has been less subject to blast than any other. It ripens in the Massachusets about 16 weeks from the sowing.

ɪences of a civilized life, equal to the like tracts of improved country in other parts of the globe. History affords us no instance of so great improvements in so short a time. The same passion still continues, and affords a prospect of the like happy effect for ages yet to come.

A natural history of the country will afford a volume of itself, and it is a work much wanted, and would entertain the curious. The botanical part would be very useful. I have not leisure, and if I had, I have not a genius for such an undertaking. I wish some person, who has both the one and the other, would undertake it.

APPENDIX.

NUMBER I.

The humble Request of his Majesties loyall Subjects, the Governour and the Company late gone for New-England; to the rest of their Brethren in and of the Church of England.

Reverend FATHERS and BRETHREN,

THE generall rumour of this solemne enterprise, wherein ourselves with others, through the providence of the Almightie, are engaged, as it may spare us the labour of imparting our occasion unto you, so it gives us the more incouragement to strengthen ourselves by the procurement of the prayers and blessings of the Lord's faithful servants: For which end wee are bold to have recourse unto you, as those whom *God* hath placed nearest his throne of mercy; which as it affords you the more opportunitie, so it imposeth the greater bond upon you to intercede for his people in all their straights; we beseech you therefore by the mercies of the LORD JESUS to consider us as your Brethren, standing in very great need of your helpe, and earnestly imploring it. And howsoever your charitie may have met with some occasion of discouragement through the misreport of our intentions, or through the disaffection, or indiscretion, of some of us, or rather amongst us: for wee are not of those that dreame of perfection in this world; yet we desire you would be pleased to take notice of the principals, and body of our company, as those who esteeme it our honour to call the *Church* of *England*, from whence wee rise, our deare Mother, and cannot part from our native countrie, where she specially resideth, without much sadness of heart, and many tears in our eyes, ever acknowledging that such hope and part as we have obtained in the common salvation, we have received in her bosome, and suckt it from her breasts: wee leave it not therefore, as loathing that milk wherewith we were nourished there, but blessing God for the parentage and education, as members of the same body, shall alwayes rejoice in her good, and unfainedly grieve for any sorrow that shall ever betide her, and while we have breath, syncerely desire and indeavour the continuance and abundance of her welfare, with the inlargement of her bounds in the kingdome of CHRIST JESUS.

Be pleased therefore *Reverend* FATHERS *&* BRETHREN to helpe forward this worke now in hand; which if it prosper, you shall bee the more glorious, howsoever your judgment is with the LORD, and your reward with your GOD. It is an usuall and laudable exercise of your charity, to recommend to the prayers of your congregations the necessities and straights of your private neighbours: Doe the like for a Church springing out of your owne bowels. Wee conceive much hope that this remembrance of us, if it be frequent and fervent, will bee a most prosperous gale in our sailes, and prouide such a passage and welcome for us, from the GOD of the whole earth, as both we which shall finde it, and yourselves, with the rest of our friends, who shall heare of it, shall be much inlarged to bring in such daily returnes of thanksgivings, as the specialties of his Providence and Goodnes may justly challenge at all our hands. You are not ignorant, that the Spirit of GOD stirred up the Apostle *Paul* to make continuall mention of the Church of Philippi (which was a Colonie of Rome) let the same Spirit, we beseech you, put you in mind, that are the Lord's Remembrancers, to pray for us without ceasing (who are a weake Colony from yourselves) making continuall request for us to GOD in all your prayers.

WHAT we intreat of you that are the ministers of God, that we crave at the hands of all the rest of our Brethren, that they would at no time forget us in their private solicitations at the throne of Grace.

IF any there be, who through want of cleare intelligence of our course, or tendernesses of affection towards us, cannot conceive so well of our way as we could desire, we would intreat such not to despise us, nor to desert us in their prayers and affections, but to consider rather, that they are so much the more bound to expresse the bowels of their compassion towards us, remembring alwaies that both Nature and Grace, doth binde us to relieve and rescue with our utmost and speediest power, such as are deare unto us, when wee conceive them to be running uncomfortable hazards.

WHAT goodnes you shall extend to us in this or any other Christian kindnesse, wee your Brethren in CHRIST JESUS shall labour to repay in what dutie wee are or shall be able to performe, promising, so farre as GOD shall enable us, to give him no rest on your behalfes, wishing our heads and hearts may be as fountains of tears for your everlasting welfare, when wee shall be in our poore Cottages in the wildernesse, over-shadowed with the spirit of supplication, through the manifold necessities and tribulations which may not altogether unexpectedly, nor, we hope, unprofitably befall us. And so commending you to the Grace of GOD in CHRIST, wee shall ever rest,

Your assured Friends and Brethren,

From *Yarmouth*, aboord
the *Arabella, April* 7, 1630.

Io: Winthrope, Gov.	*Rich: Saltonstall.*
Charles Fines,	*Isaac Johnson.*
	Tho: Dudley.
George Phillips.	*William Coddington.*
&c.	&c.

NUMBER II.

Certain Proposals made by Lord Say, Lord Brooke, and other Persons of quality, as conditions of their removing to New-England, with the answers thereto.

DEMAND I. THAT the common-wealth should consist of two distinct ranks of men, whereof the one should be for them and their heirs, gentlemen of the country, the other for them and their heirs, freeholders.

ANSWER. Two distinct ranks we willingly acknowledge, from the light of nature and scripture; the one of them called Princes, or Nobles, or Elders (amongst whom gentlemen have their place) the other the people. Hereditary dignity or honours we willingly allow to the former, unless by the scandalous and base conversation of any of them, they become degenerate. Hereditary liberty, or estate of freemen, we willingly allow to the other, unless they also, by some unworthy and slavish carriage, do disfranchize themselves.

DEM. 2. That in these gentlemen and freeholders, assembled together, the chief power of the common-wealth shall be placed, both for making and repealing laws.

ANS. So it is with us.

DEM. 3. That each of these two ranks should, in all public assemblies, have a negative voice, so as without a mutual consent nothing should be established.

ANS. So it is agreed among us.

DEM. 4. That the first rank, consisting of gentlemen, should have power, for them and their heirs, to come to the parliaments or public assemblies, and there to give their free votes personally; the second rank of freeholders should have the same power for them and their heirs of meeting and voting, but by their deputies.

ANS. Thus far this demand is practised among us. The freemen meet and vote by their deputies; the other rank give their votes personally, only with this difference, there be no more of the gentlemen that give their votes personally, but such as are chosen to places of office, either governors, deputy governors, councellors, or assistants. All gentlemen in England have not that honour to meet and vote personally in Parliament, much less all their heirs. But of this more fully, in an answer to the ninth and tenth demand.

DEM. 5. That for facilitating and dispatch of business, and other reasons, the gentlemen and freeholders should sit and hold their meetings in two distinct houses.

ANS. We willingly approve the motion, only as yet it is not so practised among us, but in time, the variety and discrepancy of sundry occurrences will put them upon a necessity of sitting apart.

DEM. 6. That there shall be set times for these meetings, annually or half yearly, or as shall be thought fit by common consent, which meetings should have a set time for their continuance, but should be adjourned or broken off at the discretion of both houses.

ANS. Public meetings, in general courts, are by charter appointed to be quarterly, which, in this infancy of the colony, wherein many things frequently occur which need settling, hath been of good use, but when things are more fully settled in due order, it is likely that yearly or half yearly meetings will be sufficient. For the continuance or breaking up of these courts, nothing is done but with the joint consent of both branches.

DEM. 7. That it shall be in the power of this parliament, thus constituted and assembled, to call the governor and all publick officers to account, to create new officers, and to determine them already set up: and, the better to stop the way to insolence and ambition, it may be ordered that all offices and fees of office shall, every parliament, determine, unless they be new confirmed the last day of every session.

ANS. This power to call governors and all officers to account, and to create new and determine the old, is settled already in the general court or parliament, only it is not put forth but once in the year, viz. at the great and general court in May, when the governor is chosen.

DEM. 8. That the governor shall ever be chosen out of the rank of gentlemen.

ANS. We never practice otherwise, chusing the governor either out of the assistants, which is our ordinary course, or out of approved known gentlemen, as this year * Mr. Vane.

DEM. 9. That, for the present, the Right Honorable the Lord Viscount Say and Seale, the Lord Brooke, who have already been at great disbursements for the public works in New-England, and such other gentlemen of approved sincerity and worth, as they, before their personal remove, shall take into their number, should be admitted for them and their heirs, gentlemen of the country. But, for the future, none shall be admitted into this rank but by the consent of both houses.

ANS. The great disbursements of these noble personages and worthy gentlemen we thankfully acknowledge, because the safety and presence of our brethren at Connecticut is no small blessing and comfort to us. But, though that charge had never been disbursed, the worth of the honorable persons named is so well known to all, and our need of such supports and guides is so sensible to ourselves, that we do not doubt the country would

* 1636.

thankfully accept it, as a singular favor from God and from them, if he should bow their hearts to come into this wilderness and help us. As for accepting them and their heirs into the number of gentlemen of the country, the custom of this country is, and readily would be, to receive and acknowledge, not only all such eminent persons as themselves and the gentlemen they speak of, but others of meaner estate, so be it is of some eminency, to be for them and their heirs, gentlemen of the country. Only, thus standeth our case. Though we receive them with honor and allow them pre-eminence and accommodations according to their condition, yet we do not, ordinarily, call them forth to the power of election, or administration of magistracy, until they be received as members into some of our churches, a privilege, which we doubt not religious gentlemen will willingly desire (as David did in Psal. xxvii. 4.) and christian churches will as readily impart to such desirable persons. Hereditary honors both nature and scripture doth acknowledge (Eccles. xix. 17.) but hereditary authority and power standeth only by the civil laws of some commonwealths, and yet, even amongst them, the authority and power of the father is no where communicated, together with his honors, unto all his posterity. Where God blesseth any branch of any noble or generous family, with a spirit and gifts fit for government, it would be a taking of God's name in vain to put such a talent under a bushel, and a sin against the honor of magistracy to neglect such in our public elections. But if God should not delight to furnish some of their posterity with gifts fit for magistracy, we should expose them rather to reproach and prejudice, and the commonwealth with them, than exalt them to honor, if we should call them forth, when God doth not, to public authority.

DEM. 10. That the rank of freeholders shall be made up of such, as shall have so much personal estate there, as shall be thought fit for men of that condition, and have contributed, some fit proportion, to the public charge of the country, either by their disbursements or labors.

ANS. We must confess our ordinary practice to be otherwise. For, excepting the old planters, i.e. Mr. Humphry, who himself was admitted an assistant at London, and all of them freemen, before the churches here were established, none are admitted freemen of this commonwealth but such as are first admitted members of some church or other in this country, and, of such, none are excluded from the liberty of freemen. And out of such only, I mean the more eminent sort of such, it is that our magistrates are chosen. Both which points we should willingly persuade our people to change, if we could make it appear to them, that such a change might be made according to God; for, to give you a true account of the grounds of our proceedings herein, it seemeth to them, and also to us, to be a divine ordinance (and moral) that none should be appointed and chosen by the people of God, magistrates over them, but men fearing God (Ex. xviii. 21.) chosen out of their brethren (Deut. xvii. 15.) saints (1 Cor. vi. 1.) Yea, the apostle maketh it a shame to the church, if it be not able to afford wise men from out of themselves, which shall be able to judge all civil matters between their brethren (ver. 5.) And Solomon maketh it the joy of a commonwealth, when the righteous are in authority, and the calamity thereof, when the wicked bear rule. Prov. xxix. 2.

OBJ. If it be said, there may be many carnal men whom God hath invested with sundry eminent gifts of wisdom, courage, justice, fit for government.

ANS. Such may be fit to be consulted with and employed by governors, according to the quality and use of their gifts and parts, but yet are men not fit to be trusted with place of standing power or settled authority. Ahitophel's wisdom may be fit to be heard (as an oracle of God) but not fit to be trusted with power of settled magistracy, lest he at last call for 12000 men to lead them forth against David, 2 Sam. xvii. 1, 2, 3. The best gifts and parts, under a covenant of works (under which all carnal men and hypocrites be) will at length turn aside by crooked ways, to depart from God, and, finally, to fight against God, and are therefore, herein, opposed to good men and upright in heart, Psal. cxxv. 4, 5.

OBJ. If it be said again, that then the church estate could not be compatible with any commonwealth under heaven.

ANS. It is one thing for the church or members of the church, loyally to submit unto any form of government, when it is above their calling to reform it, another thing to chuse a form of government and governors discrepant from the rule. Now, if it be a divine truth, that none are to be trusted with public permanent authority but godly men, who are fit materials for church fellowship, then from the same grounds it will appear, that none are so fit to be trusted with the liberties of the commonwealth as church members. For, the liberties of the freemen of this commonwealth are such, as require men of faithful integrity to God and the state, to preserve the same. Their liberties, among others, are chiefly these. 1. To chuse all magistrates, and to call them to account at their general courts. 2. To chuse such burgesses, every general court, as with the magistrates shall make or repeal all laws. Now both these liberties are such, as carry along much power with them, either to establish or subvert the commonwealth, and therewith the church, which power, if it be committed to men not according to their godliness, which maketh them fit for church fellowship, but according to their wealth, which, as such, makes them no better than worldly men, then, in case worldly men should prove the major part, as soon they might do, they would as readily set over us magistrates like themselves, such as might hate us according to the curse, Levit. xxvi. 17. and turn the edge of all authority and laws against the church and the members thereof, the maintenance of whose peace is the chief end which God aimed at in the institution of Magistracy. 1 Tim. ii. 1. 2.

NUMBER III.

Copy of a Letter from Mr. COTTON to Lord SAY and
   SEAL in the Year 1636.

Right honourable,

WHAT your Lordship writeth of Dr. Twisse his works *de scientiâ
   mediâ*, and of the sabbath, it did refresh me to reade, that his
labors of such arguments were like to come to light; and it would refresh
me much more to see them here: though (for my owne particular) till I gett
some release from some constant labors here (which the church is desirous
to procure) I can get litle, or noe oppertunity to reade any thing, or attend
to any thing, but the dayly occurrences which presse in upon me continually, much beyond my strength either of body or minde. Your Lordships
advertisement touching the civill state of this colony, as they doe breath
forth your singular wisdome, and faithfulness, and tender care of the
peace, so wee have noe reason to misinterprite, or undervalue your Lordships eyther directions, or intentions therein. I know noe man under
heaven (I speake in Gods feare without flattery) whose counsell I should
rather depend upon, for the wise administration of a civill state according
to God, than upon your Lordship, and such confidence have I (not in you)
but in the Lords presence in Christ with you, that I should never feare to
betrust a greater commonwealth than this (as much as in us lyeth) under
such a *perpetuâ dictaturâ* as your Lordship should prescribe. For I nothing
doubt, but that eyther your Lordship would prescribe all things according
to the rule, or be willing to examine againe, and againe, all things according to it. I am very apt to believe, what Mr. Perkins hath, in one of his
prefatory pages to his golden chaine, that the word, and scriptures of God
doe conteyne a short *upoluposis*, or platforme, not onely of theology, but
also of other sacred sciences, (as he calleth them) attendants, and hand-
maids thereunto, which he maketh ethicks, eoconomicks, politicks, church-
government, prophecy, academy. It is very suitable to Gods all-sufficient
wisdome, and to the fulnes and perfection of Holy Scriptures, not only to
prescribe perfect rules for the right ordering of a private mans soule to
everlasting blessednes with himselfe, but also for the right ordering of a
mans family, yea, of the commonwealth too, so farre as both of them are
subordinate to spiritual ends, and yet avoide both the churches usurpation upon civill jurisdictions, *in ordine ad spiritualia*, and the commonwealths invasion upon ecclesiasticall administrations, *in ordine* to civill
peace, and conformity to the civill state. Gods institutions (such as the
government of church and of commonwealth be) may be close and com-

pact, and co-ordinate one to another, and yet not confounded. God hath so framed the state of church government and ordinances, that they may be compatible to any common-wealth, though never so much disordered in his frame. But yet when a commonwealth hath liberty to mould his owne frame (*scripturæ plenitudinem adoro*) I conceyve the scripture hath given full direction for the right ordering of the same, and that, in such sort as may best mainteyne the *euexia* of the church. Mr. Hooker doth often quote a saying out of Mr. Cartwright (though I have not read it in him) that noe man fashioneth his house to his hangings, but his hangings to his house. It is better that the commonwealth be fashioned to the setting forth of Gods house, which is his church: than to accommodate the church frame to the civill state. Democracy, I do not conceyve that ever God did ordeyne as a fitt government eyther for church or commonwealth. If the people be governors, who shall be governed? As for monarchy, and aristocracy, they are both of them clearly approoved, and directed in scripture, yet so as referreth the soveraigntie to himselfe, and setteth up Theocracy in both, as the best forme of government in the commonwealth, as well as in the church.

The law, which your Lordship instanceth in [that none shall be chosen to magistracy among us but a church member] [1] was made and enacted before I came into the country; but I have hitherto wanted sufficient light to plead against it. 1st. The rule that directeth the choice of supreame governors, is of like æquitie and weight in all magistrates, that one of their brethren (not a stranger) should be set over them, Deut. 17. 15. and Jethroes counsell to Moses was approved of God, that the judges, and officers to be set over the people, should be men fearing God, Exod. 18. 21. and Solomon maketh it the joy of a commonwealth, when the righteous are in authority, and their mourning when the wicked rule, Prov. 29. 21. Jab 34. 30. Your Lordship's feare, that this will bring in papal excommunication, is iust, and pious: but let your Lordship be pleased againe to consider whether the consequence be necessary. *Turpius ejicitur quam non admittitur:* non-membership may be a just cause of non-admission to the place of magistracy, but yet, ejection out of his membership will not be a just cause of ejecting him out of his magistracy. A godly woman, being to make choice of an husband, may justly refuse a man that is eyther cast out of church fellowship, or is not yet receyved into it, but yet, when shee is once given to him, shee may not reject him then, for such defect. Mr. Humfrey was chosen for an assistant (as I heare) before the colony came over hither: and, though he be not as yet ioyned into church fellowship (by reason of the unsetlednes of the congregation where he liveth) yet the commonwealth doe still continue his magistracy to him, as knowing he waiteth for oppertunity of enioying church fellowship shortly.

[1] These brackets are Cotton's or Hutchinson's; they do not indicate additional material appearing for the first time in the present edition.

When your Lordship doubteth, that this corse will draw all things under the determination of the church, *in ordine ad spiritualia* (seeing the church is to determine who shall be members, and none but a member may have to doe in the government of a commonwealth) be pleased (I pray you) to conceyve, that magistrates are neyther chosen to office in the church, nor doe governe by directions from the church, but by civill lawes, and those enacted in generall corts, and executed in corts of iustice, by the governors and assistants. In all which, the church (as the church) hath nothing to doe: onely, it prepareth fitt instruments both to rule, and to choose rulers, which is no ambition in the church, nor dishonor to the commonwealth, the apostle, on the contrary, thought it a great dishonor and reproach to the church of Christ, if it were not able to yield able judges to heare and determine all causes amongst their brethren, 1 Cor. 6. 1. to 5. which place alone seemeth to me fully to decide this question: for it plainely holdeth forth this argument: It is a shame to the church to want able judges of civill matters (as v. 5.) and an audacious act in any church member voluntarily to go for judgment, otherwhere than before the saints (as v. 1.) then it will be noe arrogance nor folly in church members, nor prejudice to the commonwealth, if voluntarily they never choose any civill judges, but from amongst the saints, such as church members are called to be. But the former is cleare: and how then can the latter be avoyded. If this therefore be (as your Lordship rightly conceyveth one of the maine objections if not the onely one) which hindereth this commonwealth from the entertainment of the propositions of those worthy gentlemen, wee intreate them, in the name of the Lord Jesus, to consider, in meeknes of wisdome, it is not any conceite or will of ours, but the holy counsell and will of the Lord Jesus (whom they seeke to serve as well as wee) that overruleth us in this case: and we trust will overrule them also, that the Lord onely may be exalted amongst all his servants. What pittie and griefe were it, that the observance of the will of Christ should hinder good things from us!

But your Lordship doubteth, that if such a rule were necessary, then the church estate and the best ordered commonwealth in the world were not compatible. But let not our Lordship so conceyve. For, the church submitteth itselfe to all the lawes and ordinances of men, in what commonwealth soever they come to dwell. But it is one thing, to submit unto what they have noe calling to reforme: another thing, voluntarily to ordeyne a forme of government, which to the best discerning of many of us (for I speake not of myselfe) is expressly contrary to rule. Nor neede your Lordship feare (which yet I speake with submission to your Lordships better judgment) that this corse will lay such a foundation, as nothing but a mere democracy can be built upon it. Bodine confesseth, that though it be *status popularis*, where a people choose their owne governors; yet the government is not a democracy, if it be administred, not by the people, but by the governors, whether one (for then it is a monarchy, though elective) or by many, for then (as you know) it is aristocracy. In which

respect it is, that church government is iustly denyed (even by Mr. Robinson) to be democratical, though the people choose their owne officers and
rulers.

Nor neede wee feare, that this course will, in time, cast the commonwealth into distractions, and popular confusions. For (under correction)
these three things doe not undermine, but doe mutually and strongly
mainteyne one another (even those three which wee principally aime at)
authority in magistrates, liberty in people, purity in the church. Purity,
preserved in the church, will preserve well ordered liberty in the people,
and both of them establish well-ballanced authority in the magistrates.
God is the author of all these three, and neyther is himselfe the God of
confusion, nor are his wayes the wayes of confusion, but of peace.

What our brethren (magistrates or ministers, or leading freeholders)
will answer to the rest of the propositions, I shall better understand before
the gentlemans returne from Connecticutt, who brought them over. Mean
while two of the principall of them, the generall cort hath already con-
descended unto. 1. In establishing a standing councell, who, during their
lives, should assist the governor in managing the chiefest affayres of this
little state. They have chosen, for the present, onely two (Mr. Winthrope
and Mr. Dudley) not willing to choose more, till they see what further
better choyse the Lord will send over to them, that so they may keep an
open doore, for such desireable gentlemen as your Lordship mentioneth.
2. They have graunted the governor and assistants a negative voyce, and
reserved to the freemen the like liberty also. Touching other things, I
hope to give your Lordship further account, when the gentleman re-
turneth.

He being now returned, I have delivered to him an answer to the rest
of your demands,* according to the mindes of such leading men amongst
us, as I thought meete to consult withall, concealing your name from any,
except 2 or 3, who alike doe concurr in a joynt desire of yeilding to any
such propositions, as your Lordship demandeth, so farre as with allowance
from the word they may, beyond which I know your Lordship would not
require any thing

Now the Lord Jesus Christ (the prince of peace) keepe and bless your
Lordship, and dispose of all your times and talents to his best advantage:
and let the covenant of his grace and peace rest upon your honourable
family and posterity throughout all generations.

Thus, humbly craving pardon for my boldnesse and length, I take leave
and rest,

Your Honours to serve in Christ Jesus,

J. C.

* Appendix No II.

NUMBER IV.

Copy of a commission for regulating Plantations.

CHARLES, by the grace of God, of England, Scotland, France and Ireland, King, defender of the faith, &c.

To the right reverend father in God, our right trusty and well beloved
counsellour, William, by the providence of God, Archbishop of Canterbury, primate and metropolitan of all England; to our right trusty and
well beloved counsellour, Thomas Lord Coventry, Lord Keeper of our
great seal of England; to our right reverend father in God, our right
trusty and well beloved counsellour, Richard, by the providence of
God, Archbishop of York, primate and metropolitan of England; to
our right trusty and well beloved cousin and counsellour, Richard
Earle of Portland, and high treasurer of England; Henry Earle of
Manchester, keeper of our privy seal; Thomas Earle of Arundell and
Surrey, Earle Marshall of England; Edward Earle of Dorset, chamberlaine to our most dear consort the Queen; and to our trusty and well
beloved counsellour Francis Lord Cottington, chamberlaine and under
treasurer of our Exchequer; Thomas Edmunds, Knt. treasurer of our
houshold, John Cook, Knt. one of our principall secretaries of state;
and Francis Windebank, another of our principall secretaries of state,
GREETING.

WHEREAS divers of the subjects of us and of our late dear father
King James, of famous memory, late, of England, King, by
vertue of our royall authority, granted not only to enlarge the territories
of our empire, but more especially to propagate the gospel of our Lord
Jesus Christ, having, with their exceeding industry and charge, deduced
great numbers of the people of England into several colonies, in severall
places of the world, either altogether desert and unpeopled, or enjoyed
by salvage and barbarous nations, voyd of all manner of knowledge of
Almighty God, wee, being graciously pleased to provide for the ease and
tranquility of the said subjects, and reposeing assured confidence in your
fidelity, wisdom, justice and providence, do constitute you, our said archbishop of Canterbury, &c. or any five or more of you, our councellours,
and to you, or to any five or more of you, do commit and give power of
protection and government, as well over the said English colonies already
planted, as over all such other colonies, which by any of our people of
England, hereafter, shall be deduced into any other like parts whatsoever,

and power to make laws, ordinances and constitutions, concerning either the state public of the said colonies, or utility of private persons and their lands, goods, debts and succession within the precincts of the same, and for ordering and directing of them, in their demeanours towards forreigne princes and their people, and likewise towards us and our subjects, as well within any forreigne parts whatsoever beyond the seas, as during their voyages, or upon the seas, to and from the same.

AND for relief and support of the Clergy, and the rule and cure of the soules of our people living in those parts, and for consigning of convenient maintenance unto them by tythes, oblations and other profits accrewing, according to your good discretion, with the advice of two or three of our bishops, whom you shall think fitt to call unto your consultations, touching the distribution of such maintenance unto the clergy, and all other matters ecclesiasticall, and to inflict punishment on all offenders or violaters of constitutions and ordinances, either by imprisonments or other restraints, or by loss of life or members, according as the quality of the offence shall require, with power also (our royall assent being first had and obtained) to remove all governors and presidents of the said colonies (upon just cause appearing) from their several places, and to appoint others in their stead, and also to require and take account of them touching their office and government, and whom you shall find delinquents, you shall punish, either by depriving them of their severall places and provinces over which they are appointed, or by pecuniary mulcts and penalties, according to the qualities of the offences; and power also to ordain temporal judges and civill magistrates to determine of civill causes, with such powers, in such a forme, as to you or any five or more of you shall seem expedient; and also to ordain judges, magistrates and officers for and concerning courts ecclesiasticall, with such power and such a forme, as to you or any five or more of you, with the advice of the bishops suffragan to the archbishop of Canterbury for the time being, shall be held meet; and power to constitute and ordaine tribunals and courts of justice, both ecclesiasticall and civill, with such power and in them forme of judicature, and manner of process and appeals from and to the said courts, in all cases and matters as well criminal as civill, both personall, reall and mixt, and touching the determination pertaining to any courts of justice, ecclesiasticall and civill, to judge thereof and determine; provided nevertheless, the said laws, ordinances and constitutions shall not be put in execution, untill our royall assent, expressed under our signe at least, be first thereunto had and obtained, the which our royall assent so obtained, together with the said laws, ordinances and constitutions, being published and proclaimed in the provinces in which they are to be executed, the said laws, ordinances and constitutions, from thenceforth, shall be in force in law; and we do hereby will and command all persons whom it shall concern, inviolably to keep and observe the same. Notwithstanding, it may and shall be lawful for you, and every five and more of you, with our royal assent, the said laws, ordinances and constitutions, (tho' so published and proclaimed as aforesaid) to alter, revoke and appeal, and other new laws, &c. in forme aforesaid, from time to time, to make and publish as aforesaid, and to new and growing evills and perills to apply new remedies, in such manner, and so often as unto you shall appear to be necessary and expedient.

KNOW YEE also, that wee do constitute you the said Archbishop of Canterbury, &c. and every five or more of you, our committees, according to your good discretions, to hear and determine all complaints, at the entrance and suit of the party grieved, whether it be against the whole colonies themselves or any governor or officer of the same, or whether complaint touching wrongs exhibited and depending, either between the whole bodies of the colonies, or any private member thereof, and to summon the persons before you, and they or their procurators or agents being on both sides heard, finally to determine thereof, according to justice. GIVING moreover and granting to you and any five or more of you, that if it shall appear, than any officer or governor of the said colonies, shall injuriously intend and usurp upon the authority, power and possessions of any other, or shall unjustly wrong one another, or shall not suppress all rebells to us, or such as shall not obey our commands, that then it shall be lawful (upon advice with ourself first had) for the causes aforesaid, or upon any other just reason, to remand and cause the offender to returne into England, or into any other place, according as in your good discretions you shall think just and necessary.

AND wee do furthermore give unto you, or any five or more of you, letters patents and other writeings whatsoever, of us or of our royall predecessors granted, for or concerning the planting of any colonies, in any countries, provinces, islands or territories whatsoever, beyond the seas, and if, upon view thereof, the same shall appear to you, or any five or more of you, to have been surreptitiously and unduly obtained, or that any privileges or liberties therein granted, be hurtful to us, our crown or prerogative royall, or to any foreign princes, to cause the same, according to the laws and customs of our realm of England, to be revoked, and to do all other thing which shall be necessary, for the wholesome government and protection of the said colonies and our people therein abideing.

WHEREFORE, wee command you, that you diligently intend the premises, at such times and places as yourselves, for that purpose shall appoint, charging also and firmely commanding all presidents of provinces within the aforesaid colonies, now planted or to be planted, and all and every the said colonies themselves, and all other persons whom it doth concerne, that they attend you in the premises, and be obedient to your commands touching the same, so often as they shall be thereunto commanded, at their peril. IN WITNESS whereof, wee caused these our letters to be made patent. Witness ourself at Westminster, 28 day of April, in the tenth year of our reign.

NUMBER V.

Copy of the General Courts Addresse, the 6th of
  September 1638.

To the Right Honourable the Lords Commissioners for foreigne Plantations.

The humble Petition of the Inhabitants of the Massachusets in New-
  England, of the Generall Court there assembled, the 6th day of Sep-
  tember, in the 14th yeare of the Reigne of our Soveraigne Lord King
  CHARLES.

WHEREAS it hath pleased your Lordships, by order of the 4th of
April last, to require our patent to be sent unto you, wee do
hereby humbly and sincerely professe, that wee are ready to yield all due
obedience to our soueraigne Lord the King's majesty, and to your Lordships under him, and in this minde wee left our native countrie, and according thereunto, hath been our practice ever since, so as wee are much
grieved, that your Lordships should call in our patent, there being no
cause knowne to us, nor any delinquency or fault of ours expressed in the
order sent to us for that purpose, our government being according to his
Majestyes grant, and wee not answerable for any defects in other plantations, &c.

THIS is that which his Majesties subjects here doe believe and professe,
and thereupon wee are all humble suitors to your Lordships, that you will
be pleased to take into further consideration our condition, and to affoord
us the liberty of subjects, that we may know what is layd to our charge;
and have leaive and time to answer for ourselves before we be condemned
as a people unworthy of his Majesties favour or protection; as for the quo
warranto mentioned in the said order, wee doe assure your Lordships wee
were never called to answer to it, and if wee had, wee doubt not but wee
have a sufficient plea to put in.

IT is not unknowne to your Lordships, that we came into these remote
parts with his Majesties licence and encouragement, under his great seale
of England, and in the confidence wee had of that assurance, wee have
transported our families and estates, and here have wee built and planted,
to the great enlargement and securing of his Majesties dominions in these
parts, so as if our patent should now be taken from us, we shall be looked
on as runnigadoes and outlawed, and shall be enforced, either to remove

to some other place, or to returne into our native country againe; either of which will put us to unsupportable extremities, and these evils (among others) will necessarily follow. (1.) Many thousand souls will be exposed to ruine, being layd open to the injuries of all men. (2.) If wee be forced to desert this place, the rest of the plantations (being too weake to subsist alone) will, for the most part, dissolve and goe with us, and then will this whole country fall into the hands of the French or Dutch, who would speedily imbrace such an oppertunity. (3.) If we should loose all our labour and costs, and be deprived of those liberties which his Majesty hath granted us, and nothing layd to our charge, nor any fayling to be found in us in point of allegiance (which all our countrymen doe take notice of and will justify our faithfulness in this behalfe) it will discourage all men heereafter from the like undertakings upon confidence of his Majestyes royal grant. Lastly, if our patent be taken from us (whereby wee suppose wee may clayme interest in his Majestyes favour and protection) the common people here will conseive that his Majesty hath cast them off, and that, heereby, they are freed from their allegiance and subjection, and, thereupon, will be ready to confederate themselves under a new government, for their necessary safety and subsistance, which will be of dangerous example to other plantations, and perillous to ourselves of incurring his Majestyes displeasure, which wee would by all means avoyd.

Upon these considerations wee are bold to renew our humble supplications to your Lordships, that wee may be suffered to live here in this wilderness, and that this poore plantation, which hath found more favour from God than many others, may not finde lesse favour from your Lordships; that our liberties should be restreyned, when others are enlarged, that the doore should be kept shutt unto us, while it stands open to all other plantations, that men of ability should be debarred from us, while they give incouragement to other colonies.

Wee dare not question your Lordships proceedings; we only desire to open our griefes where the remedy is to be expected: If in any thing we have offended his Majesty and your Lordships, wee humbly prostrate ourselves at the footstool of supreame authority; let us be made the object of his Majestyes clemency, and not cut off, in our first appeal, from all hope of favour. Thus, with our earnest prayers to the King of Kings for long life and prospereety to his sacred Majesty and his royall family, and for all honour and welfare to your Lordships, wee humbly take leave.

This is a true copie compared with the original on file, as attested.

EDWARD RAWSON, Secretary.

NUMBER VI.

The Theses of the first Class of Graduates at Harvard College, in 1642.*

Spectatissimis Pietate, et Illustrissimis Eximia Virtute Viris,
D. *Iohanni Winthropo*, inclytæ Massachusetti Coloniæ
Gubernatori, D. *Johanni Endicotto*, Vice-
Gubernatori, D. *Thom. Dudleo*, D. *Rich.*
Bellinghamo, D. *Iohan. Humphrydo*,
D. *Israel. Stoughtono.*
Nec non Reverendis pientissimisque viris *Ioanni Cottono*,
Ioan. Wilsono, Ioan. Davenport, Tho. Weldo, Hugoni
Petro, Tho. Shepardo, Collegij *Harvardensis*,
nov. *Cantabr.* inspectoribus fidelissimis,
cæterisque Magistratibus, & Ecclesia-
rum ejusdem Coloniæ Presbyteris
vigilantissimis.
Has Theses Philologicas, & Philosophicas, quas, Deo duce,
Præside *Henrico Dunstero*, palam provirili propugnare
conabuntur (honoris & observantiæ grantia) dicant
consecrantque in artibus liberalibus
initiati Adolescentes.

Benjamin Woodbrigius	*Henricus Saltonstall*	*Nathaniel Brusterus*
Georgius Downingus	*Iohannes Bulkleius*	*Samuel Bellinghamus*
Gulielmus Hubbardus	*Ioannes Wilsonus*	*Tobias Bernardus.*

* From the year 1642 to the year 1764, inclusive, 2124 persons have received degrees at Harvard College, about 40 of which were honorary degrees, the remainder were conferred upon such as had been admitted students there. In July last, 1091 of the persons graduated remained alive, the eldest of whom received his degree of Bachelor of Arts in 1698. The salary of the President, from the first foundation, has been, annually, granted by the government of the colony and province, besides annual grants which have been made, for many years past, to the several professors and instructors, where the foundations have been insufficient. The charge of the several buildings also, except the first house built principally by the legacy of Mr. Harvard, Stoughton-Hall, by lieutenant governor Stoughton, and the Chapel by Mrs. Holden, has always been born by the government. The library, consisting of five or six thousand volumes, many of them by the most celebrated authors, grew out of donations from charitable benefactors, unless any small purchases have been made out of the college stock. This valuable library, together with the apparatus, and the whole of the college, in which they were placed, were consumed by fire, in January 1764. Very generous presents have been since made, towards the library, but, as yet, far short of procuring one, equal to the former. Of the many benefactors to the college, the family of Hollis stands the first upon the list.

Theses Philologicas.

GRAMMATICAS.

L INGUARUM Scientia est utilissima.
Literæ non exprimunt quantum vocis organa efferunt.
3. Hæbræa est Linguarum Mater.
4. Consonantes & vocales Hæbreorum sunt coætaneæ.
5. Punctationes chatephatæ syllabam proprie not efficiunt.
6. Linguarum Græca est copiosissima.
7. Lingua Græca est ad accentus pronuncianda.
8. Lingua Latina est eloquentissima.

RHETORICAS.

R HETORICA specie differt a Logica.
In Elocutione perspicuitati cedit ornatus, ornatui copia.
3. Actio primas tenet in pronunciatione.
4. Oratoris est celare Artem.

LOGICAS.

U NIVERSALIA non sunt extra intellectum.
Omnia Argumenta non sunt relata.
3. Causa *sine qua non* est peculiaris causa a quatuor reliquis generalibus.
4. Causa et effectus sunt simul tempore.
5. Dissentanea sunt æque nota.
6. Contrarietas est tantum inter duo.
7. Sublato relato tollitur correlatum.
8. Genus perfectum æqualiter communicatur speciebus.
9. Testimonium valet quantum testis.
10. Elenchorum doctrina in Logica non est necessaria.
11. Axioma contingens est, quod ita verum est, ut aliquando falsum esse possit.
12. Præcepta Artium debent esse *kata pantos, kath' auto, kath' olou proton.*

Mr. Thomas Hollis of London, who died in 1731, founded two professorships, one of divinity and the other of mathematicks and natural philosophy. He gave an apparatus for experimental philosophy, and made great and frequent additions to the library. Several other branches of the family have given bountifully to the college, particularly the present Mr. Hollis of Gray's Inn, who, besides his donations to the former library, has given largely towards the new library now collecting. The general court, having caused a new college to be built in the year 1763, which cost between four and five thousand pounds sterling, it has taken the name of Hollis-Hall, in grateful remembrance of the benefactions of this worthy family. I suppose the donation of Thomas Hancock, Esq; late of Boston deceased, who gave one thousand pounds sterling towards founding a professorship for the oriental languages, is the next in value. His executor and residuary legatee, Mr. John Hancock, being informed of his testator's intention to have given five hundred pounds sterling more, towards the library, generously gave the same sum for the same purpose.

Theses Philosophicas.

ETHICAS.

PHILOSOPHIA practica est eruditionis meta.
  Actio virtutis habitum antecellit.
3. Voluntas est virtutis moralis subjectum.
4. Voluntas est formaliter libera.
5. Prudentia virtutum difficillima.
6. Prudentia est virtus intellectualis & moralis
7. Justitia mater omnium virtutum.
8. Mors potius subeunda quam aliquid culpæ perpetrandum.
9. Non injuste agit nisi qui libens agit.
10. Mentiri potest qui verum dicit.
11. Juveni modestia summum ornamentum.

PHYSICAS.

CORPUS naturale mobile est subjectum Physicæ.
  Materia secunda non potest existere sine forma.
3. Forma est accidens.
4. Unius rei non est nisi unica forma constitutiva.
5. Forma est principium individuationis.
6. Privatio non est principium internum.
7. Ex meris accidentibus non fit substantia.
8. Quicquid movetur ab alio movetur.
9. In omni motu movens simul est cum mobili.
10. Cœlum non movetur ab intelligentijs.
11. Non dantur orbes in cœlo.
12. Quodlibet Elementum habet unam ex primis qualitatibus sibi maxime propriam.
13. Putredo in humido fit a calore externo.
14. Anima non fit ex traduce.
15. Vehemens sensibile destruit sensum.

METAPHISICAS.

OMNE ens est bonum.
  Omne creatum est concretum.
3. Quicquid æternum idem & immensum.
4. Bonum Metaphysicum non suscipit gradus.

NUMBER VII.

Copy of the determination of arbitrators for settling the line between New-Haven and the Dutch, in 1650.

ARTICLES of agreement made and concluded at Hartford, upon Connecticut, Sept. 19, 1650, betwixt the delegates of the honored commissioners of the united Englishe colonies, and the delegates of Peter Stuyvesant, governor generall of Newe-Netherlands.

Concerning the bounds and lymits betwixt the Englishe united Collonies and the Dutch province of New-Netherlands, wee agree and determine as followeth.

THAT upon Long-Island, a Line, run from the westermost part of Oyster-bay, and so in a streight and direct line to the sea, shall be the bounds betweene the Englishe and Dutch there; the easterly part to belonge to the English, the westermost part to the Dutch.

2. THE bounds, upon the maine, to begin upon the west side of Greenwich bay, being about four miles from Stamford, and so to run a westerly line 20 miles up into the country, and after, as it shall be agreed by the two governments of the Dutch and Newe-Haven, provided the said line runn not within tenn miles of Hudson's river. And it is agreed, that the Dutch shall not, at any tyme hereafter, build any house or habitation within six miles of the said line, the inhabitants of Greenwich to remain (till further consideration thereof be had) under the government of the Dutch.

3. That the Dutch shall hould and enioy all the lands in Hartford, that they are actually in possession off, knowne or sett out by eertaine merkes and boundes, and all the remainder of the said lands, on both sides of Connecticut river, to be and remaine to the English there.

AND it is agreed, that the aforesaid bounds and lymyts, both upon the island and maine, shall be observed and kept inviolable, both by the Englishe of the united collonies and all the Dutch nation, without any encroachment or molestation, until a full determination be agreed upon in Europe, by mutual consent of the two states of England and Holland.

AND in testimony of our joint consent to the several foregoing conditions, wee have hereunto sett our hands this 19th day of 7ber, 1650.

| Symon Bradstreete | Tho: Willet |
| Tho: Prence | Theo: [1] Baxter. |

[1] This should be "Georg" (George), not "Theo:" Baxter. It is given incorrectly in all three editions. See this volume, p. 134; and Ebenezer Hazard, *Historical Collections*, II, 220.

NUMBER VIII.

Copy of a petition to the Parliament in 1651.

To the most honourable the parliament of the commonwealth of England,
the supreme authoritie, Greeting.

THE humble petition of the general court of the Massachusetts-Bay in
New-England.

THERE coming to our handes, not long since, a printed proclamation, prohibiting Trade with Virginea, Barbados, Bermuda and
Antego, of which we were observant (though to the great losse and
prejudice of the whole colonie) about the end thereof we found, that the
parliament had given power to the counsaile of state to place governors
and commissioners (without exception) in all the colonies of the English
in America, wherein we finding ourselves comprehended as wrapped up in
one bundle with all the other colonies; our case being different from all
other English colonies in America for ought we know or have heard: Also
since receiving information by Mr. Winslow our agent, that it is the parliaments pleasure that we should take a new patent from them, and keep
our courts, and issue our warrants in their names, which we have not used
either in the late Kinges time or since, not being able to discerne the need
of such an injunction: These thinges make us doubt and fear what is intended towards us. Let it therefore pleas you, most honourable, we humbly entreat, to take notice, hereby, what were our orders, upon what conditions and with what authority we came hither, and what we have done
since our coming. We were the first moovers and undertakers of soe great
an attempt, being men able enough to live in England with our neighbours, and being helpfull to others, and not needing the help of any for
outward thinges, about three or four and twenty years since, seeing just
cause to feare the persecution of the then bishops and high commission,
for not conforming to the ceremonies then pressed upon the consciences
of those under their power, we thought it our safest course to get to this
outside of the world, out of their view and beyond their reach. Yet before
we resolved upon soe great an undertaking, wherein should be hazarded
not only all our estates but alsoe the lives of ourselves and our posterity,
both in the voyage at sea (wherewith we were unacquainted) and in coming into a wilderness uninhabited (unless in some few places by heathen
barbarous Indians) we thought it necessary to procure a patent from the
late King, who then ruled all, to warrant our removall and prevent future

inconveniencies, and soe did. By which patent, liberty and power was granted to us to live under the government of a governour, magistrates of our owne chusing, and under laws of our owne making (not being repugnant to the lawes of England) according to which patent we have governed ourselves above this twenty-three years, we coming hither at our proper charges, without the help of the state, an acknowledgment of the freedome of our goods from custom, and having expended, first and last, in our transportation, building, fencinge, warre with the Indians, fortifying, subduing the earth in making it fit for culture, divers hundereth of thousand poundes; and have now made the place soe habitable that we are enabled to live in a mean and low condition, and alsoe to furnish other places with corne, beife, pork, mastes, clapboord, pipe staves, fish, beaver, otter, and other commodities, and hoped that our posterity should reape the fruit of our labours, and enjoy the liberties and privileges we had obteined for them, and for which we have payd soe dear and run soe great hazards. And for our carriage and demeanour to the honourable parliament, for these ten years, since the first beginning of your differences with the late King and the warre that after ensuied, we have constantly adheared to you, not withdrawing ourselves in your weakest condition and doubtfullest times, but by our fasting and prayers for your good successe, and our thanksgiving after the same was attained, in dayes of solemnity set apart for that purpose, as alsoe by our sending over useful men (others alsoe going voluntarily from us to help you) who have been of good use and done good acceptable services to the army, declaring to the world heerby, that such was the duty and love we beare unto the parliament, that we were ready to rise and fall with them; for which we have suffered the hatred and threats of other English colonies, now in rebellion against you, as alsoe the losse of divers of our shippes and goods, taken by the King's party that is dead, by others commissioned by the King of Scotts, and by the Portugalls. All which if you shall pleas justly and favourably to consider, we cannot but hope, but that, as you have formerly conferred many favours upon us, soe it shall goe noe worse with us, than it did under the late King; and that the frame of our government shall not be changed, and enstead of governour and magistrates yearly by ourselves chosen, have other imposed upon us against our wills; wherein if our hopes should deceave us (which God forbid) we shall have cause to say we have fallen into hard times, and sit downe and sigh out our too late repentance for our coming hither, and patiently bear what shall be imposed upon us; our adversity in such a case being the greater, because some of us are too old, and all our estates growne too weake (except a very few) to seek out a new corner of the world to inhabit in. But, as we said before, we hope that this most honourable parliament will not cast such as have adheared to you and depended upon you, as we have done, into soe deep despaire, from the fear of which we humbly desire to be speedily freed by a just and gracious answer; which will freshly bind us to pray and use all lawfull endeavours for the blessing of God upon you and the present government.

WE will conclude, most honourable, our humble petition with the heartie acknowledgments of the goodnes of God towards us, who hath put into your hearts graciously to conferre upon us so many undeserved favours and great privileges, from tyme to tyme, in helping on the great work of God here amongst us, in taking off the customes from us, in enlarging your fund of bountie towards us for the propagating of the gospel amongst the natives with us, which work God prospereth beyond expectation in so few years; in doing us that justice in stopping all appeals from hence to you, in sending over many servants to us, in vouchsafeing to have a tender care over us upon all occasions; for these, and for all other manifold encouragements receaved from the most honourable court of parliament, as we are bound to praise and magnify the name of our good God, so we acknowledge it our bounden dutie, not only to be heartilie thankfull to the most honourable court, but ever to pray, that the Lord (if it be his good pleasure) will so establish you the supreame authoritie of that commonwealth, that, all your enemies being subdued, you may rule in peace and prosperitie, to his glorie and your owne comfort here on earth, and everlastinglie raigne with him in glorie hereafter, which are the earnest desires and fervent prayers of

Most honourable,
Your humble servants,
J. E.
T. D.
Ed. R.
In the name and of the court.

NUMBER IX.

Copy of a Letter to OLIVER CROMWELL in 1651, from the General Court of the Massachusets.

To the right honorable his Excellence the Lord General CROMWEEL.

Right Honble.

W EE acknowledge ourselves in all dutie bound, not only to take due notice of that tender care and undeserved respect your excellence hath, upon all occasions, vouchsafed unto the poor despised colonie of the Massachusets in New-England, but also to acknowledge ourselves ever obliged to serve you, and to improve that interest which, through grace, we have obtained in Jehovah, the God of armies, to prosper you and your great and godly undertakings to his glorie and your everlasting comfort.

YOUR readines, right honorable, to doe us good, hath occasioned these lines to be presented to your excellence, to the end that no priuat information may occasion your honor (contrarie to your aymes and ends) to preiudice this colonie, by inviting over many of the inhabitants thereof to be transplanted into Ireland; wherein, although we verilie beleeve that your honor aymes at the glorie of God and the welfare of this people, yet (with fauor) we conceave it will tend to the contrarie, for these reasons following.

FIRST, We did professe, we came into these remote partes of the earth to enioy the liberties of the gospel in their puritie, which, hitherto, we have (through the grace of Christ) had, without restraint, these 23 years and above. So that there is no solid ground for any defect therein, that we know, that should occasion a remoue.

SECONDLIE, God hath blessed the countrey with plentie of food of all kindes, generallie through the land, insomuch that there are many thousands of bushels of graine, and other provisions, of beef, pork, &c. yearly transported to other places. And where there be any poore people through age, or weaknes, or losses by fire or other hand of God upon them or their estates, the churches or towns, or both, doe contribute to their wants. So that povertie cannot, truely, be alleaged to be a ground of remouall.

THIRDLIE, We know not a more healthie place in the whole world, for the general, than this land. Therefore, there can be no ground of remouing for want of health.

FOURTHLIE, We know not any countrey more peaceable and free from warre, for the present, through the mercy of God. What our unthankfullness may bring upon us, the just God onlie knowes; but we desire the Lord so to guide us, that we may not provoke the eyes of his jelosie against us. Soe that we may conceave there is no just ground of remouall in that respect.

FIFTHLIE, God is pleased hitherunto to maintayne unto us all his ordinances both in church and commonwealth, whereby, spreading errors in judgement are suppressed, and prophanenes and wickednes in practice punished according to rule and the best light God is pleased to vouchsafe unto us. So that we cannot see ground of remoueall for any defect in these particulars.

SIXTHLIE, God hath made this colonie to be instrumentall in the conversion of some of the natiues amongst us, and many more are hopefull to submitt to the gosple and beleeve in Christ Jesus. And that worke is brought to this perfection alreadie, that some of the Indians themselves can pray and prophesie, in a comfortable manner, to the rest, with great gravitie, reverence and zeale, and can write and read English and Indian comfortably. And many scores of them assemble together upon their lecture days, and are well affected to the gosple. So that although this may not seeme to be an argument sufficient to hinder some from removing, yet it might be a just ground of consideration for many to turne their backs upon so hopefull and glorious a worke.

LASTLIE, The great noise and general report of so many invited, and intending to transplant themselves into Ireland, hath occasioned some discouragement and weakening to the whole bodie of the colonie, and necessarilie brings an ill report upon the land, as if defective in that which make for a people's comfortable subsistance, which cannot be but dishonourable to our good God, who hath done so much for us as he hath done, and consequentlie not comfortable to such amongst us as have occasioned it.

YET, notwithstanding (right honourable) it is not our purpose, in laying down these reasons before your excellence, to hinder any families or persons to remoue to any partes of the world where God calleth them. And there is a law, long since established amongst us, that granteth such a libertie. But our intent onlie is to let your excellence understand the state and condition of this people, that God may have his due praises, and that your honor may not be wronged (by particular information) of the state of this colonie; that, accordingly, your excellence may act as you shall, for the future, in your wisdome, see meete.

FURTHERMORE, we humbly petition your excellence to be pleased to shew us what fauor God shall be pleased to direct you unto on our behalfe, to the most honorable parliament, unto whom we have now presented a petition. The copy of it, verbatim, we are bold to send herewith, that, if God so please, we may not be hindered in our comfortable proceedings in the worke of God heere in this wildernes. Wherein, as for other fauors, we shall be bound to pray, that the Captain of the hoast of Israell may be with you and your whole army, in all your great enterprises, to the glorie of God, the subduing of his and your enemies, and your everlasting peace and comfort in Jesus Christ. In whom we are,   Right Hon[ble,]

Your most obliged servants,

J. E.

NUMBER X.

Copy of an Address to Oliver Cromwell, in 1654.

May it please your Highness,

IT hath beene no smal comfort to us poor exiles, in these utmost ends of the earth (who sometimes felt and often feared the frownes of the mighty) to have had the experience of the good hand of God, in raisinge up such, whose endeavours have not beene wantinge to our welfare: amongst whom, we have good cause to give your highness the first place: who by a continued series of favours have obliged us, not only while you moved in a lower orbe, but since the Lord hath called your highness to supreame authority, whereat we rejoice and shal pray for the continuance of your happy government, that under your shadow not only ourselves, but all the churches may find rest and peace. The assurance of your highness's endeavours for that end wee have lately received by Major Sedgwick and Capt. Leveritt, for, notwithstanding the urgent and important occasions wherewith your highness is pressed, yet your goodness hath compelled you to be mindful of us, and to give such royal demonstration of your grace and favour, far beyond what we dared to expect or desire, upon intelligence of our condition presented to your highness by some private friends, whose well meaninge to us, must excuse their mistake; which hath made us confident, that our attendance to your pleasure, in furnishinge the said gentlemen with voluntiers, for your highness's service against the Dutch at the Manhatas, will be acceptable: with whom also, in complyance with our nation, ever since wee heard of the warr, we have debarred ourselves of all commerce; and have beene exercised with serious and conscientious thoughts of our duty in this juncture of affaires; the result whereof was in May 1653, That it was most agreeable to the gospel of peace which we profess, and safest for these colonyes, at this season, to forbeare the use of the sword; and though some of the other colonyes seemed to be of another mind, yet there wanted the concurrence of such a number of the commissioners to act accordingly, without whose consent foregoinge (by the articles of our confederation) no warr may be undertaken. Wee have nothing to add, to what was then under consideration, to put us upon that undertaking, in reference to our own interest, which we ought to understand and should attend, equally with our friends not more concerned than ourselves; wherein if wee should be mistaken, wee hope wee shall not be loosers with God or good men, by our tenderness in a case of such importance, and suspendinge our actings, till wee see cleare and satisfyinge grounds of our undertakings, so highly tendinge to the violation of our peace, the almost onely blessinge remaining to us, of all our outward comforts; the losse whereof, with the necessary consequents, would add such weight to our other sufferings as might overwhelme us in sorrow, and in that respect, render us of all men most miserable; which wee are assured is so far from your gracious intentions, that wee have no doubt, but the liberty wee have taken, of the waies proposed by your highness, to take that which is in our understandinge, the most consistent with our peace and welfare; will be most acceptable to your highness, and indeed wee cannot but acknowledge it a gracious providence of God, and a high favour and gentleness in your highness towards us, that when the object of your desire was our good, the meanes to attaine that end should no way press us: for, with all readiness, wee haue consented the said gentlemen may raise 500 volunties, armed and furnished for your service, within our jurisdiction, which is a large proportion out of our small numbers, especially at this season of the year, wherein the pressinge occasions of harvest doe call for all our hands to attend that service, least the following winter punish us for our neglect: Yet have wee willingly run this hazzard, that wee might, in some measure, manifest our devotion to your service, in what wee may. Sir, be pleased to beleeve us, that our harts and our affections to your highness are sincere, and that wee should account it our unhappiness, and ranke it amongst our greatest sufferings, to incurr your highness's displeasure, though wee should never feele the effects thereof. If, therefore, our understandings have in any thing mislead us, we most humbly crave your pardon, and that your highness be pleased to retaine us in your good opinion and favour, and wee shall ever pray the Lord, your protector in all your dangers, that hath crowned you with honor after your long service, to lengthen your daies, that you may long continue Lord Protector of the 3 nations, and of the churches of Christ Jesus. In whom we are,

Sir,

Your Highness's

devoted servants,

24th August,
1654.

The General Court of the Massatusets.

NUMBER XI.

Copy of a letter from the government of the Colony of Rhode-Island, concerning the Quakers.

Much honoured Gentlemen,

PLEASE you to understand, that there hath come to our view a letter subscribed by the honour'd gentlemen commissioners of the united coloneys, the contents whereof are a request concerning certayne people caled quakers, come among us lately, &c.

OUR desires are, in all things possible, to pursue after and keepe fayre and loving corespondence and entercourse with all the colloneys, and with all our countreymen in New-England; and to that purpose we have endeavoured (and shall still endeavour) to answere the desires and requests from all parts of the countrey, coming unto us, in all just and equall returnes, to which end the coloney have made seasonable provision to preserve a just and equal entercourse between the coloneys and us, by giving justice to any that demand it among us, and by returning such as make escapes from you, or from the other coloneys, being such as fly from the hands of justice, for matters of crime done or committed amongst you, &c. And as concerning these quakers (so caled) which are now among us, we have no law among us whereby to punish any for only declaring by words, &c. their mindes and understandings concerning the things and ways of God, as to salvation and an eternal condition. And we, moreover, finde, that in those places where these people aforesaid, in this coloney, are most of all suffered to declare themselves freely, and are only oposed by arguments in discourse, there they least of all desire to come, and we are informed that they begin to loath this place, for that they are not opposed by the civill authority, but with all patience and meeknes are suffered to say over their pretended revelations and admonitions, nor are they like or able to gain many here to their way; and surely we find that they delight to be persecuted by civill powers, and when they are soe, they are like to gaine more adherents by the conseyte of their patient sufferings, than by consent to their pernicious sayings. And yet we conceive, that their doctrines tend to very absolute cutting downe and overturning relations and civill government among men, if generally received. But as to the dammage that may in likelyhood accrue to the neighbour colloneys by their being here entertained, we conceive it will not prove so dangerous (as else it might) in regard of the course taken by you to send them away out of the countrey, as they come among you. But, however, at present, we judge it requisitt (and doe intend) to commend the consideration of their extravagant outgoings unto the generall assembly of our coloney in March next, where we hope there will be such order taken, as may, in all honest and contientious manner, prevent the bad effects of their doctrines and endeavours; and soe, in all courtious and loving respects, and with desire of all honest and fayre commerce with you, and the rest of our honoured and beloved countreymen, we rest

Yours in all loving respects to serve you,

From Providence, at the
  court of trials, held for
  the coloney, Oct. 13th,
  1657.

Benedict Arnold, *Pres.*
William Baulston,
Randall Howldon,
Arthur Fenner,
William Feild.

To the much honoured, the Generall Court, sitting at Boston, for the Colloney of Massachussitts.

NUMBER XII.

Copy of a letter from R. Cromwell, Protector, &c. to the Governor and Magistrates of the Massachusets Colony in New-England.

Loveing Friends,

WE being given to understand, that Henry Sewall of Rowley in Messey-Tusick bay in New-England, dyed about foure years since, possessed of an estate of lands and goods in the colony aforesaid, and that the said estate did and ought to descend and come to his only sonn Henry Sewall, minister of North Baddesly, in our county of Southampton in England, who now purposeing to make a voyage into New-England, there personally to make his clayme to the said estate, hath desired our lycence for his absence, as also our letters recommendatory unto you, that when (by the helpe of God) he shall be arrived in New-England, he may have speedy justice and right done him concerning the said estate, that soe he may the sooner returne to his ministeriall charge at North-Baddesly. And he being personally knowne to us to be laborious and industrious in the work of the ministry, and very exemplary for his holy life and good conversation, we doe earnestly desire, that when he shall make his addresses to you, he may receive all lawful favour and furtherance from you, for the speedy dispatch of his business according to justice and equity, that soe he may the more expeditiously returne to his said charge, where (through the blessing of God) his labours in the gospell may be further usefull and profittable; which we shall esteeme as a particular respect done to us, and shall be ready to acknowledge and returne the same upon any occasion wherein we may procure or further your good and welfare, which we heartily wish and pray for, and rest

Whitehall, the 23d   Your very louing friend,
of March, 1658.   RICHARD P.

NUMBER XIII.

The Court's Declaration of their Rights by Charter, in 1661.

At the Sessions of the Generall Court, held at Boston the 10th of June, 1661. The Answer of the Committee unto the Matters proposed to their Consideration by the honourable Generall Court.

1st, Concerning our Liberties:

1. WE conceive the patent (under God) to be the first and mayne foundation of our civil polity here, by a governour and company, according as is therein exprest.

2. The governor and company are, by the patent, a body politique in fact and name.

3. This body politique is vested with power to make freemen, &c.

4. These freemen have power to choose annually a governor, deputy governor, assistants, and their select representatives or deputies.

5. This government hath also power to sett up all sorts of officers, as well superiour as inferiour, and point out their power and places.

6. The governor, deputy governor, assistants, and select representatives or deputies, have full power and authoritie, both legislative and executive, for the government of all the people here, whether inhabitants or strangers, both concerning ecclesiastical and civil, without appeals, excepting law or lawes repugnant to the lawes of England.

7. This government is priviledged, by all fitting means, (yea if neede be) by force of armes, to defend themselves both by land and sea, against all such person or persons as shall, at any time, attempt or enterprise the destruction, invasion, detriment, or annoyance of the plantation, or the inhabitants therein, besides other privileges, mentioned in the patent, not here expressed, &c.

8. We conceive any imposition prejudiciall to the country, contrary to any just law of ours (not repugnant to the lawes of England) to be an infringement of our right.

2d, Concerning our dutyes of allegiance to our soueraigne lord the King.

1. We ought to uphold, and to our power mainteyne this place, as of right belonging to our soueraigne lord the King, as holden of his Majestyes manor of East Greenwich, and not to subject the same to any foreigne prince or potentate whatsover.

2. We ought to endeavour the preservation of his Majestyes royall person, realmes and dominions, and, so farr as lyeth in us, to discover and prevent all plotts and conspiracies against the same, &c.

3. We ought to seeke the peace and prosperitie of our King and nation, by a faithfull discharge in the governing of this people committed to our care, &c.

First. By punishing all such crimes (being breaches of the first and second table) as are committed against the peace of our soueraigne lord the King, his royall crowne and dignity.

Second, In propagating the gospell, defending and upholding the true christian or protestant religion, according to the faith given by our Lord Christ in his word: Our dread soueraigne being styled defender of the faith, &c.

The premisses considered, it may well stand with the loyalty and obedience of such subjects, as are thus priviledged by their rightfull soueraigne (for himself, his heirs and successors for ever) as cause shall require, to pleade with their prince against all such as shall at any time endeavour the violation of their privileges.

We further judge, that the warrant and letter from the King's Majesty for the apprehending of Colonell Whalley and Colonell Goffe, ought to be diligently and faithfully executed by the authority of this court.

And also that the generall court may doe safely to declare, that in case, for the future, any legally obnoxious and flying from the civil justice of the state of England, shall come over to these parts, they may not here expect shelter.

By the order and consent of the committee.

Boston,   THOMAS DANFORTH.
10 4 mo. 1661.

The court allowes and approves of the report of the committee.

This is a true copie taken out of the courts booke of records, as attests
EDW. RAWSON, Secr.

NUMBER XIV.

Copy of a letter to WILLIAM GOFFE, one of the Regicides, from his Wife, in 1662.

My dearest Hart,

I Have been excedingly refresht with your choyce and precious letter of the 29th May, 1662. Those scriptures you mention, through mercy, with many others, are a great support and comfort to me in this day of my great affliction. Through grace I doe experience the Lords presence in supporting and providing for mee and mine, in this evill day. The preservation of yourselfe and my deare father, next to the light of his own countenance, is the choycest mercy that I enjoy. For, to heare of your wellfare gives, as it were, a new life to me. Ah! what am I, poore worme, that the great God of heaven and earth should continue such merceys to mee and mine, as I at this day enjoy. Many others have lost their deare youke-fellowes, and out of all hopes to see them in this life; but that is not my condition, as yet, blessed be his holy name, for he hath made mee hope in his word. 10 Zech. 9. *And I will sow them among the people, and they shall remember me in farr countreys, and they shall live with their children and turne againe.* — Persecution begins to be high heere, the bishops courts are up as high as ever. But, wee have the promises of a faithfull God to live upon, and he hath said, *To you it is given not only to beleeve, but to suffer.* He hath alsoe promised to lay noe more upon his poore people than he will give strength to beare. Oh my hart! I doe, with my whole soule, blesse the Lord for his unspeakeable goodnes to you and your deare friend, in that he hath been pleased to appeare soe eminently for your preservation. He brings to the grave, and raises up againe. Oh that the experience that wee have dayly of his goodnes may make us trust him for the future. Wee have seene that word in the 5th of Job, in some measure, made good to you. Reade the 12th verse; from the 11th to the end of the chapter, there is much comfort to those in our condition; as alsoe in 91 Psal. O my deare, let us henceforth make the Lord our refuge and our trust, and then he shall cover thee with his feathers, and be a sanctuary to thee, wheresoever he shall cast thee. I mention these scriptures because I have found comfort in them, and I hope thou wouldest doe soe too. I shall now give you an account of your family, as farre as I dare. Through mercy, I and your little ones are in reasonable health, only Betty and Nan are weakely, and I feare will be lame a little, the others are very lusty. I am yet with my aunt, but how soon she may be forst to give up housekeeping I know not (for she is warned in to the bishops court) and wee shall be disperst; but I hope the Lord will provide for us, as he hath done hitherto. — Oh my deare, lett our trust be in the Lord alone. I do hartily wish myselfe with thee, but that I feare it may bee a meanes to discover thee, as it was to —— and therefore I shall forbeare attempting any such thing for the present, hoping that the Lord will, in his owne time, returne thee to us againe; for he hath the harts of all in his hands, and can change them in a moment. I rejoyce to heere, that you are so willing to be at the Lords disposall; indeed, we are not our owne, for wee are bought with a price, with the precious blood of the Lord Jesus: And, therefore, let us comfort ourselves with this, though we should never meete in this world againe, yet I hope, through grace, wee shall meete in heaven, and soe ever be with the Lord, and it will not be in the power of men to part us. My dear, I know you are confident of my affection, yet give me leave to tell thee, thou art as deare to me as a husband can be to a wife, and, if I knew any thing that I could doe to make you happy, I should doe it, if the Lord would permitt, though to the losse of my life. As for newes, I shall forbeare writeing of any, for I know not much, and you may heare it from better hands. My unkle Burket is dead, and my mother is with her. My brother John is gon beyond sea, but I know not whither. His father-in-law is dead. My dear, my aunt and many others are very kinde to mee, soe that, through mercy, I have noe want of food and rayment, though in a meane way. The Lord is pleased to suite my minde to my condition, and to give mee strength, in some measure, to take paines with my children, which I look upon as a great mercy. I know not whether I may ever have another opportunity to send to you this season or noe, which makes me the longer now; for I shall not send but by those I judge to be faithfull, and, I being in the country, I may not heare of every opportunity; and, though it is an unspeakeable comfort to mee to heare of thy wellfare, yet I earnestly beg of thee not to send too often, for feare of the worst; for they are very vigilant here to find out persons. But this is my comfort, it is not in the power of men to act their owne will. And now, my dear, with 1000 tears, I take my leave of thee, and recommend thee to the great keeper of Israell, who neither slumbers nor sleepes, who, I hope, will keepe thee, and my deare friend with thee, from all your enemies, both spirituall and temporall, and in his owne time return you with safety to your family. Which is the dayly prayer of thy affectionate and obedient wife, till death, F.

Many freinds here desire to be remembered to you. It will not be convenient to name them. I am sure you have a stock of prayers going for you here, which you and I reape the benefitt of. My humble duty presented to you know who.

Fredrick, and the rest of thy deare babes that can speake, present their humble duty to thee, talke much of thee, and long to see thee.

My humble duty to my dear father, and tell him I pray for him with my whole hart; but I am soe bad a scribe I dare not write to him. Pray be private and carefull who you trust.

NUMBER XV.

Copy of a Commission from King CHARLES the Second, to Col. Nichols and others, in 1664.

CHARLES the 2d, by the Grace of God King of England, Scotland, France, and Ireland, Defender of the Faith, &c.

To all whom these presents shall come, Greeting.

WHEREAS we have received several addresses from our subjects of several colonies in N. E. all full of duty and affection, and expressions of loyalty and allegiance to us, with their humble desires that we would renew their several charters, and receive them into our favourable opinion and protection; and several of our colonies there, and other our loving subjects, have likewise complained of differences and disputes arisen upon the limits and bounds of their several charters and jurisdictions, whereby unneighbourly and unbrotherly contentions have and may arise, to the damage and discredit of the English interest: And that all our good subjects residing there, and being planters within the several colonies, do not enjoy the liberties and privileges granted to them, by our several charters, upon confidence and assurance of which they transported themselves and their estates into those parts. And we having received some addresses from the great men and natives of those countries, in which they complain of breach of faith, and acts of violence and injustice, which they have been forced to undergoe from our subjects, whereby not only our government is traduced, but the reputation and credit of christian religion brought into prejudice and reproach, with the gentiles and inhabitants of those countries who know not God, the reduction of whom to the true knowledge and feare of God is the most worthy and glorious end of all those plantations. Upon all which motives, and as an evidence and manifestation of our fatherly affection towards all our subjects in those several colonies of New-England (that is to say, of the Massachusets, Connecticut, New-Plimouth, Road-Island, and Providence plantation, and all other plantations within that tract of land, known under the appellation of New-England) and to the end we may be truly informed of the state and condition of our good subjects there, that so we may the better know how to contribute to the further improvement of their happiness and prosperity.

KNOW yee therefore, that wee reposing special trust and confidence in the fidelity, wisdome, and circumspection of our trusty and well-beloved Colonel Richard Nichols, Sir Robert Carre, Knt. George Cartwright, Esq;

and Samuel Maverick, Esq; of our special grace, certain knowledge, and mere motion, have made, ordained, constituted, and appointed, and by these presents do make, ordain, constitute, and appoint the said Colonel Richard Nichols, Sir Robert Carre, George Cartwright, and Samuel Maverick, our Commissioners, and do hereby give and grant unto them, or any three or two of them, or of the survivors of them, of whom wee will the said Colonel Richard Nichols, during his life, shall be alwaies one, and upon equal divisions of opinions, to have the casting and decisive voice, in our name to visit all and every the several colonies aforesaid, and also full power and authority to heare and receive, and to examine and determine, all complaints and appeales in all causes and matters, as well military as criminal and civil, and proceed in all things for the providing for and settling the peace and security of the said country, according to their good and sound discretions, and to such instructions as they or the survivors of them have, or shall from time time receive from us in that behalfe; and from time to time, as they shall find expedient, to certify us or our privy counsel, of their actings and proceedings, touching the premisses. And for the doing thereof, or any other matter or thing relateing thereunto, these presents, or the inrolment thereof, shall be unto them a sufficient warrant and discharge in that behalf. In witness whereof, wee have caused these our letters to be made patent. Witness ourselfe at Westminster, the 25th day of April, in the sixteenth yeare of our reigne.

NUMBER XVI.

Copy of the Address of the Massachusets Colony to King CHARLES the 2d, in 1664.

To the KINGS most Excellent MAJESTIE,

The humble supplication of the General Court of the Massachusett Colony in New-England.

DREAD SOVERAIGNE,

IFF your poor subjects, who have removed themselves, into a remote corner of the earth to enjoy peace with God and man, doe, in this day of their trouble, prostrate themselves at your royal feet, and beg your favour, we hope it will be graciously accepted by your Majestie. And that, as the high place you sustein on earth doth number you here among the gods, so you will imitate the God of heaven, in being ready to maintain the cause of the afflicted, and the right of the poor, and to receive their cries and addresses to that end. And we humbly beseech your majestie, with patience and clemency, to heare and accept our plain discourse, thô of somewhat greater length than would be comely in other or lesser cases. Wee are remote, and can speake but seldom, and therefore crave leave to speake the more at once. Wee shall not largely repeat, how that the first undertakers for this plantation, having, by considerable summs, purchased the right thereof, granted to the counsel established at Plimouth by King James, your royal grandfather, did after obtain a patent, given and confirmed to themselves, by your royal father, King Charles the first, wherein it is granted to them, and their heirs, assigns, and associates for ever; not only the absolute use and propriety of the tract of land therein mentioned, but also full and absolute power of governing all the people of this place, by men chosen from among themselves, and according to such lawes as they shall, from time to time, see meet to make and establish, being not repugnant to the lawes of England (they paying only the fifth part of the oare of gold and silver that shall here be found, for and in respect of all duties, demands, exactions, and service whatsoever) as in the said patent is more at large declared. Under the encouragement and security of which royal charter, this people did, at their own charges, transport themselves, their wives and families, over the ocean, purchase the lands of the natives, and plant this colony, with great labour, hazards, cost, and difficulties, for a long time wrestling with the wants of a wildernes, and the burdens of a new plantation; having also, now above 30 yeares, enjoyed the aforesaid power and priviledge of government within themselves, as their undoubted right in the sight of God and man. And having had, moreover, this further favour from God, and from your Majestie, that wee have received several gracious letters from your royal selfe, full of expressions tending to confirme us in our enjoyments, viz. in your Majesties letter bearing date the 15th day of February 1660, you are pleased to consider New-England as one of the chiefest of your colonies and plantations abroad, having enjoyed and grown up in a long and orderly establishment; adding this royal promise, Wee shall not come behind any of our royal predecessors in a just encouragement and protection of all our loving subjects there. In your Majesties letter of the 28th of June, 1662, sent us by our messengers, besides many other gracious expressions, there is this [Wee will preserve and do hereby confirme the patent and charter heretofore granted unto them by our royal father of blessed memory, and they shall freely enjoy all the priviledges and liberties granted unto them in and by the same.]¹ As for such particulars, of a civil and religious nature, which are subjoined in the said letter, wee have applyed ourselves to the utmost to satisfy your Majestie, so far as doth consist with conscience of our duty toward God, and the just liberties and priviledges of our patent. Wee are further bound, with humble thankfulness, to acknowledge your Majesties gracious expressions in your last letter wee have received, dated April 23, 1664, as (besides other instances thereof) That your Majestie hath not the least intention or thought of violating, or, in the least degree, infringing the charter heretofore granted by your royal father, with great wisdom, and upon full deliberation, &c.

But what affliction of heart must it needs be unto us, that our sins have provoked God to permit our adversaries to set themselves against us by their misinformations, complaints, and solicitations (as some of them have made it their worke for many yeares) and thereby to procure a commission under the great seal, wherein 4 persons (one of them our knowne and professed enemy) are impowered to heare, receive, examine, and determine all complaints and appeals, in all causes and matters, as well military as criminal and civil, and to proceed in all things, for settling this country, according to their good and sound discretions, &c. Whereby, instead of being governed by rulers of our owne choosing, (which is the fundamental privilege of our patent) and by lawes of our owne, wee are like to be subjected to the arbitrary power of strangers, proceeding not by any established law, but by their own discretions. And whereas our patent gives a sufficient royal warrant and discharge to all officers and persons for executing the lawes here made and published, as is therein directed, wee shall now not be discharged, and at rest from further molestation, when wee have so executed and observed our lawes, but be liable to complaints and appeales, and to the determinations of new judges, whereby our government and administrations will be made void

¹ These brackets are in the original Hutchinson text and do not indicate new material in this edition.

and of none effect. And thô wee have yet had but a little taste of the words or actings of these gentlemen, that are come over hither in this capacity of commissioners, yet we have had enough to confirme us in our feares, that their improvement of this power, in pursuance of their commission (should the same proceed) will end in the subversion of our all. We should be glad to hope that your Majesties instructions (which they have not yet been pleased to impart unto us) may put such limitations to their busines here, as will take off much of our feare; but according to the present appearance of things we thus speake.

In this case (dread soveraigne) our refuge under God, is your royal selfe, whom wee humbly addresse ourselves unto, and are the rather emboldned therein, because your Majesties last gracious letter doth encourage us to suggest what, upon the experience we have had, and observation we have made, we judge necessary or convenient for the good and benefit of this your plantation, and because we are well perswaded that had your Majestie a full and right information of the state of things here, you would find apparent reason to put a stop to these proceedings, which are certainly disservient to your Majesties interest, and to the prosperity and welfare of this place.

If these things go on (according to the present appearance) your subjects here will either be forced to seeke new dwellings, or sinke and faint under burdens that will be to them intollerable. The vigour of all new endeavours in the several callings and occupations (either for merchandize abroad, or further subduing this wilderness at home) will be enfeebled, as we perceive it already begins to be, the good of converting the natives obstructed, the inhabitants driven to we know not what extremities, and this hopeful plantation in the issue ruined. But whatever becomes of us, we are sure the adversary cannot countervail the Kings damages. It is indeed a grief to our hearts, to see your Majestie put upon this extraordinary charge and cost about a business, the product whereof can never reimburse the one halfe of what will be expended upon it. Imposed rulers and officers will have occasion to expend more than can be raised here, so as nothing will returne to your Majesties exchequer; but instead thereof, the wonted benefit by customes, exported and imported into England from hence, will be diminished by the discouragement and diminution of mens endeavours in their several occupations; or if the aime should be to gratify some particular gentlemen by livings and revenues here, that will also fail, where nothing is to be had, the King himself will be a looser, and so will the case be found to be here; for such is the poverty and meannes of the people of this country (by reason of the length and coldnes of the winters, the difficulty of subduing a wildernesse, defect of a staple commodity, the want of money, &c.) that if, with hard labour, men get a subsistence for their families, tis as much as the generality are able to do, paying but very smal rates towards the publick charges, and yet, if all the country hath ordinarily raised by the year for all the charges of the whole government were put together, and then doubled or trebled, it would not be counted, for one of these gentlemen, a considerable accommodation.

IT is true, that the estates men have, in conjunction with hard labour and vigorous endeavors in their seueral places, do bring in a comfortable subsistence for such a mean people (we dare not diminish our thankfulnes to God that he provides for us in a wilderness as he doth) yet neither will the former stand if the latter be discouraged, nor will both ever answer the ends of those that need or seeke great things. We perceive there have been great expectations of what is to be had here, raised by some mens informations, but those informations will prove fallacious, disappointing them that have relyed upon them. And, if the taking of this course should drive the people out of the country (for to a coalition, therein, they will never come) it will be hard to find another people, that will stay long or stand under any considerable burden in it, seeing it is not a country where men can subsist without hard labour and great frugality.

THERE have also been high representations of great divisions and discontents amongst us, and of a necessity of sending commissioners to relieve the aggrieved, &c. whereas, it plainly appeares, that the body of this people are unanimously satisfied in the present government, and abhorrent from change, and that what is now offered will, instead of relieving, raise up such grievances as are intolerable. Wee suppose there is no government under heaven, wherein some discontented persons may not be found; and if it be a sufficient accusation against a government, that there are some such, who will be innocent? Yet, thrô the favour of God, there are but few amongst us that are malecontent, and fewer that have cause to be so.

SIR, the allknowing God knows our greatest ambition is to live a poor and quiet life, in a corner of the world, without offence to God or man. Wee came not into this wilderness to seeke great things to ourselves, and if any come after us to seeke them heere, they will be disappointed. Wee keep ourselves within our line, and meddle not with matters abroad; a just dependence upon, and subjection to your Majestie, according to our charter, it is far from our hearts to disacknowledge. Wee so highly prise your favourable aspect (thô at this great distance) as wee would gladly do any thing, that is within our power, to purchase the continuance of it. Wee were willing to testify our affection to your Majesties service, by answering the proposal of your honourable commissioners, of which wee doubt not but they have already given your Majestie an account. Wee are carefully studious of all due subjection to your Majestie, and that not only for wrath, but for conscience sake. And should divine providence ever offer an opportunity, wherein wee might, in any righteous way, according to our poor and mean capacity, testify our dutiful affection to your Majestie, we hope, we should most gladly imbrace it. But it is a great unhappines to be reduced to so hard a case, as to have no other testimony of our subjection and loyalty offered us but this, viz. to destroy our owne being, which nature teacheth us to preserve, or to yield up our liberties, which are far dearer to us than our lives, and which, had we had any feares of being deprived of, wee had never wandred from our fathers houses into these ends of the earth, nor laid our labours and estates therein; besides engaging in a most hazardous and difficult warre, with the most warlike of the natives, to our great charge, and the losse of some of the lives of our deare friends. Neither can the deepest invention of man find out a more certain way of consistence, than to obtain a royal donation from so great a prince, under his great seal, which is the greatest security that may be had in humane affaires.

ROYAL SIR, it is in your power to say of your poor people in New-England, they shall not die. If we have found favour in the sight of our king, let our life be given us at our petition (or rather that which is dearer than life, that we have ventured our lives, and willingly passed thrô many deaths to obtain) and our all at our request. Let our government live, our patent live, our magistrates live, our lawes and liberties live, our religious enjoyments live, so shall we all yet have further cause to say, from our hearts, let the King live for ever. And the blessing of them that were ready to perish shall come upon your Majestie; having delivered the poor that cried, and such as had none to helpe them. It was an honour to one of your royal ancestors that he was called the poor mans king. It was Job's excellency, when he sat as King among his people, that he was a father to the poor. They are a poor people (destitute of outward favour, wealth, and power) who now cry unto their Lord the King. May your Majestie please to regard their cause, and maintain their right: It will stand, among the marks of lasting honour, to after generations. And wee and ours shall have lasting cause to rejoice, that we have been numbred among your Majesties

Most humble servants
and suppliants.

25th of October, 1664.

NUMBER XVII.

Copy of a letter from the Earl of CLARENDON to the Massachusets Colony, in 1664.

Mr. GOVERNOUR and GENTLEMEN,

I HAVE received yours of the 7th of November, by the hands of Mr. Ashurst, a very sober and discreet person, and did (by his communicating it to me) peruse the petition * you had directed to his Majesty, and I do confesse to you, I am so much a friend to your colony, that if the same had been communicated to no body but my self, I should haue disswaded the presenting the same to his Majesty, who, I doubt, will not think himself well treated by it, or the singular care he hath expressed of his subjects in those parts sufficiently acknowledged; but since I found by your letter to my lord Chamberlaine and Mr. Boyle, that you expected some effect from your petition, upon conference with them wee all agreed not to hinder the deliuery of it, though I have read to them and Mr. Ashurst, euery word of the instructions the commissioners haue; and they all confessed that his Majesty could not expresse more grace and goodnesse for that his plantation, nor put it more out of their power, in any degree to invade the liberties and privileges granted to you by your charter; and therefore wee were all equally amazed to find that you demand a revokation of the commission and commissioners, without laying the least matter to their charge of crymes or exorbitances: What sense the King hath of your addresse to him, you will I presume heare from himself, or by his direction; I shall only tell you, that as you had long cause to expect that the King would send commissioners thither, so that it was absolutely necessary he should do so, to compose the differences amongst yourselves, of which he received complaint, and to do justice to your neighbours, which they demanded from his royall hands. I know not what you meane by saying, the commissioners have power to exercise government there altogether inconsistent with your charter and privileges, since I am sure their commission is to see and prouide for the due and full observation of the charter, and that all the priviledges granted by that charter may be equally enjoyed by all his Majesties subjects there: I know they are expresly inhibited from intermedling with, or instructing the administration of justice, according to the formes obserued there; but if in truth, in any extraordinary case, the proceedings there haue been irregular, and against the rules of justice, as some particular cases, par-

* Nº. XVI.

ticularly recommended to them by his Majesty, seeme to be, it cannot be presumed that his Majesty hath or will leaue his subjects of New-England without hope of redresse by an appeale to him, which his subjects of all his other kingdomes haue free liberty to make. I can say no more to you but that it is in your owne power to be very happy, and to enjoy all that hath been granted to you; but it will be absolutely necessary that you performe and pay all that reverence and obedience which is due from subjects to their King, and which his Majesty will exact from you, and doubts not but to find from the best of that colony, both in quality and in number. I have no more to add, but that I am,

Gentlemen,

Your affectionate servant,

Worcester-House,
15 March 1664.

CLARENDON C.

NUMBER XVIII.

Copy of a letter from King CHARLES the 2d. to the Colony of New-Plimouth, 1666.

CHARLES, R.

TRUSTY and well beloved, we greet you well. Having received so full and satisfactory an account from our commissioners, both of the good reception you have given them, and also of your dutifulness and obedience to us, We cannot but let you know how much we are pleased therewith; judging that respect of yours towards our officers, to be the true and natural fruit which demonstrates what fidelity and affection towards us is rooted in your hearts. And although your carriage doth, of itself, most justly deserve our praise and approbation, yet it seems to be set off with the more lustre, by the contrary deportment of the colony of the Massachusets, as if, by their refractoriness, they had designed to recommend and heighten the merit of your compliance with our directions, for the peaceable and good government of our subjects in those parts. You may therefore assure yourselves, that we shall never be unmindful of this your loyal and dutiful behaviour, but shall, upon all occasions, take notice of it to your advantage; promising you our constant protection and royal favour, in all things that may concern your safety, peace, and welfare. And so we bid you farewell. Given at our court at Whitehall, the 10th day of April, 1666, in the eighteenth year of our reign.

By his Majesty's command,

WILL. MORRICE.

NUMBER XIX.

Copy of a letter from King CHARLES the 2d. to the Massachusets Colony, in 1666.

CHARLES, R.

HIS Majesty hauing received a full information, from his commissioners who were sent by him into New-England, of their reception and treatment in the seuerall colonyes and prouinces of that plantation, in all which they have receiued great satisfaction, but only that of the Massachusets; and he hauing likewise been fully informed of the accompt sent hither by the counsell of the Massachusets, under the hand of the present gouernor, of all the passages and proceedings which haue been there between the said commissioners and them from the time of their first coming ouer; upon all which it is uery euident to his Majesty, notwithstanding many expressions of great affection and duty, that those who gouern the collony of the Massachusets doe beleiue, that the commission giuen by his Majesty to those commissioners, upon so many and waighty reasons, and after so long deliberation, is an apparent uiolation of their charter, and tending to the dissolution of it, and that in truth they doe, upon the matter, belieue that his Majesty hath noe jurisdiction ouer them, but that all persons must acquiesse in ther judgments and determinations how unjust soeuer, and cannot appeale to his Majesty, which would bee a matter of such a high consequence as euery man discernes where it must end. His Majesty therefore, upon due consideration of the whole matter, thinks fit to recall his sayd commissioners, which he hath at this present done, to the end hee may receiue from them a more particular account of the state and condition of those his plantations, and of the particular differences and debates they haue had with those of the Massachusets, that so his Majesty may pass his final judgment and determination thereupon. His Majesty's express command and charge is, that the gouernor and councell of the Masachusets doe forthwith make choice of fiue or four persons to attend upon his Majesty, whereof Mr. Richard Bellingham and Major Hathorn are to be two, both which his Majesty commands upon their allegiance to attend, the other three or two to be such as the counsell shall make choice of; and if the sayd Mr. Bellingham bee the present gouernor, another fitt person is to be deputed to that office till his return, and his Majesty will then, in person, hear all the allegations, suggestions, or pretences to right or fauour that can be made on the behalf of the sayd colony, and will there make it appear how farr hee is from the least thought of inuading or infringing, in the least degree, the royall charter granted to the said colony; and his Majesty expects the appearance of the sayd persons as soon as they can possibly repair hither, after they haue notice of this his Majesty's pleasure; and his further command is that there may bee noe alterations with reference to the government of the prouince of Mayne, till his Majesty hath heard what is alledged on all sides, but that the same continue as his Majestyes commissioners haue left the same, untill his Majesty shall further determine; and his Majesty further expresly charges and commands the gouernor and counsell there, that they immediately set all such persons at liberty, who haue been or are imprisoned, only for petitioning or applying themselues to his Majesty's commissioners. And for the better prevention of all differences and disputes upon the bounds and limits of the several colonyes, his Majestys pleasure is, that all determinations made by his Majesty's sayd commissioners with reference to the said bounds and limits may still continue to bee observed, till upon a full representation of all pretences, his Majesty shall make his own final determination; and particularly the present temporary bounds set by the commissioners between the colonyes of New Plymouth and Rhoad-Island, untill his Majesty shall find cause to alter the same. And his Majesty expects that full obedience be giuen to this signification of his pleasure, in all particulars. Giuen at the court at Whitehall, the 10th day of April, 1666, in the eighteenth year of his Majesty's reign.   WILL. MORRICE.

NUMBER XX.

SAMUEL GORTON's defence against the charges upon him in Morton's Memorial.

NATHANIEL MORTON,

I Understand you have lately put forth a book of records. — But this I know, that I am unjustly enrolled, because I was never free, nor member incorporate, in your body, or any of your territories; therefore I may not refrain to make a short return, only as it concerns myself.

AND 1st. Your peremptory judging of one you know not, for I am a stranger to you. ———

MY 2d word concerns your eminency, in assuming authority to canonize and put into the number of saints such men, when they are dead, who, in their life time, were persecutors, especially, you having acknowledged them to be such yourself; as also to thrust down under your feet, and make as bruit beasts, having only hope in this present life, such as are known to be fearers of God, worshipping him instantly, day and night; tho' they be not acknowledged to be such, by some particular sectaries as yourself.

A 3d word I have to say concerns your record: Mistake me not, I meddle not with your records further than they concern myself. I then affirm, that your record is fetched from him who is a lyar from the beginning — In that you declare I have spoken words (or to that effect) that there is no state nor condition of mankind after this life. I do verily believe that there is not a man, woman, or child, upon the face of the earth, that will come forth and say, that ever they heard any such words come from my mouth; and I appeal to God, the judge of all secrets, that there was never such a tho't entertained in my heart. —

AND whereas you say, I am become a sordid man in my life; I dare be so bold as to lay my conversation among men to the rules of humanity, with any minister among you, in all the passages of my life which God hath bro't me thro', from my youth unto this day, that it hath been as comely and innocent as his. Whose ox or whose ass have I taken, or when or where have I lived upon other mens labours, and not wrought with my own hands, for things honest in the sight of men, to eat my own bread?

A 4th word I have to say to your pamphlet, concerns the stuff, as you sottishly and contemptuously call it. You may be ashamed to put pen to paper, to publish any thing to the world in shew of religion, not acknowledging the letter of the scripture, but deriding it rather. —

FOR the rest of those expressions which you charge upon us, you falsly apply them. We never called sermons of salvation, tales; nor any ordinances of the Lord an abomination or vanity; nor holy ministers, necromancers: We honour, reverence, and practice these things. And, however you term me a belcher out of errors, I would have you know, that I hold my call to preach the gospel of Christ, not inferiour to any minister in this countrey, tho' I was not bred up in the schools of humane learning, and I bless God that I never was; least I had been drowned in pride and ignorance, thro' Aristotle's principles, and other heathen philosophers, as millions are, and have been, who ground their preaching of the gospel upon humane principles, to the falsifying of the word of God, in the ruin of mens souls. Yet this I doubt not of, but that there hath been as much true use made of the languages, within this 20 years past, in the place where I live, as hath been in any church in New-England: I know the manner of your preaching very well.

WHEN I was last in England, thro' importunity I was perswaded to speak the word of God publickly, in divers and eminent places as any were then in London, as also about London, and places more remote; many times the ministers of the place being hearers, and sometimes many together, at appointed lectures in the countrey. I have spoken in the audience of all sorts of people and personages, under the title of a bishop or a King; and was invited to speak in the presence of such as had the title of excellency; and was lovingly embraced wherever I came, in the word uttered, with the most eminent christians in the place; and for leave-taking at our departure, not unlike the ancient custom of the saints, on record in the holy scripture; and I dare say, as evident testimony of God's power, going forth with his word spoken, manifested, as ever any in New-England had; publickly and immediately after the word delivered, the people giving thanks to God that ever such a word came to be uttered among them; with intreaty for stay and further manifestation, in as eminent places as are in England; where myself did know that doctors of note had formerly preached, and, at that time, such as had more honour put upon them than, ordinarily, preachers have, who gave me the call thither, in way of loving and christian fellowship, the like abounding in the hearers: Therefore, I know not with what New-England is leavened or spirited. Indeed once in London, 3 or 4 malignant persons caused me to be summoned before a committee of parliament, because I was not a university man: I appeared, and my accusers also; one of them a schoolmaster in Christ's hospital, another or two, elders of independent or separated churches; who were questioned what they had against me. They said I had preached. Divers of the committee answered, that was true, they had heard me. The chairman asked of my accusers, what I had said? They could not repeat any thing, but said they were sure I had made the people of God sad. But the sum of all their accusation was bro't out in a book, which they said contained divers blasphemies: The book was only that which was printed at the proceedings of the Massachusets against myself and others. The honoured committee took the book, and divers of them looked upon it, and found no such thing there, as they ignorantly suggested: And, tho' my adversaries could say nothing, but only vent their spleen, crying out upon blasphemy; yet the chairman and divers of the board, knights and other gentlemen, questioned me about my call to preach, and other principal points of religion, and I answered to all of them according to my knowledge and conscience. Then my accusers desired Mr. Winslow might be called forth, whom they had procured to appear there, whom they thought would oppose me strongly, with respect to that book: When he came out of the crowd (for there was a multitude of people, the place being spacious) he spake judiciously and manlike, desiring to be excused, for he had nothing to say to me in that place, his business with me lay before another committee of parliament; which gave the table good satisfaction. My answers and arguments were honourably taken by the chairman and the rest of the committee, and myself dismissed as a preacher of the gospel. Shortly after, eminent preachers, living remote from London, then present, sent unto me kind gratulations, for my arguments used, and answers given before that committee. Which act of that committee I take to be as good an human call to preach, as any of your ministers have; and other call I know none they have. And, for a human call, I think mine to be as good as the degrees in the schools, or to pass under the hands and ceremonies of a titular bishop, or under the natural hands of a titular eldership, or to have the call of a people, by the power of stipend or contribution, without one of which no contract — all which I account as human, at the best.

A 5th word I have to say, is in that you send your reader to a book printed by Mr. Edward Winslow, for a more full and perfect intelligence. Mr. Winslow, and myself had humanlike correspondency in England, and before the honourable committee which he referred himself to, as above: and, not to wrong the dead, I saw nothing to the contrary, but that I had as good acceptation in the eyes of that committee as himself had; altho' he had a greater charter and larger commission, out of these parts, than myself then had; and, however he was a man of more eminent parts than myself, yet the goodness and justice of my cause did equalize myself unto him, in those occasions, both in the minds and demeanors of our superiors. I do profess I do not know or remember any particulars in that book he then put forth: — I saw it in London, but read little of it; and when I came over into these parts, my ancient acquaintance and friend, Mr. John Brown, discoursing with me about those affairs in England, told me he had read such a book, printed or put forth by Mr. Winslow: I told him I had seen it, but read very little of it. Mr. Brown, you know, was a man approved of among you, an assistant in your government, a commissioner for the united colonies, &c. who thus spake unto me in our discourse (I will not pervert nor alter a word of the will or words of the dead) I say, he affirmed thus unto me, *That he would maintain, that there were 40 lies printed in that book.*

per me,

SAMUEL GORTON.

Warwick, June 30, 1669.

NUMBER XXI.

Major WALLEY's Journal in the Expedition against Canada in 1692.[1]

A narrative of the proceedings to Canada, soe far as concerned the land army.

HAVING passed the isle of Percey, and being put back by a contrary wind, it was designed there to have landed our souldiers, to have settled our companys, to have called a council of warr, to have made and declared such orders as was necessary for regulating our forces, but by several of our ships and vessels being drove out of the harbour by a storm, they came not in again seasonably, and soe what was intended was prevented.

UPON the 23d of Sept. wee came to an anchor at Tarrasack,* a council of warr was called, such orders and ordinances made as was judged necessary, and ordered to be published in every vessel, and at the head of each company, which orders are upon record, and may be seen.

UPON the 27th of Sept. being about 25 leagues from Cabeck,† I went aboard each vessel in the fleet, that had souldiers, to take care that they might be all ready and fixt for the service, not knowing how soon there might be occasion; and whereas there had been complaints, that, aboard several of the vessels, the souldiers and others had near a third part of their allowance taken off without order, I then gave orders that their full allowance might be given them.

UPON the 5th Oct. wee came up with the Isle of Orleans, the whole fleet together, and having promised our men, that they should with the first convenience be landed to refresh themselves, and not having opportunity before, thought it might doe well to doe it then, proposing to the council that wee might then settle the companys, that wee might then secure the island, gaine intelligence, and upon our informations to draw up such conclusions as were necessary, and not to have appeared in sight of the town untill wee were fully ready to fall upon them; but it was over-ruled by the council, and agreed we should take the advantage of the tide, and be in sight of the town by daylight, which was accordingly done.

* Tadousack.
† Quebeck.

---

[1] The date should be 1690, though in all three editions it is given as 1692.

Upon the 6th Oct. it was concluded that a summons should be sent ashore, and, while the answer was coming, to put ourselves in the best posture wee could for landing; but by that time the messenger was returned wee found the tides did not sute, and that it would be too late to land that night. It was alsoe then agreed upon, that the army should land at the north shore, at the place we after landed at; that the small vessels, that had guns, should take in the ammunition, provision, field pieces, shovels, spades, and other necessarys for the souldiers, (that tide or the next they were to come up to Charles river, that lyes by the town,) that the ships boats should come into the river to be helpfull to carry the souldiers over, and the souldiers to be ready by the river when they came, that so they might be helpful each to other, as there had been occasion; that the field pieces should come in those vessels to be landed on the other side the river; it was alsoe agreed that, when wee were over the river, the men of warr were to sail up with the town, and when they perceived wee were upon the hill, especially if we then fired a house, they were then to land 200 men under their guns, and were to make a brisk and resolute charge to enter the town; alsoe agreed that Shute and others of the larger vessels that were not men of warr, were to goe beyond the town, that the enemy might thinke we had another army to land there; alsoe agreed that wee should have two ministers and three chirurgeons ashore.

These things being thus agreed on, on the next morning being the 7th Oct. wee attempted to land our men, but by a storm were prevented, few of the boats being able to row a head, and found it would endanger our men and wett our armes, at which time the vessel Capt. Savage was in went ashore, the tide fell, left them dry, the enemy came upon them, they manfully defended themselves. I went aboard several vessels, and, though with some difficulty, caused some small vessels that had guns to weigh, and sent some boats that endeavoured to help them, or if no other way to bring off the men, but the weather and shoals were such they could do them noe good; the enemy were awed by some guns from Sir William, that the shott flew among the thickest of them, alsoe by some guns from Capt. Eldridge. At the tides coming in they floated and all gott off safe. That night, aboard Sir William's ship, the French prisoners informed us of a place about two miles beyond the town, that would be more commodious for landing the army, which I then thought might be best, (but Capt. Davis saith since, wee should not a mended our selves) but it was said the council of warr had determined the place, and wee had not time to call them together then, and it would be safest to attend order.

The next day, being the 8th Oct. as soon as the bad weather was over, and the tides suited, wee landed our men, which considering how farr many of our vessels were from the shoar, and the helps wee had, never more men were landed in less time; but the flatts lay off soe we were forced to go into the water, some up to the knees, and some near as high as their wasts upon the flatts. I drew up the whole army, which consisted of between 12 and 1300 men, caused four companys to be drawn out as forlorns, though the ground would not admitt the forlorn and main battle to be far the one from the other; this being done, I ordered the forlorns to advance, and to march, at their open order, towards the upland, and by this time the tide was upon the ground wee stood on: The forlorn were no sooner advanced a few rods, before there was firing from both sides; upon one wing some of our men saw the enemy in the bushes, and fired first, but upon the other wing, and in most places, the enemy had the first shot at us; and from a village over a creek on our right wing, there was a party gauled us considerably; upon the charge our officers and souldiers shewed courage and resolution enough, yet some having given an order to fire and fall off, but judging under the present circumstances, ordered the whole body to shoot and run up at once, which they did with one consent, that it was hard to say which company went up first or fastest; upon which, the enemy having generally made a second shott, they gave way at once, and by the convenience of swamps and bushes, they had an opportunity to run away and secure themselves, but yet in partys out of every corner of a swamp or thicket they kept firing upon us; wee continued our chase and march towards the town, and killed some of the enemy as wee went. Being informed that the enemy had fired at our men out of a barn, and judging there were some in it, I ordered it to be fired; we come up with a house where was a hogshead of claret sett at the door, and seeing our souldiers gather about it, least it were poisoned, or might otherwise harm our men or hinder our march, I ordered the head to be knocked out; drawing nearer the town and finding the army too much scattered, and not knowing but wee might be met withall by a force from the town, I drew up a good part of our forces and marcht on; wee continued our march until it was dark, two thirds of the army took up their stand by a creek, where was a house and some other shelter, with the other part I advanced about a quarter of a mile, that we might the better secure the shoar and to see our vessels that were to come into the river; there wee took up our quarters, placed our out guards and sentinels, and did what was necessary for securing ourselves and taking notice of the motion of the enemy; wee then took the advantage of the House, barn, hay and straw, that those that were not upon duty might keep themselves as warm as they could. Making enquiry what damage wee had received from the enemy, or done to them, found wee had not above four killed outright at our landing, nor less than 60 officers and souldiers wounded, and it was judged we had killed 20, some say 30 of the enemy, and since, have been informed their hospital is full of wounded men, and it is said they had not less than 7 or 800 men that lay undiscovered to take the advantage at our landing; all things considered, it was a great mercy wee had no more damage done us. The same evening, having information of a Frenchman that had surrendered himself and was with the other part of the army, I sent for him and strictly examined him, severely threatned him if I caught him in a lye, told him wee had taken other French prisoners, and if he told us any thing that was false wee should soon find it. He told us wee should cut him in pieces if he told us any thing but what was truth; he informed that there were about 600 men that were in the swamp at our coming ashore, that there was a captain and other officers killed, besides others that he saw, that the French had 900 men from the town, more, upon their march towards us, that they were over the river, but seeing wee had landed our men soe suddainly, and beaten the French off the ground, and were marching towards the town, that they retreated, marcht back to the town, or at least to the other side of the river: He said the Earl of Fron-tenack was come down, the governor of Mount Royal and the intendant; that a great many souldiers came into Cabeck on the Thursday before, a great many with the governor upon Fryday, and more with the governor of Mount Royal on Saturday, and many since: He alsoe said he was a souldier of Mount Royal that had run away, and that they were seeking after him (which wee after found true) He alsoe said, he came by the information by a Mount Royal souldier, that he had mett withall, which acquainted him they had lost but 50 souldiers at Mount Royall, and added, that he had heard some French officers, at the next house to that wee then were at, say, that they had not less than 3000 men in the town; he alsoe said, that at the most convenient place of the souldiers goeing over they had planted 8 guns. All which, afterwards, we had confirmed. That others might not be discouraged, wee told him he was sent by the enemy to tell us a parsel of lies, but he said he had told us nothing but what we should find true.

AFTER this, I sent for the rest of the forces to come over, that wee might not be too much scattered, and sent for the majors and captains, and such as belonged to the council of warr, to consider and conclude what was farther to be done; after some discourse, it was concluded by the whole, that, for as much as the vessels were not come up the river with our sup-plyes of provision, ammunition, and other necessaries, neither the boats for transporting our men, that, as matters were thus circumstanced, wee were not in a capacity to advance, but hoped the vessels would be in with the tide, that was before day, and that if they came, wee would be ready to be helpfull to defend them, as we expected help from them; but the winds prevented their coming, as the masters after said. Before day, con-trary to order, and without my knowledge, they landed the six field pieces, at the point near which the army lay, which greatly clogg'd us, and would a made our passidge over the river very difficult. In the eve-ning, wee see Capt. Gilbert weigh anchor, and the ships of warr sail up to the town, and the several ships plying their guns upon the town, and the town upon them, with utmost diligence; but the reason of their going be-fore the land army were over the river, we understood not till afterwards. The cold of the night, and our souldiers not having opportunity to dry themselves until the next day, proved very prejuditiall to them. Upon the 9th of October, Sir William's ship returned from the town, being, as wee were informed, very much disinabled, having been very smartly en-gaged with the town, alsoe were informed, that the men of warr had not powder enough left for two rounds apeice; but, however, supposing they had secured and would supply us with what was promised, and reckning it was aboard the small vessels that were to come into the river, we still expected their coming in, and that day advanced nearer the town, where wee had better shelter for the men, and a better place for our defence, where we placed out our guards, and put ourselves in the best posture we could to defend ourselves and offend our enemies, if they had come upon us; sent out partys to gain intelligence and make discovery, and what provision came within our reach was killed for the use of the army; our provisions being so much in the masters of the vessels power, and not in the commissary generals order and dispose, proved a great damidge, by reason hereof, some souldiers were provided for and others wanted, and all the rum that could be procured, to refresh the souldiers, was only about 60 gallons, which was spared from Sir William's ship, the rest either had it not, or would not own they had.

Our souldiers dried themselves, gott what refreshment they could, and hoped the vessels might come in the evening tide, wee seeing more and more need of them, being more and more sensible of the enemies strength, and our own men, many, growing sick and unfitt for service. But the vessels not coming, we stood upon our guard that night, but found it exceeding cold, it freezing that night soe that the next morning the ice would bear a man. That night I called a council, demanded their opinion what was to be done, for it would be to no purpose to lye there; one in behalf of sundry others said, that they had been together considering thereof, and that for as much as we had not suitable supplys of provisions ashore, little or no ammunition to recruit if there should be occasion, that our men were, many, sick and wearied, that they had the difficultys of the river to deal with, neither boats nor vessels to help us in our going over, that we had 8 great guns and 1000 men at the river side that were ready for us, after that, a steep bank and narrow passage to win, up or through which wee should not a been able to have carried our great guns, neither could wee have carried them over, where we might have had them for use, without the help of our boats or vessels, after all this a well fortified town with three times our number of men within to encounter with, having but one chirurgeon ashore, though three were ordered, the increasing cold weather, the enemy being capable and had a fair opportunity, had we gone over, by reason of their men on our backs and guns by Charles river, to cut off all supplys and preventing our sending off soe much as a wounded man; after some discourse on these matters it was concluded, as I understood, by the whole, that I should goe on board that morning to Sir William, and acquaint him with our difficultys and disappointments, and that it was their agreement, if he were willing, that the army should get aboard that night or before day, and that they should rest and refresh themselves a day or two, and if they found they had ammunition suitable, they were ready to land at any other place, or under the guns at the town, if the counsel should soe conclude; there was that day two men to each gun sent ashore, a barrel of powder for the great guns, and half a barrel besides, and 100 wt. of bullets or something more.

THE 10th, before noon, I went aboard to Sir William, acquainted him how matters went ashore, and of the desire and conclusion of the officers; he said he could a been glad we had been capable to have proceeded, but consented to their coming aboard, and said the boats should be sent ashore before day; after I had been aboard a while, wee heard guns goe off ashore and perceived our out guards were charged by the enemy; I was going off, but, perceiving it was soon over, staid a while, and in the afternoon went ashore again, found our guards and some scouts had been engaged by the enemy; Major Savage sent reliefs as was necessary, but being informed that the enemy might be 1000 men over the river, he sent Capt. Corwin with orders that the souldiers should make an orderly retreat, for if the enemy were numerous it were better to prepare to meet them in the plain fields than among the swamps; wee had 4 men wounded, one died of his wounds, and, through hast in the retreat, a small drummer left his drum behind him; they did considerable damage to the enemy, but could not give a certain and particular account thereof, they fired several houses and barns, and returned, but the enemy see no cause to follow them. That night wee kept a very strong and strict watch, I acquainted the souldiers of their coming aboard; after midnight several of the commanders desired we might remove our army nearer to the place where we were to goe off, accordingly wee silently marched off the ground, carryed back our guns; when I had taken care that wee had left none behind, I went to the place where they were ordered to march, found our souldiers too many of them upon the beach ready to goe off if there had been an opportunity; I caused them to be drawn up upon the upland adjoining, and put them in a posture for service if they had been attacked by the enemy, for wee were within sight and hearing of the town. Before day the boats began to row ashore, but soe many of our men drew off without orders, that they might be ready to get in with the first, I foreseeing the confusion that was like to be, and perceiving there would not be time before it was light to get all off, I sent the boats all away and would not let any goe off at that time.

THE 11th day, being soe near as to hear them calling one to another at the town, their drumming and ringing before day, and other noises in the woods, that wee had reason to thinke they intended that day to come out against us with their whole strength; in the morning they fired several great guns at us but did us no harm, our men all that day standing to their arms, drums beating, colours flying, fair in sight of the town, we saw several of the enemy not far from us, and many on the other side of the river, besides what was in the town; it is said that Capt. Davis * reckoned, what they had in the town and that alarmed us and guarded their shoars, they were more then 4000 men; they sent out 7 or 800 fresh men dayly to

* Davis was then a prisoner at Quebec, taken at Casco bay.

alarm us and to watch our motions. Designing to goe off that night, and there being like to be a good opportunity, I called several of the officers and acquainted them that I was designed to send three parties of souldiers to beat up the swamps that were round us, and beat off these spies that we had reason to judge lay near us, accordingly ordered three 16 files to be detached out of the several companies, and sent them out commanded by Capt. Barnet, and Capt. Minot, and that party that was sent out upon our right wing were soon engaged; sent Capt. March forthwith, who had a good company, and they then soon made the enemy give back, but they continued firing briskly at each other; I sent out several companys to relieve them, in the mean time not knowing but this party might have been sent to occasion the drawing off a great part of our forces, and they might have a greater strength near us, wherefore I sent out to make discovery, and stood ready with the rest of the army to fight them if they had come up with us. The souldiers were ordered to keep firing at the enemy, in and about the swamps near us and where they saw the enemy until it was dark, which accordingly they did.

It then growing near night, I ordered the sick men to be carried aboard, which might be done by day light, because two or three boats might goe off well enough unsuspected. That day, Alexander Smart came ashore with a commission to be master gunner, and had 52 seamen under his command for to attend the guns. A little before night, I called him, and acquainted him that the army was to goe off that night, and gave him a charge about the guns, in particular ordered that three guns should goe off before any men went, or with the first, the other should be let alone to the last, and kept for to defend the soldiers if there had been occasion, and to be put aboard the last boats, which might be soon done; he made me answer, that though he was the last man aboard, he would see all the guns off; I parted with him then, and never see him afterwards that I knew of; I then acquainted Major Savage and other officers, that we would draw off half each regiment at a time, and he should draw off half his regiment first, and ordered that those that went in the first boats should be helpful to draw down those three guns that were to goe first aboard, which they did, and concluded they were gone aboard. It growing very dark, notwithstanding I had ordered the officers to keep the souldiers to their arms, many precipitately and disorderly drew down to the beach, four times more than had leave, and a very great noise was made, which I was much troubled at, and was willing to go down to see if I could still them; I called to Major Ward, ordered him he should do what he could to keep the souldiers to their arms, and not to move without order, which he soon found too hard for him to doe; I ordered some souldiers to keep the rest from crowding down until those were gone off that were upon the flats; I called to them to be silent, but either of these were little regarded, for the crowd and the noise both increased; the seamen calling out for such souldiers as belonged to their vessels, and the soldiers for such boats as came from the vessels they belonged to, hundreds in the water up to the knees and higher, pressing into boats, the seamen and they contending, by reason whereof I see boats were like to be five times longer a loading than they needed; I saw a necessity of my going off to the boats, went aboard a small boat belonging to Mr. Winser, commanded silence, ordered the boats to take the men in, as they came, and to carry them to the first vessels they came at, which was not minded by many, but as I was forced to goe from boat to boat and see it done, for otherways some of the seamen would throw the souldiers overboard if they did not belong to them, or the souldiers would have pressed into boats to have sunk them. After my being at the point not less than three hours, the men were most off, and every thing still quiet, the boats were all gone, I began to think, because I see none a coming they thought the men were all off, I questioned how many men were upon the point, some said 150, we judged about 100 or 120, I told them I would see if any boats were coming, rowed off and heard several boats rowing, went to them and ordered them to hasten to the shoar; and though I thought there might be enough to take off all the men, yet they should rather have too many than want, I told them I would go to the next vessels that had boats aboard and send them away, which I did with all speed. Being now well satisfied our men were safe off, I went on board Sir William's ship, I acquainted how matters were, told him I hoped the guns were off, for did not see them when I came away; he made answer, he questioned, for the master gunner had been aboard long before, and could not give account they were off, immediately came one of the gunners aboard, with a gun, and said that the guns were all off. I then being satisfied that both men and guns were all off, I went to my cabbin, to take my rest, having had but little for 3 days and nights before. Soon after Mr. Dearing came aboard, who came off in the last parsel of boats, and acquainted some of the officers and divers others, that there was five of the guns ashore, that they had been under water, but appeared when he came away; they did not acquaint Sir William nor myself of it, until the next morning, for wee had come off undiscovered, and there was four or five hours time that they might been easily and safely fetcht, but that was neglected; they sent in the morning, but then it was too late.

THE 12th day a council was called, several, but not all the commanders aboard, they discoursed of landing at the town, or at Orleance, many of the officers declared that many of their men were sick and unfitt for service; however, it was agreed that the men should have a day or two's time to refresh themselves, and to inquire what capacity wee were in for a further attempt, and some time should be spent on Monday in prayer, to seek God's direction, but the weather prevented our meeting, and wee necessitated to weigh and fall down to Orleance, many vessels drove from their anchors, and were in danger of being drove on upon the town; wee then sent ashore about our captives, but winds and weather after proved such, as wee had never opportunity to come together, but the whole fleet were scattered, and such exceeding hard cold and windy weather sett in for 3 weeks or a month together, as I never was in so much together.

THIS narrative given into the honourable council of the Massachusetts, this 27th Nov. 1690.

P.   JOHN WALLEY.

THE land army's failing, the enemy's too timely intelligence, lyeing 3 weeks within 3 days sail of the place, by reason whereof they had opportunity to bring in the whole strength of their country, the shortness of our ammunition, our late setting out, our long passidge, and many sick in the army, these may be reckned as some of the reasons of our disappointment.

SOME question our courage, that wee proceeded no further; as things were circumstanced, others would a questioned our prudence, if wee had; were it a fault, it was the act of a council of warr; we must undergoe the censures of many: In the mean time, our consciences doe not accuse us, neither are we most, yea allmost all, of us, afraid or ashamed to answer our actions, before any that can or shall call us to an account for the same, nor unwilling to give any farther satisfaction to any reasonable men that shall desire it.

JOHN WALLEY.

Boston, the 27th Nov. 1690.